Introduction to
Homeland Security

Second Edition

David H. McElreath
Carl J. Jensen
Michael Wigginton
Daniel Adrian Doss
Robert Nations
Jeff Van Slyke

CRC Press
Taylor & Francis Group
Boca Raton   London   New York

CRC Press is an imprint of the
Taylor & Francis Group, an **informa** business

CRC Press
Taylor & Francis Group
6000 Broken Sound Parkway NW, Suite 300
Boca Raton, FL 33487-2742

© 2014 by Taylor & Francis Group, LLC
CRC Press is an imprint of Taylor & Francis Group, an Informa business

No claim to original U.S. Government works

Printed on acid-free paper
Version Date: 20131029

International Standard Book Number-13: 978-1-4398-8752-3 (Paperback)

Visit the Taylor & Francis Web site at
http://www.taylorandfrancis.com

and the CRC Press Web site at
http://www.crcpress.com

Contents

3 Foundations of Emergency Management. 43

8 Disaster Response and Recovery . . . 159

12 Border and Transportation Security . . . 253

13 The Role of Intelligence in Homeland Security 291

Authors

David H. McElreath, PhD: Dr. McElreath's background includes professor and chair, Department of Legal Studies, University of Mississippi; professor and chair, Department of Criminal Justice, Washburn University; associate professor, Southeast Missouri State University; colonel, United States Marine Corps; and law enforcement and corrections positions with the Oxford (Mississippi) Police and Forrest County (Mississippi) Sheriff's Department. His education and training include a PhD in adult education and criminal justice, University of Southern Mississippi; MSS, United States Army War College; MCJ, University of Mississippi; BPA, University of Mississippi; and graduate of the United States Army War College. He is also the author of numerous publications on the criminal justice system. He and his wife Leisa live in Oxford, Mississippi.

Daniel Adrian Doss, PhD: Dr. Doss's background includes assistant professor, College of Business Administration, University of West Alabama; assistant professor, Belhaven College; adjunct assistant professor, Embry-Riddle Aeronautical University; and chair of graduate business and management, University of Phoenix (Memphis). His professional career consists of software engineering and analytical positions in both the defense and commercial industries. Corporate entities include full-time and contract positions with Federal Express and uMonitor.com and contract positions, via Data Management Consultants, with Loral Corporation (formerly IBM Federal Systems) and Lockheed Martin. Additional credentials include lieutenant colonel, Mississippi State Guard; graduate of the Lafayette County Law Enforcement Academy; and graduate of the Law Enforcement Mobile Video Institute. He has also coauthored a variety of peer-reviewed journal articles and conference proceedings. His education consists of a PhD in business administration, Northcentral University; MCJ in homeland security, University of Mississippi; MA in computer resources and information management, Webster University; MBA, Embry-Riddle Aeronautical University; graduate certificate in forensic criminology, University of Massachusetts (Lowell); graduate certificate in nonprofit financial management, University of Maryland (Adelphi); and a BS in computer science with a mathematics minor, Mississippi State University. He is currently pursuing a second doctorate, in police science, at the University of South Africa.

Robert Nations, MA: Director Robert (Bob) Nations, Jr., is currently the director of the Shelby County Office of Preparedness, which represents the coordination of homeland security for both the Emergency Management Agency for Memphis/Shelby County, Tennessee, and the Memphis/Shelby Urban Area Security Initiative (UASI). Bob is a career law enforcement officer and police administrator serving in those related fields from 1972 through his current position. Prior to coming to Shelby County, he served as state director of homeland security for Mississippi and was chief of operations for homeland security during Hurricane Katrina. Bob is in project management with the University of Mississippi in the Legal Studies Department and is a part-time faculty member at the University of Memphis in the Department of Criminal Justice. Bob is a graduate of the Naval Post Graduate School's Center for Homeland Security and Defense—Executive Leadership Program. He currently serves on the Homeland Security Advisory Board at Daniel Webster College in Nashua, New Hampshire. Bob is a recognized public speaker/writer at regional and national conferences.

Carl J. Jensen, PhD: Dr. Jensen is the director of the University of Mississippi's Center for Intelligence and Security Studies. He also is a member of University of Mississippi's Legal Studies Department and serves in an adjunct capacity as a senior behavioral scientist with the RAND Corporation. Dr. Jensen served as a special agent with the Federal Bureau of Investigation (FBI) for 22 years; his FBI career included service as a field agent, a forensic examiner in the FBI Laboratory, and an instructor and assistant chief of the Behavioral Science Unit. He has published extensively and lectured throughout the world. Dr. Jensen received a BS degree from the US Naval Academy, an MA from Kent State University, and a PhD from the University of Maryland. He and his family reside in Oxford, Mississippi.

Michael Wigginton, PhD: Mike Wigginton's background includes assistant professor of criminal justice and director of the University of Mississippi Master of Criminal Justice Executive Cohort Program, Department of Legal Studies, University of Mississippi; assistant professor, Southeast Louisiana University; adjunct professor, Tulane University; senior special agent, United States Customs Service; special agent, United States Drug Enforcement Administration; detective and state trooper, Louisiana State Police; police officer, New Orleans Police Department; and United States Air Force security police dog handler, with service in Vietnam. His education and training include a PhD in criminal justice, University of Southern Mississippi; MS, University of New Orleans; MS, University of Alabama; and BA. Loyola University of New Orleans. He is also the author of numerous publications on the criminal justice system.

Jeff Van Slyke, EdD: Dr. Jeff Van Slyke is a retired chief of police with an inclusive background of emergency management/crisis response, threat assessment, law enforcement services, and special security details. During his career as a chief of police, Dr. Van Slyke has experientially managed and responded to such emergencies as tornados, bomb threats, Hurricane Katrina, nor'easter storms, plane crashes, suicides/homicides, chemical spills, and residence hall fires and mitigated two credible active-shooter scenarios. Dr. Van Slyke also assisted with facilitating 21 presidential visits and was responsible for maintaining the security of a presidential library, a nuclear laboratory, a university airport, athletic events, concerts, and movie sets. While serving as chief of police at the University of Texas at Austin, Dr. Van Slyke assisted the United States Secret Service with the protective responsibilities for President George W. Bush's daughter (Jenna) and was awarded the US Secret Service Certificate of Appreciation by President Bush in recognition of his efforts. Dr. Van Slyke earned a bachelor's degree in Criminal Justice, Auburn University; a master's degree in public administration, Western Carolina University; and a doctorate in higher education, University of Texas. Dr. Van Slyke also attended the FBI National Academy and the US Secret Service National Threat Assessment Center.

Introduction to Homeland Security and Emergency Management

We will always remember. We will always be proud. We will always be prepared, so we will always be free.[1]

President Ronald Reagan

Chapter objectives:

- Familiarize readers with the concept of homeland security
- Introduce the all-hazards concept
- Discuss the complexity of homeland security
- Introduce multiple perspectives of homeland security
- Emphasize the importance of homeland security for the continuance of society and of the nation

Introduction

Over the span of a few short days in April 2013, the nation experienced two events that captured our attention and, in different ways, displayed an essential need for homeland security, law enforcement, first responders, and emergency management. The Boston Marathon bombings and the explosion of a fertilizer plant in Texas are examples of the types of events that may challenge the safety of our communities. These events of modern times are not uncommon. Throughout American history, since the founding of the nation, an innumerable array of threats and hazards has endangered society. Some of these events have affected only localities, whereas other incidents have impacted the entirety of the nation.

American society has demonstrated unique resiliency when faced with adversity. It has endured an initial separation from the British; the threats experienced with westward expansion; wars, droughts, pestilences, and diseases; attacks from both foreign terrorists and nation states; internal disputes associated with hate crimes and domestic terrorism; and a plethora of natural disasters and man-made accidents. Each experience was unique and contributed toward the improving of societal security and safety.

Each incident provided a learning experience from which the nation gleaned new methods of improving its safety and security. For example, improvements in fire technologies were spawned after tremendous disasters that resulted in mass losses of life and property. Similarly, during modern times, airports were fitted with passenger scanning devices after the events of September 11, 2001. However, despite any increase of knowledge, American society has never been completely impenetrable and impervious to natural and man-made threats. Instead, historical and contemporary experiences with calamities both show the fragility of American society.

These experiences involved varying amounts of preparedness, reaction, response, mitigation, and recovery. These primary notions represent a foundational basis for conceptualizing some of the essential components of homeland security. We must always remain vigilant regarding our preparedness for both natural and man-made incidents. We must possess a strong ability to respond, to mitigate, and to recover quickly from any adverse situation. We must learn from our experiences with disasters and apply these lessons toward reducing the chances of such incidents occurring again. If we cannot completely eliminate the chance of a disaster occurring, then we must formulate some method of mitigating the effects of such events.

Homeland security is much more than merely acknowledging the dangers of man-made and natural events. It is much more than preparedness, reaction, response, mitigation, and recovery. It is much more than applying the lessons learned from experiencing calamity. Homeland security is a complex domain. It represents endless combinations of threatening possibilities and imaginative countermeasures; integrates numerous agencies, organizations, and people; affects laws, regulations, and policies; requires a vast range of tangible and intangible resources; is viewed from a variety of different perspectives; and involves every facet of American society.

Why homeland security?

Our nation, like other nations, faces the threats of natural and man-made events that can well overwhelm the resources of local communities to respond. Whether it is a major earthquake in China, a Tsunami impacting Japan, a nuclear disaster in Russia, or a disaster at a chemical plant in India, history is filled with events that have inflicted devastation, havoc, property damage, injury, and death on a major scale. Recently, within the United States, such examples include Hurricane Sandy (2012) and the 2010 BP Gulf Coast oil spill. Endangerments also transcend the national boundaries. The perpetrators of the September 11, 2001, attacks and the perpetrators of the 2013 Boston Marathon bombings originated from foreign nations. Other threats originate internally. For example, historically, Timothy McVeigh, who perpetrated the Oklahoma City bombing, and Ted Kaczynsky, the nefarious Unabomber, were both citizens of the United States.

After the attacks of September 11, 2001, a major reexamination of domestic security occurred. A decision was made to create a new agency, the Department of Homeland Security (DHS), that was entrusted with the protecting of American society. Specifically, the vision of the DHS is to "ensure a homeland that is safe, secure, and resilient against terrorism and other hazards."[2] All missions of the DHS involve a variety of goals and objectives: to "prevent, to protect, to respond, and to recover, as well as to build in security, to ensure resilience, and to facilitate customs and exchange."[2] The DHS does not accomplish its missions alone. Instead, it involves the cooperation of a plethora of individuals, government agencies, and private entities.[2]

This global awareness of the United States made the targeting of the nation for the attack by terrorists even more symbolic to our allies and foes alike. The September 11, 2001, attacks

Figure 1.1 *Homeland security is an all-hazards concept.*

sparked an immediate reaction from the United States government on many levels. Within the United States, earlier suggestions of concentrating homeland security responsibility within a specific agency were readdressed. Within months, a decision was made to create a new agency, the DHS, which will be discussed in more detail later in this text.

Over the next decade, the DHS and the general response of the nation to terrorism and other threats would continually evolve. Especially after the 2005 disaster resulting from Hurricane Katrina, the homeland security concept changed from primarily focusing on terrorism to its contemporary emphasis concerning an "all-hazards" planning approach to homeland security.

This "all-hazards" approach is comprehensive and considers all natural and man-made threats to the nation. Therefore, regardless of origin, any mass incident or significant disaster is within the domain of homeland security. As stated before, the United States has never existed without threats. Such threats, both natural and man-made, may erupt into events that impact the safety of local communities, states, the nation, and global partners (**Figure 1.1**). Natural threats, such as major hurricanes, earthquakes, floods, or fires, will always occur. Threats to the national supplies of food or the water supply will always be of great concern, and the safety of national resources will always be a vital national interest.

What is homeland security?

Homeland security itself is diverse and complex. It can be viewed as a series of organizations, located on the federal, state, tribal, and local levels of government; it can be viewed as a process, one that today attempts to embrace preparedness, mitigation, response, and recovery; it represents an all-hazards paradigm through which American society is protected from natural and man-made events; and its implementation affects every individual within the nation. Certainly, homeland security can be viewed from a variety of perspectives. Some common views are itemized as follows:

- *Science*—Homeland security is a science. Quantitative analysis permeates homeland security in a variety of ways ranging from the financial and economic attributes of disasters to the metrics of evaluating organizational preparedness. Forensics examiners may investigate the chemical, biological, geological, and physical attributes of incidents.

- **Art**—Homeland security is also inexact and imprecise in many ways. Despite the best intelligence and best attempts to forecast and predict dangers, there is no guarantee that any estimate or projection will become reality. Further, protective and preparedness activities and measures that may be appropriate for one organization may be completely inappropriate for a different organization; no universal paradigm exists through which homeland security activities and practices may be integrated among all organizational environments.

- **Philosophy**—Homeland security may be viewed from a philosophical perspective. Morals, ethics, and values differ among cultures and societies globally. The attacks against the United States, perpetrated on September 11, 2001, are a testament to the many differences in ideological and philosophical beliefs that permeate societies around the world.

- **Strategy**—Homeland security may be viewed strategically. It involves facets of vision representing the perceived future state of existence that is desirable for the continuance of American society through time. Therefore, the federal government pursues homeland security strategically incorporating numerous missions, objectives, goals, contingencies, and evaluations through time.

- **Policy**—Homeland security may be considered from a perspective of policy. Across the nation, local, federal, state, and tribal entities have policies regarding organizational behavior and conduct that affect processes and procedures that are enacted when disaster and inclement conditions strike. For example, within the DHS, its Office of Policy provides "a central office to develop and communicate policies across multiple components of the homeland security network and strengthens the Department's ability to maintain policy and operational readiness needed to protect the homeland."[2]

- **Management**—Homeland security involves management practices representing the concepts of controlling, leading, organizing, planning, and coordinating. Most notably, the National Incident Management System (NIMS) expresses the "concepts and principles" that are necessary for determining "how to manage emergencies from preparedness to recovery regardless of their cause, size, location, or complexity."[3]

- **Economics**—Economic interests represent a salient perspective of homeland security. Simply, economics examines the allocating of scarce resources to satisfy the unlimited wants and needs of humans through time. When disasters occur, personnel, materials, and other necessary resources are not limitless; they have constraints. Therefore, practitioners of homeland security must be mindful of how to allocate their available resources to achieve the best and highest benefit of their use when experiencing inclement circumstances.

- **Creativity**—Homeland security encompasses a variety of imaginings through which possible scenarios that endanger society are expressed and examined. Examples include how terrorists might attack the nation to what may happen if a chemical spill occurs in a small town involving certain characteristics of weather (e.g., wind patterns). Crafting countermeasures is just as creative—the protecting of society, at all levels, requires much thought and imagination.

- **Chronological**—Homeland security may be viewed from a chronological perspective. Since the founding of the nation, numerous man-made and natural disasters have endangered society. A review of history easily shows acts of war in every century that succeeded the American Revolution that necessitated the involvement of the United States. Natural incidents of national severity have been recorded historically in every century since the origin of the nation. Even the outcome of the American Revolution was impacted by hurricanes (contributing to an American victory).[4] During the 1780s hurricanes, over 35,000 people died because of the storms; these hurricanes destroyed much of the British Navy, and British losses from hurricanes were more than those that occurred "from the battles fought in the Revolutionary War itself."[5]

- *Lifestyle*—Homeland security may be viewed from a lifestyle perspective. People must be vigilant to observe anything that may be threatening and report it accordingly. Before the events of September 11, 2001, people could flow through airports relatively unimpeded. However, modern times and security concerns now disallow the friends and families of travelers from meeting them directly at an airport terminal.

- *Business and commerce*—Homeland security is big business for both the commercial and government sectors of the American economy. Many organizations were created during the aftermath of September 11, 2001. Most notably, the US DHS, which is the primary example representing a government organization. Within the private sector, numerous entities have crafted business models to support homeland security endeavors. For example, numerous organizations, such as Blackwater, DynCorp, Intercon, and American Security Group have protected various American resources and interests, both domestically and internationally, with respect to both man-made and natural incidents.[6]

- *Infrastructure*—Homeland security may be considered from the perspective of critical national infrastructure. Across the nation roadways, rivers, and airlines connect American society, thereby facilitating the logistics of goods and services. Television, radio, and telephone networks provide a basis for communication within American society. Hospitals and medical laboratories provide a basis for treating people who may be harmed during inclement incidents. Many other components of critical national infrastructure (CNI) exist, and all CHI components are integrated with varying levels of extensiveness. Any failure in one area may incite cascading failures that impact related areas of CNI. Protecting the CNI is a paramount interest of homeland security to ensure the production, logistics, and availability of resources throughout the nation.

- *Individuals*—Homeland security is a matter that affects everyone. Anyone can contribute to a safer nation. For example, truck drivers may be used as the eyes and ears of the road. They may observe the actions and behaviors of others during their journeys, notice strange situations, and relay information to proper authorities when they believe they have observed something that is suspicious.

Many more perspectives may be listed if one only ponders the many ways in which homeland security influences daily life and impacts the nation. Homeland security is not relegated to the constraints of government coffers or the confines of protected offices; instead, it is a concern of every American citizen and resident. Homeland security is many things to many people and organizations, and involves a myriad of different, complex perspectives. Regardless, homeland security is an essential concept embedded within every facet of American society.

What are the threats and dangers facing the nation?

Threats facing the United States are extremely diverse. Natural events such as earthquakes or hurricanes may inflict wide-ranging damage; other events, such as deadly tornados, will normally, though not always, be limited in the area they impact. Accidents, such as industrial or transportation-related accidents, also may be devastating within the immediate area of the event, but are typically limited in scope. Regardless, the individuals whose lives are adversely impacted feel the detriments of devastation and rely upon the assistance of others to recover from inclement circumstances and events.

Accidents, such as major chemical spills, fires, or nuclear disasters, are prevented by constantly improving and monitoring a variety of safety procedures. Pandemics pose their unique threats to the population. Intentional attacks against the national infrastructure remain a possibility. The diversity of the threats facing the nation is so great that it is impossible to completely eliminate the risk of a disastrous situation occurring at any time.

Intentional attacks upon the nation may come in many forms. Possible attacks against the communications and financial systems, attacks against the industrial sector, attacks against the agricultural sector, pandemics, and transnational crime (including drug smuggling) are examples of potential dangers that challenge the nation. Those that would harm the United States are typically motivated by deeply held views that the nation, the population, and the American lifestyle should be shocked or forced into radical change. This notion is commensurate with the behavioral modification goal of terrorism. Therefore, potential aggressors define the legitimacy of targets with respect to the inciting of behavioral change.

Domestically, Timothy McVeigh viewed a federal building as a legitimate target. His choice of targets had little concern regarding the welfare of the individuals who were killed during his murderous attack resulting in the destruction of the building, city infrastructure, and the lives of many Oklahomans. His actions showed little concern regarding the effects of collateral damage.

Even the most innocuous appearances may conceal the deadliest of dangers. The 2013 bombing at the Boston Marathon (**Figure 1.2**) is another example of how the freedom of the nation makes the nation vulnerable. In the case of this attack, two young men from Europe, allowed into the United States, used the freedoms of the nation to attack the nation.

Since the origin of the American government numerous, antigovernment crimes against both property and persons have occurred. Hate crimes also have been part of the criminal element for decades. Regardless of their motivations, potential aggressors and threat elements identify their targets. The vulnerabilities of potential targets are assessed and evaluated to determine the feasibility of successfully completing an attack. Afterward, depending on the outcomes of such evaluation and assessment, strikes against the target may occur.

Figure 1.2 Boston Marathon bombing: brothers Tamerlan Tsarnaev (a) and Dzhokhar Tsarnaev (b). The FBI confirmed that the bombs were housed in pressure cookers (c) hidden inside backpacks and that the devices had fragments that may have included nails, BBs, and ball bearings (d). (Courtesy of the Federal Bureau of Investigation, Boston, Massachusetts, 2013.)

When and where does disaster strike?

In a nutshell, disaster is only a heartbeat away; it may strike anytime, anywhere. Some incidents may have little or no warning, whereas other incidents may be preceded by numerous warnings and countermeasures. For example, in 2005, Hurricane Katrina was preceded by various warnings and evacuation activities. Hurricanes may be tracked across the ocean, and their trajectories may be plotted to determine potential impact locations along the coastline. Any changes in their intensities may be observed as they travel across the ocean. These observations may be used to forecast quantitatively through time a range of possible storm strengths that may or may not occur upon landfall. Although no one can guarantee with 100% certainty that such storm intensities and landfalls will occur exactly as projected, there is generally time to issue warnings, if necessary.

In contrast, some incidents may have little or no warning. Typically, earthquakes have no warning whatsoever.[7] Although ongoing research is investigating potential methods of earthquake prediction and various warning systems, they are highly ineffective with respect to the ability of enacting any countermeasures or mitigation efforts. For example, in 2013, when an earthquake affected the region of Southern California, an experimental earthquake warning system predicted the event only 30 seconds before it actually happened.[8] This amount of time was insufficient to make a difference in the lives of the Californians who were impacted by the earthquake.

Regardless of any warning that may or may not precede incidents, human life is often affected by natural and man-made hazards both indirectly and directly. For example, a train carrying dangerous chemicals may be derailed in an uninhabited region. However, because of wind patterns, the citizens of nearby communities, towns, and cities may be endangered by poisonous fumes. Although the 2010 BP oil spill occurred unexpectedly many miles offshore in the Gulf of Mexico, it affected the residents and the economies of "hundreds of miles of coastline."[9] In any case, disasters may be devastating, may involve various amounts of warning, and can strike anywhere, anytime.

Who are the responders?

The thousands of emergency response organizations throughout the country are each unique. They have separate budgets, different levels of training and expertise, varying levels of interaction with state and federal officials, and different threat environments in which they must work. The heaviest burden in preparing for domestic emergencies falls on the emergency medical personnel, firefighters, and police officers of the "first-responder" community. Concerns about mass casualties from conventional attacks and the potential use of smallpox and other biological weapons have focused renewed attention on public health and hospital preparedness, which are thought to be woefully lacking. Behind the first responders and health care personnel are state emergency management offices, the offices of the state adjutant generals, and finally, the many federal agencies with roles to play.

All of these organizations are comprised of people. Some may have many years of experience with emergencies and disasters, whereas others may be just entering their respective occupations. An organization is only as good as the people it employs and the resources that it has available. Therefore, responders must be well trained and properly equipped to perform their respective missions and tasks.

Responders come from a variety of backgrounds. Some may be college students working part-time as law enforcement officers, whereas others may be unpaid volunteers working as

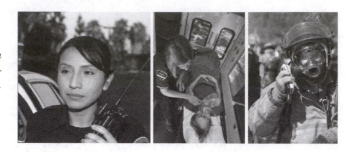

Figure 1.3 First responders come from all walks of life and different responding agencies. (Courtesy of Shutterstock. com.)

firefighters among small communities. Some responders may be full-time medical personnel working in the most notable and well-equipped hospitals, whereas others may be paramedics assigned to a rural ambulance service (**Figure 1.3**). Such individuals comprise the basic elements of all response organizations and agencies. Within the domain of homeland security, their skills, abilities, and expertise are critical during periods of calamity.

Protection of the nation

President George W. Bush proposed the creation of a new DHS. Bush stated, "America needs a single, unified homeland security structure that will improve protection against today's threats and be flexible enough to help meet the unknown threats of the future" (para. 31). The White House Office of Homeland Security was created on October 8, 2001, with Congress passing legislation mandating the DHS on November 19, 2002.

The mission of the DHS is defined in the National Strategy for Homeland Security as "a concerted national effort to prevent terrorist attacks within the United States, reduce America's vulnerability to terrorism, and minimize the damage and recover from attacks that do occur."[11] This mission statement was developed early in the evolution of the DHS. It has caused concern throughout the history of the department in that it seems to limit the scope of the mission of homeland security. It particularly causes policy questions to arise when discussing natural disasters and man-made incidents such as acts of terrorism, incidents involving weapons of mass destruction, or any other event that incites national distress. In the aftermath of the attacks on September 11, 2001, the mission statement reflected the "mood" of the country, with a focus on terrorists, acts of terrorism, and what direction American should take in the antiterrorism preparedness role. The country and its leadership, in a natural reaction to the attacks, were not focused on the natural hazards.

The department became operational on January 24, 2003, with most component agencies merging on March 1, 2003. The DHS incorporates 22 governmental agencies. Some of those agencies are the Federal Emergency Management Agency, the Coast Guard, the Secret Service, the Transportation Security Agency, the US Immigration and Customs Enforcement, and the Border Patrol, along with 16 other agencies.

This reorganization was the largest one of the federal government since the US Department of Defense was created in 1947. The mission of the office as stated by the president was as follows: "The mission of the Office will be to develop and coordinate the implementation of a comprehensive national strategy to secure the United States from terrorist threats or attacks."[12] The DHS is led by the secretary of homeland security. The former governor of Pennsylvania, Tom Ridge, was named secretary by the president to direct the office, beginning his duties on

October 8, 2001. Ridge resigned on November 30, 2004. The second secretary was Michael Chertoff, beginning on February 15, 2005.

According to the report from the DHS, in 2007, the department had 208,000 employees. Its budget for 2009 was $53 million. This makes the DHS the third largest Cabinet-level agency within the government. The department has many undersecretaries, assistant undersecretaries, administrators, and directors. All of the directorates, programs, and personnel ultimately report to the Office of the Secretary.

In the US DHS Strategic Plan, Fiscal Years 2008–2013, the language seems to address mission statement concerns. Secretary Chertoff outlines four operational objectives: (1) clarifying, defining, and communicating leadership roles, responsibilities, and lines of authority at all government levels; (2) strengthening accountability systems that balance the need for a fast, flexible response with the need to prevent waste, fraud, and abuse; (3) consolidating efforts to integrate the department's critical mission of preparedness; and (4) enhancing our capabilities to respond to major disasters and emergencies, including catastrophic events, particularly in terms of situational assessment and awareness, emergency communications, evacuations, search and rescue, logistics, and mass care and sheltering.[10] The fourth objective seems to be making a subtle shift to the natural hazards environment.

As the first phase of the development of the DHS was directed by the administration of President George W. Bush, the second phase, under President Obama, has witnessed a further evolution of the agency. During the early phases of the Obama administration, Arizona Governor Janet Napolitano was appointed director of the DHS, replacing Michael Chertoff. Secretary Napolitano initiated a review and evaluation of each function within the DHS. Under the administration of President Obama, the DHS has continued to evolve. By 2010, significant attention has been directed upon transportation and border security, responding to threats much broader than terrorism. Violence and unrest in Mexico combined with poverty in Central America are two issues that have fueled illegal immigration and violence along the nation's southwest border. As a response, the DHS strengthened enforcement and intervention efforts on the southwest border to disrupt the drug, cash, and weapon smuggling that fuels cartel violence in Mexico by adding manpower and technology to the southwest border.

Some of the programs included under the DHS include the Container Security Initiative (CSI), a program intended to help increase security for containerized cargo shipped to the United States from around the world; the National Fugitive Operations Program to enhance the apprehension and deportation of fugitive aliens from the United States, especially those who have been convicted of crimes; and Operation Community Shield, a nationwide initiative that targets violent transnational street gangs by partnering with US and foreign law enforcement agencies at all levels and making use of its authority to deport criminal aliens. Clearly, the role of the DHS continues to evolve.

Conclusion

Although most threats have limited impact upon the nation, the 9/11 attack and the damage inflicted by Hurricane Katrina converged to serve as a catalyst for homeland security. The 9/11 attacks made Americans confront the unpleasant reality that foreign terrorists could routinely operate within the United States to investigate, exploit security weaknesses, and use to their advantage the ability to strike a target at a time of their choosing. During modern times, the legacy of the terrorist attacks continues to be felt by the American public as they find themselves subjected to an increasing level of inspection at the nation's airports prior to boarding their flights. Terrorism itself is fluid; as measures are taken to remove a potential target from terrorists, the terrorists change their tactics and targets. It is a constant chess game with deadly stakes in play.

Such calamities and threats are not uncommon in American history. Since the founding of the nation, various challenges have faced the Republic, ranging from wars to natural disasters. Domestic and international events have contributed toward the maturing of the protection of American society through time. Each incident represents a unique experience from which lessons were learned that bettered the abilities of preparedness, response, mitigation, and recovery. Despite such lessons, the United States is not an invulnerable society or nation.

An all-hazards paradigm exists through which modern efforts of homeland security are instantiated. This all-hazards approach accommodates the realities of both man-made and natural disasters. Calamities may occur with varying amounts of warnings. In some cases, warnings may be sufficient to facilitate evacuations, whereas other situations may involve little or no warning. In any case, any threat, whether natural or man-made, has the potential of impacting human life.

People are the primary element of homeland security efforts. Although there are numerous organizations, both public and private, that contribute to homeland security, all organizations are comprised of people. An organization is only as good as its people and its available resources. Therefore, responders must be well trained, well equipped, and prepared to encounter both man-made and natural events. Responders come from all walks of life and have varying amounts of experience with disasters.

Homeland security encompasses a complex domain. The homeland security activities that may be appropriate for one organization may be completely inappropriate for a different organization. No solitary perspective of homeland security exists; it is many things to different organizations and people. Examples of such perspectives include policies, strategies, and philosophies. Homeland security is both an art and a science. It exhibits various attributes of uncertainty and inexactness while possessing simultaneously quantitative methods within its implementation.

Key terms

All hazards
American Revolution
Calamity
Complexity
Contingency
Creativity
Critical national infrastructure
Department of Homeland Security
Disaster
Earthquake
Event
First responder
Homeland security
Hurricane
Incident

Infrastructure
Lifestyle
Man-made incident
Management
Mitigate
Natural incident
Policy
Preparedness
Protection
Responder
Recover
Response
Security
Society
Strategy
Terrorism
Threat

QUESTIONS FOR DISCUSSION

1. Homeland security is a relatively new term that was coined after the events of September 11, 2001. However, the concept of homeland security has existed throughout the history of the United States. Review American history, and cite examples from each century of the nation's existence that involved the concept of homeland security. Write a brief essay that discusses your findings.

2. The termination of the Cold War necessitated many changes in the US homeland security philosophies. Beginning in the 1990s, how do you believe that homeland security has adapted to the complexities of modern threats? Write a brief essay that discusses your opinion.

3. Domestic threats originate from a variety of sources ranging from individual agents (e.g., Tim McVeigh, Major Nidal Hasan) to group-based and cell-based entities (e.g., Animal Liberation Front [ALF]; Earth Liberation Front [ELF]). From the perspective of domestic terrorism, please consider the actions of either an individual agent or a group/cell that has impacted American commercial or government operations. Select a case example of your choice, substantively discuss the characteristics of the case, and provide a critical analysis of the case. Within your response, please discuss the homeland security implications of your selected event.

4. Global society is dynamic through time. Now that over a decade has passed since the events of September 11, 2001, how do you believe American society views homeland security? Write a brief essay that discusses your opinion.

References

1. Reagan, R. Ronald Reagan quotes. *Brainyquote.com*. http://www.brainyquote.com/quotes/authors/r/ronald_reagan_3.html (accessed May 5, 2013).
2. U.S. Department of Homeland Security. (2013). Strategic objectives. *Office of Policy*. http://www.dhs.gov/office-policy (accessed May 2, 2013).
3. Federal Emergency Management Agency. (2013). NIMS and national preparedness. http://www.fema.gov/national-preparedness/national-incident-management-system (accessed May 2, 2013).

4. Williams, T. (2009). *Hurricane of Independence: The Untold Story of the Deadly Storm at the Deciding Moment of the American Revolution*. Naperville, IL: Sourcebooks, Inc.
5. Neely, W. (2012). *The Great Hurricane of 1780: The Story of the Greatest and Deadliest Hurricane of the Caribbean and the Americas*. Bloomington, IN: iuniverse, p. 113.
6. Scahill, J. (2005). Blackwater down. http://www.tulanelink.com/tulanelink/blackwater_box.htm (accessed May 2, 2013).
7. University of Hawaii. (2013). Earthquake mitigation hazards. http://www.uhh.hawaii.edu/~nat_haz/earth quakes/ (accessed May 3, 2013).
8. Serna, J. (2013). Quake tested warning system. *The Los Angeles Times*. http://articles.latimes.com/2013/mar/14/local/la-me-quake-early-warnings-20130314 (accessed May 3, 2013).
9. Leader, J. (2013). Gulf oil spill anniversary: 3 years later, ramifications are still felt from BP's tragedy. *The Huffington Post*. http://www.huffingtonpost.com/2013/04/20/gulf-oil-spill-anniversary_n_3118965.html (accessed May 3, 2013).
10. U.S. Department of Homeland Security. (2008). One Team, One Mission, Securing Our Homeland: U.S. Department of Homeland Security Strategic Plan Fiscal Years 2008–2013. https://www.hsdl.org/?view&did=235371 (accessed September 26, 2013).
11. The White House. "Today's Realities in Homeland Security," The White House (accessed August 25, 2013).
12. "Summary of the President's Executive Order: The Office of Homeland Security & the Homeland Security Council." 2001. Federation of American Scientist. https://www.fas.org/irp/news/2001/10/wh100801.html (accessed August 25, 2013).

2

Vital National Interests and the Defense of the Homeland

That I will support and defend the Constitution of the United States against all enemies, foreign and domestic...

US Military Officer Oath of Office

Chapter objectives:

- Understand the concept of vital national interests
- Gain an understanding of the instruments of power available to a nation
- Examine the historical evolution of the United States emerging as a major international power
- Identify the phases of the Cold War
- Recognize the impact upon the United States of the attacks of September 11, 2001, and the subsequent conflict

Introduction

The birth, growth, and development of the United States is a remarkable historical story. Moving from a set of colonies into a global superpower, over a span of two centuries, is a unique feat in world history. With the conclusion of the American Revolution, the 13 English colonies gained independence and formed the United States. The "Founding Fathers" established a nation structured as a democratic representative government, instantiated as a republic, during a period in which most powerful countries were controlled by monarchies.

Democracy would prove to be a continually evolving form of government. With its independence achieved, the young nation turned to the task of developing state and federal governments, enacting laws and establishing revenue and traffic regulations to fund the government. Being located in the northern hemisphere of the Americas, the new United States quickly realized that the location of the nation, far away from the powers of Europe, directly contributed to the homeland security and survival of the nation.

Since its founding, the United States has matured greatly as a nation. Beginning as a small collection of colonies along the eastern seashore, the nation now spans the continent, from the Atlantic Ocean to the Pacific Ocean; maintains various territories; and commands a global influence. The nation's demographics are diverse and represent a variety of different societal dimensions that have proven to be a melting pot of cultures.

For example, many different religious groups reside within the nation: "Protestant 51.3%, Roman Catholic 23.9%, Mormon 1.7%, other Christian 1.6%, Jewish 1.7%, Buddhist 0.7%, Muslim 0.6%, other or unspecified 2.5%, unaffiliated 12.1%, and none 4%."[1] The national population is approximately 313,847,465 people.[1] Its languages include "English 82.1%, Spanish 10.7%, other Indo-European 3.8%, Asian and Pacific island 2.7%, other 0.7%."[1] Economically, the nation represents "the largest and most technologically powerful economy in the world, with a per capita GDP of $49,800."[1] Rising from its humble beginnings, the United States now represents a vast amalgamation of different peoples, cultures, and philosophies.

Threats and challenges to the nation

The United States has endured, and shall continue to endure, both natural and man-made threats. Natural events, such as hurricanes, earthquakes, tornados, droughts, and floods, have caused devastation. Wars and conflicts both at home and abroad have also shaped the nation's identity. Throughout such challenges, the nation has survived and thrived. If history has any lesson for the modern practitioners and theoreticians of homeland security, it is that maintaining the security of the American homeland is both daunting and challenging.

Vital national interests and instruments of national power

The decision to exert military power should never be made lightly and should only be reached if the vital national interests are jeopardized. Vital interests are those of such importance that the nation cannot afford to compromise on their defense. The United States government has identified four such interests as vital to national security. They are survival and security, political and territorial integrity, economic stability and well-being, and national stability.[2] While these national interests are frequently discussed in vague or generalized terms by the government, they serve as the foundation for the development and implementation of national strategy and national security policies. In theory, vital national interests should be the only things that would lead a nation to engage in military action.

To ensure the safety of the nation's vital national interests, a country can call upon all its instruments of national power to influence other nations. Nations are in a constant state of change, economically, socially, and politically; they continually engage internationally with other nations. Normally, this process of change and interaction occurs peacefully because nations recognize that change is in their best interests strategically. However, there are times when peaceful change is replaced with aggression.

There are only two ways for a nation to make another nation comply with its wishes. A nation can peaceably convince the other nation through dialogue and reward. Otherwise, a nation may be influenced through threats of the use or application of force. The tools used by a nation to make another nation comply with its wishes are called "instruments of national power." There are four instruments of national power: diplomatic/political power, informational power, economic power, and military power.

Within the contexts of national security and the defense of the homeland, diplomacy is the art of employing communications and establishing global relationships to advance national objectives. The United States Department of State is the primary agency that facilitates international relations and diplomacy. The functions of diplomacy and the effects of diplomatic power are the key elements of national strategy and are the predominant instruments of national power. These diplomatic resources can be used to influence international polices, international negotiations, political recognition, treaties, and alliances. The diplomatic instrument is normally emphasized before hostilities begin and remains critical in any conflict situation.[3]

Governments should always first consider the diplomatic option to counter a threat. The costs of diplomacy are lower than those expended during military conflicts. However, the misapplication of diplomacy can amplify asymmetric threats, especially if they legitimize violence.[4] Asymmetric warfare involves leveraging inferior tactical or operational strength against the vulnerabilities of a superior opponent to achieve a disproportionate effect. This concept includes a goal of undermining the opponent's will in order to achieve the asymmetric actor's strategic objectives.

The misapplication of diplomacy contributes negatively to the resolution of problematic situations. During the months preceding World War II, one of the greatest failures of diplomacy involved the appeasement of Adolf Hitler. This appeasement included the Munich Pact of 1938. In an attempt to avoid war with Germany, the nations of France, Britain, and Italy permitted the German annexation of Czechoslovakia's Sudetenland. As parts of Czechoslovakia were absorbed under German control, the French and British leaders believed they had ensured peace. However, Germany was clandestinely preparing to invade Poland. In September 1939, the German invasion of Poland sparked a declaration of war against Germany by both France and Britain. This event proved to be the opening days of World War II in Europe.[5]

Information or informational power, the second instrument of national power, is the use of information and ideas to advance national interests. Information is used to influence opinions, views, and attitudes of both allies and adversaries. Informational resources that can be used to influence international polices include any information designed and focused to influence or shape human opinion. These informational resources include propaganda, media, news, or press releases.[3] Examples of the use of information to influence international opinion by the United States include Voice of America (VOA), Radio Free Europe (RFE), and Radio Marti (RM).

The third instrument of power is economic power. Economic power considerations remain a major concern for any nation. Economic strategies that can be employed to influence other nations include the regulation of trade practices, the provision of international loans and loan guarantees, the supplying of foreign aid and subsidies, international investment and monetary policies, and technology.[3] For example, since 1975, the heads of state or government of the major industrial democracies have been meeting annually, in what is now known as the G7/8, to deal with the economic and political issues facing their domestic societies and the international community. Six countries were represented during the first summit in November 1975. These nations consisted of France, the United States, Britain, Germany, Japan, and Italy. The G7/8 ministers and officials also meet on an ad hoc basis to deal with pressing issues such a terrorism, energy, and development. Periodically, the leaders also create task forces or working groups to focus intensively on certain issues of concern. Such issues include drug-related money laundering, nuclear safety, and transnational organized crime.

Military power is the fourth instrument of national power. It may be implemented by a government to influence international policies, but it is the instrument that should be used as a last resort. Though most of the defense of the United States centers upon the capabilities of its military, the three additional instruments of national power available to the nation are extremely important. All instruments of national power are interconnected; for example, military power is frequently dependent upon a diplomat's ability to enlist other nations in alliances, in coalitions, in obtaining basing rights, and over flight permissions. It is also directly dependent on the financial and technological strength of the nation's industrial, scientific, and economic capacities.[3]

Foundations of a nation

Over the course of two centuries, the United States rose from obscurity to global superpower, with extensive power and influence. The United States has been viewed as a nation that valued rough independence and great pride, which some observers have described as arrogance. A nation blessed with extensive resources and a population empowered with freedoms, the United States has and continues to attract refugees fleeing oppression or in search of religious tolerance, economic opportunity, or a chance for a better life.

The United States became a nation of dreamers and doers. It is a nation that would choose leaders to serve as the chief executive as diverse as the autocratic George Washington, the rough woodsman Andrew Jackson, the intellectual Thomas Jefferson and Woodrow Wilson, and the truly American Theodore Roosevelt. It became a nation that would survive an internal struggle and defeat aggressor nations, on land, at sea, and eventually in the air, who would dare to challenge and threaten the vital national interests of the country.

The United States has defined itself as a country that believed in manifest destiny, seeing itself as the primary nation in the Western Hemisphere. It is a nation that developed its unique culture and exported it globally. The United States is many things. President Ronald Reagan, drawing from the words of John Winthrop, famously said the United States remains "the shining city upon the hill with its doors open," an example to other nations that freedom is important and is something to be valued and protected. To others, the United States is a power to be feared.

For much of its history, while European powers were continually on alert from possible aggression from their neighbors, the United States was protected by the Atlantic and Pacific Oceans. With no major threat to challenge the sovereignty of the nation, investments in national defense and homeland security were limited, if not outright inadequate. Because the army served primarily as a constabulary force and the navy possessed limited power or capability, America was not perceived as a threat to stronger nations during its formative years.

Foundations of national security

At the conclusion of the American Revolution, little funds were available on the national level for national defense. The Continental Navy and Marine Corps ceased to exist. The Continental Army disbanded, and in its place, a small national army was formed, supported by local militias.

Soon realizing that the nation needed some type of naval security, on August 4, 1790, Congress authorized the formation of the Revenue Marine Service, which would serve as a coastal security force charged, among other things, with suppressing smuggling. For several years, the Revenue Marine would serve as the nation's quasi-navy until growing seagoing international commerce made it clear that the nation needed a navy.

The birth of the United States Navy did not mean and end for the Revenue Marine. Rather, the Service would prove remarkably flexible as it responded to changing needs over the next 200 years, eventually becoming what we know today as the United States Coast Guard (USCG).

Today, the coast guard operates as part of the Department of Homeland Security and serves as the nation's frontline agency for enforcing United States laws at sea, to include drug trafficking interdiction, protecting the marine environment and the United States coastline and ports, and providing emergency search and rescue operations. In times of war, or at the direction of the president, the USCG serves as directed, supplementing the Navy Department.

Today, as in the past, maritime security is important to the United States. Protection of the sea-lanes ensures that oceangoing commerce, so important to the nation, proceeds unhindered. Since the earliest colonial days, the sea has served as the highway system for much of the nation's international trade, even as the United States relied upon the British for protection in the early days of the republic.

The War of 1812, fought against the British, showed that both the United States and the Western Hemisphere were susceptible to the influences of the major European powers. The British were successful in their use of their sea power to control the sea-lanes, disrupt maritime trade, blockade ports, and land British ground forces. During this conflict, Baltimore was bombarded, Washington was burned, and Louisiana was invaded. At the end of the war, few debated the need for the United States to develop a stronger military capability.

The Monroe Doctrine

In December 1823, the administration of President James Monroe (1817–1825) established the first major United States policy toward European intervention into the Americas. In what became known as the Monroe Doctrine, the president presented a broad proclamation that was intended to define the relationship between the Americas and Europe. In this "doctrine," he warned foreign powers against interfering in the affairs of the United States and the newly independent Latin American countries, many of which had recently overthrown European rule.

The Monroe Doctrine was based upon three major principles, which would serve as the foundation for the homeland security vision of the United States for much of its history: (1) a separate sphere of influence for the Americas and Europe, (2) the cessation of European colonization of the Americas, and (3) the nonintervention of Europe into the affairs of the nations of North and South America. This was a very bold step, considering the fact that the United States did not possess the military or political power to enforce the Monroe Doctrine, nor did the nation necessarily consider the desires of the other countries in the region. No matter, the primary tents of the Monroe Doctrine established the United States as the self-proclaimed guardian of the Western Hemisphere.

Early conflicts

During the years between the War of 1812 and the turn of the century, the nation continued its expansion, fought a brief war with Mexico, and survived a major internal conflict. With the exception of the Civil War (1861–1865), the size of the United States military remained quite small and poorly funded during this period. Though these conflicts helped to shape the nation, they had little impact upon the larger world stage.

Few, if any, nations threatened the sovereignty of the United States. European powers were more concerned with expanding their influence in Africa and Asia. Beginning about 1898, the United States entered the world stage with a series of military expeditions and small wars in Cuba, the Philippines, China, Latin America, and the Caribbean, many of which, such as the small wars in Latin America and the Caribbean, would continue for decades.

The early 20th century

Many have referred to the 20th century as America's Century. In the 20th century, the United States evolved from a naive country, which was itself unaware of its potential, into the world's only global superpower. Throughout this period, the nation endured World War I, World War II, conflicts in Korea and Vietnam, and the Gulf War. It also experienced the Great Depression as well as a period of unrivaled economic prosperity. The nation invoked and repealed prohibition, experienced the New Deal, and witnessed much social change regarding civil rights. Throughout the 20th century, the face of America changed considerably.

In 1901, President Theodore Roosevelt assumed the presidency upon the assassination of President William McKinley (**Figure 2.1**). Roosevelt visualized the United States as an emerging power and expected the nation to be the leader in the Western Hemisphere and a global presence. He thought that the United States had a responsibility to maintain the Monroe

Figure 2.1 *President Theodore Roosevelt. (Courtesy of the Library of Congress.)*

Doctrine and that the nation should continue to use its power and influence to limit European involvement within the Western Hemisphere.

In 1904, Roosevelt extended the Monroe Doctrine through the proclamation of the Roosevelt Corollary. This corollary altered the original meaning of the doctrine, justifying unilateral US intervention in Latin America when deemed necessary, to include taking action to ensure nations in the Western Hemisphere fulfilled their economic obligations to international creditors. Under the corollary, foreign nations were disallowed from violating US rights or inviting "foreign aggression to the detriment of the entire body of American nations".[6]

Acting on the corollary, the United States increased its involvement in the internal affairs of other nations, using the elements of international power—diplomacy, military force, and economic outreach—to influence or shape policies in the various nations in the Americas. At various times during the early 1900s, the United States deployed military forces to Cuba, Panama, Nicaragua, Haiti, and the Dominican Republic, while simultaneously deterring European intervention.[6]

After the administration of President Roosevelt, American presidents continued to focus upon international issues, while again assuming a degree of isolationism toward Europe and European affairs. During the second decade of the century, as the First World War in Europe spread across the globe, the United States was drawn out of isolationism. By 1917, America possessed a strong navy built around a fleet of modern battleships, but the army was nothing more than a third-rate power still relying on the state militias in the event of a national emergency. The United States had not been involved in a major war for over 50 years. When drawn into World War I in the third year of the conflict, America found itself unprepared for the struggle.

Untrained and ill equipped for a European War, the involvement of the United States was limited compared to the contributions of France, Germany, Russia, and Britain. Although America engaged in World War I for less than 2 years, the conflict propelled the nation into international affairs, especially those in Europe. On the home front, espionage, domestic and international terrorism, unrest in labor, and the challenge of Communism were just a few of the things we would today call homeland security threats.

Tactically, World War I changed the way nations fought wars. Battlefields became much more lethal with the introduction of such weapons as aircraft, poison gas, machine guns, tanks, the extensive use of artillery, and a greater reliance on logistics. Much of the globe was affected by the war, and the long-term impact of the conflict was great. The "war to end all wars," as it was termed, changed the map of the world. New nations emerged from the struggle, many national borders were reshaped, and changes in governmental structures occurred among some countries. After World War I, many nations abolished their monarchial forms of government and replaced them with national governments that ranged from democracy to both Communism and fascism. Colonialism declined as independence movements gained momentum in many parts of the world. Russia experienced a revolution that resulted in the removal of its monarch and replacement with a Communist government. Germany attempted to establish a democratic government, but high unemployment and urban unrest led to its failure; Germany eventually fell under the control of the Nazis. Italy also moved toward Socialism when it adopted a fascist government under Benito Mussolini in 1922.

A significant outcome of World War I, with respect to world security, was the importance of determining diplomatic solutions to international problems. World War I inspired President Woodrow Wilson (**Figure 2.2**) to attempt the establishment of the League of Nations during the tenure of his presidency (1913–1921). Through international cooperation and diplomacy,

Figure 2.2 President Woodrow Wilson. *(Courtesy of the National Archives.)*

it was hoped that future international conflicts could be avoided. The League of Nations was formed at the end of World War I, in conjunction with the Treaty of Versailles, for the purposes of promoting "international cooperation," achieving "peace and security," and bringing nations together with the intent of avoiding future wars.[7]

President Wilson advocated American membership in the League of Nations, though the United States Senate voted not to join in 1919. Although the League of Nations was possibly doomed from its origin, it represented an attempt to find alternative solutions to international conflicts between nations.

Despite President Wilson's best efforts to expand the international role of the United States, America again reverted to isolationism and dramatically downsized its military forces. Although the League of Nations existed until 1946, its power and influence fell far short of the original vision held by its founders.[8] Despite its formation with the noblest of intentions, the League of Nations never fulfilled its potential and was disbanded. However, it was replaced with the United Nations (UN) in the hopes of forming a global alliance.

By the late 1930s, a global economic depression and a strong sense of nationalism gripped the world. Around the globe, many nations, such as Germany, Italy, the Union of Soviet Socialist Republics (USSR, also known as the Soviet Union), and Japan, witnessed their national governments fall under the control of repressive regimes intent on aggression toward their neighbors. In 1933, Japan commenced military operations in China. Germany, under the control and direction of Adolf Hitler, began an aggressive rearmament program. World War II inevitably followed these events. Even as the world lurched toward war, the United States desperately hoped it could cling to its philosophy of isolationism.

As World War II approached, America was slow to build a military from the small force that served the nation. The United States possessed a small army, limited air assets, and a poorly funded navy. In 1933, Franklin Roosevelt became president of the United States. Recognizing the dangers facing the nation, Roosevelt struggled to guide the nation out of the Great Depression and prepare the population for the possibility of war as storm clouds gathered in Europe and Asia.

World War II, challenging the spread of Communism, superpower emergence, and the competing world philosophies

Many will argue that the seeds for World War II were planted at the conclusion of World War I. During the two decades between the conflicts, Communists, Fascists, and Socialists gained control of the Soviet Union, Italy, Spain, and Germany. In Asia, Japan looked to the rich resources held by its neighbors and realized that if it were to continue as an emerging Asian power, it would have to gain control of oil, rubber, minerals, and arable land unavailable in Japan. Japan also understood that its ambitions in the region would place it on a collision with the European powers maintaining Asian colonies—the British, French, and Dutch—or the other major power in the Pacific, the United States.

In Europe and Asia, many dictators, including Mussolini in Italy, Hitler in Germany, Franco in Spain, and Stalin in the Soviet Union, looked to expand their power and influence, suppressed domestic opposition, and rearmed their nations in anticipation of future conflict. While history points to World War II beginning with Japanese aggression in Asia or the German invasion of Poland, in reality, many factors and events led to the conflict.

For the United States, support for the Allied powers, especially England, moved the nation toward war. Under President Roosevelt and against a strong sense of national isolationism, steps were slowly taken to strengthen and protect the nation.

American public opinion changed on December 7, 1941, when the Japanese naval attack upon Pearl Harbor, Hawaii, provided a harsh reality for the United States concerning the dangers of war. The Japanese attack brought America into World War II. National mobilization placed the nation on a firm war footing. By the end of the war, the United States emerged as one of two international superpowers and the only power with a nuclear capability.

World War II devastated Europe and much of China and Japan. During the years following the war, the world quickly divided under the influence of the two superpowers. The nations of Eastern Europe and much of Asia were forced to align with the USSR, whereas Western Europe and the Pacific aligned with the United States. For the first time in modern history, two distinct philosophies of government stood in direct competition with one another. Many countries, such as America, France, and England, believed that governments should be democratic and that economies should be capitalistic. In direct opposition, the USSR promoted Communism, drawing under its influence many of the nations of Eastern Europe. In 1949, the civil war in China ended with a Communist victory.[9]

As Europe divided, the United States took a bold step to rebuild its former enemies with an economic recovery effort. This economic initiative, entitled the Marshall Plan, was based on the concept that economically viable European and Asian regions would result in a safer world. The Marshall Plan stimulated the economic recoveries and stabilities of both Western Europe and Asia.[10]

Intelligence and national security

The United States government has embraced intelligence since its earliest days. President Washington believed in the value of intelligence, in both war and peace. In every conflict, commanders desire to gain insight into the mind of the enemy. Politicians and business leaders want to gain and employ intelligence to improve their decisions.

During World War II and the postwar years, both intelligence and the function of intelligence came to assume an extremely important role in homeland security. During World War II, in an effort to better collect, process, and utilize intelligence, President Franklin D. Roosevelt (1933–1945) authorized the US establishment of the Office of Strategic Services (OSS). Directed by World War I Medal of Honor recipient and lawyer William "Wild Bill" Donovan (**Figure 2.3**), the OSS conducted spectacular operations, such as assisting underground movements in Europe, gathering intelligence, and landing commando teams in Borneo. The wartime success of the OSS demonstrated its value to the nation.[11]

Between the period immediately succeeding World War II and the manifestation of the Cold War, the need for a civilian intelligence-gathering organization seemed obvious. President Harry Truman was reluctant to continue the OSS because he feared that it might become too powerful within the national government. Additionally, the president also resisted the efforts of the military and the director of the Federal Bureau of Investigation, J. Edgar Hoover, to obtain the nation's espionage mission. Instead, in 1947, President Truman authorized the creation of the Central Intelligence Agency (CIA). Today, the CIA is organized into four mission components, called directorates, which together implement "the intelligence process"—the cycle of collecting, analyzing, and disseminating intelligence.

Within the modern United States, an extensive intelligence community (IC) exists to serve the nation. The director of national intelligence (DNI) is the federal head of the IC. The DNI oversees and directs the implementation of the National Intelligence Program (NIP) and acts as the principal advisor to the president, the National Security Council (NSC), and the Homeland Security Council for intelligence matters. The goal of the DNI is to protect and defend American lives and interests through effective intelligence.

Figure 2.3 *General William J. Donovan.*
(Courtesy of the National Archives.)

World organizations promoting peace: The League of nations and the UN

The League of Nations had been created with the highest of ideals, to form an organization of nations that could provide a forum to further world peace. However, without the United States as a member, the organization was doomed to failure. Even as World War II raged, however, a decision was made to establish a new organization of nations, with many of the original goals of the League of Nations. Consequently, on January 1, 1942, the "Declaration by the United Nations" was issued. The declaration brought together representatives of 26 nations who pledged that their governments would work together in a unified effort against the Axis powers.[24] Over the next three years, the vision for the UN continued to evolve. In 1945, it formally began operations when representatives of 50 countries met in San Francisco at the United Nations Conference on International Organization to design the United Nations Charter. Over the next six decades, the membership of the UN expanded to include 192 countries, including the former Axis powers.[12]

Today, the UN is central in addressing international problems, including enhancing the cause of peace, conducting peacekeeping operations, advancing human rights, promoting economic and social development, and advancing international law.

Evolution of the Cold War

To a great extent, the Cold War defined the United States. World War II ended, and the United States emerged as one of the two existing global superpowers. Germany was divided between the Allied powers, and Japan and Italy were occupied. The nations that had worked together to defeat the Axis now viewed each other with suspicion. The United States would soon see the Soviet Union as the next major threat not only to the security of the nation but also to world peace.

On March 5, 1946, Sir Winston Churchill (**Figure 2.4**), the former British prime minister, delivered what has become known as his "Sinews of Peace" or "Iron Curtain" speech at Westminster College in Fulton, Missouri. Within this speech, Churchill spoke of "an Iron Curtain descending across Europe dividing self-governing nations of the West and those in Eastern Europe under Soviet Communist control." The insight of Churchill proved remarkable.

The Cold War became the primary focus of national security planning for both the United States and the USSR, with both nations spending enormous efforts at gaining an advantage over the other for the next 50 years. For the United States, the Cold War can be viewed in six phases: containment, mutually assured destruction (MAD), small wars and the domino theory, détente, rollback, and glasnost.

Containment

At the end of World War II, the United States and the Soviet Union took two different approaches to the postwar period. The United States demobilized much of the military, relying instead of the nation's growing nuclear arsenal to assure national safety. To avoid the economic problems that led the defeated nations at the end of World War I to move toward dictatorships, the United States pumped billions of dollars into the economies of its former enemies under the Marshall Plan. The Soviet Union took a different approach. The Soviets worked to strengthen their grip on Eastern Europe and extend their influence in Asia.

President Harry Truman (1945–1953) (**Figure 2.5**) pursued the goal of containing the USSR while increasing US quantities of nuclear, biological, and chemical armaments, believing the

Figure 2.4 British Prime Minister *Winston Churchill, 1942. (Courtesy of the Library of Congress.)*

Figure 2.5 President Harry Truman. *(Courtesy of the US Army Signal Corp.)*

threat of nuclear war would deter Soviet hostility and aggression. In 1948, the Soviets challenged the United States by blockading West Berlin, bringing the two nations to the brink of conflict. This blockade was intended to demonstrate US weakness and to force the western allies to abandon Berlin.

A strategy was quickly developed and implemented to provide West Berlin with the necessary supplies required for survival, with the US forces establishing an "air bridge," to fly daily tons of supplies to the city. Over the period of nearly a year, the siege continued. In May 1949, the Soviets abandoned the siege and reinstated a land route between West Germany and West Berlin.

This was the first, but not the last, collision between the two nations. Indeed, throughout the Cold War, both sides often pushed the other to the "brink" of conflict. During these periods, the Cold War threatened to become "hot." This so-called "brinkmanship" on multiple occasions caused the world to consider the unthinkable—a nuclear conflict that would have resulted in the deaths of millions.

While the attention of the United States primarily focused on Europe, Asia proved to be the next international flash point.[13] Within Asia, the Nationalist Chinese were driven from the Chinese mainland in 1949, and the Communist Chinese gained control of the nation. As a result, the balance of power shifted in Asia.

MAD

When World War II ended, the United States was the only nation to possess nuclear weapons. The nation's nuclear monopoly was short-lived. On August 29, 1949, the Soviets exploded their first atomic bomb. Soviet nuclear capability shocked the United States, which could no longer depend on its nuclear arsenal alone to serve as a deterrent to counter Soviet aggression. With the Soviets adding nuclear weapons to their arsenal, an arms race began that eventually included not only nuclear weapons but also chemical and biological weaponry.

The arms race produced a half-century of struggle that saw attempts to limit the spread of weapons of mass destruction (WMDs) on the one hand and, simultaneously, the span of control of both sides. The possession of significant quantities of WMDs by both the United States and the USSR contributed to the notion of MAD between these nations. The basic tenet of MAD was that both sides would be destroyed if a nuclear war occurred. Despite attempts to redefine MAD by phrasing it in contemporary terms such as *flexible response* and *nuclear deterrence,* it has remained the central theme of American defense planning for well over three decades.

By 1950, the conventional military capabilities of the United States were greatly reduced because of the downsizing that occurred following World War II. As a result, the national security ability of the United States was also weakened. Within America, naval ships were decommissioned, and military service personnel were discharged. In the first part of the decade, the international struggle for power again changed thanks to a conflict in Korea. In June 1950, Soviet-backed North Korean forces invaded South Korea, an ally of the United States. The UN condemned the North's aggression, and the Security Council authorized military support for the South.

Between 1950 and 1953, UN forces, in conjunction with the US military, conducted an attrition-based conflict limited to the Korean Peninsula, which severely tested the American will to support its allies. By the winter of 1950, the UN's forces had essentially defeated the North Korean Army and moved to occupy North Korea. With UN forces moving to the North Korean border along Communist China, the Chinese warned both the UN and the United States that it would intervene in the conflict if the UN did not leave North Korea. Ignoring the warnings, the UN forces continued their attack all the way to the Chinese border. During the month of December, 1950, the

Communist Chinese Army entered North Korea and engaged UN forces. In 1953, an armistice was reached; however, a state of war technically still exists between the North and the South.

As a result of the Korean Conflict, the Truman administration recognized the need for a stronger military and began a massive buildup of America's nuclear and conventional capabilities. In addition, the United States commenced the rearming of Western Europe and furnished its European allies with the military equipment required for defense. Under Truman's plan for the enhancement of the military, the size of the US military increased to 3.5 million personnel.[9]

Containment and continuation of MAD: Attempts to isolate the Soviet Union

The administration of President Dwight Eisenhower (1953–1961) continued the containment strategy of MAD pursued by the Truman administration. If anything, the Eisenhower administration had greater faith that the growing nuclear inventory of the United States could serve as the foundation for a defense strategy. Conceptually, this reliance upon WMDs to deter international aggression was similar to the reliance upon the national protectiveness of the Atlantic and Pacific Oceans during the 1800s.

Because of the MAD doctrine, the United States and Soviet Union could not attack each other directly. Hence, the Cold War was "war by other means." Propaganda, proxy wars, arms races, and the massive expansion of each side's intelligence capability became the battlefields.

In a further effort to deter Communist aggression, several Western nations formed the North Atlantic Treaty Organization (NATO) in 1949. During the next 60 years, NATO matured into a capable military alliance that enhanced European defenses. In a move that mirrored NATO, America and its Asian allies formed the Southeast Asian Treaty Organization (SEATO) in 1954. As with NATO, the purpose of SEATO was to further the US policy of containing Communism within Asia. SEATO member nations included Australia, Britain, France, New Zealand, Pakistan, the Philippines, Thailand, and the United States. In 1977, two years after the Communist victory in Vietnam, SEATO was dissolved.

In 1955, the USSR and other Eastern European Bloc nations responded to NATO and SEATO through the formation of the Warsaw Pact. The Warsaw Pact was a treaty between Albania, Bulgaria, Czechoslovakia, East Germany, Hungary, Poland, Romania, and the USSR; the actual treaty was signed in Poland in 1955. The official title of the agreement was the Treaty of Friendship, Co-operation and Mutual Assistance. Commencing in 1955, the Warsaw Pact and NATO would face each other, ready for war in Europe, for 35 years.[26] The Warsaw Treaty Organization was dissolved in 1991, and many of the former Warsaw Pact members joined NATO.

While it is easy to conceptualize the Cold War as merely a struggle between two superpowers, the reality is more complex; the truth is that many long-standing rivalries between nations continued. As an example, the United States military involvement in Vietnam in the 1960s is often termed a "proxy war." In fact, the Vietnamese people had struggled for centuries for unified self-government. The people of the North considered theirs a nationalistic conflict, while Americans considered it a struggle to contain Communism.

Small wars and the domino theory

The administration of President John Kennedy (1961–1963) identified regional conflicts, revolutions, and potential confrontations as "small wars." Such incidents were considered to be major threats to US national security. Kennedy was concerned with the "domino theory." The domino theory was first discussed within the Eisenhower administration following the Communist-backed

French defeat and withdrawal from Indochina. The domino theory suggests that once one nation falls to Communism, others will soon follow. Therefore, it was important to US national security to limit the spread of Soviet influence, by military means if necessary.[14]

The Kennedy administration placed an emphasis upon the development of an enhanced "special operations" capability within its military, intelligence, and diplomatic services. Special operations forces, such as the United States Army Special Forces and CIA, were committed around the world. During this period, the nuclear arms race continued, with both the United States and the USSR developing large stockpiles of weapons. Fears of nuclear conflict between the two superpowers peaked during the aftermath of the failed invasion of Cuba at the Bay of Pigs in 1961 and during the 1962 Cuban Missile Crisis. These events, combined with the weapons race, paved the way for some of the earliest agreements on nuclear arms control, including the Limited Test Ban Treaty of 1963.

President Lyndon Johnson (1963–1969) assumed the presidency upon the assassination of President Kennedy in 1963. In an effort to halt the spread of Communism in Southeast Asia, the United States found itself drawn into the conflict in Vietnam. The Vietnam Conflict proved to be a turning point regarding US national security and homeland security. Backed by the USSR, North Vietnam conducted combat operations to unify Vietnam. The conflict itself divided the American people and gave American allies a reason to question the resolve of the United States regarding its support of international and mutual defense treaties.

The administration of President Richard Nixon (1969–1974) worked to end the Vietnam Conflict. Despite massive support in materials and personnel from the United States, South Vietnam fell to the Communist North in 1975. The Vietnam Conflict greatly impacted the US national security functions. At its end, the military capability of the United States was significantly reduced. Military equipment was battle worn, and military morale was at an all-time low. It would take more than a decade to repair the damage.

Even as America and the USSR faced each other in Europe, the struggle in the Middle East between Israel and its Arab neighbors drew both of the superpowers further into Middle Eastern affairs. The Middle East was similar to Europe in that national alliances were divided between the United States and the Soviet Union. Israel, Iran, and Saudi Arabia were aligned with America, while Egypt, Syria, and Jordan sided with the USSR. Each superpower provided significant economic and military support to its allies. Perhaps the greatest issue facing the Middle East came with the formation of the state of Israel in 1948. Many Palestinian Arabs who were living within the boundaries of the newly formed state either fled or were displaced. Many settled in refugee camps throughout the Middle East, most notably in Jordan. The Palestinian cause brought together many Arab countries that immediately declared war against Israel. To the surprise of many, the small, fledgling state prevailed. To this day, the Israeli–Palestinian conflict remains a central issue in Middle Eastern politics. Since 1948, Israel has fought several wars against its Arab neighbors. To date, it has prevailed militarily, but many experts worry that, unless a solution is found, more wars will result; this is particularly worrisome, as some Middle Eastern countries appear interested in developing or obtaining nuclear weapons (e.g., Iran).

With the outbreak of each war between the Arab nations and Israel, the United States and the USSR were increasingly immersed in regional politics. Over the next 40 years, many incidents drew Soviet Union and the United States further into Middle Eastern affairs. Such events as the oil shortages of the early 1970s, the continued tension between Israel and its Arab neighbors, the USSR's invasion of Afghanistan in 1979, and America's involvement in Iraq, to name but a few, practically guarantee that the Middle East will remain a hot spot for US interests the coming years.

Détente

President Richard Nixon's national security adviser and secretary of state, Henry Kissinger, worked toward achieving détente with the USSR. Détente, or the lessening of tensions between the two superpowers, led to the reassessment of military spending and increased the sense and importance of national security for both nations. Because of the efforts of President Nixon and Secretary Kissinger, the United States and the USSR seriously commenced discussions pertaining to nuclear, biological, and chemical arms limitations. The Nixon administration also reached out to the other major powers and facilitated the American recognition of the People's Republic of China.[15] President Nixon's 1972 visit to China was a major step in formally normalizing relations between the two nations. Modern China has become a major trading partner with the United States and is in the process of becoming a global superpower.

Rollback

Eventually, a proactive strategy termed "rollback" was crafted to counter Communism. Breaking with the doctrine of "containment" that was established during the Truman administration, President Ronald Reagan's (1981–1989) foreign policy was based on John Foster Dulles's more offensive strategy from the 1950s. This mandated that the United States would actively push back or "roll back" the influence of the USSR.[27]

However, President Reagan's policy differed from that of Dulles in that it relied primarily on the overt support of those fighting Soviet dominance. This strategy was perhaps best encapsulated in the NSC's National Security Decision Directive 75. This 1983 directive stated that a central priority of the United States regarding its policy toward the USSR would be "to contain and over time reverse Soviet expansionism" particularly in the developing world.[16] An excerpt from the directive noted that

> The United States must rebuild the credibility of its commitment to resist Soviet encroachment on United States interests and those of its Allies and friends, and to support effectively those Third World states that are willing to resist Soviet pressures or oppose Soviet initiatives hostile to the United States, or are special targets of Soviet policy.[16]

Being mindful of this goal, the Reagan administration focused much of its efforts on supporting proxy armies to curtail Soviet influence. Among the more prominent examples of the Reagan Doctrine's application was one that occurred in Nicaragua, where the United States sponsored the Contra movement in an effort to force the leftist Sandinista government from power. Within Afghanistan, the United States provided material support to Afghan rebels, known as the Mujahedeen, to help them terminate the Soviet occupation of their country, which started in 1979.

Glasnost

By the 1980s, the efforts of President Reagan and Mikhail Gorbachev, general secretary of the Communist Party of the USSR (1985–1991), focused the diplomatic efforts of both nations on ending the Cold War (**Figure 2.6**). As a result of their collaboration, both nations worked to reduce tensions and open dialogue. These efforts resulted in more open, cooperative relationships between the two countries. Such openness reduced some of the tensions between the two superpowers.

Figure 2.6 *President Ronald Reagan and General Secretary Gorbachev signing the intermediate-range nuclear forces (INF) Treaty in the East Room of the White House, December 8, 1987. (Courtesy of the National Archives.)*

Within the USSR, Gorbachev introduced a policy of glasnost. This policy emphasized maximum publicity, openness, and transparency in the activities of all government institutions in conjunction with freedom of information. This openness, combined with the demands for increased freedoms across the Soviet sphere of international influence, proved contagious.

By the early 1990s, the Soviet economy could no longer support the USSR's bureaucracy. In an incredibly short period of time, the Soviet Union ceased to exist. In its place, independent countries such as Russia, the Ukraine, and Georgia emerged. The policy of glasnost raised expectations among the Russian people, some of whom believed that a democracy along the lines of the United States should be established. While that has not happened, the tensions between Russia and the United States have decreased significantly since the Cold War days. That does not mean, however, that the two countries are close friends. Just as in the Cold War days, Russian submarines armed with nuclear missiles patrol off the coast of the United States, just as American submarines patrol near Russian waters.

The complexity of the modern world

Today, we live in a complex world. The existential threat of nuclear annihilation has not disappeared, and we are faced with myriad other challenges, running the gamut from deadly pandemics, to climate change, to terrorism. New technologies have paved the way for nonstate actors to gain increasing clout in our increasingly connected world. Today, a single individual with computer savvy can wreak havoc on a scale that was once the domain of sophisticated militaries. The computer age is, in reality, a double-edged sword—while it brings with it the potential of great good, it also becomes a force multiplier for those who wish to do harm.

Although the modern world contains a variety of different threats, one would be naïve to assume that these same threats did not exist during the Cold War. Internationally, the United States experienced varying amounts of terrorism throughout the 1970s, 1980s, and 1990s. Up until the terrorist attacks of 9/11, however, a US citizen and army veteran carried out the largest terrorist attack on American soil, On April 19, 1995, Timothy McVeigh detonated a bomb outside the Murrah Federal Building in Oklahoma City; this attack claimed the lives of 168 Americans, including 19 children under the age of 6 (**Figure 2.7**).

Economic alliances and international collaborations also have the potential of challenging the United States and its allies. The combined economies of Brazil, Russia, India, and China (BRIC) are predicted to "double in the coming decade, eventually surpassing the size of the

Figure 2.7 *The bombed remains of automobiles with the bombed Murrah Federal Building in the background. (Courtesy of Staff Sergeant Preston Chasteen, Department of Defense.)*

economies of both the United States and the European Union."[17] The nation of South Africa joined this collective in 2011 (thereby necessitating the BRICS acronym).[17] In 2012, the economic potential of the BRICS nations was "ranked among the fastest-growing economies in the world," and their individual influences globally were observed to be increasing.[17] At the time of this authorship, the individual members of this alliance were struggling to determine some "common ground" through which they could "act as a unified geopolitical alliance."[17] Only time will determine the future cohesiveness and influence of the BRICS.

American society and the world are dependent upon fossil fuels for a variety of purposes. Petroleum is used to make gasoline as well as various plastics, and the United States is dependent upon a variety of foreign sources for much of its fossil fuel requirements. Given the changing dynamics of the Middle East and the forming of new governments following the Arab Spring* among various Middle Eastern nations, only time will determine the outcomes of US policies and relationships within the region.

---

* The Arab Spring was a movement of protests that commenced in 2010. It occurred among Arabic nations and resulted in changes of administration and leadership among several nations in the Middle East. Because new leaders and administrations came into power and assumed national controls, the effects of this movement are speculative regarding U.S. relationships in the Middle East.

The United States also experiences violence and much criminal activity along its border with Mexico. Organized crime entities routinely smuggle drugs and traffic humans across the border. The violence and dangerousness of the Mexican drug war affects the border region, and the corruption within the Mexican government is concerning. Some experts are concerned that Mexican violence will find its way into the United States. While this has not happened to any great extent at present, it may only be a matter of time before cartel violence relocates north.

These are but a few of the challenges presently confronting the United States. To be sure, during the Cold War, the United States faced an adversary that could threaten its very existence. However, America understood the threat posed by the Soviets. Modern times are not so black and white. Today's threats are complex and varied; no single approach is universally appropriate for handling all of the events that could negatively impact American society. Therefore, the United States must remain vigilant to protect itself from the dangerousness of many different threats arising from both known and unknown origins.

After the Cold War and the emerging of a new world

At the end of the Cold War, America's military and intelligence establishments were configured to confront an adversary that possessed a large and sophisticated military. Terrorist and criminal groups, while they existed, were seen as secondary threats to Communism. Within the United States, every governmental agency was positioned and structured to respond to a large, hierarchical enemy whose characteristics could be easily identified. "Homeland security" was primarily defined as security against the Soviets. Reconceptualizing this paradigm was difficult.

Because of changing threats, approaches to homeland security and national defense had to be reevaluated. Advancements in the areas of technology, information, communications, transportation, and international business changed the nature of the world and increased globalization. It was now difficult, if not impossible, for any nation to withdraw from the world community. The end of the Cold War found the United States as the last standing superpower. However, other nations would soon position themselves to challenge that status.

The United States further increased its international engagements after the Cold War. Support for traditional allies, such as Israel and South Korea; the "War on Drugs"; the threats of transnational crime; and both domestic and international terrorism received increased attentiveness from policy makers. Although international terrorism, specifically directed toward the United States, had been quite limited during the Cold War, several US allies, such as Britain and Israel, were engaged in a struggle with terrorists and terrorist organizations. International terrorists were evolving, increasing their recruitment efforts, and refining their tactics. Events during the final days of the Soviet Union, including aircraft hijackings, bombings, and kidnappings, focused primarily on Middle Eastern political issues. These events helped terrorists to refine their tactics and strategies.

Terrorism: The new threat to the United States

During the decade between 1980 and 1990, American international interests were increasingly affected by international terrorism. This decade was a precursor to the heinous events that affected and changed modern American lifestyles and worldviews with the attacks of September 11, 2001.

In August 1981, the Red Army Faction, a German ultraleftist terrorist group, exploded a bomb at the United States Air Force base in Ramstein, West Germany. In December 1981, three

American nuns and one lay missionary were murdered outside San Salvador, El Salvador. On the evening of December 17, 1981, United States Army Brigadier General James L. Dozier, a senior American official, present at a NATO headquarters facility in Verona, Italy, was abducted by Red Brigades terrorists.

Each of the three groups had a somewhat different motivation for their attacks, but each shared something in common—they sought to communicate a message through violence; that, in essence, is the power of terrorism.

Unlike previous terrorist activities in Italy, which had targeted senior Italian politicians, industrialists, jurists, newspaper publishers, and police officials, the kidnapping of General Dozier signaled that important foreign nationals were no longer immune from terrorists.[25] The Red Brigades held General Dozier until a team of Nucleo Operativo Centrale di Sicurezza (NOCS [*Central Security Operations Service*], a special operations unit of the Italian police) successfully implemented rescue operations and captured the terrorists.

In the 1980s, terrorist bombings became common. In April 1983, the Islamic Jihad claimed responsibility for the bombing of the United States embassy in Beirut (**Figure 2.8**). This event killed 63 people, including the Middle East director of the CIA. This attack also injured 120 individuals. In 1983, in El Salvador, the Farabundo Marti National Liberation Front (FMLN) assassinated a United States naval officer. Later in 1983, another naval officer was killed in Athens, Greece. The 1983 terrorist attacks on the Marine barracks in Beirut, Lebanon, killed 241 American service members and sent shockwaves through the marine community. The terrorist organization claiming responsibility was the Islamic Jihad later known as Hezbollah.

In early 1984, in Beirut, the Islamic Jihad kidnapped and murdered CIA Political Officer William Buckley. In 1984, 18 US servicemen were killed, and 83 people were injured during a bomb attack on a restaurant near a United States air base in Torrejon, Spain. The responsibility for this attack was claimed by Hezbollah.[18]

In February 1985, Mexican narco-trafficker Rafael Caro Quintero ordered the kidnapping, torture, and murder of Drug Enforcement Administration Special Agent Enrique Camarena

Figure 2.8 Rescue and clean-up crews search for casualties following the barracks bombing in Beirut on October 23, 1983. Suicide truck bombers attacked the Marine barracks, killing 241 American soldiers. (Courtesy of Randy Gaddo, Department of Defense.)

Salazar and his pilot, Alfredo Zavala. In 1985 Caro was arrested in Costa Rica, and extradited to Mexico to stand trial for the murders. He was convicted and sentenced to 40 years in prison.

In June 1985, US Navy diver Robert Dean Stethem was murdered by terrorists during the hijacking of the commercial airliner TWA Flight 847. The terrorists hijacked the aircraft, with 153 passengers, in Athens, Greece. They forced the pilot to fly twice to Algiers and twice to Beirut during the 17-day siege.[18] Recognizing Stethem as a member of the US military, they beat and tortured him before his murder. After the murder of Stethem, the hostages aboard the aircraft were released after Israel released 435 Lebanese and Palestinian prisoners. In June 1985, members of the FMLN fired on a restaurant in the Zona Rosa district of San Salvador. Four US Marines, who were assigned to the United States embassy security detachment, and nine Salvadoran civilians were killed during this attack.

On October 7, 1985, Leon Klinghoffer, an American tourist aboard the Achille Lauro cruise ship, was captured by Palestinian terrorists who seized the cruise ship. Once identified as an American, Klinghoffer was murdered and thrown overboard.[23]

The violence of terrorism continued during the remainder of the 1980s. In 1986, two US soldiers were killed, and 79 American servicemen were injured in a Libyan bomb attack on a nightclub in West Berlin, West Germany. This attack was launched in retaliation to the United States' attack in and around Tripoli and Benghazi, Libya. In 1987, 16 US servicemen, who were riding in a Greek Air Force bus near Athens, were injured in a bombing attack that was perpetrated by the revolutionary organization known as November 17.

One of the most gruesome attacks of the decade occurred on December 21, 1988, when a civilian airliner, Pan Am Flight 103 (**Figure 2.9**), exploded over Lockerbie, Scotland. This attack killed all 259 people onboard as well as 11 on the ground. While the flight contained passengers from 21 countries, a total of 189 were Americans. Through painstaking forensic investigation, it was determined that the attack was linked to Libya. Eventually, a Libyan intelligence agent, Abdelbaset al-Megrahi, was convicted of the crime; he was released from Greenock prison by the Scottish government and returned to Libya in 2009.

During the decade prior to the Soviet Union's collapse, the impact of terrorism upon the United States increased. The support of terrorism was initially linked to states, which were thought to sponsor activities such as the Libyan bombing of Pan Am 103, and the Soviet

Figure 2.9 *The remains of the flight deck of Pan Am 103 on a field in Lockerbie, Scotland.*

support of many leftist terrorist groups, like the Red Brigades. However, with the demise of the USSR, terrorists no longer found automatic safe havens or refuge behind the Iron Curtain.

Desert Shield and Desert Storm

In 1990, the country of Iraq invaded its neighbor, Kuwait. Under President George H. W. Bush (1989–1993), an American-led coalition was formed to force Iraq out of Kuwait and to reestablish its sovereignty. The conflict itself was short, but the major regional presence of the United States continued after the war was over. The US presence in Saudi Arabia and elsewhere in the Middle East was seen by some as an attempt by America to extend its influence throughout the region. All of this played out against a history of western involvement in Middle Eastern affairs that led many in the Arab world to believe that the United States was their enemy. For example, the establishment of the state of Israel in 1948 by the UN, which had great US support, was met with fierce Arab resistance; to this day, the issue of a Palestinian homeland has not been resolved. As well, the United States supported unpopular dictators in the Middle East, such as the Shah of Iran, who was installed in a CIA-engineered coup in 1953.

After the Soviets withdrew from Afghanistan in 1989, remnants of the Mujahedeen re-formed into a group that became known as al Qaeda, Arabic for "the base." One of its leaders was Osama bin Laden, the son of a wealthy Saudi Arabian construction company owner. Bin Laden had become a follower of a radical version of Islam while a college student. Blessed with superior organizational skills, he formed al Qaeda around this radical version of Islam. With the Soviet Union in ruins, bin Laden turned his sights on a new enemy: the United States. Between 1993 and 2001, during the aftermath of the liberation of Kuwait, the United States became the target of increased international terrorists' attacks. In 1993, the World Trade Center, located within the city of New York, was attacked for the first time. In 1998, al Qaeda carried out a series of attacks on various US embassies, which claimed over 200 lives. In October 2000, the navy destroyer *USS Cole* was attacked by suicide bombers while in the Yemeni Port of Aden, resulting in the death of 17 sailors (**Figure 2.10**). Each of these attacks signaled a new type of conflict that was quickly engaging the United States. However, unlike previous enemies, the characteristics of this new conflict were based upon global terrorism and a faceless enemy. For

Figure 2.10 *Damage inflicted against the USS Cole. (Courtesy of the Department of Defense.)*

the American military, intelligence, law enforcement and diplomatic services, this was a new type of conflict that presented new challenges.

The shock and impact of 9/11

Despite the fact that America had been in the crosshairs of terrorists for several years, most citizens of the United States felt secure within their national borders. The activities of terrorism remained largely unnoticed by the American populace. However, the State Department, the IC, and the Pentagon were observing these events with great interest and concern. Finally, on September 11, 2001, the American homeland was attacked in an unprecedented manner. Four commercial aircraft were hijacked and used as weapons targeting the World Trade Center in New York and the Pentagon in Washington, DC (**Figure 2.11**). These suicide attacks changed the rules of international terrorism. In short order, these events placed the United States and its allies on a war footing. Including the 19 hijackers, approximately 3000 people died or were missing and presumed dead as a result of the attacks. The overwhelming majority of casualties were civilians, including nationals from over 90 different countries. Because of these attacks, the vision of homeland security dramatically changed. The United States and its allies now faced a new type of threat, new tactics, and a new enemy. This threat was not linked to a specific country but, rather, to a transnational movement. In the ensuing years, American allies such as the United Kingdom, Spain, Germany, and Turkey were also attacked

This threat of terrorism presented new challenges from nonstate actors for the United States and its allies. Historically, the United States dealt with threats that were sponsored by nation–states. It soon became clear that this nonstate threat, with its lack of clear targets, structured organizations, and lines of battle, would be extremely difficult to combat.

Global war on terrorism

The attacks of September 11, 2001, revealed a divergence between military and defense philosophies. Previously, the military responded commensurately to the challenges of the Cold

Figure 2.11 New York, New York, September 25, 2001: A firefighter surveys the remaining shell and tons of debris of the World Trade Center. (Courtesy of Mike Rieger/Federal Emergency Management Agency [FEMA] News.)

War. However, the new threat of terrorism necessitated an expansion of established capabilities, such as special operations and civil affairs, and the creation of new capabilities, such as cyber warfare.[19] In the ensuing years, America and her allies have conducted major military operations in Afghanistan, Iraq, and the Horn of Africa. These operations reflected new approaches to waging war, where conventional forces, such as airpower, special operations forces, and intelligence units, are combined with law enforcement, Justice and State Department assets, and nonmilitary resources.

Role of the military in support of Homeland Security

With the heightened concern about large-scale terrorism have come efforts to involve the Department of Defense (DOD) more closely with federal, state, and local agencies in their homeland security activities. The DOD, with its active-duty and reserve forces, and the potential of federalizing National Guard units, has the largest and most diversified personnel assets in the federal government. As was demonstrated in the months after the September 2001 terrorist attacks, they can be used in a variety of security and emergency response roles. The DOD remains the greatest federal repository of resources for responding to a chemical, biological, radiological, or nuclear (CBRN) incident.

In response to Hurricane Katrina and Super Storm Sandy, DOD resources quickly deployed both active-duty and National Guard units to the area impacted and performed a wide range of mission-essential activities, including military support to civilian authorities engaged in response and recovery operations, search, rescue, and evacuation; medical and health operations; and security and emergency reestablishment of critical infrastructure.

State National Guard organizations are well positioned to represent the DOD to local emergency planners and responders. They are known in their communities and in 25 states; the state adjutant general is the state emergency management director. The National Guard has both a federal and a state mission. Its federal mission is to provide forces to the army and air force. Its state mission is to "provide trained and disciplined forces for domestic emergencies or as otherwise required by state laws."[20]

In the report of the Defense Science Board 2003 Summer Study on DOD Roles and Missions in Homeland Security, the DOD examined the potential roles and missions of the department in support of homeland security operations. This study advanced major findings and recommendations:

- In the area of information, the study recommended that new tools and capabilities be developed to enhance information collection, analysis, and sharing. This recommendation also identified the need for improved collection and integration of foreign and domestic intelligence.
- Improve the integration of cyber security and the protection of cyber-based critical infrastructure into the DOD mission.
- The DOD improves its capability against low-level airborne threats such as cruise missiles and low-flying aircraft.
- Retain the capability to surge medical assistance to aid in support of homeland security relief operations.
- Work with other law enforcement and homeland security agencies to enhance their capabilities to include training and operational planning and support those operations when needed.[20]

It is anticipated that the DOD will remain an important partner in the protection of the nation and its infrastructure well into the future.

Emerging threats

Internationally, the United States is fully engaged in the world community—economically, politically, and socially. With a stated goal of enhancing the spread of democracy and freedom, the global US presence provides potential aggressors with a wide range of potential targets. The United States will always face a wide variety of domestic and international threats. The top emerging threats, acknowledged by contemporary national security experts, are categorized as follows: (1) WMDs, including nuclear, biological, chemical, and conventional explosives that can inflict great damage; (2) terrorism, domestic and foreign; (3) narcotics trafficking and narco-terrorism, including the violence in Mexico; (4) transnational crime; (5) global conflicts and regional stability as seen in Bosnia, Kosovo, Russia, the Middle East, the Persian Gulf, South Asia, North Korea, Iran, Iraq, and the Aegean Sea; (6) the transitions occurring in Russia and China; and (7) information warfare or "netwar," including cyber warfare and cyber terrorism.[21]

Most experts believe that the greatest current threat challenging the United States is international terrorism. Terrorism becomes a tactic of choice when its potential to achieve political aims outweighs the cost of its use. Terrorism, by nature, is irregular and relatively inexpensive to perpetrate; it is a tactic employed by the weak against the strong. Like proxy wars, it can also be used by superpowers who wish to avoid direct conflict. For example, during the Cold War, the USSR sponsored both terrorist and separatist groups.[4] Currently, al Qaeda and other terror groups engage the United States in the Global War on Terror.

Homeland Defense and a new type of warfare

Few would argue that the nature of war and warfare is in a constant state of change. For the United States and its allies in the struggle against terrorism, the enemy is no longer only a state-sponsored adversary, whose military forces are organized and employed on the field of battle. This notion necessitates a consideration of the chronological dynamics of war. After the events of September 11, 2001, a new term was familiarized within American society: the "long war." The long war represents the notion that United States engagements are no longer limited to weeks, months, or a few years but may span decades (or generations). This term was used by General John Abizaid to communicate and emphasize the notion of the "judgment within the high command of the United States military that it will be engaged against terrorists and extremists for a very long time to come."[22]

The United States is now engaged with an asymmetric enemy that employs forces and tactics that are significantly different than the forces and tactics of conventional powers. Enemies, by adopting an asymmetric approach to warfare, can engage United States forces across the spectrum of political, economic, social, and military activities. Attacks against nonmilitary targets and rapid strikes against military forces are standard among enemy forces. For the United States and its allies, military forces, equipment, and tactics are constantly evolving to respond to the tactics demonstrated by the enemy. During major wars, the organized forces of two peer states seek a decisive battle outcome. Within small wars, the forces of a major power will often clash with irregular forces, and the conflict typically degenerates into guerrilla warfare or terrorism. When this event occurs, irregular troops may disregard, in part or entirely, international law and the Rules of Land Warfare when conducting hostilities.

Conclusion

Although it takes more than military strength to protect a nation's homeland, a sturdy and resilient military is an essential element. During its early years, the United States only possessed a small army with no significant navy. Because of this problem, the Revenue Marine Service was established in 1790, eventually becoming the coast guard. Because of the success of the Revenue Marine Service, Congress eventually authorized the formation of the United States Navy. During most of the 19th century, with the exception of the Civil War, the US military remained small in size and received poor funding. However, as the United States expanded its borders across the continent, it faced more enemies and international involvement.

President James Monroe established the first policy that warned Europe against meddling in US affairs and the affairs of the newly formed Latin American nations. This edict was known as the Monroe Doctrine, and it defined the relationship between Europe and America. President Theodore Roosevelt, who assumed the presidency after the assassination of President William McKinley, strongly backed the Monroe Doctrine and believed that it was the fiduciary duty and obligation of the United States to protect the Americas. He expanded the basic premise of the doctrine through the establishment of the Roosevelt Corollary of December 1904. The corollary rationalized unilateral US intervention in Latin America when necessary, and it mandated US intervention to ensure that other nations in the Western Hemisphere fulfilled their economic obligations. Foreign nations were disallowed from violating US rights, and the corollary dissuaded foreign aggression or onslaught. As time passed, the influence of the United States in the world increased, and it increasingly used diplomatic and military force to influence or shape policies among various countries throughout the world.

During the early 20th century, as the First World War spread across Europe, the United States was lured away from isolationism. At this time, the US Navy was strong, but the US Army was nothing more than a third-rate power. Although the United States was involved in World War I for fewer than 2 years, its participation integrated it among the affairs of Europe and the international arena. World War I also changed the way in which wars were fought and made battlefields much deadlier places. Many national borders were reshaped, and changes in forms of government occurred for some countries.

After World War I, President Woodrow Wilson proposed a collective organization of nations in the hope that future international conflicts could be avoided. Because of the efforts of President Wilson, the League of Nations was formed at the end of World War I under the Treaty of Versailles. It promoted Wilson's vision of unison and harmony among various nations throughout the world. However, the United States did not join the League of Nations because the US Senate voted against membership. The League of Nations was eventually dissolved in 1946 and replaced by the UN.

By the late 1930s, the United States was in the midst of the Great Depression, which continued until World War II. The 1941 attack on Pearl Harbor catapulted the United States into a war in which intelligence assumed a significant role. President Franklin Roosevelt authorized the establishment of the OSS, the precursor of the CIA. Directed by William "Wild Bill" Donavan, the OSS conducted operations such as assisting underground movements in Europe, gathering intelligence, and landing commando teams in Borneo.

World War II devastated Europe and Japan. Both the United States and the USSR emerged as superpowers. Two distinct philosophies of government, capitalism and Communism, underscored the adversarial philosophies and competitiveness between these nations. The struggles and differences between these two countries eventually instigated the Cold War, which lasted for 50 years and spanned six phases: containment, MAD, small wars and the domino theory, détente, rollback, and glasnost. During this time, both superpowers became involved in the Vietnam War and Middle Eastern conflicts. After the Soviet Union dissolved in the early 1990s, the United States became the only remaining superpower.

Since the 1970s, the United States has been targeted by international terrorism. Some examples include the kidnapping of Brigadier General James L. Dozier, the murder of 18 servicemen in Spain, the murder of Robert Dean Stethem, the murder of Leon Klinghoffer, and the downing of Pan Am Flight 103. Each attack moved the nation closer toward the Global War on Terror. In 1990, the Iraqi invasion of Kuwait integrated the United States further among the affairs of the Middle East. A radical response, from potential adversaries who wanted the United States and its influence out of the Middle East, was facilitated in conjunction with the US presence.

In 1993, the World Trade Center in New York was attacked for the first time. This attack caused extensive damage. Later, in 1998, a series of attacks against various US embassies in Africa claimed over 200 lives. During the month of October, 2000, the *USS Cole* was attacked by suicide bombers while in the Yemeni Port of Aden; 17 sailors were killed. On September 11, 2001, four commercial aircraft were hijacked and used as weapons against the World Trade Center in New York and the Pentagon in Washington, DC; the fourth airplane crashed in a field in Pennsylvania. These suicide attacks changed the rules of international terrorism and placed the United States and its allies on a war footing. Because of these attacks, international terrorism became recognized as a major threat to international peace and security. The United States and its allies commenced the Global War on Terrorism.

Since that time, the United States perspectives on the nature of war and warfare have changed. The United States is currently engaged with an enemy who is employing forces and tactics that differ significantly from those employed by America and its allies.

Four interests are vital to US national security and survival: survival and security, political and territorial integrity, economic stability and well-being, and national stability. Due to the current nature of the threats we face, the very notion of war, warfare, and response has changed in the United States. The enemy is no longer only a state-sponsored adversary, whose military forces are organized and employed on the field of battle. The principles of asymmetric warfare and the notion of a long war now characterize the new global threat, combined with other new and existing threats, such as cyber warfare, transnational crime, pandemics, earthquakes, and a whole host of other man-made and natural disasters, which will likely remain with us well into the 21st century.

Key terms

Cold War
Complexity
Containment
Desert Shield
Desert Storm
Détente

Domino theory
Emerging threats
Glasnost
Iron Curtain
Korean War
League of Nations
Low-level conflict
Murrah Building
Mutually assured destruction
Proxy War
Rollback
Strategy
Tactic
Terrorism
United Nations
USS Cole
Vietnam War
World War I
World War II

QUESTIONS FOR DISCUSSION

1. Enemies and threats against the United States were quantifiable during the Cold War. In essence, we were capable of conceptualizing, understanding, and forming strong mental models of nation–states that endangered America. Given the complexities of the modern world and the cessation of the Cold War, do you believe that conceptualizing, understanding, and forming mental models of threatening entities is more difficult during modern times? Write a brief essay that summarizes your opinion.

2. Some may consider the attack against the *USS Cole* as an act of war. Looking back through history, do you believe that the response of the United States was appropriate when its naval vessel was attacked? Why or why not? Write a brief essay that expresses and substantiates your opinion.

3. This chapter introduced various historical perspectives of national security throughout numerous presidential administrations. Given the current policies of national security, do you believe that the homeland is safer or less safe than in previous years? Why or why not? Write a brief essay that expresses and substantiates your opinion.

4. Threats against the United States may originate from any point globally. Do some research concerning current events, and formulate an opinion of what you believe are emerging threats. Write a brief essay that expresses and substantiates your opinion.

References

1. Central Intelligence Agency. (2013). The world factbook. https://www.cia.gov/library/publications/the-world-factbook/geos/us.html (accessed February 8, 2013).
2. U.S. Marine Corps. (2007). *U.S. Marine Corps Strategy*. New York: Cosimo. http://books.google.com/books?id=gJ6fvI4t78YC&pg=PA38&lpg=PA38&dq=survival+and+security;+political+and+territorial+integrity;+economic+stability+and+wellbeing;+and+national+stability.+%22vital+interests%22&source=bl&ots=mICUEAkkAd&sig=R1mfh5DM5MbnQM1qqXY8q9AfKmg&hl=en&sa=X&ei=5GEUUf2mFoie9QSBhYGg

BQ&ved=0CE8Q6AEwBg#v=onepage&q=survival%20and%20security%3B%20political%20and%20territorial%20integrity%3B%20economic%20stability%20and%20wellbeing%3B%20and%20national%20stability.%20%22vital%20interests%22&f=false (accessed February 8, 2013), p. 38.

3. United States Marine Corps. (1997). MCDP 1-1: Strategy. http://www.clausewitz.com/CWZHOME/Bibl/mcdp1_1.pdf (accessed July 28, 2008).

4. Rubin, M. (May 31, 2007). Asymmetrical threat concept and its reflections on international security. http://www.aei.org/docLib/20070502_AsymmetricalThreatConcept.pdf (accessed July 29, 2008).

5. BBC News. (September 2, 1999). Hitler's war. http://news.bbc.co.uk/1/low/special_report/1999/08/99/world_war_ii/430918.stm (accessed August 4, 2008).

6. Roosevelt Corollary to the Monroe Doctrine. (1904). MileStones: 1899–1913. *United States Department of State, Office of the Historian.* http://history.state.gov/milestones/1899-1913/RooseveltandMonroeDoctrine (accessed March 21, 2013).

7. Princeton University Library. (2003). The League of Nations: A primer for documents research. http://www.princeton.edu/~sbwhite/un/leagwebb.html (accessed July 24, 2008).

8. The League of Nations. (1920). Milestones: 1914–1920. *United States Department of State Office of the Historian.* http://history.state.gov/milestones/1914-1920/League (accessed April 29, 2013).

9. Keylor, W.R. (1992). *The Twentieth Century World: An International History* (2nd ed.). New York: Oxford University Press.

10. Eichengreen, B. (1992). The marshall plan: Economic effects and implications for Eastern Europe and the former Soviet Union. *Economic Policy, 7,* 14–75.

11. Donovan, W.J. (2013). *National Park Service.* http://www.nps.gov/prwi/historyculture/donovan.htm (accessed April 29, 2013).

12. United Nations. (2005). History of the United Nations. http://www.un.org/aboutun/unhistory/ (accessed August 6, 2008).

13. Tusa, A. (1997). *The Last Division: A History of Berlin.* New York: Basic Books.

14. Tanenhaus, S. (March 23, 2003). The world from Vietnam to Iraq: The rise and fall and the rise of the Domino theory. http://query.nytimes.com/gst/fullpage.html?res=9B05EEDF1630F930A15750C0A9659C8B63&sec=&spon=&pagewanted=all (accessed August 1, 2008).

15. United States Department of State. (n.d.). Ending the Vietnam War, 1973–1975. http://www.state.gov/r/pa/ho/time/dr/ (accessed August 2, 2008).

16. Reagan, R. (1983). National Security Decision Directive 75: U.S. relations with the U.S.S.R. http://www.fas.org/irp/offdocs/nsdd/nsdd-075.htm (accessed August 5, 2008).

17. BRICS Group. (2012). *The New York Times.* http://topics.nytimes.com/topics/reference/timestopics/organizations/b/bric_group/index.html (accessed February 7, 2013).

18. United States Department of State. (n.d.). Significant terrorist incidents. http://www.state.gov/r/pa/ho/pubs/fs/5902.htm (accessed August 2, 2008).

19. Barnett, T. (2004). *The Pentagon's New Map: War and Peace in the Twenty-First Century.* New York: G.P. Putnam's.

20. Report of the Defense Science Board 2003 Summer Study on DoD Roles and Missions in Homeland Security, United States Department of Defense. (2003). http://www.fas.org/irp/agency/dod/dsb/homelandv2.pdf (accessed January 23, 2013).

21. Garcia, M.L. (1997). Overview of emerging threats to the United States. http://engr.nmsu.edu/~etti/fall97/security/mlgarcia.html (accessed August 5, 2008).

22. Cooke, J. (2007). *Reporting the War: Freedom of the Press from the American Revolution to the War on Terrorism.* New York: Palgrave MacMillan Publishing, p. 243.

23. Rosen, G. (2005). *The Right War?: The Conservative Debate on Iraq.* New York: Cambridge University Press, pp. 108–109.

24. Nations of the World: The United Nations. (2004). *New York Times.* http://topics.nytimes.com/top/reference/timestopics/organizations/u/united_nations/index.html?inline=nyt-org (accessed August 1, 2008).

25. Phillipps, T. (2002). The Dozier Kidnapping: Confronting the Red Brigades. *Air and Space Power Journal,* http://www.airpower.maxwell.af.mil/airchronicles/cc/phillips.html (accessed August 25, 2013).

26. Soviet News. (1955). The Warsaw Pact, 1955. http://www.fordham.edu/halsall/mod/1955warsawpact.html (accessed July 28, 2008).

27. United States Department of State. (n.d.). Reagan Doctrine, 1985. http://www.state.gov/r/pa/ho/time/rd/17741.htm (accessed August 5, 2008).

3

Foundations of Emergency Management

Sometimes it's not about trying to correct the wrong thing; but rather, it's about trying to get through the wrong thing the correct way.

Jeffrey M. Van Slyke

Chapter objectives:

- Define the terminology of emergency management
- Identify principles of emergency management
- Discuss the four phases of emergency management

Introduction

On a daily basis, the United States of America, and the entire world, in general, is faced with the reality and responsibility of managing hazards, emergencies, and disasters. This chapter highlights the importance of effective emergency management.

Specifically, this chapter defines significant terms and phrases of emergency management; discusses the importance of emergency management; describes the comprehensive emergency management (CEM) concepts of hazard mitigation, disaster preparedness, emergency response, and disaster recovery; includes a brief description of the present emergency management system; and concludes with identifying effective principles of emergency management that are meant to provide fundamental best practices during an event.

Several recent natural and man-made disasters will be mentioned in this chapter along with the associated loss of life and economic cost of each. A succinct case will be made in this chapter to demonstrate that effective emergency management, utilizing the framework mapped out in later chapters, can and will reduce the lives lost and dollars spent during future such emergencies.

Definition of emergency management

Over the years, the concepts and terminology of emergency management have seemingly evolved and continue to be a work in progress based upon efforts to survive, cope, and deal with conditions and circumstances that affect the general safety and welfare of humanity. Invariably, significant events engineered by nature or mankind continue to frequent the world we live in, which result in devastating consequences including loss of life or serious injury, as well as damage and disruption to communities. Such consistently recurring incidents have served as the impetus for creating the discipline and profession commonly known as *emergency management.*

To truly understand what emergency management is, it is helpful to first break down and understand the individual meanings of *emergency* and *management.* According to the Merriam-Webster dictionary, *emergency* is defined as (1) "an unforeseen combination of circumstances or the resulting state that calls for immediate action" and (2) "an urgent need for assistance or relief."[1] According to the Merriam-Webster dictionary, *management* is defined as (1) "the act or art of managing; the conducting or supervising of something"; (2) "judicious use of means to accomplish an end"; and (3) the collective body of those who manage or direct an enterprise."[2]

While one can seemingly understand the simplistic literary explanation of *emergency management*, with respect to a practitioner-based explanation, there have been a numerous characterizations of this subject matter. Over the years, and as a result of numerous disasters, emergencies, and critical incidents, the term *emergency management* has become a profoundly interchangeable moniker. The following are examples of how the definition of emergency management has evolved over the past several decades:

1. Emergency management (1995): "Organized analysis, planning, decision-making, and assignment of available resources to mitigate (lessen the effect of or prevent) prepare for, respond to, and recover from the effects of all hazards. The goal of emergency management is to save lives, prevent injuries, and protect property and the environment if an emergency occurs."[3]
2. Emergency management (1997): "The process by which the uncertainties that exist in potentially hazardous situations can be minimized and public safety maximized. The goal is to limit the costs of emergencies or disasters through the implementation of a series of strategies and tactics reflecting the full life cycle of disaster, i.e., preparedness, response, recovery, and mitigation."
3. Emergency management (2001): "The process through which America prepares for emergencies and disasters, responds to them, recovers from them, rebuilds, and mitigates their future effects."
4. Emergency management (2002): "The process through which the Nation prepares for emergencies and disasters, mitigates their effects, and responds to and recovers from them."[4]
5. Emergency management (2003): "Activities that include prevention, preparedness, response, recovery, rehabilitation, advocacy, and legislation, of emergencies irrespective of their type, size, and location, and whose purpose is reduction in death, disability, damage, and destruction."[5]
6. Emergency management (2006): "...the term 'emergency management' means the governmental function that coordinates and integrates all activities to build, sustain, and improve the capability to prepare for, protect against, respond to, recover from, or mitigate against threatened or actual natural disasters, acts of terrorism or other man-made disasters..."[6]

7. Emergency management (2007): "An ongoing process to prevent, mitigate, prepare for, respond to, and recover from an incident that threatens life, property, operations, or the environment."[7]
8. Emergency management (2007): "Emergency management is the managerial function charged with creating the framework within which communities reduce vulnerability to hazards and cope with disasters."[8]

The primary objective of emergency management is to sustain life, minimize damage to property, and maintain the safety and welfare of a community. Fundamentally, emergency management is a twofold comprehensive process. The first part necessitates knowing what to do, which involves the coordination of persons, procedures, and provisions that are essential for the prevention of, the preparation for, the response to, and the recovery from the effects of natural disasters, acts of terrorism, man-made hazards, disasters, emergencies, and critical incidents.

The second part requires doing what you know, which involves an inclusive collaboration among all key stakeholders, including the government, the private sector, the public, and the media. The collaboration aspect must be designed to identify functions, roles, and responsibilities and requires a commitment to promote the communication and trust components, which are essential to sustain the functional effectiveness of all service deliverables during a disaster event. Comfort and Cahill[9] acknowledge the essential nature of collaboration within the emergency management function: "In environments of high uncertainty, this quality of inter-personal trust is essential for collective action. Building that trust in a multi-organizational operating environment is a complex process, perhaps the most difficult task involved in creating an integrated emergency management system." The importance of collaboration is a critical dynamic of emergency management. In essence, collaboration involves the development of mutual cooperation within a community that creates the environment in which coordination can function effectively.

Disaster response

The United States has evolved from a group of European colonies into an international superpower. Over the centuries, the growth of the United States has been an incredible testament to the benefits of democracy; modern America is a nation whose boundaries have extended beyond the continental coastlines, with highly populated cities and a well-developed national infrastructure. Although the United States has focused primarily on international terrorism as the major threat facing the nation during the last decade, there exists a much broader range of threats. This "all-hazards" approach is based upon a progressive process of risk assessment and vulnerability awareness.

For much of the history of the nation, the major threats have been natural events. Over the last three centuries, storms, earthquakes, floods, tornadoes, and fires have impacted many US cities. The damage inflicted by many of these "disasters" has been significant, but the it has been relatively localized. For the most part, recovery was carried out by state and local resources.

During the early history of the nation, the national government had limited abilities to respond to such events; nevertheless, efforts were made to ensure that the national government had a formal responsibility during disaster response. The beginning of federal disaster relief originated with the Congressional Act of 1803. This act was passed following a devastating fire in Portsmouth, New Hampshire. The Congressional Act of 1803 can be viewed as a precursor to

Figure 3.1 *Ruins of San Francisco 1906 earthquake and fire. (Courtesy of the Library of Congress.)*

the modern Federal Emergency Management Agency (FEMA). From 1803 onward, the United States experienced many events that overwhelmed the response capability of local government. The Chicago fire of 1871, which devastated much of the city; the various yellow fever epidemics of the 1870s; the Jamestown Flood in 1889; the 1900 Galveston, Texas, hurricane; the San Francisco earthquake of 1906 (**Figure 3.1**); and the 1918 Spanish influenza epidemic are examples of several of the major events that created casualties and property damage far in excess of the local community's ability to respond without external assistance.

Foundations of civil defense and emergency management

Since independence, the United States has been in a constant state of evolution. Born in the flames of conflict, the nation has faced international and domestic security threats throughout its history. During the first century and a half of the nation's existence, the United States was not a major power. During this period, European nations competed to create global empires. Britain controlled the seas. The United States experienced several small conflicts including the War of 1812, the Mexican War of the 1840s, the War Between the States, and the Spanish–American War. Over this time, the United States expanded its boundaries, reaching from ocean to ocean. The nation increased international trade and created a small navy and army to protect American interests abroad.

The protection of the nation and its interests has always remained one of the primary responsibilities of the national government. The Monroe Doctrine of 1823 informed the European powers that the United States assumed a responsibility for the Western Hemisphere, although the nation had little ability to actually enforce its intent. The nation continued its expansion. Alaska was purchased from Russia in 1867; Hawaii became a United States possession in 1898, and the nation gained control of areas including Cuba, Puerto Rico, and the Philippines as a result of the Spanish–American War. The United States was now an imperialistic power and on the threshold of international importance.

United States presidents were historically content to avoid international entanglements or push the nation onto the world stage, although enforcement of federal laws related to customs and the border became an increasing concern. In 1853, the United States Customs Border

Patrol was established when the secretary of the treasury authorized the collector of customs to hire customs mounted inspectors for patrol duty along the borders of the nation.

The border shared with Mexico had traditionally been an area of unrest. One of the driving forces behind the formation of the Texas Rangers were issues related to the border and border security. Border concerns led to many states passing their own border protection and immigration legislation. As a result, an 1875 United States Supreme Court decision ruled that creation and enforcement of immigration regulations was a federal responsibility. In 1882, the Chinese Exclusion Act and Immigration Act targeted immigration issues, putting increased emphasis upon enforcement.

By the end of the 19th century, the border-related issues had become so significant that, in 1915, the United States authorized the Bureau of Immigration to deploy mounted guards along the United States border. Border security concerns became so great that United States military forces were deployed to the Mexican border from 1916 to 1917. In 1924, Congress provided for the creation of the United States Border Patrol.

As the 20th century dawned, the vast majority of European and Asian powers were governed by some form of monarchy. The assassination of President McKinley, by the anarchist Leon Czolgosz, in 1901, led to the presidency of Theodore Roosevelt. Roosevelt, a former New York City Police commissioner, visualized the United States as an emerging world power, not only with international possessions but also with a growing global responsibility.

In 1941, with World War II unfolding in Europe and Asia, the Office of Civilian Defense (**Figure 3.2**) was established within the Office for Emergency Management to assure effective coordination of federal relations with state and local governments engaged in furtherance of

Figure 3.2 1941 civil defense poster. (Courtesy of the Library of Congress.)

war programs; to provide for necessary cooperation with state and local governments with respect to measures for adequate protection of the civilian population in war emergencies; and to facilitate participation by all persons in war programs. New York mayor Fiorello La Guardia was named as director, serving on a volunteer basis without compensation.

In August 1941, *The United States Citizens Defense Corps* was published. It gave the first complete and coordinated plan for local organization of civilian defense and was the prototype for all following civil defense (CD) organizations. With the nation in World War II, the concern for the security of the continental United States increased. The civil defense program increased in popularity and scope. In 1942, the Office of Civil Defense conducted training for civil defense police volunteers in 46 cities with the support of J. Edgar Hoover and the Federal Bureau of Investigation.

The end of World War II found the United States as one of two remaining global superpowers. In 1945, the Office of Civilian Defense was disbanded, but soon, the new threats of the Cold War, including the fear of a nuclear attack, led to renewed discussion as to the need for local-level "civil defense." In 1950, President Harry Truman signed Executive Order 10186 creating the Federal Civil Defense Administration (FCDA) within the Office for Emergency Management, Executive Office of the President. This authorized the federal civil defense program, which would continue until 1994, when it was repealed by Public Law 93-337.

During this period, the world would be dominated by the United States and the Soviet Union, which maintained an uneasy peace in what was called the "Cold War." From the earliest days of the Cold War, preparedness focused upon events such as a nuclear attack from the Soviets. Bomb drills were conducted in schools, many Americans constructed bomb shelters, and it was very common to see buildings that had been designated "fallout" shelters. Feeding, evacuation, communications, and medical response plans were also developed to be implemented in the event of an attack.

When the Cold War ended, it was hoped that the world would become a safer place and that international threats would reduce, but that proved not to be the case. New threats would challenge the nation. With the 1994 repeal of the civil defense statute, parts were retained and incorporated into the Stafford Disaster Relief and Emergency Assistance Act, including the using the term *emergency preparedness* wherever the term *civil defense* previously appeared in the statutory language.

An emergency management program examines potential emergencies and disasters based on the risks posed by likely hazards; develops and implements programs aimed toward reducing the impact of these events on the community; prepares for those risks that cannot be eliminated; and prescribes the actions required to deal with the consequences of actual events and to recover from those events. Emergency management involves participants among all governmental levels and within the private sector. Activities are geared according to phases before, during, and after emergency events. The effectiveness of emergency management rests on a network of relationships among partners in the system.

Principles of emergency management

The profession of emergency management has become an inclusive triad of process, responsibility, and discipline. First, the process of emergency management can be found in the actual response, or "boots on the ground," to an emergency, disaster, or critical incident after it happens. For the most part, every incident or event is different and will result in a profound learning moment based upon mistakes that are made and/or achievements arrived at. Because every incident/event seemingly has a life of its own, this often requires different response and recovery approaches that were not documented in standard protocol, were unforeseen, or demanded immediate modification of "best practice."

Invariably, the process or "game plan" results in the often-used paradigm of "adapt, improvise, and overcome." The four Ds can serve as a basic foundation for the emergency management process: (1) discover—lessons learned, achievements, deficiencies, effectiveness; (2) determine—what needs to be done, necessary resources, relationships, readiness; (3) develop—mitigation, preparedness, operational response/recovery methods; and (4) deploy—when, where, setout, setup, step-up, stand-down. The ever-changing dynamics associated with an adverse event will continue to develop and influence the emergency management process to the extent that there will never be a panacea or one method fits all approach.

The responsibility of emergency management involves key stakeholders including local/state/federal government agencies, first responders, and organizational entities (community businesses, volunteers, etc.). For example, during the response and recovery phases, the leadership involved must take responsibility to ensure that the necessary provisions such as personnel and supplies are adequate to the extent that the frontline responders and the public can depend upon and trust those tasked with the readiness to react when needed. Emergency managers often have few resources under their immediate control, but do have access to an incredible amount of assistance from government, nongovernmental partners, and the private sector.

Specifically, the emergency manager must act responsibly by being able to engage with those partners, understand how these other agencies work in an effort to make the best use possible of those partner-agency resources during an emergency, and then demonstrate responsible leadership. In addition, communication is the responsibility of everyone involved prior to, during, or after an incident. The absence of, or deficiency in, communication may completely hinder the responsibility of those involved with the emergency management process, including the propensity to compromise the safety and welfare of the public, responders, property, or the environment.

The profession and practices of emergency management have continued to evolve as a valid discipline and necessary subject matter that has earned its rightful place in the national headlines as well as within the mind-set of the public. Emergency management has evolved into the discipline of ensuring that communities, businesses, and organizations are able to successfully endure through all aspects of an emergency or significant critical incident. Thus, the field of emergency management has become in itself a science that does more than just "deal with" extreme events. The discipline employs methods, means, and mind-set to ensure the protection of people, property, and the environment. This goal is accomplished through mitigation, prevention, response, and recovery.

The study of previous emergency responses—as in the case of Hurricane Katrina (**Figures 3.3a and b**) of August 2005 and other such events—can help to assess areas of improvement as well as the ability to determine the causation of disasters that, if possible, may enable opportunities for prevention in the future. As disasters become more numerous and begin to encompass people from all nationalities, socioeconomic levels, races, and geographic locations, the yielded knowledge from both the experiences of a disaster and the attempt to negotiate our way through such disasters will serve as the discipline to improve and develop the distinctive phases of emergency management.

Figure 3.3 *(a) Residents are bringing their belongings and lining up to get into the Superdome, which was opened as a hurricane shelter. (Courtesy of Marty Bahamonde/FEMA.) (b) Aerial view of a flooded New Orleans neighborhood with Lake Ponchatrain in the background. (Courtesy of Jocelyn Augustino/FEMA.)*

Four phases of emergency management

The most recognized benchmark for describing the four phases of emergency management is the terminology provided by the FEMA, which includes (1) mitigation, (2) preparedness, (3) response, and (4) recovery (**Figure 3.4**).

The emergency management cycle is a description of how people, in general, respond to a major disaster. Understanding the phases is the first step in planning out a detailed response plan for any major disaster. This process follows a predictable pattern, and understanding how each component affects the other is essential in developing a well-crafted response plan.

The interdependency of the functional activities of emergency management remains its most significant characteristic. For example, the value of mitigation and preparation should not be underestimated; they are extremely constructive aspects of the entire process.

Essentially, all communities fall into in one of the established phases. Mitigation includes measures taken to prevent or subdue the effects of a disaster (securing homes, buying insurance, building levees). Preparedness includes the establishment of education and training measures (planning evacuation routes, performing emergency drills, compiling a supply list). Response occurs after the disaster and maintains the safety of the public (search and rescue missions, disaster response teams). The recovery phase occurs while the affected area is getting back on its feet (reducing financial stress, rebuilding, taking measures to prevent the same devastating result from future disasters). The following are definitions of each phase of emergency management:

1. **Mitigation (prevention):** Involves taking proactive measures to prevent or reduce the possibility of disaster or emergency from occurring, or marginalizing its impact within the community, by identifying and assessing risk and implementing preventative measures that may reduce the risk.
2. **Preparedness:** Involves organizing and preparing a community's response to emergencies with the foremost objective to save lives and to help response and rescue operations; includes aspects such as the development of

Figure 3.4 *Four phases of emergency management.*

Figure 3.5 Rockaway, New York, November 3, 2012—Local crews clear streets that are piled with sand due to Hurricane Sandy. (Courtesy of Jocelyn Augustino/FEMA.)

emergency response plans, the procurement of supplies, and educating the community about procedures for disaster response.

3. **Response:** Involves how a community reacts to a disaster, hazard, or emergency situation, including crisis communication and the treatment and protection of key assets, as well as managing and protecting life, property, the environment, and critical infrastructure.

4. **Recovery:** Involves the timely resumption of "normalcy" within the community; in essence, the process and measures necessary for moving from the "disaster" mode to the "normal" mode through treatment/therapy, rebuilding, reorganization, and revitalization (**Figure 3.5**).

Phase I: Mitigation/prevention

In preparing for a disaster, it is important to start with mitigation, or prevention, as it is sometimes known. In this phase, households, businesses, cities, counties, or larger organizations review the type of disaster, hazard, or emergency they expect to face. In thinking of the emergency management cycle, it is often useful to use scenarios. In this case, we will use a hurricane on the eastern coast of New York.

If a family were to move to the East Coast, they would likely already be aware of previous hurricanes and the annual threat posed by them. Mitigation begins the moment they decide to make the move. The news coverage of Hurricane Sandy (**Figure 3.6**) and the damaging winds, which were magnified by the tidal surge of 15–20 feet, would have been hard to miss. Thus, a family has to determine whether where they settle and reside may eventually compromise their safety and welfare due to prior history and the future propensity to be affected by a hurricane. Bottom line—how willingly does a family decide to settle in harm's way?

Specifically, in an effort to avoid the potential nightmare of enduring the likelihood of a hurricane, a family that is considering moving into a hurricane alley would need to determine whether the home on their radar to purchase is strong enough to endure the strike of a hurricane and/or if they would be willing to possibly evacuate northward if necessary. Bottom line, the family must decide what would best protect their safety and welfare from a storm's impact and determine their comfort level regarding whether to evacuate or shelter in place based upon home construction and location.

Figure 3.6 Hurricane Sandy satellite image. (Courtesy of the National Aeronautics and Space Administration [NASA].)

For example, factors to be considered regarding a hurricane's storm surge or damaging winds should include (1) the elevation of the house, (2) the house construction (brick, wood, or vinyl siding), and (3) whether their home may possibly be subject to a lower risk of the storm's impact based upon the proximity of the home relative to the time the hurricane strikes the area. These are not all-inclusive reasons, but considering the construction of a home and its location may well marginalize the impact and risk of a hurricane, which is the basis of a family's attempt to mitigate the adverse affects of a future storm.

Phase II: Preparedness

The second phase of emergency management is the preparedness phase. Preparedness comes in many forms, but most of the forms have a similar goal. The knowledge of how to plan for disasters is critical in emergency management. Planning can make a difference in mitigating against the effects of a disaster, including saving lives and protecting property, and helping a community recover more quickly from a disaster. During the preparedness phase, within the organization of an emergency management agency, plans will have been devised; employees will have been trained in procedures and then have actually practiced the procedural steps of a plan by conducting tabletop exercises.

In the previous scenario, the family in question would need to develop an overall plan. With a pending storm due to strike, maintaining a state of readiness is a must. The family might attend a seminar on disaster preparedness or simply go online to the numerous Web sites afforded the public regarding the groundwork. Either way, preparing for the worst and hoping for the best should be the mind-set for developing a plan. This plan should include things like what family essentials to pack other than clothing (legal documents, heirlooms, etc.), how far away from the coast to drive, which road(s) to take, and obtaining an emergency supply kit.

Finally, the family should run through their plan. Conducting a brief predisaster exercise will enable family members to determine the approximate amount of what all can actually be stored in the vehicle, map out at least three travel option destinations, and determine where to obtain gas and how much will be needed to reach final recovery point. Generally speaking, the preparedness process may be the last time a family or organization is able to modify their plan before the disaster occurs.

Phase III: Response

The third phase of the emergency management cycle is known as the response phase. The response phase is characterized by the initial response of first responders, field reps from agencies like FEMA and local law enforcement, as well as the initial actions taken by those affected by the disaster. It is during the response phase that those adversely affected by the disaster are provided emergency assistance from first responders. The nature and severity of the event/incident will determine the service deliverables necessary and expected by those who may be in need of medical care, rescue, or evacuation.

The timely response will begin once the scene and initial damage assessments are conducted to ensure that the assistance to the public by first responders is not compromised and that there is minimal risk for all involved. Once these assessments are made, additional support, known as emergency responders, is called to the scene or to support facilities, like hospitals. The resources available during this phase directly impact the success of the recovery phase (**Figure 3.7**).

In addition, what are commonly referred to as Community Emergency Response Teams (CERT) are also created within neighborhoods. A CERT can be an invaluable asset to local first responders. The CERT consists of trained volunteers who provide additional resources in times of need during a disaster and can be diligently organized during an incident. The CERT is well prepared to assist with first aid, search and rescue, performing triage, suppressing fire, and cost estimates of damage.

The CERT is also provided with training assistance from the local emergency management agency, which is an important aspect of being prepared to play an integral part in the response process. For example, one operable training component for a CERT includes an introduction to the process of the Incident Command System (ICS) and the Incident Management System (IMS). These provide a CERT with an organizational framework, roles and responsibilities, and the radio communication dynamics necessary to operate during a critical incident. In addition, other components of a CERT training program will include exposure to disaster preparedness, fire safety, disaster medical operations (first aid), light search and rescue, disaster psychology, and terrorism.

Figure 3.7 Washington, DC, October 31, 2012—President Barack Obama, left, and FEMA Administrator Craig Fugate, right, listen to members of the cabinet discuss updates on responses to Hurricane Sandy during a cabinet meeting at FEMA headquarters. (Courtesy of Jocelyn Augustino/ FEMA.)

Before the hurricane impacts the areas of risk, the local and state emergency response plans are usually initiated. This will include an initial public communication process regarding life safety, evacuation, and so forth. Likewise, along with local/state emergency managers and first responders, FEMA personnel may arrive to assist, and the emergency operations center (EOC) becomes fully staffed and operational. The family in our example will activate their evacuation plan, packing essential items and documents while preparing to move northward. It is also common, and strongly urged, that private business organizations administer evacuation plans, like airlines moving aircraft to safer airfields or businesses moving machinery out of the possible storm surge areas. It is important to note that response is handled at the local and state level, and the federal government cannot intervene unless officially requested by the local or state governments.

Phase IV: Recovery

The recovery phase will often overlap efforts during the response phase of a disaster. In most disasters, the recovery phase is characterized by two closely related parts of the recovery, namely, the short-term and long-term recovery efforts.

Short-term recovery will often be localized, such as the return of power to neighborhoods. The size and scale of the short-term recovery will differ from disaster to disaster, but the focus during the short term is the return or resolution of issues pertaining to basic survival necessities, such as food, water, and shelter (**Figure 3.8**). Short-term recovery is also the focus for emergency responders, to treat the injured, restore emergency services, and begin removing debris.

For the family, this would involve returning to their home and beginning the cleanup process, covering broken windows and damaged roofs with tarp in order to keep water out. During this time, they will boil their water and secure their home as best they can. Basic survival for the family is the most important part of the short-term recovery. For businesses, the short-term recovery is muted by the emphasis on the employees' part to secure their homes and families. Businesses will focus on securing any goods that they may have from looting as well as putting up tarps or canopies to protect their building from the elements.

Figure 3.8 Far Rockaway, New York, November 19, 2012—Members of the Army National Guard load trucks as they prepare to hand out supplies to people in need in response to Hurricane Sandy. (Courtesy of the US Navy/chief mass communication specialist Ryan J. Courtade.)

Education facilities (child care, primary, secondary, colleges/universities) must also begin the arduous process of assessing damage and then determine the prognosis for repair and restoration to normalcy prior to engaging students. In an effort to ensure that kids/students are not subjected to anything that may pose a risk to their health and safety, this process may be very labor intensive, but it is extremely necessary.

Health care facilities are also a significant function that is essential for a community to have restored during the recovery process. Without the assurance of operable health care, families with injury or illness, in need of remedial therapy, or awaiting a new born will be at risk, all of which can create a high degree of anxiety. Many hospitals in the New York City area were evacuated during Hurricane Sandy, as the result of underground transformers becoming inoperable or generators losing power due to massive flooding.

Long-term recovery, though, is the return to *normalcy*. This is characterized by the return of electricity and water and other services. Street repairs are completed, power lines replaced, and structures repaired. Normal police and fire responses resume, and employees return to work. An essential part of this phase is the lessons-learned portion. During the long-term recovery, those who felt the impact evaluate their response to the disaster, make adjustments as needed, and transition to the mitigation (preparedness) process for planning a future response, which is the first phase of the emergency management cycle.

Typically, the priorities during a family recovery process include a type of *homecoming*, whereby the return to normalcy will include learning the probable time for returning to work and school and also determining whether the local grocery stores have sustainable food items and that there will be sufficient fuel at the gas pumps. Eventually, at some point, families that have experienced the disaster elements should take the time to assess the *before*, *during*, and *after* dynamics of their journey and determine what proactive steps will be necessary in preparation for a response in the future.

Specifically, upon sizing up their learning curve, the family may come to a better understanding of what nonessential items were brought versus other items that were needed yet left behind. Also, they may check on obtaining insurance or making proper adjustments to their current policy to ensure full coverage. For businesses, the goal of the long-term recovery process would be a return to functional operability and a normal work schedule (**Figure 3.9**). Subsequently, employees can begin to concentrate more on returning to the routine of normal operations.

Figure 3.9 Little Ferry, New Jersey, November 20, 2012—Rising floodwaters in the aftermath of Hurricane Sandy caused water damage in hundreds of businesses in Bergen County, New Jersey. Businesses lost millions of dollars in inventory goods soaked with floodwaters. (Courtesy of Walt Jennings/FEMA.)

Conclusion

The maturation of the emergency management profession will continue to be a work in progress based upon consistent evaluation, constant speculation, and proactive integration of continually transformed principles, preparation, protocols, and performance-based best practices. In hindsight, we may definitively discuss the "what-ifs" as well as speculate on future "what-ifs." Yet, irrespective of such life-changing reality, and postincident experience, there will always be a degree of uncertainty and sometimes no definitive answers with respect to the outcome of a disaster, emergency, or hazardous event.

Principally, however, the four phases of emergency management remains a significant systematic representation regarding the adversarial evolution of a disaster, hazard, or emergency situation. Practically speaking, these phases can be immediate moments in action or years in length. Moreover, each phase may not have a specific start or stop point, but their intentions and related objectives are representative of our instinctive reaction to the consequences of life experience, which attempts to maintain the status quo in spite of a natural disaster, a technological crisis, or an intentional hazard. Understanding the dynamics of each phase affords a better understanding of the expectations involving the responsibility, the process, and the discipline that is emergency management.

Key terms

All hazards
Civil defense
Community Emergency Response Team (CERT)
Comprehensive emergency management
Disaster
Emergency
Emergency management
First responder
Hazard
Impact
Man-made event
Mitigation
Natural event
Preparedness
Reaction
Recovery
Response

QUESTIONS FOR DISCUSSION

1. All organizations should have some type of emergency plan that delineates the activities that must occur when disaster strikes regarding an array of possible incidents. Determine whether your organization has such a plan. If it does have such a plan, review its contents. Write a brief essay that critically analyzes its processes and procedures with respect to preparedness, mitigation, response, and recovery activities.

2. CERTs exist throughout the nation among a variety of communities. Determine whether your locality has a CERT. If it does sponsor a CERT, determine its size and capabilities. Based on the outcome of your investigation, write a brief essay that critically analyzes its potential as a responding entity during periods of disaster.
3. Preparedness for disasters is essential with respect to mitigating the effects of a catastrophe. Determine what natural events may impact your locality. Given this listing, do some research to determine how prepared your locality is with respect to your identified threats. Write a brief essay that highlights the preparedness activities of your locality with respect to these potential threats.
4. Determine the types of first-responder organizations that exist within your locality that may be called upon during periods of calamity. Write a brief essay that highlights the salient characteristics of each organization.

References

1. Merriam-Webster Dictionary. Definition of *emergency*, http://www.merriam-webster.com/dictionary/emergency (accessed January 11, 2013).
2. Merriam-Webster Dictionary. Definition of *management*, http://www.merriam-webster.com/dictionary/emergency (accessed January 11, 2013).
3. Blanchard, B.W. (2008). A tutorial on emergency management, broadly defined, past and present. *Federal Emergency Management Agency. Introduction to Emergency Management (1995)*. Emmitsburg, MD: Emergency Management Institute, FEMA, p. 344.
4. Blanchard, B.W. (2008). A tutorial on emergency management, broadly defined, past and present. *Federal Emergency Management Agency—Emergency Planning Workshop Instructor Guide*. (Drabek, Thomas, 1997). Emmitsburg, MD: Emergency Management Institute, FEMA, p. 344.
5. Blanchard, B.W. (2008). A tutorial on emergency management, broadly defined, past and present. *Toward an International System Model in Emergency Management*. Dykstra, Eelco H. 2003. Call for Papers—Public Entity Risk Institute Symposium on http://www.riskinstitute.org, p. 344.
6. Blanchard, B.W. (2008). A tutorial on emergency management, broadly defined, past and present. *Post-Katrina Emergency Management Reform Act of 2006*, pp. 1394–1433, Title VI of Public Law 109-295 (120 Stat. 1394), Department of Homeland Security Appropriations Act, 2007. Washington, DC: October 4, 2006, p. 346.
7. Blanchard, B.W. (2008). A tutorial on emergency management, broadly defined, past and present. National Fire Protection Association. NFPA 1600: Standard on Disaster/Emergency Management and Business Continuity Programs, 2007 Edition. Quincy, MA: http://www.nfpa.org/assets/files/PDF/CodesStandards/1600-2007.pdf, p. 346.
8. Blanchard, B.W. (September 11, 2007). Principles of emergency management. FEMA Emergency Management Higher Education Learning Project 2007–2011. https://training.fema.gov/EMIWeb/edu/08conf/Conference, p. 3.
9. Comfort, L.K. and Cahill, A.G. (1988). *Managing Disaster, Strategies and Policy Perspectives*. Durham, NC: Duke University Press.

4

Protection of the Homeland and the Establishment and Organization of the United States Department of Homeland Security

Chapter objectives:

- Gain an understanding of the formation of the Department of Homeland Security
- Familiarize readers with many of the major threats identified by the nation
- Review the roles and missions of the major components of the Department of Homeland Security

Introduction

The security of the nation has been and will remain an essential responsibility of our government. Since the founding of the United States, the nation has faced a wide variety of threats to its independence and sovereignty. During the formalization of the governmental infrastructure, the founding fathers recognized that the survival of the United States depended upon the developing and maintaining of appropriate diplomatic and military capabilities. In 1789, as a result, two of the first items of business for the new government were to create the Department of Foreign Affairs, which was soon renamed the Department of State, and to review the need for a small, national military. From this humble beginning, the United States would mature into the world's only superpower. Despite this powerful status, America is vulnerable to both man-made and natural threats.

Each threat, when it evolves into an event, is unique. For example, hurricanes present challenges that force responders to adapt to demanding and often-changing situations. The ability to respond as disasters unfold is the result of years of drawing from lessons learned, improving response techniques, developing new equipment, and strengthening agency cooperation and interaction.

The Department of Homeland Security

In the shadow of the attacks of September 11, 2001 (**Figure 4.1**), the United States Department of Homeland Security (DHS) was authorized in the Homeland Security Act of 2002 and was officially established on November 25, 2002, in response to the 2001 attacks upon the United States. President George W. Bush illustrated the need for the DHS by comparing it to President Truman's proposal in the National Security Act of 1947 to significantly reorganize the United States military. President Bush stated, "America needs a single, unified homeland security structure that will improve protection against today's threats and be flexible enough to help meet the unknown threats of the future."[1]

The creation of the DHS proved to be a significant move by the United States. It transformed and realigned a confusing patchwork of government activities and agencies into a single department whose primary mission was to protect the nation (i.e., the "homeland"). Some of the issues addressed when creating the DHS involved considerations of the department's mission, which agencies would be incorporated into the department, and how those agencies would be expected to interact with national, state, tribal, and local governments.

Although the 2001 attacks proved to be the event that ultimately solidified the legislative support for a major reorganization of the national response community, there were at least two primary programs that preceded the Homeland Security Act of 2002 and ultimately influenced the creation of the DHS: the Nunn–Lugar–Domenici Domestic Preparedness Program and the United States Commission on National Security/21st Century.

In 1996, President Clinton tasked the United States Department of Defense (DOD) to serve as the lead agency for domestic preparedness. That same year, the United States Congress enacted the Nunn–Lugar–Domenici Act/Domestic Preparedness Program, also known as the Defense Against Weapons of Mass Destruction Act of 1996. This act was created under Title XIV of the National Defense Authorization Act (NDAA) of 1996, Public Law 104-201. It was named for the three senators who sponsored the legislation: Senator Sam Nunn, Georgia; Senator Richard G. Lugar, Indiana; and Senator Pete V. Domenici, New Mexico.

Under this legislation, the DOD was tasked with identifying shortfalls in antiterrorism initiatives and developing recommendations to respond to those shortfalls. The DOD identified

Figure 4.1 President George Bush speaking at Ground Zero. *(Courtesy of www.whitehouse.gov.)*

over 120 major cities throughout the United States that needed antiterrorism equipment and training. Much of the initial work under this legislation concentrated on the detection and decontamination of chemical, biological, radiological, and nuclear incidents. Because the DOD had no legal authority to make grants or provide other financial assistance to local jurisdictions, the equipment program was a "loaner" initiative. Essentially, the DOD "loaned" equipment to participating jurisdictions, which then became responsible for the maintenance of the equipment.

The loan was based upon a 5-year performance cycle. At the end of the cycle, local jurisdictions would return the equipment to the DOD. However, it was apparent that no one really expected the equipment to be returned. Once the 5-year cycle was completed, it was anticipated that much of the equipment would be obsolete or used. Therefore, it would have no value or use to other organizations. Although the original idea for the Nunn–Lugar–Domenici Act was a step in the right direction, it lacked longevity because it was a difficult program for local governments to engage in, especially regarding the costs of maintaining the equipment.

In 1998, Secretary of Defense William Cohen, with the endorsement and support of President Bill Clinton and House Speaker Newt Gingrich, created the United States Commission on National Security/21st Century. It was also known as the Hart–Rudman Commission in recognition of Senator Gary Hart (Democrat, Colorado) and Senator Warren Rudman (Republican, New Hampshire). The focus of this commission was the study of the global threat environment and its impact upon the security of the United States. The commission was comprised of 14 panelists consisting of seven Democrats and seven Republicans. A little over 2 years later, on January 31, 2001, the commission submitted its report of 50 recommendations relative to combating terrorism for the 21st century. One of the recommendations was to create a National Homeland Security Agency (NHSA), but this proposal was discarded.

In March 2001, Texas representative Mac Thornberry again addressed the issue and proffered legislation to create the NHSA. In a news release on March 21, 2001, Thornberry stated:

> Based on a recent recommendation by the bipartisan Commission on National Security/21st Century, the measure would bring together four federal agencies currently on the front lines of homeland defense—the Federal Emergency Management Agency, the Coast Guard, the Customs Service, and the Border Patrol. Under this legislation, FEMA would be renamed the National Homeland Security Agency.[2]

Thornberry further described how the Critical Infrastructure Assurance Office, the Institute of Information Infrastructure Protection, the National Infrastructure Protection Center, and the National Domestic Preparedness Office would also be transferred to the NHSA. Thornberry's proposed legislation incorporated President Bush's idea that Federal Emergency Management Agency (FEMA) should lead and coordinate homeland security efforts. It also integrated recommendations of the 1998 Hart–Rudman Commission.

These were not new ideas. There was a provision, within the Defense Against Weapons of Mass Destruction Act of 1996, that allowed the president to transfer the lead agency responsibility, on or after October 1, 1999, from the DOD. The initial concept was that FEMA would be the new agency to assume the program from the DOD. However, there was little interest at the time for FEMA to assume a terrorism-focused program because their primary mission focused upon natural disaster planning and response. In 2000, the president subsequently transferred the Nunn–Lugar–Domenici program to the Department of Justice. With respect to both state and local governments, Attorney General Janet Reno realized the need for such a program to collaboratively address the response to the emerging threat of fundamentalist terrorism.

Funding and vision

Over the course of the 1990s, the nation witnessed a sudden increase in homeland security funding. In 1996, an earmark of $5 million was included within the Department of Justice's budget to develop and deliver training among metropolitan fire departments in an effort to improve their responses to chemical and other terrorism threats. Realizing that this was not a program typically found in the DOD, a decision was made to ask the Office of Justice Programs' Bureau of Justice Assistance (BJA) to administer it. The BJA section that was assigned this responsibility was headed by Director Butch Straub and Deputy Director Andrew (Andy) Mitchell. The program was designed to develop a training course for urban fire departments to enhance their response capabilities. According to Mitchell, the legislation necessitated the attorney general and the administrator of federal emergency management to coordinate the program with BJA, which developed training in conjunction with the National Fire Academy. During this same time, the Department of Justice programs received additional funding for a modest, locality equipment program and the establishment of two national training centers to train state and local personnel to respond to terrorist incidents domestically.

From 1996 to 2001, various programs and ideas were integrated to represent a common direction and vision for the 21st century. The ultimate goals were to preserve peace and to ensure security within the nation. These programs, working with state, tribal, and local governments, eventually came to be administered through the DHS. The fiscal year (FY) 2010 budget for the DHS was $42.7 billion and addressed key national security priorities ranging from border control to cyber security. FY 2010 funding priorities included initiatives involving safeguarding the transportation systems of the nation, cyber-security research and development, border security and immigration services, and state homeland security activities. The succeeding sections briefly describe each of these functions.

Safeguarding the nation's transportation systems

The 2010 budget funded key investments to reinforce public transportation, enhance maritime transportation, and accelerate the deployment of explosives detection equipment to improve airline security. Within the DHS is the Transportation Security Administration (TSA) (**Figure 4.2**). Formed shortly after the attacks of 9/11, the TSA employs approximately 50,000 people. It oversees security for highways, railroads, buses, mass transit systems, ports, and over 450 US airports where approximately 48,000 transportation security officers screen approximately 2 million people a day.

Within the 2010 homeland security budget, $50 million was provided to develop 15 new Visual Intermodal Prevention and Response (VIPR) teams, as components of the TSA, to increase additional risk-based force protection capability by deploying resources to transit hubs. The budget included another $10 million, in new DHS resources, to support integrated planning. Funding was also allocated to the Department of Transportation to modernize the intermodal freight infrastructure by developing a coastal link that would connect inland ports to highway and rail networks. Additional funding supported critical investments to strengthen the security of US airports and to add 109 bomb appraisal officers who specialize in explosives and improvised explosive device (IED) recognition and response. The budget also included $64 million to modernize the infrastructure used to screen travelers and workers.

Figure 4.2 Seal of the Transportation Security Administration. (Courtesy of the TSA.)

Enhancing cyber-security and technology research and development

The 2010 budget included $401 million to increase the resiliency and security of private and public sector cyber infrastructures. These funds supported the base operations of the National Cyber Security Division as well as initiatives under the Comprehensive National Cybersecurity Initiative to protect information networks. An amount of $36 million supported ongoing projects to improve surveillance technologies involving the detection of enhanced, emerging, and advanced biological threats. Efforts to develop next-generation BioWatch sensors that could detect bio-attacks at the earliest possible instant were also funded. The budget also supported the termination of outdated systems, such as the terrestrial-based, long-range radio navigation (Loran-C), operated by the United States Coast Guard (USCG), resulting in an offset of $36 million in 2010 and $190 million over 5 years.

The NDAA bolsters the ability of the United States to protect its technological infrastructure. In 2013, in conjunction with the NDAA, approximately $3.4 billion will be used within the US Cyber Command to ensure military readiness concerning cyberspace operations and a "full range of cyber contingencies."[3] The provisions of the NDAA facilitate communication between the public and private sectors, including the reporting of any security penetrations that occur among the computer networks of defense contractors.[3] The reporting of such incidents must include the techniques and methods used during the penetration, samples of any malicious software program code that were obtained, and the assessment of any "potentially compromised" information.[3]

Ensuring the security of the American nation cannot be accomplished solely through government interventions and activities. Instead, collaborative partnerships between the public and private sectors must exist. During the last two decades, the federal government has failed to keep pace with challenges to critical infrastructures, including technological infrastructures and technological research environments. Threats that endanger such entities may arise internally or externally. Protecting and safeguarding against them necessitates the sharing of information, cooperative efforts, and strong leadership among private sector executives and the leaders of various levels and forms of government administration.

Some experts argue that one of the most damaging security threats in recent years concerned the release of classified materials on the WikiLeaks Internet site. The releasing of this classified information within the public domain necessitated a review of security policies, processes, and procedures that were associated with the handling of such materials.[4] The outcome of this review mandated changes regarding the "oversight structure" and the implementing of stringent policies to strengthen the integrity of technological security.[4] It also mandated the forming of a "classified information sharing and safeguarding office" that provided a continuous emphasis regarding the "sharing and safeguarding of classified national security information."[4] Although these security improvements enhance internal security paradigms, the scopes and varieties of external threats also are considerable.

Cooperation between government and private entities is also a necessary aspect of technological security. For example, the DOD embraces such partnerships to exhibit a "whole-of-government cyber security strategy."[5] These partnerships involve the participation of both government entities and the defense industrial base. Entities within the defense industrial base include organizations that provide "defense technologies, weapons systems, policy and strategy development, and personnel."[5] When partnering with the DOD, organizations may voluntarily share information regarding "malicious or unauthorized cyber activity and protective cyber security measures."[5] Such collaboration involves trust and communication and may involve the use of incentives to motivate private entities to participate and cooperate with the DOD.[5] In any case, the purpose of such external collaboration is to improve cyber security and to "further the public good."[6]

Cyber security encompasses an astounding array of different components. For example, securing and maintaining the electrical power grid is absolutely essential, and the grid is monitored and controlled by a variety of different computer networks. Ensuring the safety of these networks involves protecting "privately owned corporate computer networks" against threats of "potentially intrusive" activities.[7] Although these networks are the property of private corporations and electric cooperatives, they provide electricity to the entire nation. Therefore, their protection and security are of paramount importance within the context of homeland security.

Threats against American cyber security must be taken seriously—destroying any aspect of the technological infrastructure may produce cataclysmic cascading effects throughout the nation. The potential of a massive cyber attack against the United States could impede or terminate functions of the "country's banking system, power grid, and other essential infrastructure," including the transportation system.[8] Because of American vulnerability within its technological infrastructure, great concern is expressed regarding the potential of a cyber attack whose outcomes may rival the effects of September 11, 2001.[8]

Both domestically and around the world, other events signal the potential of such a calamity. Various cyber attacks have targeted the American banking system, including "Wells Fargo, JP Morgan Chase, and Bank of America."[8] A Saudi corporation, Saudi Aramco, experienced a devastating cyber attack that "erased data on two-thirds" of its "corporate PCs."[8]

Another threatening scenario could possibly involve collaboration between nation states and factions of organized crime to attack American technological infrastructure. Such an attack could involve "a country like Iran work[ing] with Russian criminals or Chinese hackers to target banks, the power grid, and all the computers that control routing and ticketing for planes and trains."[8] This type of scenario would halt economic, electrical, and logistics functions within the American economy. Regarding such potential scenarios, the pertinent question is not whether it will happen but when it will occur, because "it is only a matter of time before the sophisticated tools needed fall into the wrong hands."[8] Although such scenarios may be unimaginable to some, the potential of such dangers must be neither discounted nor ignored.

Collaboration between the government and private entities is essential to safeguard technological infrastructure. Sharing data regarding suspicious activities is mutually beneficial and may prevent or mitigate the effects of cyber threats. Collaboration between public and private entities also improves the ability to perform risk assessment and to mitigate the consequences of cyber threats. Through collaboration, government and private entities become complements whose mutual goal is the preservation of technological infrastructure.

Strengthening border security and immigration services

The United States has attracted immigrants since its earliest days. Immigrants in search of freedom, escaping oppression, or just seeking a better life for themselves and their families have been drawn to our nation's shores. By the first decade of the 21st century, security concerns, including concerns related to terrorism, drug trafficking, and its related violence, led to a reevaluation of national policies related to immigration.

The 2010 homeland security budget included $45 million for the expansion of an exit pilot at key land ports of entry and other border security priorities. An amount of $4 billion within Customs and Border Protection (CBP) funded support for the 20,000 border patrol agents protecting nearly 6000 miles of United States borders. An amount of $112 million was provided for E-Verify, an electronic employment eligibility verification system, which helps employers comply with immigration law and ensures that American jobs are available to US citizens and those authorized to work in the United States. The budget also supported strengthening the delivery of immigration services by streamlining and modernizing immigration application processes.

The 2013 DHS budget request accommodated approximately "$39.5 billion in net discretionary funding."[9] This funding request was intended to provide 21,370 border patrol agents, 21,186 CBP personnel, and surveillance resources along the US–Mexican border.[9] It also requested funding to recapitalize assets of the USCG, including the "renovation and restoration" of some of its "shore facilities."[9] The budget request also included funding for the enforcing of US immigration laws and policies.[9] Such enforcement involves addressing the needs of changing demographics and better identification and removal of illegal aliens.[9] It also provides funding for the expanding of the E-Verify system, for the enforcing of other workplace employment laws regarding "monitoring and compliance," and for the prosecution of employers who violate legal hiring practices.[9]

Regardless of the amount of money expended toward protecting the American borders, whether land, sea, air, or virtual, from external threats, one cannot ignore the dangers that arise domestically. For example, since 2005, approximately 150 "border and immigration agents" have been either "arrested or indicted" for criminal offenses involving direct corruption charges of "drug and human smuggling."[10] Some of the corruption may be associated with shortcomings within the applicant screening process and the monitoring of agents after hiring.[10] In some cases, the Office of Internal Affairs of CBP failed to maintain and track the results of polygraph examinations, drug testing, and background checks.[10] Additionally, since 2005, approximately 2170 agents have been arrested for offenses that were not directly related to corruption, such as "domestic violence and driving while intoxicated."[10] In 2011, approximately 900 corruption allegations originated from both ICE and CBP.[10]

Ensuring the safety and the security of the American borders is an essential aspect of homeland and national security. Employing personnel who exhibit the highest caliber of integrity and personal conduct is critical in fulfilling the homeland security objectives and goals of border security. Any instance of human corruption among the ranks of those whose duties and responsibilities are to protect American society imperils the nation. For example, terrorist organizations that collaborate with Mexican organized crime, such as Hezbollah, working in conjunction with a corrupt American border agent could catastrophically endanger the United States.[10]

Other border threats are not always visible. In many cases, criminal organizations expend much time, money, and resources creating tunnels beneath the US–Mexican border through which humans and illegal items are trafficked and transported. Since 2008, over 70 tunnels have been discovered underneath the US–Mexican border.[11] These tunnels circumvent the stringent security exhibited by the "heightened enforcement" of laws "on land" along the US–Mexican border.[11] During recent years, these tunnels have demonstrated an increased level of sophistication and design. For example, in 2011, a 600-yard tunnel was discovered underneath the US–Mexican border that resulted in the seizure of approximately "32 tons of marijuana," thereby representing one of the largest "pot busts in U.S. history."[11] This tunnel contained ventilation and lighting systems and also incorporated "electric rail cars."[11] Generally, such tunnels are used for the trafficking of illegal narcotics. However, these tunnels could also act as entry routes for terrorists or other entities whose goals are to harm Americans.

Ensuring the integrity of the sea, land, air, and virtual borders of the United States is imperative within the context of homeland security. However, safeguarding the United Sates–Mexican border is rife with fallibility and imperfection. Approximately 61% of probable illegal aliens are intercepted along the US–Mexican border regardless of the manpower strength used to bolster border security.[12]

Along the border, the US CBP Office of Air and Marine (OAM) operates the Predator B unmanned aircraft system (UAS) in support of law enforcement and homeland security missions at the nation's borders (**Figure 4.3a and b**).

The system also supports disaster relief efforts of its DHS partners, including FEMA and the USCG.

Few methods exist through which the effectiveness of border security initiatives may be identified and judged.[12] Baseline concepts for new practices and methods are currently being considered.[12] Regardless, ensuring border security is inarguably a critical aspect of protecting American society.

Supporting state homeland security activities

The budget was also tasked with making the federal government a better partner to states and localities regarding key homeland security initiatives. Funding was provided to improve coordination between all levels of government, to support first responders, and to create more effective emergency response plans. A risk-based, national exercise program provided assistance to state, local, and tribal partners with respect to offsetting costs of critical homeland security activities. The budget further expanded medical surge capacity and aided in the stockpiling and storing of essential supplies. Funding of $260 million within the existing Homeland Security Grant Program fortified intelligence systems by improving information sharing and analysis through the addition of state and local intelligence analysts.

Figure 4.3 *Predator B unmanned aircraft system (a) in a hangar and (b) in the air. (Courtesy of the Customs and Border Patrol [www.cbp.gov].)*

The organizational structure and mission of the DHS

Following the attacks of 9/11, President Bush announced the creation of the Office of Homeland Security, whose mission was to develop and coordinate the implementation of a comprehensive national strategy to secure the United States from terrorist threats or attacks. The former governor of Pennsylvania, Tom Ridge, was named the first head of this organization on October 8, 2001 (**Figure 4.4**). Under the direction of Governor Ridge, the Office of Homeland Security took early, critical steps in the development of an identity that would eventually evolve into the United States DHS and cabinet-level status within the executive branch of the United States government.

In the short history of the DHS, it has been led by some extremely capable secretaries. The aforementioned Governor Ridge is generally credited with providing solid leadership and vision during the early days of the agency. Ridge worked with more than 180,000 employees from combined agencies to strengthen the borders, provide for intelligence analysis and infrastructure protection, improve the use of science and technology to counter weapons of mass destruction, and create a comprehensive response and recovery division.

Upon the resignation of Governor Ridge in November 2004, Judge Michael Chertoff accepted the position of Secretary of Homeland Security (**Figure 4.5**).

On February 15, 2005, Judge Chertoff was unanimously confirmed by the Senate and sworn in as the second secretary of the DHS. Chertoff stepped down as secretary in January 2009. Under the leadership of Judge Chertoff, the agency experienced great growth.

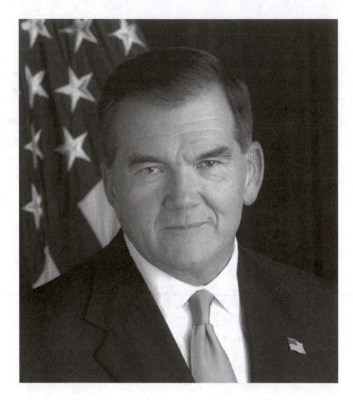

Figure 4.4 *DHS Secretary Thomas Ridge, 2003–2005. (Courtesy of the DHS.)*

Upon assuming office in January 2009, President Obama selected Governor Janet Napolitano, of Arizona, as the third secretary of homeland security (**Figure 4.6**).

Prior to joining the Obama administration, Napolitano was midway through her second term as governor of the state of Arizona. Napolitano's homeland security background is extensive. As US attorney, she helped lead the domestic terrorism investigation into the Oklahoma City Bombing. As Arizona attorney general, she helped write laws to break up human smuggling rings. As governor, she implemented one of the first state homeland security strategies in the nation, opened the first state counterterrorism center, and spearheaded efforts to transform immigration enforcement.

The DHS incorporates 22 governmental agencies. Some of those agencies are FEMA, the coast guard, the Secret Service, the Transportation Security Agency, the US Immigration and Customs Enforcement (ICE), CBP, and 16 other agencies. From its humble beginning within the DOD, by 2007, the DHS had approximately 208,000 employees. This growth and level of funding makes the DHS the third-largest cabinet-level agency within government.

By 2005, the mission of the DHS was stated to be "a concerted national effort to prevent terrorist attacks within the United States, reduce America's vulnerability to terrorism, and minimize the damage and recover from attacks that do occur." This mission statement has caused concern because it seems to limit the scope of the mission of homeland security with respect to a limited policy focus upon terrorism. In the aftermath of the attacks of September 11, 2001, the mission statement reflected the "mood" of the country. It involved a focus on terrorists, acts of terrorism, and the direction Americans should take in the antiterrorism preparedness role. The country and its leadership, in a natural reaction to the attacks, were unfocused on the threats of natural hazards.

Figure 4.5 DHS Secretary Michael Chertoff, 2005–2009. (Courtesy of the DHS.)

In 2005, Hurricane Katrina decimated the Gulf Coast, and the proverbial pendulum swung back to addressing natural hazards. The DHS's mission statement posed a challenge because it did not incorporate these natural hazards. Again, the policy and mission statements of the DHS were reviewed and revised. This review was critical, if for no other reason than that FEMA is expected to perform a vital function under the supervision of the DHS. It became an obvious concern, within the post-Katrina environment, when many felt that FEMA had failed in its mission. This scenario led to the passage of legislation called the Post-Katrina Emergency Management Reform Act of 2006. The Post-Katrina Act necessitated another major reorganization within the DHS. The nation is seven years into the reorganization that created the United States DHS. The department went through major restructuring following Hurricane Katrina with the Post-Katrina Act of 2006. The debate continues regarding whether FEMA should be in the DHS or should be returned to an independent status.

The funding appropriations and allocations are part of the homeland security debate. Some believe that funding for homeland security will "dry up." Others take the position that funding will decrease for some programs and will increase for others. However, it is agreed that local governments must be prepared to sustain projects that have been funded through the homeland security grant programs.

The United States Congress consistently asks: How prepared are we? Unfortunately, the country has not developed a method for measuring preparedness. Others ask if the nation is better off and more prepared now than it was before September 11, 2001. These questions can be

Figure 4.6 DHS Secretary Janet Napolitano. (Courtesy of the DHS.)

answered, but not everyone agrees on the answers. There are definite certainties regarding homeland security. The country will experience other hurricanes. There will be earthquakes. Other natural disasters will occur. Many believe that the nation again will be struck by terrorist attacks. The threats of natural disasters and man-made incidents exist. The response landscape has changed dramatically since the attacks of 9/11. National preparedness is a permanent part of the response environment.

The DHS has outlined four mission areas that define the goal of preparedness: prevention, protection, response, and recovery. Each of the respective response disciplines has responsibilities that support at least one of those mission areas. Federal, state, local, and tribal partnerships collaborate to secure America by supporting those four mission areas.

With the transition from the administration of President George W. Bush to that of President Barack Obama, the national strategy for securing the homeland against 21st-century threats has been reviewed and refocused. Modern strategy targets the prevention of terrorist attacks against the homeland, preparation and planning for emergencies, and investment in strong response and recovery capabilities. It is the intent of President Obama to strengthen the US homeland against all hazards, including natural or accidental disasters and terrorist threats, and to ensure that the federal government works with states, localities, and the private sector as a partner in prevention, mitigation, and response.

The highlights of the current efforts of the nation to strengthen its security include the defeat of terrorism worldwide. This goal includes the following efforts:

- Find, disrupt, and destroy al Qaeda
- Develop and apply new capabilities to defeat terrorists
- Prepare the military to meet 21st-century threats
- Win the battle of ideas by returning to an American foreign policy that is consistent with America's traditional values
- Work with moderates, within the Islamic world, to counter al Qaeda's propaganda
- Enhance American influence internationally

With respect to the prevention of nuclear terrorism, homeland security efforts include the following activities:

- Focus upon securing nuclear weapons materials and ending nuclear smuggling
- Strengthen policing and interdiction efforts: convene summits on preventing nuclear terrorism
- Eliminate Iran's and North Korea's nuclear weapons programs through diplomacy
- Strengthen the International Atomic Energy Agency (IAEA)
- Control fissile materials and prevent nuclear fuel from becoming nuclear weapons
- Set the goal of a nuclear-free world and seek reductions in international nuclear stockpiles

Within the area of the strengthening of American bio-security, the following activities are mandated:

- Prevent bio-terror attacks
- Increase capacity to mitigate the consequences of bio-terror attacks
- Accelerate the development and production capabilities of new medicines and vaccines
- Lead an international effort to diminish impact of major infectious disease epidemics

The role and function of the DHS are daunting and massive. Although the organization is experiencing its formative years, it provides valuable services to protect American society and interests from threats that impact national security. During its short history, the organization has experienced a variety of "growing pains" through organizational restructuring and resizing. However, given enough time, many believe that the DHS will mature as it serves the needs of America among dynamic environments that threaten US tranquility.

The following components make up the modern version of the DHS: (1) departmental components, (2) Office of the Secretary, and (3) various advisory panels and committees. The departmental components represent the primary factions that implement the functions of homeland security. The Office of the Secretary provides the functions of leadership. The various advisory panels and committees provide research and advice regarding homeland security issues. The succeeding sections of this chapter provide a brief synopsis of each entity and its primary components.

DHS organizational structuring and components

The modern version of the DHS is comprised of a myriad of government agencies. Three primary factions form the basis of the DHS: (1) departmental components, (2) Office of the Secretary, and (3) various advisory panels and committees. The departmental components represent the primary factions that implement the functions of homeland security. The Office of the Secretary provides the functions of leadership. The various advisory panels and committees provide research and advice regarding homeland security issues. The succeeding sections of this chapter provide a brief synopsis of each entity and its primary components.

The following entities comprise the departmental components of the DHS:

- Directorate for National Protection and Programs (DNPP)
- Directorate for Science and Technology (S&T)
- Directorate for Management
- Office of Policy
- Office of Health Affairs (OHA)
- Office of Intelligence and Analysis (I&A)
- Office of Operations Coordination and Planning (OOCP)
- Federal Law Enforcement Training Center (FLETC)
- Domestic Nuclear Detection Office (DNDO)
- FEMA
- TSA
- CBP
- USCIS
- ICE
- USCG
- United States Secret Service (USSS)

This list consists of a variety of agencies that are responsible for providing a myriad of functions within the context of homeland security (**Figure 4.7**). These responsibilities and

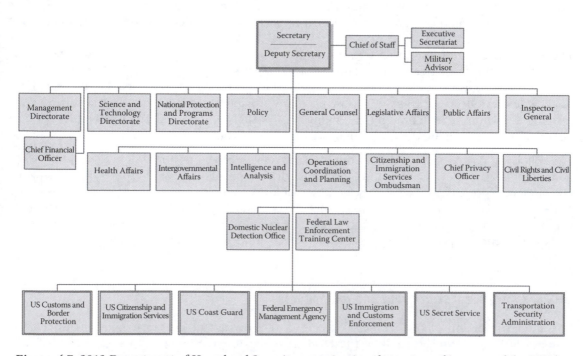

Figure 4.7 *2013 Department of Homeland Security organizational structure. (Courtesy of the DHS.)*

functions range from military to health-related fields. Regardless, each function is a critical component of facilitating the security of the American nation and its society. Unless otherwise noted, the primary source of information for each of these sections is the US DHS.[13]

DNPP

According to the DHS, the DNPP "works to advance the Department's risk-reduction mission, and reducing risk requires an integrated approach that encompasses both physical and virtual threats and their associated human elements." Reducing risk requires an integrated approach that encompasses both physical and virtual threats and their associated human elements. The DNPP is comprised of the following components:

1. Federal Protective Service (FPS)
2. Office of Cybersecurity and Communications (CS&C)
3. Office of Infrastructure Protection (IP)
4. Office of Risk Management and Analysis (RMA)
5. US-VISIT

The FPS "provides integrated security and law enforcement services to federally owned and leased buildings, facilities, properties, and other assets," and the FPS is a federal law enforcement entity. The CS&C is tasked with "assuring the security, resiliency, and reliability of the nation's cyber and communications infrastructure."[14] The IP is tasked with the "coordinated national effort to reduce risk to our critical infrastructures and key resources (CIKR) posed by acts of terrorism." Therefore, this agency "increases the nation's level of preparedness and the ability to respond and quickly recover in the event of an attack, natural disaster, or other emergency." The RMA is the departmental "Executive Agent for national risk management and analysis." The US-VISIT implements the use of "innovative biometrics-based technological solutions—digital fingerprints and photographs—to provide decision-makers with accurate information" expediently when necessary.[14]

S&T

S&T is the primary research and development entity within the DHS. According to the DHS, "it provides federal, state, and local officials with the technology and capabilities to protect the homeland." Its mission improves "homeland security by providing to customers state-of-the-art technology that helps them achieve their missions. S&T customers include the operating components of the department, and state, local, tribal and territorial emergency responders and officials." The S&T is comprised of three portfolios, six divisions, and eight offices and institutes.

The following entities comprise the portfolios of the S&T entity[13]:

- The director of research portfolio involves strategic research needs, supporting the DHS mission, providing America with a robust homeland security capability. The research portfolio contains the Office of National Laboratories, the Office of University Programs, and the Program Executive Office—Counter Improvised Explosives Devices.
- The director of Innovation/Homeland Security Advanced Research Projects Agency (HSARPA) portfolio "focuses on homeland security research and development that could lead to significant breakthroughs and greatly enhance departmental operations."
- The director of transition portfolio (DTP) focuses on delivering capabilities that satisfy the operational requirements of "Department components and first responders." The DTP includes the Commercialization Office, the Safety Act Office, the Long Range Broad Agency Announcement Program, and the Technology Transfer Program.[15]

The following entities comprise the divisions of the S&T entity:

- The Borders and Maritime Security Division "develops and transitions tools and technologies that improve the security of national borders and waterways without impeding the flows of commerce and travel."
- The Chemical and Biological Division increases national "preparedness against chemical and biological threats through improved threat awareness, advanced surveillance and detection, and protective countermeasures."
- The Command, Control, and Interoperability Division "develops interoperable communication standards and protocols for emergency responders, cyber security tools for protecting the integrity of the Internet, and automated capabilities to recognize and analyze potential threats."
- The Explosives Division "develops the technical capabilities to detect, interdict, and lessen the impacts of non-nuclear explosives used in terrorist attacks against mass transit, civil aviation, and critical infrastructure."
- The Human Factors Behavioral Sciences Division applies the social and behavioral sciences to improve detection, analysis, and understanding and response to homeland security threats.
- The Infrastructure and Geophysical Division focuses on identifying and mitigating the vulnerabilities of the 18 critical infrastructure and key assets that keep our society and economy functioning.

The following entities comprise the offices and institutions of the S&T entity:

- Business operations, services, and human capital
- Corporate Communications Division
- Interagency programs
- International cooperative programs
- Operations Analysis Division (consisting of the Homeland Security Studies and Analysis Institute and the Homeland Security Systems Engineering and Development Institute)
- Strategy, policy, and budget
- Special programs
- Test and evaluation and standards

Directorate for Management

The Directorate for Management is tasked with "budgets and appropriations, expenditure of funds, accounting and finance, procurement; human resources, information technology systems, facilities and equipment, and the identification and tracking of performance measurements." The Directorate for Management "ensures that the department's over 230,000 employees have well-defined responsibilities and that both managers and employees have effective communications methods among themselves, with other governmental and nongovernmental bodies, and with the served public."

Office of Policy

The Office of Policy is the primary policy formulation and coordination component, and it provides a centralized, coordinated focus to the development of departmental, strategic planning to protect the United States. This component develops and integrates departmental policies, planning, and programs in order to better coordinate the departmental prevention, protection, response, and recovery missions. According to the Office of Policy,[27] its basic responsibilities include the following functions:

- Leading coordination of department-wide policies, programs, and planning, which will ensure consistency and integration of missions throughout the entire department
- Providing a central office to develop and communicate policies across multiple components of the homeland security network and strengthen the department's ability to maintain policy and operational readiness needed to protect the homeland
- Providing the foundation and direction for department-wide strategic planning and budget priorities
- Bridging multiple headquarters' components and operating agencies to improve communication among departmental entities, eliminate duplication of effort, and translate policies into timely action
- Creating a single point of contact for internal and external stakeholders that will allow for streamlined policy management across the department

OHA

The OHA coordinates all DHS medical activities to ensure appropriate preparation for and response to incidents having medical significance. The OHA is tasked as the "principal agent for all medical and health matters" and is responsible for leading the development and support of a "scientifically rigorous, intelligence-based bio-defense and health preparedness architecture" to facilitate an all-hazards approach to ensuring national security. The OHA also "oversees the Department's bio-defense activities; leads a coordinated national architecture for biological and chemical Weapons of Mass Destruction (WMD) planning and catastrophic incident management; and ensures that Department employees have an effective occupational health and safety program."[16]

I&A

The I&A uses "information and intelligence from multiple sources to identify and assess current and future threats to the United States." The I&A is a member of the national Intelligence Community (IC) and facilitates the collection, analysis, and dissemination of intelligence to the full spectrum of homeland security customers in the DHS; at state, local, and tribal levels; in the private sector; and in the IC. According to the I&A, "The Under Secretary for Intelligence and Analysis, in the capacity of Chief Intelligence Officer (CINT), implements a mandate to integrate the Department's intelligence components and functions—the DHS Intelligence Enterprise (IE)—by driving a common intelligence mission."[17]

The department IE comprises I&A and the intelligence elements of the following:

- USCIS
- USCG
- CBP
- ICE
- TSA

The I&A is the "Executive Agent for the Department State and Local Fusion Center Program," and the "Under Secretary leads several additional activities for the Department, such as information sharing, stewardship of National Security Systems, and management of classified information systems security."[17]

OOCP

The OOCP is responsible for the daily monitoring of US and coordinating activities within the department, with governors, homeland security advisors, law enforcement partners, and critical infrastructure operators among all 50 states and more than 50 major urban areas nationwide. According to the OOCP, its mission is to "deter, detect, and prevent terrorist acts by coordinating the work of federal, state, territorial, tribal, local, and private sector partners and by collecting and fusing information from a variety of sources."

Through the National Operations Center (NOC), the OOCP provides real-time, national "situational awareness and monitoring of the homeland, coordinates incidents and response activities, and, in conjunction with the Office of Intelligence and Analysis, issues advisories and bulletins concerning threats to homeland security, as well as specific protective measures." The NOC daily "coordinates information sharing to help deter, detect, and prevent terrorist acts and to manage domestic incidents. Information on domestic incident management is shared with Emergency Operations Centers, at all levels, through the Homeland Security Information Network (HSIN)."[18]

FLETC

The FLETC was established in 1970 in temporary facilities in suburban Washington, DC. It began as an interagency "police academy" operating within the Department of the Treasury. Congress intended that police officers and criminal investigators of all government agencies, except the Federal Bureau of Investigation (FBI), would be trained at the new center in order to facilitate a uniform training program. The FLETC came to Georgia in the summer of 1975 and began training in September of that year.

On March 1, 2003, the FLETC formally transferred from the Treasury Department to the newly created the DHS. The FLETC provides career-long training for law enforcement professionals, to assist them in fulfilling their responsibilities both safely and proficiently. The FLETC is an "interagency law enforcement training organization for 91 Federal agencies," and it facilitates services among "state, local, tribal, and international law enforcement agencies."

In addition to Glynco, the FLETC operates other residential training centers in Artesia, New Mexico, and Charleston, South Carolina. The FLETC also conducts training at a nonresidential facility in Cheltenham, Maryland. The Cheltenham center is primarily intended for use by agencies with large concentrations of personnel in the area of Washington, DC. The FLETC maintains an office in Orlando, Florida, which provides a gateway to technology and training expertise within a nationally recognized hub for simulation and training.

According to the FLETC, it has "oversight and program management responsibilities at the International Law Enforcement Academies (ILEA) in Gaborone, Botswana, and Bangkok, Thailand. The FLETC also supports training at other ILEAs in Hungary and El Salvador."[19]

DNDO

The DNDO enhances the "nuclear detection efforts of federal, state, territorial, tribal, and local governments, and the private sector and to ensure a coordinated response to such threats." The DNDO was established on April 15, 2005, to improve the national capabilities of detecting and reporting "unauthorized attempts to import, possess, store, develop, or transport nuclear or radiological material for use against the nation, and to further enhance this capability over time." According to the DNDO, its strategic objectives are as follows[20]:

- Develop the global nuclear detection and reporting architecture
- Develop, acquire, and support the domestic nuclear detection and reporting system
- Fully characterize detector system performance before deployment
- Establish situational awareness through information sharing and analysis
- Establish operation protocols to ensure detection leads to effective response
- Conduct a transformational research and development program
- Establish the National Technical Nuclear Forensics Center to provide planning, integration, and improvements to USG nuclear forensics capabilities

FEMA

The Congressional Act of 1803 was the earliest effort to provide disaster relief on a federal level; from that point forward, assorted legislation provided disaster support. In 1979, FEMA was established by an executive order, which merged many of the separate disaster-related responsibilities into a single agency. Since then, FEMA has dedicated itself to helping communities nationwide prepare for, respond to, and recover from natural and man-made disasters— a mission strengthened when the agency became part of the DHS in 2003. Although there are over 20 agencies currently within the DHS, FEMA has primary responsibility for disaster response.

Before 1979, several governmental agencies were involved in disaster preparedness, response, and recovery. During both World War II and the period of the Cold War, Americans were familiar with the DOD program commonly known as the Civil Defense Agency (which in reality was the Civil Preparedness Agency). In the shadow of the threat of nuclear war between the United States and the Soviet Union, public awareness was at its height; for example, many school children and teachers participated in "duck-and-cover" Civil Defense drills that were conducted in schools. During these drills, children were trained to take shelter in the event of a potential attack. In hindsight, the training used to prepare for a nuclear attack was very primitive and unreliable. The Federal Disaster Assistance Administration, initially established by the Disaster Relief Act of 1974, within the Department of Housing and Urban Development (HUD), was another forerunner to FEMA. It also assisted state and local governments during disasters.

The federal approach to problem solving became especially popular in the 1930s; for example, the Reconstruction Finance Corporation was given authority to make disaster loans for repair and reconstruction of certain public facilities following an earthquake, and later, other types of disasters. In 1934, the Bureau of Public Roads was given authority to provide funding for highways and bridges damaged by natural disasters. The Flood Control Act, which gave the US Army Corps of Engineers greater authority to implement flood control projects, was also passed during this period. This piecemeal approach to disaster assistance was problematic, and it prompted legislation that required greater cooperation between federal agencies.[21]

In January 1937, the Ohio River experienced its worst flooding in history, a situation that has since been referred to as the "Super Flood." Subsequently, President Franklin D. Roosevelt signed into law the Flood Control Act of 1937. This act has been revised several times since its codification, but it remains a significant piece of legislation. Widespread discontent in the 1960s and the 1970s produced massive man-made disasters requiring assistance from the

Federal Disaster Assistance Administration, which had been established within the HUD. Events such as Hurricane Carla in 1962, the Alaskan Earthquake of 1964, Hurricane Betsy in 1965, Hurricane Camille in 1969, the San Fernando Earthquake of 1971, and Hurricane Agnes in 1972 emphasized the issue of natural disasters and necessitated increased legislation. In 1968, the National Flood Insurance Act offered new flood protection to homeowners, and in 1974, the Disaster Relief Act firmly established the process of presidential disaster declarations.[21]

The laws that were adopted during the first two centuries of US history demonstrate the piecemeal approach that the federal government took toward disaster relief. They form the foundation for the debate that facilitated the passage of the Post-Katrina Act of 2006. Undoubtedly, in 2002, when a decision was made to house FEMA under the newly formed United States DHS, it was no small policy or political task.

President Carter's 1979 executive order merged many separate, disaster-related responsibilities into FEMA, including the Federal Insurance Administration, the National Fire Prevention and Control Administration, the National Weather Service Community Preparedness Program, the Federal Preparedness Agency of the General Services Administration, and the Federal Disaster Assistance Administration. Civil defense responsibilities were also transferred to the new agency from the Defense Department's Defense Civil Preparedness Agency. During its inception, John Macy, who was the first director of FEMA, emphasized the similarities between natural hazards preparedness and civil defense activities. FEMA began development of an Integrated Emergency Management System, with an all-hazards approach, that included "direction, control and warning systems which are common to the full range of emergencies from small isolated events to the ultimate emergency—war."[21]

During its formative years, FEMA experienced unusual challenges that emphasized the complexity of emergency management. Early disasters and emergencies included the contamination of Love Canal, the Cuban refugee crisis, and the accident at the Three Mile Island nuclear power plant. Later, the Loma Prieta Earthquake in 1989 and Hurricane Andrew in 1992 tested FEMA's response capability. In 1993, President Clinton nominated James L. Witt as the new FEMA director; Witt was significant in that he became the first agency director with experience as a state emergency manager. He soon initiated sweeping reforms that streamlined disaster relief and recovery operations, placed a new emphasis regarding preparedness and mitigation, and focused agency employees on customer service. The ending of the Cold War facilitated the redirection of FEMA's limited resources from civil defense toward disaster relief, recovery, and mitigation initiatives.

In 2001, President George W. Bush appointed Joe M. Allbaugh as the director of FEMA. The attacks of September 11, 2001, necessitated an emphasis regarding national preparedness and homeland security and unprecedentedly tested the agency. The agency coordinated its activities with the Office of Homeland Security, and the FEMA Office of National Preparedness was given responsibility for ensuring that the nation's first responders were both trained and equipped to deal with weapons of mass destruction.

Once a governor has declared a disaster area or an emergency and has requested federal aid, the president can direct FEMA to administer federal disaster assistance. The magnitude and severity of the destruction must warrant federal assistance. The type of assistance offered to individuals or families includes, but is not limited to, one or more of the following: temporary housing, disaster loans, federal income tax assistance in claiming casualty losses, legal services, consumer aid, disaster unemployment benefits, crisis counseling, and both individual and family grants.

Additionally, FEMA assistance can be used for the following endeavors:

- Search and rescue
- Public hazard reduction
- Emergency communication
- Emergency shelter and temporary housing
- Food and medical assistance
- Essential repairs to homes so occupants can return
- Temporary assistance with mortgage or rental payment for people who have lost their residences because the disaster has created financial hardships for them
- Unemployment assistance
- Limited funds to pay for necessary expenses or serious needs for those unable to pay expenses not covered by other programs or means
- Loans to individuals, businesses, and farmers for repair, rehabilitation, or replacement of damaged real and personal property
- Legal services for low-income families and individuals
- Crisis counseling
- Agricultural assistance
- Veteran's assistance and adjustments
- Tax relief and casualty losses from the Internal Revenue Service (IRS)
- Penalty waiver for early withdrawal of funds from various time deposits

The mission of FEMA is to support "our citizens and first responders to ensure that as a nation we work together to build, sustain, and improve our capability to prepare for, protect against, respond to, recover from, and mitigate all hazards." FEMA has more than 3700 full time employees and 4000 standby disaster assistance employees who are available for deployment after disasters. As of November 2007, FEMA has responded to more than 2700 presidentially declared disasters. The preceding sections of this textbook provide a greater discussion of FEMA and its modern responsibilities.[13]

In 2009, W. Craig Fugate was appointed as the administrator of FEMA. An experienced emergency management professional, Fugate served as director of the Florida Division of Emergency Management (FDEM) prior to his appointment. Within that role, he managed 138 full-time staff and a budget of $745 million; his agency coordinated disaster response, recovery, preparedness, and mitigation efforts among each of the state's 67 counties and local governments.

In the aftermath of Katrina, the DHS has continued to disassemble FEMA's emergency management programs and operations. The FEMA director has, in 5 short years, gone from being a member of the president's cabinet to an office director. The many disaster programs and operations that were brought together by President Carter in 1979 from across the federal government to form FEMA have been disassembled and spread among the many agencies and directorates of the DHS.[22]

TSA

The TSA protects the nation's transportation systems to ensure freedom of movement for people and commerce. The TSA was created in the wake of 9/11 to strengthen the security of the nation's transportation systems while ensuring the freedom of movement for people and commerce. Within a year, the TSA assumed responsibility for security at the nation's airports and deployed a federal workforce to meet congressional deadlines for screening all commercial airline passengers and baggage. In March 2003, the TSA transferred from the Department of Transportation to the DHS.

The TSA is responsible for ensuring the security of all modes of transportation, including cargo placed aboard airplanes, and particularly focuses on passenger-carrying planes. By 2010, approximately 48,000 transportation security officers served in 457 US airports, screening approximately 2 million people a day.

In addition to its duties and responsibilities in the nation's airports, the TSA provides grants and facilitates law enforcement programs, security programs, and security screening within the transportation system of America.

United States CBP

The United States CBP has a long and distinguished history of service to the United States tracing back to the earliest days of the nation. In 1789, Congress passed a series of acts that established a system of tariffs and customs in order to fund the national government. Also in 1789, Congress established 59 customs collection districts under the jurisdiction of a collector of customs. Soon, the origination would be known as the United States Customs Service.

Today, CBP is a large and complex component of the DHS and has a priority mission of keeping terrorists and their weapons out of the United States. CBP "also has a responsibility for securing and facilitating trade and travel while enforcing hundreds of U.S. regulations, including immigration and drug laws." According to CBP, its strategic goals are as follows[23]:

- Preventing terrorism
- Unifying as one border agency
- Balancing trade and travel with security
- Protecting America
- Modernizing and managing for results

According to CBP, on average, it accomplishes the following every day[23]:

- Processes 989,689 passengers and pedestrians
- Processes 57,761 truck, rail, and sea containers
- Executes 2139 apprehensions between the ports for illegal entry and 107 arrests of criminals at ports of entry
- Seizes 6643 pounds of narcotics
- Seizes 454 pests at ports of entry

USCIS

The USCIS secures America's promise as a nation of immigrants by providing accurate and useful information to its customers, granting immigration and citizenship benefits, promoting an awareness and understanding of citizenship, and ensuring the integrity of the immigration system. According to the USCIS, its strategic goals include the following[24]:

- Strengthening the security and integrity of the immigration system
- Providing effective customer-oriented immigration benefit and information services
- Supporting immigrants' integration and participation in American civic culture
- Promoting flexible and sound immigration policies and programs

- Strengthening the infrastructure supporting the USCIS mission
- Operating as a high-performance organization that promotes a highly talented workforce and a dynamic work culture

United States ICE

The United States ICE, promotes homeland security and public safety through the criminal and civil enforcement of federal laws governing border control, customs, trade, and immigration.[13] ICE is the principal investigative arm of the DHS—indeed, it is the second-largest investigative agency in the federal government. The agency was created through a merger among the investigative and interior enforcement elements of separate, different government enforcement agencies. Created in 2003, ICE is a major federal agency employing more than 20,000 employees in more than 400 offices in the United States and 46 foreign countries. Its primary mission is to promote homeland security and public safety through the criminal and civil enforcement of federal laws governing border control, customs, trade, and immigration.

ICE has an annual budget exceeding $5.7 billion, and this funding is primarily allocated among the functions of Homeland Security Investigations (HSI) and Enforcement and Removal Operations (ERO).

The enforcement focus of ICE is diverse and includes, among other things, combating the smuggling of United States currency. ICE operates the Bulk Cash Smuggling Center (BCSC), which serves as a central source for information and support for identifying, investigating, and disrupting bulk cash smuggling activities around the world. Customs laws allow ICE to seize national treasures, especially if they have been reported lost or stolen. It works with experts to authenticate the items, determine their true ownership, and return them to their countries of origin. ICE is the lead US law enforcement agency responsible for fighting human smuggling and human trafficking. It also leads money laundering and financial crime investigations. In recent decades, US law enforcement has encountered an increasing number of major financial crimes, frequently resulting from the needs for drug trafficking organizations to launder large sums of criminal proceeds through legitimate financial institutions and investment vehicles. ICE investigates narcotics smuggling organizations and the methods utilized to smuggle contraband across US borders. Many of the narcotics smuggling methods ICE encounters include the use of high-speed vessels, cargo containers, aircraft, commercial trucking, commercial vessels, and human carriers.

ICE also is engaged in combating illegal weapons smuggling between the United States and foreign entities; in recent years, the focus has increasingly turned to Mexico. Weapons smuggled into Mexico from the United States often end up in the hands of the drug cartels or other illicit organizations where they can be employed against law enforcement officers and citizens in either country. These firearms continue to fuel violence along the Southwest border and in the interior of Mexico.

To combat the illicit smuggling of weapons from the United States into Mexico, ICE initiated Operation Armas Cruzadas. As part of this initiative, agencies within the US DHS and the government of Mexico have partnered on interdiction, investigation, and intelligence-sharing activities to identify, disrupt, and dismantle transborder criminal networks that smuggle weapons from the United States into Mexico.

ICE also pursues corrupt foreign officials who plunder state coffers for personal gain and then attempt to place those funds in the US financial system. The agency's Foreign Corruption Investigations Group, part of ICE HSI, is charged with spearheading investigations that hold these individuals accountable.

In June 2010, ICE issued its strategic plan for FYs 2010–2014 demonstrating its expected responsibilities for criminal investigation and civil immigration enforcement over the next 5 years. This strategic plan highlights the following goals for the agency's future[25]:

- Prevent terrorism and enhance security
- Protect the borders against illicit trade, travel, and finance
- Protect the borders through smart and tough interior immigration enforcement
- Construct an efficient, effective agency

USCG

Though the USCG was briefly discussed in Chapter 2, it is an important agency within the DHS and performs a series of vital missions for the nation. The USCG is one of the five armed forces of the United States, and it is the only military organization within the DHS (**Figure 4.8**). The USCG protects the maritime economy and the environment, defends maritime borders, and saves those in peril. The USCG originated as the United States Revenue Marine Service on August 4, 1790, when the first Congress authorized the construction of 10 vessels to enforce tariff and trade laws and to prevent smuggling. Known variously through the 19th century and the early 20th century as the Revenue Marine and the Revenue Cutter Service, the USCG expanded in both size and responsibilities as the nation grew.[26]

The USCG is one of the oldest entities within the US federal government. Until the Navy Department was established in 1798, the USCG served as the nation's only armed force afloat.

Figure 4.8 *The coast guard is the only military branch housed within DHS. Pictured here is the US Coast Guard cutter Mohawk (WMEC 913) sailing in formation during an exercise. (Courtesy of the US Navy. Photo by Mass Communications Specialist Second Class Lenny M. Francioni.)*

The coast guard is the product of five different agencies merged over time: Revenue Marine (est. 1790), the United States Life-Saving Service (est. 1848), the United States Lighthouse Service (est. 1789), the Steamboat Inspection Service (est. 1838), and the Bureau of Navigation (est. 1884).

In 1915, the USCG received its present name, under an act of Congress, when the Revenue Cutter Service merged with the Life-Saving Service to produce the nation's initial, solitary maritime service dedicated to saving life at sea and enforcing the nation's maritime laws. The USCG began to maintain the country's aids to maritime navigation, including operating the nation's lighthouses, when President Franklin Roosevelt ordered the transfer of the Lighthouse Service to the coast guard in 1939.[26] In 1946, Congress permanently transferred the Bureau of Marine Inspection and Navigation to the USCG resulting in its oversight of merchant marine licensing and merchant vessel safety.

The USCG has protected America since its inception over two centuries ago and has served in all US national conflicts. During times of peace, the USCG is an organizational component of the US DHS, whereas it serves within the Navy Department during periods of war or per the direction of the president. Regardless of its organizational structuring, the USCG is responsible for enforcing US laws at sea, protecting the marine environment, protecting the national coastline and ports, and saving life.

Throughout its history, the missions performed by the USCG have been very diverse. From the interdiction of smugglers to conducting rescues on the high seas and nation's waterways, the coast guard has proven ever vigilant. The coast guard also serves to reinforce the nation's border security initiatives by providing a layered defense to deter, detect, and interdict undocumented migrants attempting to enter the United States illegally. In 2009 alone, the coast guard interdicted nearly 3700 undocumented immigrants.[26]

In 2008, the coast guard responded to more than 24,000 search and rescue cases and saved more than 4000 lives. It conducted more than 70,000 commercial inspections of US flagged vessels, performed more than 12,000 safety and environmental examinations of foreign vessels entering United States ports, conducted nearly 4700 marine casualty investigations, boarded nearly 3700 underway fishing vessels to perform safety and compliance checks, and performed nearly 7300 dockside safety examinations.

Working with the Departments of Defense, Homeland Security, and Justice as well as other partners, in 2008, the coast guard seized nearly 185 tons of cocaine bound for the United States, interdicted nearly 5000 undocumented migrants attempting to illegally enter the United States, deployed 6 patrol boats and 400 personnel to protect Iraq's maritime oil infrastructure, trained Iraqi naval forces, enforced United Nations (UN) sanctions in the Arabian Gulf, conducted more than 1500 security boardings of high-interest vessels bound for the United States, and provided waterside security and escorts for nearly 500 military freight conveyances during Operation Iraqi Freedom and Operation Enduring Freedom.

USSS

The USSS (**Figure 4.9**) protects the president and vice president and safeguards the nation's financial infrastructure and payment systems. It also protects visiting heads of state and government at designated sites and National Special Security Events.[13] In 1865, the Secret Service Division was created to suppress counterfeit currency; Chief William P. Wood was sworn in by Secretary of the Treasury Hugh McCulloch as its first head. As time went on, Secret Service responsibilities were broadened to include "detecting persons perpetrating frauds against the

Figure 4.9 *United States Secret Service badge. (Courtesy of the USSS.)*

government," and this resulted in investigations of the Ku Klux Klan, nonconforming distillers, smugglers, mail robbers, and a number of other infractions against the federal laws.

A major national security concern is the protection of the national government from threats and the protection of the leaders of the government. The protection of the president is a major concern. Four United States presidents have been assassinated while serving in office, Presidents Lincoln, Garfield, McKinley, and Kennedy. The security protecting Presidents Lincoln, Garfield, and McKinley was either unorganized or totally absent. As a result of the 1901 assassination of President McKinley (**Figure 4.10**), the Secret Service assumed full-time responsibility for protection of the President.

The Secret Service began protecting the president-elect in 1908, and during the 1913 election, Congress authorized permanent protection of the president and the president-elect. In 1951, through Public Law 82-79, Congress enacted legislation that permanently authorized Secret Service protection of the president, his immediate family, the president-elect, and the vice president. In 1961, Congress authorized protection of former presidents for a reasonable period of time.

In 1965, Congress authorized protection of former presidents and their spouses during their lifetime and minor children until age 16. The 1970s witnessed the additional duties of diplomacy protection. During this decade, Congress authorized Secret Service protection for visiting heads of a foreign state or government, or other official guests, as directed; expanded its duties to include protection of foreign diplomatic missions located throughout the United States and its territories; and increased its responsibilities to include the protection of diplomatic missions in the area of Washington, DC (Public Law 91-217).

The Patriot Act (Public Law 107-56) increased the role of the Secret Service regarding investigating fraud and related activity in connection with computers. It authorized the director of the Secret Service to establish nationwide electronic crime task forces to assist law enforcement, the private sector, and academia in detecting and suppressing computer-based crime; increased the statutory penalties for the manufacturing, possession, dealing, and passing of counterfeit US or foreign obligations; and allowed enforcement action to be taken to protect financial payment systems while

Figure 4.10 Assassination of President McKinley, 1901. (Courtesy of the US National Library of Medicine.)

combating transnational financial crimes directed by terrorists or other criminals. The DHS was established with the passage of Public Law 107-296, which partially transferred the USSS from the Department of the Treasury to the new department effective March 1, 2003.

In 2007, protection began for presidential candidate Illinois senator Barack Obama, and this protection was the earliest initiation of Secret Service protection for any candidate in history. Presidential candidate New York Senator Hillary Clinton already received protection before she entered the race because of her status as former first lady. Since 2003, the Secret Service has made nearly 29,000 criminal arrests for counterfeiting, cyber investigations, and other financial crimes, 98% of which resulted in convictions, and seized more than $295 million in counterfeit currency. The Secret Service investigated and closed financial crimes cases where actual loss amounted to $3.7 billion and prevented a potential loss of more than $12 billion.

The modern instantiation of the Secret Service provides valuable contributions toward the facilitation of the security of the United States. Through its protection of the president, vice president, and diplomatic entities, it embellishes the concept of government continuance and the safety of elected leaders. Because of its responsibilities regarding financial crimes, the Secret Service facilitates the security and integrity of the economic and financial systems that form the basis of US commerce and trade.

Office of the Secretary of the DHS

The DHS also includes the Office of the Secretary. The Office of the Secretary consists of 11 separate agencies whose duties provide a variety of functions and services. The following entities comprise the Office of the Secretary:

- Privacy Office
- Office for Civil Rights and Civil Liberties

- Office of the Inspector General
- Office of the Citizenship and Immigration Services Ombudsman
- Office of Legislative Affairs
- Office of the General Counsel
- Office of Public Affairs
- Office of Counternarcotics Enforcement (CNE)
- Office of the Executive Secretariat (ESEC)
- Military Advisor's Office
- Office of Intergovernmental Affairs (IGA)

Each of these offices fulfills an administrative capacity that facilitates the effective and efficient functioning of the DHS. These offices collaboratively and separately perform a variety of functions, ranging from public interaction to facilitating cooperation and dialogue among peer government entities. Regardless of the function, each of these offices provides a unique service within the context of homeland security.

The Privacy Office works to preserve and enhance privacy protections for all individuals, to promote transparency of DHS operations, and to serve as a leader in the privacy community. The Office for Civil Rights and Civil Liberties provides legal and policy advice to department leadership on civil rights and civil liberties issues, investigates and resolves complaints, and provides leadership to Equal Employment Opportunity Programs. The Office of the Inspector General is responsible for conducting and supervising audits, investigations, and inspections relating to the programs and operations of the department, recommending ways for the department to carry out its responsibilities in the most effective, efficient, and economical manner possible.

The Citizenship and Immigration Services Ombudsman provides recommendations for resolving individual and employer problems with the USCIS in order to ensure national security and the integrity of the legal immigration system, increase efficiencies in administering citizenship and immigration services, and improve customer service. The Office of Legislative Affairs serves as primary liaison to members of Congress and their staffs, the White House and the executive branch, and other federal agencies and governmental entities that have roles in assuring national security. The Office of the General Counsel integrates approximately 1700 lawyers from throughout the department into an effective, client-oriented, full-service legal team and comprises a headquarters office with subsidiary divisions and the legal programs for eight department components, and it also includes the ethics division for the department.

The Office of Public Affairs coordinates the public affairs activities of all of the department's components and offices and serves as the federal government's lead public information office during a national emergency or disaster. Led by the assistant secretary for public affairs, it comprises the press office, incident and strategic communications, speechwriting, Internet content management, and employee communications. The CNE coordinates policy and operations to stop the entry of illegal drugs into the United States and to track and sever the connections between illegal drug trafficking and terrorism.

The ESEC provides all manner of direct support to the secretary and deputy secretary, as well as related support to leadership and management across the department. This support takes many forms, the most well known being accurate and timely dissemination of information and written communications from throughout the department and homeland security partners to the secretary and deputy secretary. The Military Advisor's Office advises on facilitating, coordinating, and executing policy, procedures, preparedness activities, and operations between the department and the DOD. The IGA has the mission of promoting an integrated national approach to homeland security by ensuring, coordinating, and advancing federal interaction with state, local, tribal, and territorial governments.[13]

Advisory Panels and Committees

The DHS also manifests a myriad of panels and committees, each of which provides an administrative capacity that facilitates the effective and efficient functioning of the DHS. These collaboratively and separately perform a variety of functions, ranging from issues of labor to facilitating cooperativeness and dialogues among peer government entities. Regardless of the function, each of these provides a unique service within the context of homeland security. The following entities comprise a partial list of panels and committees in the DHS:

- Homeland Security Advisory Council
- National Infrastructure Advisory Council
- Homeland Security Science and Technology Advisory Committee
- Critical Infrastructure Partnership Advisory Council
- Interagency Coordinating Council on Emergency Preparedness and Individuals with Disabilities
- Task Force on New Americans
- DHS Labor-Management Forum

Similar to the components of the Office of the Secretary, each of these panels and committees provides an administrative capacity that facilitates the effective and efficient functioning of the DHS. These entities also collaboratively and separately perform a variety of functions, ranging from issues of labor to facilitating cooperation and dialogue among peer government entities. Regardless of the function, each of these offices provides a unique service within the context of homeland security.

The Homeland Security Advisory Council provides advice and recommendations concerning homeland security matters and is comprised of leaders from state and local government, first-responder communities, the private sector, and academia. The National Infrastructure Advisory Council provides advice to the secretary of homeland security and the president concerning the security of information systems for the public and private institutions that constitute the critical infrastructure of the national economy. The Homeland Security Science and Technology Advisory Committee is a source of independent, scientific, and technical planning advice for the undersecretary for science and technology.

The Critical Infrastructure Partnership Advisory Council facilitates effective coordination between federal infrastructure protection programs and the infrastructure protection activities of the private sector and of state, local, territorial, and tribal governments. The Interagency Coordinating Council on Emergency Preparedness and Individuals with Disabilities ensures that the federal government appropriately supports safety and security for individuals with disabilities in disaster situations. The Task Force on New Americans is an interagency effort to assist immigrants when learning English, embracing the common core of American civic culture, and becoming fully American. The DHS Labor-Management Forum supports cooperative and productive labor-management relations.[13]

Committee and panel responsibilities are domain specific with respect to their individual functions. These entities are primarily responsible for analyzing situations and rendering advice regarding a myriad of topics and situations. They work collaboratively with entities of the public and private sectors to craft advice regarding strategic courses of action that impact the long-term pursuits of the homeland security community. Through the use of such entities, the DHS gains the ability to analyze a variety of issues from multiple perspectives.

Conclusion

The American Revolution was hard fought to create an independent nation. Since that time, a legacy has been preserved of protecting the borders of the United States and its territories. The most important function of government is keeping the country secure. Terrorism has a long history, but until September 11, 2001, few Americans were touched by it. The responders across the country were not unaware of the threat of terrorism; however, it was not a focus in equipment and training programs.

The 1993 bombing of the World Trade Center received short-lived attention. During this time, the Hart–Rudman idea of creating a commission to study global threats began to prick the political consciousness. The Defense Against Weapons of Mass Destruction Act of 1996 was passed in the wake of the bombing of the Oklahoma City federal building. On the domestic front, there was evidence that awareness of the threats was part of the policy and political environment.

The creation of the DHS was not simply a reaction to the events of September 11, 2001. That day of attacks was the catalyst to set the priority for government to bring a focal point in combating terrorism and securing the United States, not in the traditional military mode but in preparing the civilian response community and the citizens at large.

All of the questions relative to how the DHS should function and the clarification of its mission remain unanswered. Indeed, critics charge that many DHS programs are given little chance to mature before they are changed. It would do us well to learn from history. In 1947, President Truman indicated not that the president and the United States Congress thought the navy or the army had failed in their missions, but that there was a need to create the DOD. This seems to be the idea in creating the DHS. The optimal end product in the concept is determined by whether the function of an agency is enhanced within the incorporation of its partners. The focus should be on the function instead of the positioning.

In February 2009, then representative James Oberstar (Democrat, Minnesota) proffered legislation to bring FEMA out of the DHS and make it a standalone agency. Mr. Oberstar disagrees with the notion that disasters are local incidents. He further believes that FEMA is too restricted in its present position with the DHS to be optimally effective. Others disagree with these positions and hold the position that FEMA should stay within the DHS, reporting to the secretary. The FEMA debate is linked to perceptions created during Hurricane Katrina and the breach of the levee system in South Louisiana. It became popular to advocate the failure of the response. However, such a notion is an oversimplification. Some of the leadership at the various levels of government may have failed, but the response was not a failure in all of the jurisdictions across the Gulf Coast.

Local communities are ultimately responsible for the disasters that strike them. Long before state and federal governments are on scene to make assessments, the local governments and neighborhoods respond to the crisis. The response results are not based upon where FEMA is positioned in an organization. The assistance provided to local governments is based upon whether the function is prepared to act or not. Many first responders experienced FEMA protocols when FEMA was an independent agency and not during a period in which FEMA was a directorate within the DHS. That experience indicates that it is not the matter of positioning that is debatable; instead, it is the matter of functioning. The future will manifest transitional years for the DHS. The debate regarding the placement of FEMA will apparently occupy future instantiations of Congress.

Just as the DOD plays a significant role in homeland defense, the DHS must lead in initiatives of homeland security. It is imperative that these two models have the shared vision and the common direction to create the strongest possible stronghold against terrorism and aggression that targets the homeland, American interests, and American citizens both at home and abroad. There is a reason the American citizenry remembers and memorializes Pearl Harbor and the attacks of September 11, 2001. The history of how well prepared the nation is to endure disasters is still being written. Is the nation better prepared now than before 2001? Probably. Does the nation have more to accomplish? Definitely.

Key terms

All hazards
Border security
Civil defense
Department of Homeland Security
Domestic threat
Federal Emergency Management Agency
Government agency
Immigration
Intelligence
Intelligence analysis
International threat
Man-made threat
Natural threat
Organization
Organizational component
Threat
Transportation Security Administration
Vulnerability

QUESTIONS FOR DISCUSSION

1. The world is a dynamic place in which emerging threats may originate from both domestic and international sources. Given the all-hazards approach to homeland security that is advocated by the DHS, do you believe that it fulfills its mission and purpose both effectively and efficiently? Write a brief essay that expresses and substantiates your opinion.
2. Change is a common aspect of any organization. Given the large quantity of organizations that are contained within the DHS umbrella, with what level of ease do you believe the DHS can accommodate the changing dynamics of emerging threats? Write a brief essay that highlights your opinion.
3. The DHS was formed during the aftermath of September 11, 2001. However, this terrorist attack was not the first attack that occurred upon American soil (e.g., 1993 World Trade Center bombing). Given the history of attacks against American interests

and resources, do you believe that the DHS should have been formed much earlier in history? Why or why not? Write a brief essay that substantiates your response.

4. Each of the states has its own homeland security agency. Review your state's homeland security agency, and compare and contrast it with the federal DHS. Write a brief essay that discusses the similarities and differences that you discover.

References

1. U.S. Department of Homeland Security. (2002). Homeland security proposal delivered to congress. http://www.DepartmentofHomelandSecurity.gov/xnews/speeches/speech_0039.shtm (accessed December 12, 2008).
2. Thornberry, M. (2001). Thornberry introduces legislation to realign federal government so it is better prepared to respond to homeland security threats. http://govinfo.library.unt.edu/nssg/News/PhaseIII/press_release_thornberry.doc (accessed February 19, 2009).
3. Kincaid, M. (2013). Cybersecurity news round up: 2013 defense budget outlines new mandates to enhance cybersecurity. http://www.clearancejobs.com/defense-news/1048/cybersecurity-news-round-up-2013-defense-budget-outlines-new-mandates-to-enhance-cybersecurity (accessed January 17, 2013).
4. The White House. (2011). Fact sheet: safeguarding the U.S. government's classified information and networks. *Office of the Press Secretary*. http://www.whitehouse.gov/the-press-office/2011/10/07/fact-sheet-safeguarding-us-governments-classified-information-and-networ?utm_source=related (accessed January 17, 2013).
5. Department of Defense. (2011). *Department of Defense Strategy for Operating in Cyberspace*. Washington, DC: US Government, p. 8.
6. Department of Defense. (2011). *Department of Defense Strategy for Operating in Cyberspace*. Washington, DC: US Government, p. 9.
7. Clayton, M. (2013). *ABC News*. http://abcnews.go.com/Technology/secret-nsa-cybersecurity-program-aims-defend-us-power/story?id=18134323 (accessed January 17, 2013).
8. Taylor, P. (2012). Former US spy warns on cybersecurity. *CNBC News*. http://www.cnbc.com/id/100267883/Former_US_Spy_Warns_on_Cybersecurity (accessed January 17, 2013).
9. US Department of Homeland Security. (2013). Secretary Napolitano announces fiscal year 2013 budget request. http://www.dhs.gov/news/2012/02/13/secretary-napolitano-announces-fiscal-year-2013-budget-request (accessed January 17, 2013).
10. Kolb, J. (2013). Study finds corruption on rise among border agents, rep says security 'at risk'. *Foxnews*. http://www.foxnews.com/politics/2013/01/15/study-finds-corruption-on-rise-among-border-agents-rep-says-security-at-risk/%20?test=latestnews (accessed January 17, 2013).
11. Associated Press. (2012). Man charged with building 2 major border tunnels. http://bigstory.ap.org/article/man-charged-building-2-major-border-tunnels (accessed January 17, 2013).
12. Dinan, S. (2013). Interceptions of immigrants stubbornly low. *The Washington Times*. http://www.washingtontimes.com/news/2013/jan/9/interceptions-immigrants-stubbornly-low/ (accessed January 17, 2013).
13. Department Subcomponents. (2010). Department subcomponents and agencies. *U.S. Department of Homeland Security*. http://www.dhs.gov/xabout/structure/ (accessed November 22, 2010).
14. DNPP. (2010). Directorate for National Protection and Programs. http://www.dhs.gov/xabout/structure/editorial_0794.shtm (accessed November 22, 2010).
15. Science. (2010). Science and Technology Directorate. http://www.dhs.gov/xabout/structure/editorial_0530.shtm (accessed November 22, 2010).
16. OHA. (2010). Office of Health Affairs. http://www.dhs.gov/xabout/structure/editorial_0880.shtm (accessed November 22, 2010).
17. Office of Intelligence and Analysis. (2010). Office of Intelligence and Analysis. http://www.dhs.gov/xabout/structure/gc_1220886590914.shtm (accessed November 22, 2010).
18. OOCP. (2010). Office of Operations Coordination and Planning. http://www.dhs.gov/xabout/structure/editorial_0797.shtm (accessed November 22, 2010).
19. FLETC. (2010). *Federal Law Enforcement Training Center*. http://www.fletc.gov/ (accessed November 22, 2010).
20. DNDO. (2010). Domestic Nuclear Detection Office. http://www.dhs.gov/xabout/structure/editorial_0766.shtm (accessed November 22, 2010).

21. FEMA. (2010). *Federal Emergency Response Agency*. http://www.fema.gov/about/index.shtm (accessed November 22, 2010).
22. Haddow, G. and Bullock, J. The future of emergency management. http://www.fema.gov (accessed April 29, 2013).
23. CBP. (2010). *Customs and Border Protection*. http://www.cbp.gov/linkhandler/cgov/about/accomplish/snapshot.ctt/snapshot.pd (accessed November 22, 2010).
24. CIS. (2010). *Citizen and Immigration Services*. http://www.uscis.gov/portal/site/uscis/menuitem.eb1d4c2a3e5b9ac89243c6a7543f6d1a/?vgnextoid=2af29c7755cb9010VgnVCM10000045f3d6a1RCRD&vgnextchannel=2af29c7755cb9010VgnVCM10000045f3d6a1RCRD (accessed November 22, 2010).
25. ICE. (2010). *Immigration and Customs Enforcement*. http://www.ice.gov/about/overview/ (accessed November 22, 2010).
26. USCG. (2010). *United States Coast Guard*. http://www.uscg.mil/history/faqs/district.asp (accessed November 22, 2010).
27. Office of Policy. (2010). Office of Policy. http://www.dhs.gov/xabout/structure/editorial_0870.shtm (accessed November 22, 2010).

5

Homeland Security: Function and Operations

We need a department of Homeland Security. We've got to defend our homeland, because we have a great Navy and a great Army and a great Marine Corps and a great Air Force. But when it comes to defending America from terrorists, they can respond for us, be here in this country, defending against people like we are dealing with, that is not what we need. We need other formulations.

Warren Rudman
former US Senator, CNN's Larry King Live, 10/09/01

Chapter objectives:

- Gain an understanding of homeland security function and operations
- Understand the role and mission of Joint Terrorism Task Forces
- Review the major purpose and intent of the USA Patriot Act of 2001
- Gain an understanding of the purpose of the Public Health Security and Bioterrorism Preparedness and Response Act
- Review the major purpose of Homeland Security Presidential Directive 7
- Gain an understanding of the purpose of Presidential Decision Directive 39

Introduction

The attacks of 2001 against the United States set into motion dynamic changes in the way the nation viewed its national security. Policy makers recognized that efforts were required to bring together national, state, local, tribal, and private capabilities in an effort to reduce vulnerabilities and enhance recovery capabilities. As a major part of the efforts to enhance the nation's homeland security, a new organization, the Department of Homeland Security (DHS), was formed to more effectively orchestrate threat assessment, planning, response, and recovery efforts to both man-made and natural disasters.

This new entity represents a philosophical approach to guarding against a variety of threats both domestically and internationally. The DHS approaches its responsibilities from a per-spective of potentially experiencing a variety of hazards, thereby instantiating its "all-hazards" concept of homeland security. Therefore, it considers the potentials of both man-made and natural hazards as potential threats that may adversely impact American society.

This all-hazards perspective is massive; it necessitates considerations of numerous functions and operations both internally and externally. All of the DHS components must work together efficiently and effectively, and it must also cooperate with a variety of external entities. Within the domain of homeland security, functions and operations are not identical. This chapter explores the similarities and differences exhibited within this dichotomy. The discussions herein introduce the fiduciary responsibilities that are central to the successful performance of the DHS.

A perspective of homeland security

Homeland security is not a solitary concept. Instead, homeland security can be viewed as a function, process, discipline, and/or organization. As a function or process, one can view the anticipated threats and recovery missions that are likely to face the nation. Many of these threats are not new but, rather, natural and recurring, such as hurricanes, earthquakes, floods, and tornados. With the improvement seen in the areas of prevention, it is very unlikely that any cities in the nation will face devastation related to fire, such as that which impacted Chicago during the 1800s, unless it is related to a larger event such as a major earthquake.

As a discipline, homeland security is quickly evolving into an area of research and study similar to criminal justice, moving from an area once viewed as exclusively vocational to one in which all aspects of the sciences, management, budgeting, and planning are included within the field. Homeland security, as a discipline, is integrative regarding the functions of a wide range of first responders such as law enforcement, fire services, emergency medical technicians, and emergency management. It is typically thought to be a system of protocols and practices. The activities of a discipline exhibit these functions. The homeland security function is an extensive, comprehensive system of activities. The functions of homeland security are best identified by identifying the disciplines and the agencies that perform the activities of homeland security at each level of government. The mission of the United States DHS is to "coordinate the efforts at securing the nation."* The function of coordination is often less visible than other activities in disciplines such as police, fire, and so forth.

Organizationally, one can examine the structures, missions, functions, and characteristics of the many agencies with primary or secondary missions supporting disaster planning, response, or recovery. These agencies include the local, state, tribal, and private emergency management and emergency response agencies involved in the homeland security planning, prevention, and recovery efforts.

DHS

As we have learned, the DHS represents 22 different federal agencies of government that were integrated after the 2001 attacks. Agencies within the DHS include a wide range of agencies, including the United States Secret Service, formally under the United States Department of the Treasury and the Federal Emergency Management Agency (FEMA).

---

* http://www.DepartmentofHomelandSecurity.gov.

The DHS houses the Homeland Security Operations Center (HSOC). The Border Patrol is under the auspices of the DHS, along with the US Immigration Service, the United States Coast Guard, and the Transportation Security Agency. The DHS is part of the intelligence community through its Intelligence Unit. The DHS has many program managers in its grant and training programs. These are some of the agencies in the DHS. There are many programs and positions within the department. With approximately 200,000 employees, it is not difficult to imagine the many administrative, programmatic, and operational positions in the department.

Prevention: Disciplines, function, and operations

From a state and local law enforcement perspective, the intelligence and information-sharing capabilities were historically huge gaps throughout the United States for civilian and domestic law enforcement agencies. The gaps were identified and prioritized following the events of September 11, 2001—particularly within the 9/11 Commission study. The intelligence capability is an activity that provides the potential for interrupting man-made incidents prior to their erupting. Information sharing is the ability and capability of transmitting information to the "need-to-know" partners in the prevention mission area. Prevention capabilities move the preparedness initiatives closer to a proactive action, thereby reducing loss mitigation. Law enforcement operates within the prevention mission area as a lead discipline. This concept should be modeled throughout each level of government.

The Federal Bureau of Investigation (FBI) is the primary agency responsible for investigating suspected and overt acts of terrorism.* This status is standard protocol for the FBI. Some make the mistake of interpreting this status to mean that the FBI becomes the lead response agency. Do not be confused on this issue. Certainly, when an act of terrorism or threatened act occurs, the FBI is the lead agency in the investigation, and the US Department of Justice is the lead in the prosecution. To repeat what is a recurring theme in this text, incidents occur in local communities.

At no time, except in failed circumstances, does the federal government or its agencies take over a local community. The local law enforcement agencies are the lead in local intelligence, information sharing, and *responding* to a suspected and/or overt act of terrorism. The same is true in the local government responding to a natural disaster. However, to assist local and state governments, the president of the United States, in Presidential Decision Directive 39, followed in Presidential Decision Directive 62, identified the FBI as the lead law enforcement agency in the investigating of acts of terrorism. This structure is the same model practiced when local communities experience a robbery of a Federal Deposit Insurance Corporation (FDIC)–insured bank or other crimes having federal jurisdiction.

In 1980, the FBI, along with law enforcement partnering agencies, established the first Joint Terrorism Task Force (JTTF). Currently, there are over 100 JTTFs throughout the United States. Their membership is comprised of 2196 FBI special agents, 838 state and local law enforcement officers, and 689 other professionals. The JTTFs are designed to provide a relatively small group of subject matter experts, multidisciplined and multijurisdictional, that work with federal, state, and local agencies in information sharing, intelligence, investigations, and resource support relative to acts of terrorism and potential use of weapons of mass destruction.

The local JTTFs coordinate with the National Terrorism Task Force located in the Washington, DC, headquarters of the FBI. State and local units of law enforcement participate in the

---

* Presidential Decision Directive 39. 1995. Washington, DC.

JTTFs. In addition, many states have created intelligence fusion centers since 9/11. State and major urban area fusion centers (fusion centers) serve as focal points within the state and local environment for the receipt, analysis, gathering, and sharing of threat-related information between the federal government and state, local, tribal, territorial (SLTT), and private sector partners. Fusion centers are owned and operated by state and local entities with support from federal partners in the form of deployed personnel, training, technical assistance, exercise support, security clearances, various relationships with federal systems, technology, and grant funding.

Law enforcement, at every level of government, performs prevention initiatives. Within this discussion, the effectiveness of these initiatives is unexamined. It is important, within a discussion regarding homeland security as a function and operationally, to identify the various efforts made by law enforcement in the prevention mission area. It is also important to recognize that many federal, state, and local law enforcement agencies, other than the FBI, are involved in the homeland security prevention initiatives. The FBI has been emphasized based upon its being the lead in investigating potential and realized acts of terrorism within the United States.

The threat of use of biological weapons has been prioritized by the federal government. The lead in responding to and investigating a suspected and/or actual biological incident is directed to the US Department of Health and Human Services, which is commonly referred to as Public Health (PH). Presidential Decision Directive 39 gives the lead in a biological incident to PH. The awareness of this directive has become relevant with the heightened threat of pandemic and avian flu outbreaks (**Figure 5.1**). When preparing for a Chemical, Biological, Radiological, Nuclear, and Explosives (CBRNE) incident, the focus is not simply on some rogue laboratory creating a weapon from a benign substance, nor is the attention on a violator

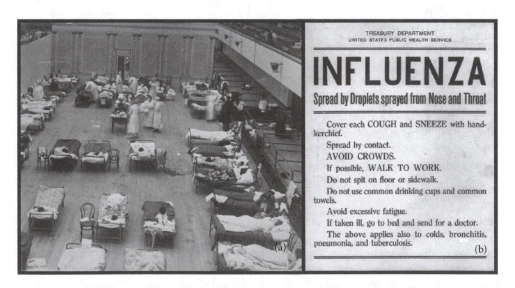

Figure 5.1 *1918 flu epidemic. (a) The Oakland Municipal Auditorium in use as a temporary hospital with volunteer nurses from the American Red Cross tending to influenza sufferers. (Courtesy of the Oakland Public Library. Material is in the public domain; there are no restrictions on use.) (b) Treasury Department, United States Public Health Service, influenza advice, 1918. (Courtesy of the Library of Congress.)*

bringing a substance into a jurisdiction. Instead, the focus concerns a potential threat element creating a weapon from an agent currently in the jurisdiction. For example, if a jurisdiction has a chemical manufacturing plant in its community, how can that facility or the product at that facility be weaponized and used against the jurisdiction? Is there a laboratory in the jurisdiction that works in the biological industry? Is there something manufactured within that entity that could be weaponized?

Suspicious substance responses among local communities are common. Local governments spend a significant amount of money and time annually in responding to "white powder" and suspicious substance incidents. Most of the incidents are related to suspected incidents involving poisonous anthrax. Most of the incidents are determined to be artificial sweeteners, baking soda, flour, and so forth. However, because governments must respond to these incidents, it is evident that it is a persistent threat that demands appropriate response.

PH, at each level of government, is the lead entity in the prevention mission relative to the plethora of threats posed by biological incidents. The Public Health Security and Bioterrorism Preparedness Response Act of 2002 continued and expanded the legal intent of PH's role in bioterrorism incidents. Excerpts of the act promote the idea of operations relative to biological incidents.

The act states its purpose: "To improve the ability of the United States to prevent, prepare for, and respond to bioterrorism and other public health emergencies." Further SEC. 2801, National Preparedness Plan, states:

"(a) in General (1) Preparedness and response regarding public health—The Secretary shall further develop and implement a coordinated strategy, building upon the core public health capabilities established pursuant to section 319A, 42 USC 300hh....."

Further the Act states, "Public Law 107-188—June 12, 2002 116 STAT. 597 for carrying out health-related activities to prepare for and respond effectively to bioterrorism and other public health emergencies, including the preparation of a plan under this section. The Secretary shall periodically thereafter review and, as appropriate, revise the plan." Regarding preparedness, the plan also indicates "(1) Providing effective assistance to State and local governments in the event of bioterrorism or other public health emergency.... (2) Ensuring that State and local governments have appropriate capacity to detect and respond effectively to such emergencies..."*

In 1984, a criminal biological incident occurred in The Dalles, Oregon. The incident involved a strain of salmonella. Salmonella is a food-borne pathogen. Its incubation period is between 6 and 72 hours. Symptoms may include diarrhea, nausea, vomiting, fever, and chills. In extreme cases, it can be fatal. The investigation involved the local health department and local law enforcement entities. Because of the preliminary concerns in the case, the Centers for Disease Control and the FBI were requested. It took well over a year for authorities to determine that this incident was an intentional act. Once this suspicion is reached in an investigation that may involve weapons of mass destruction, the guiding law is Title 18, USC Section 2332(a), which defines a weapon of mass destruction. During the investigation, a vial was discovered at the Rajneesh ranch that matched the type of agent found at the restaurants. In 1986, four people were convicted of the crime. A total of 751 people were infected by the salmonella.

Bioterrorism represents the "intentional use of infectious agents, or germs, to cause illness."[1] Much has changed since this example occurred in the 1980s. Although its basic concept

---

* Public Law 107-188. June 12, 2002. Public Health Security and Bioterrorism Preparedness Response Act of 2002. Washington, DC.

involves bioterrorism, the seriousness of bioterrorist dangers is unabated. In 2002, the Public Health Security and Bioterrorism Preparedness and Response Act was enacted by Congress. This legislation contained the following items:

- Authorization for approximately $1.5 billion of grant funding to assist "states, local governments, and healthcare facilities to improve their planning and preparedness, enhance lab capacity, and train personnel and to develop new drugs and vaccines."[2]
- Authorization for approximately $1.15 billion for expanding the "Strategic National Stockpile, including the supply of smallpox vaccine."[2]
- Authorization for approximately $300 million to support upgrade components of the Centers for Disease Control and Prevention (CDC) that deal with "public health threats."[2]
- Mandating requirements for registering "all possessors of the 36 biological agents and toxins" that are deemed the "most dangerous to humans."[2] It also necessitated "similar regulation of agents that are devastating to crops and livestock."[2]
- Authorization for approximately $545 million in funding for the Food and Drug Administration (FDA) and US Department of Agriculture (USDA) for the purpose of hiring "food-import inspectors" and developing "new methods to detect contaminated foods, and protect crops and livestock."[2]
- Empowering of the FDA to detain and inspect "suspicious foods," requiring "advance notice" of imported foods, and the gaining of improved "access to records" necessary for investigating the "source of food contamination."[2]
- Authorizing of at least $100 million in funding to assist "water utilities" when analyzing the vulnerabilities of "drinking-water systems to deliberate contamination."[2]

One must neither discount nor ignore the potential dangers of bioterrorism. In 2013, three ricin-laced letters were mailed to President Barak Obama; US senator Roger Wicker; and a local judge in Tupelo, Mississippi, Sadie Holland.[3] Initially, an Elvis impersonator, Paul Kevin Curtis, was identified as the culprit.[3] However, he was released, and charges were dropped.[3] A second individual, Everett Dutschke, a martial arts instructor, was identified as the alleged culprit.[3] Dutschke was arrested and charged with the crime.[3] This incident occurred during the time of this writing, and its outcome is pending.

As an operational concern, it is necessary for law enforcement and PH to create a model for working on the bioterrorism incident in partnership. The public health official must adapt to the protocols established and upheld by the courts as these protocols manage crime scenes, confidential information that may be under the supervision of grand juries and courts, and chain-of-custody issues. What may be considered a sample in public health is evidence to the law enforcement investigator. Evidence must be secured and preserved based on the court standard in chain-of-custody models. Conversely, law enforcement must learn the protocols mandated to public health authorities in assuming responsibilities for identification of substances, laboratory intake and analysis, and risk communications.

Law enforcement and PH have a tremendous responsibility with respect to the mission of prevention. PH becomes a significant partner in the intelligence environment and indispensable in the information-sharing component. The broad spectrum of biological incidents that can occur causes the partnership between law enforcement and the public health sector to continue to mature as the threats remain for biological incidents. This discussion emphasized the roles of law enforcement and PH regarding the prevention initiatives. Law enforcement and PH are highlighted to exemplify the operations and functions within two lead agencies relative to prevention initiatives.

Protect: Disciplines, function, operations

Homeland Security Presidential Directive 7 states, "This directive establishes a national policy for Federal departments and agencies to identify and prioritize United States critical infrastructure and key resources and to protect them from terrorist attacks." Most critical infrastructure and key assets are in local communities. The mission area of protection is one of the four mission areas that highlight the operational component in homeland security. In the mission area of protection, four target capabilities exist: critical infrastructure protection, food and agriculture safety and defense, epidemiological surveillance and investigation, and public health laboratory testing. In the mission area of protection, similar to the mission area of prevention, law enforcement and PH are lead agencies.

Operationally, one of the most critical tasks public safety undertakes is to protect critical infrastructure (**Figure 5.2**). Most of the critical infrastructure is owned and operated by the private sector. Critical infrastructure protection places a huge burden on local government. However, from a physical security perspective, protection of the critical infrastructure is a traditional role of law enforcement and public safety agencies. The traditional role has significantly changed since the 1990s. Because terrorism has been effective worldwide, a priority has been placed on protecting critical infrastructure within the United States. The following figure depicts analytical considerations that the DHS contemplates when simulating potential danger scenarios involving critical infrastructure.

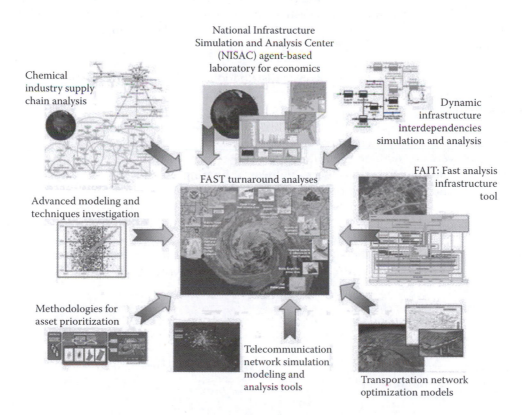

Figure 5.2 *Scenario simulation involving critical infrastructure concerns. (Courtesy of the DHS, National Infrastructure Simulation and Analysis Center.)*

In 1996, President Clinton issued Executive Order 13010. This executive order addressed the issues and concerns regarding critical infrastructure. The definition given for infrastructure in this executive order is as follows: "The framework of interdependent networks and systems comprising identifiable industries, institutions (including people and procedures), and distribution capabilities that provide a reliable flow of products and services essential to the defense and economic security of the United States, the smooth functioning of government at all levels, and society as a whole."*

Executive Order 13010 identified critical infrastructure as follows:

- Telecommunications
- Electrical power systems
- Gas and oil storage and transportation
- Banking and finance
- Transportation
- Water supply systems
- Emergency services (including medical, police, fire, and rescue)
- Continuity of government[†]

The USA Patriot Act of 2001, (Public Law 107-56) defines critical infrastructure as "systems and assets, whether physical or virtual, so vital to the United States that the incapacity or destruction of such systems and assets would have a debilitating impact on security, national economic security, national public health or safety, or any combination of those matters." This definition was adopted in the Homeland Security Act of 2002. Within Executive Order 13228 of 2001, President Bush articulated these critical infrastructures to be protected:

- Energy production, transmission, and distribution services and critical facilities
- Other utilities
- Telecommunications
- Facilities that produce, use, store, or dispose of nuclear material
- Public and privately owned information systems
- Special events of national significance
- Transportation including railways, highways, shipping ports, and waterways
- Airports and civilian aircraft
- Livestock, agriculture, and systems for the provision of water and food for human use and consumption.

In Homeland Security Presidential Directive 7, the following list identifies critical infrastructure and the agencies that are directed to act as lead in the protection mission area.

- United States DHS:
  - Information technology
  - Telecommunications
  - Chemicals
  - Transportation systems, including mass transit, aviation, maritime, ground/surface, and rail and pipeline systems

---

* Executive Order 13010. Critical Infrastructure Protection. 1996.
† Ibid.

- Emergency services
- Postal and shipping services
- USDA
  - Agriculture, food (meat, poultry, egg products)
- United States Department of Health and Human Services
  - Public health, health care, and food (other than meat, poultry, and egg products)
- Environmental Protection Agency (EPA)
  - Drinking water and wastewater treatment systems
- United States Department of Energy
  - Energy, including the production, refining, storage, and distribution of oil and gas, and electric power (except for commercial nuclear power facilities)
- United States Department of the Treasury
  - Banking and finance
- United States Department of the Interior
  - National monuments and icons
- United States Department of Defense
  - Defense industrial base

For each of the federal agencies, there is a corresponding function in both state and local governments. Banks and financial sector offices are located in local jurisdictions. The monuments and icons are in local jurisdictions. Military installations, farms, dairies, transportation systems—all are part of local jurisdictions. Disasters and acts of terrorism occur among local jurisdictions. Critical infrastructure protection is a priority in public safety for local jurisdictions.

The priority is to prevent loss incidents from occurring. Hopefully, the intelligence function will provide the capability of intervening prior to an actual loss experience. In the case that prevention is breached, the protection mission and initiatives are prioritized. To assist in protection planning and operational missions, the DHS publishes the National Infrastructure Protection Plan (NIPP). As stated in that document, the overarching goal is to "build a safer, more secure, and more resilient America by preventing, deterring, neutralizing, or mitigating the effects of deliberate efforts by terrorists to destroy, incapacitate, or exploit elements of our Nation's CIKR (Critical Infrastructure, Key Resources) and to strengthen national preparedness, timely response, and rapid recovery of CIKR in the event of an attack, natural disaster, or other emergency."* The NIPP further outlines the task for state, local, tribal, and territorial governments. It states, "Develop and implement a CIKR protection program, in accordance with the NIPP risk management framework, as a component of their overarching homeland security programs."† The risk management scheme, in simplistic terms, examines consequence, vulnerability, and threat in a matrix format.

Among local jurisdictions across the United States as a matter of routine, there are personnel assigned to the planning for protection of the critical infrastructure. They are training to protect those systems. They are equipping their first responders to ensure a safe operational environment, and they are exercising, along with the private sector, to ensure that the protection initiatives are adequate. In the risk analysis as a facility, system, or event is identified as critical infrastructure, its vulnerability to a hazard is examined against the potential threat element. Once that examination or assessment is concluded, the public and private partnership works toward "target-hardening" efforts. Therefore, one must ask what can be done to harden targets from their vulnerability to an attack.

---

* National Infrastructure Protection Plan. Washington, DC. Department of Homeland Security. 2009.
† Ibid.

To facilitate the target-hardening efforts, the US Congress, through the DHS, developed the Buffer Zone Protection Program (BZPP). The purpose of the BZPP is stated in the 2009 program guidance: "The FY 2009 BZPP provides funding to increase the preparedness capabilities of jurisdictions responsible for the safety and security of communities surrounding high-priority pre-designated Tier 1 and Tier 2 critical infrastructure and key resource (CIKR) assets, including chemical facilities, financial institutions, nuclear and electric power plants, dams, stadiums, and other high-risk/high consequence facilities, through allowable planning and equipment acquisition."* The local law enforcement jurisdiction, in which the critical infrastructure resides, is the recipient of the BZPP funds. The recipient agency or agencies work in partnership with the private sector to plan a BZPP for that site. It is a target-hardening initiative in an effort to enhance the protection for that jurisdiction and the facility.

As examined in the prevention mission area, there are an infinite number of considerations and concerns within the context of protection initiatives. The discussion has already reviewed the scenario in The Dalles, Oregon, involving intentional contamination of two restaurant salad bars. The scenario can again be applied to the protection operations and to the observation of how public health integrates into the protection mission. The protection of the food supply chain is an intricate balance between supply and demand, the free-market economy, and public safety. Restaurants are at the end of the food supply chain. Protection causes the examination of the production environment and affiliated processing environments. It is an intricate examination.

One may consider the production of cotton. Cotton is not a consumable. Primarily, one thinks of cloth and clothing as a main product from cotton. However, one may consider cottonseed oil as a derivative. Many consumable products contain cottonseeds. As cotton is harvested from the field, it is taken to a cotton gin to be ginned and processed into bales. The cottonseed is extracted from the cotton during the ginning process. Cotton gins sell the cottonseed to food processors for human and animal consumption. What is the consequence if contaminated cottonseed, used to feed cattle, is fed to a million head of cattle in a Texas feedlot? Within the food supply chain, this question would have a large impact on the beef industry and the fast-food industry.

All of these scenarios and more are assumed in the planning process to protect critical infrastructure against acts of terrorism, criminal acts, and accidental events. The laws, strategies, and preparedness documents outline and lend guidance in how the country, through its homeland security function, will develop protection initiatives to guard the food supply and the public against these types of incidents.

As evidenced in this discussion, the mission areas of prevention and protection must collaborate. Threats, whether specific or nonspecific, require federal, state, local, and tribal governments to plan, train, equip, and exercise the public safety community in protection initiatives. Further, the need to form strong partnerships between the public and private sector is evident when examining the infinite vulnerabilities that exist to the country's critical infrastructure and key resources.

Conclusion

The operational component of homeland security is performed through the mission areas of prevention, protection, response, and recovery. The capabilities within the four mission areas are performed by a myriad of disciplines and agencies at every level of local, state, and federal government. Homeland security is tasked to coordinate and support those disciplines in performing within the mission areas.

---

* FY 2009 Buffer Zone Protection Program. http://www.FEMA.gov. 2009.

Tremendous demands are placed on the first-responder community. Police, fire, and emergency services must be prepared through planning, training, equipment, and exercises to meet challenges that are infinite in scope among the myriad of potential response environments. Emergency responders, such as public health, emergency management, public works, and others, must subsequently be prepared to support the contemporary needs of the first responders.

It is awesome to consider preparing disciplines for the challenges that may be met on any given day at any given time. The threat of terrorism exists. It could be biological, an improvised explosive device, or a dirty bomb. The nation must question whether it is prepared to meet all of these challenges. Police officers, fire personnel, and emergency personnel can only spend so much money on equipment, supplies, and manpower. Training is challenging for civilian responders because they are not paid to train, although they are trained to be at work in the patrol car, at the firehouse, and in the ambulance. Within the average patrol car, fire truck, and ambulance, much more equipment is carried now than was carried 10 years ago. Another concern is responder safety and health. The first responder today must be aware of the various types of environments that may be experienced during disasters. The idea of being exposed to a weaponized, biological agent is looming. What about being contaminated with a chemical used as a weapon? Such considerations are indicative of threats that are posed to the emergency response community. Homeland security has an awesome task.

Undoubtedly, homeland security has an operational component. It is a critical component among modern preparedness environments. The function of homeland security is to plan, train, equip, and exercise the operational model for eventual deployment. Homeland security may or may not be a discipline. It is a vital function of government.

Key terms

Bioterrorism
Buffer zone
Critical infrastructure
Function
National Infrastructure Protection Plan
Operational capacity
Operation
Presidential Directive 7
Presidential Directive 39
Public health
Public Health Security and Bioterrorism Preparedness and Response Act
Responsibility
Scenario
Simulation
USA Patriot Act of 2001
Vulnerability
Weaponized

QUESTIONS FOR DISCUSSION

1. Critical national infrastructure represents the assets and resources that are absolutely vital for the functioning of the nation. Examples range from electric power plants to railway systems. Within your locale, identify assets and resources that are categorized

as critical infrastructure. Given your listing, how do you propose they be protected within the all-hazards context? Write a brief essay that summarizes your response.

2. Functions and operations differ. Define both terms, and apply these definitions within the context of homeland security. Explore Internet materials describing your state's homeland security agency, and identify several of its operations and functions. Write a brief essay that summarizes your findings.

3. This chapter introduces the concept of the public health sector. Define and explain this concept. Within your locale, identify the resources and assets that may be categorized as public health entities. Regarding the context of the all-hazards approach, how do you believe these entities could be leveraged in an emergency? Write a brief essay that summarizes your opinion.

4. This chapter discusses the relationship between law enforcement and public health entities. Within your locale, do you perceive that a strong relationship exists between these sectors? Why or why not? Write a brief essay that summarizes your opinion.

References

1. King County, Washington. (2013). Bioterrorism preparedness. http://www.kingcounty.gov/healthservices/health/preparedness/bioterrorism.aspx (accessed April 27, 2013).
2. Center for Infectious Disease Research and Policy. (2013). University of Minnesota. http://www.cidrap.umn.edu/cidrap/index.html (accessed April 27, 2013).
3. Associated Press. (2013). Feds charge Mississippi man in case of ricin-laced letter sent to Obama. *Fox News*. http://www.foxnews.com/politics/2013/04/27/feds-make-arrest-in-case-ricin-laced-letter-sent-to-obama/ (accessed April 27, 2013).

6

The Partnerships of Homeland Security

The way it's best described is DHS is the conductor of an orchestra. All of these partners … are the various musicians playing beautiful music together creating a symphony of preparedness. We've made great progress.

George Foresman
Former Undersecretary for Preparedness, US Department of Homeland Security

Chapter objectives:

- Gain an understanding of the partnerships in support of homeland security
- Identify some of the entities that partner within homeland security relationships
- Identify cooperation that exists within the public sector
- Identify cooperation that exists within the private sector
- Identify cooperation that exists between public and private entities

Introduction

No one agency or level of government can be entirely responsible for the security of the United States when one considers the wide variety of threats that potentially face the nation. As a result, successful homeland security can only be achieved through the combined efforts of many public and private agencies and organizations. Before the advent of the United States Department of Homeland Security (DHS), President Bush described the government's efforts of performing homeland security activities as "patchwork." This term referred to the many agencies and programs that were working toward ensuring the security of the United States relative to domestic preparedness but whose efforts were not effectively coordinated. One of the major purposes in creating the DHS was to establish a framework that would develop organizational coordination and collaboration among all federal agencies.

Response partnerships now exist that combine both public and private sector resources, available to provide support and assistance in the event of a disaster contingency, both large and small. That concept of partnerships in government has a long history and is reflected in the

Declaration of Independence. Partnerships, both domestic and international, are essential to the successfulness of the national domestic preparedness program called homeland security.

Although the DHS is demonstrative of a myriad of partnerships that facilitate homeland security initiatives, it is a federal government entity. Given the advent and proliferation of globalization, any consideration of homeland security must also incorporate some attributes of the private sector with respect to both for-profit and nonprofit entities. Numerous alliances, not-for-profit charitable organizations, and nongovernment agencies exist that provide America with the ability to prepare for disasters, respond to disasters, and recover from disasters.

The notion of securing the homeland is not a new concept. The basic premise of ensuring the safety and security of American communities and localities originates during the Colonial period. A foundational cornerstone of achieving such safety and security exists among all American communities: the individual. Each day, a myriad of individuals volunteer their time, skills, and material resources for the betterment of society and the pursuits of safety and security. Individuals perform volunteer duties among the partnering entities of the DHS. These entities include the Fire Corps, USAonWatch (UOW), the Citizen Corps, the Medical Reserve Corps (MRC), and the Volunteers in Police Service (VIPS). Each of these organizations contributes positively and meaningfully toward the goals of homeland security preparedness and response initiatives. These organizations demonstrate national capacities to affect local communities through training, preparation, planning, and implementation of services during periods of distress. Through such efforts, local communities demonstrate the ability to provide security and safety for their citizenry.

A unique characteristic shared by each of these organizations is the land-based approach they all manifest regarding potential disasters. However, threats may not always be land based. Instead, they may involve aerial or maritime attributes that impact America negatively. Although disasters may occur inland, aerial functions (e.g., aerial photography) or maritime functions (e.g., blockades) may be necessitated during occurrences of disasters or during their aftermaths. Two organizations exist that provide such services and functions: (1) the Civil Air Patrol (CAP, the US Air Force Auxiliary) and (2) the US Coast Guard Auxiliary (USCGA). Both of these organizations utilize volunteers in support of homeland security initiatives.

Another observation of homeland security partnerships involves the basic nature of the relationships that define and govern the partnered entities. Partnerships may be either willful or mandated. Within the government architecture, DHS partnerships may be mandated through legislation or through the creation and implementation of various government agencies. With respect to the private sector, partnerships may be willful and may be exercised through the use of contracts, various agreements, or memorandums of understanding (MOUs) to govern the basic attributes of the relationships among the participating entities. Regardless of the construct, relationships exist, among both governmental and private factions, that facilitate the effective and efficient conveyance of preparedness and responsiveness among American communities and localities.

Ensuring homeland security is not the solitary responsibility of any one individual, agency, or organization. Instead, the manifestation of security and safety occurs through collaboration and the sharing of information and resources. Therefore, many partnerships exist that provide opportunities for both organizations and individuals to participate in a myriad of activities and roles, which are commensurate with their skills, abilities, and resources.

Building preparedness partnerships

The DHS is the lead agency for disaster response at the federal level. Through the Federal Emergency Management Agency (FEMA) Directorate, collaborative response efforts are coordinated among the various state, local, and tribal response agencies. Government operations and the private sector are, in today's global environment, codependent and inseparable. A simple example of this codependency can be illustrated by the requirement in most of the governmental agencies for employees to receive their pay and reimbursements through direct deposits. This requires a partnership between the government entity, the financial sector partner (banks), and the individual. And, the financial sector is dependent upon government to protect their infrastructure from attack and/or damage.

Resilient and prepared communities understand the importance of building preparedness partners in keeping with the idea of engaging the "whole" community in the partnership. Electronic technologies demand strong partnerships. These technologies operate our communications systems and social media, and they support and maintain health providers, emergency services, commerce, and economies. The strength of preparedness results from such partnerships.

One of the oldest models of a partnership between the private sector and government is in the practice of law. Government, through the legislative branch, creates laws. From that simple premise, attorneys in private practice present their cases to a judge and/or jury. The government, through elections or by appointments, provides the judges; maintains courtrooms; summons and pays the jurors; and maintains a record of legal proceedings. The government also provides prosecutors, defense counsel, and other legal assistance to the citizenry. Lessons could be learned in a study of this historical model.

One partnership model created in 2003 through the DHS is the regional partnerships in the Urban Area Security Initiative (UASI) Program. The UASI Program was created to foster regional partnerships in the urban areas across the United States. By 2010, there were 64 UASIs operating. This has been one of the most effective programs in homeland security. In 2010, the DHS reduced and defunded 34 of the UASIs. However, the reduction does not reflect poor modeling. This is an excellent model in building partnerships across the public and private domains, integrating multiple disciplines in multijurisdictional venues.

Another example of a formidable partnership model in many communities is faith-based partnerships. The effective ones are inclusive of all faiths and are instrumental in providing long-term shelters, food, clothing, and often, additional financial assistance.

Since Hurricane Katrina (2005), the partnership between civilian authorities and the military has been enhanced. The Department of Defense (DOD) can activate significant quantities of personnel and equipment that can operate in the most difficult of environments, and even more importantly, military units can sustain themselves while assisting in major recovery operations. Generations of Americans have become accustomed to the marines, navy, army, air force, coast guard, and National Guard being deployed in short-term and longer-term conflicts throughout the world. Americans have also witnessed Army National Guardsmen work side by side with civilian responders in filling sandbags along river levees, providing security during national emergencies, and assisting in maintaining law and order at scenes of civil unrest.

Partnerships and posse comitatus

Hurricanes, terrorist attacks, and other threats toward the United States have renewed a historical challenge. The challenge involves a rather basic law called the Posse Comitatus Act of 1878. It states in its original version,

> From and after the passage of this act it shall not be lawful to employ any part of the Army of the United States, as a posse comitatus or otherwise, for the purpose

of executing the laws, except in such cases and under such circumstances as such employment of said force may be expressly authorized by the Constitution or by an act of Congress; and no money appropriated by this act shall be used to pay any of the expenses incurred in the employment of any troops in violation of this section, and any person willfully violating the provisions of this section shall be deemed guilty of a misdemeanor and on conviction thereof shall be punished by fine not exceeding ten thousand dollars or imprisonment not exceeding two years or both such fine and imprisonment (ref. 1, para. 2).

According to Baker,[2] the original posse comitatus provision was a rider to an appropriations bill, Chapter 263, Section 15, Army as Posse Comitatus (Title 18, USC Section 1385). A shorter version states:

Whoever, except in cases and under circumstances expressly authorized by the Constitution or Act of Congress, willfully uses any part of the Army or Air Force as a posse comitatus or otherwise to execute the laws shall be fined under this title or imprisoned not more than two years, or both (ref. 1, para. 4).

The Posse Comitatus Act was passed in 1878 after a controversial election. Rutherford B. Hayes became President by one electoral vote. The act was passed to resolve conflict in the southern states caused by military personnel being used to enforce civil law during the period of reconstruction. In the western frontier, county sheriffs often called upon the military to assist in enforcing civilian laws or to conduct other law enforcement duties. Some of these duties were necessary considering that the military force was the most immediate and largest authority available to assist local law enforcement.

During modern times, some hold the belief that posse comitatus is no longer useful, arguing that it has been rendered irrelevant and obsolete. Often, in the argument, Title 10, USC Chapter 18, is cited as support for the position that the Congress has rendered posse comitatus irrelevant. It states, "The military is authorized to provide support to civilian law enforcement agencies for counter drug operations and in emergencies involving chemical or biological weapons of mass destruction" (para. 1).[3] Distinctions are made relative to duties of active-duty military personnel, reservists, the National Guard, and the state guard. Certain presidential exceptions exist to provide military support to law enforcement and other response agencies at the state, local, and tribal levels of government. State governors can activate the National Guard to support response efforts and to maintain law and order.

The renewed interest in posse comitatus is partially caused by the priority placed on building partnerships and the questions that continually arise regarding the use of the military for civilian purposes during disasters and in matters pertaining to homeland security. John Binkerhoff[4] states, "… new rules are needed to clearly set forth the boundaries for the use of federal military forces for homeland security. The Posse Comitatus Act is inappropriate for modern times, and needs to be replaced by a completely new law" (para. 3).

Why would the US Congress not assign the military as the lead agency for the federal government in response to national disasters and significant events? Within the Declaration of Independence, Thomas Jefferson stated[5]:

The King of England] has kept among us, in times of peace, Standing Armies without the consent of our legislatures….He has affected to render the Military independent of and superior to the Civil Power…For quartering large bodies of armed troops among us:

For protecting them, by mock Trial from punishment for any Murders which they should commit on the Inhabitants of these States (para. 13–16).

When the declaration was written, there was fear of military rule that would potentially allow an abuse of power with no oversight. The vision of the founding fathers was that there would be a distinct separation between the government and military rule, the fortification of individual liberties, and protection from tyranny. The fathers further envisioned the need to have military support but civilian rule and oversight. Thus far, throughout the history of the American Republic, the US Congress has upheld the ideology articulated in 1776.

Care must be taken to maintain the system of American democracy during times of crisis. It would be catastrophic to create any protocol that would threaten or usurp the system that upholds the autonomy of state and local governments. In creating a national preparedness program, it is necessary to respect the system of American democracy and the organizational missions of the collaborative partnerships. When incidents occur in local communities, the local governments are the first boots on the ground. Only when local governments are overwhelmed and request assistance should the other partners respond. As the country continues the evolution and maturation of homeland security through building partnerships, it is essential to safeguard the basic principles governing "these United States."

Operational partnerships

The National Response Framework (NRF) outlines and gives explanation to the National Incident Management System (NIMS). The response, operational model, and partnerships are well defined and well rehearsed. The response system outlined in the NRF has been institutionalized. It is a national model replicated from federal, to state, to local emergency management agencies. The FEMA activates a National Operations Center (NOC). Each state has a state emergency operations center (SEOC). Local governments have one or more emergency operations centers (EOCs). Usually, at the local government level, the state statutes will recognize one local EOC as the primary point of coordination. When activated, these tiered operation centers are hubs of coordination for the resources and assets, communications, and collaborative management of the incident. This system provides immediate connection with the local, state and federal officials, and response personnel in coordination of the event. Although this is an oversimplification of the greater system, it provides a high-level survey of the basic operational function. There is even a National Business Emergency Operations Center (NBEOC) that regularly meets with FEMA leadership to discuss operational planning and preparedness (**Figure 6.1**).

Within the NIMS, there exist Emergency Support Functions (ESFs). ESFs represent the primary partnerships in response. There are some differences among jurisdictions in the assignment of ESFs, but most are common. The system is a simple one. Its design makes it easy to move from one jurisdiction to another and recognize the functions without requiring extensive training. Some jurisdictions have functions that other jurisdictions do not. However, the ESF model remains consistent regardless of the number of ESFs identified and/or the tasks within the designated ESFs. The DHS's[6] NRF identifies 15 ESFs and the disciplines that operate within those categories (pp. 58–59):

- ESF 1: Transportation
- ESF 2: Communications

Figure 6.1 Washington, DC, April 23, 2013—Members of the National Business Emergency Operations Center (NBEOC) participate in an operational summit with Administrator Fugate and other FEMA operational leadership. (Courtesy of Brittany Trotter/ FEMA.)

- ESF 3: Public Works and Engineering
- ESF 4: Firefighting
- ESF 5: Emergency Management
- ESF 6: Mass Care, Emergency Assistance, Housing, and Human Services
- ESF 7: Logistics Management and Resource Support
- ESF 8: Public Health and Medical Services
- ESF 9: Search and Rescue
- ESF 10: Oil and Hazardous Materials Response
- ESF 11: Agriculture and Natural Resource
- ESF 12: Energy
- ESF 13: Public Safety and Security
- ESF 14: Long-Term Community Recovery
- ESF 15: External Affairs

It requires little imagination to envision the many disciplines and tasks associated with each one of the ESFs. Each of the ESFs is coordinated by emergency support coordinators (ESCs). ESCs are personnel assigned to the operation centers upon activation by their respective agencies. Within agencies, the personnel designated as ESCs are uniquely trained in the emergency management system. In order to understand how the partnership works, there must be an understanding of the relationship between ESFs and ESCs.

There is little knowledge on the part of the public and in some response agencies regarding the work of the ESCs and the integration of the operations centers. The lack of knowledge probably is caused by the inherent lack of visibility to this part of the system. The media and public information officers generally report from the incident scene(s). The Operations Centers and the ESCs are behind the scenes. The EOCs are usually in a low-traffic area and in as secure environment as available to the jurisdiction.

When the operations center is activated, the respective ESCs respond to that location. Each ESC represents a discipline as outlined and suggested in the NRF. These centers are the link from operations to the scene and all other logistical support. The operation centers offer an excellent snapshot of the preparedness partners at work in a coordinated and cohesive effort. The ESC at the local government EOC has a counterpart at the state EOC. The state ESC has a counterpart at the NOC. This system offers a foundation for clear, concise, and orderly management of resources and assets needed to resolve the incident. Communications are critical and essential during a response. This system enhances the ability to communicate and remain orderly in potentially chaotic environments.

At the local EOC, the local response partners are coordinated, and command and control is established. As needs arise, the local EOC contacts the SEOC, and state resources are coordinated. If further needs arise, the SEOC contacts the NOC where the federal resources are coordinated. Each of these centers can be operational from fixed or mobile locations. The emergency operations system is an excellent venue to capture who the preparedness partners are and how the multidisciplined, multijurisdictional partnerships integrate into a single mission organism.

The intelligence partnership

One of the critical observations coming from the *9/11 Commission Report* was the lack of information sharing and intelligence among agencies. At the time of the September 11, 2001, attacks, intelligence mechanics and fusion centers were not common at state and local levels of law enforcement. It became a priority in the earliest stages of the evolving DHS. The mission statement from the DHS Office of Intelligence and Analysis[7] states, "To provide homeland security intelligence and information to the Secretary, other federal officials, and our state, local, tribal, and private sector partners." According to the Office of Intelligence and Analysis[7], 58 fusion centers are operating throughout the United States. According to the DHS, from 2004 through 2007, approximately $254 million were allocated to states and local governments to support fusion centers.

Fusion centers assemble a corps of preparedness partners to collect, analyze, and disseminate information relative to the threat priorities. The fusion centers are represented by a diverse group of partners depending on the needs and resources available to the state or local jurisdiction. The centers generally are staffed by federal, state, and local personnel, including the private sector. Centers are in various phases of development but will perform similar functions when they are completed.

The need for information and information sharing is common to both the public and private sectors. The information-sharing partnership is one of the most essential in planning and prevention. It is critical to the partnership between industry and law enforcement.

Regional information sharing systems

The Regional Information Sharing Systems (RISS) is a tool through which an integration of information resources exists to support the collaborative activities and efforts of law enforcement entities. It may also be used to support homeland security initiatives. According to the RISS Web site,[8] the primary categories of its organizational functions are information sharing, analysis, equipment loans, confidential funds, training, technical assistance, provision of disaster information for first responders, conflict management for officer safety, and intelligence functions concerning gang-related crimes. Each of these categories contributes toward the fulfillment of the functions of criminal analysis.

The RISS defines as a "major goal" the provision of "law enforcement member agencies with the necessary tools to share information about known or suspected criminals and criminal activity."[8] Based on the writings of Boba[9] and the RISS[8], this function of the RISS is commensurate with homeland security functions and may be accomplished through the use of computerized, electronic, and software technologies. Because of such shared information, the efficiency and effectiveness of homeland security initiatives may be improved.

Based on the descriptions of the RISS services,[8] these services have the potential of impacting the strategic, tactical, and operational decisions that influence homeland security functions and environments. Based on the writings of Sweet[10] (p. 267), such decision attributes, with respect to shared resources, support "threat analysis and warning functions" and influence "national decision-makers responsible for securing the homeland from terrorism." This consideration is commensurate with the writings of Baker[11] regarding terrorism and counterterrorism activities. The RISS functions provide emergency responders with support for the performance of their duties through the use of "RISS Automated Trusted Information Exchange (ATIX)," in which pertinent information regarding incidents is provided.[8] Therefore, the RISS services demonstrate the capacity for embellishing the homeland security function with respect to decisions regarding addressing threat assessment and terrorism response activities.

Further, both Boba[9] and Baker[11] indicate that various forms of quantitative analysis are components of the criminal analysis function. Based on the contents of the RISS site,[8] the RISS may support the implementation of such forms of mathematical analysis (e.g., trend analysis, forecasting, etc) through its provision of a unique "compilation and analysis of investigative data to develop analytical products as requested by the member agency."[8] Therefore, the RISS manifests the potential of contributing toward the successful achievement of the functions of homeland security initiatives.

Planning, training, equipment, and exercise partnerships

In the administration of the homeland security program, planning, training, equipment, and exercise partnerships are referred to as solution areas. There is a fifth solution area, called organization, which is not part of the discussion within this section. It has been ill defined and has many interpretations.

Partnerships in the solution areas require participation by the public sector and the private sector. Preparedness cannot be accomplished by the public sector alone. All of the preparedness efforts are corporately organized by joint partnerships through these solution areas. For example, local responders in partnership with private partners conduct scheduled risk assessments identifying critical infrastructure that include special events and vulnerabilities to natural and man-made incidents. Risk assessments are part of the master-planning tasks. Data assimilated from those assessments are used to develop strategic plans, operational plans, and tactical plans.

These plans are then incorporated into the Continuity of Operations and Continuity of Government Plans as part of the recovery mission area. It is impossible to develop these plans in the absence of police, fire responders, emergency medical services (EMS), emergency medical administration (EMA), public health, and government administration. It is equally impossible to develop these plans in the absences of the private sector, including financial, industrial, and business partners. These integrated plans outline the guidelines for prevention efforts, protection efforts, and response and recovery initiatives. Proper planning then supports the training, equipment, and exercise programs.

Training is incredibly demanding. The core competencies are conducted in the various service academies (e.g., the police and fire academies). Other disciplines have their own requirements for meeting the professional requirements in core competencies. The core competency prepares personnel for basic functions of the anticipated job function. Because of professional certification requirements, the basic competencies are regulated by legislative bodies. It is often difficult to change training protocols once laws are adopted that regulate course requirements and number of training hours allocated. Training then becomes a funding issue. The US Congress, through the US DHS, has attempted through the grants program to satisfy some of the training gaps by funding specific training in antiterrorism efforts. Grants from the Departments of Justice, Health and Human Services, and Fire assist in filling other training gaps and complement the preparedness mission.

Training moves well beyond the basics. The public and private responders must be prepared to respond to potentially lethal chemical incidents that may be accidental or intentional. There is a continued nonspecific threat of biological agents being employed as a weapon. Among some jurisdictions, biological agents are developed, stored, and used in laboratories. The entire chemical, biological, nuclear, radiological, and explosive spectrum must be integrated into the planning, training, equipment, and exercise tasks for emergency response personnel. In addition, the public health partnership has training demands that require participation of the response partnership. The threat of pandemic and avian flu causes contingency planning and training to prepare for the consequences associated with these potential health incidents. This consideration is further exacerbated by concerns with exposure to smallpox and other contagious outbreaks.

The private partners are concerned with these contingencies, and they engage in training programs. Potential incidents, if realized, will impact their ability to operate. This broad spectrum of threat response is demanding and costly for police, fire, EMS, EMA, and health responders. The training is costly and time consuming but necessary. Many private enterprises that manufacture, use, transport, store, or otherwise handle hazardous materials, biological agents, and explosives have highly trained personnel who work with the public safety personnel in planning, training, exercise, and equipment programs on a continuous schedule.

A critical partnership exists with vendors that make and sell the infinite number of categories of equipment necessary in the contemporary preparedness environment. Training and equipment are inseparable. Equipment needs range from highly sophisticated software for intelligence, detection, and management purposes to personal protection equipment and hand sanitizers. The National Fire Protection Association works with the DHS toward equipment safety and standardization. These standards are not always without challenge but generally are accepted and adopted for use.

Technology has advanced the development and the utility of response equipment. Not too many years ago, the traditional "gas mask" had been in use for decades. Today, that has evolved into masks designed to keep responders safe in chemical and biological environments. Software for detecting chemical and biological agents has matured through several product generations and is now used routinely among incident scenes. To assist federal, state, local, and tribal partners in examining this huge array of equipment, the US Congress, within the Homeland Security Science and Technology Enhancement Act of 2006, adopted homeland security equipment standards.

The last solution area is exercise. This consideration again integrates entities to rehearse the plans, training, and equipment and evaluates, through exercise, the effectiveness of those solution areas. There are three types of exercise: tabletop, functional, and full scale. The most cost effective types are tabletop and functional, with tabletop being the most inexpensive. The tabletop exercise is generally accomplished by designing an incident and talking through the scenario with the group to be exercised. The functional exercise is somewhat larger because it may require the activation of the EOC or other operational components. It does not necessitate an actual field response. Instead, it is accomplished through messages or a simulator, or in some virtual environment. The full-scale exercise is a full deployment of the disciplines and jurisdictions being evaluated.

The civilian response community traditionally struggled with conducting exercises because of funding issues. It is difficult, within local budgets, to allocate funds for exercise. Again, the US Congress, through the DHS, has made an attempt to resolve such issues by funding the Homeland Security Exercise and Evaluation Program (HSEEP). For many local agencies, it is difficult to release personnel for the time frame some of the exercise programs require, and many jurisdictions do not have personnel trained in exercise design and management. As the national preparedness program matures, more jurisdictions are being trained in exercise development and are able to participate in exercise programs more frequently.

Out of these four solution areas, the civilian response community has been able to support planning and equipment initiatives more effectively than the training and exercise programs. Herein is identified another distinctive difference between the military and the civilian environment. The military is paid on a 24-hour clock. They are paid to train and exercise. Training and exercise are substantial programs for the military. The civilian community is paid to be on patrol, respond to fires, attend to injured victims, and so forth. Although training and exercise participation and capability are expanding, they remain a challenge for civilian responders.

Private partnership sector

Enough cannot be said about the equal partnership between the government and the private sector. This partnership in the national preparedness program is an essential collaborative effort. In 2006, John McCarthy stated, "As 80 to 90 percent of the critical infrastructure in the United States is owned and operated by the private sector... Learning to manage this public private intersection is at the heart of our homeland security discussion today" (para. 5).[12] Undersecretary Asa Hutchinson, following McCarthy, stated, "...I think the right strategy is assessments, knowing where we are, and identifying the critical assets and infrastructure that needs to be protected... Partnerships are an important part of that cooperation... our emphasis should be on building the support in the private sector..." (para. 23).[12]

The application of risk management, through assessment models, is a binding task between the public and private sector. It is not difficult to establish a priority when 80% to 90% of America's infrastructure is privately owned. This statistic alone should cause focus on the planning, training, equipment, and exercise value where critical infrastructure is located. It also should guide government in prioritizing efforts in developing and maintaining private sector partners.

Because of such considerations, the DHS created the Private Sector Office in the Office of Policy. The DHS[13] articulates the responsibilities in the Private Sector Office as follows:

- Advises the Secretary on the impact of the department's policies, regulations, processes, and actions on the private sector
- Creates and fosters strategic communications with the private sector to enhance the primary mission of the department to protect the American homeland
- Interfaces with other relevant federal agencies with homeland security missions to assess the impact of these agencies on the private sector

- Creates and manages private sector advisory councils composed of representatives of industries and associations designated by the secretary to (1) advise the secretary on private sector products, applications, and solutions as they relate to homeland security challenges and (2) advise the secretary on homeland security policies, regulations, processes, and actions that affect the participating industries and associations
- Works with federal laboratories, federally funded research and development centers, other federally funded organizations, academia, and the private sector to develop innovative approaches to address homeland security challenges to produce and deploy the best available technologies for homeland security missions
- Promotes existing public–private partnerships and development of new public–private partnerships to provide for collaboration and mutual support to address homeland security challenges
- Assists in the development and promotion of private sector best practices to secure critical infrastructure
- Coordinates industry efforts regarding department functions to identify private sector resources that could be effective in supplementing government efforts to prevent or respond to a terrorist attack
- Consults with the various DHS elements and the Department of Commerce on matters of concern to the private sector, including the travel and tourism industries

Just as incidents originate in local jurisdictions, the private sector encompasses most of the local communities. Because the private sector represents the economic health of local communities, the priority in building public–private partnerships is obvious.

Building community partnerships

Community preparedness has been and continues to be a national priority. Community preparedness is synonymous with community recovery. The age-old idea that the best defense and offense are the eyes and ears continues to support preparedness efforts. It is neighbor helping neighbor. During most incidents, community citizens act to assist their neighbors. The volunteer spirit is characteristically strong throughout the United States. Government understands that preparedness starts at the neighborhood level. The DHS, through the FEMA Directorate, funds many citizen-based programs. Some of those programs are the following:

Citizens Corps—According to DHS, currently, there are 2342 Citizen Corps Councils operating across the United States serving 78% of the population. The Citizens Corps program assists in the coordination and development of community awareness and preparedness programs. The Community Emergency Response Team (CERT) program trains community people in basic emergency preparedness skills, enabling them to assist in the workplace and communities in preparing for disasters. The Citizens Corps is funded through the DHS.

Fire Corps—This is a fire advocacy program focused on citizenry participation in support of fire safety. This program is also funded through the DHS.

UOW—This program is funded through the Department of Justice and indicates the expansion of the Neighborhood Watch Program.

MRC—This program is funded through the US Department of Health and Human Services. The MRC represents professional health care personnel volunteering to support community health preparedness needs and requirements.

VIPS—VIPS are funded through the Department of Justice. The program is administered by the International Association of Chiefs of Police (IACP). This program represents advocates for law enforcement volunteer programs and initiatives funded by governmental departments. One example of an organization is the Voluntary Organizations Active in Disasters (VOAD), which is nationally organized and coordinates the venue to bring volunteer groups together for information sharing and networking.

The Citizen Corps

According to the Citizen Corps, its mission to "harness the power of every individual through education, training, and volunteer service to make communities safer, stronger, and better prepared to respond to the threats of terrorism, crime, public health issues, and disasters of all kinds."[14] Accomplishing this mission is facilitated through the use of a variety of councils nationwide. The Citizen Corps Councils are networks of state, local, and tribal entities to "implement preparedness programs and carry out a local strategy to involve government, community leaders, and citizens in all-hazards preparedness and resilience."[14] **Figure 6.2** shows the extensiveness and distribution of Citizen Corps Councils throughout the United States and its territories.

Participating individuals are volunteers who prepare themselves for calamities and render assistance during periods of distress. The services provided by the Citizens Corps include first aid, emergency services, the support of emergency response personnel, disaster relief activities, and community safety.[14] The Citizen Corps is coordinated nationally by the FEMA in accordance with the DHS.

When compared with peer organizations that provide similar services, the Citizens Corps is a relatively new entity. It was founded during the aftermath of the September 11, 2001, attacks. In January 2002, President Bush enacted the Citizen Corps in an effort "to capture the spirit

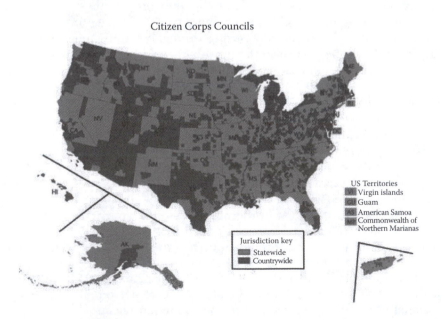

Citizen Corps Councils

US Territories
VI Virgin islands
GU Guam
AS American Samoa
MP Commonwealth of Northern Marianas

Jurisdiction key
Statewide
Countrywide

Figure 6.2 Citizen Corps Councils. (Courtesy of www.citizencorps.gov.)

of service that emerged throughout our communities following the terrorist attacks."[14] Both state and local governments sponsor "opportunities for citizens to become an integral part of protecting the homeland and supporting the local first responders" through Citizens Corps programs.[14] Although it is a relatively new entity, the Citizens Corps spans a national audience of served communities within American society.

Ensuring the safety and security of communities, both rural and urban, involves much "preparedness, training, and citizen involvement in supporting first responders."[14] The benefit of the Citizen Corps is manifested through its capacity to coordinate volunteerism and sponsor activities that contribute toward the security and safety of American communities. It integrates existing programs and infrastructures to improve the quality of responses affiliated with the existence and manifestation of any occurring incidents that impact community safety and security. Local innovation is a primary catalyst for the development of Citizens Corps programs.

The Fire Corps

According to the Fire Corps,[15] its mission is to "increase the capacity of volunteer, career, and combination fire and emergency management services departments through the use of citizen advocates. Fire Corps provides resources for departments to utilize citizen advocates in nonoperational roles so they can develop, implement, and sustain programs and services that will help their department meet the needs of their community." According to the Fire Corps,[15] within the context of this mission, the Fire Corps seeks to do the following:

- Learn about promising practices being used in existing nonoperational volunteer programs
- Share this information with departments that want to expand or improve their programs
- Increase the use of nonemergency volunteers in existing programs
- Help citizens learn about and get involved in Fire Corps programs in their communities
- Help agencies without a program to get one started

This organization provides willing volunteers whose services complement and supplement existing fire departments locally among American communities. The Fire Corps is a collaborative entity that is contained within the organizational structure of the Citizen Corps and the FEMA. It provides an integration of both community and government leaderships with respect to the all-hazards emergency preparedness and response goals of homeland security. The Fire Corps was originated in 2004 and collaborates with a myriad of organizations that comprise the Fire Corps National Advisory Committee.[15] The Fire Corps is managed by the National Volunteer Fire Council, receives support from the United States Fire Administration, and received funding through both the Citizen Corps and the DHS.[15]

Personnel from each major fire service organization comprise the membership of the Fire Corps, and they "provide valuable input, critical feedback, and supplementary ideas as to the direction of the program."[15] These personnel "perform non-emergency tasks and roles," thereby allowing firefighters to concentrate on "emergency response and training."[15] As a result, this use of Fire Corps volunteers enables fire departments to increase their offered services (e.g., educational programs). These volunteers also "gain a greater understanding of fire and emergency services" and improve their ability to render quality services during periods of emergency.[15]

UOW

The primary emphasis of the UOW program involves neighborhood watch programs. Through the use of such programs, neighborhoods become empowered to provide their own levels of safety and security locally among individual communities. According to UOW,[16] such watch programs have integrated the efforts of "law enforcement agencies, private organizations, and individual citizens in a nation-wide effort to reduce crime and improve local communities." This UOW initiative, regarding local neighborhood watch programs, was initiated in 1972 and has matured into the "the nation's premier crime prevention and community mobilization program." The "information, training, technical support, and resources, provided to local law enforcement agencies and citizens," are foundational characteristics of the Neighborhood Watch initiative.[16] The training paradigm enhances the potential of law enforcement entities to collaborate with citizens with respect to the identification, reporting, and deterring of criminal activities.

The involvement of community citizens is paramount to the success of neighborhood watch programs. Further, the use of such programs embellishes community-oriented policing initiatives and provides a tool that facilitates improved communications between law enforcement entities and their served communities. Because citizens become engaged actively within their communities, they experience bonding through neighborhood watch programs. The visibility of the initiative is manifested through the use of "street signs, window decals, community block parties, and service projects."[16]

In 2002, a collaborative approach was implemented among government entities and local communities to improve and strengthen neighborhood watch programs. According to UOW,[16] the "NSA—in partnership with USA Freedom Corps, Citizen Corps, and the U.S. Department of Justice—launched USAonWatch, the face of the revitalized Neighborhood Watch initiative, which represents the expanded role of watch programs throughout the United States." Through the use of neighborhood watch programs, local communities become active participants in "homeland security efforts."[16]

The MRC

In 2002, the MRC was created to motivate American citizens "to volunteer in support of their country."[17] The composition of the MRC includes "organized medical and public health professionals, who serve as volunteers to respond to natural disasters and emergencies" and serve through assisting "communities nationwide during emergencies and for ongoing efforts in public health."[17] The MRC resulted from the terrorist events of September 11, 2001. Because of the scope and magnitude of these events, the need for "trained, supplemental medical and public health personnel, to assist with emergency operations," was manifested (**Figure 6.3**).[17] A typical MRC poster and recruiting announcement is shown in **Figure 6.3**.

Although a myriad of medical personnel and public health personnel supported the emergency response efforts of September 11, 2001, there existed "no organized approach to channel their efforts."[17] This shortcoming is resolved through the organizational structure, processes, and procedures of the MRC. The structuring of the MRC facilitates organized deployments of "medical and public health personnel in response to an emergency, as it identifies specific, trained, credentialed personnel available and ready to respond to emergencies."[17]

Within the United States, each individual community is a unique entity. Because of such variances among communities, an array of "alternative approaches to natural disasters and emergencies" is necessary regarding the disasters that may impact American society.[17] According to

Figure 6.3 *South Central Missouri MRC volunteers respond to the 2011 EF5 tornado in Joplin, Missouri, providing tetanus vaccinations to volunteers clearing debris. (Courtesy of the Medical Reserve Corps.)*

the MRC,[17] the "terms 'medical' and 'reserve' indicate that trained personnel are available to respond to emergencies requiring support to the community's health and medical resources," and the "term 'Corps' refers to an organized body of individuals with a similar function" that is commensurate with the requirements of the Citizen Corps. According to the MRC,[17] the "term 'medical,' in Medical Reserve Corps, does not limit MRC units to medical professionals," and "individuals without medical training can fill essential, supporting roles."

The MRC's units are localized among US communities. This localization forms the basis of 10 MRC regions.[17] Within these regions, coordination occurs between local MRC units and state-level personnel. Local MRC units are "responsible for implementing volunteer capabilities, for emergency medical response and public health initiatives, to match specific community needs."[17] According to the MRC, its direction exists among the "nation, state, and local levels," and "each level has key personnel responsible for overseeing activities at their respective level".[17] The local MRC units are led by unit coordinators, who match "community needs—for emergency medical response and public health initiatives—with volunteer capabilities" and who are "also responsible for building partnerships, ensuring the sustainability of the local unit, and managing the volunteer resources."[17]

According to the MRC, the "Office of the Civilian Volunteer Medical Reserve Corps (OCVMRC) oversees activities of the 10 MRC Regional Coordinators," who collaborate with national, state, and local emergency preparedness, response, and medical and health care personnel.[17] Nationally, the OCVMRC, "functions as a clearinghouse for information and best practices to help communities establish, implement, and maintain MRC units nationwide," and it also "sponsors an annual leadership conference; hosts a Web site; and coordinates with local, state, regional, and national organizations and agencies to help communities achieve their local visions for public health and emergency preparedness"[17] Through the use of the MRC, response initiatives may be efficiently and effectively supplemented by competent medical personnel during periods of distress.

The VIPS

Another component of the Citizen Corps is the VIPS. According to the VIPS,[18] "the IACP manages and implements the VIPS Program in partnership with, and on behalf of, the White

House Office of the USA Freedom Corps and the Bureau of Justice Assistance, Office of Justice Programs, US Department of Justice." The goal of the VIPS is to "enhance the capacity of state and local law enforcement to utilize volunteers," and it pursues this goal through the provision of "support and resources for agencies interested in developing or enhancing a volunteer program and for citizens who wish to volunteer their time and skills with a community law enforcement agency."[18]

According to the VIPS,[18] through the implementation of the VIPS Program, its personnel strive to do the following:

• "Learn about promising practices being used in existing VIPS programs and share this information with law enforcement agencies that want to expand their programs"
• "Increase the use of volunteers in existing programs"
• "Help citizens learn about and become involved in VIPS programs in their communities"
• "Help agencies without volunteer programs get them started"

Police entities sponsor VIPS programs and may register their programs. Additionally, regarding the VIPS Program registration, "volunteers must work directly within the agency, through an in-house volunteer program or with an organization operating in concert with a law enforcement agency, such as a citizens' police academy alumni association or a Retired and Senior Volunteer Program (RSVP), to place volunteers."[18]

Additional volunteer entities

The programs and initiatives of the VIPS, the Fire Corps, UOW, the MRC, and the Citizen Corps were created and instigated as responses to the terrorist events of September 11, 2001. Although these entities perform necessary roles and provide valuable services for the United States, their basic premise is not a new paradigm. Throughout the history of the United States, a variety of volunteers and volunteer entities have served the nation admirably during periods of distress. Two such entities that continue to serve the nation and manifest partnerships with the US military are the CAP (US Air Force Auxiliary) and the USCGA. Both organizations augment the capabilities of preparedness and responses affiliated with emergency services and disaster scenarios.

The CAP (US Air Force Auxiliary)

According to the US Air Force,[19] the Civil Air Patrol (CAP) is a "congressionally chartered, federally supported, non-profit corporation that serves as the official auxiliary of the US Air Force." The CAP performs a variety of missions per the request of the US Air Force, and many of these missions entail homeland security functions. The mission of the CAP involves three functions: (1) emergency services, (2) aerospace education, and (3) cadet training. The modern existence of the CAP embellishes homeland security services and functions, but its origin occurred in 1941 in conjunction with World War II. Historically, regarding World War II, the CAP allowed "private pilots and aviation enthusiasts to use their light aircraft and flying skills in civil defense efforts."[19] This wartime service included target towing to allow military personnel to practice aerial marksmanship, coastal patrols, ferrying of aircraft, search and rescue missions, and logistics missions to facilitate the movement of material resources and personnel. The CAP "became a permanent peacetime institution July 1, 1946, when President Harry S. Truman signed Public Law 476 establishing it as a federally chartered, benevolent, civilian corporation."[19]

During the 1990s, the CAP experienced an increasing quantity of missions that necessitated its involvement during disaster situations. These events included the 1991 San Francisco earthquake, the Midwest floods, and major hurricanes.[20] The US Congress again altered and modified the CAP in 2000 with the enacting of the Floyd D. Spence National Defense Authorization Act, which "clarified auxiliary status as a conditional state dependent on CAP performing actual services for a federal department or agency" and "specified the funding mechanisms the Air Force must use to provide funds to CAP for operations, maintenance, and procurement of property."[19]

After the terrorist attacks of 2001, in 2003, the US Congress "amended the Omnibus Crime Control and Safe Streets Act of 1968 to make members of the Civil Air Patrol eligible for Public Safety Officer death benefits."[20] Because of this legislation, when CAP personnel perish or become permanently disabled in the line of duty, they become "eligible for the same federal death benefit provided to other public safety personnel."[20] This legislation also was known as the Civil Air Patrol Homeland Security Benefits Act (HR 3681).

During the 2005 hurricane season, the benefit of the CAP during disasters was demonstrated along the Gulf Coast. During this period, "CAP serviced dozens of locations across the region—more than 1500 CAP members volunteered to provide support ranging from aircraft missions such as search and rescue, transportation of critical personnel and supplies, and aerial imagery of flood damaged areas for civil authorities to ground team missions such as house to house searching of neighborhoods and passing out emergency supplies. In total, the CAP flew nearly 1000 aircraft missions in support of the hurricane relief efforts."[19] The air force funds the "purchase and maintenance of 530 aircraft and more than 950 vehicles to support the organization."[19]

The infrastructure of the CAP is significant regarding its capacity to support disaster relief operations. It deploys air and ground transportation, an extensive communications network, and an aerial platform for responder agencies, and its aircraft "are equipped with slow-scan video technology that enables them to transmit damage assessment photos, flood stage observations, and traffic conditions" within seconds of recording a photographic image.[20] The communications infrastructure of the CAP is substantial because it encompasses the nation with "a data and voice net built to survive the loss of civil communications."[20] This communications system involves the use of frequencies that are dedicated solely for CAP use, and its systems also "coordinate and track" a variety of "search flights" through the use of a "sophisticated data-link."[20]

Although the organizational attributes of the CAP are commensurate with those of the US Air Force, there are dissimilarities between the organizations. The CAP personnel quantities consist of "approximately 23,000 cadets and more than 34,000 adult volunteers" who wear "the Air Force uniform, but with distinctive CAP emblems and insignia."[19] The CAP organizational structure involves the operation of "eight geographic regions" that are comprised of "52 wings" representing each state, the District of Columbia (Washington, DC), and Puerto Rico.[19] Analogous to the US Air Force, CAP wings are comprised of groups, squadrons, and flights across "1600 individual units."[19] Maxwell Air Force Base, located in Alabama, is the headquarters of the CAP, and it is "staffed with 100 full-time civilian employees who provide administrative and logistics support to 57,000 CAP members nationwide." These personnel receive financial compensation from the US Air Force, but, "neither Air Force civil servants nor contractors, they are employees of the CAP Corporation."[19]

The CAP maintains a close relationship with the US Air Force. The Civil Air Patrol–United States Air Force (CAP–USAF), which provides an administrative function, is "collocated with the CAP headquarters and assigned to Air University," and its personnel consists of both "Military and Air Force civilian personnel."[19] Additional CAP–USAF liaisons, consisting of Air Force Reserve personnel, are assigned to both CAP regions and wings to advise and assist individual CAP units.

The emergency services role of the CAP includes "air and ground search and rescue, disaster relief, counterdrug, and an increasing role in homeland security. Its members fly more than 95 percent of the inland search and rescue missions directed by the Air Force Rescue and Coordination Center at Langley Air Force Base, Virginia. The Civil Air Patrol flew more than 3000 search and rescue missions and was credited with saving 73 lives in 2005."[19] The CAP renders additional services among agencies of the US government. According to the CAP,[19] it assists the "U.S. Customs Service, Drug Enforcement Administration and Forest Service in their counterdrug efforts. In 2005, CAP aircrews flew more than 12,000 hours in support of the nation's war on drugs and were credited with contributing to the confiscation of more than $400 million of illegal drugs."

The homeland security applications of the CAP are varied regarding the performance of its mission. According to the CAP,[19] its aircrews fly noncombat homeland security missions such as surveillance of critical infrastructure, airborne communications relay, and airlift of critical cargo. These missions are flown under the authority of the US Northern Command, the Joint Command responsible for the continental United States. The CAP receives tasking from the air component of Northern Command, First Air Force, with headquarters at Tyndall Air Force Base, Florida. Examples of such tasking and missions include "disaster relief and emergency services following natural and manmade disasters, including such phenomena as 9/11, Hurricane Katrina, Texas and Oklahoma wildfires, tornadoes in the south and central U.S., North Dakota flash flooding and the October 2006 earthquake in Hawaii, as well as humanitarian missions along the U.S. and Mexican border."[21]

The USCGA

The USCGA is another volunteer-based organization whose presence serves the maritime interests of American communities and coastlines. Therefore, the CAP is not the sole military auxiliary whose mission includes homeland security components. Similar to the CAP, the USCGA also contributes toward homeland security endeavors. The USCGA maintains presences among each of the "50 states, Puerto Rico, the Virgin Islands, American Samoa, and Guam."[22] The USCGA, through its relationship with the US Coast Guard, is a component of both the US DHS and the US Coast Guard that provides maritime services for the benefit of the American public.[22]

The USCGA originated during the period of World War II. According to the USCGA,[22] "When the Coast Guard 'Reserve' was authorized by act of Congress on June 23, 1939, the Coast Guard was given a legislative mandate to use civilian volunteers to promote safety on and over the high seas and the nation's navigable waters." During this period, "the Coast Guard Reserve was then a non-military service comprised of unpaid, volunteer U.S. citizens who owned motorboats or yachts."[22] The auxiliary was created 2 years later, in 1941, when the US Congress "amended the 1939 act with passage of the Auxiliary and Reserve Act of 1941" that designated the Coast Guard Reserve as a "military branch of the active service." As a result of this legislation, the array of civilian volunteers, who were "formerly referred to as the Coast Guard Reserve, became the Auxiliary."[22]

The entry of America into World War II witnessed the joining of "50,000 Auxiliary members" within the "war effort."[22] These volunteers performed a variety of missions that supplemented wartime security activities and search and rescue activities. The organization "guarded water-fronts, carried out coastal picket patrols, rescued survivors from scuttled ships," and performed a myriad of other assignments.[22] Many private vessels were used during this period.

After the end of World War II, the USCGA was tasked with missions and duties involving "recreational boating safety."[22] According to the USCGA,[22] the auxiliary's four primary missions, consisting of vessel examination, education, operations, and fellowship, "were established and remained the Auxiliary's pillars into the 1990s." After the passage of the Coast Guard Authorization Act of 1996, the USCGA supplemented the coast guard, as "authorized by the Commandant, in performance of any Coast Guard function, duty, role, mission or operation authorized by law."[22] The modern functions of the USCGA involve the operation of "safety and regatta patrols," and it is "an integral part of the Coast Guard Search and Rescue team."[21] Auxiliary personnel also perform "communication watches, assist during mobilization exercises, perform harbor and pollution patrols, provide platforms for unarmed boarding parties, and recruit new people for the service."[22]

According to the USCGA,[23] the modern USCGA is "a force multiplier of vetted and trained volunteers devoted to the support of Coast Guard missions and provides a broad inventory of vital skills, assets, and experience." The USCGA is the "leading volunteer organization" within the US DHS and is an "essential component of daily operations and an effective resource primed to prevent and respond to catastrophes in the maritime region."[23] According to the USCGA,[23] the "core strategic purpose of the Auxiliary is to continuously hone its expertise to perform three prioritized functions." These functions are to "promote and improve recreational boating safety," to "support Coast Guard maritime homeland security efforts," and to "support the Coast Guard's operational, administrative, and logistical requirements."[23]

The USCGA, through its Incident Management Division (IMD), provides a variety of services that embellish disaster preparedness, response, and relief initiatives. The primary goal of the USCGA IMD is to "foster communication, standardization, and interoperability in USCG Auxiliary planning, response, and incident management systems" using a variety of models that "promote alignment with Coast Guard mechanisms and procedures to improve communication, coordination and cooperation in planning and response activities."[22] The USCGA IMD provides "tools, training, and assistance to Auxiliary leadership and members to improve our overall planning, readiness and response capability for all-hazard scenarios, including acts of terrorism, wild-land and urban fires, floods, hazardous materials spills, nuclear accidents, aircraft accidents, earthquakes, hurricanes, tornadoes, typhoons, war-related disasters, and others."[22]

Complementing the USCGA IMD is the USCGA aviation component (AUXAIR). The AUXAIR units perform a variety of missions that support homeland security initiatives. According to the USCGA,[22] the AUXAIR entity supports many coast guard missions, including the following:

- Search and rescue
- Ports
- Waterways and coastal security
- Marine safety
- Pollution response
- Aids to navigation
- Ice reconnaissance
- Logistic transport

The personnel within the USCGA AUXAIR complete "auxiliary aviation training" that is required for the completions of levels of qualification. Upon the approval of their knowledge and skills by an auxiliary flight examiner, USCGA AUXAIR personnel "may be certified by the District Director of Auxiliary (DIRAUX) as Pilots, Observers or Air Crew in the AUXAIR Program."[22] Air patrol orders are issued among air facility operations in a fashion that is analogous to the dissemination of orders among surface operations. According to the USCGA, "Orders are issued based on schedules created by crew and facility availability and the needs of the Coast Guard," and the "Coast Guard Air Stations are the Order Issuing Authority for AUXAIR."[22] This type of organizational structuring is demonstrative of the "squadron concept because aviation orders and directions flow directly between the air station and the district aviation staff."[22]

The organizational structuring of the USCGA is similar to the structuring of the US Coast Guard. Although it operates in accordance with the "authority of the Commandant of the U.S. Coast Guard," the USCGA represents an "internally autonomous" structuring.[22] The basic structures of the USCGA are (1) flotilla, (2) division, (3) district/regions, and (4) national. Each of these levels provides both complementary and supplementary services to internal and external factions of coast guard and USCGA entities. According to the USCGA,[22] below are synopses of each organizational level:

- Flotilla—The flotilla is the basic organizational unit of the auxiliary. A flotilla is comprised of at least 15 qualified members who carry out auxiliary program activities. Each of the auxiliary personnel is assigned to a billet within a local flotilla. Each flotilla is headed by a flotilla commander (FC).
- Division—For maximum administrative effectiveness in carrying out auxiliary programs, flotillas are grouped into divisions. These divisions are comprised of the flotillas in the same general geographic area. The division provides administrative, training, and supervisory support to flotillas and promotes district policy. Each division is headed by a division captain (DCP) and division vice captain (VCP) and usually consists of five or more flotillas.
- District/region—Flotillas and divisions are organized in districts, which are comparable to the coast guard districts and must be assigned the same district number. Some districts are further divided into regions. The district/region provides administrative and supervisory support to divisions and promotes policies of both the district commander and national auxiliary committee. All districts and regions are governed by a district commodore (DCO), district vice commodore (VCO), and district rear commodore (RCO) under the guidance of the coast guard district commander. At this level, coast guard officers are assigned to oversee and promote the auxiliary programs.
- National—The auxiliary has national officers who are responsible, along with the commandant, for the administration and policy making for the entire auxiliary. These officers comprise the National Executive Committee (NEXCOM), which is composed of the chief director of auxiliary (an active-duty officer), the national commodore, and the national vice commodores. NEXCOM and the National Staff make up the Auxiliary Headquarters organization. The chief director is a senior coast guard officer and directs the administration of the auxiliary on policies established by the commandant. The overall supervision of the Coast Guard Auxiliary is under the assistant commandant for operations (G-O), who reports directly to the commandant.

The geographic distribution of USCGA districts is presented in **Figure 6.4**.

The significance of USCGA contributions was highlighted during Hurricane Katrina. In 2005, when Hurricane Katrina impacted the American Gulf Coast, numerous active-duty coast guard resources were damaged and became inoperable.[24] This deficiency was rectified through the

Figure 6.4 *US Coast Guard Auxiliary districts. (Courtesy of the United States Coast Guard Auxiliary.)*

use of USCGA personnel who provided "radio and boat assets, and the trained manpower" that was necessary to embellish operations during both the progression and aftermath of the storm.[24] Coast Guard Auxiliary members provided a communications and manpower infrastructure that resulted in the locating and rescuing of victims who were trapped within the affected region. Such abilities of the USCGA are not uncommon. During the 2010 storm season, a member of the Coast Guard Auxiliary, located near Philadelphia, Pennsylvania, received a distress signal that was broadcast from a vessel that was "located on the Mississippi River, just south of New Orleans."[25]

This ability to intercept messages from such a great distance and to route the necessary assistance is demonstrative of the strength of the communications network maintained by the USCGA. Such a robust network provides the capacity to communicate efficiently and effectively during homeland security training scenarios and incidents. Through the maintaining and operating of such a networked communications resource, the USCGA establishes itself as a robust, first-responder entity during emergencies.

Maritime administration

During the preceding two centuries, the US fought a variety of wars successfully and overcame numerous challenges that threatened its existence, and it now exists as the solitary superpower upon the face of the earth. Although a myriad of agencies and organizations have come and gone, their legacy and conceptual basis continue to influence modern homeland security paradigms. During World War II, the US Merchant Marine protected ocean sea routes to ensure that the oceanic shipping of men and materials was successful. However, this organization ceased to exist after the conclusion of the war. During modern times, its basic principles of protecting and facilitating American shipping and logistics remain an important consideration within the context of homeland security.

The modern instantiation of shipping fleet security is facilitated through the US Department of Transportation and the Maritime Administration. Within the US Department of Transportation, the Maritime Administration is the agency that oversees waterborne transportation. The

Maritime Administration "promotes the use of waterborne transportation and its seamless integration with other segments of the transportation system, and the viability of the U.S. Merchant Marine." The Maritime Administration encompasses many functions and services "involving ships and shipping, shipbuilding, port operations, vessel operations, national security, environment, and safety." Its additional duties include "maintaining the health of the merchant marine" because "mariners, vessels, and intermodal facilities are vital for supporting national security." Therefore, the Maritime Administration supports the needs of both current and future mariners as well as providing a variety of educational programs to inform the public regarding the importance of the "maritime industry."[26]

Within the context of maritime administration, the National Defense Reserve Fleet (NDRF) exists as a resource through which maritime resources may be maintained and accessed during periods of calamity. The NDRF was established within Section 11 of the Merchant Ship Sales Act of 1946. According to the Maritime Administration,[27] "At its height in 1950, the NDRF consisted of 2277 ships at the following eight anchorages: Stony Point, New York; Fort Eustis, Virginia; Wilmington, North Carolina; Mobile, Alabama; Beaumont, Texas; Benicia, California; Astoria, Oregon; and Olympia, Washington."

Many changes have occurred regarding the NDRF during the preceding 60 years. The characteristics of the modern instantiation of the NDRF are radically different from those it manifested during the 1950s. The modern NDRF fleet is significantly smaller and consists of three of its "original eight anchorages located at: Fort Eustis; Beaumont; Suisun Bay in Benicia, California, and at designated port facility berths."[27] The NDRF primarily consists of vessels representing "dry cargo ships," "some tankers," and "military auxiliaries."[27] In 2010, the array of NDRC vessels consisted of 163 ships.[27]

In 1976, a Ready Reserve fleet component was established to provide rapid deployment of military equipment.[27] This entity later became the Ready Reserve Force (RRF), and its modern reserve quantity consists of 49 vessels.[27] Two NDRF ships are sponsored for "missile tracking" activities of the Missile Defense Agency, and the NDRF also maintains ships for the US Transportation Command (USTRANSCOM).[27] Additionally, a total of 16 vessels are maintained for "other government agencies on a cost-reimbursable basis."[27]

In 2010, a total of 31 vessels were in a status of retention and were "preserved" to ensure that their integrity remained in the "same condition as when they entered the fleet."[27] The retarding and controlling of "corrosion of metal and growth of mold and mildew" occurs effectively through the "dehumidification of air-tight internal spaces."[27] The implementation of a "cathodic protection system," involving an "impressed current of DC power," is distributed through an array of "anodes to the exterior underwater portions of the hull, resulting in an electric field that suppresses corrosion and preserves exposed hull surfaces."[27]

After 1950, a variety of NDRF vessels supported "emergency shipping operations during war and national emergencies."[27] A total of 540 vessels were activated to support military forces and operations during the Korean War of the 1950s. Between 1951 and 1953, because of a global "shortfall" in vessel "tonnage," more than 600 "ship activations" were necessary to "lift coal to Northern Europe and grain to India."[27] In 1956, the closure of the Suez Canal occurred, and it necessitated the activation of "223 cargo ships and 29 tankers" as a response to the additional ensuing "tonnage shortfall."[27] Between 1955 and 1964, an additional "698 ships were used to store grain for the U.S. Department of Agriculture."[27] The Berlin crisis occurred in 1961. This crisis necessitated the activation of 18 vessels, which actively "remained in service until 1970.[27] During the Vietnam War, an NDRF total of "172 vessels were activated" to support the initiatives of the U.S. military."[27]

Title 10 of the *US Code*

Section 10 of the *US Code* governs the US military. Within this section are requirements specifying the tenets of general military law, the army, the navy and Marine Corps, the air force, and the reserve components of the US military. Within Section 10, Subtitle A, Part IV, Chapter 148, Subchapter V, are delineated the parameters regarding national defense, technology and industrial base, defense reinvestment, and defense conversion. Although the entirety of contents of the preceding passage is a salient aspect of homeland security, various excerpts may be examined within the context of this chapter regarding homeland security partnerships. Specifically, these sections are given as follows:

"§ 2531. Defense memoranda of understanding and related agreements"

"§ 2533b. Requirement to buy strategic materials critical to national security from American sources; exceptions"

"§ 2535. Defense Industrial Reserve"

"§ 2536. Award of certain contracts to entities controlled by a foreign government: prohibition"

Defense memoranda of understanding and agreements

The preceding chapters discussed the necessity of worldwide collaboration given the advent and proliferation of globalism. Although the United States seeks to actively participate within the global economy, it must still acknowledge its sovereignty with respect any agreements and partnerships among which it may enter as a salient consideration of homeland security. Given below is an excerpt from the *US Code*, that highlights the scope and limitations that are associated with MOUs and national agreements.

These concepts are highlighted within Title 10 of the *US Code*. Specifically, the following excerpt of the *US Code* expresses the ability of the United States to ensure that its resource needs and requirements are satisfied during any periods of distress. Unless otherwise noted, the contents of the following excerpt were obtained from Cornell University Law School.[28]

"§ 2531. Defense memoranda of understanding and related agreements

(a) Considerations in Making and Implementing MOUs and Related Agreements.—
In the negotiation, renegotiation, and implementation of any existing or proposed memorandum of understanding, or any existing or proposed agreement related to a memorandum of understanding, between the Secretary of Defense, acting on behalf of the United States, and one or more foreign countries (or any instrumentality of a foreign country) relating to research, development, or production of defense equipment, or to the reciprocal procurement of defense items, the Secretary of Defense shall—

(1) Consider the effects of such existing or proposed memorandum of understanding or related agreement on the defense technology and industrial base of the United States; and

(2) Regularly solicit and consider comments and recommendations from the Secretary of Commerce with respect to the commercial implications of such memorandum of understanding or related agreement and the potential effects of such memorandum of understanding or related agreement on the international competitive position of United States industry.

(b) Inter-Agency Review of Effects on United States Industry.—Whenever the Secretary of Commerce has reason to believe that an existing or proposed memorandum of understanding or related agreement has, or threatens to have, a significant adverse effect on the international competitive position of United States industry, the Secretary may request an inter-agency review of the memorandum of understanding or related agreement. If, as a result of the review, the Secretary determines that the commercial interests of the United States are not being served or would not be served by adhering to the terms of such existing memorandum or related agreement or agreeing to such proposed memorandum or related agreement, as the case may be, the Secretary shall recommend to the President the renegotiation of the existing memorandum or related agreement or any modification to the proposed memorandum of understanding or related agreement that he considers necessary to ensure an appropriate balance of interests.

(c) Limitation on Entering into MOUs and Related Agreements.—A memorandum of understanding or related agreement referred to in subsection (a) may not be entered into or implemented if the President, taking into consideration the results of the inter-agency review, determines that such memorandum of understanding or related agreement has or is likely to have a significant adverse effect on United States industry that outweighs the benefits of entering into or implementing such memorandum or agreement."

Purchasing requirements

The maturation of global markets presents a variety of opportunities for American entities to purchase goods and services from a myriad of nations globally. These goods and services may be solely available from overseas sources, or overseas suppliers may be attractive because their prices may be lower than those prices offered by domestic producers. However, the United States must be mindful of this concept with respect to ensuring national security and its ability to generate resources during periods of distress. Therefore, it is prudent to obtain critical resources from domestic suppliers. Through the use of domestic suppliers, the United States practically guarantees the ability to produce critical resources during period of distress. Because of such independence, the United States avoids dependencies that could impede its ability to obtain critical resources.

This concept is not unnoticed by the US Congress. Within Section 10 of the *US Code* are requirements that constrain the purchasing of critically strategic materials to sources that are within the domestic United States. Specifically, the *US Code* expresses the ability of the nation to ensure that its resource needs and requirements are satisfied during any periods of distress. The *US Code* provides constraints and guidelines regarding acquisitions. These considerations include rules, exceptions, and constraints associated with the purchasing of strategic materials that support a range of functions ranging from combat operations to transfers of electronic devices. Certainly, regarding any perspective of acquisitions, considerations of national security influence purchasing decisions. Therefore, certain transactions may be allowed or disallowed.

The Defense Industrial Reserve

Within the preceding chapters of this textbook, the essential dependence of the US economy upon butter as well as munitions was conceptually both identified and explained within the context of homeland security. It is imperative that America retain and maintain the ability to design, develop, test, produce, and implement an industrial base that is capable of supply resources that are necessary components of national defense and national security. This concept is relevant with respect to maintaining the current American status among the myriad of allied and adversarial nations that exist within the global society. Given the necessity of safeguarding America against any aggressors, the Defense Industrial Reserve (DIR) represents a concept through which the capacity to provide resources and materials, during periods of distress, is retained and maintained.

These concepts are highlighted within Title 10 of the *US Code*. The *US Code* provides rules, constraints, and exceptions regarding DIR transactions. Therefore, certain transactions may be allowed or disallowed. Regardless, any DIR transactions occur to bolster national security and provide a means of ensuring that necessary resources are obtainable and available during periods of calamity. The *US Code* encompasses a range of DIR considerations ranging from financial obligations to industry categorization to ensure the presence of resources.

The essence of the DIR provides a basis for ensuring the industrial capacity of the United States during periods of distress. It also pertains to the government ownership and control of any such resources that are mandated during emergencies and periods of distress. Therefore, partnerships among such government organizations may not necessarily be willful. Instead, they may be mandated by government decree and direction unless these organizations contemplate collaboration with entities within the private sector. Regardless, this portion of the *US Code* is an essential aspect of providing the ability to generate materials and resources that satisfy the requirements of emergency situations.

The United States must consider the integrity of its national security with respect to the characteristics of its trading partners. Therefore, a variety of prohibitions exist that affect the awarding of contracts. Section 10 of the *US Code* constrains the awarding of contracts with respect to characteristics of entities that are controlled by foreign governments.

Conclusion

The homeland security program is a national preparedness program. It is national because it is dependent on local communities. It is a partnership program. The number of partnerships, at the federal, state, and local levels, is difficult to estimate. The military, federal agencies, state agencies, and local and tribal agencies tasked to provide support for preparedness initiatives are incredible. These partnerships recognize their interdependency with one another. That idea is further recognized in partnering with the private sector. Among modern environments, the public and private sectors are interdependent and cannot support planning, training, equipment, and exercise initiatives without the partnership. The information-sharing efforts cannot perform optimally without the partnerships. The public and private sectors must operate in the proverbial "hand-in-glove" relationship. Their interests are common: to prevent incidents from occurring, to protect the citizens and critical infrastructure, to respond as necessary to reduce the consequences, and to recover the vitality of the community when disaster has interrupted its routine.

Citizen partners have the same common interests. The myriad of volunteer groups and individuals are working to make their neighborhoods safe. They are making tremendous efforts in providing public awareness and training. Citizens are participating in training programs that prepare them in activities that will aid them in surviving and also assist them in helping their community survive.

Partnerships must also be considered within the long-term, strategic context of national security. The United States must maintain as much control as is possible over its ability to produce critical resources. Such independence eliminates dependencies that could impede the ability of the nation to wage war or to respond during periods of distress. Section 10 of the *US Code* delineates a variety of tenets that facilitate the long-term, strategic perspective of national security and national sovereignty.

The United States government is a partnership. The founders captured that vision and incorporated it into the fundamental document describing the anticipated American Republic. "These United States" provided the partnership to break away from the potential threat caused by abuse of power, tyranny, and oppression. That partnership has survived many military campaigns, both inside its borders and on foreign soils. It has survived periods of civil unrest and disagreements that threatened its existence. The partnership of the United States is a lesson in resiliency. It keeps recovering. Preparedness is a partnership.

Key terms

Citizens Corps
Civil Air Patrol
Defense Industrial Reserve
Emergency Support Functions
Fire Corps
Medical Research Corps
National Defense Reserve Fleet
Operations Center
Regional Information Sharing Systems
US Air Force Auxiliary
US Coast Guard Auxiliary
USAonWatch
Volunteer
Volunteers in Police Service

QUESTIONS FOR DISCUSSION

1. This chapter introduces two paramilitary organizations: the US Air Force Auxiliary and the US Coast Guard Auxiliary. Both organizations are comprised primarily of unpaid citizen volunteers. Perform some research regarding the missions and functions of both organizations. Write a brief essay that compares and contrasts these two entities. Further, within your essay, provide a commentary describing how these entities contribute to homeland security.
2. This chapter introduced a variety of groups that exist throughout the nation. Practically anyone can volunteer to become a member of an organization that contributes meaningfully to homeland security. Review each of the volunteer organizations discussed herein, and provide a commentary regarding their benefits. Which of these organizations would you have an interest in joining? Why? Write a brief essay that summarizes your opinion.
3. This chapter introduced the Volunteers in Police Service. How does membership in this organization differ from serving as a part-time or reserve law enforcement officer within one's locality? Write a brief essay that summarizes your response.
4. Perform some research within your locality. Determine which of the organizations discussed herein have a presence within your community. If any are present, contact one organization and determine how the organization serves your locality. Write a brief essay that summarizes your findings.

References

1. U.S. Department of Justice. (n.d.). The Posse Comitatus Act of 1878. http://www.dojgov.net/posse_comitatus_act.htm (accessed March 23, 2009).
2. Baker, B. (1999). The origins of the Posse Comitatus. *Aerospace Power Chronicles*. http://www.airpower.maxwell.af.mil/airchronicles (accessed January 22, 2013).
3. U.S. Congress. (2007). Title 10, Subtitle A, Chapter 18, § 382: Emergency situations involving chemical or biological weapons of mass destruction. http://www.law.cornell.edu (accessed March 21, 2009).
4. Binkerhoff, J.R. (2002). The Posse Comitatus Act and Homeland Security. *Journal of Homeland Security*, http://www.homelandsecurity.org (accessed February 12, 2009).
5. Jefferson, T. (July 4, 1776). Declaration of independence. http://www.ushistory.org/Declaration/document/index.htm (accessed March 21, 2009).
6. Department of Homeland Security. (2008). National Response Framework. http://www.fema.gov (accessed March 20, 2009).
7. Department of Homeland Security. (n.d.). Office of Intelligence and Analysis. http://www.dhs.gov (accessed March 20, 2009).
8. RISS. (2009). *Regional Information Sharing Systems*. http://www.riss.net/services.aspx (accessed September 26, 2009).
9. Boba, R. (2005). *Crime Analysis and Crime Mapping*. California: Sage Publications.
10. Sweet, K. (2006). *Transportation and Cargo Security: Threats and Solutions*. New Jersey: Pearson Prentice-Hall Publishing.
11. Baker, T. (2005). *Introductory Criminal Analysis: Crime Prevention and Intervention Strategies*. New Jersey: Pearson Prentice Hall Publishing.
12. The National Press Club. (2003). Protecting America's critical infrastructure: from war room to boardroom. http://cip.gmu.edu (accessed March 20, 2009).
13. Department of Homeland Security. (2009). About the Private Sector Office. http://www.dhs.gov (accessed March 20, 2009).
14. Citizens Corps. (2010). *Citizens Corps: About Citizen Corps*. http://www.citizencorps.gov (accessed November 22, 2010).
15. Fire Corps. (2010). *The Fire Corps*. http://www.firecorps.org (accessed November 22, 2010).
16. USAonWatch. (2010). *USAonWatch*. http://www.usaonwatch.org (accessed November 25, 2010).
17. Medical Reserve. (2010). *Medical Reserve Corps*. http://www.medicalreservecorps.gov (accessed November 25, 2010).
18. VIPS. (2010). Volunteers in Police Service. http://www.policevolunteers.org (accessed November 25, 2010).
19. Civil Air. (2010). Civil Air Patrol. http://www.af.mil/information/factsheets/factsheet.asp?id=163 (accessed November 22, 2010).
20. Military. (2010). Military Civil Air Patrol. http://www.globalsecurity.org (accessed November 26, 2010).
21. Carr, MG Charles. (2013). "An Introduction from the National Commander," Civil Air Patrol, http://www.gocivilairpatrol.com/about/from_the_national_commander/ (accessed August 25, 2013).
22. USCGA. (2010). *United States Coast Guard Auxiliary*. http://www.cgaux.org/about.html (accessed November 26, 2010).
23. Allen, T. (n.d.). U.S. Coast Guard Auxiliary Policy Statement. http://www.auxnaco.org/documents/Auxiliary_Policy_Statement.pdf (accessed November 27, 2010).
24. Westcott, R. (n.d.). Auxiliarists play key role in Coast Guard mission in Hurricane Katrina aftermath. http://www.teamcoastguard.org (accessed November 27, 2010).
25. O'Hagan, J. (2010). A brush with Hurricane Earl. http://www.teamcoastguard.org (accessed November 27, 2010).
26. Maritime Administration. (2010). *Maritime Administration*. http://www.marad.dot.gov/ (accessed November 27, 2010).
27. NDRF. (2010). National Defense Reserve Fleet. http://www.marad.dot.gov/ships (accessed November 27, 2010).
28. Defense Industrial. (2010). Defense Industrial Reserve. http://www.law.cornell.edu (accessed November 28, 2010).

7

Disaster Preparedness and Mitigation Strategies

Nevertheless, there are gaps in receiving funding or planning for emergency preparedness. We must identify and address them, because these issues will remain with us for years to come. Unfortunately, there is no quick fix.

Micheal Shea

Chapter objectives:

- Examine the 15 planning scenarios identified by the US Department of Homeland Security
- Discuss the prodromal cycle
- Review the homeland security planning model
- Gain an understanding of the roles of local, state, and federal governments in the development of disaster preparation and mitigation strategies
- Emphasize the importance of homeland security for the continuance of society and of the nation
- Identify some of the major challenges encountered in disaster planning

Introduction

Homeland Security planning is a national priority in the programs funded by the US Congress and administered by the US Department of Homeland Security (DHS). Not long ago, *terrorism* was a vague and unknown term to most Americans. Acts of terrorism were remote to the continental United States. Primarily, local communities prepared for conventional weather-related hazards. Typically, the priority of first responders consisted of fire prevention and suppression and law enforcement anticrime, antidrug, and antigang efforts. Emergency management went about the business of planning for natural disasters, which included tornadoes, hurricanes, and floods. High-profile incidents that captured the nation's attention were school shootings, gang violence, and hate crimes. Grants and programs were designed to combat these types of activities.

Leadership was indifferent to the idea that status quo is history. What is today is not tomorrow. Apparently, some of the nation's leadership understood this concept, as cited in Burton[1]:

> In the 1970s, the National Governor's Association adopted a common framework for describing these functions, in part to facilitate governments of neighboring states coming to each other's aid in disaster situations. The four functions sometimes referred to as phases in the all-hazards management approach, are mitigation, preparedness, response and recovery. It is collectively described as the all-hazards approach....

This citation is particularly interesting as it illustrates a national discussion taking place when the response community was a collection of stovepiped disciplines. Public response agencies rarely addressed integrated planning and collaborative initiatives. It is also interesting to note the use of the term *all-hazards* within the national conversation during the 1970s.

At each level of government response, agencies operated within their respective institutionalized system. This "stovepipe" response culture was identified within the contents of the *9/11 Commission Report*. One of the most critical observations of the *9/11 Commission Report* included targeting the intelligence community for its lack of collaboration with partnering agencies. Joint responses did occur as a matter of routine. Once the scene was secured, each response discipline retreated to its respective duties with little integration in the planning scheme. Communications and information sharing were relegated to internal support. However during modern times, the world moves toward globalization. The information age evolves, matures, and adapts.

It was into this setting that the events of September 11, 2001, changed. According to Christopher Bellavita (2005),[22] "We have been at war with the terrorists since September 11, 2001. They have been at war with *us* (emphasis added) since October 23, 1983, when 241 U.S. service members were killed in Lebanon.... A relatively small group of people were alarmed by the rising threat of terrorism. As has been well documented in the post 9/11 era, most of those calls to pay attention were ignored." In 1983, the Marine barracks in Beirut, Lebanon, was bombed, resulting in the deaths of 241 US service personnel, which included 220 marines, 18 sailors, and 3 soldiers, and injury to 60 others in the largest 1-day death toll experienced by the United States military since World War II.

In 1993, the World Trade Center in New York City was bombed, and in 1995, the Murrah Federal Office Building was bombed in Oklahoma City, resulting in the deaths of 168 men, women, and children. Next, the attacks of 9/11 occurred.

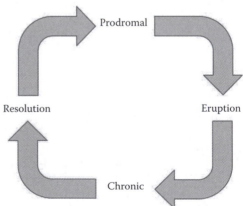

Steven Fink[2] uses the word prodrome to describe predictors. Its root meaning is "things that come before." Fink describes the "prodromal cycle" as an environment in which the routine life is lived. It is also described as one part of a four-part cycle of crisis. The prodromal cycle comes before the eruption (incident) and follows the resolution (closure) cycle. This cycle is in perpetual motion. **Figure 7.1** shows the conceptual relationships within the prodromal cycle.

Figure 7.1 The prodromal cycle. (From Fink, S., Crisis Management: Planning for the Inevitable, *American Management Association, New York, 1986*.)

Within the prodromal environment, avoidance and prevention initiatives can be optimized if global experiences are observed and integrated into organizational objectives. It requires the recipient to borrow from the profit and loss experience and the economy of the global partners. Simply illustrated, if an event occurs in California today, it will occur in Florida tomorrow. The question would then be: Is anyone in Florida observing and reacting?[2]

Historically, public safety leadership, elected officials, and emergency management leaders did not deny the presence of terrorists or the potential consequences posed by catastrophic, natural disasters. These were incidents experienced elsewhere or so infrequently that decades could pass without an occurrence. Catastrophic events were not the priority. However, that priority has changed.

Homeland Security Presidential Directives

The White House announced Homeland Security Presidential Directive 5 (HSPD-5) on February 28, 2003. The purpose of HSPD-5 is to manage domestic incidents, as duly noted in the first paragraph of HSPD-5: "[The purpose is] to enhance the ability of the United States to manage domestic incidents establishing a single, comprehensive national incident management system." The directive further states, "The Secretary [of DHS] will also provide assistance to State and local governments to develop all-hazards plans and capabilities including those of greatest importance to the security of the United States, and will ensure that State, local and Federal plans are compatible."[3]

HSPD-8 was announced by the White House on December 17, 2003. The purpose of HSPD-8 is national preparedness. Paragraph 1 of the directive describes how policies are established that strive to bolster the ability of the United States to prevent and respond to terrorist attacks, natural disasters, and all other emergencies. The directive states that this will be accomplished through "… requiring a national domestic all-hazards preparedness goal, establishing mechanisms for improved delivery of Federal preparedness assistance to State and local governments, and outlining actions to strengthen preparedness capabilities of Federal, state and local entities."[4]

Paragraph 2(a) of this directive further describes the meaning of the term *all-hazards preparedness* and explains that "…all-hazards preparedness refers to preparedness for domestic terrorist attacks, major disasters, and other emergencies." It was later decided that there were some additions that needed to be made to the original HSPD-8 in order to foster its effectiveness. An important addition to the directive included establishing a "standard and comprehensive approach" to any and all national planning and preparedness, while also providing direction on how to comply with the Homeland Security Management System of the National Strategy for Homeland Security of 2007.[5] The following are key terms and phrases to be extracted from HSPD-5 and HSPD-8:

- All-hazards plans and capabilities
- Ensure plans are compatible
- All-hazards preparedness goal
- All-hazards preparedness refers to…domestic terrorist attacks, major disasters, and other emergencies
- Formally establishing a standard and comprehensive approach to national planning

There are 21 HSPDs issued as of January 2009. This text examines two of these directives that were published in 2003. The language in these directives might cause one to conclude that a comprehensive planning model exists. Supposedly, between 2001 and 2006, the DHS met the preparedness goal by reducing vulnerabilities and enhancing, from a measurable perspective, the capabilities of the first responders. However, research indicates otherwise. The American Disaster Preparedness Foundation Inc.,[6] in its 2006 study of 30 top metropolitan areas, cited this finding:

> Overall results from the study indicate a poor prognosis for future disaster response efforts unless actions are taken to make significant improvements in emergency planning. Preparedness in at least half of all major metropolitan areas was rated worse than a 'C' while the highest ranked city, Phoenix, received only a B+ to its position at the top of the list.

Local officials may give little attention to the planning model chosen for preparedness planning. Conversely, they may give an inordinate amount of attention to the end product, especially the funding model. Risk analysis identifies gaps in capabilities. Funding is required to build, enhance, and sustain capabilities. Planning is the tool designed to guide the execution process, which includes a funding model.

Planning: Strategies and operations

The US DHS suggests the use of 15 planning scenarios within the planning cycle by those planners tasked to create preparedness plans. Below are listed the 15 planning scenarios identified by the US DHS:

- Improvised nuclear device
- Aerosol anthrax
- Pandemic influenza
- Plague
- Blister agent
- Toxic industrial chemicals
- Nerve agent
- Chlorine tank explosion
- Major earthquake
- Major hurricane
- Radiological dispersal device (RDD)
- Improvised explosive device (IED)
- Food contamination
- Foreign animal disease
- Cyber attack

These planning scenarios represent a conflict within the all-hazards planning model. The all-hazards planning approach, relative to the current capabilities-based planning model, exemplifies the planning and policy conflicts and inconsistencies present within the homeland security program. The issue with the 15 planning scenarios is attempting to compare natural disasters with man-caused incidents within a threat matrix. Some jurisdictions do not choose to use these scenarios within their planning scheme. According to the definition of the mission of homeland security within the national strategy, it is difficult to encompass natural disasters. Some are concerned that the inconsistency can be minimized by using these scenarios. Planning initiatives within the homeland security and preparedness program migrate from the federal government and trickle down to state, local, and tribal governments. However, it is common for the US DHS to be flexible and to not prescribe for state, local, and tribal partners specific scenarios. Although the model causes some debate, these 15 scenarios can be considered as suggestions for planning purposes.

Two foundational documents, related to the planning task in the national homeland security and preparedness program, are considered within the scope of this textbook. Those two documents are the National Homeland Security Strategy and the National Response Framework (NRF). The National Homeland Security Strategy states that the purpose of our strategy is to guide, organize, and unify our nation's homeland security efforts.[7] The strategy goes on to list areas of concern that the United States and its people should acknowledge:

- Preventing and disrupting terrorist attacks
- Protecting the citizens, infrastructure, and key resources
- Responding to all incidents that occur, terrorist acts or otherwise
- Continuing to make improvements in order to ensure triumph

The strategy stresses the importance of planning and proactive initiatives. There must be collaboration between local, state, and federal agencies for the strategy to be effective. The safety of the nation improves in conjunction with greater amounts of available tools and resources. There must be a clear and concise set of rules and regulations that every agency must follow, as well as precisely thought-out scenarios that can assess our nation's ability to respond to any event. With all that being said, the most important characteristic for agencies to possess is flexibility and the ability to adapt to any situation, as not every possible scenario can be imagined before it occurs. Every incident will be different and have its own characteristics and obstacles that must be overcome.[7]

The NRF is a rudimentary document that outlines the operational and response system that is institutionalized to assist federal, state, local, and tribal governments in the planning for response. Within the National Homeland Security Strategy (2007), roles and responsibilities were identified in the following manner: (1) community response, (2) state response, (3) federal response, and (4) private and nonprofit sector responses.

Community response

All emergencies are local. By this we mean that no matter the scope of an event, to each citizen impacted, recovery is personal. One of the fundamental response principles is that all incidents should be handled at the lowest jurisdictional level possible. The initial response to the majority of incidents typically is handled by local responders within a single jurisdiction and goes no further. When incidents exceed available resources, the local or tribal government may rely on mutual aid agreements with nearby localities or request additional support from the state. It is worth noting that for certain types of federal assistance, tribal nations work with the state, but as sovereign entities, they can elect to deal directly with the federal government for other types of assistance. One of the greatest challenges for the local responders is the decisions resulting in actions in the initial stages of an event. First responders can easily become casualties responding to an incident.

Local preparation is important. As an example, the Community Emergency Response Team (CERT) training program is a positive and realistic approach to prepare citizens for emergency and disaster situations. Through training, citizens learn basic disaster response skills such as fire safety, light search and rescue, team organization, and disaster medical operations. CERT members can assist others in their neighborhood or workplace when professional responders are not immediately available to help during a disaster or emergency.

State response

State governments have the primary responsibility for assisting local governments to respond to and recover from disasters and emergencies. When an incident expands to challenge the resources and capabilities of the state to coordinate requests for additional support, the state may request support from the private and nonprofit sector, turn to other states for support through the Emergency Management Assistance Compact, or call upon the federal government for assistance. States also may collaborate with one another to ensure a broader, more effective regional response.

Within the assets of the states are the forces contained in military departments, including the National Guard, air guard, and, in over 20 states, the state guard—state-level law enforcement assets and state-level emergency management assets, each of which may be called upon in the event of an emergency.

Federal response

The federal government maintains a wide array of capabilities and resources that may be made available to states and local governments. Federal assistance is provided, when needed, to support state and local efforts or to lessen or avert the threat of a catastrophe within the United States. Accordingly, federal response efforts are designed to complement and supplement, rather than supplant, the state and local response. The federal government also maintains relationships with private and nonprofit sector entities to aid in facilitating additional support.

Private and nonprofit sector

The private and nonprofit sectors fulfill key roles and collaborate with communities, states, and the federal government. The private sector plays an essential role when implementing plans for the rapid restoration of commercial activities and critical infrastructure operations. This activity can help to mitigate consequences, improve quality of life, and accelerate recovery for communities and the nation.

A 2009 review of the 25 leading homeland security contractors reflected the increasing emphasis upon border security and a decreasing focus upon the post-Katrina recovery. The top 10 homeland security–related vendors included Boeing, IBM Corporation, Accenture, General Dynamics, Cooperative Personnel Services, Science Applications International Corporation, Unisys, L-3 Communications Holdings, Lockheed Martin Corporation, and Integrated Coast Guard Systems.

Nonprofit organizations serve a vital role by performing essential services within communities in times of need, such as mass sheltering, emergency food supplies, counseling services, or other vital support services. Increasingly, it is common for the faith-based community to become robust partners in these functions.

Special circumstances

There are special circumstances where the federal government exercises a larger, more proactive role. Such situations include catastrophic incidents when local and state governments require significant assistance. They also include incidents where federal interests are directly implicated, such as those involving primary federal jurisdiction or authorities. For example, the federal government leads response efforts to render weapons of mass destruction (WMDs) safe and coordinate related activities with state and local partners, as appropriate.

The National Homeland Security Strategy and the NRF promote and support the comprehensive efforts in national preparedness. It is not absent conflict. However, prior to a discussion regarding areas of conflict within the planning task, it is necessary to examine the current planning model. **Figure 7.2** is a visual concept of the current model.

Preparedness is the goal, as shown in **Figure 7.2**. The goal of preparedness is supported by four mission areas. The four mission areas are performed by the appropriately identified response disciplines. The Target Capabilities List (TCL) assists in matching identified capabilities to the appropriate response discipline, which is then matched to one or more of the four mission areas. Superimposed upon the model are the 15 National Planning Scenarios. This model engages the idea that the response will be a multidisciplined, multijurisdictional effort. Within this model, the planning unit or team chooses a scenario and applies it to the TCL.

What capabilities are necessary for a jurisdiction to respond to this incident? **Table 7.1** lists many of the capabilities necessary. There are many response disciplines [e.g., fire, police, Emergency Medical Services (EMS) etc.] that are required to perform one or more of the mission areas related to this scenario. Once these activities are accomplished, the supposition is that the planner should have a product that will support risk analysis, resulting in determinations of gaps in capabilities.

This model should be a cyclic exercise that becomes a process in continuum. According to its framers, it should enhance capabilities, reduce vulnerabilities, and provide information relative to consequence management. There are three overarching elements in risk management employed by the DHS: threat, vulnerability, and consequence (**Figure 7.3**).

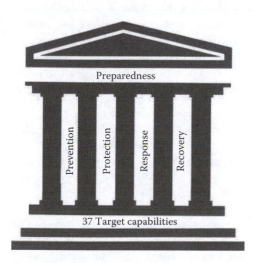

Figure 7.2 Homeland security planning model.

Within his testimony to the United States Congress in February of 2007, William O. Jenkins, Jr., stated, "While risk-based allocation decision making is still evolving, GAO has proposed a systematic risk management approach for allocating resources that reflects an assessment of threats, vulnerabilities, and the potential consequences of terrorist attacks and other risks." Jenkins further testified, "Full adoption of a risk management framework is essential for DHS to assess risk by determining which elements of risk should be addressed in what ways within available resources."[8] Planning and risk management are identified as common capabilities in the TCL. Planning is the critical capability. Risk management strategies and models cannot be effectively integrated absent a strong planning program.

The organizational planner or the planning unit is usually considered a function that assimilates disparate

Table 7.1 Target Capabilities List Categorized by Mission Area

Common Mission Area	Recover Mission Area
Communications	Economic and community recovery
Community preparedness and participation	Restoration of lifelines
Planning	Structural damage assessment
Risk management	**Respond Mission Area**
Intelligence/information sharing and dissemination	Animal health emergency support
Prevent Mission Area	Citizen evacuation and shelter in place
CBRNE detection	Critical resource logistics and distribution
Information gathering and recognition of indicators and warnings	Emergency operations center management
Intelligence analysis and production	Emergency public information and warning
Counterterror investigations and law enforcement	Environmental health
Protect Mission Area	Explosive device response operations
Critical infrastructure protection	Fatality management
Epidemiological surveillance and investigation	Fire incident response support
Food and agriculture safety and defense	Isolation and quarantine
Laboratory testing	Mass care (sheltering, feeding, and related services)
On-site incident management	Mass prophylaxis
Emergency public safety and security response	Medical supplies management and distribution
Responder safety and health	Medical surge
Emergency triage and pre–hospital treatment	
Search and rescue (land based)	
Volunteer management and donations	
WMD/hazardous materials response and decontamination	

CBRNE, chemical, biological, radiological, nuclear, and explosive agents and devices.

particles, reduces them to a cohesive collection of ideas that mature into the goals and objectives, identifies the mission of the organization, and guides it toward the intent of its existence. Those disparate particles may be thoughts and ideas, products, designs, resources, or assets, both tangible and intangible. The planning function is transparent to the obvious and visible parts of the organization. Certainly, it seems unusual or rare to find planning being the tip of the spear for controversy or being the catalyst for crisis. Planning synchronizes by integrating ideas and resources. However, there are conflicts within the framework of homeland security and preparedness guidance planning guidelines.

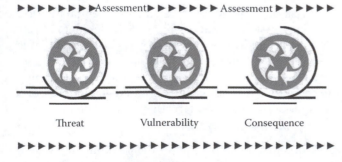

▶▶▶▶▶▶▶Assessment▶▶▶▶▶▶ Assessment ▶▶▶▶▶▶

Threat   Vulnerability   Consequence

▶▶▶▶▶▶▶▶▶▶▶▶▶▶▶▶▶▶▶▶▶▶▶▶▶▶▶▶▶▶▶▶

Figure 7.3 Threat assessment.

As we have stated earlier in the text, the DHS is a very robust department, including 22 agencies of government. One of the agencies placed under the DHS is the Federal Emergency Management Agency (FEMA). The integration with FEMA has been one of the most conflicting transitions during the history of the DHS. The definition of the DHS does not offer any resolution to this conflict. In fact, until Hurricane

Katrina occurred in 2005, the national focus emphasized terrorism. This emphasis seemed to coalesce with the rationale in creating the DHS and the definition describing its function. It simultaneously seems to conflict with the mission and function of FEMA in its responsibilities in natural disasters. This conflict was unresolved when Hurricane Katrina came ashore.

Shortly before Hurricane Katrina struck the Gulf Coast, a meeting occurred in Washington, DC, with state homeland security advisors, state emergency management directors, the DHS (including the FEMA director), and DHS Secretary Michael Chertoff. The secretary had requested the meeting for the purpose of discussing the all-hazards environment. The other, less visible agenda item related to the positioning of FEMA. The secretary listened very attentively for 2 days. His closing remarks were resolute. The all-hazards approach was the model, and FEMA would remain within the DHS. A few days, later Hurricane Katrina impacted the nation. Hurricane Katrina provided the opportunity that FEMA needed to make its case. The proponents, who believed there had been too much emphasis on terrorism, felt some vindication. This certainly was obvious during the post-Katrina testimonies before the US Congress and associated congressional inquiries. The DHS went through another change as a result of the reaction to Hurricane Katrina.

Planning: The challenges

As a result of Hurricane Katrina, Congress passed the Post-Katrina Emergency Management Reform Act of 2006. The DHS/FEMA conflict is further exacerbated within this legislation. The NRF is not reconciled with the legislation. The fundamental question regarding this conflict is: Who is in charge? The legislation states: "[The administrator of FEMA] shall lead the Nation's efforts to prepare for, protect against, respond to, recover from, and mitigate against the risks of natural disasters, acts of terrorism, and other man-made disasters."[9] This statement would appear to reconcile the conflict. However, the NRF indicates that the secretary of the DHS is the federal official responsible for coordinating the response and reporting to the president. This conflict trickles down to state, local, and tribal governments. It impacts the effectiveness at each level. Therefore, the conflict remains unresolved.

The DHS-versus-FEMA conflict impacts the definitions of terms. The use of the term *all-hazards* is involved within the conflict. Therefore, one may question whether hazards may be interchanged with threat. Many risk assessment methods encompass a standard of measure that provides equity in the natural hazard versus the man-made events (i.e., act of terrorism). Do the all-hazards planning characteristics (of the current model) adequately engage natural disasters as opposed to acts of terrorism? Twelve of the 15 National Planning Scenarios are terrorism based.

Further planning and management conflicts are indicated within the incident command level of the model. The current model identifies four mission areas: (1) prevention, (2) protection, (3) response, and (4) recovery. A model from the 1970s, which remains within contemporary literature and conversations, identifies four functions in the all-hazards approach: (1) mitigation, (2) preparedness, (3) response, and (4) recovery. Mitigation is used within the earlier model, rather than prevention. Using mitigation would not be compatible with the current TCL. The other obvious conflict between these two models involves preparedness as one of the four mission areas. Preparedness is either a goal or the goal—otherwise, it is a function. Within the current model of the DHS, preparedness is the goal.

The current DHS model is a capabilities-based planning model. This model is borrowed from the Department of Defense (DOD). Borrowing from the DOD is not new for the DHS. It does pose a few challenges in attempting to adapt a DOD model into the civilian response agency. Similar to other federal, state, and local partnership enterprises, homeland security has to be adapted to its working environment. State and local responders are challenged by laws and ordinances that are not applicable to federal agencies. The civilian responders are well rehearsed in civil rights and constitutional safeguards among their relationships with the citizens of their state and local communities. These constraints cause some differences between state/local and federal/military partners.

Other challenges for state and local responders are the finite number of personnel that can be deployed at any given time. Deployment and budgetary issues, such as backfill, overtime, number of hours worked, skills sets, as well as many other issues, are considerations for both state and local response agencies.

When using the capabilities-based planning model, as outlined by the DHS, these considerations integrate within the overall process of planning. There has been hesitancy on the part of local jurisdictions to fully accept the current model. For local jurisdictions, it is often difficult to work within the target capabilities. One of the more obvious challenges is selecting a capability that is not sustainable by local appropriations, which means that the capability is only in place for the performance period of the grant funds allocated.

The current capabilities-based planning encourages regional collaboration and multijurisdictional partnerships. This situation is often challenging. It is naïve to consider that because language exists promoting the idea of an integrated plan, it will be produced or duplicated. The funding challenge is caught in the conflict when collaboration is at stake. It is inherent in the system that jurisdictions first take care of their own needs and then consider the collaborative partnerships. However, mutual aid agreements have been an effective utility for many years. Those agreements continue to provide capabilities in cross-jurisdictional boundary incidents.

Two of the most formidable challenges in identifying capabilities, or gaps in capabilities, from a regional approach are geographic and demographic differences. Many of the regionally based programs place rural, less populated jurisdictions within the regional model among large metropolitan communities. The relationship is often tense. Because there are limited, prescriptive guidelines and policies from the DHS related to state and local government confusion is rampant within the programmatic objectives. Within the capabilities-based model, a planning unit, comprised of representatives from both large and small jurisdictions, can find it difficult to work their way through the process of identifying capabilities and disciplines to support the TCLs. The process easily becomes a funding strategy rather than a planning model.

Sharon Caudle[10] testified regarding regional approaches: "Moreover, it will be difficult to develop and implement regional approaches where core capabilities can be supported and supplemented by other jurisdictions in the region." Caudle further testified: "…risk assessment is not defined and presented as an integral part of homeland security CBP decision-making." Capabilities-based planning may be the model as the national homeland security program progresses. If so, it must result in a method to measure preparedness.

No model has provided the answer to the prevailing question regarding the level of preparedness. Therefore, one may continue to ask a simple question: How prepared are we? US representatives Bennie G. Thompson, chairman of the US House of Representatives Committee on Homeland Security, and Howard L. Berman, chairman of the US House of Representatives Committee on Foreign Affairs, issued a report in September 2008. This report was their evaluation of the Bush administration's performance regarding homeland security. The report examined the following 10 areas of interest: (1) aviation security, (2) rail and public transportation security, (3) port security, (4) border security, (5) information sharing, (6) privacy and civil liberties, (7) emergency response, (8) bio-surveillance, (9) private sector preparedness, and (10) national security.

The Bush administration assessment did not receive passing or high marks within this report. The report states, "…the Bush Administration has not delivered on a myriad of critical homeland and national security mandates set forth in the 'Implementing the 9/11 Commission Recommendations Act of 2007'. Without them, the Administration has failed to provide the American people the security they expect and deserve."[11] Similarly, on September 11, 2007, the Brookings Institute released the following statement: "A just released Government Accountability Office report bashed DHS for making limited progress on emergency-response capabilities and the management of human capital."[12]

The all-hazards approach to capabilities-based planning is immersed in controversy and conflict. Some of the conflict is inherently political and bureaucratic. Some of the conflict is definitional. Some of the conflict is also based on the question of whether planning, relative to homeland security and preparedness, can be employed as a universal model or whether it is better employed on a jurisdiction-by-jurisdiction basis. For example, the TCL may not be the model for each jurisdiction, and it may not be the model for the civilian response community.

Barry R. Rosen states, "As has often been pointed out, the United States and most developed, democratic countries are extremely vulnerable to terrorist attacks. These are open societies…. Dangerous activities occur in modern society every day. Prosaic means can be employed against everyday targets to produce catastrophic results."[13] For now, the preparedness planner is guided by the all-hazards approach to capabilities-based planning. It is the driver to funding allocations and programmatic priorities. Regardless of whether it is ultimately deemed as effective or successful, it is the current planning model used by the DHS. The planner must encompass the natural disasters and the man-made incidents in the comprehensive basic preparedness plans within his jurisdiction.

Risk management and assessments

The model for national preparedness is designed by the DHS. The *National Preparedness Guidelines*[20] are published by the DHS to facilitate a suggested planning format. Congress and the DHS agree that risk management principles must be employed within the threat and that both vulnerability and consequence assessments are promulgated within the DHS policy and program. It may not be obvious to the practitioner, but underlying and supporting the assessments are the principles of risk management. The practitioner may only be trained in the use of the planning model and not necessarily the principles embedded in the design model.

According to Jenkins,[8] during his testimony to Congress, "…adoption of a comprehensive risk management framework is essential for DHS to assess risk by determining which elements of risk should be addressed in what ways within available resources." Contemporary discussions will continue to focus upon the all-hazards approach to capabilities-based planning. It is vital that jurisdictions incorporate a uniform planning model within their preparedness programs. It is also critical that jurisdictions within the United States and territories consistently assess threats, vulnerabilities, and consequences.

Practically anything can be considered from the perspectives of risk and risk management. **Figure 7.4**, from an article entitled "Threat/Vulnerability Assessments and Risk Analysis" by Nancy A. Renfroe and Joseph L. Smith,[23] depicts a typical methodology employed by the federal government when contemplating security risk.

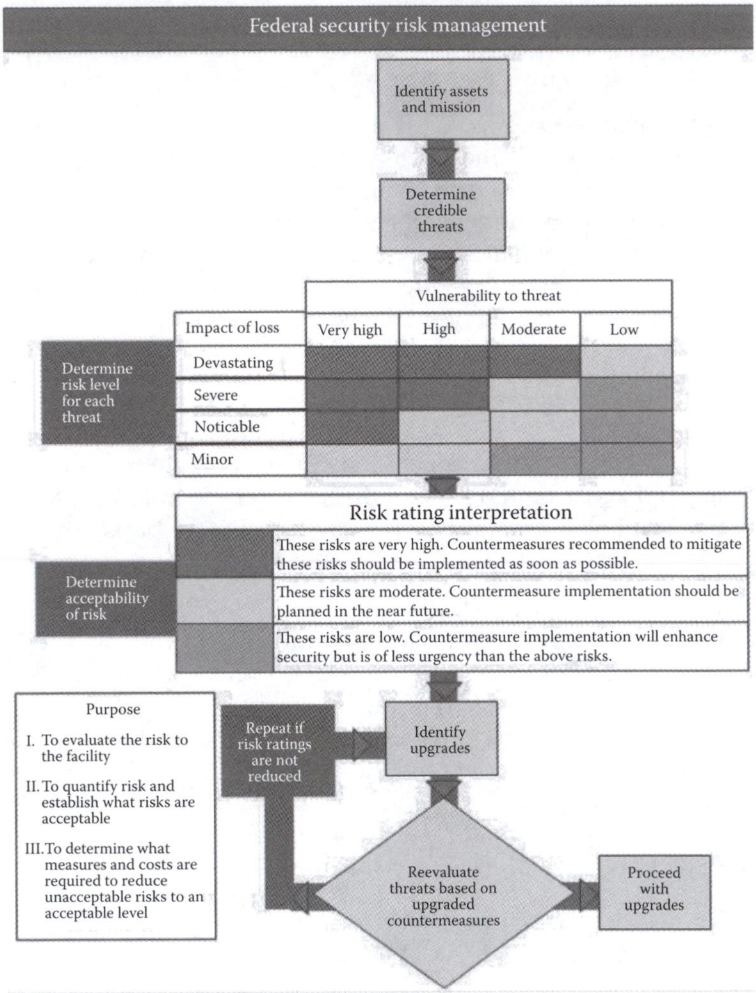
Federal security risk management
Identify assets and mission
Determine credible threats
Vulnerability to threat
Impact of loss
Very high
High
Moderate
Low
Determine risk level for each threat
Devastating
Severe
Noticable
Minor
Risk rating interpretation
Determine acceptability of risk
These risks are very high. Countermeasures recommended to mitigate these risks should be implemented as soon as possible.
These risks are moderate. Countermeasure implementation should be planned in the near future.
These risks are low. Countermeasure implementation will enhance security but is of less urgency than the above risks.
Purpose
I. To evaluate the risk to the facility
II. To quantify risk and establish what risks are acceptable
III. To determine what measures and costs are required to reduce unacceptable risks to an acceptable level
Repeat if risk ratings are not reduced
Identify upgrades
Reevaluate threats based on upgraded countermeasures
Proceed with upgrades

Figure 7.4 *Flowchart depicting the basic risk assessment process. (Courtesy of Nancy A. Renfroe, PSP, and Joseph L. Smith, PSP, of Applied Research Associates. Used with permission.)*

Threat assessments

Threat assessments examine a full spectrum of incident types. The *National Preparedness Guidelines*,[20] assimilated and published by the DHS in 2007, contain 15 National Planning Scenarios that suggest both natural and man-made hazards. The local official all-hazards preparedness executive handbook emphasizes catastrophic planning and federal emergency management of low-probability versus high-consequence hazards. With respect to these 15 National Planning Scenarios, a question arises regarding the use of the term *hazards*: Can the terms *hazards* and *threat* be used interchangeably? Can a consistent assessment methodology be employed to assess threat as it relates to natural disasters and acts of terrorism? James Carafano[16] asserts that "...hurricanes are not national security threats."

Within the threat assessment, the practitioner will examine, among a myriad of threats, the threat of chemical, biological radiological, nuclear, and explosive agents and devices (CBRNE). Explosives remain the weapons of choice for terrorist groups. CBRNE is closely related to WMDs. One rudimentary question when surveying CBRNE and WMD threats is: What is in a jurisdiction that can be used as weaponry? This question is not solely focused on what might be brought into a jurisdiction. Instead, it questions the identification of what is already present that can be used against the jurisdiction. An example is the 9/11 weapons. The terrorists did not purchase the fuel or the airplanes that were used as weapons. Instead, they used the airplane as a weapon.

Chemical agents are common to everyday life. Some are harmful, and some are lethal. Common chemicals can become effective weapons. Chlorine, gasoline, and alcohol are examples of common chemicals that can be used as weaponry. Others are designed for injury and death. An example of a deadly chemical agent is sarin nerve gas. In March 1995, a terrorist group, Aum Shinrikyo (now using the name Aleph), released the sarin nerve agent onto three trains in Japan. Eight people died, hundreds were injured, and a total of 5,000 people were treated for injuries.

The potential consequence caused by a bio-terrorism incident is unfathomable. In 2001, five people died after handling mail contaminated with anthrax. Bruce Ivins, a bio-defense researcher, became the primary suspect. He committed suicide in 2008. Within the United States and throughout the world, anthrax is common in some soils. It is associated with animals, such as horses, goats, and cattle. Any form of anthrax can be used as a lethal weapon.

The "dirty bomb" is a commonly used planning scenario relative to the use of a radiological agent in conjunction with a RDD. This weapon combines a conventional explosive (e.g., TNT) with radioactive materials. Experts consider the conventional explosive agent within the RDD to be the most harmful. The radiological agent is used more as a psychological weapon to instill panic, fear, and hysteria within a population.

The nuclear threat is such an overwhelming incident that local jurisdictions struggle with accomplishing threat assessments on the nuclear incident potential. The use of a nuclear weapon would immediately require all federal resources available for response. The threat assessment is useful in determining the risk factors associated with the use of a nuclear weapon. Information derived from the threat assessment assists local jurisdictions and states in prevention and protection planning.

Explosive and incendiary devices, and the associated modus operandi, are the weapons of choice for acts of terrorism. The World Trade Center bombings of 1993, the Murrah Building bombing of 1995, and the attacks of September 11, 2001, are tragic examples of the effectiveness of these weapons.

The IED is used frequently and effectively. The vehicle-borne IED (VBIED) has been very effective in Afghanistan and Iraq. The DHS has prioritized deterrence and detection training for IED interventions within the 2008 homeland security program. The uses of IEDs (e.g., roadside bombs and suicide car bombs) have caused over 60% of all American combat casualties in Iraq and 50% of combat casualties in Afghanistan.[21] These figures include both killed and wounded individuals.[21]

Within a threat-based scenario, the CBRNE agents and devices are the weapons of choice identified with the threat element. The threat element is the individual or group identified as the threat. The threat-based assessment identifies the threat element, linking that identification to the preferred weapons of choice and method of employing the weapons and subsequently linking those findings to the vulnerability data.

Vulnerability assessments

Vulnerability assessments may be one of the most difficult of the assessment activities. Within these assessments, a simple question is posed: What are the vulnerabilities within the jurisdiction relative to all-hazards planning? The chemical plant that is located on the coastal waterfront may be more vulnerable to the hurricane than if it were located 25 miles north of the coastline. However, it may be equally vulnerable to man-made attacks in either location. The relationship of threat to vulnerability is that in the absence of a threat, there is no vulnerability. If the jurisdiction has no railway, the jurisdiction is not threatened by a train derailment. It is interesting; however, that, within its 2008 funding awards for the Urban Area Security Initiatives across the nation, the DHS considered all of the urban areas equally vulnerable to similar types of threats. In so doing, the DHS may have solved a funding challenge, but it weakened the integrity of vulnerability assessments.

Consequence assessments

Consequence assessments continue the assessment process. Consequence is a comprehensive impact assessment. It is a concentric process. Consequence assessments pose more queries: What is the impact to the local jurisdiction? What is the impact to the state, the nation, and the international community? Consequence assessments, from a proactive perspective, enhance the efforts of each of the mission areas. They aid in designing prevention strategies and protection practices, such as target-hardening initiatives. Consequence assessments also support response and recovery planning. The consequence assessment is the data source for resiliency strategies. The data assimilated from the assessment process guide jurisdictions in planning, management, and most importantly, prioritization of funding allocations.

National observations following major disasters

In 2006, 5 years after the events of September 11, 2001, and 1 year after the devastating hurricane season of 2005, which included Hurricanes Katrina, Rita, and Wilma, the United States Conference of Mayors (USCM) disseminated a survey that investigated the levels of preparedness and homeland security that existed within the United States. Given the preceding discussions regarding planning and preparedness, this survey yielded some interesting findings regarding the statuses of American cities in terms of these characteristics of homeland security.

According to the USCM,[19] this survey was disseminated among 183 cities in 38 states, the District of Columbia (Washington, DC), and Puerto Rico. According to the USCM,[19] three categories of cities were examined: (1) populations ranging up to 100,000 individuals; (2) populations ranging between 100,001 and 300,000 individuals; and (3) populations exceeding 300,000 individuals. A total of 104 respondents represented the first category; a total of 49 respondents represented the second category; and a total of 30 respondents represented the third category.

Overall, the survey responses demonstrated some levels of preparedness and some levels of unpreparedness. Although it is impossible to imagine and predict each and every combination and permutation of events that may devastate an urban area, the outcomes of the study are demonstrative of functions that necessitate improvements regarding emergency planning and responsiveness. Admittedly, the survey outcomes are dated, given that 4 years have passed since the dissemination of the survey instrument. However, regardless of this passage of time, the survey queries and findings present issues that all urban areas must contemplate with respect to emergency and contingency planning. It is anticipated that readers will heed these issues and consider the best and highest use of planning initiatives to enhance public safety.

The cost of federal homeland security

Homeland security is expensive. Within the DHS, the 2011 fiscal year (FY) budget is approximately $56.3 billion. The succeeding sections highlight the salient attributes of this budget. The contents of the succeeding sections, unless otherwise noted, were obtained from the DHS.[13]

Federal: Preventing terrorism and enhancing security

A variety of functions occur involving the deterrence of terrorism and other acts of crime. These functions necessitate both human and technological infrastructures and resources. Deterrence efforts include initiatives that vary widely. Such activities include the inspection of individuals during transit and the provision of law enforcement officers among aviation routes. Regardless of the function, the deterrence of terrorism and the provision of security are both costly functions within the DHS. This section describes the entities that perform the functions of terrorism prevention and security enhancement. The contents of the succeeding paragraphs, unless otherwise noted, were obtained from the DHS.[14]

Advanced imaging technology (AIT): An increase of $214.7 million is requested to procure and install 500 advanced imaging technology machines at airport checkpoints to detect dangerous materials, including nonmetallic materials. This request, along with planned deployments for 2010, would provide AIT coverage at 75% of Category X airports and 60% of the total lanes at Category X through II airports.

Transportation security officers (TSOs) to staff AITs: An increase of $218.9 million is requested for additional TSOs, managers, and associated support costs to operate additional AITs at airport checkpoints. Passenger screening is critical to detecting individuals carrying dangerous or deadly objects and preventing them from boarding planes.

Federal air marshals (FAMs): An increase of $85 million is requested for additional FAMS to increase international flight coverage. FAMs must operate independently without backup and rank among those federal law enforcement officers that hold the highest standard for handgun accuracy. They blend in with passengers and rely on their training, including investigative techniques, criminal terrorist behavior recognition, firearms proficiency, aircraft-specific tactics, and close-quarters self-defense measures to protect the flying public.[15]

Portable explosive trace detection (ETD): An increase of $60 million is requested to purchase approximately 800 portable ETD machines ($39 million) and associated checkpoint consumables ($21 million).

Canine teams: An increase of $71 million is requested to fund an additional 275 proprietary explosives detection canine teams, 112 teams at 28 Category X airports and 163 teams at 56 Category I airports.

Behavior detection officers (BDOs): An increase of $20 million is requested to further enhance the Transportation Security Administration's (TSA's) Screening Passengers by Observation Techniques program. The FY 2011 request includes a total of 3,350 officers to enhance coverage at lanes and shifts at high-risk Category X and I airports and expand coverage to smaller airports.

Domestic Nuclear Detection Office Systems Engineering and Architecture: An increase of $13.4 million is requested to fund systems engineering efforts to address vulnerabilities in the global nuclear detection architecture, the multilayered system of detection technologies, programs, and guidelines designed to enhance the nation's ability to detect and prevent a radiological or nuclear attack.

Radiological/nuclear detection systems: An increase of $41 million is requested for the procurement and deployment of radiological and nuclear detection systems and equipment to support efforts across the department.

Law enforcement detachment teams: An increase of $3.6 million is requested to bring deployable US Coast Guard Law Enforcement Detachment (LEDET) teams to full capacity. LEDETs help prevent terrorism, secure US borders, disrupt criminal organizations, and support counterdrug missions overseas. In FY 2009, for example, LEDETs aboard US naval and partner nation assets accounted for more than 50% of total maritime cocaine removals.

2012 presidential campaign: Total funding of $14 million is requested for start-up costs associated with the 2012 presidential campaign, including training for candidate/nominee protective detail personnel. The Secret Service also began to procure and preposition equipment, services, and supplies to support candidate/nominee protective operations throughout the country.

Secret Service information technology (IT): Total funding of $36 million is requested for the Information Integration and Transformation program. This funding will allow the Secret Service to successfully continue its comprehensive IT transformation and provide a multiyear, mission-integrated program to engineer a modernized, agile and strengthened IT infrastructure to support all aspects of the Secret Service's mission.

Federal: Securing and managing our borders

The United States shares national borders with the nations of Canada and Mexico. The expansiveness of these borders provides unique challenges and dangers regarding homeland security functions. The preceding chapters of this textbook highlighted the dangers that are presented by the physical borders of the nation. However, it must be noted that borders are not necessarily defined geographically. Instead, borders exist among airports and seaports through which many travelers arrive via aircraft and ships. Regardless of whether a national border is tangible or intangible, it must be secured. Therefore, the DHS performs a myriad of functions involving border security. This section describes the salient functions associated with border security and border management. The contents of the succeeding paragraphs, unless otherwise noted, were obtained from the DHS.

Journeyman pay increase: In the spring of 2010, DHS implemented the journeymen pay increase, raising the journeyman grade level for frontline Customs and Border Protection (CBP) officers, border patrol agents, and agricultural specialists from the GS-11 level to the GS-12 level. An adjustment to base of $310.4 million will fund the full-year impact of the salary and benefit requirements associated with this implementation.

CBP officers: An increase of $44.8 million is requested to fund 318 CBP officers full-time employee (FTEs) within the Office of Field Operations and 71 support FTEs for CBP. The decline in the number of passengers and conveyances entering the United States in FY 2009 resulted in an almost 8% decrease in revenues from inspection user fees. CBP, therefore, has fewer resources to maintain critical staffing levels for CBP officers. The proposed funding will allow CBP to maintain staffing for critical positions to protect the United States at its ports of entry.

Border enforcement security task forces (BESTs): An additional $10 million is requested to establish BESTs in three additional locations: Massena, New York; San Francisco, California; and Honolulu, Hawaii. These multiagency teams work to identify, disrupt, and dismantle criminal organizations posing significant threats to border security, including terrorist groups, gang members, and criminal aliens.

Intellectual property rights (IPR) enforcement: An increase of $25 million is requested to support CBP IPR enforcement efforts, including IT systems that support IPR activities and implementation of the 5-year IPR plan. An increase of $5 million is also requested for the Immigration and Customs Enforcement (ICE)–led National Intellectual Property Rights Coordination Center (IPR Center). The IPR Center brings key US government agencies together to combat IPR violations that threaten our economic stability, restrict the competitiveness of US industry, and endanger the public's health and safety. ICE will also use these funds to focus on disrupting criminal organizations through the Internet and support for anticounterfeiting efforts.

Intelligence analysts: An increase of $10 million is requested to fund 103 intelligence analysts for CBP. This staffing increase will support 24/7 operations of CBP Intelligence Watch, operations coordination, and the Commissioner's Situation Room.

Coast guard asset recapitalization: A total of $1.4 billion is requested to continue recapitalization of aging coast guard surface and air assets. Included in this request is $538 million for production of the coast guard's fifth National Security Cutter to continue replacement of the 378-foot High Endurance Cutters fleet. Also included is $240 million for production of four Fast Response Cutters to continue replacement of the 110-foot Class Patrol Boat fleet. The Fast Response Cutters have enhanced capability, high readiness, speed, and endurance, which will allow them to quickly and effectively respond to emerging threats. Additionally, $40 million is requested to purchase one maritime patrol aircraft (MPA), HC-144A. The HC-144A will address the coast guard's MPA flight hour gap by providing 1200 hours every year per aircraft. Finally, $13.9 million is requested for improvement and/or acquisition of housing to support military families.

Federal: Enforcing and administering our immigration laws

Each day, a myriad of individuals enter the nation through both its tangible and intangible borders. These individuals arrive both legally and illegally. Although legal immigrants are welcomed, the arrival of illegal aliens is demonstrative of porous borders. Immigration is a paramount consideration within the homeland security function. This section describes the resources that are affiliated with immigration. The contents of the succeeding paragraphs, unless otherwise noted, were obtained from the DHS.

E-Verify: A total of $103.4 million is requested for the E-Verify Program. In FY 2011, US Citizenship and Immigration Services (USCIS) developed and implemented an E-Verify portal that provides a single-user interface for the program's products and services. In addition, USCIS will enhance E-Verify's monitoring and compliance activities through analytical capabilities that will support more robust fraud detection and improved analytic processes and will continue developing system enhancements in response to customer feedback, surveys, mission requirements, and capacity needs.

Secure Communities: Total funding of $146.9 million is requested to continue FY 2010 progress toward nationwide implementation of the Secure Communities program, which involves the identification, apprehension, and removal of all Level 1 criminal aliens in state and local jails through criminal alien biometric identification capabilities. Secure Communities, in cooperation with federal, state, and local law enforcement agencies, will provide a safeguard to American communities by removing those criminal aliens from the United States that represent the greatest threats to public safety and by deterring their reentry through aggressive prosecution.

Immigrant integration: A total of $18 million is requested to fund the USCIS Office of Citizenship initiatives, including expansion of the competitive Citizenship Grant Program to support national and community-based organizations preparing immigrants for citizenship, promote and raise awareness of citizenship rights and responsibilities, and enhance English language education and other tools for legal permanent residents. The Office of Citizenship will support the implementation of the immigration integration program and lead initiatives to educate aspiring citizens about the naturalization process, monitor and evaluate the administration and content of the new naturalization test, and develop educational materials and resources for immigrants and the organizations that serve them.

Federal: Safeguarding and securing cyberspace

The preceding sections of this textbook described the salient security considerations of both physical reality and virtual reality. Because the national infrastructure depends heavily upon digital technologies, it is imperative to ensure the security of the virtual environment. This section describes resources that are necessary for embellishing the security of the virtual environment. The contents of the succeeding paragraphs, unless otherwise noted, were obtained from the DHS.

National Cyber Security Division (NCSD): Total funding of $379 million is requested for the NCSD to support the development of capabilities to prevent, prepare for, and respond to incidents that could degrade or overwhelm the nation's critical IT infrastructure and key cyber networks. These funds will identify and reduce vulnerabilities, mitigate threats, and ensure that cyber intrusions and disruptions cause minimal damage to public and private sector networks.

National Cyber Security Center (NCSC): A total of $10 million is requested for the NCSC to enhance cyber security coordination capabilities across the federal government including mission integration, collaboration and coordination, situational awareness and cyber incident response, analysis and reporting, knowledge management, and technology development and management.

Federal: Ensuring resilience to disasters

Any consideration of homeland security must include the robustness of responsiveness regarding any incidents that impact the nation. Regardless of the scope, magnitude, or type of event, the characteristics of responsiveness must be robust to facilitate public safety. This section describes resources that enhance the robustness of responsiveness. The contents of the succeeding paragraphs, unless otherwise noted, were obtained from the DHS.

Disaster Relief Fund (DRF): The budget seeks funding of $1.95 billion, an increase of $0.35 billion, for the DRF. The DRF provides a significant portion of the total federal response to victims in declared major disasters and emergencies.

FEMA facilities: An additional $23.3 million is requested to address critical FEMA real-estate needs. It was projected that by FY 2011, the capacity of FEMA facilities would be unable to accommodate key mission responsibilities and staff. FEMA also faces a critical need to maintain and repair aging and deteriorating national facilities. To address these needs, FEMA has developed a 5-year capital plan to begin critical regional facility acquisitions and repairs.

Pre-Disaster Mitigation Grants: Total funding of $100 million is requested to provide program support and technical assistance to state, local, and tribal governments to reduce the risks associated with disasters, support the national grant competition, and provide the required allocation of $500,000 per state. Resources will support the development and enhancement of hazard mitigation plans, as well as the implementation of predisaster mitigation projects.

Flood map modernization: A total of $194 million is requested to analyze and produce flood hazard data and map products and communicate flood hazard risk. The funding will support the review and update of flood hazard data and maps to accurately reflect flood hazards and monitor the validity of published flood hazard information.

Rescue 21: $36 million is requested for the Rescue 21 system, enabling the US Coast Guard to enhance preparedness, ensure efficient emergency response, and rapidly recover from disasters. The Rescue 21 system replaces the US Coast Guard's legacy National Distress and Response System and improves communications and command and control capabilities in the coastal zone. The system is the foundation for coastal search and rescue and enhances maritime domain awareness through increased communications ability with mariners and interagency partners.

Federal: Maturing and strengthening the homeland security enterprise

The DHS is a new organization relative to the existences of other state and federal government entities. However, through time, it will mature and identify itself as a unique component of the national security infrastructure. This section considers a variety of resources that embellish national security efforts. The contents of the succeeding paragraphs, unless otherwise noted, were obtained from the DHS.

St. Elizabeth's headquarters consolidation: To streamline the department's core operations, $287.8 million is requested to consolidate executive leadership, operations coordination, and policy and program management functions in a secure setting at St. Elizabeth's. The department's facilities are currently dispersed over more than 40 locations throughout the National Capital Region (NCR). This consolidation at St. Elizabeth's will reduce the fragmentation of components and will improve communications, coordination, and cooperation across all DHS headquarters organizations.

Lease Consolidation—Mission Support: A total of $75 million is requested to align the department's real-estate portfolio in the NCR to enhance mission performance and increase management efficiency.

Data center migration: A total of $192.2 million is requested for the continuation of system and application migration of legacy data centers to two enterprise-wide DHS data centers to meet current and anticipated data service requirements. Funding will also be utilized for upgrading infrastructure requirements.

Acquisition workforce: The FY 2011 request included an increase of $24 million to strengthen the department's acquisition workforce capacity and capabilities. The increase was requested to mitigate the risks associated with skill gaps of the acquisition workforce, ensure that the department achieves the best terms possible in major acquisitions, and improve the effectiveness of the workforce.

Science and Technology (S&T) Safe Container (SAFECON)/Time Recorded Ubiquitous Sensor Technology (TRUST) research and development (R&D): A total of $8 million is requested for the S&T SAFECON and TRUST programs. These initiatives develop high-reliability, high-throughput detection technologies to scan cargo containers entering the country for WMDs, explosives, contraband, and human cargo.

Grants: A total of $4 billion is requested for grant programs to support our nation's first responders. This funding assists state and local governments in the prevention of, protection against, response to, and recovery from incidents of terrorism and other events.

Federal: Comments regarding the budget

Although the preceding budgetary allocations are demonstrative of functions that contribute toward the maximization of public safety and enhance national security, the financing of homeland security is not without debate. According to Miller and Carafano,[18] issues of "pork barrel spending" were considered regarding the early homeland security finances. Warnings ensued concerning "earmarks" that could potentially "take funding from building a truly national homeland security system and addressing the highest priority risks and divert it to the special interests of individual legislators."[16] Such debates questioned the methodology through which early funding of homeland security was accomplished.

Arguments occurred regarding the allocations and disseminations of funds among the American states. Homeland Security Secretary Michael Chertoff made a powerful appeal to the senators to distribute the money based on risk. A foundation of such arguments indicated that funds were allocated to low-risk settings without regard to areas of higher risk and probability of attack.

Government financing is comprised of taxpayer dollars and foreign investment. American leaders have a fiduciary obligation and responsibility to ensure that their financial decisions are rendered toward the best interests of American society, the nation, and its stakeholders. Therefore, these decisions must be conducted and rendered according to achieving the highest and best use of financial resources. These concepts are applicable to all years of homeland security accounting, budgeting, and finance.

The DHS is experiencing its stages of infancy and is a maturing organization. However, despite its newness, it must be mindful of its use of monies with respect to the benefits of national interests. In 2009, this concept was emphasized during the testimony of Secretary Napolitano before the Senate Appropriations Committee Subcommittee on Homeland Security. According to Secretary Napolitano, "As the Department highlights its spending priorities in this Budget, it is simultaneously conducting a bold and far-reaching Efficiency Review initiative to ensure that taxpayer dollars are spent in the most effective way possible. Efficiency Review encompasses both simple, common-sense reforms and longer-term, systemic changes that will, over time, make DHS a leaner, smarter department better equipped to protect the nation."[17]

This commentary provided the basis for conducting evaluations to optimize the performance of the DHS, through time, toward the benefit of national interests. The basis of Secretary Napolitano's evaluations involved the use of 30-day, 60-day, 90-day, and 120-day periods to implement a variety of improvement initiatives. According to the DHS, these initiatives are given as follows[17]:

- 30 days:
  - Eliminate non–mission-critical travel and maximize use of conference calls and Web-based training and meetings.
  - Consolidate subscriptions to professional publications and newspapers.
  - Minimize printing and distribution of reports and documents that can be sent electronically or posted online.
  - Maximize use of government office space for meetings and conferences in place of renting facilities.
- 60 days:
  - Implement an electronic tracking tool for fleet usage data to identify opportunities for alternative fuel usage; heighten vigilance for fraud, waste or abuse; and optimize fleet management.
  - Conduct an assessment of the number of full-time and part-time employees and contractors to better manage the workforce.
  - Utilize refurbished IT equipment (computers and mobile devices) and redeploy the current inventory throughout the DHS.
  - Leverage buying power to acquire software licenses for department-wide usage (estimated savings of $283 million over the next 6 years).
- 90 days:
  - Develop cross-component training opportunities for employees.
  - Develop a process for obtaining preliminary applicant security background data for candidates referred for final consideration (savings of up to $5500 per avoided full background check).
  - As replacements are needed, convert new printers, faxes, and copiers into all-in-one machines (estimated savings of $10 million over 5 years).
  - Streamline decision-making processes in headquarters offices to eliminate redundancies.
- 120 days:
  - Establish a plan to ensure that the DHS workforce has employees sufficient in number and skill to deliver the core mission.
  - As replacements are needed for non–law enforcement vehicles, initiate acquisition and leasing of hybrid vehicles, or alternative-fuel vehicles in cases where hybrids are not feasible (estimated mileage improvement of above 30%).
  - Maximize energy efficiencies in facility management projects (estimated savings of $3 million a year).
  - Standardize content for new-employee orientation and mandatory annual training modules department-wide.

The preceding evaluation periods contribute toward the strategic optimizing of government resources regarding the performance of the homeland security function. Therefore, these evaluations are designed to minimize wastefulness, improve efficiency, and either maintain or improve the effectiveness of the homeland security function. Further, through the allocating of monies for specific tasks and purposes, the use of such evaluations facilitates accountability regarding the allocation and use of monies for homeland security. Through the use of such methods, various arguments, associated with unjustified pork barrel and preferential allocations of financial resources, may be dissuaded and avoided because of the accountability resulting from periodic evaluations.

Hurricane Katrina: A case study

On August 29, 2005, Hurricane Katrina struck the Gulf Coast. Southern Louisiana, Mississippi, and Alabama were heavily damaged. Communities in Hancock, Harrison, and Jackson Counties, in Mississippi, were decimated. Before Hurricane Katrina, the 1969 Hurricane Camille was the most devastating hurricane to occur on the Gulf Coast. Katrina came ashore with sustained winds of 140 mph and was classified as a Category IV storm. Its sustained winds were less than Camille's at 190 mph. However, Katrina was a much larger storm. For the Mississippi Gulf Coast, Camille was the benchmark storm until Katrina struck.

Consider the following planning questions as both predisaster and postdisaster considerations that a public safety and emergency management planner might use in developing contingency plans for their jurisdiction:

- Did anyone wake up on August 29, 2005, a day after Katrina made landfall, surprised to find that Mississippi was a Gulf Coast state?
- Did anyone awaken surprised to discover that Gulf Coast states experience hurricanes?
- If Camille is the benchmark, what changed on the coast in the past 30 years? Were there more businesses? Were they located with a vulnerability to hurricanes?
- Had the population increased or decreased?
- Had there been any residential areas established that were different than in 1969? What about highways, bridges, airports, and utility infrastructure?
- What changes had occurred in Waveland, Bay St. Louis, or Pass Christian?
- How many casinos were operating at the time of Camille compared to Katrina?
- What industry and business interests are most threatened by this hazard?
- How much of the population is threatened?

These are questions the planner would be continuing to ask when the state, local, and tribal jurisdictions have identified such a massive vulnerability. When answering these questions, consider the following queries:

- Would knowledge of vulnerabilities enable the planner, within the predisaster environment, to make some preliminary determinations?
- Could risk assessments be conducted that would assist in determining potential economic impact if the region sustained a catastrophic hurricane?
- Would predisaster planning assist response agencies in identifying the types of equipment necessary to respond to a major hurricane on the coast?
- What about training?
- What about exercise?
- Would employing the DHS planning model assist in mitigating this storm?
- Are the vulnerabilities today different on the Mississippi Gulf Coast than in August 2005?
- Does the threat of a tropical storm or hurricane exist in the Gulf Coast region?
- Has planning since 2005 changed any risk factors on the coast?
- Are response agencies better prepared today than in 2005?

Additional questions may be posed regarding the allocation of resources:

- What happens during the planning scenario if assets and resources are focused on the Gulf Coast and hurricanes, and the New Madrid Seismic region erupts, causing catastrophic damage in the mid-south region that includes northern Mississippi and western Tennessee?
- What considerations does this pose for the planner?

The planner must consider these and many other questions. For example, once risk assessment data are analyzed, planning actions must be taken to integrate any new threat information into the plan. The planner must impose upon the four mission areas the following questions:

- Can this incident be prevented?
- Can the population and critical infrastructure be protected against the threat/hazard?
- What is required in the response?
- Also, what will it take for the community to recover from the impact of this threat/hazard?

It is a daunting task to consider planning for the safety and protection of a community when having to consider catastrophic natural disasters such as Katrina and incidents such as the attacks of September 11, 2001. This case study presents a mere subset of the issues that must be considered regarding such events.

Conclusion

Homeland security as a function and as a bureaucracy is new to the American system of government. It is evolving. Planning for preparedness in the all-hazards environment is a reality. Risk assessments must be a fixed function within the response community. Planning, by any model or means, must engage risk management principles and integrate the results into the preparedness initiatives. All of the efforts should be concentrated on local units of government to facilitate a national preparedness program instead of a federal program ignoring the needs of the heartland of America.

Preparedness is performed in the execution of initiatives in the four mission areas. These mission areas, consisting of prevention, protection, response, and recovery, demand their unique planning considerations. Within the modern public safety environment, the planner must engage the complexities of the four mission areas and the infinite categories of threats and hazards that have become a very real possibility, if not probability.

Appropriate planning uses risk assessment data in the prodromal cycle to optimize both strategic and operational planning. Strategic planning promotes a high-level vision of the goals and objectives to be reached by the operational plans. Strategic planning will cause planners to consider the potential threat/hazard; the resources required to prevent and protect from those threats; and the "what ifs" in the consequence experience.

Planning guides jurisdictions in the predisaster and postdisaster environment. Employing a risk assessment model and integrating the resultant data into the strategic and operational plans optimizes strategic and operational planning. Regardless of the best plans possible, there are always contingencies that impact the implementation of emergency plans. Leaders must be mindful of events that could transpire that impede the anticipated progression and performance of any expressed emergency plans. Further, regardless of the best efforts of planning initiatives, it is impossible to imagine, predict, and calculate the permutations and combinations of events that necessitate emergency responses.

Homeland security is an expensive component and function of local, state, tribal, and federal governments. Although the federal budget provides a large amount of monies to support these functions, financial decisions must be rendered with respect to the benefit of the nation, American society, and its stakeholders. Therefore, homeland security leaders have a fiduciary obligation to render decisions that exploit the highest and best uses of homeland security funding.

Key terms

Assessment
Budget
Disaster
Emergency
Evaluation
Federal
For-profit sector
Funding
Local
Mitigation
Nonprofit sector
Planning
Preparedness
Priority
Prodromal cycle
Recovery
Relationship
Response
Stakeholder
State
Strategy
Tactic

QUESTIONS FOR DISCUSSION

1. Planning is an essential activity that must be thoroughly contemplated within the context of homeland security. Consider the preparedness level of your organization regarding both man-made and natural threats. How strongly has your organization planned regarding such endangerments? Write a brief essay that details your response.
2. Homeland security is a necessary expense. Obtain a copy of your locality's municipal budget, and examine the amount of funds that it expends toward homeland security endeavors. Do you believe that this level of funding is sufficient? Why or why not? Write a brief essay that substantiates your opinion.
3. Threat assessment is a valid consideration of planning and preparedness. Converse with the leaders of your municipality, and determine the types of threats that they contemplate when performing tasks of preparedness planning. Do you believe that their assessments are thorough enough? Why or why not? Write a brief essay that substantiates your opinion.
4. Given your response to the preceding question, identify some unique planning and preparedness challenges that impact your locality. Write a brief essay that describes these challenges.

References

1. Burton, L. (2008). The constitutional roots of all-hazards policy, management, and law. *Journal of Homeland Security and Emergency Management, 5*(1), Article 35.
2. Fink, S. (1986). *Crisis Management: Planning for the inevitable*. New York: American Management Association.

3. Bush, G.W. (February 28, 2003). Homeland Security Presidential Directive/HSPD. http://www.whitehouse.gov/news/releases/2003/02/20030228-9.html (accessed August 15, 2008).

4. Bush, G.W. (December 17, 2003). Homeland Security Presidential Directive/HSPD-8. http://www.whitehouse.gov/news/releases/2003/12/20031217-6.html (accessed August 15, 2008).

5. U.S. Department of Homeland Security. (September 9, 2007). Homeland Security Presidential Directive 8 Annex 1. http://www.dhs.gov/xabout/laws/gc_1199894121015.shtm#content (accessed August 15, 2008).

6. American Disaster Preparedness Foundation. (January 2006). *A Study of the Preparedness of the Largest Metropolitan Areas in the U.S: How Prepared is Your City?* Illinois.

7. Homeland Security Council. (2007). The national homeland security strategy. http://www.dhs.gov/xlibrary/assets/nat_strat_homelandsecurity_2007.pdf (accessed August 18, 2008).

8. U. S. Government Accountability Office. (February 7, 2007). Statement of William O. Jenkins Jr.: Testimony before the Subcommittee on Homeland Security, Committee on Appropriations, House of Representatives. http://www.gao.gov/new.items/d07386t.pdf (accessed August 15, 2008).

9. Stockton, P. (September 2007). *Readiness in the Post Katrina and Post 9/11 World: An evaluation of the New National Response Framework (Speech)*. Stanford University.

10. Caudle, S.L. (2005). Homeland security capabilities-based planning: lessons from the defense community. *Homeland Security Affairs*, *1*(2), Article 2.

11. Committee on Homeland Security and Committee on Foreign Affairs. (September 2008). *Wasted Lessons of 9/11: How the Bush Administration Has Ignored the Law and Squandered Its Opportunities to Make our Country Safer*. Washington D.C.: U.S. House of Representatives.

12. Byman, D.L. (September 11, 2007). Homeland insecurities: six years after 9/11 we're still not thinking strategically. *Brookings Institute*. http://www.brookings.edu/articles/2007/0911defense_byman.aspx (accessed August 15, 2008).

13. Rosen, B. (2002). The struggle against terrorism, grand strategy, strategy and tactics. *International Security, 26*(3), pp. 39–55.

14. Fact Sheet. (2010). Fact sheet: secretary Napolitano announces fiscal year 2011 budget request. http://www.dhs.gov/ynews/releases/pr_1265049379725.shtm (accessed November 21, 2010).

15. Transportation Security Administration. (2013). Federal Air Marshals. http://www.tsa.gov/about-tsa/federal-air-marshals (accessed August 26, 2013).

16. Carafano, J.J. (October 10, 2007). New homeland security strategy misses the mark. http://www.heritage.org/research/HomelandDefense/wm1659.cfm (accessed August 15, 2008).

17. Testimony. (2009). Testimony of secretary Napolitano before the senate appropriations committee subcommittee on homeland security, "FY 2010 budget request" (written testimony). http://www.dhs.gov/ynews/testimony/testimony_1242246808937.shtm (accessed November 22, 2010).

18. Miller, K. and Carafano, J. (2005). The specter of pork barrel homeland security. *The Heritage Foundation*. http://www.heritage.org/Research/Reports/2005/04/The-Specter-of-Pork-Barrel-Homeland-Security (accessed November 22, 2010).

19. USCM. (2006). *United States Council of Mayors*. http://www.usmayors.org/pressreleases/documents/disasterpreparednesssurvey_2006.pdf (accessed November 21, 2010).

20. U.S. Department of Homeland Security. (2007). *National Preparedness Guidelines*. Washington D.C.: U.S. Department of Homeland Security, p. 31, Fig. B-1.

21. Wilson, C. (Updated August 28, 2007). CRS report for congress: improvised explosive devices (IEDs) in Iraq and Afghanistan: effects and countermeasures. http://www.fas.org/sgp/crs/weapons/RS22330.pdf (accessed August 15, 2008).

22. Bellavita, C. (2005). Changing homeland security: The issue-attention cycle. *Homeland Security Affairs*, http://www.hsaj.org/?fullarticle=1.1.1 (accessed August 26, 2013).

23. Renfroe, N. and Smith, J. (2011). Threat/vulnerability assessments and risk analysis. *Whole Building Design Guide*, http://www.wbdg.org/resources/riskanalysis.php (accessed August 25, 2013).

8

Disaster Response and Recovery

As for the enemies of freedom, those who are potential adversaries, they will be reminded that peace is the highest aspiration of the American people. We will negotiate for it, sacrifice for it; we will not surrender for it, now or ever.

President Ronald Reagan
1981 Inaugural Address

Chapter objectives:

- Gain an understanding of disaster response
- Gain an understanding of disaster recovery
- Gain an understanding of disaster recovery assistance
- Gain an understanding of civil defense
- Gain an understanding of emergency management and homeland security

Introduction

The American first-response community has changed significantly since 2001. The relationship between law enforcement, emergency management, and public health is one example of how dynamically the first-response environment has adapted to change within a decade. Historically, it was common for local law enforcement and the fire services, usually through the emergency medical services, to respond to scenes together. However, as recorded in the *9/11 Commission Report*, gaps in communications and information sharing remained. Homeland security initiatives cause the disparate response community, especially from a local perspective, to become a cooperative, collaborative function encompassing the whole body of first responders within a jurisdiction. That collaborative effort demonstrates the current relationship among law enforcement, fire services, emergency medical services, public health, private health care providers, emergency management, the private sector, and government administration. Through presidential directives, each of these disciplines has enhanced its capacities and expanded its functions in the post-9/11 response environment.

Each of the first-response disciplines maintains its primary mission. However, in the contemporary first-response community, roles and missions adapt to the "all-hazards" environment to meet the needs of the community in prevention, protection, mitigation, response, and recovery. The new and expanded roles illustrate a "new normal" for responders.

Since the earliest days of Colonial America, communities have experienced devastating disasters caused by weather, enemy attacks, and epidemic outbreaks. Whether these disasters occur in smaller communities or in the densely populated urban areas makes little difference—the focus remains on the safety and welfare of citizens. The early night watchmen walked the streets of their towns, watchful for dangers, such as fire, which could quickly spread through the buildings of the community, impacting lives and property.

As communities grew into cities, the public services available within those communities also increased and improved. Communities developed more sophisticated fire response, expanded law enforcement, and improved medical capabilities to better serve its citizens. As a result, responders today find themselves serving as a critical component in an emergency/disaster response network, which includes other homeland security assets, resources, and agencies.

Historical events, such as the Chicago fire of 1871, the Galveston hurricane of 1900, and the San Francisco earthquake of 1906 show how communities can quickly be devastated in an "event." More recent events, such as the Oklahoma City bombing, the attacks of September 11, 2001, Hurricane Katrina, Hurricane Sandy, and the Boston Marathon bombing demonstrate that even with an increased capability, a major incident can have a great impact on the public and the community of first responders.

Foundations: The role of law enforcement and emergency management

Although the focus of this chapter is homeland security, it is important not to lose sight that law enforcement plays a much larger role for our nation, both domestically and internationally. While the law enforcement profession has traditionally focused its efforts domestically, it is not unusual to find law enforcement agencies serving overseas, performing duties ranging from training law enforcement counterparts in emerging nations, assisting in the development of legal systems, and providing assistance to international joint task forces, to developing intelligence in the struggles against international crime and other criminal activity. Law enforcement today is a dynamic profession.

The traditional role of local law enforcement is one of community service. Local and tribal law enforcement, which includes tribal police, urban police, and sheriff's offices, typically possesses enough capabilities, personnel, and equipment to meet the normal needs of its communities. Few communities have the fiscal resources or desire to stockpile extensive supply reserves, such as food, medical equipment, or temporary housing, in anticipation of the catastrophic event. Therefore, in the case of a major incident that overwhelms local resources, communities must partner with other organizations, agencies, or elements of government to enable an expansion or incident response surge.

During any major incident, local jurisdictions initially seek assistance from mutual aid partners. This usually comes from neighboring or contingent jurisdictions where pre-event agreements have been executed. If mutual aid is exhausted, the jurisdiction seeks state assistance. Although states can provide assistance, they have limited capabilities to respond to a major event. State-level enforcement agencies are staffed and equipped for specific missions (e.g., highway safety for state highway patrol or wildlife enforcement). Being mission specific, they possess a limited capability to surge and sustain operations over a long period of time. As a result, states rely extensively on the resources possessed, sourced, or that can be acquired by organizations such as the National Guard, state emergency management, or state-level homeland security. These resources, typically state based, can be called upon or activated by the state governor and deployed as needed. In many cases, the ultimate cost of their activation and deployment will be covered by federal funds upon direction by the president.

Disasters, mutual assistance, and command and control

Most communities will never be impacted by a disaster. Most emergencies that do occur are limited in scope and do not need or receive federal disaster declarations. This scenario does not eliminate the need for communities to examine their community-based vulnerabilities and to develop contingency plans if an incident does occur. In any event, the initial efforts to respond are very important. Confusion and uncertainty often inhibit the first efforts to gain a clear assessment of the extent of damage. Incident response is always difficult but is even more so if event contingency planning has not been conducted. Part of contingency planning is the development of mutual aid and assistance agreements with adjacent communities. These are of great importance in ensuring that adequate resources can be made available quickly in response to an event.

Law enforcement, in its role as a first responder, is one of the first, if not the first, agencies on the scene of an event. If the event is localized, command and control of the event may be relatively informal. If the event is larger, some type of incident command function will be established. In this case, responders may not be working for their day-to-day supervisors, or they may be assigned in work areas outside of their normal routine. Event responders must be capable of functioning as part of a larger system. Whether the event is a natural or man-made disaster, law enforcement personnel, with other first responders, such as fire and medical personnel, will typically find themselves working together to mitigate the damage and facilitate event recovery.

In some cases, state and federal resources may be available. For example, the National Guard may be activated following an extremely heavy snow, in the case of wildfire, during the aftermath of a hurricane, or following a terrorist incident. Federal resources including Disaster Medical Assistance Teams (DMATs) and Disaster Mortuary Teams (DMORTs) may be activated following a mass casualty incident.

The terrorist attacks of September 11, 2001, were an extreme example of how all levels of government, the private sector, and nongovernmental agencies will have to work together to prepare for, protect against, respond to an event that exceeds the capabilities of any single entity.[7] Although the probability of an attack commensurate with the scope and magnitude of 9/11 is rare, the potential for major events, such as a natural disaster, can pose challenges to first responders on a level as great or greater. This chapter examines some of the famous incidents that have impacted the nation.

Law enforcement finds itself as just one part of a homeland security response team. Depending on the impact and scope of the event, agencies providing response and recovery support may be drawn from federal, state, local, tribal, or private assets. Therefore, the need exists to conduct jurisdictional risk, vulnerability, and needs assessments that guide incident management relationships, strategies, and the operational/tactical planning necessary for effective response and recovery once an incident or event has occurred.

Major incidents: A brief historical examination

The United States has faced and experienced many challenges. From the perspective of homeland security, several "incidents" or "events" can be examined to provide a brief but valuable insight into an incident as it unfolds and its impact. This chapter examines briefly a wide range of incidents, including earthquakes, fires, floods, hurricanes, disease, and terrorist attacks, to demonstrate the diversity of dangers faced by our nation. Some of these incidents resulted in extensive injury, loss of life, and property damage; others had the potential but did not inflict human injury. Although major events are relatively uncommon, they can and do occur.

The role of the federal government regarding disaster response has evolved throughout the past 200 years. The Congressional Act of 1803 was the earliest effort to provide federal disaster relief after a fire devastated a New Hampshire town. From that point forward, assorted legislation provided disaster support. Between 1803 and 1950, the federal government intervened in approximately 100 incidents (earthquakes, fires, floods, and tornadoes).[1] Within this same period, the US Congress passed 128 laws dealing with emergencies.[2]

Incidents such as the New Madrid earthquake of 1811–1812, the Chicago fire of 1871, the Memphis yellow fever epidemic of the 1870s, the Johnstown flood of 1889, the Galveston hurricane of 1900, and the San Francisco earthquake and fire of 1906 are several major incidents that impacted the nation and overwhelmed local capabilities. Among each of these cases, with the exception of the New Madrid earthquake, significant loss of life and extensive property damage occurred. Each incident, again with the exception of the New Madrid earthquake, exceeded the capabilities of local resources to respond. This chapter briefly examines each of these incidents, placing them in historical context and identifying those lessons painfully gained.

New Madrid earthquakes of 1811–1812

Several parts of the United States rest upon fault lines that are prone to earthquakes. These areas include California, Alaska, and the central part of the nation running north and south along the Mississippi River. It was along the Mississippi River, during the period of 1811–1812, that a series of earthquakes, now known as the New Madrid earthquakes, occurred. This fault line between St Louis, Missouri, and Memphis, Tennessee, was sparsely populated. As a result, it inflicted little personal injury but did cause property damage, including the destruction of the town of New Madrid, Missouri, on February 12, 1812. In a letter dated January 13, 1814, Missouri Territorial Governor William Clark asked for federal relief for the "inhabitants of New Madrid County." This was one of the earliest, if not the first, examples of a request for disaster relief from the United States federal government.

This incident is not the largest recorded earthquake to strike the United States. The largest event was the Prince William Sound, Alaska, earthquake and ensuing tsunami that caused $300 million in property damages and claimed around 128 lives. Another New Madrid earthquake, along the same fault line, would inflict property damage and fatalities estimated to range from Memphis, Tennessee, in the south, to St. Louis in the north, clearly overwhelming local, state, and federal response capabilities.

Chicago fire of 1871

Major fires are common in the west, especially in California, where dry conditions lead to fires that may consume thousands of acres of land. With the advancement in fire protection, it is hard to imagine a major part of a city in the nation burning out of control. During the 1800s, as cities rapidly expanded, with little control regulating the construction of the buildings themselves, it appeared to be a matter of time before a major disaster related to urban fire occurred. Many cities around the world had experienced, in some cases more than once, their destruction because of fire. London burned in 1666; Boston burned the year after Chicago in 1872; Seattle, Washington, lost its central business district to fire in 1889; Jacksonville, Florida, lost over 2,300 buildings in a 1901 fire that left approximately 10,000 homeless; and Baltimore, Maryland, lost about 1,500 buildings in a 1904 fire. One of the very interesting aspects of the Baltimore fire was that even though nearby cities sent firefighters to assist, many of the responding firefighters discovered that their equipment, specifically the hose couplings, did not fit the fire hydrants used in Baltimore.

A significant fire was the Great Chicago Fire. There is still discussion as to the actual cause of the fire, but what is known is that the city burned from October 8 to early October 10, 1871. In the wake of the fire, the center of the city, including the central business district, was destroyed. It was estimated that the fire destroyed an area about 4 miles long and averaging 3/4 mile wide, encompassing more than 2,000 acres. Destroyed were more than 17,500 buildings and $222 million in property—about a third of the city's valuation. Of the 300,000 inhabitants, an estimated 300 were dead and 90,000 homeless. General Philip Sheridan was present during the fire and coordinated military relief efforts. The mayor, to calm the panic, placed the city under martial law and issued a proclamation placing Sheridan in charge. Because there were no widespread disturbances, martial law was lifted within a few days. Relief operations began immediately. The Great Chicago Fire demonstrated how rapidly local resources can be overwhelmed in a major incident.

Memphis yellow fever epidemic of the 1870s

Epidemic diseases have always posed a great threat. The bubonic plague of the Middle Ages devastated Europe. The Spanish influenza epidemic of 1918–1919 killed an estimated 20 to 40 million people. Advancement in medical care has reduced the impact of epidemics, but American cities have been impacted by disease, including outbreaks of cholera, smallpox, and dysentery. Prior to the modern advancements in medicine, people lived with the reality of disease-induced death, especially in the growing urban areas, where sanitation was often poor. For residents of West Tennessee, and particularly Memphis, yellow fever posed the greatest threat.

Memphis experienced yellow fever outbreaks in 1828, 1855, and 1867, but the yellow fever outbreaks of the 1870s devastated the city. The 1873 epidemic claimed 2,000 in Memphis, a number that constituted, at the time, the most yellow fever victims in an inland city. Five years later, as the city tried to recover, the mild winter of 1878, combined with a long and gentle spring, sparked the resurgence of the fever. Panic gripped not only Memphis but also nearby communities, who feared its spread as an estimated 25,000 Memphians fled the city to escape the danger. New Orleans newspapers reported the epidemic in late July as Memphis officials established checkpoints to control entry into the city. The fever raged in Memphis until mid-October infecting over 17,000 and killing 5,150. The yellow fever epidemic that devastated Memphis demonstrated how disease can impact a community, including creating panic.

Johnstown flood of 1889

In 1889, Johnstown, Pennsylvania, was devastated by the worst flood in the nation's history. In a town with a population of about 30,000, over 2,200 were dead, with many more homeless when the South Fork Dam ruptured, sending 20 million tons of water rushing toward the town. The impact of the flood destroyed the town and overwhelmed the local ability to recover. The nation responded to the disaster with a spontaneous outpouring of time, money, food, clothing, and medical assistance.

Figure 8.1 On September 9, 1900, a powerful hurricane hit Galveston Island. At the time, it was the largest city in Texas. It is still the deadliest natural disaster ever to strike the United States. The 4-mile lone, 17-foot-high Galveston Sea Wall was erected in the wake of the disaster.

Galveston hurricane of 1900

The Galveston hurricane (**Figure 8.1**) inflicted great damage and loss of life. It was estimated that over 3,600 homes were destroyed, and the death toll was between 6,000 and 12,000 individuals,[14] giving the storm the third-highest number of casualties of any Atlantic hurricane. The Galveston hurricane of 1900 is, to date, the deadliest natural disaster ever to strike the United States. By contrast, the second-deadliest storm to strike the United States, the 1928 Okeechobee hurricane, caused more than 2,500 deaths, and the deadliest storm of recent times, Hurricane Katrina, claimed the lives of approximately 1,800 people.

San Francisco earthquake of 1906

In April 1906, the San Francisco area experienced an earthquake and fire that resulted in over 500 deaths, the destruction of over 28,000 buildings, and an estimated 225,000 people left homeless. The earthquake shook the city. Buildings fell, roads crumbled, power lines severed, and gas lines ruptured. Almost immediately, fires, fueled by debris and gas escaping from broken lines, sprang up in various sections of the city. Waterlines, so important in combating the fires, were severed. As police and fire responders struggled in the recovery effort, fires spread throughout the city. In a desperate attempt to halt the flames, city officials decided to dynamite buildings to create fire lanes. Realizing that the extent of the disaster overwhelmed law enforcement and fire responders, local authorities asked for the help of the army forces stationed in the area.

Brigadier General Frederick Funston, commanding the Military Department of California and a resident of San Francisco, had already decided that the situation required the use of troops. During the first few days, soldiers provided valuable services, including general security; patrolling streets to discourage looting; guarding buildings such as the US Mint, post office, and county jail; assisting the fire department in dynamiting to demolish buildings in the path of the fires; and providing critical support in feeding, sheltering, and clothing the tens of thousands of displaced residents of the city. On July 1, 1906, civil authorities assumed responsibility for relief efforts, and the army withdrew from the city.

The San Francisco earthquake and fire is a great example of how when local authorities are overwhelmed by the extent of a disaster, federal resources, in this case, the military, can provide a rapid and effective response with the intent to limit further loss of life and property damage.

The 1993 World Trade Center attack

Although overshadowed by the attacks of September 11, 2001, the World Trade Center was the target of international terrorists in 1993 (**Figure 8.2**). On February 26, 1993, terrorists detonated a truck bomb in the parking area under Tower One of the World Trade Center with the intent of bringing down the structure in the hope that as Tower One fell, it would also fall into and destroy Tower Two. The explosion killed 6 people and injured over 1000. Those responsible were identified, arrested, and convicted. This attack brought what would

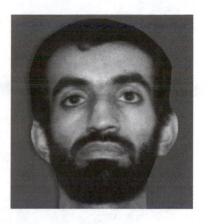

Figure 8.2 *Photo of Ramzi Yousef.*

become known as the "Global War on Terror" home to the United States. An investigation led to a Pakistani named Ramzi Yousef (**Figure 8.2**), the nephew of Khalid Sheikh Mohammed, who would later help Osama bin Laden plan the 9/11 attacks. Yousef was arrested February 7, 1995, and indicted in January 1996 for his role in the 1993 World Trade Center bombing.

Oklahoma City bombing of 1995

Inspired by his ultra-right-wing beliefs, Timothy McVeigh perpetrated one of the deadliest terrorist attack on United States soil when he detonated a truck bomb in front of the Alfred P. Murrah Federal Building in Oklahoma City on April 19, 1995, killing 168 people. This attack shocked the nation and demonstrated that areas in the nation well away from our coasts or major cities could become the target of an attack. Probably more disturbing was the fact that the attack was executed by an ultra-right-wing "lone wolf."

Terrorist attacks of September 11, 2001

The coordinated suicide attacks by al Qaeda upon the United States on September 11, 2001, shocked the nation and put into motion what became known as the "Global War on Terrorism." On that morning, 19 al Qaeda terrorists hijacked four commercial passenger jet airliners. The hijackers intentionally crashed two of the airliners into the Twin Towers of the World Trade Center in New York City, killing everyone on board and many others working in the buildings. Both buildings collapsed within 2 hours, destroying nearby buildings and damaging others. The hijackers crashed a third airliner into the Pentagon in Arlington, Virginia, just outside Washington, District of Columbia. The fourth plane crashed into a field in rural Pennsylvania after some of its passengers and flight crew attempted to take control of the plane, which the hijackers had redirected toward Washington, District of Columbia.

Hurricane Katrina

In 2005, Hurricane Katrina decimated the Gulf Coast (**Figure 8.3**). The storm damage caused massive loss of capabilities/assets in many of the response agencies in the path of the storm. Resources quickly flowed into the area. The National Guard, active military,

Figure 8.3 New Orleans, Louisiana, August 31, 2005: A photo of residents being evacuated from their homes by a FEMA Urban Search and Rescue team from Florida. (Courtesy of Jocelyn Augustino/FEMA.)

law enforcement, firefighters, and emergency responders from across the nation provided their assistance. There was a huge response by the faith-based community, nonprofit, and relief organizations, providing temporary shelter, food, and clothes to displaced citizens. Significant efforts were directed to the initial short-term recovery: opening roads; removing debris; providing supplies and shelters; and reestablishing communications, banking, water and power, and other basic services. Long-term recovery has extended into years, reestablishing governmental services, revitalizing the economic infrastructure and housing.

At the time of Katrina, the Department of Homeland Security's (DHS's) mission statement did not include natural hazards. This observation is critical, if for no other reason than the Federal Emergency Management Agency (FEMA) being a vital function under the supervision of the DHS. It became a more obvious concern in the post-Katrina environment, when many felt that FEMA had failed in its mission. This notion led to the passage of legislation called the Post-Katrina Emergency Management Reform Act of 2006. The Post-Katrina Act called for yet another major reorganization within the DHS.

The Post-Katrina Emergency Management Reform Act of 2006 (Public Law 109-295) returned most preparedness powers to the FEMA and renamed the undersecretary for Federal Emergency Management as the administrator of FEMA, effective March 31, 2007. The act also elevated the administrator to the same level of authority as a deputy secretary. Additionally, the president may designate the administrator to serve as a member of the cabinet in the event of natural disasters, acts of terrorism, or other man-made disasters.[11]

Civil defense, emergency management, and homeland security

The formation of the United States was the result of a revolution. There has always been the threat, both internationally and domestically, to the safety and security of the United States and its territories. As a fledgling country and republic, the United States struggled to survive and prosper. It was not always a global superpower.

The early developmental years of the United States witnessed several significant conflicts. European nations competed to create global empires. Britain controlled the seas. The United States experienced several small conflicts including the War of 1812, the Mexican War of the 1840s, the War Between the States, and the Spanish–American War. Over this time, the United States expanded its boundaries, reaching from ocean to ocean. The nation increased international trade and created a small navy and army to protect American interests abroad.

The protection of the nation and its interests has always remained one of the primary responsibilities of the national government. The Monroe Doctrine of 1823 informed the European powers that the United States assumed a responsibility for the Western Hemisphere, although the nation had little ability to actually enforce its intent. The nation continued its expansion. Alaska was purchased from Russia in 1867; Hawaii became a United States possession in 1898, and the nation gained control of areas including Cuba, Puerto Rico, and the Philippines as a result of the Spanish–American War. The United States became an imperialistic power and was becoming a nation of international importance.

United States presidents were historically content to avoid international entanglements or push the nation onto the world stage, although enforcement of federal laws related to customs and the border became an increasing concern. In 1853, the United States Customs Border Patrol was established when the secretary of the treasury authorized the collector of customs to hire customs mounted inspectors for patrol duty along the borders of the nation.[12]

The border shared with Mexico had traditionally been an area of unrest. One of the driving forces behind the formation of the Texas Rangers was issues related to the border and border security. Border concerns led to many states passing their own border protection and immigration legislation. As a result, an 1875 United States Supreme Court decision ruled that creation and enforcement of immigration regulations was a federal responsibility. In 1882, the Chinese Exclusion Act and Immigration Act of 1882 targeted immigration issues,[12] putting increased emphasis upon enforcement.

By the end of the 19th century, the border-related issues had become so significant that, in 1915, the United States authorized the Bureau of Immigration to deploy mounted guards along the United States border. Border security concerns became so great that United States military forces were deployed to the Mexican border from 1916 to 1917. In 1924, Congress provided for the creation of the United States Border Patrol.[12]

As the 20th century dawned, the vast majority of European and Asian powers were governed by some form of monarchy. The assassination of President McKinley by the anarchist Leon Czolgosz in 1901 led to the presidency of Theodore Roosevelt. Roosevelt was a former New

York City police commissioner who visualized the United States as an emerging world power, not only with international possessions but also with a growing global responsibility.

In 1941, with World War II escalating in Europe and Asia, the Office of Civilian Defense was established within the Office for Emergency Management to assure effective coordination of federal relations with state and local governments engaged in furtherance of war programs; to provide for necessary cooperation with state and local governments with respect to measures for adequate protection of the civilian population in war emergencies; and to facilitate participation by all persons in war programs. New York Mayor Fiorello La Guardia was named director, serving on a volunteer basis without compensation.

In August 1941, *The United States Citizens Defense Corps* was published. It gave the first complete and coordinated plan for local organization of civilian defense and was the prototype of all subsequent Civil Defense (CD) organizations. With the nation at war, the threat level relative to an enemy attack increased within the borders of the United States, and there emerged a growing concern for the safety and security of the country. The civil defense program increased in popularity and scope. In 1942, the Office of Civil Defense conducted training for civil defense police volunteers in 46 US cities with the support of J. Edgar Hoover and the Federal Bureau of Investigation.

The end of World War II found the United States as one of two remaining global superpowers. In 1945, the Office of Civilian Defense was disbanded, but soon, the new threats of the Cold War, including the fear of a nuclear attack, led to renewed discussions regarding the need for local-level "civil defense." In 1950, President Harry Truman signed Executive Order 10186 creating the Federal Civil Defense Administration (FCDA) within the Office for Emergency Management, Executive Office of the President.[8] This authorized the federal civil defense program, which would continue until it was repealed by Public Law 93-337 in 1994. With the 1994 repeal of the civil defense statute, some parts of the law were incorporated into the Stafford Disaster Relief and Emergency Assistance Act, including the use of the term *emergency preparedness* wherever the term *civil defense* previously appeared in the statutory language.

Following World War II, the world was dominated by the United States and the Soviet Union. The two nations maintained an uneasy peace in what was called the "Cold War." From the earliest days of the Cold War, preparedness focused upon events such as a nuclear attack from the Soviets. Bomb drills were conducted in schools, many Americans constructed bomb shelters, and it was very common to see buildings that had been designated "fall-out" shelters. Feeding, evacuation, communications, and medical response plans were also developed to be implemented in the event of an attack.

When the Cold War ended, it was hoped that the world would become a safer place and that international threats would diminish; however, that proved not to be the case. New threats would challenge the nation.

An emergency management program examines potential emergencies and disasters based on the risks posed by likely hazards; develops and implements programs aimed at reducing the impact of these events on the community; prepares for those risks that cannot be eliminated; and prescribes the actions required to deal with the consequences of actual events and to recover from those events. Emergency management involves participants among all governmental levels and within the private sector. Activities are geared according to phases before, during, and after emergency events. The effectiveness of emergency management rests on a network of relationships among partners in the system.

The DHS

The DHS emerged from the ashes of September 11, 2001, and redefined itself after Hurricane Katrina; it became a major component of a national effort to respond to the evolving global dynamics of the post–Cold War period. The world would face a new and very sinister threat: the threat of global terrorism. This threat targeted the United States and changed the roles of the first-response community in America.

President George W. Bush proposed the creation of a new DHS. Bush stated, "America needs a single, unified homeland security structure that will improve protection against today's threats and be flexible enough to help meet the unknown threats of the future."[15] The White House Office of Homeland Security was created on October 8, 2001, which became the precedent to creating the DHS on November 19, 2002. The mission of the DHS is defined in the National Strategy for Homeland Security as "a concerted national effort to prevent terrorist attacks within the United States, reduce America's vulnerability to terrorism, and minimize the damage and recover from attacks that do occur."[9]

This mission statement was developed early in the evolution of the DHS. It has caused concern throughout the history of the department in that it seems to limit the scope of the mission of homeland security. It particularly causes policy questions to arise when discussing natural disasters and man-made incidents such as acts of terrorism, incidents involving weapons of mass destruction, or any other event that incites national distress. In the aftermath of the attacks on September 11, 2001, the mission statement reflected the "mood" of the country with a focus on terrorists, acts of terrorism, and what direction American should take in the antiterrorism preparedness role. The country and its leadership, in a natural reaction to the attacks, were not focused on the natural hazards.

The department became operational on January 24, 2003, with most component agencies merging on March 1, 2003. The DHS incorporates 22 governmental agencies. Some of those agencies are the FEMA, the coast guard, the Secret Service, the Transportation Security Agency, the US Immigration and Customs Enforcement, and the Border Patrol, along with 16 other agencies.

This reorganization was the largest one of the federal government since the US Department of Defense was created in 1947. The mission of the office as stated by the president was "to develop and coordinate the implementation of a comprehensive national strategy to secure the United States from terrorist threats or attacks."[9] The Department of Homeland Security is led by the secretary of homeland security. The former governor of Pennsylvania, Tom Ridge, was named by the president to direct the office, beginning his duties on October 8, 2001. Ridge became the first secretary of homeland security following the creation of the department in 2002. He resigned on November 30, 2004. The second secretary was Michael Chertoff, beginning February 15, 2005. The department has many undersecretaries, assistant undersecretaries, administrators, and directors. All of the directorates, programs, and personnel ultimately report to the Office of the Secretary.

In the US Department of Homeland Security Strategic Plan, Fiscal Years 2008–2013, the language seems to address mission statement concerns. Secretary Chertoff outlines four operational objectives: (1) clarifying, defining, and communicating leadership roles, responsibilities, and lines of authority at all government levels; (2) strengthening accountability systems that balance the need for fast, flexible response with the need to prevent waste, fraud, and abuse; (3) consolidating efforts to integrate the department's critical mission of preparedness; and (4) enhancing our capabilities to respond to major disasters and emergencies including catastrophic events, particularly in terms of situational assessment and awareness, emergency communications, evacuations, search and rescue, logistics, mass care, and sheltering.[13] The fourth objective seems to be making a subtle shift to the natural hazards environment.

As the first phase of the development of the DHS was directed by the administration of President George W. Bush, the second phase under President Obama has witnessed a further evolution of the agency. During the early phases of the Obama administration, Arizona Governor Janet Napolitano was appointed secretary of the DHS, replacing Michael Chertoff. Secretary Napolitano initiated a review and evaluation of each function within the DHS. Under the administration of President Obama, the DHS has continued to evolve.

By 2010, significant attention was directed toward transportation and border security, responding to threats much broader than terrorism. Cybersecurity is also strong area of attention and is also a homeland security priority. Violence and unrest in Mexico combined with poverty in Central America are two issues that have fueled illegal immigration and violence along the nation's Southwest border. As a response, the DHS strengthened enforcement and intervention efforts on the Southwest border to disrupt the drug, cash, and weapon smuggling that fuels cartel violence in Mexico by adding manpower and technology to the Southwest border.

Some of the programs included under the DHS include the Container Security Initiative (CSI), a program intended to help increase security for containerized cargo shipped to the United States from around the world; the National Fugitive Operations Program to enhance the apprehension and deportation of fugitive aliens from the United States, especially those who have been convicted of crimes; and Operation Community Shield, a nationwide initiative that targets violent transnational street gangs by partnering with US and foreign law enforcement agencies at all levels and making use of its authority to deport criminal aliens. Clearly, the role of the DHS continues to evolve.

Homeland security vision, mission, goals, and objectives

During the aftermath of the 9/11 attacks, the first National Strategy for Homeland Security contained the following goals (Office of Homeland Security 2002, p. vii):

- Prevent terrorist attacks within the United States
- Reduce America's vulnerability to terrorism
- Minimize the damage and recover from attacks that do occur

The 5 years between 2002 and 2007 witnessed changes in the definition and goals of homeland security. Although terrorism was still a major issue, several other issues also began to take precedence. including natural disasters, such as Hurricanes Katrina and Rita; border problems, including smuggling and illegal immigration; increased violence along the border; and diverse concerns such as pandemics and the security of the nation's food supply. The nation's awareness level was heightened, and it became blatantly obvious that threats to the security of the United States could be both natural and man-made. This realization and recognition has been pivotal in the continual evolution of the DHS. Thus, the United States has the enormous responsibility of preparedness as it relates to natural and man-made incidents and disasters. This mission is now an all-hazards mission.

In 2003, President Bush issued Homeland Security Presidential Directive 8 (HSPD-8). The purpose of this directive was to "...establish policies to strengthen the preparedness of the United States to prevent and respond to threatened or actual domestic terrorist attacks, major disasters, and other emergencies by requiring a national domestic all-hazards preparedness goal."[16]

By 2007, the 2002 goals of the DHS had changed to reflect a much broader definition of threats (p. 1)[9]:

- Prevent and disrupt terrorist attacks
- Protect the American people, critical infrastructure, and key resources
- Respond to and recover from incidents that do occur
- Continue to strengthen the foundation to ensure long-term success

The term *all hazards* has been the traditional language used to communicate the idea that preparedness would encompass natural and man-made hazards. The term *all-hazards* is now used routinely in training materials and guidelines published by the DHS. For some reason, the phrase has not found its way into the formal mission statement of the DHS, but it is the planning concept used by state, local, and tribal governments. Further, within the 2008 Strategic Plan, the mission states, "We will lead the unified effort to secure America. We will prevent and deter terrorist attacks and protect against and respond to threats and hazards to the nation. We will secure our national borders while welcoming lawful immigrants, visitors, and trade" (p. 3).[13] The phrase "respond to threats and hazards to the Nation" indicates a subtle policy shift that is necessitated by politics and practice.

The DHS must remain vigilant as a forward-thinking entity with respect to both contemporary and emerging threats. This notion is expressed within its statements of vision and mission expressed in 2013. **Figure 8.4** shows a continued commitment to unequivocally pursuing the all-hazards approach organizationally within DHS.

Our Mission

Overview

The vision of homeland security is to ensure a homeland that is safe, secure, and resilient against terrorism and other hazards.

Three key concepts form the foundation of our national homeland security strategy designed to achieve this vision:

- Security,
- Resilience, and
- Customs and Exchange.

In turn, these key concepts drive broad areas of activity that the Quadrennial Homeland Security Review (QHSR) process defines as homeland security missions. These missions are enterprise-wide, and not limited to the Department of Homeland Security. These missions and their associated goals and objectives tell us in detail what it means to prevent, to protect, to respond, and to recover, as well as to build in security, to ensure resilience, and to facilitate customs and exchange.

Hundreds of thousands of people from across the federal government, state, local, tribal, and territorial governments, the private sector, and other nongovernmental organizations are responsible for executing these missions. These are the people who regularly interact with the public, who are responsible for public safety and security, who own and operate our nation's critical infrastructures and services, who perform research and develop technology, and who keep watch, prepare for, and respond to emerging threats and disasters. These homeland security professionals must have a clear sense of what it takes to achieve the overarching vision articulated above.

Figure 8.4 DHS 2013 vision and mission statements. (Courtesy of the DHS.)

Pursuing such a vision involves multiple missions throughout the spectrum of individual organizations that comprise the cumulative DHS entity. These missions are itemized as follows:

- Preventing terrorism and enhancing security
- Securing and managing the national borders
- Enforcing and administering immigration laws
- Safeguarding and securing cyberspace
- Ensuring resiliency to disasters

The DHS now exists as a complex, multifaceted organization that is comprised of various entities that all serve specific purposes. Through time, it will continue to change and mature with respect to the needs and challenges of future threats. Certainly, the influences of future government administrations will impact the DHS with respect to its capacity as a responding entity during periods of catastrophe. Regardless, the DHS shall continue to maintain a fiduciary obligation to safeguard the American nation and its society.

Future of the DHS

The department went through major restructuring following Hurricane Katrina and in compliance with the Post-Katrina Act of 2006. The debate continues regarding whether FEMA should be in the DHS or should be returned to an independent status.

The funding appropriations and allocations are part of the debate. Some will say that the funding for homeland security will "dry up." In 2010, there were major reductions in funding for state and local governments for homeland security programs. Others take the position that funding for some programs will be decreased, whereas that for others will be increased through time. However, it is agreed that local governments must be prepared to sustain projects that have been funded through the homeland security grant programs. This becomes a challenge at a time when local and state governments struggle in sustaining essential government functions while revenue is substantially diminished.

The US Congress consistently asks: How prepared is the nation? Unfortunately, the country has not developed a method for measuring preparedness. Others ask if the nation is better off or more prepared now than it was before September 11, 2001. These questions can be answered, but not everyone would agree on the answers.

There are definite certainties. The country will experience other hurricanes. There will be earthquakes. Natural disasters will occur. Domestic acts of terrorism continue, and the threats of international attacks remain. The first-response landscape has changed dramatically since 9/11. National preparedness is a permanent part of the response environment.

Emergency operations centers and response

During periods of calamity, an emergency operations center (EOC) is often necessary to support an emergency response to natural and man-made incidents. An EOC represents a nexus through which coordination of efforts and resources occurs when responding to an incident. The EOC is a central location where agency representatives can coordinate and make decisions when managing an emergency response. Within the EOC, numerous agencies may have representatives. This paradigm exhibits a process that allows all levels of government and all disciplines to work together more efficiently and effectively. Multiagency coordination occurs across the different disciplines involved in incident management, across jurisdictional lines, or across levels of government.

An EOC generally exhibits various characteristics: (1) survivability, (2) redundancy, (3) communications, (4) flexibility, (5) open architecture, and (6) security.[3] The first is quite important. Any EOC must be capable of surviving an incident and becoming and remaining operational. Redundancy of resources is necessary as a method of implementing fault tolerance. If a primary system fails, then a backup system must be present to ensure that a loss of capability does not occur. Communication is absolutely necessary for a variety of purposes and should be implemented with redundancy. Communication provides a means of both transmitting and receiving pertinent information and intelligence and serves as the tool for informing others to ensure that a mutual understanding exists among responding entities.

EOCs must be flexible. In other words, they must be capable of scaling the scope and magnitude of their activities to suit the needs of the incident and its response. Therefore, EOCs must be capable of responding efficiently and effectively to both small-scale and large-scale incidents in a timely fashion. They must be capable of either expanding or shrinking their operations in accordance with mission and operational needs of the response. Flexibility also must accommodate any changes of mission that may occur during a response.[3] Therefore, the resources of the EOC must be capable of changing quickly to the dynamics of an incident.

Open architecture is another salient consideration of the EOC. Essentially, the design and construct of an EOC influences its operation. Through time, technologies change and advance, and new technologies emerge. An EOC must be capable of integrating a variety of technologies through time to support its mission and response activities. This notion is not constrained solely to technology. The physical design and construct of an EOC must be considered from an architectural standpoint. For instance, raised floors may be used to support wiring for a number of communications systems and electronic devices.[3]

Security must be present within an EOC environment. Security mechanisms must be applied to both tangible and intangible entities within and near the EOC. Tangible characteristics may include the use of security guards and video surveillance systems, whereas intangible characteristics may include passwords necessary to access computer systems. In some cases, certain information may not be immediately released to the general public and must remain clandestine. In any case, security is a paramount consideration of any EOC to ensure the integrity of the working environment and its assets and the capacity to continue unimpeded operations.

The EOC is the focal point of incident response and may integrate a variety of agencies and resources. During Hurricane Sandy, EOCs were necessary to coordinate response activities and efforts. This incident exhibited the use of the Internet to announce various operations and to disseminate responsibilities for the participating entities via the EOC. **Figure 8.5** shows the EOC Internet presence for Long Beach Island.

The Long Beach Island EOC Internet site displayed various statistics regarding operational regions, including debris removal from the affected location. It also announced various statuses regarding response operations within the incident region. For example, the figure shows that debris recovery in Mill Creek and other areas was completed. Accessing this information provides both responders and the general public with some understanding of which tasks were completed and which were remaining. Further, the Internet presence was leveraged to disseminate chronological information regarding a mandatory evacuation of the incident area.

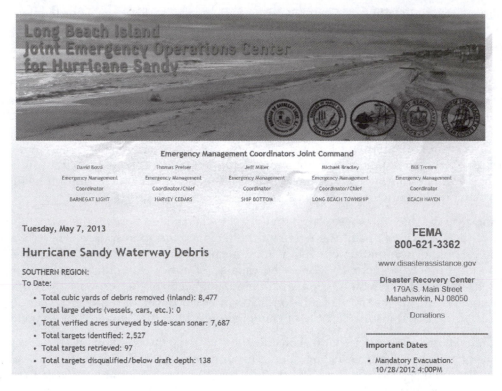

Figure 8.5 Long Beach Island EOC. (Courtesy of http://www.lbieoc.org/2013/04/hurricane-sandy-waterway-debris.html.)

Not all EOCs generate such a sophisticated method of leveraging the Internet during an incident response. Further, no two EOCs are exactly alike, but they all have a common purpose as a focal point during emergency incidents. Regardless of the location or resources, the EOC represents an entity through which coordination occurs to facilitate disaster response.

Disaster recovery and assistance

Incident recovery represents the development, coordination, and execution of service restoration and site restoration plans for impacted communities and the reconstitution of government operations and services through individual, private-sector, nongovernmental, and public assistance programs. In many cases, these resources are crucial for the survivors and refugees of calamities. When disaster strikes, humans may perish, and physical infrastructure may be destroyed. The economies of the affected areas are also impacted adversely. When such conditions arise, disaster recovery assistance is often necessary to restore some sense of normalcy and to facilitate recovery efforts within the incident area.

In 2011, a storm spawned a system of tornadoes that ravaged much of the South.[4] As a result, the city of Tuscaloosa, Alabama, was devastated by a tornado within 6 minutes.[4] This tornado "destroyed 12 percent of the city, killed dozens, injured hundreds and left hundreds of millions of dollars in property damage."[4] The need for recovery assistance was inevitable. Cumulatively, as a form of recovery assistance, the state of Alabama now anticipates receiving approximately $120 million in funding in addition to approximately "$56 million that HUD

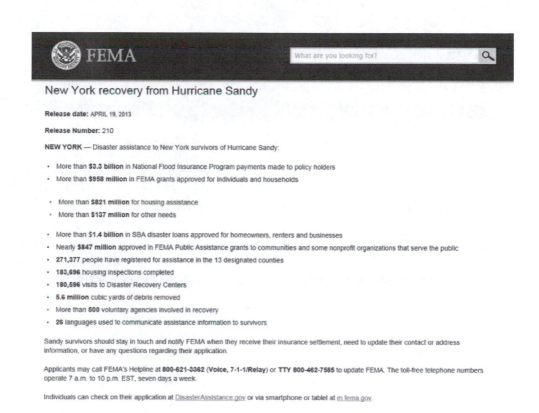

Figure 8.6 New York Hurricane Sandy recovery assistance. (Courtesy of http://www.fema.gov/news-release/2013/04/19/new-york-recovery-hurricane-sandy.)

allocated to Alabama in January 2012."[4] The city of Tuscaloosa expects to receive approximately $43.9 million in funding as a form of recovery assistance.[5]

During the aftermath of Hurricane Sandy in 2012, recovery assistance was also necessary. **Figure 8.6** shows the extensiveness of New York recovery assistance that was associated with this storm.

Recovery assistance exists as a method of obtaining government help during the aftermath of disasters. Such assistance is often available from a variety of government agencies. Agencies sponsoring assistance range from the Department of Agriculture and the Department of the Interior to the Small Business Administration and the Social Security Administration.[6] Recovery assistance provides a means for states, municipalities, organizations, and communities to endure the aftermath of calamity toward the goal of becoming vibrant again.

Conclusion

The American Revolution was hard fought to create an independent nation. Since that time, a legacy has been preserved of protecting the borders of the United States and its territories. The most important function of government is keeping the country secure. Terrorism has a long history, but until September 11, 2001, few Americans were touched by acts of terrorism. The responders across the country were not absent knowledge relative to terrorism, but it was not a focus in equipment and training programs.

The 1993 bombing of the World Trade Center received short-lived attention. In 1995, Timothy McVeigh detonated the deadly bomb in Oklahoma City. During this time, the Hart-Rudman idea for creating a commission to study global threats began to prick the political consciousness. The WMD Defense Act of 1996 was passed. The Department of Justice domestic preparedness program had begun. On the domestic front, there was evidence that awareness of the threats was part of the policy and political environment.

The creation of the DHS was not a reaction to the events of September 11, 2001. That day of attacks was the catalyst to set the priority for government to bring a focal point in combating terrorism and securing the United States, not in the traditional military mode but in preparing the civilian response community and the citizens at large. These attacks occurred in local jurisdictions not as military attacks but, rather, as acts of international terrorism on the civilian population.

The DHS has outlined four mission areas that define the goal of preparedness. Those four mission areas are prevention, protection, response, and recovery. Each of the respective response disciplines has responsibilities in support of at least one of those mission areas. The partnerships at the federal, state, local, and tribal levels of government are working to secure America by supporting those four mission areas.

All of the questions relative to how the DHS should function and clarification of its mission are not answered. The programs are given little chance to mature before they are changed. The internal structure of the department has not matured into a stable posturing. In February 2009, Representative Oberstar, (Democrat, Minnesota) proffered legislation to again bring FEMA out of the DHS and make it a stand-alone agency, Representative Oberstar disagrees with the notion that disasters are local incidents. He further holds the position that FEMA is too restricted in its present position within the DHS to be optimally effective. Others disagree with these positions and hold the position that FEMA should stay within DHS, reporting to the secretary.[10]

It would do us well to learn from history. In 1947, it does not seem that President Truman was saying that the president and the US Congress thought the Navy or Army had failed in their mission, and thereby, there was a need to create the Department of Defense. It does seem that the statement and subsequent actions were attempting to pull together a disparate system to enhance its resources, capabilities, and collaboration. This seems to be the idea in creating the DHS. The optimal end product in the concept is determined by whether the function of an agency is enhanced within the incorporation of its partners. The focus should be on the function, not the positioning.

The FEMA debate is linked to perceptions created during Hurricane Katrina and the breach of the levee system in south Louisiana. It became popular to take the position that the response failed. That is an oversimplification. Some of the leadership at the various levels of government may have failed, but the response was not a failure in all of the jurisdictions across the Gulf Coast. Local communities respond to the disasters that strike their communities. Long before state and federal governments are on scene to make assessments, the local governments and neighborhoods are responding to their crisis. The response results are not based upon where FEMA is positioned in an organization. The assistance provided to local governments is based upon whether the function is prepared to act or not. Many first responders have had a career working with the FEMA protocols with FEMA as an independent agency and with FEMA as a directorate within the DHS. That experience indicates that it is not the positioning; it is the functioning. The year 2011 was another transitional year for the DHS. The debate as to the placement of FEMA occupied another round of Congress.

A variety of volunteer personnel serve during times of distress. These individuals often serve among state guard or state defense force units. Such military organizations are supplements to the National Guard and are authorized constitutionally among each state of the republic. Their functions vary according to their individual missions. Their rendered services include an array of functions ranging from military police roles to providing emergency shelter management.

Just as the Department of Defense plays a significant role in homeland defense, the DHS must lead in initiatives of homeland security. It is imperative that these two models have the shared vision and the common direction so as to create the strongest possible stronghold against terrorism and aggression that targets our homeland and the American citizen at home and abroad.

Experiencing a disaster is very traumatic. Regardless, locales must be capable of instigating recovery operations and facilitating an EOC. Through the EOC, coordination efforts of the response occur as well as the integrating of resources to support the recovery efforts. During the aftermath of calamity, damage may be very extensive. Numerous recovery assistance programs exist through which states, municipalities, and communities may begin to recover from a calamity.

Key terms

Disaster
Emergency
Emergency management
Emergency operation center (EOC)
Hazard
Mitigation
Multiagency coordination
Preparedness
Prevention
Recovery
Recovery assistance
Response
Risk

QUESTIONS FOR DISCUSSION

1. Disaster can strike at any time and may inflict varying amounts of damage. Consider your organization with respect to the experiencing of either a man-made or a natural disaster. Do some research, and determine whether your organization has a recovery plan. If so, write a brief essay that critically analyzes your organization's recovery plan.
2. Some abuses of recovery assistance programs occur during the aftermaths of incidents. Do some research, and determine how extensive you believe these abuses are regarding federal funding. Write a brief essay that substantiates your opinion.
3. This chapter highlights several historical incidents that necessitated recovery operations and that influenced American emergency management. Review some of these events, and consider how these experiences improved the ability to respond to disasters. Write a brief essay that summarizes your findings.
4. This chapter lists some federal agencies that provide disaster recovery assistance. Do some research, and determine whether any state agencies exist that provide similar services and assistance. Write a brief essay that summarizes your findings.

References

1. Wamsley, G. (1993). *Coping with Catastrophe: Building an Emergency Management System to Meet People's Needs in Natural and Man-Made Disasters*. Washington, DC: National Academy of Public Administration, p. 10.
2. O'Leary, R., van Slyke, D. and Kim, S. (2010). *The Future of Public Administration Around the World: The Minnowbrook Perspective*. Washington, DC: Georgetown University Press, p. 118.
3. Holdeman, E. (2013). EOC design considerations. http://www.disaster-resource.com/articles/08p_136.shtml (accessed May 8, 2013).
4. Roney, M. and Pesce, C. (2011). Dozens of tornadoes kill at least 297 people in south. *USA Today*. http://usatoday30.usatoday.com/weather/storms/tornadoes/2011-04-28-deadly-tornado-south_n.htm (accessed May 8, 2013).
5. Associated Press. (2013). Alabama getting more tornado recovery aid. *Claims Journal*. http://www.claimsjournal.com/news/southeast/2013/03/29/225943.htm (accessed May 8, 2013).
6. Partners. (2013). *DisasterAssistance.gov*. http://www.disasterassistance.gov/about-us/partners#.UYr4g8rZm9I (accessed May 8, 2013).
7. Federal Emergency Management. (2010). Fundamentals of Emergency Management Independent Study 230.a. January 14, 2010.
8. Harris, M.U. (1975). Significant events in United States civil defense history. Defense Civil Preparedness Agency, Washington, DC. http://www.civildefensemuseum.com/history.html (accessed October 30, 2010).
9. Homeland Security Council. (October 2007). National strategy for homeland security. http://www.dhs.gov/xlibrary/assets/nat_strat_homelandsecurity_2007.pdf (accessed February 19, 2009).
10. McCarter, M. (March 18, 2009). Post Katrina Reform Act augments both FEMA and DHS, experts say. http://www.hstoday.us/content/view/7676/149/ (accessed March 30, 2009).
11. U.S. Department of Homeland Security. (2008). *Senior Leadership, The First Five Years*: 2003–2008. http://www.hsdl.org/?view&did=37028 (accessed August 26, 2013).
12. United States. (2010). *United States Customs and Border Protection Timeline*. http://nemo.customs.gov/opa/TimeLine_062409.swf (accessed October 27, 2010).
13. U.S. Department of Homeland Security. (2008). *One team, one mission, securing our homeland: U.S. Department of Homeland Security strategic plan fiscal years 2008–2013*. http://www.dhs.gov/xlibrary/assets/DHS_StratPlan_FINAL_spread.pdf (accessed February 20, 2009).
14. Weems, J. (2013). Galveston hurricane of 1900. *Texas State Historical Association*, http://www.tshaonline.org/handbook/online/articles/ydg02 (accessed August 26, 2013).
15. CNN News. (2002). White House Statement on Homeland Security. http://archives.cnn.com/2002/ALLPOLITICS/06/06/white.house.homeland/ (accessed August 26, 2013).
16. Fairfield County Emergency Management and Homeland Security. (2013). State Homeland Security Program. http://www.fairfieldema.com/shsp/index.html (accessed August 26, 2013).

9

Principle Natural Hazards and Accidents Facing the United States

The likelihood of a major natural disaster, flood, hurricane, or earthquake, affecting our communities was inevitable.

George Haddow and Jane Bullock
Institute for Crisis, Disaster and Risk Management

Chapter objectives:

- Gain an understanding of the primary natural threats facing the United States
- Categorize various natural hazards that cause disasters
- Examine some of the major accidents that have resulted in significant damage and loss of life
- Examine the major natural hazards facing the nation and identify those threats most likely to occur

Introduction

Nations around the globe, including the United States, face a wide range of national safety and security threats. Some of these threats result from naturally occurring events, such as severe weather or earthquakes, that can quickly devastate a community or a region. Other threats are the result of the acts of man, some of which are intentional, such as attacks by radicals, as was witnessed in the attacks of September 11, 2001, whereas other events are accidental, such as the 2010 oil spill along the Mississippi Gulf Coast or the chemical disaster that occurred in Bhopal, India, in 1984.

The United States is one of the most open nations in the world. Sharing an international border that stretches 8000 miles with Canada to the north and Mexico to the south, the United States also has over 13,000 miles of open coastal waters, power grids, ports, rail stations, airports, and river bridges, and each is a potential target. These entities are representative of critical national infrastructure. They must be protected and maintained to ensure the survival and continuity of the nation. Although one may contemplate a variety of both natural and man-made events that may endanger these constructs, it is impossible to predict every type of scenario that poses different hazards for the critical national infrastructure. Regardless, ensuring the soundness of the integrity of the critical national infrastructure is a paramount concern of American homeland security. Within the context of homeland security, one must be cognizant of the threats posed by nature that may impact negatively various components of critical national infrastructure.

Nature often wreaks unparalleled havoc surprisingly or with little warning. Individuals and communities may experience irreparable harm resulting from the experiencing of natural calamities. Although some amount of preparedness may be achieved to mitigate the potential consequences of natural disasters and calamities, some amount of varying risk is always associated with the forces of nature. Across the United States, numerous natural threats endanger localities. **Figure 9.1** shows considerations of possible natural threats that have the potential of impacting negatively American society.

Natural events occur globally in varying magnitudes and scopes. Some nations and societies are better prepared than others to experience and mitigate the consequences of natural disasters and calamities. In many cases, the responses to natural disasters are comprised of participants representing the international community. Such efforts and collaborations are generally influenced by international and global politics.[1] Natural disasters involving international efforts often have high levels of volatility and complexity that also impact international efforts and collaborations.[1] Regardless, depending upon the severity of the incident and the resources of the nation, humanitarian assistance is often rendered internationally during the aftermath of natural calamities.[1]

Earthquake

Tornado

Hurricane

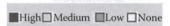

Figure 9.1 Tornado, hurricane, and earthquake risk maps. (Courtesy of the National Network of Libraries of Medicine, Emergency Preparedness & Response Initiative.)

No nation is insusceptible to the dangers of natural disasters and calamities. Numerous disasters impacted the globe in 2012. The United States experienced Hurricane Sandy, and it experienced a drought that was acknowledged as having approximately a "99 percent chance of being the warmest ever recorded" within the nation.[2] The nations of Afghanistan, Italy, Iran, and the Philippines experienced earthquakes.[2] Typhoon Bopha also affected the Philippines.[2] Regardless of the location, natural disasters may strike with little or no warning and may inflict various amounts of damage, ranging from minor impediments to utter destruction.

Similarly, accidents may involve both lethality and varying levels of complexity. Their effects may involve long periods of detrimental consequences within society. For instance, the coal mine fire of Centralia, Pennsylvania, has burned unceasingly for over 43 years.[3] Throughout the preceding four decades, this accident has resulted in the baking of "surface layers" of the earth, the venting of "poisonous gases," and the opening of "holes large enough to swallow people or cars."[3] This fire may continue to burn for approximately another 250 years, underneath nearly 3700 acres of land, until it expends the underground coal supply that represents its source of fuel.[3]

Regardless of the origin of an incident, either man-made or nature, various complexities and dynamics exist that may interject unpredictability regarding its outcomes and long-term effects. Nature is a tremendous force that often strikes with speed, surprise, and violence and whose potential endangerments are continuous. Accidents may arise from any number of reasons ranging from mechanical equipment failure to human error, and their effects may be commensurate with those of natural disasters. In any case, American society must acknowledge and respect the dangerousness that is posed by both man-made and natural events.

Overview of domestic safety and security

The lines between domestic and international security for the United States are not clear and distinct. At one extreme, the Department of Defense operated within the executive branch of government under the command of the president of the United States. At the other extreme, local communities relied on the services of their state and local law enforcement, fire and emergency services, sheriffs, and corrections officials. In the middle are agencies including the Federal Bureau of Investigation, Drug Enforcement Administration, and the Central Intelligence Agency (which maintained both domestic and international missions). Although recovery from disaster is unique to each community, depending on the amount and type of damage caused by the disaster and the resources that the community has ready or can receive, state governments have the legal authority for emergency response and recovery and serve as the point of contact between local and federal governments.

With the end of the Cold War, the United States found itself as the world's only remaining superpower, but challenged on multiple fronts: economically, diplomatically, scientifically, and militarily. The threats of the Cold War disappeared and were replaced with an explosion of new threats: illicit drug production, trafficking, and consumption; illegal immigration; global terrorism; and natural and accidental disasters. Various nations became battlefronts, centers of drug production, or havens from those deemed terrorists or drug czars. Natural and accidental events resulted in great damage and impacted the lives of citizens across multiple states.

As a response to these threats, National Guard personnel found themselves deployed to support border security initiatives. The coast guard and navy responded to the Gulf oil spill, the Drug Enforcement Administration accepted a global mission (as did most other federal law enforcement agencies), and states established emergency management and homeland security organizations. States challenged the national government on immigration. This was the world in which the United States faced new dangers, and to respond, new solutions had to be developed. One of the national responses, to these evolving threats and challenges, was the development of the Department of Homeland Security.

Modern threats, hazards, and challenges

Emergency management planning today faces many critical obstacles, such as an imbalance of focus between homeland security and natural disaster management, the challenge of involving the public in preparedness planning, the lack of an effective partnership with the business community, cuts to emergency management funding, and questions surrounding the evolving organizational structure of the nation's emergency management system. Such obstacles need to be overcome if emergency management activities are to be successful in the years ahead.[4]

Natural disasters

The United States has faced and experienced many challenges. From the perspective of homeland security and emergency management, "incidents" or "events" can be examined to provide a valuable insight into an incident as it unfolds. Following its impact, an array of efforts are made to begin the process of recovery.

Natural disasters that have impacted the United States include, but are not limited to, drought and subsequent dust storms, earthquakes, extreme heat, fires, floods, landsides and debris flow, severe weather, and storms. Other examples include hurricanes and tornadoes, tsunamis, volcanoes, wildfires, winter storms, extreme cold and heat, and disease. Though some events have caused extensive property damage, rarely has the United States experienced extensive loss of life as a result of a natural disaster.

Incidents such as the New Madrid earthquake of 1811–1812, the Memphis yellow fever epidemic of the 1870s, the Johnstown flood of 1889, the Galveston hurricane of 1900, and the San Francisco earthquake and fire of 1906 are several major incidents that impacted the nation and overwhelmed local capabilities. Among all of these cases, with the exception of the New Madrid earthquake, losses of life and extensive property damages occurred and exceeded the capabilities of local resources to respond.

Not all endangerments result from human origins. Nature is full of deadly surprises and harmful calamities. Natural threats and hazards are continuous and may involve localized events as well as events that impact the entirety of the nation. One need only review news articles to learn the details of natural disasters that impact the nation throughout most any given year. Natural disasters are defined as follows:

> A natural disaster is a serious disruption to a community or region caused by the impact of a naturally occurring rapid onset event that threatens or causes death, injury or damage to property or the environment and which requires significant and coordinated multi-agency and community response. Such serious disruption can be caused by any one, or a combination, of the following natural hazards: bushfire; earthquake; flood; storm; cyclone; storm surge; landslide; tsunami; meteorite strike; or tornado.[5]

Certainly, many more natural events may be listed within the context of this definition. Regardless of the type of natural disaster, society is imperiled with loss of life occurring in the worst cases. Natural disasters have the potential of disrupting supply lines and logistics, impacting economic functioning, and impacting agricultural functions. Many natural disasters have impacted the United States throughout its history. Below are described a variety of natural disasters that are within the domain of emergency management and homeland security.

Drought

Drought is defined as "a period of dryness especially when prolonged" and a period that "causes extensive damage to crops or prevents their successful growth."[6] Drought has often affected the United States throughout its history locally, regionally, and nationally. During the last century, three of the worst droughts were the Dust Bowl of the 1930, the 1950s drought, and the drought between the years 1987 and 1989.[7] During the 1930s, drought conditions were so severe that "soil, depleted of moisture, was lifted by the wind into great clouds of dust and sand which were so thick they concealed the sun for several days at a time."[7] The 1950s drought resulted in "crop yields in some areas" being reduced by approximately 50%.[7] The

Pursuing such a vision involves multiple missions throughout the spectrum of individual organizations that comprise the cumulative DHS entity. These missions are itemized as follows:

- Preventing terrorism and enhancing security
- Securing and managing the national borders
- Enforcing and administering immigration laws
- Safeguarding and securing cyberspace
- Ensuring resiliency to disasters

The DHS now exists as a complex, multifaceted organization that is comprised of various entities that all serve specific purposes. Through time, it will continue to change and mature with respect to the needs and challenges of future threats. Certainly, the influences of future government administrations will impact the DHS with respect to its capacity as a responding entity during periods of catastrophe. Regardless, the DHS shall continue to maintain a fiduciary obligation to safeguard the American nation and its society.

Future of the DHS

The department went through major restructuring following Hurricane Katrina and in compliance with the Post-Katrina Act of 2006. The debate continues regarding whether FEMA should be in the DHS or should be returned to an independent status.

The funding appropriations and allocations are part of the debate. Some will say that the funding for homeland security will "dry up." In 2010, there were major reductions in funding for state and local governments for homeland security programs. Others take the position that funding for some programs will be decreased, whereas that for others will be increased through time. However, it is agreed that local governments must be prepared to sustain projects that have been funded through the homeland security grant programs. This becomes a challenge at a time when local and state governments struggle in sustaining essential government functions while revenue is substantially diminished.

The US Congress consistently asks: How prepared is the nation? Unfortunately, the country has not developed a method for measuring preparedness. Others ask if the nation is better off or more prepared now than it was before September 11, 2001. These questions can be answered, but not everyone would agree on the answers.

There are definite certainties. The country will experience other hurricanes. There will be earthquakes. Natural disasters will occur. Domestic acts of terrorism continue, and the threats of international attacks remain. The first-response landscape has changed dramatically since 9/11. National preparedness is a permanent part of the response environment.

Emergency operations centers and response

During periods of calamity, an emergency operations center (EOC) is often necessary to support an emergency response to natural and man-made incidents. An EOC represents a nexus through which coordination of efforts and resources occurs when responding to an incident. The EOC is a central location where agency representatives can coordinate and make decisions when managing an emergency response. Within the EOC, numerous agencies may have representatives. This paradigm exhibits a process that allows all levels of government and all

By 2007, the 2002 goals of the DHS had changed to reflect a much broader definition of threats (p. 1)[9]:

- Prevent and disrupt terrorist attacks
- Protect the American people, critical infrastructure, and key resources
- Respond to and recover from incidents that do occur
- Continue to strengthen the foundation to ensure long-term success

The term *all hazards* has been the traditional language used to communicate the idea that preparedness would encompass natural and man-made hazards. The term *all-hazards* is now used routinely in training materials and guidelines published by the DHS. For some reason, the phrase has not found its way into the formal mission statement of the DHS, but it is the planning concept used by state, local, and tribal governments. Further, within the 2008 Strategic Plan, the mission states, "We will lead the unified effort to secure America. We will prevent and deter terrorist attacks and protect against and respond to threats and hazards to the nation. We will secure our national borders while welcoming lawful immigrants, visitors, and trade" (p. 3).[13] The phrase "respond to threats and hazards to the Nation" indicates a subtle policy shift that is necessitated by politics and practice.

The DHS must remain vigilant as a forward-thinking entity with respect to both contemporary and emerging threats. This notion is expressed within its statements of vision and mission expressed in 2013. **Figure 8.4** shows a continued commitment to unequivocally pursuing the all-hazards approach organizationally within DHS.

Our Mission

Overview

The vision of homeland security is to ensure a homeland that is safe, secure, and resilient against terrorism and other hazards.

Three key concepts form the foundation of our national homeland security strategy designed to achieve this vision:

- Security,
- Resilience, and
- Customs and Exchange.

In turn, these key concepts drive broad areas of activity that the Quadrennial Homeland Security Review (QHSR) process defines as homeland security missions. These missions are enterprise-wide, and not limited to the Department of Homeland Security. These missions and their associated goals and objectives tell us in detail what it means to prevent, to protect, to respond, and to recover, as well as to build in security, to ensure resilience, and to facilitate customs and exchange.

Hundreds of thousands of people from across the federal government, state, local, tribal, and territorial governments, the private sector, and other nongovernmental organizations are responsible for executing these missions. These are the people who regularly interact with the public, who are responsible for public safety and security, who own and operate our nation's critical infrastructures and services, who perform research and develop technology, and who keep watch, prepare for, and respond to emerging threats and disasters. These homeland security professionals must have a clear sense of what it takes to achieve the overarching vision articulated above.

Figure 8.4 *DHS 2013 vision and mission statements. (Courtesy of the DHS.)*

1980s drought was severe and represented one of the most expensive natural disasters in US history. Cumulatively, the costs of the 1980s drought were approximately $39 billion.[7]

At the turn of the 21st century, China found itself suffering from a rapid deterioration of cropland resulting in part from decades of programs instituted to increase agricultural output and an expansion of urbanization and industrial development. The urbanization and industrial development have contributed to the reduction in forestation and other vegetation that once provided moisture to the region. Additionally, three decades of satellite imagery from those areas of northern China has revealed the loss of thousands of lakes due to the reduction in annual rainfall and increased demands on the available water.[8]

During modern times, drought is a natural force that impacts communities across the nation.

Heat wave

A heat wave represents a "prolonged period of excessive heat, often combined with excessive humidity" involving extreme heat.[9] During such conditions, temperatures may "hover 10 degrees or more above the average high temperature for the region and last for prolonged periods of time."[9] Heat waves are extremely dangerous and are associated with losses of life. Within the United States, events of "excessive heat" are responsible for claiming "more lives each year than floods, lightning, tornadoes, and hurricanes combined."[10] Across the nation, during the 1980 heat wave, approximately 1250 people perished; among them, 700 were in the city of Chicago.[10] In 2003, during the month of August, a heat wave resulted in approximately 50,000 deaths.[10] Heat waves affect all segments of the nation.

Tsunami

The word *tsunami* is derived from the Japanese language.[11] It is comprised of two parts: "tsu, meaning harbor, and nami, meaning wave."[11] A tsunami is generally caused by landslides or earthquakes beneath the ocean.[12] The symptoms of a tsunami include "a strong earthquake lasting 20 seconds or more near the coast" and "a noticeable rapid rise or fall in coastal waters."[13] Although many individuals may think of Asian disasters involving large ocean waves, the United States is susceptible to the dangers of tsunamis. The states of Alaska and Hawaii, and other United States territories in the Pacific Ocean, have felt the impacts of tsunamis, as has the US West Coast[12] (**Figure 9.2**). The deadliest tsunami to impact the United States occurred in 1964 off the coast of Alaska, and it resulted in "many casualties."[12]

Figure 9.2 2009 Samoa tsunami: A car sits upside down among other debris that was caused by the September 29, 2009, 8.1-magnitude submarine Samoa earthquake and resultant tsunami in American Samoa. The tsunami spread debris throughout the village of Leone. (Courtesy of the Federal Emergency Management Agency [FEMA].)

Earthquake

An earthquake is a quick displacement of "land/rock mass, which typically occurs along a fault line," that result in the forming of "seismic waves from the origin outward" and the releasing of energy.[14] Earthquakes are one of the most costly natural hazards faced by the nation and pose a risk to 79 million Americans in 39 states.[15] The severity of earthquakes is often expressed according to the characteristics of magnitude and intensity.[16] Incidences of earthquakes represent approximately "20% of insured catastrophic losses" and approximately one-third of "economic losses" that result from "natural hazards."[17]

Very common after an earthquake are aftershocks. An aftershock is an earthquake of similar or lower intensity that follows the main earthquake. Aftershocks may continue for some time after the main shock and can well cause additional damage. The epicenter of an earthquake is the location on the earth's surface directly above the point on the fault where the earthquake rupture began.[15]

Several parts of the United States rest upon fault lines that are prone to earthquakes (see **Figure 9.3a and b**). These areas include California, Alaska, and the central part of the nation running north and south along the Mississippi River. It was along the Mississippi River, during the period of 1811–1812, that a series of earthquakes, now known as the New Madrid earthquakes, occurred. This fault line, between St. Louis, Missouri, and Memphis, Tennessee, was sparsely populated. As a result, it inflicted little personal injury, but it did cause property damage, including the destruction of the town of New Madrid, Missouri, on February 12, 1812. In a letter dated January 13, 1814, Missouri Territorial Governor William Clark asked for federal relief for the "inhabitants of New Madrid County." This was one of the earliest, if not the first, examples of a request for disaster relief from the United States federal government.

This incident is not the largest recorded earthquake to strike the United States. The largest was the Prince William Sound, Alaska, earthquake and ensuing tsunami that caused $300 million in property damages and claimed around 128 lives. Another New Madrid earthquake, along the same fault line, would inflict property damage and fatalities estimated to range from Memphis, Tennessee, in the south, to St. Louis, Missouri, in the north, clearly overwhelming local, state, and federal response capabilities.

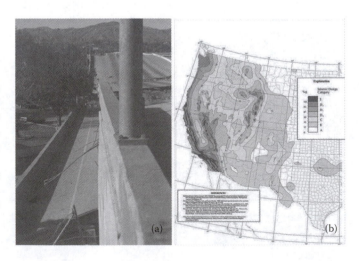

Figure 9.3 (a) Many roads, including bridges and elevated highways, were damaged by the 6.7-magnitude Northridge earthquake on January 17, 1994. Approximately 114,000 residential and commercial structures were damaged, and 72 deaths were attributed to the earthquake. Damage costs were estimated at $25 billion. (b) US West Coast earthquake hazards. (Courtesy of FEMA.)

Volcano

Though most Americans do not consider the pos-sibility of volcanic action to be a major threat, the reality is that volcanic activity is ongoing. A vol-cano is defined as "a vent in the crust of the earth or another planet or a moon from which usually molten or hot rock and steam issue" or "a hill or mountain composed wholly or in part of the ejected material."[18] Most volcanoes exist at the boundaries of the Earth's plates. It is estimated that about 550 volcanoes have erupted on the Earth's surface since recorded history.

Figure 9.4 *Map of North American Plate and volcanoes. (Courtesy of the United States Geological Survey.)*

History is full of examples of the impact of volcanic action upon communities. The famous eruption of Mount Vesuvius in AD 79 buried the towns of Pompeii and Herculaneum and resulted in an estimated loss of over 3000 lives. The most lives lost to volcanic action are related to the 1815 volcanic eruption in Tambora, Indonesia, which ultimately resulted in the death of as many as 92,000; the 1883 eruption and tsunami in Krakatau, Indonesia, that is estimated to have killed over 36,000; and the 1902 eruption of Mount Pelee in Martinque that may have resulted in the deaths of over 29,000.[19]

Notably, within the United States, a significant volcanic eruption occurred in 1980, when Mount St. Helens erupted in the state of Washington. This event was "the most studied vol-canic eruption of the twentieth century."[20] **Figure 9.4** shows monitored volcanic presences within the United States.

Tornado

Tornadoes are common throughout the United States. It is estimated that as many as 1000 tor-nadoes annually occur in the nation.[20] A tornado is defined as "a violently rotating column of air extending between, and in contact with, a cloud and the surface of the earth."[21] Tornadoes are usually associated with thunderstorms and may involve "speeds that exceed 200 mph" and that may "approach 300 mph" in "extreme cases."[21] The deadliest tornado in world history was the Daultipur–Salturia Tornado in Bangladesh on April 26, 1989, which killed approximately 1300 people.

For homeland security and emergency response personnel, tornadoes always pose a great challenge. Often quickly forming and with the potential to both move rapidly and change course, large tornadoes can create a wide path of destruction over a vast area. As a result, search and rescue operations may be hampered, not only by poor weather but also by downed power lines, trees, and other various debris, including the wreckages of buildings and vehicles (see **Figure 9.5**).

Blizzard

According to the National Weather Service, a blizzard occurs when the following conditions are observed over a period of 3 or more hours: "sustained wind or frequent gusts to 35 miles an hour or greater; and considerable falling and/or blowing snow (i.e., reducing visibility frequently to less than 1/4 mile)."[22] Blizzards occur throughout various geographic segments within the United States. In 2013, a blizzard occurred among the New England states that

Figure 9.5 On May 22, 2011, volunteers and debris fill the streets of Joplin, Missouri, after an EF5 tornado struck the city killing 161 residents and devastating one-third of the city. (Courtesy of Photo by Steve Zumwalt/ FEMA.)

deposited well over 2 feet of snow and resulted in death, destruction, and calamity for many people and organizations.[23] This event generated over 3 feet of snow, necessitated the cancelling of approximately "5000 flights," and "knocked out power to more than 635,000 customers."[24] It also necessitated the evacuating of "coastal regions" and the suspending of postal service in "seven states."[24]

Fire

Throughout the history of the United States, the nation has faced the challenges and dangers of fire. In 2011, there were 1,389,500 fires reported in the United States. These fires caused 3005 civilian deaths, 17,500 civilian injuries, and $11.7 billion in property damage. Of those, an estimated 484,500 were structure fires, causing 2640 civilian deaths, 15,635 civilian injuries, and $9.7 billion in property damage.[25]

Any region of the United States is susceptible to incidents of fire. In 1871, 1500 to possibly as many as 2500 people were killed as a result of what became known as the Peshtigo Fire. Occurring the same day as the Great Chicago Fire, it burned over 1875 square miles and destroyed 12 communities. In terms of lives lost, the Peshtigo Fire was the worst natural disaster to strike the United States.[26]

As for property damage and loss, the National Fire Protection Association identifies the Oakland Fire Storm of 1991 as the costliest wildland fire in the United States, with damage estimated at over $1.5 billion.[25] Even today, with the resources available to combat them, major fires still pose great challenges to emergency management professionals. In 2012, the US wildfire season was so extreme that "the U.S. Department of Agriculture Forest Service ran out of money to pay for firefighters, fire trucks, and aircraft that dump retardant on monstrous flames."[27] This funding situation necessitated the transferring of funds from fire prevention programs to satisfy outlying costs.[27] Eventually, congressional intervention was necessary to generate approximately $400 million toward fire prevention.[27] The United States is not the only nation that has experienced the impact of uncontrolled fires; in 1987, the Black Dragon fire in China burnt a total of 18 million acres of forest along the Amur River.

Flood

Flash floods occur when excessively large quantities of rain occur "within a short period of time," generally less than 6 hours, thereby causing water levels to increase and decrease

Figure 9.6 Braithwaite, Louisiana, September 6, 2012: A house lies in water after floodwaters topped the levee in Braithwaite, Louisiana, during Hurricane Isaac. (Courtesy of by Patsy Lynch/FEMA.)

quickly.[28] Flooding also occurs when mass amounts of water, originating from "a river or other body of water," either cause damage or represent a threat.[28] Flooding impacts many regions throughout the United States annually. According to the National Hurricane Center, inland flooding has been responsible for more than half the deaths associated with tropical cyclones in the United States over the last 30 years.[29]

Some of the major flooding that has impacted the nation includes the 1913 Ohio flood that resulted in over 450 deaths and over 100 million in property damage and the 1927 Mississippi River flood that impacted states from Missouri down to Louisiana and sparked a national-level debate on finding solutions to combat flooding.[30] In 2013, Hurricane Isaac impacted the American Gulf Coast region. **Figure 9.6** shows the flooding that occurred in Braithwaite, Louisiana, during the aftermath of the storm.

Hailstorm

Hail is defined as "precipitation in the form of small balls or lumps usually consisting of concentric layers of clear ice and compact snow."[31] Therefore, a hailstorm represents "a storm accompanied by hail."[31] Damages from hail are not insignificant both economically and financially. Hail may fall to the Earth with speeds as fast as 100 mph and may also "contain foreign matter, such as pebbles, leaves, twigs, nuts, and insects" within their icy content.[32] Annually, hail inflicts approximately $1 billion in damages to both crops and property.[32] In 2003, the largest hailstone ever discovered within the United States was found in Aurora, Colorado.[32] It was nearly the size of a soccer ball and was measured to be approximately 7 inches wide.[32]

Hail has impacted the outcomes of historical events. In 1360, a hailstorm affected the Hundred Years' War that occurred between the nations of England and France.[33] Hail killed "thousands of horses" and "hundreds of English troops" near Paris.[33] During modern times, the effects of hail are just as deadly and severe. In 2013, within a period of 20 minutes, in the nation of India, nine people were killed, and both crops and homes were destroyed when a hailstorm deposited a "snow like blanket" among "seven villages in Chevella, Moinabad, and Shankarpally."[34]

Dust storm

A dust storm is an event that may arise surprisingly and without warning and generally has the appearance of an "advancing wall of dust and debris which may be miles long and several thousand feet high."[35] Dust storms are quite dangerous even though they may require short periods of time for completion. The conditions of dust storms often include blinded or extremely limited visibility, thereby increasing the dangers of travel. During the 1930s, the famous Dust Bowl represented one of the "worst environmental disasters of the twentieth century" globally.[36] It resulted in 3 million people abandoning their Great Plains farms approximately 500,000 people migrating to the western states.[36]

Landslide

A landslide represents the mass wasting of materials. Mass wasting is defined as the "down slope movement of soil and/or rock under the influence of gravity."[37] This movement occurs because of slope failure involving a moment in which "gravity exceeds the strength of the earth materials."[37] Notably, landslides have often occurred in the western United States, where residents have endured much damage, including the loss of homes and property. In 2011, in the state of California, entire sections of roadways slid into the Pacific Ocean because of landslides.[38]

Sinkhole

Sinkholes are "depressions or holes in the land surface" that result from "the dissolving of the underlying limestone."[39] Sinkholes may occur in open areas as well as underneath structures or roadways. The damages that result from sinkholes may be both excessive and costly.[39] Within the state of Florida, many lakes are actually "relic sinkholes."[39]

Cyclone

Cyclones are analogous with rotating storms (e.g., hurricanes, tornadoes, etc.). A cyclone is defined as "a storm or system of winds that rotates about a center of low atmospheric pressure, advances at a speed of 20 to 30 miles (about 30 to 50 kilometers) an hour, and often brings heavy rain."[40]

The deadliest natural disaster to impact the United States was the Galveston hurricane of 1900. Striking on September 8, 1900, it caused between 6000 and 12,000 deaths and devastated the city, destroying approximately 3600 homes and buildings.[41] The 1926 Miami hurricane is considered the costliest hurricane to strike the United States.[42] During the first decade of the 21st century, the most notable example of a cyclone storm was Hurricane Katrina.

In 2012, hurricane Sandy devastated the eastern seaboard of the United States and caused significant destruction among regions of New York and New Jersey that rarely experience hurricane activity.[43] This storm "killed more than 100 people, destroyed whole communities in coastal New York and New Jersey, left tens of thousands homeless, crippled mass transit, triggered paralyzing gas shortages, inflicted billions of dollars in infrastructure damage and cut power to more than 8 million homes, some of which remained dark for weeks."[43] This event impaired the regional economy and impacted numerous organizations around the nation that had relationships with the impacted area.

Whirlpool

A whirlpool is a "swirling body of water usually produced by ocean tides," and more powerful whirlpools are known as maelstroms.[44] During the 15th century, it is conjectured that a Malian fleet of ships was destroyed by a whirlpool when attempting to explore the Atlantic Ocean.[45] Out of the 200 vessels that were deployed, only one returned.[45] Although their occurrences may not be well known, whirlpools are dangerous entities. In 2010, in the nation of India, a total of 36 people drowned in conjunction with a whirlpool, and another 25 remained missing after the incident.[46] The incident occurred when an overcrowded boat was caught in a whirlpool and then capsized.[46]

Limnic eruption

Limnic eruptions occur rarely. However, they represent situations in which carbon dioxide erupts suddenly from "water, posing the threat of suffocating wildlife, livestock, and humans."[44] The conditions that generate these events are rare.[47] In 1986, in the Cameroon region, a limnic eruption occurred that expelled approximately "1.6 million tons" of carbon dioxide from a lake at a speed of roughly 60 mph.[47] The resulting cloud "displaced all the oxygen in several small villages, suffocating between 1700 and 1800 people, not counting all their livestock."[47]

Major accidents

The emergency management community must be prepared to respond to a wide range of accidents, both major and minor. Over the last several decades, major events such as the tragic 1984 Union Carbide industrial accident in Bhopal, India; the 1986 disaster at the Chernobyl Nuclear Power Plant in the Soviet Union; the 1989 *Exxon Valdez* oil spill in Prince William Sound, Alaska; the Deepwater Horizon oil spill in 2010; and the 2011 Fukushima Daiichi nuclear disaster have demonstrated the potential scope of an accidental disaster. Each of these events presented unique and very grave challenges to responders.

Triangle Shirtwaist Factory fire of 1911

On March 25, 1911, a fire broke out on the eighth floor of the Triangle Shirtwaist Company located in New York City. Employing approximately 500 workers, this company's environment was primed for catastrophe.[48] It offered low pay and difficult working conditions, and the unsafe work environment increased the danger of fire.[48] Fire rescue arrived but found their ladders too short to reach the trapped women on the eighth and ninth floors. Workers found that the main stairwell was too engulfed in smoke and fire to exit. The door to the only other exit door was locked, thereby trapping the workers. About 20 escaped down the outside fire escape before it collapsed, killing several workers.[48] Some tried to escape using the elevators, until they quit, trapping other workers. Sixty-two workers jumped from the eighth and ninth floors to their death on the street below.[48] The fire resulted in the deaths of 146 young women.[48] Prior to the terrorist attacks of 9/11, the Triangle Shirtwaist fire was the largest mass casualty event in New York City history. The owners were placed on trial, but no convictions resulted. Many lessons were learned from this disaster that resulted in the crafting of regulations related to workplace safety.[48]

Texas City explosion of 1947

The worst industrial disaster in United States occurred on April 16, 1947, in Texas City, Texas, when initially, the cargo of the SS *Grandcamp* and then that of the SS *High Flyer* exploded. The SS *Grandcamp* was loaded with 2300 tons of explosive-grade ammonium nitrate, the same type of explosive that would be used years later in the bombing of the Murrah Federal Building in Oklahoma City. The SS *High Flyer* held a cargo of over 2000 tons of sulfur.

As the ship burned, firefighters were called to respond. As they battled the fire, onlookers gathered, including a group of schoolchildren. When the explosions occurred, all of the firefighters and practically all of the onlookers on their pier were killed, as were many employees in the Monsanto Chemical Company and throughout the dock area.

There were 362 freight cars in the Texas City Terminal Co. yards, all of which were damaged and many of which were totally destroyed. Approximately 600 automobiles in the Monsanto parking lot and the dock area were practically a total loss. It is estimated that over 500 people were killed and over 2000 were injured, thereby making the Texas City explosion the worst industrial disaster in United States.[49]

1984 Union Carbide industrial accident

The 1984 Union Carbide industrial gas leak in Bhopal, India, is considered the world's worst industrial disaster. Bhopal is a city of approximately 1 million. In 1984, the plant was manufacturing Sevin at one-quarter of its production capacity due to decreased demand for pesticides. At 11:00 p.m., on December 2, 1984, while most of the 1 million residents of Bhopal slept, an operator at the plant noticed a small leak of methyl isocyanate (MIC) gas and increasing pressure inside a storage tank. The vent gas scrubber, a safety device designed to neutralize toxic discharge from the MIC system, had been turned off 3 weeks before.[50]

Over 500,000 people were exposed to MIC gas and other chemicals. The toxic substance made its way in and around the communities located near the plant. Even though Bhopal had four major hospitals, there was a shortage of physicians and hospital beds and no plan for mass casualty emergency response. As casualties filled the hospitals, health care professional desperately searched to identify the cause and soon linked the illness back to the Union Carbide plant. More than 20,000 people required hospital treatment for symptoms including swollen eyes, frothing at the mouth, and breathing difficulties. As with many accidents, the Union Carbide industrial gas leak resulted from a series of events and failure to implement safety measures that were expected to neutralize any potential industrial hazard.

Following the disaster, environmental awareness and activism in India increased significantly. In 1986, the Indian government enacted the Environment Protection Act, creating the Ministry of Environment and Forests and strengthening India's commitment to the environment. Under the new act, the Ministry of Environment and Forests was given overall responsibility for administering and enforcing environmental laws and policies. It established the importance of integrating environmental strategies into all industrial development plans for the country.

1986 Chernobyl Nuclear Power Plant explosion

The Chernobyl Nuclear Power Plant disaster was a catastrophic nuclear accident that occurred on April 26, 1986, at the Chernobyl Nuclear Power Plant in Ukraine. The Chernobyl disaster is widely considered to have been the worst nuclear power plant accident in history and is one of only two classified as a level 7 event on the International Nuclear Event Scale.

The Chernobyl accident in 1986 was the result of a flawed reactor design that was operated by inadequately trained personnel. The resulting steam explosion and fires released at least 5% of the radioactive reactor core into the atmosphere and downwind. This resulted in the largest uncontrolled radioactive release into the environment ever recorded for any civilian operation, and large quantities of radioactive substances were released into the air for about 10 days.

The response to the fire and explosion reflected the confusion that is often typical during major disasters. First responders had no idea of the degree of danger they faced. Two

Chernobyl plant workers died on the night of the accident, and 28 more people died within a few weeks as a result of acute radiation poisoning.

The scope of the disaster combined with the secrecy in the Soviet Union at the time further impacted operations to first stabilize the disaster and then implement steps toward recovery. Within the first few days of the disaster, the decision was made to evacuate the approximately 45,000 residents of the town of Pripyat. Later, other evacuations occurred, with as many as 200,000 people being permanently displaced from their homes.[51] The legacy of Chernobyl remains as more nations look to the use of nuclear power as an alternative to other traditional sources of fuel.

1989 *Exxon Valdez* oil spill

On March 24, 1989, The *Exxon Valdez* oil spill occurred in Prince William Sound, Alaska, spilling into the sound between 260,000 and 750,000 barrels of crude oil. In response to the spill, the United States Congress passed the Oil Pollution Act of 1990 (OPA). The legislation included a clause that prohibits any vessel that, after March 22, 1989, has caused an oil spill of more than 1 million US gallons in any marine area from operating in Prince William Sound.[52] Although this accident occurred almost 25 years ago, the disaster site remains tainted with lingering traces of oil.[53] It is estimated that the remaining oil contaminants are "decreasing at a rate of approximately 0%–4%" annually.[53] Given this rate, it will necessitate decades to centuries for the contaminants to be completely eliminated.[53]

2010 Deepwater Horizon oil spill

This oil spill, along with response and cleanup activities, caused extensive damage to marine and wildlife habitats and the Gulf's fishing and tourism industries (**Figure 9.7**). It surpassed the severity of the *Exxon Valdez* incident and represented the worst US "offshore oil spill" in American history.[54] It resulted in the spillage of approximately 206 million gallons of oil,

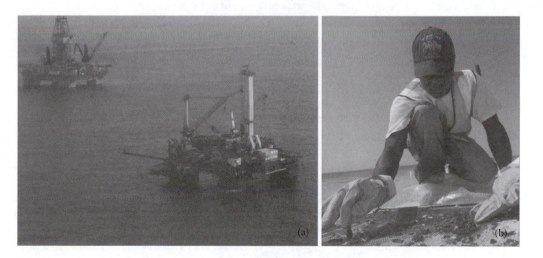

Figure 9.7 *2010 Deepwater Horizon oil spill. (a) Rigs drilling a relief well and preparing the static kill are shown in the Gulf of Mexico on July 31, 2010, over the Deepwater Horizon well 40 miles from the southern coast of Louisiana. (Courtesy of Petty Officer First Class Sara Francis, US Coast Guard.) (b) An oil recovery technician sifts through tar balls at a beach in Pass Christian, Mississippi, on July 31, 2010, as part of the Deepwater Horizon oil spill response effort. (Courtesy of Petty Officer Third Class Brandyn Hill, US Coast Guard.)*

whereas the *Exxon Valdez* incident involved a spillage of approximately 11 million gallons.[55] The US Coast Guard was an integral component of the "federal response" to the incident, which involved the spillage of "hundreds of millions of gallons of oil."[56] This oil spill also resulted in the deaths of 11 workers.[54]

This incident resulted in the passing of the RESTORE Act in 2012. This legislation represented a mechanism through which the penalties associated with the Clean Water Act could be implemented.[57] It also provided a foundation for creating the Gulf Coast Environmental Restoration Council.[57] As a result of this incident, the BP Corporation "pled guilty to felony misconduct" and was tasked with paying approximately $4.5 billion in "penalties."[54] Additionally, this financial amount included approximately a $1.256 billion "criminal fine" that represented the largest such fine in American history.[54]

Although 3 years have passed since this incident, environmental concerns remain important topics within the affected region and nationally. Both crustaceans and fish were discovered to have various abnormalities, including "skin lesions."[55] The dispersant used to treat the affected region is also known to alter the DNA of organisms and is known to be carcinogenic.[55]

2011 Fukushima Daiichi earthquake, tsunami, and nuclear disaster

Though technically a result of an act of nature, the Fukushima Daiichi earthquake, tsunami, and nuclear disaster revealed how a natural disaster could be compounded. The Fukushima Daiichi earthquake, tsunami, and nuclear disaster is the largest nuclear disaster since the Chernobyl disaster of 1986 and only the second disaster, along with Chernobyl, to measure level 7 on the International Nuclear Event Scale. There were no casualties caused by radiation exposure, though approximately 25,000 died because of the earthquake and tsunami. With an analysis of the quantity of radiation released and the number of people exposed, the range is 0 to 100 cancer deaths in the coming decades. Researchers affiliated with Stanford University have estimated initially that approximately 130 deaths and 180 incidents of cancer may occur within the populace near the affected locality.[58] However, recent research indicates that these initial estimates regarding the health effects associated with the incident may have been underestimated. Instead, it is now estimated that approximately 1000 cancer deaths may occur.[59]

Aftermath of incidents

The aftermath of any incident, whether natural or man-made, may have various risks and unpredicted effects. Although rare in developed nations, various infectious diseases may occur within the environments of undeveloped countries.[60] Examples include cholera, typhoid fever, dysentery, hepatitis, balantidiasis, leptospirosis, malaria, and dengue fever.[60] Such diseases may be spread through the drinking of contaminated water that is infected with animal waste or through insect and animal bites.[60] Various venoms may be experienced from insect and animal bites.[60] Among disaster relief shelters, diseases such as measles, tuberculosis, gastroenteritis, and hepatitis may be communicable between humans.[60] Such diseases and the effects of venoms may result in death or severe health consequences for survivors if they are untreated.

Other outcomes may involve the effects of poisonous gases following incidents. In 2005, in Graniteville, South Carolina, a train wreck resulted in the releasing of toxic gases when two trains collided, "leaving 16 cars derailed."[61] The wreck involved the releasing of approximately

120,000 pounds of chlorine gas.[61] A total of 9 people were killed, over 500 people were injured, and approximately 5400 people were evacuated from the town.[63] During the aftermath of the incident, many people suffered damage to their respiratory tracts and vocal chords.[61] A year after the accident, some people also suffered from memory loss and pulmonary disease.[62] This accident represented the "deadliest train wreck involving hazardous material since 1978."[62]

Nuclear accidents often involve long-term, detrimental effects associated with radiation and contamination. After the Chernobyl incident, the city was abandoned. It remains abandoned and uninhabitable to this day. Twenty-five years after the accident, the health effects remained unascertained.[63] Since the accident, approximately 6000 instances of thyroid cancer were detected within the affected region near Chernobyl.[63] It is unclear whether all of these diagnoses were related to the nuclear accident.[63]

The dynamics of natural disasters and accidents are often complex and unpredictable. They may have long-term implications for the economies of the affected regions, involve long-term damage ecologically, and have long-term health consequences for people near the location of the incident. Despite the best efforts to mitigate the effects of calamities, there is no guarantee that detrimental consequences will not occur during the aftermaths of events. In many cases, only time will reveal the effects of natural disasters and accidents.

Conclusion

The role of the federal government regarding disaster response has evolved throughout the past 200 years. The Congressional Act of 1803 was the earliest effort to provide federal disaster relief after a fire devastated a New Hampshire town. From that point forward, assorted legislation provided disaster support. Between 1803 and 1950, the federal government intervened in approximately 100 incidents (earthquakes, fires, floods, and tornadoes).

Such events are severe reminders of the potency of natural hazards and disasters to affect negatively not only the impacted area but also entire segments of the nation. These calamities necessitate emergency management and response and also involve various amounts of preparedness, depending upon location and resources. Although they do not result from human activities, these natural events are just as deadly and as powerful as any threat that could be unleashed from human origins. This notion represents a dichotomy of threats: man-made events and natural disasters. Although these categories may differ with respect to their origins, their potentials to cause mass death, destruction, and suffering are comparable. Modern American society must acknowledge the dangerousness of both categories and must craft methods to mitigate the effects of a range of incidents that may arise from many different origins.

The United States experiences a variety of natural disasters. Depending upon one's locality, the types of disasters may be different. For example, it is highly unlikely that someone living in Florida will experience a blizzard, whereas someone in Montana may well prepare for much snowfall annually. Regardless of the type of event or incident, all natural calamities have some amount of risk and potential of lethality. Deaths may result from landslides just as easily as they may result from volcanic explosions. One must not discount the dangerousness of nature.

Each natural incident represents a learning experience locally, regionally, and nationally, often resulting in the crafting of legislation to improve the ability of preparedness, mitigation, and recovery regarding the potential hazards of future natural calamities. For instance, the events involving the *Exxon Valdez* and the Deepwater Horizon resulted in congressional legislative activities. Such legislation often improves the enforcing of regulations and imposing of punitive measure that may be necessary during the aftermaths of events. It also provides a framework for supporting preparedness and mitigation initiatives.

The United States possesses a large landmass that exhibits a variety of different ecological, meteorological, and geological attributes. Dangers may arise from storms, volcanoes, earthquakes, floods, fires, blizzards, and many other natural factors. Given the size of the nation, these dangers are unequally distributed within American society. Each locality is susceptible to the unique threats that endanger its region within the nation.

The United States also exhibits a complex variety of roadways, airways, railways, and waterways. It also possesses complex municipal infrastructures. Accidents may occur among any of these venues. After any such accidents, the resulting consequences may be detrimental in many ways. Long-term health effects may impair the functioning of the human body and may result in death. The aftermath of many incidents, both accidental and natural, may also involve considerations of numerous diseases.

In any case, it is undeniable that American society faces many dangers representing both natural and man-made origins. These dangers are not constrained solely to the United States. Instead, any nation is susceptible to man-made and natural disasters. Such events may occur with speed, surprise, and violence and have differing levels of lethality. All practitioners and theoreticians of homeland security must acknowledge and respect the potentials of such incidents to impact American society. If such events occur, society must evaluate and assess these instances as a method of crafting betterments that may improve its ability to prepare for, mitigate, and recover from future calamities.

Key terms

Accident
Consequences
Disaster
Fumes
Hazard
Hazardous materials (HAZMAT)
Maritime disaster
Nuclear incident
Natural disaster
Poisonous
Weather

QUESTIONS FOR DISCUSSION

1. Throughout the nation, the types of natural threats that may impact locales differ according to geographic location. Do some research and determine what natural hazards exist within your locale. Write a brief essay that summarizes your findings.
2. Given your findings regarding the preceding question, how well prepared do you believe you locale is to experience a natural disaster? Write a brief essay that substantiates your opinion.

3. Consider your organization or locale with respect to the potential of experiencing a natural disaster. Do some research, and determine whether a recovery plan exists. If such a plan exists, write a brief critical essay that analyzes this recovery plan.

4. The experiencing of natural hazards may occur through much time. For example, the Dust Bowl of the 20th century occurred over a period of years. Do you believe that American society is better prepared for such a calamity during modern times? Why or why not? Write a brief essay that explains your opinion.

References

1. Veenema, T. (2007). *Disaster Nursing and Emergency Preparedness: For Chemical, Biological, and Radiological Terrorism and Other Hazards* (2nd ed.). New York: Springer Publishing, p. 575.
2. Worst Natural Disasters of 2012. (2012). *The Huffington Post*. http://www.huffingtonpost.com/2012/12/28/worst-natural-disasters-of-2012_n_2349311.html#slide=more270588 (accessed April 2, 2013).
3. Krajick, K. (2005). Fire in the hole. *Smithsonian Magazine*. http://www.smithsonianmag.com/travel/firehole.html (accessed April 2, 2013).
4. Haddow, G. and Bullock, J. (2010). *The Future of Emergency Management*. Burlington, MA: Butterworth-Heinemann.
5. Australian Emergency Management. (2002). *Natural Disasters in Australia: Reforming Mitigation, Relief, and Recovery Arrangements*. http://www.em.gov.au/Documents/Natural%20Disasters%20in%20Australia%20-%20Review.pdf (accessed February 11, 2013).
6. Drought. (2013). *Merriam-Webster Dictionary*. http://www.merriam-webster.com/dictionary/drought (accessed February 12, 2013).
7. National Oceanic and Atmospheric Administration. (2013). North American drought: a paleo perspective. http://www.ncdc.noaa.gov/paleo/drought/drght_history.html (accessed February 12, 2013).
8. Royston, R. (October 28, 2010). China's dust storms raise fears of impending catastrophe. *National Geographic News*. http://news.nationalgeographic.com/news/2001/06/0601_chinadust.html (accessed March 18, 2013).
9. Federal Emergency Management Agency. (2013). Community Emergency Response Team Appendix 1-A: Hazard Lesson Plans. training.fema.gov/EMIWeb/downloads/04-Heat-PM-Rev2.doc (accessed February 12, 2013).
10. National Oceanic and Atmospheric Administration. (2013). Heat: a major killer. http://www.nws.noaa.gov/os/heat/index.shtml (accessed February 12, 2013).
11. Dudley, W. and Lee, M. (1998). *Tsunami!* (2nd ed.). Honolulu, HI: University of Hawaii Press, p. 51.
12. Geist, E., Earle, P. and McCarthy, J. (2005). Could it happen here? Tsunamis that have struck U.S. coastlines. http://soundwaves.usgs.gov/2005/01/fieldwork2.html (accessed February 12, 2013).
13. American Red Cross. (2013). Tsunami. http://www.redcross.org/prepare/disaster/tsunami (accessed April 2, 2013).
14. Banks, E. (2005). *Catastrophic Risk Management: Analysis and Management*. West Sussex, England: John Wiley & Sons Publishing, p. 19.
15. Fact Sheet Earthquakes. FEMA. (December 2007). US Department of Homeland Security. Catalog No. 07337-7.
16. U.S. Geological Survey. (2013). The severity of an earthquake. http://pubs.usgs.gov/gip/earthq4/severitygip.html (accessed February 12, 2013).
17. Oliveira, C., Roca, A. and Goula, X. (2008). *Assessing and Managing Earthquake Risk Geo-Scientific and Engineering Knowledge for Earthquake Risk Mitigation: Developments, Tools, and Techniques*. Dordrecht, The Netherlands: Springer Publishing, p. 388.
18. Volcano. (2013). *Merriam-Webster Dictionary*. http://www.merriam-webster.com/dictionary/volcano (accessed February 12, 2013).
19. The Deadliest Volcanic Eruptions. (2013). http://www.chm.bris.ac.uk/webprojects2003/silvester/Page6Famous.htm, Bristol University. (accessed March 24, 2013).
20. Mt. St. Helens Eruption (1980). (2013). *San Diego State University*. http://www.geology.sdsu.edu/how_volcanoes_work/Sthelens.html (accessed February 13, 2013).
21. The Weather Channel. (2013). Tornadoes: definition & prevalence. http://www.weather.com/outlook/wxready/articles/id-54 (accessed February 13, 2013).

22. National Weather Service. (2013). Blizzard. http://w1.weather.gov/glossary/index.php?letter=b (accessed February 12, 2013).
23. PHOTOS: Blizzard 2013 Blasts Through Northeast. (2013). *Fox News Insider*. http://foxnewsinsider.com/2013/02/09/photos-blizzard-northeast-nemo-2013/ (accessed February 12, 2013).
24. Snow, M., Ford, D. and Ariosto, D. (2013). Northeast digs out after deadly blizzard. *CNN News*. http://www.cnn.com/2013/02/09/us/northeast-blizzard (accessed February 11, 2013).
25. Deadliest/large-loss Fire. (2012). *National Fire Protection Association* (2/12). http://www.nfpa.org/itemDetail.asp?categoryID=954&itemID=44745&URL=Research/Fire%20statistics/Deadliest/large-loss%20fires (accessed March 30, 2013).
26. Hemphill, S. (November 27, 2002). Peshtigo: a tornado of fire revisited. *Minnesota Public Radio*. http://news.minnesota.publicradio.org/features/200211/27_hemphills_peshtigofire/ (accessed March 30, 2013).
27. Fears, D. (2012). U.S. runs out of funds to battle wildfires. http://articles.washingtonpost.com/2012-10-07/national/35500576_1_battle-wildfires-wildfire-suppression-worst-wildfire-season (accessed February 13, 2013).
28. Flash Flood. (2013). *U.S. Geological Survey*. http://ks.water.usgs.gov/waterwatch/flood/definition.html (accessed February 12, 2013).
29. Fact Sheet Floods. FEMA. (December 2007). US Department of Homeland Security. Catalog No. 07337-3.
30. Perry, C. (12/10/10). (2010). Significant floods in the United States during the 20th Century–USGS measures a century of floods. *USGS*. http://ks.water.usgs.gov/pubs/fact-sheets/fs.024-00.html#HDR1 (accessed March 30, 2013).
31. Hail Storm. (2013). *Merriam-Webster Dictionary*. http://www.merriam-webster.com/dictionary/hail%20storm (accessed February 12, 2013).
32. Largest Hailstone in U.S. History Found. (2013). *National Geographic*. http://news.nationalgeographic.com/news/2003/08/0804_030804_largesthailstone.html (accessed February 13, 2013).
33. May 8th: A Hail of a Day. (2012). *Accuweather*. http://www.accuweather.com/en/weather-news/may-8th-a-hail-of-a-day/64926 (accessed April 3, 2013).
34. Reilly, J. (2013). Nine people killed as freak hailstorm rains massive boulders down on Indian villages. *The Daily Mail*. http://www.dailymail.co.uk/news/article-2271147/Nine-people-killed-freak-hailstorm-rains-massive-boulders-Indian-villages.html (accessed April 3, 2013).
35. National Oceanic and Atmospheric Administration. (2013). Motorist Beware! http://www.nws.noaa.gov/om/brochures/duststrm.htm (accessed February 12, 2013).
36. Cook, B., Miller, R. and Seager, R. (2011). Did dust storms make the Dust Bowl drought worse? *Columbia University–Lamont-Doherty Earth Observatory*. http://www.ldeo.columbia.edu/res/div/ocp/drought/dust_storms.shtml (accessed April 2, 2013).
37. What is a Landslide? (2013). *University of Wisconsin*. http://www.geology.wisc.edu/courses/g115/projects03/emgoltz/definition.htm (accessed February 13, 2013).
38. California Road Slides into Ocean After Landslide. (2011). *BBC News*. http://www.bbc.co.uk/news/world-us-canada-15819302 (accessed February 12, 2013).
39. State of Florida. (2013). Sinkholes. http://www.swfwmd.state.fl.us/hydrology/sinkholes/ (accessed February 12, 2013).
40. Cyclone. (2013). *Merriam-Webster Dictionary*. http://www.merriam-webster.com/dictionary/cyclone (accessed February 12, 2013).
41. Ripley, A. (September 15, 2008). The 1900 Galveston hurricane. *Time*. http://www.time.com/time/nation/article/0,8599,1841442,00.html (accessed April 1, 2013).
42. Barnes, J. (1998). *Florida's Hurricane History*. The University of North Carolina Press, Chapel Hill.
43. Hurricane Sandy: Covering the Storm. (2012). *The New York Times*. http://www.nytimes.com/interactive/2012/10/28/nyregion/hurricane-sandy.html (accessed February 11, 2013).
44. Bhagat, S.B. (2009). *Foundations of Geology*. New Delhi, India: New Vision Publishing House, p. 532.
45. Wright, E. (2008). *Lost Explorers: Adventurers that Disappeared off the Face of the Earth*. St Leonards, NSW Australia: Murdoch Books, p. 11.
46. At Least 36 Killed After Indian Boat Sinks in Whirlpool. (2010). *Thaindian News*. http://www.thaindian.com/newsportal/india/at-least-36-killed-after-indian-boat-sinks-in-whirlpool_100442672.html (accessed April 3, 2013).
47. Frater, J. (2010). *Ultimate Book of Bizarre Lists*. Berkeley, CA: Ulysses Press, p. 52.
48. Rosenberg, J. Triangle shirtwaist factory fire. (2013). *About.com 20th Century History*. http://history1900s.about.com/od/1910s/p/trianglefire.htm (accessed March 30, 2013).
49. Fire Prevention and Engineering Bureau of Texas. (2013). Texas City Disaster. http://www.local1259iaff.org/report.htm (accessed March 31, 2013).
50. Shrivastava P. (1987). *Bhopal: Anatomy of a Crisis*. Cambridge, MA: Ballinger Publishing, p. 184.

51. Chernobyl Accident. (1986). *World Nuclear Association*. http://www.world-nuclear.org/info/Safety-and-Security/Safety-of-Plants/Chernobyl-Accident/#.UU8whVfyCSp (accessed March 24, 2013).

52. Oil Pollution Act of 1990–Summary. *Federal Wildlife and Related Laws Handbook*. August 18, 1990. (accessed March 10, 2008).

53. Oil Remains: The Persistence, Toxicity, and Impact of Exxon Valdez Oil. (2013). State of Alaska. http://www.evostc.state.ak.us/recovery/lingeringoil.cfm (accessed April 3, 2013).

54. Hubert-Allen, O. (2013). A look back at the BP Deepwater Horizon oil spill. *The Baltimore Sun*. http://darkroom.baltimoresun.com/2012/11/a-look-back-at-the-bp-deepwater-horizon-oil-spill/#1 (accessed April 2, 2013).

55. Ecological Impacts of Deepwater Horizon Oil Spill. (2012). http://ihrrblog.org/2012/05/08/ecological-impacts-of-deep-water-horizon-oil-spill/ (accessed April 2, 2013).

56. Carden, M. (2010). Military support to mitigate oil spill continues. http://www.defense.gov/news/newsarticle.aspx?id=60040 (accessed April 3, 2013).

57. Florida Department of Environmental Protection. (2013). Deepwater horizon oil spill response and restoration. http://www.dep.state.fl.us/deepwaterhorizon/ (accessed April 2, 2013).

58. McClure, M. (2012). Stanford researchers calculate global health impacts of the Fukushima nuclear disaster. http://news.stanford.edu/news/2012/july/fukushima-health-impacts-071712.html (accessed April 2, 2013).

59. Brodie, R. (2013). Reassessing the health effects of the Fukushima Daiichi nuclear accident. http://www.rsc.org/chemistryworld/2013/01/reassessing-health-effects-fukushima-daiichi-nuclear-accident (accessed April 2, 2013).

60. Disaster Aftermath: The Risk of Epidemic Diseases. (2010). *CBC News*. http://www.cbc.ca/news/health/story/2008/05/16/f-health-disaster-diseases.html (accessed April 2, 2013).

61. Toxic Train, Deadly Crash. (2006). *ABC News*. http://abcnews.go.com/Primetime/story?id=2375087&page=1#.UVuoRDdXqYo (accessed April 2, 2013).

62. Jarvie, J. (2006). Effects of deadly train crash still rumble through town. *Los Angeles Times*. http://articles.latimes.com/2006/jan/16/nation/na-graniteville16 (accessed April 3, 2013).

63. Vengerowsky, K. (2011). Chernobyl impact felt 25 years later. *USA Today*. http://usatoday30.usatoday.com/news/world/2011-04-26-chernobyl-anniversary-nuclear-radiation.htm (accessed April 2, 2013).

10

International Terrorism and Threat Groups

The threat posed by international terrorism, and in particular from al Qaeda and related groups, continues to be the gravest we face.

FBI Director Robert S. Mueller, III
Testimony before the Senate Committee on Intelligence, February 16, 2005

Chapter objectives:

- Gain an understanding of the concept of international terrorism
- Examine historical and modern facets of international terrorism
- Identify terrorist groups that endanger the United States

Introduction

The decade between 2001 and 2011 has been a remarkable time in world history. On September 11, 2001, the world's unquestioned superpower experienced a series of attacks by a stateless agent. These attacks ignited a response that has resulted in billions of dollars expended, thousands of lives lost, countless injured, national governments changing, and a physical and psychological clash of cultures that continues to this day.

Almost 10 years later, in the early morning hours of May 2, 2011, a United States military force, which included members of the United States Navy's elite SEAL Team 6, brought to an end a global search that had lasted a decade to find Osama bin Laden. The death of Osama bin Laden (**Figure 10.1**) did not end the threat to the nation posed by international terrorism, but it did demonstrate the ability of the United States to use its wide range of capabilities in the search to hold him accountable for the 9/11 attacks.

Global struggle against international terrorism

The events of September 11, 2001, shocked the United States and sent the nation on a path of a global engagement with what we view as international terrorism. Prior to these attacks,

Figure 10.1 Osama bin Laden. Killed by special forces in Pakistan on May 2, 2011, in a raid on his compound.

potential enemies and threats to our nation appeared to be both identifiable and quantifiable. However, the events of September 11, 2001, and the succeeding years, were indicative of the multipolar world in which various threats arose from both man-made and natural origins.

Although these events were devastating and tragic, they were both catalysts for influencing and changing the US security models and mechanisms through which the facilitation of security occurs through time. Further, these events incited an epiphany among the American population and the US government: Modern threats arise quickly; they may be unexpected; and they may be violent. The effects of such events may be long lasting. They may also severely impede the immediate and short-term capacities of government and civilian response agencies.

Across the United States, significant resources have been directed to homeland security since the terrorist attacks of 2001. While the attacks of 2001 demonstrated national vulnerabilities to attack, the following decade awakened the nation to a deeper understanding of homeland security and threats that face the nation. Threats facing the United States today include not only the terrorism that struck the nation so deeply on September 11, 2001.

For many Americans who were born during the 1960s or before, the date that marked their first exposure to international terrorism was not September 11, 2001. Instead, it was another late summer day, almost 30 years earlier. On September 5, 1972, people from around the world were enjoying the second week of what had been a joyous and successful Olympics in Munich, Germany. US athletes, such as swimmer Mark Spitz, were winning medals and setting records. Suddenly, sports coverage was interrupted and replaced by much more serious news: Terrorists, from the Palestinian group Black September, had taken the Israeli Olympic team hostage. During a drama that played out live, broadcast over international TV, for the next several hours, German authorities attempted to resolve the crisis. Ultimately, after a botched rescue, 11 Israelis, 5 Palestinians, and 1 German police officer lay dead.[1]

Although many Americans have a narrow view of international terrorism, which conceptualizes a few groups or movements, that is not the reality. The US Department of State has designated 42 groups as foreign terrorist organizations and 4 countries as state supporters of terror.[2] Within this chapter, an overview of international terrorism is provided that includes how the US government defines it; how it designates groups and individuals as international terrorists; and the scope of modern, international terrorism. This chapter also examines various groups involved in international terrorism and includes discussions of their histories and motivations.

International terrorism defined

There is no universally accepted definition of terrorism. While definitions vary from agency to agency and nation to nation, intelligence and law enforcement agencies recognize that one way terrorism and terrorist activity can be viewed is as either domestic or international in nature and origin. The Federal Bureau of Investigation (FBI) defines international terrorism as that which occurs "primarily outside the territorial jurisdiction of the United States or transcend[s] national boundaries in terms of the means by which they are accomplished, the persons they appear intended to intimidate or coerce, or the locale in which their perpetrators operate or seek asylum."[3] Therefore, even though they occurred inside the United States, the FBI considers the attacks of September 11, 2001, to be acts of international terror because the origins of al Qaeda and its operations are primarily outside of US borders.

Designating a terrorist group as either domestic or international is not merely a matter of semantics—it has significant ramifications for those groups and individuals under investigation. For example, the FBI has two sets of guidelines, one for international groups and one for domestic ones, that outline the conditions under which investigations can be opened and carried out and the techniques permitted under each. The two sets of guidelines differ markedly. In addition, the State Department has the authority to restrict US financial activities for groups designated as foreign (international) terrorist entities. To place restrictions on an organization, the State Department must first designate an organization as a foreign terrorist organization before the United States Treasury can impose any financial sanctions.

Beginnings

Until the 20th century, most activities that could remotely be considered acts of international terrorism directed against the United States are better described as acts of war. These events include the burning of the White House by the British during the War of 1812 and the sinking of the USS *Maine* in Havana Harbor in 1898. The cause of the sinking of the USS *Maine* remains a source of controversy to this day. Despite two official inquiries and two major private investigations, a definitive explanation for the explosion that killed 266 US sailors has yet to emerge. The two leading theories suggest that either an external mine or an accidental coal fire sparked the conflagration.[4] During the 20th century, the Japanese bombing of Pearl Harbor qualifies as such an event.

The first acts that could reasonably be considered as international terror, inside the United States, came at the hands of the world anarchist movement and occurred with regularity in the early part of the 20th century. There was no distinction between international and domestic terrorism at this point in history. The acts of the anarchists are categorized as international because the movement had its intellectual genesis and conducted many of its first acts of violence overseas and because many of its actors within the United States were from outside the country. By 1914, anarchists began a series of bombings and violent activities that lasted through 1920. Numerous police departments, churches, and government buildings were targeted, which resulted in several deaths.[5]

As a response to these attacks, Attorney General A. Mitchell Palmer, himself a target of the anarchists, carried out a series of raids, between 1919 and 1921, against suspected subversives. Dubbed the Palmer Raids, they were led by a young attorney who worked at the Department of Justice named John Edgar Hoover. Hoover, who never lost his zeal for investigating suspected subversives, would later go on to serve as the director of the FBI from 1924 until 1972. Public support for the Palmer Raids soon diminished. With respect to modern connotations regarding responses, they are considered an overreaction by the federal government because numerous quantities of innocent people were arrested and deported.[6] Violent anarchist activity subsided in the United States after the Palmer Raids. From the 1920s until the 1970s, external terrorist threats to the United States consisted primarily of unsuccessful Nazi sabotage during World War II.

1972: A watershed year

Before 1972, the United States had plenty of opportunities to become acquainted with international terrorism from a distance. Israel, its strongest ally in the Middle East, had been the target of military and terrorist attacks since its founding in 1947, and longtime friend Great Britain had been violently victimized by the Irish Republican Army (IRA) throughout much of the 20th century.

Sensing that its natural borders and intelligence agencies would somehow keep it safe, America had been lulled into a false sense of security. Interestingly, it was not a direct attack on the US homeland that first caused the United States to seriously pay attention to international terrorist threats. Instead, it was the aforementioned Black September attack, against the Israelis, during the 1972 Olympics, that prompted heightened US concern.

Shortly after the attack, President Richard Nixon established the Office for Combating Terrorism, within the Department of State, to provide day-to-day counterterrorism coordination activities and to develop policy initiatives and responses for the United States government.[7] Since that time, international counterterrorism operations of the State Department have increased significantly. During modern times, the coordinator for counterterrorism oversees all State Department efforts aimed at countering international terrorism.

Starting in the 1970s, both the Central Intelligence Agency (CIA) and the FBI gradually expanded their roles in pursuing international terrorists. As the decade progressed, each agency realized the need to redirect more resources to counterterrorism. Beginning in the 1970s, the world was shaken by numerous terrorist events that were perpetrated by individuals and groups who promoted various causes. US interests were attacked with regularity overseas and occasionally within the United States. Finally, the 2001 terrorist attacks on the World Trade Center and Pentagon forcefully drove home the point that innocent Americans were vulnerable in their homeland. Natural barriers, law enforcement, and intelligence agencies were seemingly insufficient to keep the nation safe and unharmed.

The state department's list of foreign terrorist organizations

The laws of the United States require the secretary of state to provide Congress with an annual report that identifies countries and groups that the United States believes to be involved with international terrorism. This list is used to help craft sanctions, direct investigative and diplomatic efforts, and guide immigration policies. The two primary parts of the list are (1) state sponsors of terrorism and (2) US government designated foreign terrorist organizations. Taken together, this report provides the best listing of international terrorist threats facing the United States.

State sponsors of terror

Unless otherwise noted, information contained in this section was taken from the US Department of State. State sponsors of terror are those countries the State Department believes support terrorist groups and movements against US interests. Countries that finance and otherwise support terror are especially worrisome to the United States because they generally have access to significant funding, weapons, materials, and safe havens from which groups can operate. Also, some have the capability to manufacture weapons of mass destruction (WMDs). The State Department lists the following four countries as state sponsors of terror (listed in order of the date they were designated as such):

Syria (designated as a state sponsor of terrorism on December 29, 1979)—Syria continues its long-time support for terrorist organizations such as Hezbollah, the Islamic Resistance Movement (HAMAS), Palestinian Islamic Jihad (PIJ), the Popular Front for the Liberation of Palestine (PFLP), and the Popular Front for the Liberation of Palestine–General Command (PFLP-GC). Syria also stands accused of attempting to undermine Lebanon's sovereignty and security and is being investigated for involvement in the assassination of former Lebanese prime minister Rafiq Hariri in 2005. In addition, it is estimated that nearly 90% of all foreign terrorists known to be in Iraq used Syria as an entry point.

Cuba (designated as a state sponsor of terrorism on March 1, 1982)—The government of Cuba provides safe haven to individuals from such terrorist groups as the Basque Fatherland and Liberty (ETA) and the Revolutionary Armed Forces of Colombia (FARC). It also allows more than 70 US fugitives, some whom have murdered US citizens, to live legally in Cuba and has refused almost all US requests for their return.

Iran (designated as a state sponsor of terrorism on January 19, 1984)—Since the installation of a theocracy hostile to the United States in 1979, Iran has been considered an enemy of the United States. Recently, the State Department believes Iran has engaged in the following activities: (1) supported terrorist groups like HAMAS and Hezbollah; (2) provided logistical support, to include deadly explosively formed projectiles (EFPs), to anti-US militants in Iraq and Afghanistan; and (3) refused to turn over or identify senior al Qaeda militants currently detained in Iran.

Sudan (designated as a state sponsor of terrorism on August 12, 1993)—Despite its inclusion on the list, State Department officials have applauded recent efforts by Sudan to crack down on terrorist activity. However, al Qaeda–like groups, such as the PIJ, HAMAS, and the Lord's Resistance Army (LRA), continue to operate in Sudan. In 2011, after years of violence, the southern part of Sudan attained independence as the nation of South Sudan.

US government designated foreign terrorist organizations

Unless otherwise noted, information contained in this section was taken from United States Department of State.[8] Because of space limitations, not every group designated by the State Department as a terrorist organization is discussed within this textbook. However, readers who wish to learn more about these organizations are encouraged to consult the listing provided by the US Department of State.

Organizations within this list represent the most significant international terrorist threats challenging the United States. Unlike the countries listed above, which would likely not launch a direct attack against the United States for fear of retaliation, many of these groups show no such restraint. Although many of the organizations listed below have, to date, not attacked the United States, they have either expressed enmity toward US policies or those of our close allies or shown a willingness to indiscriminately engage in violence. Therefore, the State Department considers them a threat or potential threat. As of 2012, the United States Department of State had designated 51 organizations and groups as foreign terrorist organizations.

Palestinian groups

Although the re-formation of the state of Israel had always existed as a distant goal for many Jewish people over the years, it was not until 1898, when Austrian journalist Theodor Herzl published *Der Judenstaat* (*The Jewish State*), that a vision for the modern state of Israel emerged. However, after the end of World War II, the British, who controlled the area of Palestine, were weary of the terrorism directed at them by radical Zionist groups. Convinced that they would never settle the dispute between the Jews and Palestinians, Britain persuaded the newly formed United Nations to partition Palestine into two countries. One nation was designated as the Jewish state of Israel, whereas the other nation was to remain under Arab control.

Although this division was acceptable to the Jews, it was rejected immediately by the Palestinian people and all Arab countries in the region. As a result, war was immediately declared against Israel. In 1948, Arab armies invaded Israel, expecting to win a quick victory. Instead, Israel prevailed. Subsequent to that conflict, there were three other major wars between Israel and her Arab neighbors: the Sinai War (1956), the Six-Day War (1967), and the Yom Kippur War (1973). There were also numerous smaller conflicts. Over the years, Israel made peace with some Arab countries despite remaining, technically, at war with others. Many Palestinians, however, have never accepted the right of Israel to exist. They believe that their lands were stolen by the Zionists and have pledged to do whatever it takes to win them back, including engaging in terrorist and insurgent activities.

Palestinian terrorism can be viewed as a progression of various groups and movements. Over time, some embraced Communism, others pursued strictly nationalistic goals, and others adhered to a radical vision of Islam. Usually, each group begins with the premise that Israel must be destroyed and Palestine reestablished under Arab control. While many groups never have strayed far from this core concept, others, over the years, have recognized the Israeli right to exist and have engaged in peace talks.

The United States is a strong ally of Israel and provides it with money, arms, and other support. Often, the United States is the only country in the world to vote with Israel in the United Nations. As such, many Palestinians and other Arabs view the United States as an enemy almost as great as Israel. Therefore, while Palestinian groups generally do not directly attack US interests, officials worry that this situation could easily change, particularly if some sort of major catastrophe further befalls the Palestinians. Because of this reason, America's closeness to Israel, and the fact that Americans have died at the hands of Palestinian terrorists over the years, the State Department continues to include many Palestinian groups on its list of designated terrorist organizations.

During the 1970s and 1980s, Palestinian terrorist groups were among the most prolific in the world. Their activities included engaging in airline hijackings, bombings, and other acts of violence. Four of these groups, the Popular Liberation Front (PLF), the PFLP, the PFLP-GC, and the Abu Nidal Organization (ANO), remain on the State Department's list of designated terrorist organizations.

A new wrinkle in Palestinian terrorism involves the emergence of religiously based groups. Most of the groups that formed during the 1960s and 1970s were secular. Some groups considered themselves to be Marxist–Leninist and eschewed religion completely. However, during the 1970s, the PIJ, a group with a decidedly radical Islamic agenda, was formed. Its example provided the impetus for one of the most important Islamic-based organizations to emerge: the Islamic Resistance Movement, better known as HAMAS.

HAMAS was formed in 1987. It was largely an outgrowth of the Muslim Brotherhood, a Sunni Islamic group first established in Egypt in the 1920s. Before 2005, it engaged in numerous attacks against Israeli targets, which included mortar attacks, rocket attacks, and suicide bombings. However, while it continues to conduct attacks, any modern categorization of HAMAS as merely a terrorist group would be incorrect. In fact, it has a large political arm and engages in numerous educational, charitable, and service activities in the West Bank and Gaza. Although its military operatives number in the thousands, HAMAS enjoys wide support among many Palestinians. In 2006, it won a stunning victory against Yasser Arafat's party in the Palestinian parliamentary elections. Although Arafat died in 2004, his legacy continues to influence Palestinian politics. At one time, Arafat's popularity among his people was without peer. However, during his latter years, Arafat and Fatah were accused of corruption and mismanagement of the Palestinian National Authority (PNA). Many experts believe that this helped to facilitate the HAMAS victory in 2006.

The issues in the Israeli–Palestinian conflict are both complex and multifaceted. Any resolution to their disputes and issues shall not occur soon. Therefore, while the United States is generally not a primary target of Palestinian groups, it could easily become their target because of its close relationship with Israel.

Radical Islamic organizations

For many Americans, international terrorism starts and ends with al Qaeda. While it is true that the United States government sees al Qaeda and its leader, Osama bin Laden, as "Public Enemy #1," the State Department list above should make clear the fact that many violent, radical groups with an Islamic orientation exist in the world today. Many have little interest in attacking the United States and instead strive to replace the governments of the countries in which they exist with theocracies based on their interpretation of Islam.

A brief history of radical Islam

Many Americans are unsure whether Islam is a "violent" religion. This confusion necessitates the following query: Is there anything inherent in Islam that would logically convince its adherents to engage in acts of unspeakable violence, often against innocents? Columnist Fareed Zakaria made the following observation just after the 9/11 attacks:

> Nothing will be solved by searching for "true Islam" or quoting the Quran. The Quran is a vast, vague book, filled with poetry and contradictions (much like the Bible)....You can find in it condemnations of war and incitements to struggle, beautiful expressions of tolerance and stern strictures against unbelievers. Quotations from it usually tell us more about the person who selected the passages than about Islam.[9]

Religion is often used to justify violence, and radical Islam is not the only example of this concept. The Ku Klux Klan and other white supremacist groups have also developed their own interpretation of the Bible to justify their views regarding non-Aryan peoples. The vast majority of modern Muslims would no more clothe themselves with a suicide belt than would most Christians. Therefore, the following question may be posed: How did bin Laden and his followers arrive at their own peculiar version of Islam?

The origins of Islam

Like Judaism and Christianity, with whom it shares a common ancestry, Islam is a monotheistic religion. The history of Islam begins with Mohammed, whom Muslims believe to be God's final and most significant messenger on Earth. In AD 570, Mohammed was born in the Arabian trading town of Mecca. There was nothing in Mohammed's early life that suggested he would become a prophet. When he was 25, he married a wealthy 40-year-old widow. This arrangement allowed him to live as a prosperous businessman for a number of years. When Mohammed was 40 years of age, he was said to have begun receiving regular visits from the angel Gabriel. The teachings of Gabriel, as revealed to Mohammed, became the Quran, the holiest book in Islam, which Muslims believe to be the literal words of God.

Soon after Mohammed began to reveal these teachings to the people of Mecca, he was forced to flee to the city of Medina. However, by AD 624, Mohammed had gained a sufficient following to return to Mecca and challenge the town militarily. Initially, surprising victory was followed by defeat, and Mohammed was wounded during battle. However, during AD 629, Mohammed and his followers prevailed, and they returned triumphantly to Mecca. Mohammed remained in Mecca and continued to preach until his death in AD 632.

When he died, Mohammed had not designated a successor. Ultimately, there was considerable disagreement over who should rule the Muslim nation upon Mohammed's death. This situation created a schism that continues during modern times. Those who thought that Mohammed's successor should be elected became the Sunnis, while those who favored the appointment of Mohammed's closest male heir became the Shi'a. Islam spread very rapidly after the death of Mohammed. At its zenith, Muslim culture was unrivaled. At a time when Europe was mired in the Dark Ages, Islamic scholars were making contributions in all fields of endeavor, including mathematics, philosophy, science, medicine, and law. It is said by some that their contributions sped up the onset of the Enlightenment by several years.

Jihad

One of the most controversial aspects of Islam, even among Muslims, is the concept of jihad. Although many in the West translate the word as "holy war," its literal meaning is "struggle," and its practical meaning varies widely among Muslims. Mohammed was a man of both peace and war. His justification for engaging in warfare concerned the defense of the faith: Surely, God would not object to His followers engaging in a defensive war, provided they were not the aggressors and followed certain rules. During modern times, many Muslims view jihad from a perspective of it being the defense of the faith if Islam or the Muslim nation is attacked. Osama bin Laden uses this logic to justify his attacks on the United States. Certainly, many Muslims reject bin Laden's arguments. They emphasize that his wanton disregard for life, including the murder of innocents, is opposite to the true meaning of Islam.

However, among a significant number of Muslims, the importance of the lesser jihad (defensive warfare) is superseded by the greater jihad. This interpretation is indicative of a belief that jihad is the internal struggle that each Muslim endures to make himself a better Muslim. In this case, jihad has nothing to do with fighting an external enemy. Instead, it involves resisting the temptations of life and the inner demons that constantly strive to lead good Muslims off course.

The road to radicalism

Some trace the roots of al Qaeda all the way back to a 13th-century legal scholar and theologian named Taqi al-Din Ahmad ibn Taymiyya (usually known simply as Ibn Taymiyya). Taymiyya lived in Syria and adhered to a very stern version of Islam. He believed that anyone who disagreed with him were apostates and were traitors to Islam deserving of death (Esposito 2002). In the 18th century, an Arabian religious scholar, named Mohammed ibn Abd al-Wahhab, used Ibn Taymiyya as his spiritual model to preach a fiery version of Islam. Al-Wahhab and his religious visions might have come and gone like so many others, except for one fact: He aligned himself with a tribal chief named Mohammed ibn Saud, who later ruled the oil-rich nation of Saudi Arabia.

Al-Wahhab's teachings reached a wide audience. One who listened was a 20th-century Egyptian named Sayyid Qutb. Qutb served a 3-year assignment in the United States for the government of Egypt. Shocked by what he considered to be moral depravity, racial discrimination, and rampant materialism, he returned to Egypt in 1951. Upon his return, he assumed a significant role in the radical Muslim Brotherhood. This organization was determined to replace Egypt's secular government with one based on Islamic law (Esposito 2004). Among those whom he influenced was the Ayatollah Khomeini. In 1979, Khomeini later established an Iranian Islamic state after the ouster of the Shah, and for both Osama bin Laden and his right-hand man, Ayman al-Zawahiri, Qutb's treatise served as the blueprint for al Qaeda.

The birth of al Qaeda

After the Soviet Union invaded Afghanistan in 1979, many young Muslims globally heeded the call to fight against the Soviets. One of these recruits was the 17th child of a rich engineer who enjoyed a close relationship with the Saudi royal family: Osama bin Laden. During the 1980s, bin Laden formed an organization, the Maktab al-Khidimat (MAK), to globally recruit Islamic soldiers for the Afghan resistance. Bin Laden directly credited the defeat of the Soviets to the will of God.

In spite of American support for the Mujahideen, bin Laden was not a fan of the West. Taking his lead from Sayyid Qutb, bin Laden wanted nothing more than to rid Muslim countries of western influence. He was willing to accomplish this goal by any means necessary. After the Afghan war, bin Laden returned to Saudi Arabia, a country that granted permission for the United States to station troops inside the kingdom in preparation for the first Gulf War in 1990. Bin Laden was outraged because he considered infidels in the land of Islam's two most sacred sites (Mecca and Medina) tantamount to the invasion by the Crusaders in the 12th century. Adding to his anger was a sense of personal frustration and disappointment. As a response to the invasion of Kuwait, he had first approached the royal family with a plan to assemble an army of jihadists to oust the invading Iraqis, but his plan was summarily rejected. Soon, bin Laden was writing political tracts denouncing both the Americans and the Saudi royals.

Criticizing the Saudi royal family was a dangerous maneuver. In 1991, bin Laden was forced to flee from Saudi Arabia to Sudan, just ahead of the authorities. In 1992, he issued his first fatwa (religious decree) against America, principally for the "occupation" of Arab lands. He named his group "al Qaeda," which is Arabic for "the base." In 1994, Saudi Arabia revoked his citizenship.

By 1993, bin Laden was not the only radical Muslim to have the United States in his sights. On February 26, 1993, a bomb exploded in the basement of Tower One of the World Trade Center in New York City, and it killed 6 people and injured 1040 others. When one of the bombers attempted to retrieve the security deposit for the rental truck that was used in the bombing, he was arrested. The investigation quickly led to the apartment of a Pakistani named Ramzi Yousef. He was the nephew of Khalid Shaikh Mohammed, who would later help bin Laden plan the 9/11 attacks. Eventually, bin Laden was expelled from Sudan. He later visited Afghanistan as the guest of the Taliban regime. Supported and protected by the Taliban, he established training camps for Mujahideen from all over the world.

During the progression of the 1990s, bin Laden formulated ambitious plans to attack American interests. In 1998, al Qaeda operatives blew up United States embassies in Nairobi and Dar es Salaam. In what would become an al Qaeda signature, the embassies were attacked simultaneously by suicide bombers. Within these events, attacks occurred through the use of truck bombings that resulted in the deaths of over 200 individuals and the injuries of another 5000 people. Two years later, a small boat, carrying al Qaeda suicide bombers, exploded adjacent to an American Naval destroyer, the USS *Cole,* during a Yemeni port visit. This attack resulted in the deaths of 17 American sailors and almost sank the ship.

By the summer of 2001, American intelligence and law enforcement agencies were observing "chatter," or nonspecific communications, that convinced many that another al Qaeda attack was imminent. However, most experts believed that al Qaeda would strike American interests overseas as it had in 1998 and 2000.

Little did anyone realize that, by early September 2001, an al Qaeda attack team was emplaced within the United States and waiting to strike against the nation. The operational leader of the attack team was Mohammed Atta, an Egyptian engineer who spent many years in Germany. Atta led 18 others in a plot that was remarkable for its reliance on both simple and complex technologies and its keen understanding of American security procedures and protocols for airline hijackings.

The attacks of September 11, 2001, changed the way homeland security is viewed and approached in the United States. In late 2001, America embarked on "Operation Enduring Freedom," a joint military venture with Afghan dissidents, in which the Taliban government, which had supported and hosted bin Laden, was overthrown. The United States also created the Northern Command, a military unit dedicated to protecting US territory. In 2002, in direct response to the 9/11 attacks, several US government agencies were brought together in the newly created Department of Homeland Security. Perhaps most significantly, the United States and a small coalition of other countries invaded Iraq in 2003. The stated reason for this invasion was the belief that Iraq President Saddam Hussein had acquired or was attempting to acquire WMDs including nuclear weapons. It was assumed that Hussein intended to pass along these weapons to terrorist groups.

The al Qaeda attacks did not end with 9/11. In 2004, the organization attacked trains in Madrid, Spain, killing 191 individuals. Up to that point, Spain was an ally of the United States in Iraq. However, immediately after the bombings, a new Spanish government was elected. Among its first acts was the withdrawal of all Spanish troops from Iraq.

In 2005, a group with philosophical ties to al Qaeda, bombed trains in London, which resulted in the deaths of 57 individuals. Other bombings linked to al Qaeda include a 2007 attack in Algiers and a 2008 bombing at the Danish embassy in Pakistan. Al Qaeda also set up operations, within Iraq, to attack US troops following the invasion of 2003. For a time, al Qaeda enjoyed significant success in Iraq. However, in 2007, Sunni leaders began to turn against them, fearing that the group would attempt to install its harsh version of Islam if successful.

There is considerable debate regarding the true character of al Qaeda. Most experts agree that, as an organization, it was significantly weakened by US military and intelligence efforts. However, by late 2008, intelligence suggested that al Qaeda had reopened terrorist training camps within the largely ungoverned wilderness of northwestern Pakistan. This location was where bin Laden was believed to be hiding. Some believed that al Qaeda has regained its pre-9/11 strength.

Most experts agree that al Qaeda also exists as a movement in which bin Laden serves as a spiritual and political advisor. Although he does not directly command many of his adherents, they are expected to discern and follow his general principles, which include striking out at the United States wherever and whenever possible. Law enforcement officials are concerned about these "homegrown" terrorists who use bin Laden as a model. During recent years, al Qaeda–inspired cells have been discovered and broken up in such places as Lackawana, New York; and Miami, Florida. Additionally, many of the groups included within the State Department listing of terrorist organizations use al Qaeda as a model to oppose secular governments in their own countries.

Political and nationalistic attributes

During the 1960s, many terrorist groups had a Marxist orientation. Inspired by the revolution in Cuba, led by Fidel Castro during the 1950s, and supported and often funded by the Soviet Union, the goal of these groups was to overthrow the existing government in the countries in which they operated and replace it with one based on Socialist principles. Some of these groups have operated for years. For example, the ETA was founded in 1959. Its goal has been to oust the Spanish government from the Basque region in Spain and replace it with one based on Communism. Others are quite large and operate along the lines of armies. The FARC is estimated to have between 9000 and 12,000 "soldiers." It raises significant funds through kidnapping-for-profit and drug trafficking activities.

Not every group interested in overturning existing governments has a Marxist orientation. The Continuity Irish Republican Army (CIRA) and the Real IRA (RIRA) are descendants of the IRA. The IRA was originally formed during the early part of the 20th century to overthrow English rule of Ireland. Between 1919 and 1921, the IRA fought a brutal war against English forces. In 1921, England signed a truce with the IRA, which led to the establishment of an independent Irish state in all but the six northern counties of Ireland. The source of the conflict between England and Ireland was both political and religious. A majority of the Irish population was Catholic and favored independence, whereas the population in the northern part of the country was predominantly Protestant and desired to remain affiliated with England. In order to reach a compromise, the northern part of the country became the state of Northern Ireland and remained under British control.

This partition was disagreeable among Irish Catholic elements, who desired a single, independent state. Beginning in the 1960s, the IRA staged a series of violent attacks against British authorities in Northern Ireland. Eventually, both Protestants and Catholics mustered insurgent forces, which battled one another. IRA violence was not constrained to Ireland. Terrorists staged spectacular bombings in London and assassinated Louis Mountbatten, a popular member of the British royal family and hero of World War II.

Over the course of its existence, the IRA received much funding from Americans sympathetic to its cause. Eventually, the IRA signed a cease-fire with British authorities, which it has largely followed. However, the two groups included on the State Department list, the CIRA and the RIRA, do not recognize this cease-fire. In 1997, the RIRA was formed from disaffected members of the IRA. It continues to attack British authorities, using both guns and firebombs as weapons. The CIRA, which formed in 1994, is small, with perhaps 50 members. It also engages in small and sporadic attacks against authorities.

Although most Americans equate suicide bombers with al Qaeda or HAMAS, the Liberation Tigers of Tamil Eelam (LTTE or Tamil Tigers), a group at war with the Sri Lankan government, utilized this tactic well before either group. However, the LTTE is not an Islamic group. The LTTE was founded in 1976, and its goal is to acquire a Tamil homeland in the north and east of Sri Lanka. Its most famous attack occurred in 1991, when a female operative assassinated Indian Prime Minister Rajiv Gandhi in a suicide attack. During modern times, the LTTE is a formidable fighting force and has both an amphibious component and an air component. Its membership is estimated to number between 8000 and 10,000.

Other religious groups

As mentioned previously, radical Islamic groups are not the only religiously motivated organizations that embrace terrorism. Two others, Aum Shinrikyo and Kahane Chai, have also been placed on the State Department list. Established in Japan, in 1987, by blind acupuncturist Shoko Asahara, Aum Shinrikyo's philosophy is a mixture of Asahara's interpretation of Buddhism, yoga, Taoism, and other religious practices. Over the years, Asahara's goals have ranged from taking over Japan and the world to preparing his group for Armageddon, which he believes will be caused by the United States. On March 20, 1995, followers of Asahara released deadly sarin gas into the Tokyo subway system. This attack killed 12 people and injured thousands of others. Experts believe that the attacks would have been much deadlier had the group designed a better system for distributing the gas.

Kach and Kahane Chai are Jewish terrorist groups that operate primarily in the West Bank and Gaza strip, while enjoying support from some individuals in the United States. Kach was founded by radical Rabbi Meir Kahane during the 1970s. It advocated discrimination against Arabs and was blamed for various acts of violence aimed primarily at Arabs. In 1990, Kahane was assassinated after a speech in New York City. His son, Binyamin, founded Kahane Chai ("Kahane Lives") even as others took over Kach.

The special case of Hezbollah

In 1982, Hezbollah was formed as a response to the Israeli invasion of Lebanon. Unlike most other radical Islamic groups, Hezbollah is Shi'a and takes its ideological inspiration, along with significant logistical aid, from Iran. It also receives Syrian assistance and is operationally based in Lebanon. Americans probably know Hezbollah best as the organization that US authorities believe orchestrated the bombing of the US Marine barracks in Lebanon in 1983. This attack resulted in the deaths of 241 service personnel, and it prompted President Ronald Reagan to remove troops from Lebanon.

Although the United States, Canada, and Israel have designated Hezbollah as a terrorist organization, many Middle Eastern countries consider it to be a legitimate armed force. Indeed, Hezbollah has changed significantly over the years. In its early days, it behaved like many other terrorist entities because it implemented tactics involving suicide bombings, assassinations, and kidnappings. The modern version of the group possesses a significant arsenal of sophisticated weapons that include Katyusha rockets. The US Department of State has described Hezbollah as the most technically capable terrorist group in the world today.

Hezbollah has demonstrated its significant military capability. In both 2000 and 2006, its soldiers fought fierce battles against the Israeli Defense Force near Lebanon's border with Israel. On each occasion, Hezbollah did remarkably well, fighting the Israelis to a tactical standstill. Its military prowess is but one element of Hezbollah's capabilities. Evidence of its considerable political clout can be seen in its recent victories in Lebanon: It currently holds 14 elected seats in the 128-seat Lebanese National Assembly. Hezbollah continues to be fervently anti-Israeli and, by extension, fervently anti-American. In 2007, in Iraq, a high-ranking Hezbollah official was apprehended for providing training to Shi'a fighters. Because of its considerable capabilities and hatred toward the United States, American officials are deeply worried by Hezbollah. Some scholars claim that the War on Terror cannot be won until its terrorist inclinations are somehow curtailed.

The US border with Mexico, drug violence, and Mexican terrorism

Throughout the last half-century, terrorism influenced a variety of other nations. The preceding listing contains the events that primarily affected US interests. However, despite such an array of examples, numerous events occurred that were not listed. During the last decade, the violence of the US–Mexican border has increased dramatically. The Mexican drug conflict has affected law enforcement activities along the border and among the communities of both the United States and Mexico. Although the Mexican drug wars are primarily affiliated with drug cartels, the possibility of other international terrorist organizations infiltrating the US–Mexican border must not be discounted. The chief of the National Guard Bureau, General Craig McKinley, recognizes the dangers of the US–Mexican border through observing that "the link between terrorism and drug cartels along the United States' border with Mexico is increasingly clear" because of the financial associations between drug cartels, other criminal organizations, and terrorist organizations.[10] These observations are not insignificant regarding the security of America. The US–Mexican border represents a portal through which a variety of unwanted resources could enter the United States for the purposes of causing death and destruction within the American infrastructure. Therefore, considerations of border dangers must not be ignored.

The tactics of Mexican drug cartels are analogous to those of international terrorist organizations. Both organizations incite fear and attempt to modify the behavior of their targeted individuals and populations. Both organizations frequently employ kidnappings, threats, murders, bodily mutilations, bombings, grenade attacks, torture, beheadings, smuggling operations, tunneling, and fraudulent financing as tools through which they perpetrate their criminal activities. Both organizations desire political influence and control of government factions. Both organizations seek to operate with impunity.

These situations are extremely dangerous because they facilitate recruiting efforts, between organized crime and terrorist organizations, through which jihadists could be interjected within American society.[11] Numerous terrorist organizations have the potential of strategically partnering with Mexican organized crime factions financially and politically. Such collaboration is the framework through which terrorist organizations gain the capacity of logistically transporting both humans and materials for the purposes of terrorism. Through the use of networking and the creation of individual cells within America, such terrorist organizations strengthen the ability to strike inside the domestic United States. The US–Mexican border represents a dangerous intermediary through which such initiatives are facilitated and the goals of terrorist organizations are pursued.

Mexican Al Shabaab presence

According to Winter,[11] the US Department of Homeland Security alerted Texan "authorities to be on the lookout for a suspected member of the Somalia-based Al Shabaab terrorist group who might be attempting to travel to the U.S. through Mexico." The Al Shabaab organization espouses the implementation of Sharia law, is cooperating with al Qaeda, and has stated the intent to inflict harm against the United States. Winter also indicates that Al Shabaab recruits American Somalis for the purpose of traveling to Somalia, "where they are often radicalized by more extremist or operational anti-American terror groups, which Al Shabaab supports." If they return to the American society, these individuals represent significant risks of being actors among terrorist events.

In 2010, two indictments occurred regarding the smuggling of Somalis into the United States via the US–Mexican border. These indictments were issued against Ahmed Muhammed Dhakane and Anthony Joseph Tracy. The case against Dhakane involved his leadership of a Somali "human smuggling ring" that trafficked "East Africans, including Somalis with ties to terror groups," through the nation of Brazil and "across the Mexican border and into Texas." The case against Tracy involved his "alleged role in an international ring that illegally brought more than 200 Somalis across the Mexican border" through the use of a "Kenya-based travel business as a cover to fraudulently obtain Cuban travel documents for the Somalis."[11] The locations of these smuggled individuals are unknown, and they pose a significant security risk within American society. Their potentials for enacting events of terror raise concerns within both rural and urban areas of the United States as well as the international community.

In 2010, Nima Ali Yusuf, of San Diego, California, rendered assistance to Al Shabaab. According to Watson and Forliti,[12] Yusuf was the fourth person from San Diego who rendered assistance to Al Shabaab, and her radicalization may have occurred in Minnesota. This Minnesota association is pertinent because it is believed that approximately 20 individuals were radicalized in Minnesota and later provided assistance to Al Shabaab.[12] Given the distance between San Diego, California, located near the US–Mexican border, and Minnesota, such observations are salient regarding the networking ability of terrorist organizations within the borders of America. Such observations are also salient regarding the potential of Al Shabaab to penetrate the US–Mexican border and leverage these networks for the purposes of terrorism.

The case of Nima Ali Yusuf is not the only recent determination of international terrorist organizations gaining assistance within the domestic United States. According to Temple-Raston,[13] "the Department of Justice unsealed indictments charging 14 people with helping the group with everything from money to people; that seems to be only the beginning," and "in Minneapolis alone, there are 19 defendants." Temple-Raston indicates that "nine have been arrested, five have already pleaded guilty to terrorism charges and 10 are still at large."[13] Although arrests and indictments occurred, such scenarios are indicative of the capacity of international terrorists to permeate American society.

This dangerousness is recognized and acknowledged by the US government. According to Gurwitz,[14] US officials "cannot exclude the possibility that U.S. persons aligned with Al Shabaab in the Horn of Africa may return to the U.S., possibly to carry out acts of violence." The seriousness of this scenario must not be underestimated because Al Shabaab is a subset of al Qaeda. Given the demonstrated capacity of al Qaeda to strike the United States, it is imperative that the nation evaluate seriously the potential dangers posed by Al Shabaab and the dangerousness of the permeability of the US–Mexican border.

Mexican Hezbollah presence

The dangers of Al Shabaab are not the only concerns of international terrorism that involve the US–Mexican border. According to Phillips,[15] US senator Sue Myrick requested for "Department of Homeland Security head Janet Napolitano to investigate the Hezbollah's presence on the U.S.'s southern border, particularly in light of the increasing number of gang members arrested in southwestern states who have tattoos in Farsi."[15] In 2001, Kourani "paid to be smuggled across the US–Mexico border." The Anti-Defamation League highlights the association between Kourani and Hezbollah and indicates that Kourani provided "material support" for the terrorist organization.[16]

The comments of Senator Myrick also are commensurate with the findings of the Mexican government regarding the dangerousness of Hezbollah among the nations of Latin America. The nation of Mexico discovered and nullified the attempts of Hezbollah to implement a South American network. According to Khoury,[17] Jameel Nasr, a resident of Tijuana, Mexico, was arrested for assisting Hezbollah. During his period of assistance, Nasr "made frequent trips to other countries in Latin America, including a two-month stay in Venezuela in the summer of 2008." Such associations are indicative of the potential influences of Middle Eastern nations within the region of Latin America.[17]

During the time of the authorship of this textbook, the nation of Mexico is experiencing chaotic and lethal drug wars. Such factions of organized crime involve associations between drug trafficking and terrorist organizations. According to Myrick, "An indictment was handed down August 30, 2010 by the Southern District Court of New York that shows a connection between Hezbollah—the proxy army of Iran and a designated terrorist organization—and the drug cartels that violently plague the US–Mexico border." Myrick also observes that the tactics of drug organizations are becoming increasingly similar to the tactics of terrorist organizations. According to Myrick, after the arrest of Nasr, two car bombs exploded near the US–Mexican border. These bombings used cell phone detonations and were demonstrative of "an evolution in the tactics being used by the drug cartels and bear a strong resemblance to those employed by Hezbollah, raising questions as to who trained the cartels."[18]

Other tactics are comparable between Mexican drug organizations and terrorist organizations. According to the *Washington Times*, the Hezbollah organization uses the "same southern narcotics routes that Mexican drug kingpins do to smuggle drugs and people into the United States, reaping money to finance its operations and threatening U.S. national security." Although Hezbollah has operations among the nations of South America, it leverages the assistance of Mexican drug organizations to smuggle both humans and materials into the United States. In 2002, Mexican authorities sentenced Salim Boughader Mucharrafille, a "Mexican of Lebanese descent," who was a resident of Tijuana, to 60 years of imprisonment "for smuggling 200 people, said to include Hezbollah supporters, into the U.S." Such collaborations, between terrorist organizations and drug trafficking organizations, provide financial cash flows to support terrorism globally.[19]

This concept is not unnoticed by the US government. According to Gato and Windrem,[20] a variety of Middle Eastern individuals are often intercepted among illegal aliens who attempt to access America via the US–Mexican border. Associations exist between Hezbollah and South American nations (i.e., Paraguay, Argentina, and Brazil), and the nation of Mexico, along with other nations of Latin America, presents intermediary access to the United States. These relationships involve the movements of "large sums of money to militia leaders in the Middle East and [finance] training camps, propaganda operations and bomb attacks in South America"; they also pose a danger to the United States because "poorly patrolled borders and rampant corruption in the Tri-border region," among the nations of South America, "could make it easy for Hezbollah terrorists to infiltrate the southern U.S. border." This type of US infiltration could occur because terrorists have the capacity of "booking passage" through the nation of Brazil into Mexico and then entering the United States from the nation of Mexico "by posing as tourists."[20]

These observations are quite concerning regarding the security and safety of America. According to the US government, members of Hezbollah have already entered the United States via the US–Mexican border.[21] Because of the existing trade routes exploited by drug traffickers, terrorist organizations have the capacity of expanding their operations globally from the Middle East into the Western Hemisphere. Therefore, their ability to access the United States is increased substantially from both logistics and financial perspectives. The partnerships between organized crime and terrorist organizations present strategic considerations that must neither be ignored nor underestimated among US government entities, individual US states, and law enforcement organizations. Through leveraging these existing drug routes, terrorist organizations logistically gain the capacity to smuggle both humans and materials into the United States, thereby potentially instigating acts of terrorism within the American borders.

Mexican HAMAS presence

HAMAS is another terrorist organization that may leverage Mexican resources to access the United States. According to Mora,[22] the HAMAS organization also exploits Mexican and South American drug trafficking activities to support its financial requirements. Analogous to the activities of Hezbollah, within South America, HAMAS leverages drug trafficking activities, among the nations of Paraguay, Argentina, and Brazil, to finance its operations and perpetrate international terrorism. Although Hezbollah and HAMAS have presences within South America, Hezbollah is the dominant entity, whereas HAMAS is a secondary organization.[22] However, both organizations collaborate with organized crime to facilitate their terrorist strategies and tactics.

Terrorist organizations finance their activities through a variety of illegal methods among these nations. According to Levitt and Ross,[23] these methods include counterfeiting, "wire fraud, trademark violations, alien smuggling, harboring of illegal aliens, narcotics smuggling, and visa fraud." These illegal activities also transcend the US–Mexican border. According to Levitt and Ross, in 2004, a group of individuals in Los Angeles, California, was arrested for "violating state trademark regulations related to adulterated oil." The membership of this group was believed to have a relationship with HAMAS.[23] Additional arrests included "Omar Okour, Mahmoud Khalil, and Ziad Saleh for unlawful presence in the United States," and "Khalil and Saleh claim to have paid $10,000" to a Mexican smuggler for transporting them into the United States. Similar to Hezbollah, this example is demonstrative of the ability of terrorist organizations to penetrate the US–Mexican border.

This example is demonstrative of terrorist organizations leveraging the US–Mexican border to perpetrate criminal activities. These organizations have little respect for those whom they exploit and seek to access the United States internally. Terrorist organizations have attempted to internally harm the nation since September 11, 2001, but these attempts have been unsuccessful. However, there is no guarantee that any future attacks will be unsuccessful. Therefore, each of the border states and the federal government seriously examine the US–Mexican border as a dangerous intermediary for the perpetuating of terrorism.

Mexican al Qaeda presence

The events of the September 11, 2001, were demonstrations of the ability of international terrorists to permeate the borders of the nation, manipulate resources for its advantage, and perpetrate mass acts of terror that have altered both national policies and American lifestyles. Although the US–Mexican border was not the primary source of entry for these al Qaeda terrorists, their ability to transcend the US national boundaries was unprecedented with respect to the scope and magnitude of their terrorist acts of 2001. The results of their actions are not lingering, shadowy memories—each day, the American populace experiences a variety of policies, processes, and procedures that are the result of the terrorist acts of September 11, 2001.

During the years succeeding 2001, the al Qaeda organization has not relinquished or abandoned its goals of inflicting terror globally despite the current War on Terror. The United States remains a target of this organization. Therefore, it continuously seeks methods through which it may inflict terror within the United States, against US interests globally, and against American allies regardless of geographic location. Hence, the US–Mexican border must be considered as both a feasible and viable method through which access to the US mainland may be accomplished by this organization.

This consideration is not unnoticed within the United States. According to *The Washington Times*, in 2009, the threat of smuggling bioweapons across the US–Mexican border, by al Qaeda, for the purpose of a mass-casualty attack, was authenticated by US officials. This authentication substantiated the notion that al Qaeda continuously seeks to "exploit weaknesses in U.S. border security" and to ally itself with "anti-government" entities or hate groups domestically.[24] Although the threat was substantiated, no evidence was determined to be indicative of the organization's actual securing of weaponry. However, the potential of al Qaeda gaining access to the domestic United States via its border with Mexico and staging additional attacks must be considered seriously among homeland security and law enforcement agencies.

According to Whitaker,[25] the tactics involved within the Mexican drug wars are increasingly reflective of those tactics implemented by al Qaeda. In 2010, "43 people were indicted in San Diego for murder and kidnapping, including a Mexican government official" in conjunction with such violence. This violence involves the use of car bombings as tactics of drug organizations. According to Whitaker, a decoy person was used to lure first responders to the bomb and then to explode the bomb upon their arrival and inspection of the decoy. Whitaker indicates that such tactics are indicative of the methods used by the al Qaeda organization.[25]

Although this consideration involved a small-scale event, the goals of al Qaeda involve the implementing of large-scale, strategic attacks that rival or surpass the lethality of the events of September 11, 2001. In 2005, speculation regarding such attacks involved with respect to the "American Hiroshima" initiative. This initiative involved the smuggling of suitcase nuclear devices into the United States through the US–Mexican border and exploding these devices within urban areas of the domestic United States.[26] However, this initiative did not come to fruition. Nevertheless, such considerations of the potential of al Qaeda nuclear devices must not be discounted. According to Mowatt-Larssen,[27] in 2008, Ayman al-Zawahiri, a leader within the al Qaeda organization, issued a fatwa that advocated the use of WMDs, thereby providing the basis for an attack that is commensurate with the lethality of the events of September 11, 2001.[27]

The US border with Mexico represents a portal through which such devices could enter the nation. Therefore, US officials must be mindful of this danger and remain vigilant to deter any such events from occurring. However, given the declared intentions of al Qaeda, it must be noted that an al Qaeda presence was observed along the US–Mexican border during the years succeeding 2001. According to the Alabama Policy Institute,[48] an "al Qaeda operative was captured by Mexican officials and turned over to the Brewster County, Texas, sheriff's department." This individual was an Iraqi national, listed on the FBI's terrorist list, and he was tasked with conducting surveillance of the US–Mexican border.[28]

The dangerousness of the US–Mexican border encompasses organized crime, drug wars, and terrorist organizations. Although terrorist groups have not implemented an attack that rivals the events of 2001, it is not impossible for such events to occur again. The US border with Mexico represents a portal through which both al Qaeda personnel and materials may enter America. Because of the desire and demonstrated ability of al Qaeda to implement large-scale attacks of terror, the US–Mexican border must be considered as a resource through which such terrorism may be facilitated.

Drug cartels and violence

Gangs located on both sides of the Southern border of the United States present a homeland security threat to our nation. Drug-related violence in Mexico has claimed over 70,000 lives in the last decade as criminal organizations struggle to gain control of the lucrative drug business. Linked to the drug violence are other crimes including, but not limited to, weapons trafficking, kidnapping, sexual assault, theft, corruption of public officials, and of course, money laundering.

Mara Salvatrucha (MS-13), continues to expand its influence in the United States. FBI investigations reveal that it is present in almost every state and continues to grow its membership, now targeting younger recruits more than ever before. Members of Mara Salvatrucha, better known as MS-13, who are mostly Salvadoran nationals or first-generation Salvadoran Americans, but also Hondurans, Guatemalans, Mexicans, and other Central and South American immigrants.

MS-13 members engage in a wide range of criminal activity, including drug distribution, murder, rape, prostitution, robbery, home invasions, immigration offenses, kidnapping, carjackings/auto thefts, and vandalism. To counteract this growth, the FBI formed the MS-13 National Gang Task Force in December 2004. Based at FBI headquarters, this intelligence-driven task force combines the expertise, resources, and jurisdiction of federal agencies that investigate this violent international street gang. It focuses on maximizing the flow of information and intelligence, coordinating investigations nationally and internationally, and helping state and local law enforcement improve operations and prosecutions targeting MS-13.[29]

Law enforcement efforts to battle the threats

Law enforcement organizations constantly attempt to thwart the activities of international endangerments. The following sections provide a brief glimpse regarding these activities.

International Law Enforcement Academies

On October 22, 1995, President Clinton called for the establishment of a network of International Law Enforcement Academies (ILEAs) throughout the world to combat international drug trafficking, criminality, and terrorism through strengthened international cooperation. The United States and participating nations have expanded this program to include four ILEAs: Europe (Budapest), Africa (Gaborone), Central and South America (San Salvador), and Asia (Bangkok). A regional training center has also been established in Lima and an academic ILEA in Roswell, New Mexico. The ILEAs serve a broad range of foreign policy and law enforcement purposes for the United States and the world by supporting emerging democracies within the regions.[30]

International Narcotics and Law Enforcement Affairs Program

The Department of States's Bureau of International Narcotics and Law Enforcement Affairs (INL) advises the president, secretary of state, and other agencies within the US government on the development of policies and programs to combat international narcotics and crime. INL programs aim to reduce the entry of illegal drugs into the United States and minimize the impact of international crime on the United States and its citizens. INL's counternarcotics and anticrime programs also complement the war on terrorism, both directly and indirectly, by promoting modernization of and supporting operations by foreign criminal justice systems and law enforcement agencies charged with the counterterrorism mission.[31]

Central American Law Enforcement Exchange

The Central American Law Enforcement Exchange, known as CALEE, is a joint FBI and State Department initiative that brings US and Central American agencies together to share information and intelligence in the fight against the growing gang problem.[32]

Terrorism from Canada

Although the US–Canadian border is not engrossed in the violence and deadliness of a drug war, it is a method of entry into the domestic United States that must be considered as a resource that terrorist organizations may leverage to accomplish their goals and strategic pursuits. According to Leiken and Brooke, "Canada is the most worrisome terrorist point of entry, and al Qaeda training manuals advise agents to enter the U.S. through Canada rather than through France."[33] This observation highlights the dangerousness of the US–Canadian border with respect to the potentials of terrorist organizations seeking to inflict harm and damages against the United States.

In 1999, Ahmed Ressam, an Algerian terrorist, was captured when he attempted to cross the US–Canadian border, in Port Angeles, Washington, and had an allotment of explosives contained within his vehicle. Ressam was a member of a Canadian terrorist cell, based in Montreal, which was affiliated with the Armed Islamic Group (GIA) and al Qaeda organizations. This organization was planning a "millennium attack" at the Los Angeles International Airport. In 2001, Ressam was "convicted in Los Angeles of conspiracy to commit terrorism, document fraud and possession of deadly explosives." The investigation revealed that Canada is home to approximately 150 terrorist organizations.[34]

The event associated with Ressam is not the only instance of a terrorist presence within the nation of Canada. According to BBC News, in 2005, Abdullah Khadr, was arrested in Canada, per the request of the United States, for the purpose of extradition associated with charges of terrorism. These charges include "procuring weapons, including mine components and rocket-propelled grenades, for al Qaeda to use against coalition forces in Afghanistan. Khadr returned to Canada from Pakistan, and was arrested by the Royal Canadian Mounted Police." However, a Canadian judge refused the extradition of Khadr.[35]

These events are indicative of the potential lethality that is posed by the US–Canadian border. A variety of terrorist organizations have presences within the nation of Canada. According to the Anti-Defamation League,[34] "Islamic extremists and their supporters from al Qaeda, HAMAS, Islamic Jihad, Hezbollah, GIA, and Egyptian Islamic Jihad are among those suspected of operating in Canada." Given this observation, the US–Canadian border must be considered as a dangerous entry point for terrorist organizations seeking to inflict destruction within the United States.

Canadian al Qaeda presence

The al Qaeda organization has a Canadian presence. According to Levine,[36] in 2009, Mohammed Warsame, a Somali who later became a naturalized Canadian citizen, entered a court guilty plea regarding charges involving his assistance to the al Qaeda organization. In 2000, Warsame attended Afghani al Qaeda training and met with bin Laden. He later traveled to both Pakistan and Canada and facilitated the sharing of information among al Qaeda associates between 2002 and 2003.[36]

According to Vasudevan,[37] Canadian law enforcement authorities thwarted an al Qaeda plot to "blow up hydroelectric plants and transmission lines to hit the U.S."[37] This operation posed a serious threat to the United States because of the American dependency on Canada to provide various amounts of electric power within New York. This incident is indicative of the potential of terrorist organizations to strike the United States from inside the nation of Canada.

This incident is not the only Canadian terrorist operation. According to the CBC News, Fahim Ahmad received a sentence of 16 years of imprisonment for his participation within a terrorist group. He was guilty of assembling an al Qaeda type of terrorist cell and foundationally supported the creation of "two training camps in Ontario where he assessed recruits' ability to attack various targets in Toronto and Ottawa, including Parliament." A total of 18 individuals were charged with involvement in the terrorist activities of this group. However, "seven saw their charges dropped or stayed," and "four were found guilty and seven pleaded guilty."[49] According to French,[38] Zakaria Amara, the leader of the group, received a life sentence of imprisonment for his involvement within this terrorist organization. The Toronto 18 sought to "detonate truck bombs near targets such as the Toronto Stock Exchange, the CN Tower, an Ontario military base, and the Toronto offices of the national spy agency."[38]

According to the Anti-Defamation League,[34] "Egyptian-born longtime Canadian resident Ahmad Sa'id Al-Khadr left Toronto for Pakistan to become the regional coordinator for the Canadian-based Human Concern International, a charity that has allegedly diverted funds to al Qaeda." Al-Khadr was "detained by Pakistani authorities for his alleged involvement in the 1995 bombing of the Egyptian Embassy in Islamabad but was later released, reportedly, after the personal intercession of Canadian Prime Minister Jean Chretien."[34] However, in 2001, the "U.S. froze his assets and placed him on a list of nine al Qaeda members most wanted by the U.S."[34]

These events are representative of the reality of Canadian terrorism. Although the nations of the United States and Canada peaceably coexist, various terrorist factions seek to harm both nations internationally and domestically. Through leveraging the US–Canadian border, terrorist groups may perpetrate terrorist acts against not only the United States but also the nation of Canada. Therefore, the both the US and Canadian governments must be mindful of the potential ability of terrorists to incite significant damage within both nations.

Canadian HAMAS presence

The nation of Canada hosts the activities of other terrorist groups and organizations. According to the Anti-Defamation League,[34] in 2003, "the Israeli government announced that it had arrested in November a Palestinian-born Canadian man, Jamal Akkal, 23, who confessed to being recruited and trained by HAMAS' military wing in Gaza." The Anti-Defamation League further indicates that "Akkal reportedly had orders to kill Israeli officials and Jews in Canada and the U.S."

Other aspects of HAMAS must be considered within the context of the Canadian nation. In 2009, the nation of Canada banned George Galloway, a British lawmaker, from entering the nation because it deemed him as a security risk. According to the Associated Press,[39] Galloway was denied access to Canada because of statements alleging his provision of financial support for HAMAS and because of his allegedly supporting Taliban endeavors. However, Benari[40] indicates that the Canadian officials relented and allowed Galloway to enter the Canadian nation, where he appeared in a variety of public venues.

HAMAS has used the Canadian nation as a monetary resource through which it financed its international terrorist activities and Canadian terror activities. Before the 2002 banning of the Holy Land Foundation in Canada, it fraudulently obtained charitable Canadian donations. According to the Anti-Defamation League,[34] the Holy Land Foundation "raised hundreds of thousands of dollars in Canada." This observation is salient regarding the ability of HAMAS to secure fraudulent Canadian financing among its operations.

The presence of HAMAS among Canadian settings is demonstrative of its global capacity as a terrorist organization and potential to obtain resources to facilitate acts of terror globally. Regardless of whether these resources are human, material, or financial, the presence of HAMAS within Canada must not be understated or downplayed by the Canadian or the US government.

Canadian Hezbollah presence

Hezbollah is another terrorist organization that manifests a Canadian presence. Again, analogous to the descriptions of the preceding terrorist organizations, Hezbollah demonstrates a global capacity for financing its operations, distributing its resources, and cultivating supportiveness among nations and peoples. The nation of Canada is not insusceptible to the presence of Hezbollah and its activities of terrorism. A variety of events and activities highlight the presence of Hezbollah within Canada. According to the Anti-Defamation League,[34] the nation of Canada is a significant origin of Hezbollah funding. Canada is also a significant aspect of Hezbollah recruitment and is a "key component of the group's international network." Such activities involve a myriad of crimes that support the organization globally.

According to Hagmann,[41] within Canada, Hezbollah "raises money, recruits terrorists, purchases military supplies, and forges travel documents in Canada," and that "money is raised in Canada in much the same fashion as in the Unites States—through credit card scams and counterfeit rings." Hagmann[41] also indicates that "in two cases, alleged Hezbollah agents wanted for terrorist activities overseas were found hiding in Canada" and that "Hezbollah theft rings have stolen luxury cars in Canada and sent them to Lebanon for use by senior Hezbollah officials." These activities are representative of the global capacity to launder money and logistical capacity of transporting materials that support the initiatives of Hezbollah.

In 2002, a Hezbollah presence impacted both the nations of Canada and the United States. According to the Anti-Defamation League,[34] the following event transpired:

> Two members of a North Carolina–based Hezbollah terror cell were convicted of providing material support to the terrorist organization. Their cell was part of a larger Hezbollah network that raised funds and procured dual-use technologies for Hezbollah. The Canadian part of the network was allegedly run by Mohammed Hassan Dbouk and his brother-in-law Ali Adham Amhaz, who allegedly received money from Hezbollah officials in Lebanon and engaged in credit card and banking scams in Canada in order to finance the purchase in Canada and the U.S. of night-vision goggles, global positioning systems, stun guns, laser range finders and other military items which were then smuggled into Lebanon. Amhaz was indicted in North Carolina in March 2001 on charges of providing material support to Hezbollah. In October 2001, Canadian authorities arrested him based on an American arrest warrant calling for his extradition. Amhaz was freed in December 2001 after the U.S. dropped the arrest warrant; the U.S. indictment against him still stands. Dbouk fled to Lebanon.

In 2008, much speculation occurred regarding the potential of a Hezbollah terrorist attack involving Canadian sleeper terrorist cells. According to Esposito and Ross,[42] Hezbollah associates "conducted recent surveillance on the Israeli embassy in Ottawa, Canada and on several synagogues in Toronto." It was assumed that these activities were precursors for retaliatory attacks as revenge for the assassination of Imad Mugniyah. Mugniyah was a Hezbollah military commander. The Hezbollah organization instructed its members to send their families home to Lebanon, and "as many as four sleeper cells were activated." These activities also witnessed the presence of high-level "Hezbollah weapons experts" in Canada and were coordinated with the assistance of the Iranian Revolutionary Guard.[42] However, despite these activities, no attack came to fruition.

Additional Hezbollah initiatives were manifested in 2009. According to Bell,[43] in 2009, Hezbollah conducted intelligence operations within Canada as potential measures involving any conflict with the nations of the Western Hemisphere. These activities could have been "rearming and recruiting" efforts to prepare for war with Israel and as preparatory measures for any attack against the nuclear infrastructure of Iran.[43] The Iranian nuclear sites were not attacked, and a Hezbollah response was never manifested.

These activities are indicative of a strong Hezbollah presence in Canada. The dangerousness of a Canadian Hezbollah presence must be considered seriously as a threat to the security of both the United States and Canada. Although Hezbollah is determined to be a terrorist organization by both nations, its influence exists within both the United States and Canada. Its ability to garner supportiveness and raise both financial and material capital must not be discounted by either government.

Canadian Tamil Tigers presence

Another terrorist organization impacting Canada is the LTTE (i.e., Tamil Tigers). According to the Anti-Defamation League, the nation of "Sri Lanka is Canada's leading source of refugees." Further, an estimated 250,000 Tamils exist within Canada, and Toronto, boasting an estimated 200,000 Tamils, is the "largest Tamil city outside of Sri Lanka." The Anti-Defamation

League indicates, "Canadian intelligence believes that there are 8,000 former LTTE guerrillas in Toronto."[34]

Similar to the efforts of other terrorist organizations, the LTTE obtains a significant amount of funding in Canada. It is estimated that the LTTE obtains approximately $120 million annually, and approximately "a quarter of this amount" is derived from Canadian sources. The methods of LTTE funding within Canada include "donations, organized crime, and LTTE front organizations" in addition to the illegal functions of "drug trafficking, human smuggling and passport forgery and fraud." The financing capacity of LTTE is acknowledged as being the "most sophisticated of any terrorist organization" operating within the nation of Canada.[34]

Canada banned the LTTE organization in 2006. Despite the Canadian ban against the LTTE and other terrorist organizations, suspected terrorists affiliated with such organizations continue to enter the nation. In 2010, much debate occurred regarding the influx of Tamils into Canada. During the period of the authorship of this textbook, debate is occurring regarding whether the maritime arrival of a cargo ship, manifesting an estimated "200 Sri Lankans, toward British Columbia, is being managed by the Tamil Tigers" because the vessel "may be carrying a number of its members."[44] The LTTE was devastated by Sri Lankan forces during 2009 conflicts. These debates are concerned with whether these arrivals of refugees are truly seeking asylum or are clandestinely hoping to perpetrate terrorist functions. Fears regarding the influx of refugees also involve considerations that the group may be attempting to re-form itself using Canada as a base of operations.

Although the 2009 conflict between Sri Lanka and the LTTE resulted in an LTTE defeat, the group may be seeking to establish some method of reinvigorating itself using Canadian resources. During the time of the authorship of this textbook, no resolution has occurred regarding the debates concerning whether refugees are truly seeking asylum or are terrorist entities seeking to revive their organization. Only time and experience shall divulge the underlying intentions of such refugees. Regardless, the presence of LTTE survivors presents a dangerous scenario for Canadian and American authorities.

International ecoterrorism

The preceding chapters considered the definition and concept of ecoterrorism. Within these chapters, a variety of organizations, such as the Animal Liberation Front (ALF) and the Earth Liberation Front (ELF), were highlighted as terrorist organizations whose ideologies emphasized either animalistic or environmental tenets. Therefore, a lengthy discourse regarding these ecoterrorist entities shall not be repeated within this chapter. However, additional considerations of the international characteristics of ecoterrorist activities are briefly delineated within this chapter.

Within the United States, ecoterrorism is identified as a primary threat that impacts national security and safety. Although the ALF and ELF conduct land-based operations against their targets, organizations exist that perpetrate ecoterror crimes along oceanic sea-lanes. In 2008, the nation of Japan accused Animal Planet, a US television network, of crimes associated with ecoterrorism. These accusations involved activities that occurred during the filming of the voyages of "ships owned and operated by the militant animal rights group, Sea Shepherd Conservation Society (SSCS), as it launched a series of criminal attacks on the high seas in January, February, and March 2008 against vessels operated" by the Institute of Cetacean Research (ICR). The tactics of the SSCS involve "sabotage fishing operations by attacking vessels at sea beyond national boundaries, thereby avoiding prosecution." In 2008, the SSCS implemented "propeller fouling devices constructed from steel cables, throwing acid, smoke bombs, and bottles onto the decks of the ICR vessels and attempted collisions," and it also "welded a seven foot steel blade to its ships to open the hulls of the vessels it attacked."[45] Such events were televised during Animal Planet television programs.

The forms of ecoterrorism vary and are not limited to any solitary domain of environmentalism. Among a variety of global markets, the prices of natural resources are affected by acts of ecoterrorism. Within the Nigerian Niger Delta, "insurgent groups" have influenced oil prices through the destruction of "flow stations and other industrial installations." Further, Onduku[46] indicates that expatriates employed within the oil industry of the region are the victims of kidnappings, thereby inciting oil corporations to relocate their operations among neighboring nations because of such "insecurity." Further, according to Onduku, "although Nigeria is the world's eighth largest oil exporter, the bombings of oil platforms and kidnappings of oil workers have cut Nigerian production by a fifth since early 2006, helping push world oil prices to record highs."[46] Given these observations, crimes of ecoterrorism have the potential of impacting national security because of the prices associated with petroleum products.

A salient consideration of ecoterrorists involves the basic premise of ecoterrorism. Many of the tenets of ecoterrorist organizations espouse the notion that the actions and functions of humans are damaging and harmful to the earth and its animal inhabitants and that such harmful actions and functions must be terminated. This notion was espoused during the recent Discovery Channel hostage crises, when Jason Jay Lee held hostage several employees of the corporation before he was killed by police.[47] This ideology is not limited to any one nation or geographic location. Instead, it has the capacity to permeate all nations globally, thereby facilitating international crimes of ecoterrorism.

Conclusion

Hundreds of billions of dollars have been spent on homeland security since September 11, 2001, and numerous models have been developed to study the strategic interactions between defenders and adversaries (e.g., attackers or terrorists). Unfortunately, few if any models have yet been validated using empirical data, limiting the application of those models in practice, but what we do know is that we are in an on-going struggle. While most experts believe that the greatest terrorist threat facing the United States today comes from international organizations, the threats posed by domestic terrorist groups present a real danger. Additionally, the violence along the United States and Mexican border is real and not only threatens the security of both nations but also poses a regional danger as its influence continues to spread.

Our struggle with international terrorism continues. Though bin Laden is dead, his influence continues. Al Qaeda has now morphed into a "loose jihadist ideological movement" that spawned the Boston marathon bombing, Bergen said, and it is this "Binladenism" that is still very much a threat to Americans.[50]

As the primary government agency dealing with international relations and diplomacy, the State Department is responsible for designating which organizations and countries pose the greatest terrorist threat to America. Therefore, the State Department lists four countries that it believes support terrorism worldwide: Sudan, Cuba, Iran, and Syria. A much longer list includes those groups that have been designated as foreign terrorist organizations. This can have significant impact on a group, including making it a crime to support it logistically or financially. Although many groups, involving a variety of different orientations, exist within the State Department list, they may be categorized with respect to the different ideologies or movements they represent.

Palestinian groups, in general, oppose the right of the state of Israel to exist. Because the United States is a staunch ally of Israel, many of these groups also pose a potential threat to America. Some groups have attacked US interests, including murdering its citizens. Palestinian terrorism has changed greatly over the years, as some groups that once engaged in acts of significant violence now recognize Israel's right to exist. Palestinian terrorism was especially extreme in the 1970s and 1980s. During that time, attacks were mounted against cruise ships, airliners, buses, and other public institutions. Possibly the most infamous attack occurred during the 1972 Munich Olympics, when Black September massacred the Israeli Olympic team. Palestinian groups on the State Department list include HAMAS and the PFLP.

Justifying violence based on views of Islam, which encompasses several centuries, radical Islamic groups such as al Qaeda, demonstrate a ruthless disregard for civilian or even Muslim lives. Inspiration for this movement comes from the Iranian revolution of 1979 and the victory of the Mujahideen over the Soviet Army in Afghanistan during the 1980s. Such Islamic terrorist organizations continue to impact the world through their sponsorship of a variety of terrorist functions.

Other international groups have a nationalist orientation, seeking to overthrow the governments of the countries in which they operate. Some of these groups, like the FARC in Colombia and the Shining Path in Peru, have a Marxist/Maoist/leftist orientation. Therefore, they wish to replace current governments with Communism or Socialism. Additional organizations, such as the RIRA and LTTE, are primarily interested in independence and self-rule. Two non-Islamic religious groups also appear on the list: Aum Shinrikyo, a group that released sarin gas in the Tokyo subway system in 1995, and Kahane Chai (Kach), a radical Jewish movement that has attacked Arabs throughout the world.

Perhaps the most capable terrorist group in the world today is Hezbollah, a Lebanese-based Shi'a organization that receives support from both Iran and Syria. Hezbollah has attacked American interests and has demonstrated a significant military capability in its mini-wars with Israel. It also holds significant political clout, with 14 of its members serving in the Lebanese National Assembly.

Previous chapters have discussed the phenomenon of globalization, or the "shrinking" of the world. This concept means that the capability of international groups to strike inside the United States is at an all-time high. Globalization will continue to pose a major challenge for those entrusted with the responsibility of keeping America safe. Striking the right balance between safety and openness is a daunting, but essential, task.

The United States shares its national boundaries with the nations of Canada and Mexico. These borders present national security concerns for all three nations. Within Canada, active presences of al Qaeda, HAMAS, Islamic Jihad, Hezbollah, GIA, Egyptian Islamic Jihad, and the Tamil Tigers form the basis of a dangerous environment that is supportive of terrorist entities. Within Mexico, the influences of drug cartels, coupled with the influences of HAMAS and Hezbollah, are problematic and form the basis of environments that are supportive of terrorism. Given these observations, it is evident that the Western Hemisphere manifests a variety of dangers and threats that infringe upon US national security and the safety of American society.

Although ecoterrorism is not based upon religious ideology, it does espouse ideological tenets that denote humanity as a harmful entity to the earth and its animal inhabitants. Both the ALF and the ELF are examples of organizations whose origins transcend national boundaries. Ecoterrorism is not limited to land-based crimes. Instead, maritime aspects of ecoterrorism also impact nations. Ecoterrorism has the potential of transcending national borders and affecting national security.

Key terms

Al Qaeda
Border
Ecoterrorism
Gang
HAMAS
Hezbollah
International collaboration
International terrorism
Jihad
Organized crime
Radicalism
State sponsor of terror
Tactics
Tamil Tigers
Terrorist organization

QUESTIONS FOR DISCUSSION

1. This chapter introduces a variety of international terrorist organizations representing a variety of different ideologies. Do some research, and identify two other terrorist organizations that are not contained herein. Write a brief essay that describes the characteristics of your discovered organizations.
2. State sponsors of terror endanger international society. Do some research, and determine how US foreign policy addresses various issues associated with state sponsors of terror. Write a brief essay that highlights your findings.
3. Gang violence often employs terrorist tactics. Do some research, and determine how terrorist tactics are used during gang violence. Given your findings, what suggestions do you have to counter these activities? Write a brief essay that summarizes and substantiates your opinion.
4. Gangs are an ever-increasing problem that affects US society adversely. Do some research, and determine how your locality is impacted by gang activities. Given your findings, what suggestions do you have to counter these activities? Write a brief essay that summarizes and substantiates your opinion.

References

1. Beyer, L. (December 2005). The myths and reality of Munich. *Time Australia*, *49*, 24.
2. United States Department of State. (2008). State sponsors of terrorism overview: country reports on terrorism, 2007. http://www.state.gov/s/ct/rls/crt/2007/103711.htm (accessed September 6, 2009).
3. Federal Bureau of Investigation. (n.d.). Terrorism 2000/2001. http://www.fbi.gov/publications/terror/terror2000_2001.htm (accessed August 6, 2008).
4. Allen, T.B. (Ed.). (1998). What really sank the Maine? *Naval History*, *11*, 30–39.
5. Baily, T.A. and Kennedy, D.M. (1994). *The American Pageant* (10th ed.). Washington, D.C.: Heath and Company.

6. Murray, R.K. (1955). *The Red Scare*. Westport: University of Minnesota Press.
7. United States Department of State. (n.d.). Office of the coordinator for counterterrorism. http://www.state.gov/s/ct/on 09/06/2008 (accessed September 8, 2008).
8. United States Department of State. (2008). Terrorist organizations: country reports on terrorism, 2007. http://www.state.gov/s/ct/rls/crt/2007/103714.htm (accessed September 6, 2008).
9. Zakaria, F. (October 15, 2001). The politics of rage: why do they hate us? *Newsweek*. http://www.fareedzakaria.com/articles/newsweek/101501_why.html (accessed August 18, 2005).
10. General. (2010). General: drug cartels linked to terrorism. *United Press International*. http://www.upi.com/Top_News/Special/2009/03/09/General-Drug-cartels-linked-to-terrorism/UPI-23681236628976/ (accessed November 19, 2010).
11. Winter, J. (2010). Feds issue terror watch for the Texas/Mexico border. *FOX News*. http://www.foxnews.com/us/2010/05/26/terror-alert-mexican-border/ (accessed November 18, 2010).
12. Watson, J. and Forliti, A. (2010). California woman accused of aiding Somali terrorists. http://www.kansas.com/2010/11/16/1590852/california-woman-accused-of-aiding.html (accessed November 20, 2010).
13. Temple-Raston, D. (2010). Al-Shabaab becomes magnet for would-be jihadists. http://www.npr.org/templates/story/story.php?storyId=129021164 (accessed November 20, 2010).
14. Gurwitz, J. (2010). Border security must be viewed with an eye on terrorists. http://www.mysanantonio.com/opinion/columnists/jonathan_gurwitz/border_security_must_be_viewed_with_an_eye_on_terrorists_98634369.html (accessed November 20, 2010).
15. Phillips, J. (2010). Hezbollah in Mexico stocking terrorism fears. http://motherjones.com/mojo/2010/08/hezbollahs-mexican-cartel-connection (accessed November 19, 2010).
16. Dearborn. (2005). Dearborn man pleads guilty to supporting Hezbollah. *Anti-Defamation League*. http://www.adl.org/main_Terrorism/tnews_dearborn_40105.htm (accessed November 20, 2010).
17. Khoury, J. (2010). Mexico thwarts Hezbollah bid to set up south American network. http://www.haaretz.com/news/diplomacy-defense/mexico-thwarts-hezbollah-bid-to-set-up-south-american-network-1.300360 (accessed November 20, 2010).
18. Myrick, S. (2010). Hezbollah car bombs on our border. *The Washington Times*. http://www.washingtontimes.com/news/2010/sep/1/hezbollah-car-bombs-on-our-border/ (accessed November 20, 2010).
19. Hezbollah Uses. (2009). Hezbollah uses Mexican drug routes into U.S. *The Washington Times*. http://www.washingtontimes.com/news/2009/mar/27/hezbollah-uses-mexican-drug-routes-into-us/ (accessed November 20, 2010).
20. Gato, P. and Windrem, R. (2007). Hezbollah builds a western base. *MSNBC*. http://www.msnbc.msn.com/id/17874369/ns/world_news-americas (accessed November 20, 2010).
21. McCaul, M. (n.d.). A line in the sand: confronting the threat at the southwest border. *Majority Staff of the House Committee on Homeland Security Subcommittee on Investigations*. http://www.house.gov/sites/members/tx10_mccaul/pdf/Investigaions-Border-Report.pdf (accessed November 21, 2010).
22. Mora, E. (2010). Hezbollah, Hamas raise money for 'terrorist activities' from drug trade in south America. http://www.cnsnews.com/news/article/67377 (accessed November 20, 2010).
23. Levitt, M. and Ross, D. (2006). *Hamas: Politics, Charity, and Terrorism in the Service of Jihad*. Washington, D.C.: The Washington Institute for Near East Policy.
24. Al Qaeda Eyes. (2009). Al Qaeda eyes bio attack from Mexico. *The Washington Times*. http://www.washingtontimes.com/news/2009/jun/03/al-qaeda-eyes-bio-attack-via-mexico-border/ (accessed November 21, 2010).
25. Whitaker, B. (2010). Mexico's drug war adopts al Qaeda tactics. *CBS News*. http://www.cbsnews.com/stories/2010/07/23/eveningnews/main6707471.shtml (accessed November 21, 2010).
26. Farah, J. (2005). Al-Qaeda nukes already in U.S. http://www.wnd.com/?pageId=31232 (accessed November 21, 2010).
27. Mowatt-Larssen, R. (2010). Al Qaeda's nuclear ambitions. *Foreign Policy*. http://www.foreignpolicy.com/articles/2010/11/16/al_qaedas_nuclear_ambitions (accessed November 21, 2010).
28. Al-Qaida Operative. (2005). Al-Qaida operative nabbed near Mexican border. *Newsmax.com*. http://archive.newsmax.com/archives/ic/2005/11/20/151654.shtml (accessed November 21, 2010).
29. The MS-13 threat: a national assessment. *The Federal Bureau of Investigation*. http://www.fbi.gov/news/stories/2008/january/ms13_011408 (accessed May 1, 2013).
30. International Law Enforcement Academy (ILEA) program overview. *CBP.gov*. http://www.cbp.gov/xp/cgov/border_security/international_operations/international_training/law_enforce.xml (accessed May 1, 2013).
31. International Narcotics and Law Enforcement Affairs (INL) program. *CBP.gov*. http://www.cbp.gov/xp/cgov/border_security/international_operations/international_training/inl.xml (accessed May 1, 2013).

32. United against MS-13, our Central American partnerships. (2009). *Federal Bureau of Investigation.* http://www.fbi.gov/news/stories/2009/november/calee_111009 (accessed April 28, 2013).
33. Leiken, R. and Brooke, S. (2006). The quantitative analysis of terrorism and immigration: an initial exploration. *Terrorism and Political Violence, 18*(4), 503–521.
34. Canada. (2004). Canada and terrorism. *Anti-Defamation League.* http://www.adl.org/terror/tu/tu_0401_canada.asp (accessed November 21, 2010).
35. Canadian Accused. (2010). Canadian accused of buying weapons for al Qaeda freed. *BBC News.* http://www.bbc.co.uk/news/world-us-canada-10875652 (accessed November 20, 2010).
36. Levine, M. (2010). Feds deport al Qaeda associate to Canada. http://liveshots.blogs.foxnews.com/2010/10/08/feds-deport-al-qaeda-associate-to-canada/ (accessed November 21, 2010).
37. Vasudevan, R. (2010). Al-Qaeda bombing plot in Canada busted. *Asian Tribune.* http://www.asiantribune.com/news/2010/08/27/al-qaeda-bombing-plot-canada-busted (accessed November 21, 2010).
38. French, C. (2010). Toronto 18 mastermind gets life for bomb plot. http://www.reuters.com/article/idUS TRE60H3PN20100118 (accessed November 21, 2010).
39. Canada Bans. (2009). Canada bans British lawmaker for financing Hamas. *Associated Press.* http://www.foxnews.com/story/0,2933,509957,00.html (accessed November 21, 2010).
40. Benari, E. (2010). Canada backtracks and lets pro-Hamas Galloway in country. http://www.israelnationalnews.com/News/news.aspx/140690 (accessed November 21, 2010).
41. Hagmann, D. (2006). Confirmed: Hezbollah terror operatives, "sleeper cells" poised in the U.S. *Canada Free Press.* http://www.canadafreepress.com/2006/hagmann071806.htm (accessed November 21, 2010).
42. Esposito, R. and Ross, B. (2008). Exclusive: Hezbollah poised to strike? *ABC News.* http://abcnews.go.com/Blotter/story?id=5203570&page=1 (accessed November 21, 2010).
43. Bell, S. (2009). Canada may be terror target. *National Post.* http://www.nationalpost.com/news/story.html?id=1818339 (accessed November 21, 2010).
44. Ship Nearing. (2010). Ship nearing Canada run by Tamil Tigers: expert. *CTV News.* http://www.ctv.ca/CTVNews/TopStories/20100810/sri-lankans-ship-100810/ (accessed November 21, 2010).
45. BYM. (2008). *BYM Marine Environment News.* http://www.bymnews.com/news/newsDetails.php?id=45087 (accessed November 21, 2010).
46. Onduku, A. (2008). The global repercussions of Nigeria's Niger delta insurgency. http://www.jamestown.org/programs/gta/single/?tx_ttnews[tt_news]=5082&tx_ttnews[backPid]=167&no_cache=1 (accessed November 21, 2010).
47. Unruh, B. (2010). Eco-terrorist pursued 'core manifesto' of 'green' movement. http://www.wnd.com/?pageId=198433 (accessed November 18, 2010).
48. Alabama Policy Institute. (2010). Sessions' border security bill will protect U.S. http://www.alabamapolicy.org/gary_blog/article.php?id_art=175 (accessed November 20, 2010).
49. Toronto 18. (2010). Toronto 18 ringleader gets 16 years. *CBC News.* http://www.cbc.ca/canada/toronto/story/2010/10/25/toronto-toronto-18-terrorism-sentence.html (accessed November 20, 2010).
50. Bergen, P. (2013). From bin Laden to Boston. *CNN News,* http://www.cnn.com/2013/04/30/opinion/bergen-bin-ladenism (accessed August 26, 2013).

Domestic Threats, Threat Groups, and Terrorism

The Folk, namely the members of the race, are the Nation. Racial loyalties must always supersede geographical and national boundaries. If this is taught and understood, it will end fratricidal wars. Wars must not be fought for the benefit of another race.[56]

Aryan Nations Web site

Chapter objectives:

- Understand the issues created by domestic threat groups in relation to domestic terrorism
- Recognize the diversity of domestic threat groups
- Explore the history and origins of domestic threat groups

Introduction

Domestic-related fringe and hate groups pose a threat not only to law enforcement and governmental authorities but also to citizens in general. While the United States embraces diversity, fringe elements, those who use violence and the threat of violence to advance their agenda, pose a danger. In recent years, while many have fixed their attention on international threat groups, such as al Qaeda, there remains a domestic element, varied and diverse, that also poses a threat to our communities and nation.

In the 1920s and again in the 1950s, the United States worried about the influence of Communism upon the nation. The Red Scare of the 1920s spawned thousands of investigations by the Department of Justice (DOJ) of United States citizens, in an effort to identify subversives. In the immediate post–World War II period, another Red Scare occurred in which again, thousands were investigated. By the 1960s, the nation's security focus had moved away from Communism as a major internal threat.

During the 1960s, as the United States was deeply embroiled in the Vietnam Conflict and the struggle for civil rights, many domestic groups, generally on the far left of the political spectrum, gained prominence. Some of these included the Weather Underground, the Black Panthers, and the Symbionese Liberation Army.

As the radicalism of the far left receded following the Vietnam War, groups on the far right of the extremist spectrum and those with an interest in single issues emerged. During the 1980s and 1990s, law enforcement dealt with a resurgence of white supremacists, radical survivalists, so-called constitutionalists and freemen, violent antiabortionists, and extreme environmentalists. Some of these groups and movements continue to persist and thrive within American society.

What is domestic terrorism?

Domestic terrorism and hate crimes can take on many forms. From the actions of the Ku Klux Klan (KKK) in the post–Civil War period to the actions of the Unabomber as he waged a decade-long terror campaign or the 2002 Beltway Sniper killings carried out by Lee Malvo and John Muhammed, the nation and our communities have proven to be vulnerable.[1]

The Federal Bureau of Investigation (FBI) defines domestic terrorism as follows:

> ...the unlawful use, or threatened use, of force or violence by a group or individuals based and operating entirely within the United States or Puerto Rico without foreign direction committed against persons or property to intimidate or coerce a government, the civilian population, or any segment thereof in furtherance of political or social objectives.[2]

When discussing terrorist and extremist movements, careful consideration must be given to differentiating between citizens involved in legitimate protest and those who cross the line into terrorism. For example, many Americans are not in favor of abortion and participate in peaceful protest activities outside of clinics. These citizens are definitely not terrorists. On the other hand, some antiabortionists have taken it upon themselves to assassinate doctors who perform abortions and plant bombs outside of clinics. These actions could definitely be classified as terrorism.

Many definitions of the term *terrorism* exist. One generally accepted by experts holds that terrorism is a

> ...pre-meditated and unlawful act in which groups or agents of some principal engage in a threatened or actual use of force or violence against human or property targets... [These entities] engage in this behavior intending the purposeful intimidation of governments or people to affect policy or behavior with an underlying political objective.[3]

Gerstenfeld[4] expands this definition and identifies such variables as "power," "racial separatism," "religion," "common antipathy for the same groups," and a "common antipathy for particular beliefs and actions" as components of terrorist characteristics.

Because of the many varieties of domestic terrorism that exist today, some experts craft definitions specifically designed for certain movements. For example, Chalk et al.[5] define ecoterrorism as "the use of or threat to use violence in protest of harm inflicted on animals and the world's biosphere." Bennett[6] indicates that ecoterrorism is the "use or threatened use of violence of a criminal nature against innocent victims or property by an environmentally oriented, sub-national group for environmental–political reasons, or aimed at an audience beyond the target, often of a symbolic nature." Hall[7] reinforces this notion and indicates that environmental and animal-advocacy groups were recently considered by law enforcement to be threats in the United States. According to Hall, both the Animal Liberation Front (ALF) and the Earth Liberation Front (ELF) are representative members of such groups. Further, he indicates that

> …[during] 2002, FBI domestic-terrorism section chief James Jarboe said the FBI had ranked the ALF and ELF as the top domestic-terrorism threat, and told Congress they had committed more than 600 criminal acts in the United States since 1996, resulting in damages topping $43 million.[7]

The economic potential of such acts of terror must neither be ignored nor understated. Jackson et al.[8] provide additional financial and economic considerations regarding the United States. According to them,

> …since 1976, 1,100 criminal acts have been committed in the United States by radical environmentalist groups, resulting in more than $110 million in property damage alone, a figure that does not include the significant additional costs associated with lost research, increased security, and dampened productivity.[8]

Deshpande[9] also describes "pyro-terrorism" incidents and crimes, among the nations of Israel, Greece, Spain, Estonia, and the United States, that have environmental attributes and significant consequences. Given the discussions of Deshpande and Jackson, both the economic and financial potentials of ecoterrorism are significant concerns.

Although both the ALF and ELF have different origins, many of their ideological beliefs and much of their threat potentials are similar. Walsh and Ellis[10] indicate that the ALF and the ELF have "close ties" because of their common ideological beliefs and "respective agendas."[10] Hall[7] provides similar observations of commonness regarding the prosecution of crimes committed by the ALF and the ELF. Alexander[11] indicates that both the ALF and the ELF "have attacked business interests as they view Corporate America as harming the environment and animals" and caused approximately "over $42 million in damages" during the period of "1996–2002."

These observations of ecoterrorism demonstrate just how difficult it is to craft a "one-size-fits-all" definition of domestic terrorism. While violence and murder can certainly be key components of such a definition, damaging infrastructure and impeding societal functions can also be considered "terroristic."

As the next section makes clear, the United States has witnessed myriad examples of terrorism throughout its history. There is little reason to believe that these dangers will not prove problematic for future generations.

Domestic terrorism and threat groups

The United States has a long history of democracy. Its national history is replete with the contributions of a variety of individuals and groups whose efforts and works provided benefits within society. However, despite such positive events, American history also contains the blemishes and crimes of domestic terrorism. In an effort to understand the dynamics of domestic terrorist activity within the United States, it is important to categorize groups based upon the inherent motivation that serves as the adversarial norm of each group. Basically, there are three main categories of domestic terrorist groups: hate-motivated, right-wing patriot militia, and special-interest groups.[12]

1. Hate-motivated groups consist of movements such as the following:
   a. White supremacy—These groups maintain an ideology of cultural supremacy and antigovernment sentiment (KKK, neo-Nazi, Aryan Brotherhood, Posse Comitatus). They are characterized by intolerance, racism, and religious dogma.
   b. Racial–religious—These groups adhere to radical religious beliefs that are distinctly either non-Christian or anti-Christian (White Aryan Resistance, World Church of the Creator [COTC], Odinism). They are characterized as terrorism based upon interrelated religious ideas that are subordinated to political, ethnic, or ideological objectives.
   c. Black separatism—These groups advocate racial separatism, ethnocentricity, and antigovernment sentiment (Nation of Islam, New Black Panther Party [NBPP]). They are characterized by anti-Semitism, strict racial separation, and government opposition.
2. Right-wing patriot militia—These groups consist of movements that are characterized as sovereign citizen groups that maintain conspiracy beliefs that the federal government is tyrannical in having compromised or is trying to dissolve constitutional rights and that the government has become anti-Christian, and anti-American. Basically, such groups are organized cells motivated by their beliefs that the condition of America's present political, economic, and judicial status is meant to strip them of their constitutional right to bear arms, tax the nation into poverty, and diminish the value of the nation's currency.[12]
3. Special interest—These groups consist of prominent movements committed to a particular cause that focuses on the resolution of a specific issue. Special-interest groups are well-organized groups that engage in direct forms of action characterized as either extremist or terrorist. Their respective actions range on a continuum from legal forms of civil disobedience (protests) to illegal forms of activity (arson, vandalism, murder), comprising both extremist and terrorist actions. Extremist groups include animal rights (e.g., People for the Ethical Treatment of Animals [PETA]); prolife and antiabortion; and ecological (environmentalists, e.g., Earth First and Greenpeace) groups.[12]

Terrorism has been used against the domestic United States for a variety of reasons. Some of the contributing factors include economic, political, and religious philosophies.

The radical right: A variety of perspectives

The term *radical right* is applied to a wide-range of groups and movements, including white supremacists, so-called sovereign citizens and freemen, tax protestors, antiabortionists, and militia groups. To the extent that one assumes groups categorized as "radical right" all follow a conservative or ultraconservative agenda, the term can be misleading. For example, most militia groups believe in a strict, idiosyncratic interpretation of the United States Constitution, whereas many white supremacists are true revolutionaries, enamored with the overthrow of the American government or intent on the establishment of a "whites-only" nation.

Nevertheless, for sake of simplicity, this textbook adheres to the generally understood classification scheme referred to as "radical right." Readers, however, are cautioned to approach each group as an individual entity and not to read anything into a group's political orientation just because it is classified as belonging to the "radical right." The following section will examine some groups considered to be "right-wing extremist."

Supremacy groups

As the name implies, supremacy groups believe that their race or ethnicity is superior to all others. Of course, the First Amendment guarantees that individuals are free to hold these beliefs and espouse them publically. However, history has demonstrated that these views propel some to believe they have the right, indeed the responsibility, to act out violently against others to "protect" their race. When the word "supremacy" is mentioned, many people automatically assume that this refers to white supremacist groups, like the KKK and Aryan Nations. However, there are many such groups, with diverse racial, religious, and ethnic orientations.

KKK

Perhaps the longest-surviving domestic threat group is the KKK, which has proven remarkably adept at reconstituting itself over the years. The KKK is one of the best-known ultra-right-wing groups in the United States. When first formed, the Klan was a single organization that quickly spread across major portions of the South. The nature of the organization, built on a foundation of the secrecy of a loosely connected confederation, quickly saw it evolve into highly independent, locally based groups. Today, there are over 150 Klan groups, of various sizes, located in over 30 states.

The Klan was founded in 1865 in Pulaski, Tennessee, and was initially a social organization. By 1867, the Klan had shifted its emphasis. Quickly spreading across much of the South, the Klan selected former Confederate cavalry general Nathan Bedford Forrest as its leader. During this period of the late 1860s and early 1870s, the Klan terrorized citizens.[13] By the late 1870s, with the conclusion of Reconstruction in the South, the first era of the Klan concluded, and the organization lay dormant for the next three decades.

In the early 1900s, a series of events led to the second incarnation of the Klan. Massive immigration occurred in which thousands of eastern Europeans, many of whom were Catholic and Jewish, flooded into the United States. Also, African Americans migrated from the agricultural South to the industrial North in record numbers. Because of such events, many people felt threatened and believed that their lifestyles were under assault.

In 1915, while these events were occurring, filmmaker D.W. Griffith produced *The Birth of a Nation*. Based on Thomas Dixon's 1905 novel, *The Clansman*, *Birth of a Nation* portrayed the KKK in a sympathetic and heroic light. The movie made a huge impact; it was screened in the White House and became wildly popular with many audiences. The movie was considered to be one of the most innovative films ever made.

By the 1920s, Klan membership was estimated to be approximately 5 million (**Figure 11.1**). Its anti–African American orientation had expanded to include anti-Catholic, anti-Semitic, and anti-immigrant biases. In some locations, the Klan existed as a social organization instead of a terrorist group. During this time, it was common for politicians to join the KKK if they wished to hold office.[14] Less than 10 years later, mismanagement, outrage by various media outlets and politicians, and a series of sensational sexual and criminal scandals had decimated the ranks of the Klan. It would not regain its power and influence until much later in the 20th century.

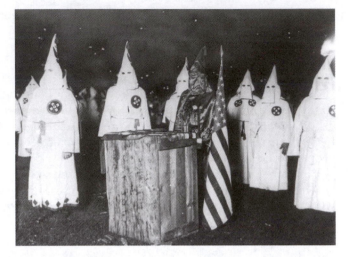

Figure 11.1 *Altar with Kleagle in black robe at a meeting of nearly 30,000 Ku Klux Klan members from Chicago and northern Illinois (c. 1920). (Courtesy of the Library of Congress.)*

The third incarnation of the KKK started during the 1950s in response to civil rights groups that were attempting to secure rights for African Americans. A series of sensational bombings and murders gripped the South during the 1950s and 1960s. Very often, perpetrators were never brought to justice. Eventually, law enforcement efforts, on the federal and state levels, began to erode the power of the Klan. Ironically, the largest attack on the Klan came not in criminal court but in civil actions. Groups like the Southern Poverty Law Center (SPLC) won judgments of millions of dollars against various KKK members and groups.

The Ku Klux Klan continues to exist within American society. Groups today tend to be small and engage primarily in attempting to gain members or in spreading their message through public protests, Internet postings, and publications. Perhaps ironically, the American Civil Liberties Union (ACLU) has defended the Klan in various lawsuits and has successfully argued that the First Amendment of the US Constitution guarantees KKK and members of other fringe organizations the right to free speech. Today, it is estimated that there are between 5,000 and 8,000 Klan member in the United States.[15]

Neo-Nazi and Aryan movement

The Nazi movement in the United States predates World War II. In 1936, the German American Bund was established as a pro-Nazi, quasi-military organization that was most active in the years immediately preceding the United States' entry into World War II. The Bund's members were mostly American citizens of German ancestry. The organization received covert guidance and financial support from the German government. Military drill and related activities were provided for adults and youths at Bund-maintained camps: Camp Siegfried, Yaphank, New York, and Camp Nordland, Andover, New Jersey.[16] With the United States entry into World War II, the German American Bund lost public support.

After World War II, an American Nazi movement reemerged under, most noticeably, the leadership of George Lincoln Rockwell. Rockwell was a United States Naval officer in World War II who, in March 1959, founded the World Union of Free Enterprise National Socialists (WUFENS), a name selected to denote opposition to state ownership of property. In December, the name was changed to the American Nazi Party (ANP), and the headquarters relocated to Arlington, Virginia. In 1967, Rockwell was assassinated.[17]

While some neo-Nazi groups emphasize simple hatred, others are more focused on the revolutionary creation of a fascist political state. Nazism, of course, has roots in Europe, and links between American and European neo-Nazis are strong and growing stronger. American neo-Nazi groups, protected by the First Amendment, often publish material and host Internet sites that are aimed at European audiences—materials that would be illegal under European antiracism laws. Similarly, many European groups put up their Internet sites on American servers to avoid prosecution under the laws of their native countries.

By the 1960s, the American Nazi Party and the KKK found much common ground in their views. Both organizations advocated similar agendas. Many of the leaders of radical right-wing organizations at one time or another were affiliated with one of these organizations.

Several major leaders of the neo-Nazi movement emerged from the influence of the American Nazi Party and the KKK. After Rockwell's assassination in August 1967, Pierce became one of the principal leaders of the National Socialist White People's Party (NSWPP), the successor to the ANP. In 1970, Pierce left the NSWPP and joined the National Youth Alliance. By 1974, Pierce formed the National Alliance and led it until his death in 2002. One of the most significant impacts Pierce had on the radical right was the authorship of *The Turner Diaries*. *The Turner Diaries*, published in 1978, were the fictional diaries of Earl Turner, a member of an underground white supremacist army, involved in an Aryan revolution that overturns the United States government in the near future. In the book, Turner's guerrilla unit detonates a homemade bomb at FBI headquarters, killing hundreds—a passage that came to be seen as foreshadowing, and as an inspiration, to Oklahoma City bomber Timothy McVeigh. The book is one of the most widely read and cited books on the far right.

Other extreme-right leaders have also emerged from the foundations of the neo-Nazi movement. Richard Butler led the Aryan Nations and the Church of Jesus Christ Christian, the nation's most well-known bastion of neo-Nazism and Christian Identity. In 2000, the Aryan Nations lost its church and 20-acre compound in northern Idaho after a $6 million civil judgment led to a bankruptcy filing. Butler's use of religion as a foundation to advance his agenda would be seen in others.[18]

The neo-Nazi and Aryan Nations movements have a major presence in the nation's correctional system. As an example, the Aryan Brotherhood is a highly organized prison gang and one of the most violent white supremacist groups in the nation. It has been linked to over 100 murders throughout its existence. Aryan Brotherhood leaders have been the recent target of the FBI, Drug Enforcement Agency (DEA), and Alcohol, Tobacco, and Firearms (ATF), who are trying to dismantle the ruthless gang. The Aryan Brotherhood also has been linked to a series of murders and assaults on law enforcement officials. The Aryan Brotherhood is one of the largest prison gangs in the nation and has branches in California, Nevada, Arizona, New Mexico, Texas, Missouri, Arkansas, Alabama, Florida, Mississippi, Georgia, Kansas, Ohio, and Colorado.[19]

The sovereign citizen movement

Sovereign citizens are antigovernment extremists who believe that even though they physically reside in this country, they are separate or "sovereign" from the United States. As a result, they believe they do not have to answer to any government authority, including courts, taxing entities, motor vehicle departments, or law enforcement.

Sovereign citizens are often confused with extremists from the militia movement. But while sovereign citizens sometimes use or buy illegal weapons, guns are secondary to their antigovernment, antitax beliefs. On the other hand, guns and paramilitary training are commonly associated with to militia groups.[20]

The ideas behind the movement originated during the 1970s with a group known as the Posse Comitatus and enjoyed some popularity in extremist circles during the 1980s and 1990s. Early on, the movement featured white supremacist elements, but this has not kept some African Americans from subscribing to its ideals in recent years. In the 1990s, the movement attracted 250,000 followers and was marked by the FBI's standoff with a group known as the Montana Freemen that lasted 81 days. Current estimates suggest a membership of 300,000.

Sovereign citizens have, in some instances, created fictitious entities and used fake currency, passports, license plates, and driver licenses. In 2009, a federal jury found three men guilty of conspiring to use and sell fraudulent diplomatic credentials and license plates that they believed allowed "their customers to enjoy diplomatic immunity and to no longer pay taxes."[21]

Militias and the militia movement

A militia is a military force composed of citizens designed to provide defense, law enforcement, and other services during a time of emergency. The primary militia in the United States is the National Guard. The National Guard, along with reserve forces and state defense forces, supplements the active-duty military. Additionally, these units serve their state governments during the response cycles to natural disasters—hurricanes, floods, tornados, forest fires—and during emergency circumstances such as riots and episodes of civil unrest.

The Militia Act of 1903 created the National Guard and the "unorganized" militia that consists of all males between the ages of 17 and 45 (with certain exceptions). For most of the 20th century, the unorganized militia did not exist in any real sense.

However, during the 1990s, a confluence of factors convinced many private citizens to take up arms and form their own militia units. Like the patriot movement, citizens who gravitated toward the militia believed that the United States was in extreme danger. They were convinced that "black helicopters" and other sinister forces from outside America were about to take over the country. Some of these groups had a strong religious orientation, while others did not. Some were racist, but many had no racial bias. Many militia members were average American citizens concerned about the future of the United States. They believed that they were the last line of defense for their government and community, and they prepared themselves to resist efforts by both foreign subversives and those who would commit treason from within.

When the new millennium began, many computer specialists believed that a global economic and physical catastrophe would occur. It was called the Year Two Thousand (Y2K) phenomenon, and it was believed that most computers would fail during the early hours of the new year, 2000. Stories of cataclysm were common. This sensationalism, unfortunately, fed the hyperbole around the militia movement, and many American citizens, fearing financial disasters, global crop failures, and abuses against private citizens by what they considered to be an oppressive government, joined militia units to ensure their own safety from the predicted disaster.

Fortunately, very few terrorists have come out of militia brigades, or even the patriot movement, for that matter. To some degree, these units became a catharsis for those Americans who had extreme concerns about the government. However, during the 1990s, there was great concern that a single incident could trigger a violent reaction from militia personnel, thereby setting off a firestorm.

Racist skinheads

In the United States, racist skinheads have a legacy stretching back to the early 1980s. However, skinhead culture originated in the United Kingdom in the late 1960s and today has a global reach. Since the early 2000s, the movement in the United States has been characterized by a proliferation of regional groups or crews rather than a united core organization. In law enforcement circles, racist skinheads have a reputation for violence. This is reinforced by hate-filled white-power music and literature. In the mid-1990s, many US-based racist skinhead groups allied with one another to form the Hammerskin Nation (HSN). HSN eventually developed chapters throughout the United States and in Europe.[21]

Black separatists

The definition of *separatist* is often misconstrued with respect to threat groups. Basically, a separatist is a person, or movement composed of a group of individuals, that seeks to withdraw, secede, or be separate from others in society. The main beliefs that motivate separatists include all or several of the following: sectarianism, which is an attitude of bigotry, discrimination, and hatred; ethnic ideologies; ideologies on gender, economic, or social status; and religious beliefs. For example, per the position of the SPLC, "Black separatists typically oppose integration and racial intermarriage, and they want separate institutions—or even a separate nation—for black people in America. Most contemporary forms of black separatism are strongly antiwhite and anti-Semitic, and a number of religious versions assert that blacks—not Jews—are the Biblical 'chosen people' of God."[22]

For example, the NBPP is a black separatist group that believes black Americans should have their own nation. The NBPP is a virulently racist and anti-Semitic organization whose leaders have encouraged violence against whites, Jews, and law enforcement officers. The NBPP claims to have been founded in 1989, although the group was not active until 1990. That year, Aaron Michaels, a Dallas radio personality, assembled a group of black citizens to engage in community activism. He called the group the New Black Panther Party.[23]

The NBPP characterizes itself as a militant, modern-day expression of the black-power movement. Its leaders have blamed Jews for the 9/11 terrorist attacks and for the slave trade. The NBPP demands that blacks be given a country or state of their own, within which they can make their own laws. They demand that all black prisoners in the United States be released to "the lawful authorities of the Black Nation." They claim to be entitled to reparations for slavery from the United States, all European countries, and "the Jews."[23]

The NBPP also holds black supremacist religious beliefs and is most notable for its antiwhite and anti-Semitic hatred. NBPP members believe that blacks are God's true "chosen people" and that the people normally called "Jews" actually are impostors. (This ideology is remarkably similar to the white racist theology of Christian Identity, which says whites are God's real chosen people.) They believe that blacks are naturally superior to people of other races.[23]

A document on the NBPP Web site entitled "The Nationalist Manifesto" claims that white men have a secret plan to commit genocide against the nonwhite races. It also refers to black people who condone mixed-race relationships as the "modern day Custodians [sic] of Uncle Tom's Cabin." The now-deceased Khalid Abdul Muhammad, who formerly served as the NBPP chairman, emphatically stated, "There are no good crackers, and if you find one, kill him before he changes."[23]

Interestingly, members of the original Black Panther Party, which has no connection to the NBPP, have heavily criticized the NBPP. An open letter from the Dr. Huey P. Newton

Foundation, which is run by members of the original Black Panther Party, decries the NBPP for being a hateful and unconstructive group. Bobby Seale, a famous founding member of the original Panthers, calls the organization "a black racist hate group."[23]

Patriot groups

The SPLC Intelligence Project identified 1,360 antigovernment "patriot" groups active in 2012. Generally, patriot groups define themselves as opposed to the "New World Order," engage in conspiracy theorizing, or advocate or adhere to extreme antigovernment doctrines. The philosophical roots of the patriot movement are derived from those of the John Birch Society (during the 1950s and 1960s) and the Posse Comitatus. Patriots are sometimes called "constitutionalists." It is their position that they—and, perhaps, they alone—represent the ideals intended by the authors of the Constitution and its Bill of Rights.

Internationally, they are isolationists. Domestically, patriots believe very strongly in independent speech protected by the First Amendment and the right to bear all types of firearms and weaponry, as they believe the Second Amendment intended. They favor small government and resent the intrusion of public policies that influence their lives on a daily basis.

Most of the men and women of the patriot movement believe that the Federal Personal Income Tax Law (the Sixteenth Amendment of the United States Constitution) and the application of the tax through the Internal Revenue Service are unconstitutional. The Federal Reserve Banking System is also challenged regarding its constitutionality. Many believe that a vast conspiracy is underway to establish a "new world order." Author Michael William Haga[24] provides a glimpse of this mindset in *Taking Back America:*

> Are there different levels of conspirators? Are there people who control and others who simply collaborate without even knowing, half the time that they are collaborating with a conspiracy? Although some theories are delusional, it's also just as much of a mistake to brand all theories about any conspiracy as being delusional. For example: The Federal Reserve Banking System was created at a secret meeting among Congressmen and bankers at Jekyll Island, Georgia, in 1913. It wasn't a plan to save the United States banking system, it was a plan to consolidate power, monetary power, in the hands of a few bankers. They did it secretly. It was a conspiracy. And it affects us to this very day.

For many, if not most, patriots, the government is not to be trusted. This charge is directed primarily at the federal government and includes state and local governments. The idea of a world government, such as one run by the United Nations, is anathema to the patriot. In 1991, President George H.W. Bush made a speech discussing the "new world order." Insofar as the patriot movement was concerned, he might as well have said that the apocalypse was beginning the following week. A gauntlet had been thrown down by a casual reference to what President Bush considered a better world.

Patriot movement members believe that the government of the United States no longer represents the people's interests and has become increasingly intrusive in private and business matters. According to some supporters, law enforcement officers have gone too far and are, in fact, state terrorists. Many patriots continue to recognize only elected sheriffs and their deputies as constitutional law enforcement officers. Likewise, the patriot membership does not recognize many of the federal and state courts. In response to these beliefs, the movement has created its own court system, known as the common law court. Mirroring the courts of state and federal governments, the common law court issues its own subpoenas, facilitates court proceedings, and issues judgments. However, the verdicts are clearly unbinding. Further, some common law adherents have misled county officials and had liens placed on properties owned by individuals who have been successfully "sued" in these pseudo-courts.

As well, because they believe in the legitimacy of their own system, common law adherents have been violently confrontational to state and local law enforcement officials when subjected to traffic stops or in the routine service of warrants. Additionally, there have been ideological confrontations with members of the National Park Service, the Bureau of Land Management, and the Federal Emergency Management Agency, which is considered to be a "shadow government," with citizen prisons located on military reservations.

Inspiration, leaderless resistance, and the lone wolf

Many things drive radical ideas and individuals and groups to radical action. Two of the major events that have most recently inspired the radical actions of some have been the Randy Weaver and Waco sieges.

In August 1992, Randy Weaver and his family were engaged in an 11-day standoff with federal law enforcement agents. Randy Weaver had failed to appear in court on firearms-related charges in 1991. Subsequently, an unsuccessful operation to arrest Weaver led to the death of his 14-year-old son and a US Marshal. It also precipitated the standoff. During the standoff, Weaver and a friend were shot and wounded. An FBI sniper also shot and killed Weaver's wife, Vicki.

On February 28, 1993, an unsuccessful attempt by ATF agents to arrest the sect's leader, David Koresh, initiated a 51-day siege near Waco, Texas. Koresh was wanted on suspicion of federal firearms and explosives violations. Four ATF agents and six Branch Davidians died in a gunfight during the operation. Protracted discussions followed between federal negotiators and Koresh. These failed. On April 19, federal agents assaulted the Davidian compound, which caught fire. At least 75 Branch Davidians perished in the assault. The sieges of the Weaver home and the Branch Davidian compound stimulated many on the radical right, including the militia and sovereignty movements.[21]

Louis Beam, a Vietnam War veteran, became Grand Dragon of the Texas KKK during the 1980s. Considered an intellectual of the white supremacist movement, Beam studied the right-wing terror organizations that failed or were harmed by law enforcement and United States Justice Department efforts. He soon realized that the large bureaucracy of an organization, such as the Ku Klux Klan of the 1960s and 1970s, was itself a weakness. Too many Klansmen were privy to confidential knowledge of criminality, and infiltration by undercover operatives was relatively easy. Individual Klan units had sought various solutions to this problem. For example, the Mississippi White Knights of the KKK had a specialty unit called the "wrecking crew." This unit was separated from the normal Klan organization.

Beam expanded the initial concept. He proposed the creation of a "leaderless cell" network where individuals would take their inspiration, but not their orders, from leaders in the movement. Each cell would act independently, without knowing the identity of individuals in other cells. These cells would be invisible for the large part and answerable to few, if any, individuals. The leaderless resistance concept is not limited to white supremacists. Indeed, ecoterrorists and international groups have employed this structure. Another term that has been used to describe this concept is *phantom cells*. Closely related to this notion is the concept of the *lone wolf*, which denotes an individual who acts totally on his or her own.

Eric Rudolph (**Figure 11.2**) is a good example of a lone wolf. During the 1990s, he bombed abortion centers and set off a bomb at the Atlanta Olympics. Rudolph operated alone and

Figure 11.2 *Olympic park bomber Eric Rudolph.*

independently. Once he began his terrorist activities, he ceased using credit cards, bank accounts, and his social security number. Instead, he paid his rent and other bills with cash or a money order. In essence, he rejected the political values of America. This rejection is sometimes referred to as *severation*. This term was first used by the tax protesters of Posse Comitatus as a plan to "retire from America."

Acting and living by himself, Rudolph was able to evade capture for many years despite a massive manhunt by the FBI. His survivalist skills and his elimination of communications with outsiders made him difficult to apprehend. Despite his lone-wolf status, Rudolph claimed that he carried out his acts on behalf of the "Army of God." This entity is a shadowy, antiabortion movement that follows the tenets of leaderless resistance. Although the true motivation for his crimes remains unknown, Rudolph had an extended exposure to ideological teachings that affected his behavior.

Another example of leaderless resistance may be found in the 1995 bombing of the Oklahoma City Federal Building by Timothy McVeigh (**Figure 11.3**). McVeigh was a former army enlisted man who claimed he was "radicalized" by the government actions at Waco in 1993 and Ruby Ridge in 1992; in both of those incidents, individuals died after standoffs with the federal government. On the morning of April 19, 1995, McVeigh parked a rented truck, loaded with approximately 5000 pounds of ammonium nitrate and motor racing fuel, in front of the federal building. Shortly after 9:00 a.m., his homemade bomb exploded, obliterating the front of the building and killing 168 people. McVeigh was ultimately convicted and sentenced to death, and his army buddy, Terry Nichols, was convicted of assisting him in the plot.

Former FBI Agent Mike German, who spent years undercover with white supremacist groups, cautions that even lone wolves may receive assistance and support from others. German notes:

Figure 11.3 Oklahoma City bomber Timothy McVeigh.

Tim McVeigh seemed able to find a militia meeting wherever he went. He was linked to militia groups in Arizona and Michigan, white supremacist groups in Oklahoma and Missouri, and at gun shows he sold copies of *The Turner Diaries*, a racist novel written by the founder of a neo-Nazi organization. No one finds such groups by accident.[25]

The notions of leaderless resistance and lone-wolf actors are both deadly and dangerous. These methods provide an effective means through which a variety of organizations can perpetrate acts of terror without detection. Because of these basic tenets, terrorist entities need not be large or necessitate a large quantity of resources to cause significant damage.

Right to life: Revolutionary reaction to abortion

In 1973, the United States Supreme Court legalized abortion in the *Roe v. Wade* decision. Almost immediately, groups and individuals started protesting the decision. Recently, a movement calling itself the "Army of God" emerged with a mandate to violently oppose abortion. This mandate included the assassination of doctors and the bombing of clinics.

Although two different groups claim the title "Army of God," or "Soldiers of God," the first group is a prolife group established to stop abortion, and the second is the name that some in the Christian Identity movement have given to themselves. The Christian Identity movement represents an amalgamation of white supremacy groups and those that adhere to ideologies of anti-Semitism.[26] Although both of these groups occasionally target abortion centers, they perpetrate attacks for different reasons.

The Christian Identity members believe that abortion is racial treason because white children are aborted in numbers greater than those of other races. The Army of God members oppose all abortions for any reason. Sometimes, the movement is called "antichoice." The Army of God was most active during the 1980s, indicated by the frequent bombings of abortion clinics throughout the United States. During the mid-1990s, support for the group began to grow exponentially because increasing numbers of Americans objected to abortion.

The Army of God has an active Web site, and it publishes a manual containing instructions for the sabotage, arson, or bombing of abortion clinics. Operating in the shadowy network of the right-wing underground, they are antigovernment to the degree that they believe that any government authorizing the murder of innocent children does not have the right to exist. Two examples of Army of God "warriors" include Eric Rudolph and Paul Hill. On July 29, 1994, Hill killed three people, including an abortion doctor, at a clinic in Pensacola, Florida.[27]

Other organizations that pose a domestic threat

Outlaw motorcycle gangs (OMGs) are organizations whose members use their motorcycle clubs as conduits for criminal enterprises. OMGs are highly structured criminal organizations whose members engage in criminal activities such as violent crime, weapons trafficking, and drug trafficking. There are more than 300 active OMGs within the United States, ranging in size from single chapters with five or six members to hundreds of chapters with thousands of members worldwide. The Hells Angels, Mongols, Bandidos, Outlaws, and Sons of Silence pose a serious national domestic threat and conduct the majority of criminal activity linked to OMGs, especially activity relating to drug trafficking and, more specifically, to cross-border drug smuggling. Because of their transnational scope, these OMGs are able to coordinate drug smuggling operations in partnership with major international drug-trafficking organizations (DTOs).[28]

The radical left: Ecological and animal rights

Ecological militants are "single-issue" terrorists. Many such groups exist, one of which involves ecoterrorism. The goal of ecoterrorism is to preserve the environment through direct action and engage in activities to protect biological and ecological diversity. Domestic ecological terror is primarily focused on preserving the environment and protecting animal life. The two primary groups who practice ecoterrorism today are the ELF and the ALF, both of which are labeled as terrorist groups by the FBI.

According to Best and Nocella,[29] the ELF was formed in 1992 in England. In 2001, the FBI added the ELF to its domestic terrorist list because it was involved in militant criminal activities. A prime example of the ELF's activities is their attack on a ski resort near Vail, Colorado, which caused $12 million in damage.[30] The ELF opposes oil drilling, the timber industry, genetic research, and the development of recreation and housing construction sites. Their attack on the ski resort occurred because it encroached on the habitat of the Canadian lynx.

Like the ELF, the ALF was also formed in England. However, the ALF can trace its philosophical roots at least as far back as 19th-century England when a group that called itself the "Band of Mercy" formed to oppose fox hunting. During the 1970s, Band of Mercy was resurrected to oppose fox hunting. However, the scope of the group began to expand to include opposition to medical research involving animals. Around 1976, Ronnie Lee, a member of Band of Mercy, founded the spin-off group ALF. Within a short period of time, ALF activities, which include damaging animal research laboratories, releasing animals from farms and ranches, and attacking private meat-packing plants, began to occur throughout the United States.[29]

The ELF and ALF, as well as groups like them, commonly use property damage and vandalism to further their cause. Both the ALF and ELF have proven to be elusive adversaries for law enforcement. Because individuals act on their own initiative without direct guidance from higher officials (a practice termed "leaderless resistance"), it has been quite difficult to infiltrate and investigate these groups. Given their close ties and willingness to work together, there is debate about whether the ALF and ELF, in fact, represent two separate entities or are one and the same. As stated in a 2006 article by the FBI, "In 2004, [it was] estimated that ELF, ALF and related extremist groups had committed more than 1,100 criminal acts since 1976 with damage estimates over $100 million."[75]

Despite this success, the FBI considers ecoterrorists and animal rights extremists as "one of the most serious domestic terrorism threats in the U.S. today" (para. 5).[76] According to the FBI,[76] individuals involved in these activities are especially dangerous given the huge volume of the crimes they commit, their large economic impact, and the wide range of victims affected. The FBI is also worried about what it calls the increasingly violent rhetoric and tactics demonstrated by eco-extremists.[76] The violence perpetrated by these groups is varied. The targets of the ALF have included research laboratories at the University of California at Los Angeles and employees of the New York Stock Exchange. Other ALF targets were located at the University of Minnesota and the University of California at San Francisco.[31] The financial impacts of these attacks were in the millions of dollars.

Ecoterrorist groups attempt to leverage strategically "leaderless resistance" to "avoid state detection, infiltration, and prosecution by powerful government agencies" during the course of their terrorist activities.[32] Walsh and Ellis[10] indicate that both the ALF and the ELF share this structuring and strategy of "leaderless resistance" and have "close ties" regarding agendas and ideological tenets. According to Leader and Probst,[33] the ecoterror events of both the ALF and the ELF "have been perpetrated in virtually every region of the US against a wide variety of targets." Further, Leader and Probst indicate that, in 1993, the ELF and ALF declared "solidarity" and that increasing amounts of "convergence of leadership, membership, agendas and funding" have occurred between these organizations.[33]

The global and international aspects of the ALF are considerable and demonstrate terror incidents among a variety of nations. Flükiger describes ALF attacks in Germany and Switzerland involving the use of arson,[34] while Marris and Simonite[35] document ALF movements, organizations, and events among nations representing the United Kingdom, Sweden, Switzerland, the Netherlands, Germany, and the United States.

The ELF also demonstrates a history of ecoterrorism and violence. According to Leader and Probst (p. 38),[33] in 1992, the ELF originated in the United Kingdom (Brighton, England) and was a derivative of the "activist environmental group, 'Earth First!' who believed criminal acts would better advance their environmentalist agenda than would legal protest." Further, Leader and Probst indicate that the "American branch announced its creation in October, 1996 with an arson attack on a US Forest Service truck in Oregon's Willamette National Forest." Perlstein[36] acknowledges a paradigm shift occurrence, over time, regarding the types of targets selected by the ELF, which demonstrates a change from rural settings (e.g., farms, crops, etc.) to urban settings (e.g., apartment complexes, warehouses, etc.). These instantiations of the ELF demonstrated its organizational tenets of "direct action and revolutionary violence."[33]

According to the ELF literature, a goal of its ideology is to "defend and protect the Earth for future generations by means of direct actions," using approaches that were manifested by its predecessor ecoterrorist entities (e.g., Environmental Life Force) that involved the use of "eco-guerilla" tactics.[37] The ELF manifests "small cells consisting of anywhere from one to several people without a central command structure" and maintains the anonymity of its members through such cells; "one cell does not know the members or plan of another cell." This organizational structuring, using "leaderless resistance," increases the difficulties of law enforcement when attempting to infiltrate "cells."[38]

The targets of the ELF are also varied. They range from a Colorado ski resort to a car dealership in California that sold sport-utility vehicles. Additional targets of the ELF include research laboratories and logging corporations.[33] Two examples of such activities include perpetrating arson at a meat-packaging facility in Oregon and an act of arson at Michigan State University.[39] The financial damages of such terrorist acts also range in the millions of dollars.[11] Similar to the ALF, the activities and ideologies of the ELF are not constrained solely to the United States and are pervasive among nations. The activities of the ELF have been observed also in England, Scotland, and Canada, and also among international waters.

Major law enforcement agencies battling terrorism and hate

Federal agencies

The DOJ and the FBI do not officially list domestic terrorist organizations, but they have openly delineated domestic terrorist "threats." These include individuals who commit crimes in the name of ideologies supporting animal rights, environmental rights, anarchism, white supremacy, antigovernment ideals, black separatism, and antiabortion beliefs.[21]

The FBI and the Department of Homeland Security (DHS) have recently popularized the phrase "homegrown violent extremist." It separates domestic terrorists from US-based terrorists motivated by the ideologies of foreign terrorist organizations. According to DHS and the FBI, a "homegrown violent extremist" is "a person of any citizenship who has lived and/or operated primarily in the United States or its territories who advocates, is engaged in, or is preparing to engage in ideologically motivated terrorist activities (including providing support to terrorism) in furtherance of political or social objectives promoted by a foreign terrorist organization but is acting independently of direction by a foreign terrorist organization."

State, local, and tribal agencies

The DHS has fully understood the necessity of integrating its policies, practices, and procedures within state, local, and tribal jurisdictions. The obvious rationale is the danger posed by both domestic threat groups and international terrorists. As duly noted in 2011, Los Angeles Deputy Police Chief Michael P. Downing included "black separatists, white supremacist/ sovereign citizen extremists, and animal rights terrorists" among his chief counterterrorism concerns.[40]

Although the federal government maintains a plethora of law enforcement agencies, such resources cannot take on and operate the functions of state, local, and tribal agencies (SLTA). During its evolution process, DHS fully recognized and acknowledged within its sphere of influence the shared responsibilities it has with SLTA. With respect to the diversity of roles and resources, the federal government and SLTA must remain decentralized but progressively interoperable. Thus, in an effort to create a synergistic landscape of operability between DHS and SLTA, President Bush issued Homeland Security Presidential Directive 5 (HSPD-5), which mandated the following:

The Federal Government recognizes the roles and responsibilities of State and local authorities in domestic incident management. Initial responsibility for managing domestic incidents generally falls on State and local authorities. The Federal Government will assist State and local authorities when their resources are overwhelmed, or when Federal interests are involved. The Secretary will coordinate with State and local governments to ensure adequate planning, equipment, training, and exercise activities. The Secretary will also provide assistance to State and local governments to develop all-hazards plans and capabilities, including those of greatest importance to the security of the United States, and will ensure that State, local, and Federal plans are compatible.[41]

Subsequently, with the development of the DHS, the objective remained to apply the recommendations within HSPD-5 in a collaborative and integrative manner that would complement the autonomy of SLTA but also provide the continuity necessary to apply the homeland security initiatives. Thereafter, DHS created the State, Local, Tribal, and Territorial Government Coordinating Council (SLTTGCC), which sought SLTA membership based upon the following requirements[42]:

- A state, local, tribal, or territorial homeland security director or equivalent with relevant programmatic planning and operational responsibilities
- Accountable for the development, improvement, and maintenance of critical infrastructure protection policies or programs at the state, local, and tribal level
- Recognized among his or her peers as a leader
- Committed to acting as a national representative regarding homeland security practices relevant to states and localities[42]

More often than not, the federal system takes the lead by creating laws, regulations, and policies. Invariably, the crutch to successful implementation remains in the hands of the states and localities, which must cooperate and operate by adopting policies and practices consistent with, and equivalent to, the principles of the homeland security directives within the operational guidelines of DHS.

Shortly, after the events of 9/11, every state created its own office of homeland security in an effort to be as prepared as possible for terrorist attacks as well as to monitor and manage domestic threat groups. Basically, the governor of each state was responsible for the creation of its office of homeland security and designated an individual to provide the leadership to create the organizational structure necessary to protect a state's infrastructure by coordinating the various needs, resources, and operations of the state emergency management office; various state agencies (law enforcement, health, public safety functions); local governments; the private sector; nongovernment organizations (NGOs); and the federal government.[43]

Most state homeland security offices are organized to include an advisory panel consisting of various agencies so that there is constructive and proactive collaboration and communication regarding preparation and response. In addition, some states have also fully integrated into their homeland security design other existing agencies such as the National Guard, specialized task forces like the FBI Joint Terrorism Task Force (JTTF), and data fusion centers within regional and major metropolitan areas for the primary purpose of maintaining a unified effort to report, track, access, and analyze intelligence and other information deemed to be relevant to the mission of homeland security.[43]

With respect to the local level, the operational integration is of equal importance and just as necessary to promote and maintain the objectives and strategic initiatives of the federal and state entities. Given the complexities of working within the scope of the federal and state nexus, local governments have, either on their own initiative or through state-mandated guidelines, become fully integrated into the collaborative operational demands of the federal and state levels.

As of now, there remain very few, if any, organizational boundaries regarding homeland security operations. For example, in an effort to develop and maintain efficient operability, many states have restructured their homeland security operations by creating regional operational programs with the following objectives[43]:

- Develop county task forces
- Develop regional counterterrorism task forces
- Integrate federal/state/local response
- Institutionalize mutual aid in the region
- Establish standing regional response groups
- Encourage and develop regional networking

Such regional design is a geographical composition of local, state, and federal agencies, which share a working operation within a specific part of the state. Included within the scope of such a regional structure, and depending upon availability, a regional homeland security program may consist of state and local agencies that partner with such federal entities as the FBI; Bureau of Alcohol, Tobacco, and Firearms; Environmental Health and Protection Agency; DEA; and the United States Marshals.[43]

Nongovernmental agencies battling terrorism and hate

While most Americans expect federal law enforcement officials in the DHS, the FBI, and the Bureau of Alcohol, Tobacco, Firearms and Explosives (BAFTE) to protect the nation from both foreign and domestic terrorists, there are some American groups that have remarkably impacted hate crimes, anti-Semitism, and direct violence against minorities. These groups include the SPLC, the ACLU, and the Anti-Defamation League (ADL).

SPLC

This organization based in Montgomery, Alabama, has had significant success in dealing with radical, racist, and terrorist groups. Perhaps more than any other agency, the SPLC has protected the weak and oppressed. Using the federal statute known as Racketeer Influenced and Corrupt Organizations Act (RICO), it has taken many radical organizations to civil court, recovering buildings, grounds, bank accounts, and many other forms of assets for their clients. The SPLC office building was formerly the United Klans of America headquarters. The building was seized by the federal court, as the result of a lawsuit against that Klan chapter.

The SPLC has its own intelligence arm that tracks hate groups across the country. Its intelligence reports have aided law enforcement officials and district attorneys all across the United States, giving them the background they needed on particular groups and individuals. Although this function is representative of the modern SPLC mission, the SPLC historically championed civil rights causes.

According to the SPLC (2010),[132] "It has dismantled institutional racism in the South, reformed juvenile justice practices, shattered barriers to equality for women, children and the disabled, and protected low-wage immigrant workers from abuse." Further accomplishments include eliminating "some of the nation's most dangerous hate groups by winning crushing, multimillion-dollar jury verdicts on behalf of their victims." According to the SPLC (2010), examples of these victories include the following court cases:

Keenan v. Aryan Nations: Victoria and Jason Keenan were chased and shot at by members of the Aryan Nations in Coeur d'Alene, Idaho. Held at gunpoint, the mother and son feared for their lives. The center sued and obtained a $6.3 million jury verdict; Aryan Nations was forced to turn its compound over to the victims it had terrorized.[44]

Macedonia v. Christian Knights of the Ku Klux Klan: On a summer evening in 1995, members of the Christian Knights of the KKK set a fire, completely destroying a 100-year-old black Baptist church in South Carolina. The center sued the Klan on the church's behalf, winning the largest judgment ever awarded against a hate group.[45]

Austin v. James: In 1995, Alabama corrections officials brought back the barbarity of chain gangs. The center sued, claiming that chaining men in groups of five and putting them on busy highways was cruel and dangerous. The lawsuit put an end to the Alabama chain gang and another torturous practice called the "hitching post".[46]

Mansfield v. Church of the Creator: For killing an African American Gulf War veteran, a white supremacist "reverend" received an award of honor from the leaders of the racist COTC. In the wake of this horrible crime, the center sued the COTC for inciting violence against African Americans.[47]

The SPLC also monitors active hate groups within the domestic United States. According to the SPLC, in 2012, it tracked the activities of 1,007 hate groups. The SPLC disseminates its findings publically via the use of an online, interactive map that delineates the geographical locations and activities of its monitored groups. Such tools provide the public with information regarding the activities of hate organizations within their locales. This monitoring provides law enforcement with demographic information that is necessary for the combating of these organizations. Further, the SPLC pursues lawsuits against such organizations for the purpose of destroying "networks of radical extremists".[48]

The ADL

The ADL was established to protect the interests of Jewish people who were often discriminated against in unlawful ways. The ADL, like the SPLC, is always ready to consider lawsuits against those who would discriminate or attack members of the Jewish community. The ADL has an excellent intelligence division, and it issues a quarterly news report alerting their membership of civil or criminal dangers.

The ADL serves a variety of purposes. According to the ADL, its mission involves the following functions[49]:

- Scrutinizes and exposes extremists and hate groups
- Monitors hate on the Internet
- Provides expertise on domestic and international terrorism
- Probes the roots of hatred
- Develops and delivers educational programs
- Fosters interfaith/intergroup relations
- Mobilizes communities to stand up against bigotry

The consistent performance of the above functions provides the ADL with a strong basis for effectively combating a variety of terrorist actions and other crimes that impact American society. The ADL maintains and operates the Center on Extremism, which exposes and documents the "groups and individuals whose ideologies and activities perpetuate hatred and extremism."[49] This function contributes toward the diminishing of criminal activity within America and the raising of awareness regarding such entities within US society.

The ADL tracks the primary extremist groups that impact American society. Each synopsis contains discussions regarding the recent, known activities of various extremist organizations; ideology and leadership characteristics; known affiliations; organizational tactics; and organizational history. The ADL does not monitor any specific type of extremism. Instead, it monitors a variety of categories ranging from the activities of the Aryan Nations and the New Black Panther Party for Self-Defense to the activities of the National Socialist Movement and the Little Shell Pembina movement.

The ADL also enjoys a strong relationship with law enforcement entities. Within the state of California, the ADL provides training for the San Bernadino County and Kern County law enforcement personnel. This training encompasses the "distinction between hate crimes and hate incidents, identifying and recognizing hate motivated behavior, the California white-power subculture and recognizing hate symbols."[49] Additional law enforcement relationships include California Department of Corrections and Rehabilitation, California Highway Patrol, and the Bureau of Land Management.[49]

ACLU

The ACLU sees itself as a champion of the Constitution. Through the years, it has staunchly defended the rights of free speech, even for unpopular groups, like the neo-Nazis. The ACLU also has developed intelligence databases, which they have provided to public authorities when appropriate. The ACLU also publishes intelligence reports and gives information to the public about entrenched domestic radical groups seeking to limit the activities of others and to use violence.

The domain of the ACLU is not limited solely to terrorism; they champion a variety of issues. Examples include voting rights, human rights, capital punishment, prisoners' rights, drug law reform, and women's rights. Regardless of the issue considered, the ACLU provides a myriad of information outlets through which it facilitates public awareness of sensitive issues that impact American society. Historically, privacy was a primary issue considered by the ACLU. Given the proliferation of antiterrorism and counterterrorism activities mandated by the US Government, privacy aspects of the liberty-versus-security argument remain salient ACLU issues.

During the time of the authorship of this textbook, American airports are implementing full-body x-ray scanners as a method of dissuading crime and terrorism. A variety of arguments indicate that these full-body scans are unacceptably perverse invasions of privacy. Arguments also involve the dangers of these scanners regarding the potential of contributing to the development of cancer, the diminishing of human reproductive potential, the developing of cataracts and impaired vision, and other health concerns. Although such scanning systems are preventive measures to thwart the potential of unwanted items entering an aircraft, they are controversial with respect to the liberty-versus-privacy argument.

At present, the ACLU is collecting data to "determine the scope of this problem and evaluate future action" of scanning technologies.[51] Although these technologies have had limited use within the United States, their use among other nations has sparked vigorous debates regarding the basic premise of security versus liberty. Within the United States, the ACLU has not announced any actions or positions regarding the implementation of these scanning systems. The ACLU has been a controversial organization historically. During modern times, its challenges to homeland and national security efforts have incited much debate within the legal system. Currently, the ACLU is challenging the Foreign Intelligence Surveillance Act (FISA) Amendments Act (FAA) of 2008.

According to the ACLU,[51] "This controversial piece of legislation not only effectively legalized the secret warrantless surveillance program that President Bush had authorized in late 2001, it gave the NSA new power to conduct dragnet surveillance of Americans' international telephone calls and e-mails en masse, without a warrant, without suspicion of any kind, and with only very limited judicial oversight." The ACLU pursued a lawsuit to "enforce a Freedom of Information Act (FOIA) request for records related to government agencies' implementation of the invasive FAA surveillance power" with respect to "information about how the FAA spying power is being interpreted and used, how many Americans are affected, and what safeguards are in place to prevent abuse of Americans' privacy rights." Further, the ACLU is currently challenging the constitutionality of the FAA.

Conclusion

As we have seen, terrorists are typically driven by particular ideologies. In this respect, domestic terrorists are a widely divergent lot, drawing from a broad array of philosophies and worldviews. Over the years, the nation has witnessed terrorism from both the left and the right. While left-wing groups, such as the Weather Underground and Symbionese Liberation Army, no longer exist, other entities, like the ALF and ELF, have taken their place.

The 1980s and 1990s saw a resurgence of groups on the radical right. In some instances, these groups have engaged in acts of terror and murder. As well, single-issue groups, such as the anti-abortion Army of God, escalated their use of violence to include assassination and bombing.

In addition, the patriot and militia movements emerged to protect America from what was perceived to be an impending takeover by hostile foreign interests and domestic traitors. Although domestic terrorism has fallen from the radar screens of many, replaced by the all-too-real danger of international entities like al Qaeda, many experts fear that current realities, including an economic crisis, runaway illegal immigration, and the fear of massive gun control, could easily inspire the movement.

Domestic terrorism is a bona fide threat within the United States. Recent American history records the horrific results of this reality. The strength of American society is its freedom to pursue life, liberty, and happiness. This open lifestyle is also its greatest vulnerability, one that has been exploited over the years and will be exploited again.

Key terms

Anti-Defamation League
Black separatist
Domestic terrorism
Hate group
Ideology
Neo-Nazi
Outlaw motorcycle gang
Southern Poverty Law Center
White supremacy

QUESTIONS FOR DISCUSSION

1. This chapter presents only a few of the domestic terror groups that pervade the United States. Do some research, and identify two others that are not discussed herein. Write a brief essay that summarizes your findings.

2. This chapter presents numerous ideologies that underlie domestic terrorist organizations. Compare and contrast some of these ideologies. Based on your observations, do you believe there is an increased possibility of coalitions forming among these groups? Why or why not? Write a brief essay that summarizes and substantiates your opinion.

3. This chapter introduces the concept of outlaw motorcycle gangs. Do some research, and determine the pervasiveness of this problem throughout America. Write a brief essay that highlights your findings.

4. Domestic terrorist organizations exist throughout the United States. Based on the descriptions presented within this chapter, how do you believe that law enforcement deals with and attempts to counter the activities of these organizations? Write a brief essay that summarizes and substantiates your opinion.

References

1. Malvo. (2006). Malvo takes the stand in beltway sniper trial. *FOX News*. http://www.foxnews.com/story/0,2933,196606,00.html (accessed November 14, 2010).
2. Federal Bureau of Investigation. (2002). Congressional testimony of James F. Jarboe: The threat of eco-terrorism. http://www.fbi.gov/congress/congress02/jarboe021202.htm (accessed March, 15, 2009).
3. Martin, G. (2010). *Understanding Terrorism: Challenges, Perspectives, and Issues* (3rd ed.). Thousand Oaks, CA: Sage Publishing, p. G-22.
4. Gerstenfeld, P. (2010). *Hate Crimes: Causes, Controls, and Controversies*. Thousand Oaks, CA: Sage Publishing, pp. 143–151.
5. Chalk, P., Hoffman, B., Reville, R. and Kasupski, A. (2005). *Trends in Terrorism: Threats to the United States and the Future of the Terrorism Risk Management Act*. Arlington, VA: RAND Corporation Publication, p. 47.
6. Bennett, B. (2007). *Understanding, Assessing, and Responding to Terrorism: Protecting Critical Infrastructure and Personnel*. Hoboken, NJ: Wiley Publishing, p. 45.
7. Hall, L. (2009). Disaggregating the scare from the greens. *Vermont Law Review*, 33(4), 689–715.
8. Jackson, B., Baker, J., Cragin, K., Parachini, J., Trujillo, H. and Chalk, P. (2005). *Aptitude for Destruction: Case Studies of Organizational Learning in Five Terrorist Groups*. Arlington, VA: RAND Corporation Publication, p. 142.
9. Deshpande, N. (2009). Pyro-terrorism: recent cases and the potential for proliferation. *Studies in Conflict & Terrorism*, 32(1), 36–44.
10. Walsh, A. and Ellis, L. (2007). *Criminology: An Interdisciplinary Approach*. Thousand Oaks, CA: Sage Publishing, p. 357.
11. Alexander, D. (2004). *Business Confronts Terrorism: Risks and Responses*. Madison, WI: The University of Wisconsin Press, pp. 24.
12. Bolden M., Raymer, G. and Whamond, J. (2001). *Domestic Terrorism and Incident Management*. Springfield, IL: Thomas Publisher, Ltd, p. 15.
13. The Various Shady Lives of the Ku Klux Klan. (1965). *Time Magazine*. http://www.time.com/time/magazine/article/0,9171,898581-3,00.html (accessed March 21, 2009).
14. Lay, S. (2005). Ku Klux Klan in the Twentieth Century. http://www.georgiaencyclopedia.org/nge/Article.jsp?id=h-2730 (accessed March 21, 2009).
15. Ku Klux Klan. (2013). *Southern Poverty Law Center*. http://www.splcenter.org/get-informed/intelligence-files/ideology/ku-klux-klan#.UYB8lsryCSo (accessed January 23, 2013).
16. German American Bund. (2013). *Encyclopedia Britannica*. http://www.britannica.com/EBchecked/topic/230640/German-American-Bund (accessed April 30, 2013).
17. Clark, C.S. Death of an Arlington Nazi. (2010). *North Virginia Magazine*. http://www.northernvirginiamag.com/entertainment/entertainment-features/2010/12/30/death-of-an-arlington-nazi/ (accessed January 23, 2013).

18. Associated Press. (September 9, 2004). White supremacist Richard Butler dies. *The Washington Post*. http://www.washingtonpost.com/wp-dyn/articles/A6967-2004Sep8.html. (accessed January 23, 2013), p. B05.

19. Aryan Brotherhood. (Website). http://www.prisonoffenders.com/aryan_brotherhood.html (accessed April 30, 2013).

20. FBI. (2010). Domestic terrorism: the sovereign citizen movement. *The Federal Bureau of Investigation*. http://www.fbi.gov/news/stories/2010/april/sovereigncitizens_041310/domestic-terrorism-the-sovereign citizen-movement (accessed April 29, 2013).

21. Bjelopera, J.P. (January 17, 2013). The domestic terrorist threat: Background and issues for congress. *Congressional Research Service*. http://www.fas.org/sgp/crs/terror/R42536.pdf (accessed February 22, 2013).

22. Black separatist. (2013). *Southern Poverty Law Center*. http://www.splcenter.org/what-we-do/hate-and-extremism (accessed May 1, 2013).

23. New Black Panther Party—Intelligence Files. (2013). *Southern Party Law Center*. http://www.splcenter.org/get-informed/intelligence-files/groups/new-black-panther-party#.UYU-dowo6M8 (accessed May 2, 2013).

24. Haga, M.W. (1995). *Taking Back America: The Revolution Begins*. New York: Acclaim Publishing Company, p. 34.

25. German, M. (June 5, 2005). Behind the lone terrorist, a pack mentality. *Washington Post*, p. B01.

26. Wright-Neville, D. (2010). *Dictionary of Terrorism*. Malden, MA: Polity Press, p. 61.

27. Mullins, W.C. (1997). *A Sourcebook on Domestic and International Terrorism: An Analysis of Issues, Organizations, Tactics, and Responses* (2nd ed.). Illinois: Charles Thomas Publishers, p. 233.

28. Motorcycle Gangs. (2013). *The United States Department of Justice*. http://www.justice.gov/criminal/ocgs/gangs/motorcycle.html (accessed April 12, 2013).

29. Best, S. and Nocella, A.J. II. (2006). *Terrorists or Freedom Fighters? Reflections on the Liberation of Animals*. New York: Lantern Books.

30. Swanson, C.R., Territo, L. and Taylor, R. (2008). *Police Administration*. New Jersey: Pearson/Prentice Hall.

31. Lamberg, L. (1999). Researchers urged to tell public how animal studies benefit human health. *The Journal of the American Medical Association*, *282*(7), 619–621.

32. Joosse, P. (2007). Leaderless resistance and ideological inclusion: The case of the Earth Liberation Front. *Terrorism & Political Violence*, *19*(3), 351–368.

33. Leader, S. and Probst, P. (2003). The Earth Liberation Front and environmental terrorism. *Terrorism & Political Violence*, *15*(4), 37–58.

34. Flükiger, J. (2008). An appraisal of the radical animal liberation movement in Switzerland: 2003 to March 2007. *Studies in Conflict & Terrorism*, *31*(2), 145–157.

35. Marris, E. and Simonite, T. (2005). Animal-rights militancy exported to United States and Europe. *Nature*, *438*(7096), 717–717.

36. Perlstein, G. (2003). Comments on Ackerman. *Terrorism & Political Violence*, *15*(4), 171–172.

37. ELF. (2010). *Earth Liberation Front*. http://earth-liberation-front.org/ (accessed June 18, 2010).

38. McCann, J. (2006). *Terrorism on American Soil: A Concise History of Plots and Perpetrators from the Famous to the Forgotten*. Boulder, CO: Sentient Publications.

39. Coombs, T. (2008). *PSI Handbook of Business Security,* Volume One. Westport, CT: Greenwood Publishing.

40. Gertz, B. (2011). L.A. Police use intel networks against terror, *The Washington Times*, http://www.washingtontimes.com/news/2011/apr/11/la-police-use-intel-networks-against-terror/?page=all (accessed August 26, 2013).

41. US Department of Homeland Security. (2003). Homeland Security Presidential Directive 5 (HSPD-5). http://www.fas.org/irp/offdocs/nspd/hspd-5.html (accessed May 1, 2013).

42. US Department of Homeland Security. (2013). State, Local, Tribal and Territorial Government Coordinating Council. http://www.dhs.gov/state-local-tribal-and-territorial-government-coordinating-council (accessed May 2, 2013).

43. Nemeth, C. (2013). *Homeland Security: An Introduction to Principles and Practice* (2nd ed.). Boca Raton, Florida: Taylor & Francis Group, LLC.

44. Keenan v. Aryan Nations. (2013). *Southern Poverty Law Center*. http://www.splcenter.org/get-informed/case-docket/keenan-v-aryan-nations#.UYB14cryCSo (accessed February 1, 2013).

45. Macedonia v. Christian Knights of the Ku Klux Klan. (2013). *Southern Poverty Law Center*. http://splcenter.org/get-informed/case-docket/macedonia-v-christian-knights-of-the-ku-klux-klan#.UYB2osryCSo (accessed February 1, 2013).

46. Austin v. James. (2013). *Southern Poverty Law Center*. http://www.splcenter.org/get-informed/case-docket/austin-v-james#.UYB3SMryCSo (accessed February 1, 2013).

47. Mansfield v. Church of the Creator. (2013). *Southern Poverty Law Center*. http://www.splcenter.org/get-informed/case-docket/mansfield-v-church-of-the-creator#.UYB6rcryCSo (accessed April 1, 2013).

48. Hate Map. (2013). *Southern Poverty Law Center*. http://www.splcenter.org/get-informed/hate-map (accessed April 29, 2013).
49. ADL. (2010). *Anti-Defamation League*. http://www.adl.org/home.asp?s=topmenu (accessed November 17, 2010).
50. 16 Bombs. (1998). 16 Bombs, three deaths. *The Washington Post*. http://www.washingtonpost.com/wp-srv/national/longterm/unabomber/bkgrdstories.ted.htm (accessed November 16, 2010).
51. ACLU. (2010). *American Civil Liberties Union*. http://www.aclu.org (accessed November 17, 2010).
52. ADL Applauds. (2008). ADL applauds law enforcement for preventing killing spree and Obama assassination attempt. *Anti-Defamation League*. http://www.adl.org/PresRele/NeoSk_82/5380_82.htm (accessed November 17, 2010).
53. ALF. (2010). *Animal Liberation Front*. http://www.animalliberationfront.com/MediaCenter/flash/AR_logic/index.html (accessed June 15, 2010).
54. Green, K. (2008). Animal rights activists defend firebombing attacks against US researchers. http://www.guardian.co.uk/world/2008/aug/04/usa1 (accessed November 16, 2010).
55. Appignanesi, L. and Maitland, S. (1990). *The Rushdie File*. United States: Institute of Contemporary Arts.
56. Aryan Nations. (2009). Web site. www.aryan-nations.com (accessed April 23, 2009).
57. Associated Press. (2009). US agency helped uncover 1973 NYC plot to kill Golda Meir. http://www.ynetnews.com/articles/0,7340,L-3665848,00.html (accessed November 13, 2010).
58. Barnard. (2010). Barnard: the liberal arts college for women in New York City. http://www.barnard.edu/bc1968/exhibit.html (accessed November 12, 2010).
59. Bath. (2010). Bath massacre. http://www.press.umich.edu/pdf/9780472116065_qa.pdf (accessed November 14, 2010).
60. Bhattacharjee, Y. (2010). FBI closes anthrax case, says Bruce Ivins was sole culprit behind letter attacks. *Science Magazine*. http://news.sciencemag.org/scienceinsider/2010/02/-fbi-closes-anthrax-case-says-br.html (accessed November 16, 2010).
61. Bohacik, A. (2008). When activists attack. *Risk Management, 55*(3), 30–34.
62. Byte. (2007). A byte out of history–'63 Baptist church bombing. *Federal Bureau of Investigation*. http://www.fbi.gov/news/stories/2007/september/bapbomb_092609 (accessed November 14, 2010).
63. CIA Intelligence. (2000). CIA Intelligence report tied Penochet to Letelier assassination. http://www.gwu.edu/~nsarchiv/news/letelier/index.html (accessed November 15, 2010).
64. College Student. (2002). College student charged in pipe bomb cases. *CNN News*. http://articles.cnn.com/2002-05-07/us/mailbox.pipebombs_1_luke-john-helder-pipe-bomb-james-bogner?_s=PM:US (accessed September 16, 2010).
65. Homicide. (2010). Congressman Scott Garrett proudly serving the 5th District of New Jersey. http://garrett.house.gov/News/DocumentSingle.aspx?DocumentID=156106 (accessed November 13, 2010).
66. Crime. (1970). Crime: A good deal. *Time Magazine*. http://www.time.com/time/magazine/article/0,9171,909181,00.html (accessed November 15, 2010).
67. Davis, P. and Glod, M. (2002). CIA shooter kasi, harbinger of terror, set to die tonight. *The Washington Post*. http://www.washingtonpost.com/ac2/wp-dyn/A55638-2002Nov14 (accessed November 15, 2010).
68. Delafuente, C. (2004). Terror in the age of Eisenhower: recalling the mad bomber whose rampage shook New York. http://query.nytimes.com/gst/fullpage.html?res=9C05E4DF1530F933A2575AC0A9629C8B63&sec=health&spon=&pagewanted=all (accessed November 12, 2010).
69. Discovery. (2007). Discovery of CIA tip of Israeli envoy's killer could revive 1973 case. http://www.haaretz.com/news/discovery-of-cia-tip-on-israeli-envoy-s-killer-could-revive-1973-case-1.224465 (accessed November 14, 2010).
70. Discovery Gunman. (2010). Discovery gunman James Lee's sordid past as a human smuggler. *ABC News*. http://abcnews.go.com/US/discovery-channel-attack-inside-james-lee-takedown/story?id=11541307&tqkw=&tqshow=WN&page=2 (accessed November 16, 2010).
71. Dowd, M. (1994). Crash at the white house: The overview: unimpeded, intruder crashes plane into white house. *The New York Times*. http://query.nytimes.com/gst/fullpage.html?res=9903E1D6173BF930A2575AC0A962958260&sec=health&spon=&pagewanted=all (accessed November 16, 2010).
72. Explosion. (2000). Explosion and fire at temple prompt an inquiry in Syracuse. *New York Times*. http://www.nytimes.com/2000/10/15/nyregion/explosion-and-fire-at-temple-prompt-an-inquiry-in-syracuse.html (accessed September 14, 2010).
73. Extremism. (2006). Extremism in the news. *Anti-Defamation League*. http://www.adl.org/learn/extremism_in_the_news/Other_Extremism/seattle_jewish_federation_shooting.htm?LEARN_Cat=Extremism&LEARN_SubCat=Extremism_in_the_News (accessed November 16, 2010).
74. FBI. (2005). Murder and mayhem in the Osage Hills. *Federal Bureau of Investigation*. http://www.fbi.gov/news/stories/2005/january/osage_012605 (accessed November 15, 2010).

75. Federal Bureau of Investigation. (2006). Eco-Terror indictments: 'Operation backfire' nets 11. http://www.fbi.gov/page2/jan06/elf012006.htm (accessed March 15, 2009).

76. Federal Bureau of Investigation. (2008). Putting intel to work against ELF and ALF terrorists. http://www.fbi.gov/page2/june08/ecoterror_063008.html (accessed February 12, 2009).

77. Fort Hood. (2009). Fort Hood and the growing Muslim extremist threat. http://www.adl.org/main_Terrorism/fort_hood_shooting.htm (accessed November 16, 2010).

78. Gage, B. (n.d.). Business as usual: The 1920 Wall Street explosion and the politics of forgetting. http://www.newschool.edu/nssr/historymatters/papers/beverlygage.pdf (accessed November 14, 2010).

79. George, J. and Wilcox, L. (1996). *American Extremists: Militias, Supremacists, Klansmen, Communists, and Others*. New York: Prometheus Books.

80. Gilliam, C. (2009). Suspect captured in killing of Kansas abortion doctor. *Reuters*. http://www.reuters.com/article/idUSTRE54U1JW20090601 (accessed November 16, 2010).

81. Green, K. (2008). To stop global warming, end eco-extremism: Pragmatic solutions provide the best options. *Fraser Forum*, 2008(April), 11–13.

82. Gross, G. (2008). FBI: Courthouse bomb was simple, but deadly. http://legacy.signonsandiego.com/news/metro/20080505-1503-bn05bomb.html (accessed November 16, 2010).

83. GTD. (2010). *Global Terrorism Database–University of Maryland*. http://www.start.umd.edu/gtd/search/Results.aspx?expanded=no&casualties_type=&casualties_max=&success=yes&perpetrator=20147&ob=GTDID&od=desc&page=1&count=100#results-table (accessed November 15, 2010).

84. Malvo. (2006). Malvo takes the stand in beltway sniper trial. *FOX News*. http://www.cnn.com/US/9702/24/empire.shooting/ (accessed November 15, 2010).

85. Hamilton, N. (2002). *Rebels and Renegades: A Chronology of Social and Political Dissent in the United States*. New York: Routledge.

86. Heining, A. (2010). Who is Joe Stack? http://www.csmonitor.com/USA/2010/0218/Who-is-Joe-Stack (accessed November 16, 2010).

87. Hertzberg, A. (1992). *Jewish Polemics*. New York: Columbia University Press.

88. History. (2010). Bomb explodes in capitol building. http://www.history.com/this-day-in-history/bomb-explodes-in-capitol-building (accessed November 12, 2010).

89. Homicide. (2010). *Homicide in Chicago*. http://homicide.northwestern.edu/crimes/haymarket1/ (accessed November 14, 2010).

90. Imperial. (2004). Imperial Kleagle of the Ku Klux Klan in Kustody. *Federal Bureau of Investigation*. http://www.fbi.gov/news/stories/2004/march/kkk031104 (accessed November 14, 2010).

91. Jersey City. (2010). Jersey City: Past and present. http://www.njcu.edu/programs/jchistory/pages/b_pages/black_tom_explosion.htm (accessed November 14, 2010).

92. Jewish Militant. (2004). Jewish militant faces bomb trial. *BBC News*. http://news.bbc.co.uk/2/hi/americas/3808015.stm (accessed November 15, 2010).

93. Kansas City. (n.d.). Kansas City massacre–Charles Arthur "Pretty Boy" Floyd. *Federal Bureau of Investigation*. http://www.fbi.gov/about-us/history/famous-cases/kansas-city-massacre-pretty-boy-floyd (accessed November 15, 2010).

94. Kaplan, J. and Loow, H. (2002). *The Cultic Milieu: Oppositional Subcultures in an Age of Globalization*. Walnut Creek, CA: Altamira Press.

95. Kushner, H. (2002). *Encyclopedia of Terrorism*. Thousand Oaks, CA: Sage Publishing.

96. Mullins, W.C. (1997). *A Sourcebook on Domestic and International Terrorism: An Analysis of Issues, Organizations, Tactics, and Responses*. Springfield, IL: Charles C. Thomas Publishing.

97. Liddick, D. (2006). *Eco-Terrorism: Radical Environmental and Animal Liberation Movements*. Westport, CT: Praeger Publishing.

98. Liddy, T. (2008). Three cops honored for '82 bomb heroics. *The New York Post*. http://www.nypost.com/p/news/regional/item_ArLTi4UFYqQnl2ctyQz3pN;jsessionid=1FFD71CA124AEDA0E8D916CA95C8A1DD (accessed November 15, 2010).

99. Nemeth, C. (2013) Homeland Security. An Introduction to Principles and Practice (2nd edition). Taylor & Francis Group, LLC. Boca Raton, Florida.

100. Mansfield, D. (2008). Rampage attributed to hatred of liberalism. *The Washington Post*. http://www.washingtonpost.com/wp-dyn/content/article/2008/07/28/AR2008072802314.html (accessed November 16, 2010).

101. Markon, J. (2010). After 40 years, search for University of Wisconsin bombing suspect heats up again. *The Washington Post*. http://www.washingtonpost.com/wp-dyn/content/article/2010/09/21/AR2010092106588.html (accessed November 14, 2010).

102. Mauro, J. (2010). A forgotten July 4 bombing at the world's fair. *National Public Radio*. http://www.npr.org/templates/story/story.php?storyId=128216755 (accessed November 15, 2010).

103. McNamara Brothers. (2010). The McNamara Brothers. http://www.libraries.uc.edu/libraries/arb/exhibits/mcnamara/bombing.html (accessed November 14, 2010).

104. McPheters, M. (2009). *Agent Bishop: True Stories from an FBI Agent Moonlighting as a Mormon Bishop.* Springville, UT: Cedar Fort.

105. Mississippi Burning. (2007). Mississippi burning. *Federal Bureau of Investigation.* http://www.fbi.gov/news/stories/2007/february/miburn_022607 (accessed November 14, 2010).

106. National Commission. (2004). National commission on terrorist attacks upon the United States. http://www.9-11commission.gov/report/911Report_Notes.htm (accessed November 16, 2010).

107. MSNBC. (2003). MSNBC–T is for terror. http://www.msnbc.msn.com/id/3070093 (accessed November 14, 2010).

108. News. (n.d.). News headlines from 1933. http://www.historic-newspapers.co.uk/Old-Newspapers/1933-Newspapers (accessed November 14, 2010).

109. No Bail. (2009). No bail for suspect in recruiter killing. http://www.upi.com/Top_News/2009/06/02/No-bail-for-suspect-in-recruiter-killing/UPI-97771243966695/ (accessed November 16, 2010).

110. Palmer Raids. (2007). The Palmer raids. *Federal Bureau of Investigation.* http://www.fbi.gov/news/stories/2007/december/palmer_122807 (accessed November 13, 2010).

111. Patty. (n.d.). The Patty Hearst kidnapping. *Federal Bureau of Investigation.* http://www.fbi.gov/about-us/history/famous-cases/patty-hearst-kidnapping (accessed November 14, 2010).

112. Pence, G. (2002). *Brave New Bioethics.* Lanham, MD: Rowan & Littlefield Publishers.

113. Redden, J. (2002). Tumultuous times fattened the files: Unprecedented activism and real crimes kept intelligence officers busy. *The Portland Tribune.* http://www.portlandtribune.com/news/story.php?story_id=13719 (accessed November 14, 2010).

114. Reid, T. (2009). White supremacist James W. Von Brunn kill guard at holocaust museum. *The Times.* http://www.timesonline.co.uk/tol/news/world/us_and_americas/article6473316.ece (accessed November 16, 2010).

115. Rudacille, D. (2001). *The Scalpel and the Butterfly: The Conflict between Science and Animal Protection.* Berkeley, CA: University of California Press.

116. Section Two. (n.d.). Section Two. http://prop1.org/park/pave/rev6.htm (accessed November 16, 2010).

117. Smith, C. (2010). Ayers' talk kept quiet at pitt. *Pittsburgh Tribune Review.* http://www.pittsburghlive.com/x/pittsburghtrib/news/s_673673.html (accessed November 14, 2010).

118. Springer, J. (2002). La Guardia Christmas bombing remains unsolved 27 years later. http://archives.cnn.com/2002/LAW/12/24/ctv.laguardia/ (accessed November 12, 2010).

119. Statement. (1999). Statement of special agent (Ret.) Richard S. Hahn before the senate committee on the judiciary hearing on FALN clemency September 15, 1999. http://www.latinamericanstudies.org/puertorico/hahn.htm (accessed November 15, 2010).

120. Stein, B. (2009). Point of view: punishing an act of bigotry. *The Riverdale Press.* http://www.riverdalepress.com/stories/Point-of-view-Punishing-an-act-of-bigotry,40679 (accessed September 14, 2010).

121. Stock, C.M. (1996). *Rural Radicals: From Bacon's Rebellion to the Oklahoma City Bombing.* New York: Penguin Books.

122. Switzer, J. (2003). *Environmental Activism: A Reference Handbook.* Santa-Barbara, CA: ABC-CLIO Publishing.

123. Tao, D. (2009). Police say 'fight club' inspired a bomber. *The New York Times.* http://www.nytimes.com/2009/07/16/nyregion/16starbucks.html?_r=1 (accessed November 16, 2010).

124. Terrorism Chronology. (2010). Terrorism chronology. *Australian Broadcasting Corporation.* http://www.abc.net.au/4corners/stories/s368066.htm (accessed November 15, 2010).

125. Terrorists Take. (2001). Terrorists take to Arizona. *CBS News.* http://www.cbsnews.com/stories/2001/10/26/attack/main316077.shtml (accessed November 15, 2010).

126. Time. (1965). New York: The monumental plot. *Time Magazine.* http://www.time.com/time/magazine/article/0,9171,833472-2,00.html (accessed November 14, 2010).

127. Tokar, B. (2001). *Redesigning Life: The Worldwide Challenge to Genetic Engineering.* London: Zed Books, Ltd.

128. Tulsa. (2010). The Tulsa Race Riot of 1921. http://www.montgomerycollege.edu/Departments/hpolscrv/VdeLaOliva.html (accessed November 12, 2010).

129. UMWA. (2010). *United Mine Workers Association.* http://www.umwa.org/?q=content/ludlow-massacre (accessed November 14, 2010).

130. UNC. (2006). UNC Grad in court on alleged hit and run. *FOX News.* http://www.foxnews.com/story/0,2933,186946,00.html (accessed November 16, 2010).

131. Webb, C. (2009). Counterblast: How the Atlanta temple bombing strengthened the civil rights cause. http://www.southernspaces.org/2009/counterblast-how-atlanta-temple-bombing-strengthened-civil-rights-cause (accessed November 14, 2010).

132. Southern Poverty Law Center. (2013). SPLC History, http://www.splcenter.org/who-we-are/splc-history (accessed August 26, 2013).

12

Border and Transportation Security

We must secure nearly 7500 miles of land border with Canada and Mexico, across which more than 500 million people, 130 million motor vehicles, and 2.5 million rail cars pass every year. We also patrol almost 95,000 miles of shoreline and navigable waters, and 361 ports that see 8000 foreign flag vessels, 9 million containers of cargo, and nearly 200 million cruise and ferry passengers every year. We have some 422 primary airports and another 124 commercial service airports that see 30,000 flights and 1.8 million passengers every day. There are approximately 110,000 miles of highway and 220,000 miles of rail track that cut across our nation, and 590,000 bridges dotting America's biggest cities and smallest towns. That is just a thumbnail of the vast infrastructure that supports the largest and most efficient economy in the world—with more than $11 trillion in Gross Domestic Product.

Remarks by former Deputy Secretary of Homeland Security, James Loy
at the National Cargo Security Council Annual Convention

Chapter objectives:

- Understand the concept of border security
- Gain an overview of the critical issues facing the nation in the areas of transportation and border security
- Examine the historical evolution of border security
- Identify the threats associated with air, land, maritime, and virtual borders

Introduction

Transportation security involves moving commerce and people safely and quickly. Each day, a myriad of goods and services are exchanged among global, national, regional, and local markets. Regardless of the economic systems that are advocated among nations, markets are the entities that manifest the exchanges of limited services and goods toward the satisfaction of unlimited human wants and needs through time. Given the proliferation of globalism during the preceding century, few of these markets facilitate exchanges in which goods and services are exclusively produced among any solitary nation. Instead, globalism interjects and integrates the provision of countless goods and services among destination markets that exist around the world, which are separate from their considered points of origin.

According to the United Nations, "Industrialized countries, with 19% of the world's population, account for 71% of global trade in goods and services, 58% of foreign direct investment, and 91% of all Internet users."[1] The United States conducts and participates in a signification amount of global and international trade. According to the US Department of Commerce, Bureau of Economic Analysis (BEA), recent examinations of the US economy, performed in October 2010, indicated that the US monthly international trade deficit decreased "from $44.6 billion (revised) in September to $38.7 billion in October, as exports increased and imports decreased."[2] Further, according to the BEA,[38] during the third quarter of 2010, US real gross domestic product (GDP) increased 2.6 percent in the third quarter of 2010 after increasing "1.7 percent in the second quarter."

Other considerations of US trade may be considered. According to the US government, in 2010, when measured in millions of US dollars on a nominal basis, and not seasonally adjusted, US export values to China were $72,276.2 million, and US imports from China were $299,026.0 million, thereby demonstrating a trade balance of –$226,749.8 million.[3] According to the US government, in 2010, when measured in millions of US dollars on a nominal basis, and not seasonally adjusted, US export values to Canada were $207,393.6 million, and US imports from Canada were $229,423.1 million, thereby demonstrating a trade balance of –$22,029.5 million.[4]

Finally, according to the US government, in 2010, when measured in millions of US dollars on a nominal basis, and not seasonally adjusted, US export values to Mexico were $133,961.4 million, and US imports from Mexico were $189,987.7 million, thereby demonstrating a trade balance of –$56,026.4.[5] These figures are demonstrative of a massive economic function, globally and internationally, through which goods and services are exchanged around the Earth.

Given these observations, it is obvious that these global exchanges of goods and services, which cross national borders, must be facilitated through some mechanisms of transportation. During modern times, three intermediaries exist through which these exchanges occur: (1) air, (2) sea, and (3) land. Air transportation involves the use of both passenger and cargo airlines. Maritime transportation encompasses oceangoing vessels that sail the world's oceans and barges that traverse American rivers and waterways. Land transportation involves the myriad of trucks and delivery vehicles that travel along roadways and interstates and the networks of railways that connect the American infrastructure.

Each of these intermediaries must function effectively and efficiently to facilitate their respective business and economic functions within modern society. Any impediments could interrupt the provision of services and goods among an array of settings. Because of just-in-time logistics, economic integration internationally and globally, the inability of some nations to produce the goods and services that are consumed within their economies, and the numerous economic dependencies that have resulted from globalization, it is imperative that these intermediaries be secured against the myriad of threats that endanger their operations.

Because of globalism, the US depends on other nations to supply many of the goods and services that are consumed within the American economy. Therefore, it is obvious that such goods and services must cross some form of national boundary (i.e., border) that separates America from its national neighbors and the remainder of the world. The penetrating of the US border involves the use of each of the preceding intermediaries. Once goods cross the American borders, they must be disseminated among their destination markets. Therefore, questions and considerations of border and transportation securities are of paramount importance regarding the safety and protection of American society.

Overview: Border and transportation security

The United States exhibits four types of borders: (1) land, (2) sea, (3) air, and (4) virtual. The land borders of the United States represent its national boundaries with the nations of Mexico and Canada, through which pass many individuals, vehicles, and goods. The sea borders of the United States include the myriad of ports through which massive quantities of goods and people enter and depart the nation. The borders of the United States represent a line of demarcation that intangibly separates it from other nations. For example, a foreign traveler may enter the United States via an airline, but must pass through a border that exists within the confines of an American international airport whose location may be deep inside the geographic expanse of the nation. This type of border is a virtual border.

Securing the borders and transportation systems of American society is a critical concern of homeland security. The events of September 11, 2001, were demonstrative of the necessity of maintaining the integrity of aviation transportation and having a good knowledge of the individuals that enter the United States. Along the US–Mexican border, the effects of drug wars impact American towns and citizens and interject their lethality among US and Mexican citizens. Further, numerous tunnels exist that connect the United States with Mexico, through which pass illegal aliens, narcotics, and a myriad of other entities. During the 20th century, Ted Kaczynski leveraged the logistics of the postal system to deliver his bombs among an unsuspecting audience. Each of these examples demonstrates some aspect of the American infrastructure that is characteristic of imperfect security.

Further, these examples are indicative of the notion that threats may originate both externally and internally. The events of September 11, 2001, were externally perpetrated by the al Qaeda organization, whose operatives entered America solely for the purpose of inflicting devastation and deadliness, to further the terrorist goals and agendas of the organization.

Many border and transportation security improvements occurred after the tragic events of September 11, 2001. The response to the 2001 attacks included the enactment of the Transportation Security Act of 2001, the creation of the Transportation Security Administration (TSA), and the passage of laws to strengthen border security. Such legislation included immigration policies, with respect to the admission of foreign nationals, and the strengthening of security within the maritime domain. The response also included the creation of the Department of Homeland Security (DHS) and its responsibilities of protecting American society and critical infrastructure against perilous threats.

However, despite the best efforts of the government and commercial sectors, no guarantee exists that security breaches shall not occur in due time. Because of the gigantic quantities of goods, services, individuals, and vehicles that cross the American borders daily, involving some form of transportation, the task of protecting American society is vast and challenging.

Historical perspective: Aviation and aerospace security

The uses of aviation and aerospace resources have long been associated with the notion of security. Within the United States, some of the earliest uses of such entities were demonstrated during the War for Southern Independence. During this conflict, both the Union and Confederate militaries employed the use of balloons for the purposes of reconnaissance. According to the United States Centennial of Flight Commission, these events represented the initial uses of balloons "in the United States for reconnaissance." Although the Union Army successfully completed the construction of a balloon, it was unused because "it escaped its tethers and was shot down to prevent it from falling into Confederate hands."[6]

From the perspective of homeland security, the notions of aerial reconnaissance and surveillance continue to be salient resources through which modern intelligence efforts are implemented and accomplished. The concept of transporting and delivering aviation resources, via waterborne vessels, continues to be a significant aspect of naval aviation and intelligence functions that facilitate aerial reconnaissance and surveillance.

Modern perspective: Aviation and aerospace security

Air carriers en route to the United States from a foreign country are required to submit passenger manifests before their arrival at a US port of entry (POE). While inspections are done on US soil, such advance notification alerts the Customs and Border Protection (CBP) inspectors to which travelers will need closer scrutiny. The manifest is transmitted electronically, via the Advanced Passenger Information System (APIS), which is integrated with the Interagency Border Inspection System (IBIS), a component of the US-VISIT program.[7]

The attacks of September 11, 2001, dramatically demonstrated the vulnerability of aviation security. The plot aboard Northwest Airlines (NWA) flight 253, on December 25, 2009, was unsuccessful when passenger Umar Farouk Abdulmutallab tried and failed to detonate concealed explosives. Another failed plot occurred on October 28, 2010, when aircraft were used to conceal and ship explosive devices. These events highlight the fact that the terrorist threat is a global challenge and that ensuring aviation security is a shared responsibility.

Although extensive efforts have been directed toward aviation passenger security, an additional area of major concern is cargo security among airlines. To highlight the crucial role of the private sector in this area, it is important to note that FedEx, UPS, DHL, and TNT together employ more than 1 million people around the world and own or operate more than 1700 aircraft. Each of these companies has operations in more than 200 countries. In 2008, air merchandise trade comprised almost 30% of US exports by value, totaling approximately $390 billion, and almost 20% of US imports by value, totaling more than $417 billion. Combined, that represents more than $800 billion of US–international merchandise trade.[56] These figures are not inclusive of the passenger airlines that carry cargoes within the underbellies of their aircraft (e.g., Delta, American, etc.). Regardless, such quantities are demonstrative of the economic saliency and relevancy of cargo airlines. Any impeding of their services and functions has the potential of affecting the US, international, and global economies.

In 1994, the Federal Express Corporation experienced the hijacking of one of its cargo airliners, flight 705. This event represented the terrorizing of an aircraft crew by one of their fellow employees of the corporation. This situation is unique because it involves the hijacking of a cargo aircraft solely for suicidal reasons. Historically, passenger airliners were hijacked for a variety of reasons and were routed to a myriad of destinations. Such reasons included inciting terrorist agendas; inciting political change; financial motivations; securing the release of various and sundry prisoners globally; or the unusual case of D.B. Cooper, in which the perpetrator parachuted from the aircraft, taking with him a large sum of money (**Figure 12.1**).

The attacks of September 11, 2001, although tragic, were indicative of aviation threats, posed by terrorist factions, whose origins were external to American society. The case of FedEx flight 705 is representative of a different threat, whose potential lethality also could have drastically affected numerous aspects of American society. In the case of FedEx flight 705,

Figure 12.1 The Federal Bureau of Investigation (FBI) wanted poster for D.B. Cooper. (Courtesy of the FBI.)

the threat represented an origin that was internal to American society. From the perspectives of homeland security and aviation, both events demonstrate that aviation threats exist that may be either external or internal to America and that such threats involve radically different motivations. Regardless, in both cases, the intent involved the use of commandeering aircraft to perform devastating acts of lethality.

The events of September 11, 2001, necessitated the cessation of all aviation flights, other than military and emergency aircraft, from occurring over the United States. Because of this interruption in the air transportation system, cargo airlines were unable to deliver their payloads for a period of time. As a result, many businesses and government entities, which relied upon just-in-time delivery supply chains, were impacted adversely. The agrarian sector also was impacted because of the inability to perform the aerial tasks of crop-dusting. This restriction also applied to passenger airlines. Many travelers were delayed, and passenger airlines that also carried cargo goods within the underbellies of their aircraft were unable to transport both their passengers and cargo payloads. Although alternative forms of transportation and logistics were implemented, the economic, financial, and personal impacts of ceased aviation transportation impacted countless individuals and organizations. As an interesting note, the Armed Cargo Pilot Program was discontinued 2 days prior to the attacks of September 11, 2001.

The accounts of FedEx flight 705 and September 11, 2001, provided lessons that served to improve American security functions within the aviation sector. Because of the FedEx event, corporate security and airport security were enhanced. These changes are representative of localized improvements that may be made to bolster security. Because of the 2001 events, the entirety of American aviation was impacted through the passing of legislation and operational embellishments that improved aviation security. Although such improvements are controversial and have incited much debate, their intent is to protect American society and its transportation infrastructure.

During modern times, aviation security may be considered from the perspective of National Security Presidential Directive 47/Homeland Security Presidential Directive 16 (NSPD-47/HSPD-16). It represents the national strategy of the United States regarding aviation security through which the "coordination and integration of government-wide aviation security efforts" are optimized.[8] A primary thrust of the strategy involves integration and cooperation between the public and private sectors toward coordinating an "effort to detect, deter, prevent, and defeat threats to the Air Domain, reduce vulnerabilities, and minimize the consequences of, and expedite the recovery from, attacks that might occur."[9]

Although this strategy expresses the foundational aspects of aviation security, it is supplemented by additional plans. Brief descriptions of these plans are given as follows:

- *Aviation transportation system security plan*—Uses a risk-based paradigm for "developing and implementing measures to reduce vulnerabilities within the aviation transportation system."[10]
- *Aviation operational threat response plan*—Establishes an array of "protocols to assure an effective and efficient United States Government response to air threats" that endanger national interests.[10]
- *Aviation transportation system recovery plan*—Expresses a variety of strategies regarding the "operational and economic effects" of an aviation domain attack, including measures to "enable the aviation transportation system and other affected critical government and private sector aviation-related elements to recover from such an attack as rapidly as possible."[10]
- *Air domain surveillance and intelligence integration plan*—Facilitates the coordination of "requirements, priorities, and implementation of national air surveillance resources" and the methods of sharing these resources with "appropriate stakeholders."[10]
- *International aviation threat reduction plan*—Expresses the "U.S. international activities to counter illicit acquisition and use by terrorists, other criminals, and other hostile individuals or groups of stand-off weapons systems" that represent the highest endangerments "to lawful civilian and military use of the air domain."[10]
- *Domestic outreach plan*—Facilitates the participation of stakeholders regarding the "implementation of the supporting plans and related aviation security policies" and expresses foundational "guidelines for outreach in the event of a threat to, or an attack

on, the United States or another disruptive incident to the aviation transportation system."[10]

- ***International outreach plan***—Represents a "comprehensive framework to solicit international support for an improved global aviation security network."[10]

Individually, each plan has its own goals regarding the safety of American society and protecting the nation from the risks of harmful events. Collectively, these plans approach aviation security from a robust perspective that accommodates a variety of risks and catastrophic events that must be acknowledged as potential endangerments to the American air domain. Their totality provides measures for the preparedness, mitigation, response, and recovery phases of operations that may be necessary in the event of an aviation event leveraged against the United States. Implementing these plans cumulatively facilitates much cooperativeness between domestic and international entities and both government and private organizations through which information is shared regarding any potential aviation threats. Regardless of the perspective, either cumulative or individual, these plans all share a common theme— deterring the chances of an attack against the United States, mitigating the effects of any incident that may occur, and facilitating a speedy recovery during the aftermath of any catastrophic incident.

Additional commentary: Aircraft hijacking

The cases of September 11, 2001, and FedEx flight 705 demonstrate two hijackings that served different purposes. The former was the result of radical Islamists, whose hijackings propagated terrorist agendas, whereas the latter was the result of a disgruntled employee, whose dishonesty resulted in a failed hijacking endeavor. In both instances, an aspect of the intent of the hijackers was to leverage the aircraft itself as a weapon through which their respective goals could be accomplished. However, these two instances are not the only events of aircraft hijacking that have occurred since the beginning of modern flight.

Hijacking events have occurred over approximately a half-century and have affected a myriad of nations and societies. Among these hijackings are examples of both the internal threats and external threats that endanger America and its allies. Within these examples are demonstrated a variety of motivations for performing the hijacking of aircraft: political, religious, economic, financial, revenge, and so forth. These examples are a testament to the modern necessities of attempting to ensure the integrity and safety of aviation environments, through security embellishments and improvements, which affect the infrastructures of American flight.

Because of the risk of hijacking, the necessity of security among aviation settings must be neither ignored nor discounted. Therefore, aviation environments must strive to ensure their safety and security through multiple methods. Based on the writings of Sweet,[51] one potential method of bolstering aviation security involves a layered methodology. According to Sweet,[51] the different security measures that comprise the layered security effect, with respect to the approach of countering hijacking, are as follows: (1) enhanced cargo, baggage, and passenger screening (**Figure 12.2**); (2) perimeter security and terrorism watch list (i.e., no-fly list); (3) cockpit door enhancement; (4) flight deck officers (voluntary); and (5) air marshals (i.e., sky marshals).[11]

The category of enhanced cargo, baggage, and passenger screening provides a security mechanism through which contraband materials and individuals that pose potential threats may be discovered before boarding aircraft. This activity provides a tool through which potential

Figure 12.2 Airport security screening. (Courtesy of Shutterstock.com, copyright James Steidl.)

weapons may be discovered and neutralized before any aircraft damage or criminal activity may occur. Various arguments are associated with this issue. Rudner[57] considers passenger screening from the perspective of identity fraud and potential threat and indicates that such procedures and processes hamper the movement of potential terrorists across borders. Ackleson[25] emphasizes the importance of screening cargo and items for safety purposes, but also notes the necessity of facilitating a strong level of unimpeded economic commerce that occurs through transportation networks. Given these considerations and perspectives, it may be concluded that airport screening provides a valid mechanism through which undesirable entities may be discovered, thereby dissipating potential catastrophes, and it also provides a perception of safety, real or imagined, within the mental models of air travelers and air personnel.

The categories of perimeter security and passenger watch lists (i.e., no-fly lists) also contribute toward the potential of stronger security among air environments. According to Rudner,[57] such methods may identify individuals who may pose risk or represent danger. Martonosi and Barnett (2006) advocate such examinations as a method of improving the probability of identifying individuals who may pose serious threats. Given such arguments, it may be concluded that such examinations may deter and prevent criminal activity from occurring through the potential identification of individuals who are wanted by law enforcement or who represent a high risk to flight safety.

Cockpit and flight crews are a component of aviation security and safety. Security of the cockpit area may occur through the use of weapons or strengthened doors to avoid any undesired cockpit access that may compromise the flight status of the aircraft. The category of cockpit door enhancement provides a safety mechanism that heightens the security of the cockpits and the safety of flight crews of aircraft as a method of diminishing the impacts of hijackings and other criminal activities that may occur during takeoff, flight, or landing. The category of voluntary flight deck officer status provides the means through which armaments may be provided to flight crew members as a safety and security attribute of air travel. Regardless of the method(s) selected, debate is associated with the use of weapons among such fragile and complex environments with respect to the damaging of equipment or interference with the operations of the aircraft.[12]

The category of air marshals (i.e., sky marshals) represents the presence of law enforcement among air routes and serves as a method through which the physical presence of a commissioned officer may address criminal situations that may arise during the course of travel. This program is commensurate with the writings of Gesell[40] regarding the legality of the presence of armed law enforcement officers among aircraft environments. Through the use of such personnel, individuals may be detained, apprehended, and arrested prior to the landing of the aircraft as a method of countering dangerous situations.

Based on the aforementioned discussions, it may be concluded that on-ground security is the dominant characteristic of airline safety and security. Based on the writings of Rudner[57] and Martonosi and Barnett (2006), screening may identify undesirable entities during the initial accessing of airport environments and thereby eliminate them from boarding aircraft as a method of avoiding danger.[73] However, such screening is not the only consideration of airline security.

The necessity of ensuring the security and safety of airport operations environments cannot be emphasized enough. For example, aircraft maintenance and review (e.g., preflight checks) must be performed to ensure the robustness and flight potential of the aircraft before terminal departure. Fuel areas must remain secure. Control towers, radars, and other electronic systems must be secure. Baggage areas and loading mechanisms must be secure as a method of avoiding dangerous items that may be carried among cargo-hold environments. Although the safety and security of the aircraft environment must be considered during all phases of flight (departure, travel, and disembarking), such an environment is merely a subset of the overall superset of airport and aerospace operations. Given the greater quantity of threat risks posed by the overall superset of aviation operations environments, it may be concluded that on-ground security is the dominant characteristic of airline safety and security because it provides the opportunity to counter dangerous situations prior to the departing of aircraft and lends itself to the safety and security of the overall aerospace and aviation operations environment.

Historical perspective: Maritime security

The concept of maritime security is not new. Maritime security has been an American concern since the creation of its original colonies and the founding of the United States. During modern times, American maritime interests must be maintained and protected to ensure the effective, efficient functioning of commerce activities. They must also be maintained and protected to ensure the logistical flow of vessels and goods among the earth's oceans. They must be maintained and protected to guard against the potential of hostile entities that may seek to leverage political agendas against the United States and its allies. Further, given the modern dangers of terrorism and the influences of organized crime, they must be maintained and protected to guard against such hostile entities.

Another example, the grounding of the *Exxon Valdez* along the Alaskan shore, in Prince William Sound, Alaska, in 1989 caused one of the worst maritime oil spills in American history. The economic and financial losses, incurred because of the *Exxon Valdez* accident, were tremendous. A variety of research studies examined the adverse impacts that affected the fishing industry, sport fishing sector, tourism, recreation, and replacement costs. According to the EVOSTC (n.d.),[67] the estimated value of "lost passive use" was $2.8 billion dollars. The lessons learned from the incident were varied. Skinner and Reilly[60] emphasize the notion that better preparedness could have improved the quality of the response regarding its efficiency and effectiveness. Further, Skinner and Reilly[60] indicate that better preventive measures are salient attributes of avoiding such catastrophic events. Further, because of the *Exxon Valdez* incident, numerous improvements regarding infrastructure were recommended, through which betterments in communications, logistics, environmental cleaning, and coordination occurred.

With respect to the modern application of homeland security initiatives, the lessons learned from the *Exxon Valdez* are timeless and are clearly appropriate regarding the contemporary issues concerning the efficiency and effectiveness of disaster responses. The incident shows that human imperfections and human errors may cause disasters of massive proportions. Although technologies have changed during the preceding 20 years, human nature remained unchanged. The potential for another incident, comparable to the events of the grounding of and succeeding oil spillage from the *Exxon Valdez*, resulting from human imperfections, exists among modern maritime environments.

Another timeless lesson involves nature itself. Although technologies changed during the decades that succeeded the *Exxon Valdez* incident, nature remains unchanged. Mountains still impede radio communications if electronic repeaters are not present to strengthen the transmissions and conveyances of radio signals. Stormy weather still necessitates the grounding of aircraft that may be necessary during response initiatives. Rough seas still may impede the provision of maritime resources and other supplies that are necessary during responses. Modern practitioners of homeland security must be aware of this lesson and its representative constraints of nature.

During modern times, America must ensure that its maritime abilities of conducting global and international trades are unimpeded because of the current manifestations of economic integrations that exist between America and a myriad of nations. These relationships provide foreign products for consumption within the American economy and provide American products for consumption among other economies globally. Hence, given the historical growth of globalization, modern America has many partners—and is dependent upon each of them as they commensurately depend upon America to facilitate mutual economic benefits.

Accidents happen. This notion is certainly appropriate for any field of endeavor—especially the disciplines and vocations of homeland security. Modern practitioners of homeland security must be prepared to implement quality disaster responses both effectively and efficiently. However, prevention is certainly a core component of both avoiding and mitigating the potential risks associated with a variety of accident scenarios. During modern times, American infrastructure must be committed to the prevention of accidents, thereby avoiding costly responses and impediments regarding the provision of resources that are necessary attributes of economic functioning and national security. If accidents do happen, then homeland security practitioners must be prepared to render appropriate responses. Both preparedness and responsiveness not only must accommodate the logistics of a situation but also must consider the characteristics of nature that may affect the disaster response.

Modern perspective: Maritime security

More than 80% of the world's trade, by volume, is conducted by ship, and 99% of overseas trade, by volume, enters or leaves the United States by ship. Such a vast transportation system can only be secured through the combined efforts of federal, state, and local governments and the contributions of private industry. The US Coast Guard (USCG) is the primary federal agency in securing the maritime transportation mode, and the US CBP also shares much of this responsibility. The TSA's Port and Intermodal Division is engaged in this unified, national effort, primarily by providing expertise in credentialing as well as passenger and vehicle screening techniques and procedures.[55]

Although America boasts such government organizations regarding the protection and security of shipping, national coasts, and waterways, external threats exist that may affect the provision of seaborne goods and services. The preceding section considered the accounts of the Barbary pirates, whose piracy impeded international trade during the 19th century. Over two centuries later, the concepts and deeds of piracy continue to endanger maritime environments. During recent years, acts of sea piracy have gained notoriety among a myriad of national media outlets. According to the US Department of State, Bureau of Consular Affairs (BCA), "Piracy at sea is a worldwide phenomenon which has affected not only the coasts of Africa, but also Indonesia, Malaysia, the Philippines, Yemen, Venezuela, and the Caribbean. American citizens considering travel by sea should exercise caution when near and within these coastal areas."[46]

During recent years, significant acts of piracy have occurred near the continent of South America, within the Gulf of Aden, within the regions of Asia and the Pacific Ocean, and near the continent of Africa (**Figure 12.3**). Although acts of piracy may occur anywhere, US agencies and organizations perform a masterful job of ensuring the safety of American waters. However, regarding other nations, such protections either are limited or are nonexistent.

According to the BCA, "Incidents of piracy off the coast of Venezuela are a serious concern."[46] These acts of piracy involved "violent attacks" against "private vessels" that included the "severe beating of an American citizen, the fatal shooting of an Italian citizen, and a machete attack on a U.S. citizen."[46] In 2008, an act of piracy "resulted in the death of one American citizen and injury to another when pirates boarded their private boat."[46]

The BCA also provides warnings regarding the Asian and Pacific regions. According to the BCA, the Strait of Malacca, which is located between Indonesia and Malaysia, "was long considered to be the world's most dangerous waters for pirate attacks."[46] However, since 2005, within this region, piracy has decreased because of "increased military patrols and vessel security."[46] The BCA also indicates that the International Maritime Bureau (IMB) "reported 25 pirate attacks in the Straits of Malacca in 2004, 10 in 2005, and only two through the third quarter of 2008."[46]

Additional considerations involve the region surrounding Tioman Island near Malaysia. According to the BCA,[46] four piracies were reported in 2008. However, this area is "not

Figure 12.3 US Navy and Marine Corps visit, board, search, and seizure team members stationed aboard the guided missile cruiser USS San Jacinto (CG 56) stand guard over suspected pirates on board a dhow as they travel the waterways of the Gulf of Aden on May 27, 2010. USS San Jacinto is part of a multinational task force established in January 2009 to conduct counterpiracy operations under a mandate to actively deter, disrupt and suppress, and protect global maritime security and secure freedom of navigation for all nations. (Courtesy of the US Navy. Photo by Mass Communication Specialist Second Class Ja'lon A. Rhinebart.)

historically known for piracy."[46] Further, it is advisable for "all ships transiting the South China Sea, off Tioman Island" to "maintain a strict watch" because "pirates, armed with guns and machetes, robbed three vessels and hijacked a tugboat and barge."[46]

Piracy within the Gulf of Aden, especially near Somalia, received much attention among media outlets during recent years because of its tenacity, scope, and magnitude. According to the BCA, "In some instances attacks have occurred as far as 300 nautical miles out in international waters," and the majority of the piracies were conducted against "cargo vessels."[46] Although most of these piracies occur against cargo ships, others are also perpetrated against cruise vessels. According to the BCA,[46] "Recent incidents in the region include an attack on Oceania Cruises' premium cruise ship, the Nautica, in the Maritime Safety Protection Area in the Gulf of Aden; an attempted attack on Transocean Tour's cruise ship MS Astor in the Gulf of Oman; the hijacking of a 50-foot yacht resulting in the kidnapping of the two French citizens aboard; and the seizure of a French luxury yacht and its 30 crew members."

Piracy within the Pacific Ocean is a concern for America. Because the United States conducts a vast amount of trade with China, the Pacific Ocean is the primary intermediary through which goods and vessels travel between the two nations. Any interruption of the maritime logistics system could impede the flow of goods that are consumed within the American economy. This concept is not exclusive to the American relationship with China. Instead, it is also applicable regarding any nation with which the United States manifests a logistical system of imports or exports. Therefore, the monitoring of sea-lanes and vessels is a paramount consideration of maritime security.

The Office of Law Enforcement of the National Oceanic and Atmospheric Administration (NOAA) maintains a vessel monitoring system (VMS) that currently tracks over 5900 small vessels, with an anticipated expansion of another 2500 vessels this calendar year. In addition, NOAA maintains law enforcement information on small vessels through its Law Enforcement Accessible Database System (LEADS), which tracks investigations, incidents, activities, and outreach. An additional resource is the International Chamber of Commerce, which also records transactions of piracy among the Earth's oceans.

The preceding section considered the accident of the *Exxon Valdez*. Although the accident occurred over 20 years ago, accidents continue to impact American society. In 2010, another spillage of oil occurred that impacted America. This incident occurred on April 20, 2010, when a British Petroleum (BP) oil well exploded within the Gulf of Mexico and caused a continuous, undersea spillage of oil to escape from an undersea oil well. This event "easily eclipsed the *Exxon Valdez* as the biggest oil spill in U.S. history."[29] Similar to the events and consequences of the *Exxon Valdez*, the Gulf of Mexico spillage adversely affected the environmental and economic facets of the region along the American coastline.

The volume of the spillage manifested a "rate of between 12,000 to 19,000 barrels a day—much higher than the initial estimate of 5000 barrels a day."[58] Containment of the spillage was attempted multiple times and involved the application of "heavy drilling liquids" and "dubbed mud" within the "fractured wellhead to beat back the flow of oil, before sealing it with concrete."[58]

The cause of the accident demonstrated a myriad of factors that contributed toward the manifesting of the catastrophe. According to the National Commission on the BP Deepwater Horizon and Offshore Drilling,[54] the accident occurred as a combination of the following characteristics of the problem domain:

> The well blew out because a number of separate risk factors, oversights, and outright mistakes combined to overwhelm the safeguards meant to prevent just such an event from happening. But most of the mistakes and oversights at Macondo can be traced

back to a single overarching failure—a failure of management. Better management by BP, Halliburton, and Transocean would almost certainly have prevented the blowout by improving the ability of individuals involved to identify the risks they faced, and to properly evaluate, communicate, and address them. A blowout in deepwater was not a statistical inevitability.

According to Salazar-Winspear,[58] as part of the disaster response effort, the Obama administration terminated further drilling and exploration initiatives within the Gulf of Mexico, which included "suspending 33 deepwater exploratory wells being drilled in the Gulf." This action affected the economic functions of a variety of organizations and individuals whose dependence upon the oil industry facilitated their livelihoods. The economic impacts were also unconstrained to the immediate region of the incident. Salazar-Winspear[58] indicates that additional exploration and drilling restrictions were also implemented that suspended "planned exploration in two locations off the coast of Alaska" and oil facility lease sales near the coast of Virginia.

The lessons of the *Exxon Valdez* encompassed the facets of both human imperfections and nature that must be observed among members of the homeland security community. Humans are imperfect and are susceptible to errors and mistakes that cause accidents. Nature, through its innate characteristics of weather and geography, also must be considered with respect to incident preparedness and disaster responses. Similar lessons are learned from the Gulf of Mexico oil spillage disaster. According to the National Commission on the BP Deepwater Horizon and Offshore Drilling,[54] these concepts are expressed as follows:

> Deepwater drilling provides the nation with essential supplies of oil and gas. At the same time, it is an inherently risky business given the enormous pressures and geologic uncertainties present in the formations where oil and gas are found—thousands of feet below the ocean floor. Notwithstanding those inherent risks, the accident of April 20 was avoidable. It resulted from clear mistakes made in the first instance by BP, Halliburton, and Transocean, and by government officials who, relying too much on industry's assertions of the safety of their operations, failed to create and apply a program of regulatory oversight that would have properly minimized the risks of deepwater drilling. It is now clear that both industry and government need to reassess and change business practices to minimize the risks of such drilling.

Because of the recentness of the event, it is currently impossible to know the full scope and magnitude of the effects of the disaster strategically. However, within the coming decades, a better realization and understanding of the effects and the consequences of the Gulf oil spillage will be attained. However, during the current period of time, initial observations are commensurate with the lessons learned from the *Exxon Valdez* disaster: Humans are imperfect, nature is challenging, and any economic activity is not without risk. Practitioners of homeland security must observe and affirm these lessons. Regarding the Gulf oil spillage, the rendering of decisions was imperative to providing an effective, efficient response. However, the rendering of decisions was also an important component of prevention. Based on the preceding excerpts, the disaster may have been prevented if better decisions and actions had occurred before the explosion.

Petroleum is a natural resource. A large portion of the American transportation system is fueled by this natural resource. Ensuring the integrity, security, and safety of its current production mechanisms is a paramount aspect of homeland security because of the fuel dependencies that exist within the American economy. Therefore, preventive measures must be acknowledged as a salient consideration of preserving the integrity, effectiveness, and efficiency of obtaining and processing natural fuels. In the event that catastrophes occur, responses must be done quickly, efficiently, and effectively in accordance with any disaster plans that exist federally or among the states.

The Gulf incident also has another implication: market alternatives. Petroleum is a natural resource and is finite. Therefore, its quantities are limited. From a perspective of homeland security, this constraint impacts facets of both the economy and national security. Not only is petroleum the basis of producing fuels for the American transportation system (e.g., gasoline); it is also used to produce pharmaceutical, medical, plastic, and roadway-paving products. Although the American economy depends upon its availability, its limitation, as natural resource, must be considered within the context of market alternatives (e.g., fuel cells, solar power, etc.) as a method of satisfying the American demands within its transportation system.

Throughout history, various concepts and lessons are unchanging regarding their implications for homeland security. During the Jeffersonian period of the 19th century, and during modern times, maritime piracies affected, and continue to affect, American interests adversely. The Jefferson administration fought against the Barbary pirates, whereas modern presidents are concerned with the issues of piracy among the maritime regions of South America, within the Gulf of Aden, within the regions of Asia and the Pacific Ocean, and near the continent of Africa. The 20th century witnessed the catastrophe of the *Exxon Valdez*, whereas the 21st century now witnesses the Gulf of Mexico disaster. Both incidents provided lessons regarding nature and the imperfections of humans.

Within the context of homeland security, from a maritime perspective, both the set of historical examples and the set of modern examples provide much insight regarding the concepts of transportation and border security. American interests must not be impeded by hostile actors that attempt any forms of extortion toward the furtherance of their agendas. The infrastructure of the American economy must also be secure, and its safety and integrity must not be compromised. However, despite the best and highest attempts to protect American infrastructure and economic functions, accidents happen that necessitate disaster responses. When responses are implemented, their lessons must be observed to influence preparedness functions as a method of potentially avoiding future cataclysms or of improving the quality of future disaster responses.

Historical perspective: Mass transit and railway security

Historically, mass transit matured with the growth and the expansion of American society, especially the construction of the nation's railroad system. Mass transit also changed in conjunction with the technological advancements that improved society through time. According to Schrag,[59] the origins of American mass transit are among the introductions of "horse-drawn omnibuses and streetcars in Eastern cities" during the 1830s. Throughout 19th century, American mass transit systems created and expanded rail services and subway systems.

Although such technological advancements in transportation provided numerous benefits within society, their existence and use also presented a variety of risks. In 1866, the Reno gang successfully accomplished the "first robbery of a moving train in the U.S., making off with over $10,000 from an Ohio and Mississippi train in Jackson County, Indiana."[36] Before the implementation of this "innovation in crime," train robberies occurred "only on trains sitting at stations or freight yards."[36] This tactic quickly expanded toward the American west, where "the recently constructed transcontinental and regional railroads made attractive targets."[36] During this period, trains "often carried" large cash reserves, thereby making them "attractive targets for thieves."[36]

Such attacks prompted security improvements among the railway infrastructures. Railroad companies began to resist these attacks and fortified their boxcars. During this period, security improvements included "protecting their trains' valuables with large safes" employing "armed guards."[36] These security improvements increased the difficulties of train robbery and altered the risks and dangers associated with robbing trains.[36] Historically, such train robberies are indicative of the human greed that motivated acts of crime among railways.

However, other dangers existed that threatened railway systems historically. During the 19th century and the 20th century, numerous railway accidents occurred that were caused accidentally. Among these accidents was the death of a notable figure in American history: Casey Jones. In 1900, a train collision occurred in Vaughn, Mississippi, which claimed the life of Jones.[43] Jones was employed with the Illinois Central Railroad (ICR) as an engineer.[43] During inclement weather, consisting of fog, Jones was the engineer aboard a passenger train, the *Cannonball Express*, when it collided with a stationary freight train in Vaughn.[28,43] Jones attempted to halt the forward movement of his train but was unsuccessful. Although his actions saved the lives of his passengers, Jones died during the incident.[43]

These historical accounts are representative of two categories of threats that endangered American railways. First, railways were susceptible to attacks perpetrated by humans. Regardless of the motivations for such violence, susceptibilities existed among railways that were indicative of poor, if any, security features. Such attacks could impede the economic functioning of American society through the impeding of the transportation system and the thefts of cash reserves. Second, railways were susceptible to accidents. Regardless of the severity of the outcomes, accidents existed that damaged the railway infrastructure and were lethal.

Commensurate with the timelessness of the historical lessons learned from the maritime and aviation sectors, the American railway system also demonstrates lessons that are timeless. The lack of security among railway settings facilitated the easiness of train robbery, thereby allowing hostile entities to perpetrate their agendas against society. Because of absent security features, attacks against the railway system impeded the economic flows of goods and impeded the functioning of the railway system. During modern times, railways are a sizeable component of the national transportation infrastructure. Therefore, railways must implement security features to bolster their integrity and quality of service. Railways must also ensure that the integrity and functions of their infrastructure are unimpeded and that they perform efficiently and effectively.

Railway accidents were indicative of human error, mechanical failures, or inclement weather. Regardless of the cause, modern railway environments are susceptible to threats identical to those that existed during the 19th century. During modern times, equipment may malfunction, inclement weather may affect railway infrastructure, or human errors may cause severe accidents. Therefore, modern railway environments must consistently and continuously evaluate their infrastructures to maximize both security and safety attributes.

Modern perspective: Mass transit and railway security

Within the United States, approximately 6000 mass transit systems serve about 15 million riders daily. In comparison, the nation's airlines carry about 2 million passengers per day. The systems include everything from small-town bus services to massive transit systems that include integrated bus and rail service.[52] White[66] indicates, "There are roughly 140,000 miles of active track in the national freight rail network comprised of the Class Is and about 600 short line railroads; 23,000 miles of track used for rail passengers; 7100 miles of urban rail transit systems; 165,000 miles of bus routes; and more than 4 million miles of interstate, national highway and other roads open to the trucking industry within America's surface transportation system." The use of mass transit, combined with the limited security designed to detect or record criminal activity within the systems, makes mass transit a prime target for threat groups. Given the vastness of the American mass transit infrastructure, it is impossible to completely and totally ensure its security (**Figure 12.4**).

However, among segments of this system, security may be improved. Such improvements are not without challenges. Guerrero[42] indicates that mass transit systems exhibit the characteristics of open systems, in which security mechanisms are few, because of the necessity of transporting "large numbers of people quickly." Although the aviation industry has significantly improved its security mechanisms through the use of scanners, searches, and other methods, the remaining components of American mass transit do not demonstrate such tenacity. Examples of such openness include the ability of passengers to access and travel within buses, subways, and trains with few, if any, security mechanisms and restrictions. Further, such openness facilitates vulnerabilities because of the general inability to "monitor or control who enters or leaves the systems."[42]

The manifesting of such openness increases the attractiveness of mass transit systems as potential targets for damage or destruction. Additional target attractiveness is manifested because such systems exhibit the characteristics of "high ridership, expensive infrastructure, economic importance, and location (e.g., large metropolitan areas or tourist destinations)."[42] The impracticalness of implementing security features is demonstrated through the high quantity of passengers that rely upon mass transit for transportation; the costs associated with developing, testing, and implementing security features; and the costs of securing the quantity of "access points" along routes.[42] Obviously, the American mass transit system is susceptible to attacks.

However, even if these systems manifested stringent security features, the risk of accidents, necessitating disaster responses, would persist. Such risks are unavoidable and have affected American mass transit during the preceding decades. According to the National Transportation Safety Board (NTSB),[31] in 1993, the derailing of Amtrak Train 2, the Sunset Limited, traveling between Los Angeles, California, and Miami, Florida, occurred in Mobile, Alabama, when it collided with a displaced bridge. This accident caused the deaths of 47 people (42 passengers and 5 members of the train crew) and injured 103 passengers.[31] The implications of this

Figure 12.4 Due to the high volume of people, and the fact that transit systems need to be open and accessible, they are a prime target for threat groups. (Courtesy of Shutterstock.com, copyright Christian Mueller.)

accident must be acknowledged regarding the security, safety, and integrity of railways within the American mass transit system. This accident necessitated the improving of the mass transit infrastructure among American railways.

It is impossible to eliminate completely the risks of accidents that may affect the railway system. Therefore, practitioners of homeland security must be mindful of the potential for such accidents among the myriad of railway networks that connect American cities. Although the Alabama tragedy occurred in conjunction with a passenger railroad carrier (i.e., Amtrak), freight railroad entities are susceptible to identical risks of accidents.

Within the United States, freight railroads represent a significant component of the transportation system that facilitates the functioning of the American economy. According to the American Association of Railroads,[32] in 2008, freight railroads employed approximately 184,000 personnel and generated approximately "$265 billion in total economic activity" annually that included "direct, indirect, and induced effects." Freight railroads demonstrate greater fuel efficiency than roadway trucks. In 2009, "U.S. railroads moved a ton of freight an average of 480 miles per gallon of fuel" and were "four times more fuel efficient than trucks."[32] Given the preceding considerations regarding the limitations of petroleum fuels, this consideration is significant because of the contributions provided by railroads within the American economy. Further, according to the American Association of Railroads,[32] a "train can carry the freight of 280 or more trucks," thereby reducing "highway gridlock, the costs of maintaining existing highways, and the pressure to build costly new highways." This observation is also relevant given the necessity and costs of maintaining the American highway system.

Based on data obtained from the American Association of Railroads,[32] the following observations are demonstrative of the economic potency of the freight railway system:

- The main freight of railroads is bulk cargo, such as coal, heavy equipment, and iron ore.
- Annually, railroads transport approximately "1.7 million carloads of wheat, corn, soybeans, and other agricultural products, plus another 1.5 million carloads of animal feed, beer, birdseed, canned produce, corn syrup, flour, french fries, frozen chickens, sugar, wine, and countless other food products."
- Annually, the "2 million carloads of chemicals that America's railroads carry" assist to clean American water, fertilize farms, package food, build cars and homes, protect health, and enhance well-being "in thousands of other ways."
- Approximately "half of America's electricity is produced from coal, and railroads haul 70 percent of America's coal." Further, the amount of "electricity produced from rail-delivered coal is enough to meet the power needs of every home in America." Therefore, because of contributions toward "keeping coal-based electricity affordable," freight railroads "reduce the dependence on imported energy and save money."
- Annually, "America's freight railroads carry 1.3 million carloads of lumber and paper products—including wood to build our homes, newsprint and magazine paper, and cardboard for packaging. Railroads also haul tens of thousands of carloads of recycled paper each year."
- "Intermodal service (moving shipping containers and truck trailers on rail cars) transports a huge variety of consumer goods, from electronics and greeting cards to clothing and furniture, as well as industrial and agricultural products. Approximately 60 percent of rail intermodal traffic consists of imports or exports, reflecting the vital role railroads play in international trade."

- Annually, freight railroads "deliver millions of new cars and trucks and many of the parts and accessories used to build them."
- "Railroads also carry millions of carloads of raw materials and industrial products that are critical to our way of life, including metallic ores (such as iron ore and bauxite for aluminum), steel and other metal products, petroleum, crushed stone and gravel, cement, scrap metal for recycling, and much more."

The preceding facts are indicative of the notion that American railroads represent a mode of transportation that contributes toward the satisfaction of the demand that exists for goods and services within the American economy. It is imperative that this system function effectively and efficiently without impediments. Any damage or destruction within this system could easily delay or prohibit the delivery of a myriad of products within the American economy. If this system were disrupted, the delivery of pharmaceutical products, fuels, and an array of other necessary products would be hampered. Therefore, practitioners of homeland security must be mindful of the importance and significance of the American railway system regarding both consumer interests and national security.

The railway system is a critical component of American transportation. The integrity of the railway system must be monitored and maintained to ensure its functioning effectively and efficiently. American railways serve the purposes of transporting people and transporting freight among urban and rural areas. Although it is susceptible to incidents of both accident and attack, some levels of security mechanisms exist within its infrastructure. However, these security features are less stringent when compared with those of the aviation sector. During modern times, the events of September 11, 2001, gained attention regarding short-comings within the aviation sector, thereby facilitating numerous security improvements within its infrastructure. However, the importance of the railway system is comparable to the importance of the aviation system: Both are intermediaries for transporting people and freight. Given this realization, from a homeland security perspective, railway entities must be mindful of incident preparedness and must facilitate disaster recovery and response efforts.

Following the events of September 11, 2001, numerous alterations occurred to improve railway security. Although the TSA was tasked with aviation security after its creation, it was also tasked with protecting American ports, highways, and railways.[13] In addition to the influences of government organizations, private railway entities also undertook the analyses of strengths, weaknesses, opportunities, and threats (SWOT) as methods of assessing and evaluating their operational vulnerabilities.[13] Some of these activities, in conjunction with government regulations, also fostered the crafting of detailed railway operational maps that could be shared with emergency responders if an incident occurs.[13] New tracking technologies were developed that located the real-time positions of railway cars among railroad networks.[13] Railway corporations forged collaborative agreements with emergency responders and provided access to railway cars for emergency responder training.[13]

Changes following the events of September 11, 2001, have affected and permeated all of the states within the Union. For instance, within Texas, specific attention is given to the routing of hazardous materials, bridge management, and tank car safety.[14] Specifically, these changes incorporated the rerouting of hazardous materials along rail lines to diminish the risk of catastrophic incidents near populated areas.[14] Texas also gives specific attention to inspecting railway operations and resources to ensure their integrity and to ensure the safety of society. Such inspections may identify "defects requiring repair within a specified time limit or serious defects requiring immediate repair or removal from service."[14]

The economic, logistical, and strategic importance of railways must be acknowledged with respect to their contributions to critical national infrastructure. Given the vast quantities of people, materials, and resources that flow throughout railway networks, maintaining their performance is of paramount importance to the nation. Railways carry goods and people from ports to inland regions nationally. Conversely, they ferry goods and people from inland origins to seaside destinations. Railways are resources through which mass quantities of numerous goods, ranging from medicines to munitions, may be transferred and distributed throughout the nation. Because of the dangerousness of hazardous materials that may be lethal or severely damaging to human health and the ecosystem, railways are a resource for transporting these items through routes that may reduce the chances of endangering human life. Maintaining the integrity of the railway system is a significant goal of homeland security.

Container and cargo security

Much of the recent US maritime security efforts have focused on regulating cargo containers and large vessels at official POEs. The US maritime system consists of more than 300 sea and river ports with more than 3700 cargo and passenger terminals, with most ships calling at US ports being foreign-owned. Container ships have been the focus of much of the attention on seaport security due to the potential of terrorists infiltrating them. More than 12 million marine containers enter US ports each year (**Figure 12.5**), and while all cargo information is analyzed by CBP officers for possible targeting for closer inspection, only a fraction is actually physically inspected. CBP works in tandem with the USCG at sea POEs. Efforts such as the coast guard's requirement that ships provide a 96-hour notice of arrival and CBP's Container Security Initiative (CSI) program aid in preventing more harmful things from getting into the United States.[7]

Figure 12.5 Billions of dollars' worth of cargo is shipped globally, and a staggering 12 million marine containers enter US ports each year. (Courtesy of Shutterstock.com, copyright Artens.)

Container and cargo container security initiatives address the threat to border security and global trade posed by the potential for terrorist use of a maritime container to deliver a weapon and to expand the border so that our ports will not be the first line of defense, by proposing a security regime to ensure that all containers that pose a potential risk for terrorism are identified and inspected at foreign ports before they are placed on vessels destined for the United States. CBP has stationed multidisciplinary teams of US officers from both CBP and Immigration and Customs Enforcement (ICE) to work together with our host foreign government counterparts.

The three core elements of CSI are (1) the identification of high-risk containers (CBP uses automated targeting tools to identify containers that pose a potential risk for terrorism, based on advance information and strategic intelligence); (2) prescreening and evaluation of containers before they are shipped (i.e., containers are screened as early in the supply chain as is possible; generally at the port of departure), and (3) the use technology to prescreen high-risk containers to ensure that screening can be done rapidly without slowing down the movement of trade. This technology includes large-scale x-ray and gamma-ray machines and radiation detection devices.

These notions of cargo security are vital to protecting American society from threats that may be present among items that enter the nation through its airports and seaports. Given the advent and proliferation of globalism, the United States imports many goods and services from foreign nations and exhibits numerous dependencies regarding the importing of items externally. The United States imports a tremendous quantity of items from other nations. Such items range from clothing and toys to petroleum and electronics. These items must reach American consumers throughout the nation. Therefore, maintaining the securities of logistics systems and their cargoes is significantly important. Numerous methods of securing these systems and cargoes exist, ranging from the use of security guards among seaports and airports to the implementing of closed-circuit camera systems. Because this text is an introductory discussion of such topics within the context of homeland security, only a few concepts are introduced herein. Readers desiring a greater knowledge and understanding of these concepts are encouraged to consult texts in security management, transportation security, and border security.

One method of securing cargo and logistic systems involves the use of security guards among airport and seaport locations. These personnel may be either government or private employees. The TSA is tasked with protecting American transportation systems, thereby representing government resources that are dedicated to protecting logistics systems and their respective cargoes.[15] Specifically, with "discretion," the DHS mandates that "motion detectors" and patrolling security guards may be used as security methods.[16] From the perspective of private entities, the use of security companies, such as Wackenhut, may be used as security resources.[17]

In both cases, the primary actor of security is the human. All personnel must undergo some form of background investigation.[18] Various levels of personnel screenings must be "consistent" with the "responsibilities" of the position and situation.[18] For candidates who are considered for positions necessitating high security, personnel interviews must complement screening and background investigations.[18] Depending upon the situation, one should "never use" any reference information that is "provided by candidates."[18] All providers of security personnel must be reviewed and evaluated to ensure that they are "legitimate service providers."[18]

Another mechanism through which cargo and logistics system security is embellished involves the use of satellite technologies and systems. Within this type of security paradigm, both transmitters and wireless sensor devices are placed within cargo containers.[19] These mechanisms perform data collection regarding "container condition, security, humidity, internal temperature, and radiation."[19] In some cases, they exhibit levels of sensitivity that allow them to determine whether a container was "dropped by a crane."[19] The collected data are transmitted to a processing center for analysis.[19] The use of such systems contributes toward reductions in "theft and tampering" while simultaneously "increasing supply chain efficiency."[19] Such systems also reduce the chances of containers being used for terrorist purposes.[19]

Satellite systems are also used for tracking purposes. Through such tracking systems, the locations of vehicles and cargoes may be queried using real-time computer systems. Vehicles that are transporting cargoes may be tracked using satellite systems.[20] If any service disruptions occur, then law enforcement entities may be notified and summoned.[20] Such abilities are beneficial, especially regarding the transporting of hazardous materials.[20]

The use of Radio-Frequency Identification (RFID) technology bolsters cargo and container security within logistics systems. After the events of September 11, 2001, the DHS embraced the use of RFID systems as a method of improving "security protection" among both the "borders and ports of entry" into the United States.[21] RFID technologies may be used for a variety of purposes, including the authentication and identification of individuals and the crafting of "biometric passports."[21] From the perspectives of cargoes and logistics systems, the use of RFID technology provides a means of identifying containers, acting as "smartseals," and tracking items through logistics systems.[21] Through the use of RFID materials, any breach of container security may be detected instantly.[21]

Certainly, awareness and prevention are relevant factors when considering container and cargo security within logistics systems. These considerations are aspects of the CSI. The CSI is a structured attempt to improve security with respect to the potential of terrorists using a "maritime container to deliver a weapon."[22] It involves the deployment of "multidisciplinary teams" to foreign locations for the purpose of examining "high-risk cargo" prior to its being stored within vessels whose destination is the United States.[23]

Within logistics systems, container and cargo security are not merely considerations of ports of departure and ports of destination. Instead, security concerns permeate the entirety of the logistics system through which goods are transported to America from foreign nations. Security activities may commence within the factory settings where goods are produced and continue through the intermediary points of distribution, shipping, and transit and among exit points where they are finally distributed to consumers within American society. **Figure 12.6** highlights these concerns of cargo and container security within logistics systems.

American consumers enjoy daily the benefits of safe and secure logistics systems in which cargoes and containers are protected. Such protection not only safeguards the goods that are destined to eventually arrive in the United States but also protects society and national infrastructure from endangerments ranging from terrorist activity to instances of theft and smuggling of contraband within supply chains. Although this chapter presents an introductory consideration of security methods that protect containers and cargoes within logistics systems, many more protective mechanisms exist domestically and internationally. In any case, the importance and relevancy of such protections must neither be discounted nor ignored. Without such protections, the chances of harm being levied against American society are much greater.

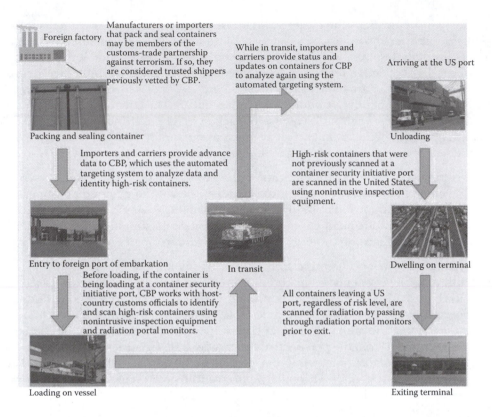

Foreign factory

Manufacturers or importers that pack and seal containers may be members of the customs-trade partnership against terrorism. If so, they are considered trusted shippers peviously vetted by CBP.

While in transit, importers and carriers provide status and updates on containers for CBP to analyze again using the automated targeting system.

Arriving at the US port

Packing and sealing container

Unloading

Importers and carriers provide advance data to CBP, which uses the automated targeting system to analyze data and identity high-risk containers.

High-risk containers that were not previously scanned at a container security initiative port are scanned in the United States using nonintrusive inspection equipment.

Entry to foreign port of embarkation

In transit

Dwelling on terminal

Before loading, if the container is being loading at a container security initiative port, CBP works with host-country customs officials to identify and scan high-risk containers using nonintrusive inspection equipment and radiation portal monitors.

All containers leaving a US port, regardless of risk level, are scanned for radiation by passing through radiation portal monitors prior to exit.

Loading on vessel

Exiting terminal

Figure 12.6 *Global supply chain process. (Courtesy of the US Government Accountability Office.)*

The Mexican border and violence

The basic shape of the current US–Mexican border was established in conflict more than 150 years ago and has been challenged ever since. Creation of the Texas Republic from Mexican territory by force of arms in 1836, its subsequent annexation by the United States in 1845, the 1846–1847 war with Mexico, and the resulting Treaty of Guadalupe Hidalgo in 1848 collectively led to "more than half the territory of Mexico becoming one third of the territory of the United States."[69]

Over the next 160 years, the relationship between the United States and Mexico would prove to be volatile. On February 24, 1913, fighting commenced along the border near Brownsville, Texas, and on March 2, Mexicans attacked US troops along the border near Douglas, Arizona. In response, in 1914, US forces invaded Mexico and occupied Veracruz for over 6 months. In 1916, General John J. Pershing (1860–1948) was ordered by the president to lead a punitive expedition into Mexico in pursuit of Francisco "Pancho" Villa. In February 1917, once the relationship between the two nations improved, United States forces were withdrawn from Mexico, though minor clashes would continue until 1919.

Efforts to establish security and stability along the US–Mexican border are not exclusive issues for the United States. In December 2006, President Calderon of Mexico launched a sweeping initiative to crack down on the drug cartels that operate in that country and supply a great deal of the illegal drugs used throughout our state. The cartels are fighting back, leading to a dangerous uptick in violence on both sides of the border. Mexican drug trafficking organizations have battled it out with the Mexican government, the US government, and each other, with violence escalating on both sides of the US–Mexican border.

According to a *New York Times* article,[70] it is estimated that more than 70,000 people have been killed in the nearly 4 years since President Felipe Calderón began his offensive against the Mexican drug organizations, with the gangs escalating fights over turf and dominance as the federal police and military try to stamp them out. Of those, over 2000 were local, state, or federal police officers, according to the Mexican Public Security Ministry.[53] The majority of the weapons used in the violence in Mexico were obtained in the United States. According to National Public Radio, since 2006, more than 60,000 of the weapons used in Mexican crimes have been traced back to the United States.[41]

Some US officials who specialize in counternarcotics worry that al Qaeda and other terrorist organizations may realize and exploit the porous nature of the Central American–US corridor. They suggest that America's border problems do not end at border cities like El Paso and Brownsville, Texas. They say the border problem begins in Colombia and must be tackled in Guatemala, where it is easier to intercept the drugs and people before they make their way too far north.

During the administration of President Ronald Regan, the United States "declared a war on drugs." Since that time, billions of dollars have been directed toward combating the challenges presented by illicit drug trafficking, marketing, and use. Drug trafficking in the US is fueled by the demand for the drugs by Americans. According to the 2007 National Survey on Drug Use and Health, approximately 20 million Americans use illicit drugs. Drug trafficking across the world exists as a $400 billion trade, with drug traffickers earning gross profit margins of an estimated 300%.

In what some have termed as America's Third War, drug trafficking continues to expand, with networks including cross-border cooperation and international connections. This growth and increased organization results not only from an expanding consumer market but also from poverty. The upsurge in drug-related violence is traced to the end of 2006, when the government launched a frontal assault on the cartels by deploying tens of thousands of soldiers and federal police to take them on.[53]

The Mexican cartels have come to dominate global cocaine trafficking (**Figure 12.7**). Mexico also has become the world's largest exporter of marijuana. Estimates of the revenue generated by the Mexican drug cartels range from $18 billion to $40 billion a year. They use their cash to bribe local public officials and purchase arsenals of military-style weapons.[27]

Latin American drug smugglers have used aircraft, surface, and undersea assets to transport drugs to the United States. Between 2001 and 2007, the USCG reported detecting 23 mini submarines attempting to transport drugs toward the United States. After 2007, the production and use of the mini submarine surged, with over 60 encountered in 2008. Most of these vessels are small, but they have become increasingly sophisticated. Engines and exhaust systems are typically shielded to make their heat signatures nearly invisible to infrared sensors used by United States and allied aircraft trying to find them. If encountered by law enforcement authorities, it is not uncommon to see the mini submarines scuttled.

In 2009, United States law enforcement officials identified 230 cities, including Anchorage, Atlanta, Boston, and Billings, Montana, where Mexican cartels and their affiliates "maintain drug distribution networks or supply drugs to distributors," as a Justice Department report stated. Although Justice Department officials indicated that the figure rose from 100 cities

Figure 12.7 The drug cartels' lucrative trade in cocaine, marijuana, and other drugs—and their capability to heavily arm—results in an increasingly dangerous and deadly combination.

as reported 3 years earlier, they concluded that this may be a result of better data collection methods as well as the spread of the organizations.

Human trafficking

In 2000, the US Congress signed the Victims of Trafficking and Violence Protection Act into law, representing the beginning of a large-scale, coordinated effort by the United States government to fight human trafficking. There are at least 12.3 million enslaved adults and children around the world "at any given time." Of these, at least 1.39 million are victims of commercial sexual servitude, both internationally and within national borders. More than half, 56%, of all forced labor victims are women and girls.

Human trafficking often occurs to enslave individuals to act as forced laborers. According to the US Department of State,[49] this situation often occurs because slave traders take advantage of "gaps in law enforcement to exploit vulnerable workers." Attributes that contribute toward the enslaving of humans consist of "unemployment, poverty, crime, discrimination, corruption, political conflict, and cultural acceptance of the practice."[50] Within this category is also the concept of bonded labor (i.e., debt bondage), in which the "use of a bond, or debt" is used to maintain human "subjugation."[50] This activity is "criminalized under U.S. law and included as a form of exploitation related to trafficking" with respect to the protocols of the United Nations.[49]

According to the US Department of State,[49] "Sex trafficking comprises a significant portion of overall trafficking and the majority of transnational modern-day slavery." Many sex slaves are used to provide prostitution services. The act of prostitution is "inherently harmful and dehumanizing, and fuels trafficking in persons."[49] The government of the United States is opposed to acts of "prostitution and any related activities, including pimping, pandering, or maintaining brothels as contributing to the phenomenon of trafficking in persons, and maintains that these activities should not be regulated as a legitimate form of work for any human being. Those who patronize the commercial sex industry form a demand which traffickers seek to satisfy."[49]

Among many nations, children may be legally employed as laborers in accordance with existing laws. However, in many cases, children are often used as slave laborers among a variety

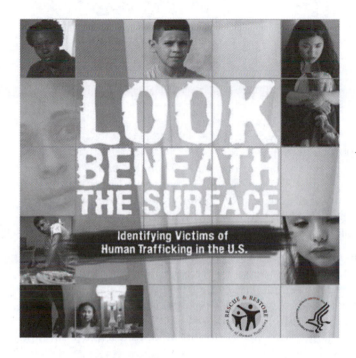

Figure 12.8 *Human trafficking aware-ness poster. (Courtesy of the US Department of Health and Human Services, http://archive.acf.hhs.gov/trafficking/about/form.htm.)*

of national settings. According to the US Department of State, "Any child who is subject to involuntary servitude, debt bondage, peonage, or slavery through the use of force, fraud, or coercion is a victim of trafficking in persons regardless of the location of that exploitation."[49] Illegal child labor is also found among areas of conflict globally. This form of child enslave-ment may be perpetrated by "government forces, paramilitary organizations, or rebel groups," and child soldiers, on average, range "between the ages of 15 and 18," with some being "as young as 7 or 8 years of age."[49]

Such considerations of human trafficking often cross national boundaries and are relevant aspects of American border security. According to the US Department of State,[33,65] annually, between 600,000 and 800,000 individuals are trafficked across global, international borders, and approximately 50% of these individuals are less than 18 years of age. With respect to the US borders, the US Department of State[65] estimates that approximately between 14,500 and 17,500 individuals are trafficked across the American border annually.

Such quantities of trafficked humans are both disturbing and alarming. Because trafficking occurs clandestinely, there is little information regarding the identities of those who are traf-ficked or the entities that perpetrate the trafficking activities. Further, there is a relationship between human trafficking and terrorist organizations. According to Keefer,[47] "Terrorists use the transportation networks of smugglers and traffickers to move operatives." This obser-vation is salient because of the dangerousness posed by terrorist organizations that desire American destruction. Therefore, homeland security practitioners much seriously consider human trafficking as a significant national security threat (**Figure 12.8**).

Transportation and border security initiatives

The concerns of US transportation and border security are mission-critical aspects of ensur-ing the safety of American society. Therefore, many initiatives exist through which the risk of hostile entities who desire to enter the United States and impose devastation may be diminished. The goals and objectives of these initiatives vastly differ with respect to their intended functions through time. Given below are summaries of the primary initiatives that currently contribute toward the provision of American security.

Border permeability

The United States shares its national borders with Mexico and Canada. The United States also manifests virtual borders among its airports and seaports. Regardless of whether a border is tangible or intangible, entities that may endanger the nation may pass through American borders. During the time of the authorship of this textbook, the nation of Mexico is enduring a drug war in which numerous cartels are competing for illegal markets. Within Mexico, the presences of international terrorist organizations are manifested both openly and clandestinely. Although the nation of Canada appears to be peaceful, it also hosts a variety of terrorist organizations.

The chief of the National Guard Bureau, General Craig McKinley, recognizes the dangers of the US–Mexican border, observing that "the link between terrorism and drug cartels along the United States' border with Mexico is increasingly clear," because of the financial associations between drug cartels, other criminal organizations, and terrorist organizations. Examples of international terrorist entities operating within Mexico include Hezbollah, HAMAS, al Shabaab, and al Qaeda. Each of these organizations demonstrates an anti-American bias and represents dangerousness that must not be ignored.

Similarly, the US–Canadian border also presents a variety of dangers that must not be ignored. The U.S. border with Canada is a most troublesome entry point, and Al-Qaida documentation emphasizes that a terrorist entity may enter the U.S. through this border.[74] Although the United States and Canada enjoy a mutually peaceful relationship, there exist a variety of terrorist presences within Canada. According to the Anti-Defamation League, "Islamic extremists and their supporters from Al Qaeda, HAMAS, Islamic Jihad, Hezbollah, Armed Islamic Group (GIA), and Egyptian Islamic Jihad are among those suspected of operating in Canada."[68] Further an estimated 250,000 Tamils exist within Canada and Toronto, boasting an estimated 200,000 Tamils, is the "largest Tamil city outside of Sri Lanka."[68] According to the Anti-Defamation League, it is estimated that approximately 8000 former Tamil Tigers are present within Canada.[68]

Border security: Immigration

Border security is not an issue exclusively concerning the United States. The desire to seek opportunities and a better life has continually driven human movement from one area to another. It is estimated that between 400,000 and 1 million undocumented migrants try to clandestinely cross the rivers and deserts along the 2000-mile (3200-km) US–Mexican border with an estimated 350,000 successfully entering illegally. In 2005, over 1.2 million illegal aliens were apprehended by the Border Patrol.

The US government has employed a number of strategies and programs to make the nation's borders more secure. The following actions are set in a framework that suggests different types of possible policy actions: (1) pushing the border outward to intercept unwanted people or goods before they reach the United States; (2) hardening the border through the use of technology and the presence of more agents at the border; (3) making the border more accessible for legitimate trade and travel; (4) strengthening the border through more effective use of intelligence; and (5) multiplying effectiveness through the engagement of other actors in the enforcement effort (including engaging Canada, Mexico, state and local law enforcement resources, and the private sector).[7]

Border security: Searches

According to Gesell,[40] with respect to the requirements regarding search and seizure, probable cause must be established before initiating any form of search followed by any succeeding seizure. Gesell indicates that any such searches must not be "unreasonable," and the goal of searching is to determine and locate "incriminating evidence" (p. 41). Further, to avoid protection for the "rights of the innocent," the establishment and adherence to "proper procedures" must be observed when searching and seizing any resulting evidence (p. 41).[40] Otherwise, if such procedures are not followed, evidence may be inadmissible regardless of its incriminating nature.[40] Further, the necessity and importance of search warrants must not be understated with respect to the concepts of search and seizure.[40] However, given the contents of class discussions, warrants are immaterial when conducting border searches.

Based on the writings of Gesell,[40] it may be concluded that the requirements necessary for search and seizure represent a dichotomy concerning the rights, liberties, and freedoms of individuals versus the potentials of government power. Through the Fourth Amendment, citizens are protected against unreasonable search and seizure. Through the Fourth Amendment, law enforcement agencies are provided the authority and operational scope to conduct searches and seizures per the dictates of appropriate warrants. Therefore, a unique balance is provided that ensures the rights of the individual and establishes power and authority among law enforcement entities.

According to Davidson and Kim (2009),[71] the locations and activities associated with border searching may transpire upon "land entry" from both the Canadian and Mexican border entry points; upon the dockage of a ship upon its arrival, provided it has visited a "foreign port"; and within the first airport where "international flights" land. Additional locations and timings include searches conducted among the "functional borders" (e.g., "international airports," etc.) that represent the "first practical detention point" after surpassing an established border or entry point. (p. 1) Searches conducted among these "functional borders" are equivalent to searches conducted among "physical borders" because of the impracticality associated with the routing of aircraft or sea vessels to established points of entry among "physical borders." (p. 1)

With respect to the border searches, three types of searches are prevalent: (1) routine, (2) nonroutine. and (3) extended. Davidson and Kim (2009)[71] indicate that routine searches are not significantly invasive with respect to the privacy of the individual (e.g., searching purses, computers, etc.) but may necessitate the instigation of a nonroutine search depending upon the establishment of reasonable suspicion. Nonroutine searches demonstrate a greater privacy invasion of the individual (e.g., strip searching). Extended searches may transpire beyond both the physical and virtual borders provided that reasonable suspicion exists regarding "criminal activity," reasonable knowledge and certainness exist that a type of border was surpassed, and characteristics of the subject of the search are unchanged. (p. 2)

Further, based upon the class discussions and the writings of Davidson and Kim (2009),[71] it may be concluded that border searches demonstrate a pyramidal structure with respect to their conceptual design and complexity. The relationship among these entities ranges from a level of low complexity (e.g., routine) to a level of greater complexity (e.g., extended).

Considerations of the Fourth Amendment must be examined from the perspective of border searches. The necessities of warrantless border search and seizure activities are valuable within the domain of homeland security. Because border searches contribute to the national security of the United States, it may be concluded that such searches are a necessity given the risks posed by traveling people and other entities entering the nation. Such searches protect against criminal entry, smuggling of weapons, disease, or other forms of undesirable paraphernalia. Given these thoughts, regardless of Fourth Amendment tenets, it may be concluded that border searches are imperative to ensure national security and to contribute toward the greater benefit and overall good of American society.

Border security: US–Mexican border fence

Chairman of the House Armed Services Committee Duncan Hunter proposed building two parallel steel and wire fences running from the Gulf of Mexico to the Pacific Coast. Hunter called for building a reinforced, two-layer 15-foot fence, separated by a 100-yard gap, along the entire length of the US border with Mexico. It would include additional physical barriers, powerful lighting, and sensors to detect illegal border crossers. Some envision a wall or a fence. Others foresee a "virtual" fence of cameras, lighting, and sensors along the US–Mexican border.[64]

As of 2013, approximately 750 miles of border fences have been completed. As border fences along the US–Mexico border get stronger, smugglers are attempting to dodge increased security by tunneling and sailing their way into the United States; tunneling activity has increased 65% in the past 2 years, and a multiagency team made over 800 sea smuggling arrests in 2010, up from just 400 in 2009.[63]

Border security: Aviation surveillance and reconnaissance

The DHS has used unmanned aerial vehicles (UAVs) to observe the US–Mexican border since June 2004, among certain border sectors. The fiscal year 2008 Consolidated Appropriations Act (P.L. 110-161) directed the DHS to explore the use of UAVs in the marine environment in addition to the border and appropriated $15 million for the DHS's UAV program, resulting in the modified "Guardian" Predator B UAV.

Within the DHS, aerial assets are operated by the U.S. CBP's Office of Air & Marine (A&M). CBP utilizes advanced technology to augment its US Border Patrol (USBP) agents' ability to patrol the border. The technologies used include, but are not limited to, sensors, light towers, mobile night vision scopes, remote video surveillance systems, directional listening devices, various database systems, and UAVs.[44]

Small vessel security strategy

The Small Vessel Security Strategy addresses the risk that small vessels might be used to smuggle terrorists or weapons of mass destruction (WMDs) into the United States or might be used as either a standoff weapon platform or as a means of a direct attack with a waterborne improvised explosive device (WBIED). This strategy also describes the small vessel community and the environment in which it operates. Since the terrorist attacks of September 11, 2001, maritime security efforts have focused primarily on large commercial vessels, cargoes, and crew. Efforts to address the small vessel environment have largely been limited to traditional safety and basic law enforcement concerns. Small vessels are, however, readily vulnerable to potential exploitation by terrorists; smugglers of WMDs, narcotics, aliens, and other contraband; and other criminals. Small vessels have also been successfully employed overseas by terrorists to deliver WBIEDs.

Federal flight deck officers

Federal flight deck officers are trained by the Federal Air Marshal Service regarding the use of firearms, use of force, legal issues, defensive tactics, the psychology of survival, and program standard operating procedures.[34] Because of the events of September 11, 2001, the necessity of securing commercial aircraft was realized. As a result of the 2001 attacks, the Flight Deck Officer (FDO) program was implemented as a voluntary program, supervised by US sky marshals, to train aircrews to employ defensive measures, when necessary, to ensure the safety and security of their airliners. Crew members are trained to "use firearms to defend against an act of criminal violence or air piracy attempting to gain control of an aircraft."[34] Personnel who undergo this program may be "a flight crew member," for instance, a "a pilot, flight engineer, or navigator assigned to the flight."[34]

Terrorist watch list and the no-fly list

The TSA is mandated by law to maintain a watch list of names of individuals who are suspected of posing "a risk of air piracy or terrorism or a threat to airline or passenger safety." The watch list was created in 1990 and was initially administered by the Federal Bureau of Investigation. Later, it was administered by the Federal Aviation Administration before the TSA finally assumed the administrative responsibility. Individuals whose names are on these lists are subjected to additional security measures, with a "no-fly" match requiring the individual to be detained and questioned by federal law enforcement and a "selectees" match requiring additional screening. Currently, P.L. 108-458 sets forth procedures for appealing erroneous information or determinations made by TSA with respect to the aforementioned records.[7]

Legislation pertaining to transportation and border security

During the preceding 50 years, much legislation was drafted and passed that enhanced the security of US ports, railways, airports, and borders. Sadly, much of this legislation resulted from catastrophic events that signaled the need for security improvements. Other legislation resulted from realizing the need for improvement without the manifestation of a precursory event. Regardless of the origin, much legislation exists that contributes toward the security and safety of American society. Given below are short descriptions of the primary pieces of legislation that bolster homeland security aspects of American society.

The Magnuson Act of 1950

The Magnuson Act of 1950 provides the USCG with the authority to ensure the protection and security of vessels, harbors, and waterfront facilities against sabotage or other subversive activities. It authorizes the USCG to establish security zones to prevent damage or injury to any vessel or waterfront facility and to safeguard ports, harbors, territories, and waters of the United States.

Ports and Waterways Safety Act of 1972

The USCG is the lead agency for port security per the Maritime Security Act. According to the USCG,[50] the Ports and Waterways Safety Act (PWSA) of 1972 is described as follows:

> The purpose of the PWSA (33 USC 1221 et seq.) is to increase navigation and vessel safety, to protect the marine environment, and to protect life, property, and structures in, on, or immediately adjacent to the navigable waters of the United States. The PWSA does not provide for personnel screening programs or for emergency security powers, but does provide for the protection and 'safe use' of the port and for protection against the degradation of the marine environment. It specifically provides for the establishment, operation, and maintenance of vessel traffic services (VTS), control of vessel movement, establishment of requirements for vessel operation, and other related port safety controls.

Port and Tanker Safety Act of 1978

According to the USCG,[50] the Port and Tanker Safety Act of 1978 is described as follows:

> The Port and Tanker Safety Act of 1978 amended the PWSA, and provides the Coast Guard with broader, more extensive, and explicitly stated authority. The Act addresses improvements in the supervision and control over all types of vessels, foreign and domestic, operating in the U.S. navigable waters, and in the safety of all tank vessels, foreign and domestic, which transport and transfer oil or other hazardous cargoes in U.S. ports. Additionally, the Act addresses improvements in the control and monitoring of vessels operating in offshore waters near our coastline, and vessel manning and pilot age standards. The Act also includes regulatory authority over areas not previously covered, such as participation with neighboring nations in coordinated vessel traffic systems in boundary waters, lightering operations in offshore areas, and discouraging activities such as tank wash dumpings at sea in preparation for loading cargoes in U.S. ports. The Act now serves as the strongest authority for the Marine Safety and Security (MSS) Program, and is the basis for the navigation safety regulations and the Marine Safety Information System (MSIS).

International Maritime and Port Security Act

The International Maritime and Port Security Act amended the PWSA by adding a new section: port, harbor, and coastal facility security. This section authorizes the secretary to carry out measures to prevent or respond to an act of terrorism against an individual, vessel, or public or commercial structure that is subject to the jurisdiction of the United States and located within or adjacent to the marine environment, or a vessel of the United States or an individual onboard that vessel.

Maritime Transportation Security Act of 2002

The Maritime Transportation Security Act of 2002 (MTSA) is designed to protect the nation's ports and waterways from a terrorist attack. This act directs initial and continuing assessments of maritime facilities and vessels that may be involved in a Transportation Security Incident (TSI). It requires vessels and port facilities to conduct vulnerability assessments and develop security plans that may include passenger, vehicle, and baggage screening procedures; security patrols; establishing restricted areas; personnel identification procedures; access control measures; and/or installation of surveillance equipment.

Developed using risk-based methodology, the MTSA security regulations focus on those sectors of maritime industry that have a higher risk of involvement in a TSI, including various tank vessels, barges, large passenger vessels, cargo vessels, towing vessels, offshore oil and gas platforms, and port facilities that handle certain kinds of dangerous cargo or service vessels.

The MTSA also required the establishment of committees in all the nation's ports to coordinate the activities of all port stakeholders, including other federal, local, and state agencies; industry; and the boating public. These groups, titled the Area Maritime Security Committees, are tasked with collaborating to develop plans to secure their ports so that the resources of an area can be best used to deter, prevent, and respond to terror threats.

Security and Accountability for Every Port Act of 2006 (SAFE Port Act)

In an effort to further the progress made through the MTSA of 2002, the Security and Accountability for Every Port Act (SAFE Port Act) was passed and became effective in October 2006. The SAFE Port Act created and codified new programs and initiatives and amended some of the original provisions of MTSA.

The Oil Pollution Act of 1990

According to the USCG,[50] the Oil Pollution Act of 1990 is described as follows:

> The Oil Pollution Act of 1990 (OPA 90) amended the PWSA and imposes new requirements on the operation of oil tankers in the U.S.; addresses shortcomings in the navigation safety in Prince William Sound, Alaska; and enhances the Coast Guard's authority to effectively regulate the conduct of oil tankers and merchant marine personnel in the U.S. OPA 90, section 4107, amended the PWSA's vessel operating requirements broadening the Coast Guard's authority so that they '... may construct, operate, maintain, improve or expand vessel traffic services....' In addition, section 4107 requires mandatory participation for "appropriate vessels" which operate in a VTS area.

The Illegal Immigration Reform and Immigrant Responsibility Act of 1996

This complex piece of legislation was enacted in 1996. Germain and Stevens[39] provide a synopsis of the salient aspects of this legislation as follows:

> It directly addresses border patrol and upgrades needed for border patrol enforcers, equipment, and the overall patrolling process. It also details an increase in interior enforcement and practices with regard to INS and investigators monitoring visa applications and visa abusers. Illegal activities were a central concern in this bill and penalties for racketeering, alien smuggling and the use or creation of fraudulent immigration-related documents are high on the priority list. Other crimes and immigration-related offenses committed by aliens and the consequences, including deportation, are addressed in the sections following. Employment programs and employment eligibility issues are incorporated into the bill, which includes sanctions threatened on employers and the regulation

of unfair immigration-related employment practices. The title of the next section of IIRAIRA points to restrictions placed on alien benefits, which includes but is not limited to state and federally funded programs. Some miscellaneous provisions mentioned relate to medical services, pilot programs, and reporting. Alien residence (housing) and financial issues regarding the same are addressed including a plethora of miscellaneous provisions. These further miscellaneous provisions are directed towards refugees, parolees, and the reform of asylum, while the Immigration and Nationality Act was amended under many different topics. Without belaboring the miscellaneous provisions, they covered visa processing, consular efficiency, as well as but not limited to schooling, religious (criminal-related) offenses, mail-order brides, H-2A nonimmigrant worker program, and other broadly ranging issues.

Aviation and Transportation Security Act of 2001

The Aviation and Transportation Security Act (ATSA) provides broad federal authority for security in all modes of transportation. The authorities of the ATSA are delegated by the secretary of homeland security to the administrator of the TSA. The administrator "shall be responsible for security in all modes of transportation," including civil aviation security, and all "security responsibilities over other modes of transportation that are exercised by the Department of Transportation." The administrator is given an array of specific authorities, which carry out this broad responsibility.

Critical Infrastructure Information Act of 2002

Enacted as part of the Homeland Security Act, this legislation creates a framework that enables members of the private sector to voluntarily submit sensitive information regarding the nation's critical infrastructure/key resources to the DHS with the assurance that the information, if it satisfies certain requirements, will be protected from public disclosure.

Border Protection, Antiterrorism, and Illegal Immigration Control Act of 2005 (H.R. 4437)

This legislation includes a provision requiring the construction of security fencing along portions of the southern border that have high rates of illegal border crossing. Additionally, the DHS was required to conduct a study and report back to Congress on the use of physical barriers along the northern border. An amendment was adopted during consideration on the floor that requires the construction of an estimated $2.2 billion worth of fences along part of the southern border. The secretary of homeland security was required to provide for least two layers of reinforced fencing, the installation of additional physical barriers, roads, lighting, cameras, and sensors.

Conclusion

The security of the United States has been a primary concern of American society since the founding of the nation. Throughout history, numerous examples exist that highlight the relevancy of maintaining a strong national power within the context of international and global societies. Historically, the security of American transportation and borders has encompassed four categories: (1) air, (2) sea, (3) land, and (4) virtual. During modern times, the security of these categories remains a mission-critical function of American government and among the citizenry of the United States.

Given these notions, American society must be protected from threats that originate both externally and internally. The use of modern technologies embellishes the ability of government and commercial entities to contribute toward such protection. However, despite the best efforts of the government and commercial sectors, no guarantee exists that security breaches shall not occur in due time. Because of the gigantic quantities of goods, services, individuals, and vehicles that cross the American borders daily, involving some form of transportation, the task of protecting American society is vast and challenging.

Examples of external and internal threats have been manifested within the aviation sector. The attacks of September 11, 2001, although tragic, were indicative of aviation threats, posed by terrorist factions, whose origins were external to American society. The case of FedEx flight 705 is representative of a different threat whose potential lethality also could have drastically affected numerous aspects of American society. In the case of FedEx flight 705, the threat represented an origin that was internal to American society. From the perspectives of homeland security and aviation, both events demonstrate that aviation threats exist that may be either external or internal to America and that such threats involve radically different motivations. Regardless, in both cases, the intent involved the use of commandeering aircraft to perform devastating acts of lethality.

Dangers also exist regarding the maritime and the railway sectors of American society. Historically, the Barbary pirates represented an external maritime threat. During modern times, maritime hijackings occur among the earth's oceans and continental coastlines. Human errors also endanger American interests. With respect to this category, the incident of the *Exxon Valdez* represents such an incident. Further, the constructs of the American transportation infrastructure are susceptible to mechanical faults and failures as well as natural conditions.

The American economy depends on the monitoring and maintaining of its transportation systems. Such systems include the maritime sector, aviation sector, rail systems, and mass transit systems that daily integrate their functions to provide transportation for humans and the goods that are consumed by Americans. Certainly, the transportation system is representative of the services that are consumed within the American economy. Therefore, its security is of paramount importance to homeland security practitioners.

Homeland security also encompasses legislation and a variety of accompanying programs that complement the efforts to ensure America's safety. Such legislation encompasses the three facets of the American transportation system: land, sea, and air. Various programs exist to bolster American security, including such activities as training aircrews regarding defensive safety measures, the construction of border fences, and immigration policies and programs. Certainly, many other examples may be identified, and a subset of such programs is discussed within this chapter.

Overall, the security of the national borders and the transportation system must not be compromised. Both entities are mission-critical aspects of national security and the continued existence of the United States. Hostile entities exist that seek to cross America's national borders and either destroy or damage its infrastructure—including the transportation system. Although it is impossible to secure completely each and every facet of the transportation system, its security must be maximized. Striving to ensure that hostile entities do not penetrate American borders and impact the transportation system is a primary challenge and responsibility of the practitioners of homeland security.

Key terms

Airport security
Airway
Aviation border
Border
Border security
Cargo
Cargo security
Maritime
Maritime border
Maritime security
Land border
Logistics
Logistics security
Piracy
Port security
Railway
Railway security
Trafficking
Transportation
Transportation security
Virtual border

QUESTIONS FOR DISCUSSION

1. This chapter introduces the notion of transportation security. Certainly, most travelers are well aware of the security mechanisms and protocols that exist when progressing through an airport. These resources are stringent. However, when traveling via railway, subway, buses, and so forth, there is less emphasis regarding the examining of passengers before they board the respective mode of transportation. Why do you believe less emphasis exists? Write a brief essay that highlights the salient points of your response.

2. Trafficking organizations demonstrate a variety of routes across the national borders, thereby representing methods of accessing the United States. These passages are useful logistics routes for smuggling and trafficking a variety of goods ranging from illegal drugs to humans. Given this notion, do you believe it is possible for factions of organized crime to cooperate with terrorist entities to collaboratively use these routes? Why or why not? Write a brief essay that substantiates your opinion.

3. The use of airport security mechanisms has spawned a variety of disputes regarding the freedoms guaranteed within the Fourth Amendment. Do some research, and explore some lawsuits that have resulted from the use of airport security protocols and resources. Write a brief essay that reviews your findings.

4. A vast quantity of ships enter and leave US harbors daily, carrying a variety of materials and people. Do some research, and explore the quantities of vessels that must be inspected before docking in a US port. Given the contents of this chapter and your own personal research, how is it possible to reduce the chances that harmful items and people do not enter the United States? Write a brief essay that highlights your response.

References

1. Vital Statistics. (2011). Vital statistics. *United Nations.* http://www.un.org/cyberschoolbus/briefing/globalization/index.htm (accessed January 9, 2011).
2. October 2010. (2010). October 2010. *U.S. Department of Commerce. Bureau of Economic Analysis.* http://www.bea.gov (accessed January 9, 2011).
3. Trade with China. (2010). Trade with China: 2010. *U.S. Census Bureau.* http://www.census.gov/foreign-trade/balance/c5700.html#2010 (accessed January 9, 2011).
4. Trade with Canada. (2010). Trade with Canada: 2010. *U.S. Census Bureau.* http://www.census.gov/foreign-trade/balance/c1220.html#2010 (accessed January 9, 2011).
5. Trade with Mexico. (2010). Trade with Mexico: 2010. *U.S. Census Bureau.* http://www.census.gov/foreign-trade/balance/c2010.html#2010 (accessed on January 9, 2011).
6. CFC. (2010). Balloons in the American civil war. U.S. Centennial of Flight Commission. http://www.centennialofflight.gov (accessed January 9, 2011).
7. Seghetti, L.M., Lake, J., Robinson, W. and Lisa M. (2005). Border and transportation security: selected programs and challenges. *CRS Report for Congress.* (March 29, 2005). http://www.fas.org (accessed on January 7, 2011).
8. U.S. Department of Homeland Security. (2013). Aviation Security Policy, National Security Presidential Directive 47/Homeland Security Presidential Directive 16, http://www.dhs.gov/hspd-16-aviation-security-policy (accessed April 3, 2013).
9. Federation of American Scientists. (2007). National strategy for aviation security. http://www.fas.org/irp/offdocs/nspd/nspd-47.pdf (accessed April 3, 2013), p. 2.
10. U.S. Department of Homeland Security. (2007). Aviation transportation system security plan. http://www.dhs.gov/xlibrary/assets/hspd16_transsystemsecurityplan.pdf (accessed April 3, 2013), p. i.
11. Sweet, K. (2006). *Transportation and Cargo Security: Threats and Solutions* (1st ed.). New Jersey: Pearson Prentice Hall.
12. Tasers Take. (2004). *Tasers Take Off—New Scientist.* http://www.newscientist.com/article/mg18424730.500-tasers-take-off.html (accessed August 9, 2009).
13. Rodriguez, B. (2011). Freight rail transportation in the post-9/11 era: balancing safety and freedom in a corporate setting. *Florida Coastal Law Review, 13*(113), 119.
14. State of Texas. (2013). Chapter 5–Rail safety and security. http://ftp.dot.state.tx.us/pub/txdot-info/rail/plan/ch5.pdf (accessed April 3, 2013).
15. Dempsey, J. (2011). *Introduction to Private Security.* Belmont, CA: Wadsworth Publishing.
16. Abbot, E. and Hetzel, O. (2010). *Homeland Security and Emergency Management: A Legal Guide for State and Local Governments.* Chicago, IL: ABA Publishing, p. 137.
17. Maggio, E. (2011). *Private Security in the 21st Century: Concepts and Applications.* Burlington, MA: Jones and Bartlett Publishing.
18. Brandman, B. (2007). The 7 deadly sins of logistics security. *The NCLC Annual Conference,* http://www.nclcworld.com/pdf/Deadly%20Sins%20of%20Logistics%20Security%20by%20Brandman.ppt.pdf (accessed April 3, 2013).
19. Plunkett, J. (2009). *Plunkett's Transportation, Supply Chain, and Logistics Industry Almanac.* Houston, TX: Plunkett Research, Ltd., p. 31.
20. Deans, P.C. and Karwan, K. (1994). *Global Information Systems and Technology: Focus on the Organization and Its Functional Areas.* Harrisburg, PA: The Idea Group, p. 339.
21. Hunt, V.D., Puglia, A. and Puglia, M. (2007). *RFID: A Guide to Radio Frequency Identification.* Hoboken, NJ: John Wiley and Sons Publishing, p. 69–71.
22. Customs and Border Protection. (2013). CSI: Container Security Initiative. http://www.cbp.gov/xp/cgov/trade/cargo_security/csi/ (accessed April 4, 2013).
23. Customs and Border Protection. (2013). Fact sheet. http://www.cbp.gov/linkhandler/cgov/trade/cargo_security/csi/csi_factsheet_2011.ctt/csi_factsheet_2011.pdf (accessed April 4, 2013), p. 1.
24. 95-6206. (1997). 95-6206. United States Court of Appeals, Sixth Circuit. *United States of America v. Auburn Calloway.* http://bulk.resource.org (accessed January 9, 2011).
25. Ackleson, J. (2005). Border security technologies: Local and regional implications. *Review of Policy Research, 22*(2), 137–155.
26. Archibold, R. (2009). U.S. Adds Drones to Fight Smuggling. *The New York Times,* http://www.nytimes.com/2009/12/08/us/08drone.html?_r=0 (accessed August 26, 2013).
27. Beaubien, J. (2009). Violence continues as drug wars rage in Mexico. (March 23, 2009). *National Public Radio.* http://www.npr.org (accessed January 7, 2011).

28. Casey. (2008). The legend of Casey Jones. *Casey Jones Home and Railroad Museum*. http://www.casey-jones.com/caseyjones/legend.htm (accessed January 11, 2011).

29. Chronology. (2010). Chronology of news events in 2010. *News 24*. http://www.news24.com (accessed January 10, 2011).

30. Department of Homeland Security Small Vessel Security Strategy. (April 2008). http://www.dhs.gov (accessed January 6, 2011).

31. Derailment. (1994). Derailment of Amtrak Train No. 2 on the CSXT Big Bayou Bridge near Mobile, Alabama, September 22, 1993. *National Transportation Safety Board*. http://www.ntsb.gov/publictn/1994/RAR9401.htm (accessed January 10, 2011).

32. Economic. (2010). The economic impact of America's freight railroads. *Association of American Railroads*. http://freightrailworks.org (accessed January 9, 2011).

33. Facts About. (2005). The facts about human trafficking for forced labor. *U.S. Department of State*. http://www.state.gov (accessed January 9, 2011).

34. Federal Flight. (n.d.). Federal flight deck officers. *Transportation Security Administration*. http://www.tsa.gov (accessed January 9, 2011).

35. FedEx 705. (n.d.). FedEx 705. Cockpit Voice Recorder Database: a database containing CVR transcripts of aviation accidents and incidents. http://www.tailstrike.com (accessed January 9, 2011).

36. First. (n.d.). First U.S. train robbery. *History Channel*. http://www.history.com/this-day-in-history/first-us-train-robbery (accessed January 9, 2011).

37. Gawalt, G. (2011). America and the Barbary pirates: an international battle against an unconventional foe. *U.S. Library of Congress*. http://memory.loc.gov/ammem/collections/jefferson_papers/mtjprece.html (accessed January 9, 2011).

38. GDP Growth. (2010). GDP growth picks up in third quarter. *U.S. Department of Commerce. Bureau of Economic Analysis*. http://www.bea.gov (accessed January 9, 2011).

39. Germain, K. and Stevens, C. (n.d.). 1996 Illegal Immigration Reform & Immigrant Responsibility Act. *U.S. Immigration Legislation Online*. http://library.uwb.edu/guides/USimmigration (accessed January 9, 2011).

40. Gesell, L. (1996). *Aviation and the Law*. (2nd ed.). Lorton, VA: Coast Aire Publications.

41. Grimaldi, J. (2011). How thousands of U.S. guns fuel crime in Mexico. *National Public Radio*. http://www.npr.org (accessed January 7, 2011).

42. Guerrero, P. (2002). Mass transit: challenges in securing transit systems. *Testimony Before the Subcommittee on Housing and Transportation, Committee on Banking, Housing, and Urban Affairs, U.S. Senate*. http://www.gao.gov (accessed January 10, 2011).

43. Gurner, J. (2006). The real Casey Jones story. *Water Valley Casey Jones Railroad Museum*. http://www.watervalley.net/users/caseyjones/casey.htm (accessed January 9, 2011).

44. Haddal, C. and Gertler, J. (2010). Homeland security: unmanned aerial vehicles and border surveillance. *Congressional Research Service*. http://www.fas.org/sgp/crs/homesec/RS21698.pdf (accessed January 7, 2011).

45. Intelligence. (n.d.). Intelligence's new tools. *Central Intelligence Agency*. https://www.cia.gov (accessed January 9, 2011).

46. International Maritime. (2011). International Maritime Policy. *U.S. Department of State. Bureau of Consular Affairs*. http://travel.state.gov (accessed January 9, 2011).

47. Keefer, S. (2006). Human trafficking and the impact on national security for the United States. *USAWC Strategy Research Project*. http://www.dtic.mil/cgi-bin/GetTRDoc?Location=U2&doc=GetTRDoc (accessed January 11, 2011).

48. Lake, J., Robinson, W. and Seghetti, L. (March 29, 2005). Border and transportation security: The complexity of the challenge. *CRS Report for Congress*. http://www.fas.org/sgp/crs/homesec/RL32839.pdf (accessed January 7, 2011).

49. Major. (2008). Major forms of trafficking in persons. *U.S. Department of State*. http://www.state.gov/g/tip/rls/tiprpt/2008/105377.htm (accessed January 11, 2011).

50. Marine Safety. (1996). Marine safety manual. *United States Coast Guard*. http://www.uscg.mil (accessed on January 10, 2011).

51. Sweet, K. (2006). How effective is security screening of airline passengers? *Interfaces, 36*(6), 545–552.

52. Transportation Security Administration. (2011). Mass transit ensures security for 6000 systems, protects 15 million riders a day. http://www.tsa.gov/press/happenings/mt_security.shtm (accessed January 5, 2011).

53. Reuters. (2010). Gunmen Ambush Mexican Officers, Killing 8. *The New York Times*, http://www.nytimes.com/2010/10/12/world/americas/12mexico.html?_r=0 (accessed August 27, 2013).

54. National. (2010). *National Commission on the BP Deepwater Horizon and Offshore Drilling*. http://www.oilspillcommission.gov (accessed January 10, 2011).

55. Port and Intermodal: Transportation Sector Network Management. (n.d.). *Transportation Security Administration*. http://www.tsa.gov (accessed January 5, 2011).

56. Reeder, V. (2010). Testimony before the Senate Commerce Committee on International Aviation Screening Standards. http://www.tsa.gov (accessed January 7, 2011).

57. Rudner, M. (2008). Misuse of passports: Identity fraud, the propensity to travel, and international terrorism. *Studies in Conflict and Terrorism, 31*(2), 95–110.

58. Salazar-Winspear, O. (2010). Obama defends government response to oil spill. http://www.france24.com/en/20100527-obama-defends-government-response-oil-spill-gulf-mexico-bp (accessed January 11, 2011).

59. Schrag, Z. (2010). Urban mass transit in the United States. http://eh.net/encyclopedia/article/schrag.mass.transit.us (accessed January 10, 2011).

60. Skinner, S. and Reilly, W. (1989). The *Exxon Valdez*: A report to the president. *The National Response Team*. http://www.akrrt.org/Archives/Response_Reports/ExxonValdez_NRT_1989.pdf (accessed January 11, 2011).

61. Timelines. (2010). *Timelines of History*. http://timelinesdb.com (accessed January 11, 2011).

62. Turbiville, G. (1999). US–Mexican border security: Civil-military cooperation. *Military Review.* (July–August 1999). http://fmso.leavenworth.army.mil/documents/border/border.htm (accessed January 7, 2011).

63. Tunnels, Boards Used to Defeat Stronger Border Security. (2010). *Homeland Security Newswire*, http://www.homelandsecuritynewswire.com/tunnels-boats-used-defeat-stronger-border-security (accessed August 27, 2013).

64. U.S.–Mexico Border Fence/Great Wall of Mexico Secure Fence, Global Security, http://www.globalsecurity.org/security/systems/mexico-wall.htm (accessed August 27, 2013).

65. Victims. (2000). *Victims of Trafficking and Violence Protection Act of 2000: Trafficking in Persons Report.* U.S. Department of State. Washington, DC: U.S. Government Printing Office.

66. White, C. (2007). Guest viewpoint: developing railroad security. *Institute for Supply Management*. http://www.tuck.dartmouth.edu/cds-uploads/publications/pdf/Pub_ISM_RailroadSecurity.pdf (accessed January 9, 2011).

67. Monterey Institute of International Studies. (2008). *How Non-Market Values Influence Public Policy*, http://www.oceaneconomics.org/nonmarket/pubPolicy.asp (accessed August 26, 2013).

68. Gamage, D. (2005). Canadian police arrest two Tamils of Sri Lankan origin connected with LTTE front group WTO for counterfeiting. *Asian Tribune*, http://www.asiantribune.com/news/2005/05/12/canadian-police-arrest-two-tamils-sri-lankan-origin-connected-ltte-front-group-wto-c (accessed August 26).

69. Turbiville, G. H. Jr. (1999). "US-Mexican Border Security: Civil Military Cooperation." *Military Review*, 79(3), pp. 37–38.

70. Aguilar, J. (2013). Texas officials oppose new controls, despite gun smuggling to Mexico. *The New York Times*, http://www.nytimes.com/2013/01/20/us/texas-officials-oppose-new-controls-despite-gun-smuggling-to-mexico.html (accessed August 27, 2013).

71. Davidson, D. and Kim, G. (2009). Additional powers of search and seizure at and near the border. Western Washington University, http://www.wwu.edu/bpri/files/2009_Summer_Border_Brief.pdf (accessed August 26, 2013), pp. 1–4.

72. United Press International. (2009). General: drug cartels linked to terrorism. http://www.upi.com/Top_News/Special/2009/03/09/General-Drug-cartels-linked-to-terrorism/UPI-23681236628976/ (accessed August 26, 2013).

73. Martonosi, S. and Barnett, A. (2006). How effective is security screening of airline passengers. *Interfaces*, 36(6), pp. 545–552.

74. Blumenthal, L. (2007). US Canada Border is a Security Nightmare: Increased Illegal Crossings Feared Along Wide-Open Northern Border, http ://circ.jmellon.com/docs/view.asp?id=1166 (accessed October 3, 2013).

13

The Role of Intelligence in Homeland Security

[No] analytic work foresaw the lightning that could connect the thundercloud to the ground.[1]

9/11 Commission
quoting an unnamed government official (p. 7)

Chapter objectives:

- Understand the concept of intelligence
- Gain an understanding of the role of intelligence in homeland security
- Give an overview of the critical issues facing the nation in the areas of transportation and border security
- Examine the historical evolution of intelligence analysis
- Identify the salient aspects of the intelligence cycle

Introduction

The inability to detect the terrorist attacks of September 11, 2001, before the fact and the flawed National Intelligence Estimate (NIE) regarding Iraq's supposed 2003 possession of weapons of mass destruction (WMDs) are widely considered intelligence failures. That is, neither scenario provided decision makers with the accurate and timely assessments they needed to carry out operations and formulate policy. Given modern dangers, it is essential that the United States maintain a robust, competent intelligence capability that can help its leaders understand the world around them and the threats they face. But, just what is intelligence? What is its role in homeland security? Finally, which agencies in the United States are responsible for carrying out this important function? This chapter investigates such questions and provides an introduction to the concepts of intelligence and intelligence analysis.

What is intelligence?

Perhaps the best way to define intelligence is to describe what it is not. Intelligence is not merely information or data. Within the modern world, there are billions of bits of information surrounding humans all the time. One may consider the Internet, which contains untold volumes of information and whose capacity grows by the minute. Certainly, some of this information is accurate, while some of it is inaccurate. As well, buried among all this "noise" may be pieces of information that, when properly addressed, might assist the nation in knowing the intentions and plans of national enemies. In order to get to the "wheat" of information, however, it must first be separated from the considerable "chaff" that exists, and then integrated to gain a fuller understanding of its characteristics. These concepts, in essence, are what intelligence collection and analysis are all about.

Many entities of the US government are engaged in intelligence, and each has its own unique definition for the term. The Department of Defense has a two-part definition for intelligence:

1. The product resulting from the collection, processing, integration, analysis, evaluation, and interpretation of available information concerning foreign countries or areas
2. Information and knowledge about an adversary obtained through observation, investigation, analysis, or understanding (pp. 15–16)[2]

The Central Intelligence Agency (CIA), which functions as the primary civilian intelligence service in the United States, provides a more informal definition: "Reduced to its simplest terms, intelligence is knowledge and foreknowledge of the world around us—the prelude to decision and action by US policymakers" (para. 14).[3]

Each of the above definitions emphasizes a different and important facet of good intelligence; the DOD version explains that intelligence is produced by a specific process, whereas the CIA makes clear that intelligence should be "actionable" or helpful to decision makers as they choose between various courses of action.

Generally, intelligence agencies engage in four activities: collection, analysis, covert operations, and counterintelligence. Collection and analysis will be discussed in the next section. Covert operations are those carried out against other countries or enemies in secret. In many cases, these activities would be considered highly embarrassing if they could be traced back to their country of origin. Some famous covert operations, carried out by the United States, include the attempted assassination of Cuban leader Fidel Castro during the 1960s and the successful coup against Iranian prime minister Mohammad Mosaddeq in 1953. Counterintelligence involves the hunt for spies. Within the United States, the Federal Bureau of Investigation (FBI) has primary responsibility for counterintelligence. However, even the FBI was famously penetrated by spies such as Earl Pitts and Robert Hanssen.

Contemplating intelligence

According to Lowenthal[4] (p. 4), intelligence "largely refers to issues related to national security" involving "defense and foreign policy and certain aspects of homeland and internal security"; such notions of intelligence became increasingly relevant during the aftermath of the events of September 11, 2001. Domestically, Lowenthal[4] (p. 4) indicates that intelligence is comprised of three categories: "foreign, domestic, and homeland security." However, the discussions of Lowenthal[4] (p. 5) indicate that these categories are not mutually exclusive and demonstrate ambiguity regarding their unique discernments among "practitioners."

According to Lowenthal[4] (p. 5), the intelligence domain is limited to neither a solitary scope nor a single perspective. Instead, it encapsulates an array of "areas of concern" that include the "actions, policies, and capabilities of other nations and of important non-state groups"

(p. 5).[4] Further, Lowenthal[4] articulates that activities within the intelligence domain must also monitor and evaluate the characteristics of "powers that are neutrals, friends or even allies, but are rival in certain contexts." Therefore, intelligence is unrestricted regarding its scope and limitations of observing entities within the intelligence domain, and is not solely limited to considerations of aggressive entities or "enemies" (p. 5).[4]

Given these considerations, Lowenthal[4] defines intelligence as the "process by which specific types of information important to national security is requested, collected, analyzed, and provided to policy makers, the products of that process, the safeguarding of these processes, and this information by counterintelligence activities, and the carrying out of operations as requested by lawful authorities" (p. 8).

To be sure, "intelligence is not what is collected; it is what is produced after collected data is evaluated and analyzed" (p. 3).[5] Further, "field operations generally collect information (or data)" even though "intelligence may be collected by and shared with intelligence agencies and bureaus" (p. 3).[5] The conceptual differentiation between information and intelligence concerns the processing of information into a product that supports decision making. Therefore, intelligence is derived from processed information. Intelligence products rarely supply "the" answer; that is because the information on which they are based can be fragmentary, incomplete, contradictory, or just plain wrong.

While most people think of intelligence in the context of national security, it serves other functions as well. Businesses, for example, employ analysts to understand the markets and to gain a competitive advantage over rivals. According to McElreath et al.[6] (p. 32), "Our security depends as much upon butter as it does upon guns; few would argue today that 'security' depends upon stable, reliable financial markets." This observation invokes mental connotations of the economic and financial ramifications of national security.

Economic and financial characteristics are salient aspects of intelligence with respect to the crafting of national policy and strategy through time. Therefore, contemporary definitions of intelligence must encompass considerations of the characteristics and demographics of international economics and finance. However, such characteristics are not the only considerations of regional, national, and international entities that are within the domain of intelligence functions. Economic intelligence and financial intelligence may be enhanced through the use of political intelligence.

According to Shulsky and Schmitt[7] (p. 55), political intelligence "consists of information concerning the political processes ideas, and intentions of foreign countries, factions, and individual leaders." Blakeney and Borins[8] (p. 61) indicate that political intelligence serves as a measure of the strengths of responses to "policies and programs." However, it must be noted that an amount of instability exists regarding political intelligence because of the dynamics of political change among regions, nations, and internationally.

Such change is considered by Heuer[9] (p. 180) through observations regarding "political judgments" affiliated with intelligence functions. According to Heuer[9] (p. 180), "Political judgments are generally couched in imprecise terms, and are generally conditional upon other developments," and "there are no objective criteria for evaluating the accuracy of most political intelligence judgments as they are presently written." Treverton, on the other hand, views intelligence from the perspective of a service-oriented industry. The service perspective is "designed to serve American foreign policy" and is "charged with providing information for its 'customers' in both the executive branch and Congress" (p. 20).[10] The service approach is influenced by changes within the intelligence domain and is influenced by the "redefining" of customer objectives.

Intelligence does not just support the economic or political decision maker; it is of critical importance to the military as well. According to Warner[11] (p. 27), military intelligence involves the interpretation of evaluated observations regarding "information of the enemy and of the terrain over which operations are to be conducted." Similarly, Austin and Rankov[12] (p. 1) indicate that military intelligence is "that which is accepted as fact, based on all available information about an actual or potential enemy or area of operations." These notions transcend time with respect to necessities of intelligence among military organizations. Austin and Rankov,[12] for example, discuss military intelligence in a historical context, describing its use by the Romans.

By now, it should be obvious that there are many definitions of intelligence; each is mediated by the specific end user. So, for example, a law enforcement agency would define intelligence in terms of understanding criminal groups, while a military unit would describe it in terms of providing advantage on the battlefield. Each of the aforementioned definitions is representative of the notion that intelligence encompasses a variety of domains and is characterized among a myriad of perspectives among these domains. This notion is commensurate with the writings of former CIA analyst Mark Lowenthal[4] (p. 5) because such an array may consist of domains involving areas of "political, economic, social, environmental, health, and cultural" considerations and applications.

Intelligence is also important in the business world,[13] the medical community,[14] and myriad other areas. Lowenthal provides perhaps the most comprehensive definition of intelligence, noting that at least three perspectives are relevant to its definition (p. 8)[4]:

- Processes—"Intelligence can be thought of as the means by which certain types of information are required and requested, collected, analyzed, and disseminated, and as the way in which certain types of covert action are conceived and conducted."
- Products—"Intelligence can be thought of as the product of these processes, that is, as the analyses and intelligence operations themselves."
- Organizations—"Intelligence can be thought of as the units that carry out its various functions."

Given the variety of definitions noted above, the authors postulate another, which has applicability to the wide variety of situations that involve homeland security:

- Intelligence—That which is derived from the interpretation of processed facts and information; it facilitates decision making across time and a variety of problem domains, for the purpose of achieving a desired end state.

This definition is purposely generic; it embodies many of the concepts of noted intelligence professionals as well as the dynamic facets of multiple domains of application. Nevertheless, we recognize that such a definition is imperfect. Indeed, the creating of a "model" definition, acceptable to all, continues to elude the profession.

The intelligence cycle

Over the years, analysts and researchers have worked to improve the manner in which they produce intelligence. Most agencies employ some version of the "intelligence cycle." The intelligence cycle is a process that specifies all aspects of how information is turned into intelligence and provided to those who need it for a specific purpose. This process has developed over the years. Army publications from World War I describe a process that incorporated a variety of techniques (e.g., collection, analysis), but it is not until 1948 that authors Robert Glass and Philip Davidson used the term "intelligence cycle" for what appears to be the first time.[15] The most current version of the intelligence cycle was dissemination by the director of national intelligence (DNI), the leader of the US Intelligence Community (IC), in 2011. It appears in **Figure 13.1**.

Yet what exactly do the terms means? In the words of the DNI[16] (p. 11):

- "Planning and direction: Establish the consumer's intelligence requirements and plan intelligence activities accordingly.

  The planning and direction step sets the stage for the intelligence cycle. It is the springboard from which all intelligence cycle activities are launched. Oftentimes, the direction part of the step precedes the planning part. Generally, in such cases, the consumer has a requirement for a specific product. That product may be a full report, a graphic image, or raw information that is collected, processed, and disseminated but skips the analysis and production step. Given the customer's requirement, the intelligence organization tasked with generating the product will then plan its intelligence cycle activities.
- Collection: Gather the raw data required to produce the finished product.

  Data collection is performed to gather raw data related to the five basic intelligence sources (geospatial intelligence [GEOINT], human intelligence [HUMINT], measurement and signature intelligence [MASINT], open-source intelligence [OSINT], and signals intelligence [SIGINT]). The sources of the raw data may include, but are not limited to, news reports, aerial imagery, satellite imagery, and government and public documents.
- Processing and exploitation: Convert the raw data into a comprehensible format that is usable for production of the finished product.

  The processing and exploitation step…involves the use of highly trained and specialized personnel and technologically sophisticated equipment to turn the raw data into usable and understandable information. Data translation, data decryption, and interpretation of filmed images and other imagery are only a few of the processes used for converting data stored on film, magnetic, or other media into information ready for analysis and production.

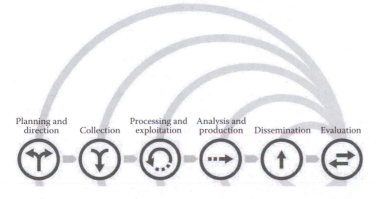

Figure 13.1 *The intelligence cycle. (From the Director of National Intelligence, U.S. National Intelligence: An Overview 2011, 2011.)*

- Analysis and production: Integrate, evaluate, analyze, and prepare the processed information for inclusion in the finished product.

   The analysis and production step also requires highly trained and specialized personnel (in this case, analysts) to give meaning to the processed information and to prioritize it against known requirements. Synthesizing the processed information into a finished, actionable intelligence product enables the information to be useful to the customer. Note that, in some cases, the intelligence cycle may skip this step (for example, when the consumer needs only specific reported information or products such as raw imagery). This was the case during the Cuban Missile Crisis (October 1962), when President Kennedy needed only the actual number of pieces of Soviet equipment in Cuba and facts concerning reports on observed Soviet activity with no analysis of that information.

- Dissemination: Deliver the finished product to the consumer that requested it and to others as applicable.

   The consumer that requested the information receives the finished product, usually via electronic transmission. Dissemination of the information typically is accomplished through such means as Web sites, e-mail, Web 2.0 collaboration tools, and hard-copy distribution. The final, finished product is referred to as "finished intelligence." After the product is disseminated, further gaps in the intelligence may be identified, and the intelligence cycle begins all over again.

- Evaluation: Continually acquire feedback during the intelligence cycle and evaluate that feedback to refine each individual step and the cycle as a whole.

   Constant evaluation and feedback from consumers are extremely important to enabling those involved in the intelligence cycle to adjust and refine their activities and analysis to better meet consumers' changing and evolving information needs."

According to Richelson[17] (p. 5), seven primary domains of applications exist in which the use of the intelligence cycle is leveraged for such strategic and tactical benefits: "political, military, scientific and technical, economic, sociological, and environmental. Cumulatively, the intelligence cycle provides a methodical process through which intelligence is provided, among a variety of organizations and individuals, to support a variety of decisions that influence national policies and strategies. However, the intelligence cycle is no better than the fallible humans who manage its stages or perform necessary activities within its stages, and there is no guarantee that the consumers of intelligence services and products will render wise or prudent decisions. Indeed, the intelligence cycle is rarely used in its pure form. Decision makers often request "real-time" raw data that shortcuts the very important analysis phase; as well, analysts may go back to collectors on a regular basis to obtain additional information if there are "gaps." Nevertheless, the cycle provides a useful model to understand how, in a perfect world, the production and use of intelligence unfolds.

The United States IC: History

Today, the 17 federal agencies that perform the bulk of intelligence gathering and analysis on the national and international level refer to themselves as the US "intelligence community." They strongly emphasize the notion of "community," implying that they work together well and share information freely. However, this concept of a "community" is a relatively recent innovation. In order to understand how and why the IC is set up in its present form, it is important to understand the history of intelligence activities since the earliest days of the republic.

IC history: The Revolutionary War to World War II

Up until World War II, the United States did not have a permanent, civilian agency devoted to intelligence gathering and analysis. This was a sharp contrast to the rest of the world, where spy agencies had been in service for years. For example, England, France, and Russia all had intelligence organizations by the 1600s.[4] Protected by its oceans and surrounded by nonthreatening neighbors, American administrations did not see the need for a permanent intelligence capability. In addition, the constitutional protections afforded to US citizens made spying appear unseemly and undesirable. In 1929, for example, Secretary of State Henry Stimson made the famous statement that "gentlemen don't read each other's mail" to justify discontinuing a State Department code-breaking operation.[18]

That is not to say that the United States did not engage in spying; it did so in earnest during times of war. Indeed, one of the biggest proponents of intelligence throughout US history was George Washington, who formed secret committees during the Revolutionary War to carry out sabotage and spy on British troop and ship movements. During the War Between the States, both sides employed spies. The Union in particular received a great deal of information by interviewing escaped slaves who had found their way north; in some cases, African Americans who had escaped slavery voluntarily returned south to engage in espionage.

By the late 19th century, it became clear to the military that it needed to remain abreast of technological advancements by other armies and navies. As a result, the Office of Naval Intelligence was formed in 1882, followed by the army's Military Information Division in 1885.[4]

However, despite the presence of numerous warning signs, neither agency nor any other governmental entity accurately predicted the attacks on Pearl Harbor in 1941. As it had in other wars, the United States immediately reinstituted intelligence gathering—only this time, the organization it created, the Office of Strategic Services (OSS), would survive the end of the war in an altered form as the CIA.

IC history: World War II and the Cold War

The OSS was established by a presidential military order issued by President Roosevelt on June 13, 1942, to collect and analyze strategic information required by the Joint Chiefs of Staff and to conduct special operations not assigned to other agencies. During the War, the OSS supplied policy makers with facts and estimates, but the OSS never had jurisdiction over all foreign intelligence activities. The head of the OSS was William "Wild Bill" Donovan, a lawyer, army major general, and World War I Medal of Honor recipient. At its height, the OSS had a $10 million budget and engaged in covert operations in both Europe and the Pacific.[19]

World War II also saw enhanced counterintelligence activities by the FBI. In 1942, the Bureau disrupted "Operation Pastorious," a German operation in which prospective saboteurs were transported clandestinely to the United States by U-boat. Soon after they landed, one of the saboteurs turned himself in to startled FBI agents in Washington, DC. Thanks to information he provided, the others were soon arrested.

Following the end of World War II, the United States found itself in a "Cold War" against the Soviet Union and its allies. Realizing the need for a permanent civilian intelligence service but wary of the power possessed by the OSS, President Harry Truman established the CIA in 1947. Because he did not want to create a US "Gestapo," Truman watered down the authority of the CIA, specifically denying it law enforcement powers and forbidding it to conduct activities inside the United States.[20]

From its formation until the fall of the Soviet Union, the primary mission of the CIA was to engage in intelligence activities directed against Communist countries. It was soon joined by other agencies like the National Security Agency (NSA), founded in 1952, whose mission was to intercept and analyze foreign communications.

During the Cold War, the CIA and its sister intelligence agencies enjoyed both success and failure. For example, while the IC did not foresee the invasion of South Korea by the North in 1950, they were remarkably prescient in predicting the difficulty of defeating the North Vietnamese. As well, the CIA could not dislodge Castro from Cuba, but it successfully supplied the mujahedeen in Afghanistan with weapons that led to the Soviet withdrawal from that country in 1989.

By the early 1990s, the Soviet Union had collapsed. Unfortunately, the IC was slow to retool itself to fight other enemies, such as al Qaeda, despite its brazen attacks on two US embassies in 1998 and the USS *Cole* in 2000. All of that changed, however, when commercial jets slammed into the World Trade Center and Pentagon on September 11, 2001. Even as the fires in New York and Arlington raged, experts realized that the IC had failed in a catastrophic way. It was clear that changes would have to be made in the manner the United States gathered and analyzed intelligence; however, the decision on exactly what should be done was far from unanimous.

IC history: Iraq to the present

In the wake of the 9/11 attacks, the national commission formed to ascertain why the attacks were not prevented, directed significant criticism at the IC.

The IC struggled, throughout the 1990s up to 9/11, to collect intelligence on and analyze the phenomenon of transnational terrorism. The combination of an overwhelming number of priorities, flat budgets, an outmoded structure, and bureaucratic rivalries resulted in an insufficient response to this new challenge (p. 12).[1]

The 9/11 Commission made several recommendations for reforming the IC. Chief among these was the creation of a DNI, a cabinet-level position responsible for coordinating all federal-level intelligence activities; prior to this, the director of the CIA served in this capacity.

Around the same time that the 9/11 Commission was releasing its report, another governmental agency was finding further fault with the IC. In October 2002, the IC had delivered a secret report, called a National Intelligence Estimate, to the president detailing its findings on Iraq's alleged possession of WMDs. In short, the NIE concluded that Iraq was continuing its WMD programs in defiance of United Nations (UN) resolutions and restrictions. Saddam Hussein's regime was alleged to possess both chemical and biological weapons and missiles with ranges in excess of UN restrictions. The NIE further concluded that Iraq would likely have a nuclear weapon before 2010.[21]

After the invasion of Iraq in 2003, the expected stockpiles of WMDs were not located. As a result, the Senate began an investigation into the preparation of the Iraq WMD NIE. In part, it concluded that most of the key judgments in the NIE were overstated or not supported by the intelligence at hand. The Senate Committee further reported that faulty analysis had led to the erroneous conclusions.[21]

In response to IC failures, Congress passed the Intelligence Reform and Terrorism Prevention Act of 2004, which President Bush signed into law on December 17 of that year. That act called for the creation of the Office of the Director of National Intelligence (ODNI), which is responsible for overseeing all federal intelligence activities, including making sure that agencies work well together and share intelligence.[22]

The modern US IC

There are 16 agencies that currently report to the DNI. Regardless of the agency, each is responsible for ensuring that timely, objective, accurate intelligence is provided to the president and other decision makers. **Figure 13.2** depicts this relationship.

The ODNI is relatively new and occurred as a response, during the aftermath of the events of September 11, 2001, and the "fruitless search for weapons of mass destruction (WMD) in Iraq."[23] Such events raised concern regarding the robustness, effectiveness, and efficiencies of US intelligence efforts. Prior to the establishment of this new office, the head of the US IC had been the director of central intelligence, a role held by the director of the CIA. The DNI position is not without critics; some contend it does nothing more than add a layer of unnecessary bureaucracy that only serves to slow US efforts. However, others argue that such a position is necessary to ensure that agencies work well together and that there is a single individual responsible for intelligence efforts. The missions of the remaining 16 agencies are as follows:

- **CIA:** Independent agency responsible for providing national security intelligence to senior US policy makers
- **Defense Intelligence Agency:** Department of Defense combat support agency that produces foreign intelligence in support of the military
- **Department of Energy Office of Intelligence and Counterintelligence:** Provides technical intelligence analyses on all aspects of foreign nuclear weapons, nuclear materials, and energy issues worldwide

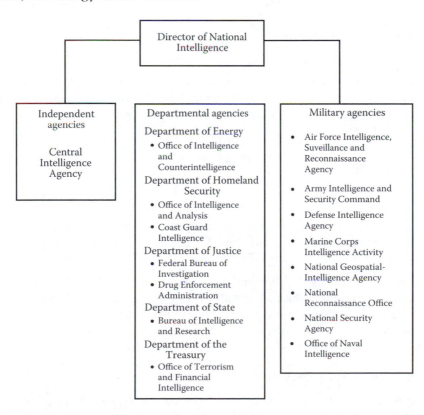

Figure 13.2 *Agencies reporting to the DNI. (From the Office of the Director of National Intelligence,* An Overview of the United States Intelligence Community for the 111th Congress, *2009.)*

- **DHS Office of Intelligence and Analysis:** Responsible for using information and intelligence from multiple sources to identify and assess current and future threats to the United States
- **Department of State Bureau of Intelligence and Research:** Provides the Secretary of State with analysis of global developments as well as real-time insights from all-source intelligence
- **Department of Treasury Office of Intelligence and Analysis:** Responsible for foreign intelligence and foreign counterintelligence related to the operation and responsibilities of the Department of the Treasury
- **Drug Enforcement Administration Office of National Security Intelligence:** Responsible for providing drug-related information responsive to IC requirements
- **FBI National Security Branch:** Conducts counterterrorism and counterintelligence activities inside and outside of the United States
- **National Geospatial-Intelligence Agency:** Provides geospatial intelligence in support of national security objectives
- **National Reconnaissance Office:** Designs, builds, and operates the nation's reconnaissance satellites.
- **NSA/Central Security Service:** Coordinates, directs, and performs highly specialized activities to protect US information systems; produces intelligence information on foreign signals
- **United States military (air force, army, coast guard, marine corps, and navy):** Have intelligence components that support each service's mission

State and local intelligence efforts

Up to this point, this textbook has focused on the federal government's efforts in intelligence matters. However, to leave it at that would miss the significant role that state and local agencies play in collecting, analyzing, and sharing intelligence. Two of the areas in which intelligence is proving crucial include intelligence-led policing and the creation of fusion centers; both are described below.

Intelligence-led policing

Intelligence has always been important in policing. During the early years of the Cold War, most large departments had "red squads" that were created to keep tabs on dissidents and radicals. By the 1970s, however, a series of commissions revealed that police agencies at all levels—federal, state, and local—had abused their authority and impinged upon citizens' rights. In response to this, many police departments disbanded their intelligence divisions.

However, that was not the case in the United Kingdom. In the 1990s, the Kent Constabulary experimented with a strategy it dubbed "intelligence-led policing" to combat a series of motor vehicle thefts. Kent's use of systematic analysis led to the arrest of a small number of offenders who were responsible for a majority of the thefts.[24] The success of the Kent experiment convinced British authorities that intelligence should drive investigations rather than the other way around. Until the attacks of September 11, 2001, however, most American agencies ignored the intelligence-led approach.

Today, organizations such as the International Association of Law Enforcement Intelligence Analysts and the Law Enforcement Intelligence Unit have been pushing to have intelligence-led policing adopted by all US agencies. Shortly after the 9/11 attacks, the International

Association of Chiefs of Police (IACP) established the National Criminal Intelligence Sharing Plan (NCISP). In effect, the NCISP is a blueprint for a US variant of the British model.

The US Department of Justice (DOJ) has joined forces with the IACP to promote the adoption of intelligence-led policing. The DOJ established the Regional Intelligence Sharing System (RISS), a computer network designed to enable intelligence to be shared between the 18,000 law enforcement agencies that serve the United States.[25]

Some local agencies have needed little or no incentive from the federal government to institute their own version of intelligence-led policing. Perhaps the most significant example of this involves the New York City Police Department, which has taken a number of steps to enhance its intelligence capabilities, including hiring a number of analysts, stationing officers overseas, and appointing a former CIA deputy director as its deputy commissioner of intelligence.

Fusion centers

One difficulty in sharing intelligence between law enforcement and intelligence agencies is the sheer number of police and sheriff's departments that exist in the United States: The number exceeds 18,000. This is a unique situation in the world. In many countries, policing is a federal concern, which limits the number of agencies that a country will house. In the United States, however, policing is primarily a state and local function. Hence, most agencies tend to be small and serve a particular community.

Sharing information between 18,000 agencies, many of whose computers cannot "talk" to one another, approaches the nightmarish. As a result, many states have taken an intermediate approach: They have established fusion centers to coordinate the analysis and sharing of intelligence (see boxed text). While the jury is still out regarding whether fusion centers work, the concept seems practical and necessary.

Legal guidelines pertaining to intelligence collection

The United States makes a strong distinction between intelligence that can be gathered on US citizens and that which can be gathered on non-US persons. In general, it is much more difficult to open a case and gather evidence against US citizens than it is against non-US citizens,

---

EXCERPT FROM THE NATIONAL CRIMINAL INTELLIGENCE SHARING PLAN: "WHAT IS A FUSION CENTER?"

A fusion center is an effective and efficient mechanism to exchange information and intelligence, maximize resources, streamline operations, and improve the ability to fight crime and terrorism by merging data from a variety of sources. In addition, fusion centers are a conduit for implementing portions of the *National Criminal Intelligence Sharing Plan* (NCISP).

Global Justice Information Sharing Initiative. (2003). Fusion centers. *National Criminal Intelligence Sharing Plan*. http://www.iir.com/global/products/NCISP_Plan.pdf (accessed November 29, 2008).

who are not afforded the protections of the United States' Constitution. That is one of the major reasons the FBI is so careful to classify groups as either "domestic" or "international."

When US intelligence abuses were revealed in the 1970s, there was an outcry to pass legislation that would strictly regulate intelligence-gathering activities. One of the first pieces of legislation to pass was the Foreign Intelligence Surveillance Act of 1978 (FISA), which describes procedures and requirements necessary to obtain authority for the physical and electronic surveillance of suspected agents of "foreign powers." In other words, agents and police officers cannot merely seize evidence against suspected terrorists on a whim; as in conventional criminal cases, they must articulate reasons for their surveillance, and these must pass muster with a specially appointed FISA judge.[26]

The overriding legal authority that determines what law enforcement agencies may or may not do in terms of intelligence collection is Title 28 of the Code of Federal Regulations (CFR) Part 23. 28 CFR Part 23 contains standards for operating federally grant-funded multijurisdictional criminal intelligence systems. It provides guidance in five areas: submission and entry of criminal intelligence information, security, inquiry, dissemination, and reviewing and purging files.

Finally, the passage of the Uniting and Strengthening America by Providing Appropriate Tools Required to Intercept and Obstruct Terrorism Act of 2001, commonly referred to as the USA PATRIOT Act, increased the ability of law enforcement agencies to engage in various acts of electronic and physical surveillance, eased restrictions on regulating suspected terrorist-related financial transactions, and expanded immigration authority in detaining and deporting immigrants suspected of terrorism-related acts.[27]

Foreign intelligence services

The nature of transnational threats in a globalized world means that cooperation must occur between countries. Many allies of the United States have developed intelligence agencies that serve the unique cultural and legal requirements of their respective governments. Since the attacks of 9/11, the sharing of intelligence between these agencies has reached unprecedented levels.

Perhaps America's greatest ally in the war on terror has been the United Kingdom. Like the United States, Britain has separate agencies that deal with international and domestic threats. Military Intelligence 6 (MI6) is England's equivalent of the CIA, dealing with external threats. Military Intelligence 5 (MI5), like America's FBI, deals with threats inside the country. However, unlike the FBI, MI5 lacks law enforcement powers.

Israel also divides domestic and external intelligence gathering between two agencies: the Mossad (external) and Shin Bet (internal). Given the extreme level of threat facing Israel on a daily basis, both organizations enjoy excellent reputations as effective, if sometimes ruthless, intelligence agencies.

Like the United States, Canada did not establish a formalized intelligence service until the 20th century. The Canadian Security Intelligence Service, formed in 1984, is the primary intelligence agency of the Canadian government, responsible for collecting, monitoring, and analyzing intelligence on threats to Canada and for conducting covert operations.[28]

The list of international intelligence services could continue for quite some time: Most countries have some intelligence capability. Of interest, even as belligerents, it is not unusual for intelligence agencies to communicate with one another. Even at the height of the Cold War, the United States and the Soviet Union communicated in secret, in the hope that nuclear catastrophe could be avoided.

The function of intelligence in homeland security

Most readers will clearly understand the role of intelligence in such things as countering foreign spies and preventing the next big terrorism event. However, this represents only the tip of the iceberg with regard to intelligence and homeland security. Consider law enforcement. Today's transnational criminal organizations differ markedly from those of the past. Some years ago, the typical gang consisted of a handful of mostly young males who attempted to exert control over a geographical area of a few city blocks. Contrast that with today's notorious gangs, like Mara Salvatrucha, whose membership includes many thousands who operate across several countries. Without robust intelligence efforts, it would be impossible to understand the operations of the group, its leadership, and the extent of its criminality.

Intelligence is especially important in understanding the lifeblood of any organization: its finances. Warde[29] indicates that money trails "yield invaluable clues and unmask vast conspiracies." The case of Al Capone is instructive. According to Warde[29] (p. 25), in 1931, Capone, was "perhaps the best-known gangster of his time" and "was convicted for tax evasion and sent to jail." Further, Warde[29] (p. 26) indicates that law enforcement was unable to prosecute him for his more heinous criminal offenses, such as murder, but was able to send him to prison on charges of tax evasion. During this period, Capone "avoided paying income taxes by investing illegal profits in legitimate businesses" (p. 445).[30] Such funds were earned through illegal activities; "prostitution, drug trafficking, and the production and distribution of alcohol were invested in legitimate, cash-based businesses, such as clothes laundries and restaurants" (p. 445).[30]

The downfall of Capone was based on evidence regarding his claimed net worth versus his actual net expenditures. Because Capone was spending more than he claimed to be taking in, he was obviously underreporting his income to the Internal Revenue Service. Upon conviction, he was sent to prison for 8 years, the longest time anyone up to that point had served on tax charges.

A very specific analytical function, and one that mirrors the intelligence process, is crime analysis. Students familiar with such TV shows as *Criminal Minds* are aware of the "profiling" conducted by the FBI's Behavioral Analysis Units (BAU). In reality, the bureau doesn't use the term profiling; it instead refers to the process as criminal investigative analysis. Agents assigned to the BAUs use the criminal investigative analysis protocol to help them understand the "what, why, and who" of violent criminal acts.

Rossmo[31] describes how law enforcement authorities utilized criminal analysis in the case of the Zodiac Killer, who murdered five people in the San Francisco area between 1968 and 1969. The Zodiac taunted the police by sending them coded and cryptic notes about the killings.

According to Rossmo[31] (p. 194), "a letter to the *Chronicle* newspaper postmarked June 26, 1970, included a cipher and a map providing clues to the location of a bomb intended for a school bus." Additional details were provided, within a second note, which was received on July 26, 1970.[31] According to Rossmo[31] (p. 194), the geographic map "focused on Mt. Diablo ('Devil's Mountain') in Contra Costa County, across the Bay from San Francisco." Further, a "compass symbol was hand drawn in the middle of the map, the center of which contained the Naval

Radio Station" (p. 194).[31] Rossmo[31] (p. 194) indicates that despite analysis, "the bomb was never found, the mystery of the map never solved, and the Zodiac Killer never apprehended."

Cryptanalysis is another activity that occurs within the intelligence function. Especially important during wartime, Shulsky and Schmitt[7] note that, among other things, the deciphering of Japanese military codes provided the means through which intelligence was used to significantly sway the course in favor of the United States during the Midway battle. The Allies were also able to decode German traffic, thereby shortening World War II.

Intelligence gathering versus privacy

A quick reading of the Constitution reveals the strong importance Americans place on limiting the power of their government (e.g., in most cases, the police need a warrant before they can search your home). This notion of privacy, which was ultimately recognized by the Supreme Court, is deeply imbedded in the American psyche. How, then, does one reconcile the right to privacy against the potential intrusiveness of intelligence gathering? To be sure, it is a difficult balancing act, and one that has not always been carried out well by the agencies of the IC. For example, beginning in the 1950s and lasting until the early 1970s, the FBI engaged in a program called COINTELPRO (Counterintelligence Program) that targeted individuals who had not necessarily broken the law but who were deemed subversive (e.g., Communists, white supremacists, members of far-left political organizations). The bureau both spied on these individuals and engaged in "dirty tricks" to try to destabilize their organizations. In some cases, COINTELPRO proved quite effective. Upon the public's discovery of the program in the early 1970s, the FBI was sharply criticized. New laws were passed that significantly curtailed what law enforcement could do in the intelligence arena. However, the FBI was not the only organization that had overstepped its proper boundaries. Lawmakers also discovered that both the military and the CIA had spied on American citizens during the Vietnam War, an unprecedented breach of the law.

Of course, in today's digitized world where the amount of data increases at an exponential rate, it is essential that a method be available to understand what is happening and to "separate the wheat from the chaff." Only a proper, robust intelligence and analysis function will provide that. At the same time, agencies must remain vigilant in protecting civil liberties. This can be especially problematic during a time of national struggle, such as what occurred immediately after the 9/11 attacks. At that time, people were understandably afraid, and many were willing to trade a certain amount of privacy for a feeling of security. As the attacks have receded into history, the pendulum has swung back toward the direction of privacy. This is a natural and inevitable phenomenon and one that helps maintain the stability of the republic. According to Foxman[32] (p. 1043), the "best way to fashion effective and appropriate security measures is to rely on the constitutional structure that those measures are designed to protect" as a method of facilitating "the right balance between safety and civil liberty."

Intelligence challenges for the new century

A primary goal of intelligence is to preempt, or prevent, tragedy. Today, the foremost priority of the FBI is to prevent the next 9/11; this stands in sharp contrast to the FBI's historic mission of solving crimes after they have occurred. Prevention implies the ability to foresee future threats. In his publication titled *Vision 2015*, the DNI[33] looked to the probable future rather than merely current challenges. Interestingly, his concerns were not confined to just crime or terrorism; they covered a wide range of threats. This implies that intelligence agencies can no longer concentrate their field of vision on a single area, as they did in the Cold War. Instead, they must be prepared to deal with many different challenges simultaneously. The emerging threats identified by the DNI are contained within **Figure 13.3**.

Perhaps the most salient part of *Vision 2015* was the introduction by then DNI J.M. McConnell, who noted:

> We are engaged in a dynamic global environment, in which the pace, scale, and complexity of change are unprecedented. It is a networked world where what happens in Peshawar affects Peoria—and vice versa…[a]dapting the Community to this new environment is our fundamental challenge.[33]

Attempting to anticipate the future is a major function of the IC. Every few years, the National Intelligence Council (NIC), the DNI's "think tank," produces its latest addition to its *Global Trends* series. Among other things, the NIC forecasts that certain resources (e.g., water) will become increasingly scarce and that nontraditional powers (e.g., China and India) will emerge as superpowers.

Certain environmental factors "drive" change. The main four "drivers" that will likely affect the future are

- Technology
- Demographics
- Economics
- Politics/governance

The most rapidly changing driver in the world today is technology. Think of the many new technologies that did not exist just 10 years ago; consider how things may change over the

Figure 13.3 Persistent threats and emerging missions. (From the Office of the Director of National Intelligence, 2008.)

course of the next 10 years. Things like nanotechnology (the manipulation of atomic and subatomic particles), artificial intelligence (computers that can "think" like humans), and the emergence of human/machine interfaces that will prolong human life for significant periods are but a few of the technologies experts think may soon arrive. The intelligence function must remain at the forefront of technology. Many law enforcement experts believe that the most significant threat we will soon face will come not from terrorists with bombs but from terrorists, criminals, rogue states, and others operating in the cyber arena. Talk of a "Cyber Pearl Harbor" is becoming more and more common; some experts believe that it is not a matter of *if* but *when* such attacks will come. Considering how many things are linked together and dependent on the Internet, the results could prove catastrophic.

Technology will have a significant effect on the future; so will demographics. By 2025, the world's population should reach 8 billion; Africa and East Asia will account for the majority of that growth. The population of developed countries will continue to "age." That is, the average age of the population will increase. This phenomenon is already occurring in the United States, producing much angst with regard to health care and entitlements, such as Social Security. Other parts of the world, such as Africa and the Middle East, are expected to have "youth bulges" where the high birth rates will produce large numbers of young people.

Unfortunately, these same countries have some of the world's worst economies; they likely will not be able to support the young populations. This situation most likely will lead to unprecedented levels of immigration. America may less resemble a melting pot of gradual assimilation into the culture than a salad bowl, where individuals representing many different ethnicities, religions, and cultures will be living side by side.

US intelligence agencies are especially concerned with border security, or lack of the same. America's borders, especially those with Mexico, have grown exceptionally porous as a result of lucrative smuggling opportunities for both humans and illicit goods. Terrorists could exploit both legal and illegal immigration to introduce themselves and/or WMDs into the United States.

The last two drivers—economics and politics—are related. Experts realize that "globalization" (the linking together of economies and cultures) has caused the world to shrink. National borders are becoming increasingly irrelevant, which allows people to form allegiances with entities other than their country of origin—things like their religion or ethnic heritage, for example. Globalization has provided some definite benefits. Consider, for example, the low prices one pays for goods manufactured in China as a result of their cheap labor costs. It has also provided significant dividends for countries like China and India who have managed to exploit globalization to their advantage.

Role in homeland security

Critics charge that the national vulnerability to terrorism is increased through a lack of communication and sharing of information, bureaucratic inertia, failed systems, and competing agencies. Such considerations were debated after the initial attack against the World Trade Center during the 1990s. Because the manifestation of mass terrorism only recently arrived within the US, its intelligence infrastructure is continuously adapting and changing to accommodate the dynamics of this threat. However, many other countries have had a long-standing tradition of intelligence that dates back centuries. Because their histories contain a myriad of experiences with terrorism, other nations are significantly experienced with the integration of military, international, and domestic security information.

Before the events of September 11, 2001, the State Department primarily possessed coordination authority regarding terrorism. Neither the Justice Department nor the Department of Defense possessed such coordination authority. Various agencies collected and processed information to provide intelligence. Prior to 9/11, 56 federal law enforcement agencies as well as the Army, Air Force, Navy, Marines, and Coast Guard produced intelligence and clandestine terror activity reports.

Most federal agencies that deal with any type of investigative function possess some type of audit or enforcement authority. The State Department employed its own security analysts. The Drug Enforcement Administration studied drug movements, money transfers involving narcotics, and narco-terrorism. The NSA and the Defense Investigative Agency (DIA) also were in the information pipeline. The military, with its orbiting communications and spy satellite capability, received dynamic information worldwide in terms of signal, electronic, and photographic resources. The FBI served the domestic home front, integrating the information gleaned from the legal attachés assigned to American embassies with information regarding international and domestic terrorist groups operating in the United States. The CIA performed a similar function internationally, albeit without law enforcement powers. The intelligence capabilities were extremely limited at the state and local levels of law enforcement. Most local communities had no means of connecting to the global information pipeline.

These conditions of disparate agencies functioning in silos became obvious in the post 9/11 investigations. Recognizing these deficiencies influenced historical reorganization of government, including the creation of the US Department of Homeland Security. While the idea of a single office for the Department of Homeland Security (DHS) is laudable, the question remains whether it can overcome the politics and turf battles that have raged in Washington since the beginning of the republic. Conversely, other skeptics argue that the way to streamline agencies and increase efficiency is not accomplished by adding another layer to an already bloated bureaucracy.

Conclusion

In today's world, it is essential that every country have a robust, competent intelligence capability that can help its leaders understand the world around them and the threats they face. Policy makers need to understand that intelligence is not merely information or data. Instead, it is the product of a specific process that generally involves collecting, planning and direction, processing/collation, analysis, dissemination, and reevaluation. This process is often referred to as the "intelligence cycle."

Today, 17 federal agencies make up what is termed the US "intelligence community." However, up until World War II, the United States did not have a permanent, civilian agency devoted to intelligence gathering and analysis. That varied greatly with the rest of the world, where spy agencies had been in service for years. In the early days of the republic, US spying was generally confined to periods of war. However, after America failed to predict the Pearl Harbor attacks in 1941, it was decided that the United States needed a permanent, civilian intelligence capability. After the war, the OSS was remade into the CIA, which led US intelligence efforts during the Cold War.

After the collapse of the Soviet Union in the 1990s, the IC was slow to retool itself to fight other enemies, such as al Qaeda. In the wake of the attacks of 9/11, however, it was recognized that US intelligence required a major overhaul. The 9/11 Commission recommended that a central DNI be appointed to oversee all activities of the IC. In 2004, the ODNI was established. Currently, all IC agencies report to the DNI.

The federal government is not the only entity that engages in intelligence matters. Through fusion centers, intelligence-led policing, and the NCISP, state and local authorities also have a major role to play. In addition, a great deal of cooperation currently exists between the intelligence services of the United States and its foreign allies. This is essential in combating transnational terrorist and criminal organizations. Intelligence professionals today must adhere to a series of laws and guidelines that dictate what can be done in investigations. These laws include FISA, the USA PATRIOT Act, and 28 CFR 23.

Key terms

Assessment
Central Intelligence Agency
Director of national intelligence
Emerging threats
Fusion center
Intelligence
Intelligence analysis
Intelligence cycle
Intelligence failure
Intelligence report
Intelligence-led policing
Observations
Real time
Technology
Threats

QUESTIONS FOR DISCUSSION

1. Intelligence analysis and information processing are two separate entities. Write a brief essay that defines both entities and that discusses the salient characteristics of both concepts. Compare and contrast these terms within your response.
2. Historically, intelligence analysis has a long history within the United States. It has experienced a myriad of successes and failures. One of the most shocking events of the Cold War occurred when an intelligence ship, the USS *Pueblo*, was captured by North Korea during the 1960s. Do some historical research, and write a brief essay that summarizes the scenario. Given your findings, write a brief essay that speculates how extensive the damage was to US intelligence efforts regarding this loss?
3. Intelligence is used by large government organizations and small-town police departments. Consult your local law enforcement agency, and determine how they leverage intelligence and intelligence analysis to solve crimes. Write a brief essay that highlights your findings.
4. When discussing intelligence with your local agency, determine whether they participate in any type of fusion center. Within your essay, include a description of how your local law enforcement agency leverages a fusion center relationship to solve cases and to deter crime.

References

1. 9/11 Commission. (2004). The 9-11 commission report: final report of the national commission on terrorist attacks upon the United States (Executive Summary). http://www.9-11commission.gov/report/911Report_Exec.pdf (accessed November 29, 2008).
2. Waltz, E. (2003). *Knowledge Management in the Intelligence Enterprise*. Norwood, MA: Artech House Publishing.
3. Warner, M. (2007). Wanted: A definition of 'intelligence.' https://www.cia.gov/library/center-for-the-study-of-intelligence/csi-publications/csi-studies/studies/vol46no3/article02.html#author1 (accessed November 30, 2008).
4. Lowenthal, M. (2009). *Intelligence: From Secrets to Policy* (4th ed.). Washington, DC: CQ Press.
5. Intelligence-Led. (2009). National Criminal Justice Reference Service. *Intelligence-Led Policing: The New Intelligence Architecture*. http://www.ncjrs.gov/pdffiles1/bja/210681.pdf (accessed July 11, 2010).
6. McElreath, D., Quarles, C., Jensen, C. and Nations, R. (2010). *Introduction to Homeland Security*. Tulsa, OK: K & M Publishers, Inc.
7. Shulsky, A. and Schmitt, G. (2002). *Silent Warfare: Understanding the World of Intelligence*. Dulles, VA: Brassey's Publishing, Inc.
8. Blakeney, A. and Borins, S. (1998). *Political Management in Canada: Conversations on Statecraft* (2nd ed.). Toronto, Canada: University of Toronto Press.
9. Heuer, R. (1999). Psychology of intelligence analysis. https://www.cia.gov/library/center-for-the-study-of-intelligence/csi-publications/books-and-monographs/psychology-of-intelligence-analysis/PsychofIntelNew.pdf (accessed July 12, 2010).
10. Treverton, G. (2003). *Reshaping National Intelligence for an Age of Information*. Cambridge, UK: Cambridge University Press.
11. Warner, M. (2009). Intelligence as risk shifting. In Gill, P., Marrin, S. and Pythian, M. (eds.) *Intelligence Theory: Key Questions and Debates*. New York: Routledge Publishing, pp. 16–32.
12. Austin, N. and Rankov, N. (1995). *Exploration: Military and Political Intelligence in the Roman World from the Second Punic War to the Battle of Adrianople*. New York: Routledge Publishing.
13. Seah, M., Hsieh, M. and Weng, D. (2010). A case analysis of Savecom: the role of indigenous leadership in implementing a business intelligence system. *International Journal of Information Management, 30*(4), 368–373.
14. Oliver, W. (2007). Medicine looks back at intelligence. *International Journal of Intelligence & Counter Intelligence, 20*(3), 564–566.
15. Wheaton, K.J. (2011). Let's kill the intelligence cycle. *Sources and methods*. May 20, 2011. http://sourcesandmethods.blogspot.com/2011/05/lets-kill-intelligence-cycle-original.html (accessed December 24, 2011).
16. Director of National Intelligence. (2011). U.S. national intelligence: an overview 2011. http://www.odni.gov/IC_Consumers_Guide_2011.pdf (accessed January 25, 2012).
17. Richelson, J. (1999). *The U.S. Intelligence Community* (4th ed.). Boulder, CO: Westview Press.
18. Brainyquote. (n.d.). Henry Stimson quotes. http://www.brainyquote.com/quotes/quotes/h/henrylsti295174.html (accessed November 30, 2008).
19. Smith, R. (2005). *OSS: The Secret History of America's First Central Intelligence Agency*. Guilford, CT: Lyons Press.
20. Zegart, A. (2007). License to fail. *Los Angeles Times*. http://articles.latimes.com/2007/sep/23/opinion/op-zegart23 (accessed November 30, 2008).
21. Select Committee on Intelligence. (2004). Report on the U.S. intelligence community's prewar intelligence assessments on Iraq. http://www.gpoaccess.gov/serialset/creports/iraq.html (accessed November 30, 2008).
22. Office of the Director of National Intelligence. (n.d.). Who we are. http://www.dni.gov/index.html (accessed November 30, 2008).
23. Tucker, N. (2008). The cultural revolution in intelligence: interim report. *Washington Quarterly, 31*(2), 47–61.
24. McGarrell, E.F., Freilich, J.D. and Chermak, S. (2007). Intelligence-Led policing as a framework for responding to terrorism. *Journal of Contemporary Criminal Justice, 23*, 142–158.
25. Institute for Intergovernmental Research. (2008). Regional information sharing systems. http://www.iir.com/riss/ (accessed November 30, 2008).
26. Federation of American Scientists. (n.d.). Foreign Intelligence Surveillance Act. http://www.fas.org/irp/agency/doj/fisa/ (accessed November 30, 2008).
27. U.S. Congress. (2001). Uniting and Strengthening America by Providing Appropriate Tools Required to Intercept and Obstruct Terrorism (USA PATRIOT ACT) Act of 2001. http://epic.org/privacy/terrorism/hr3162.html (accessed November 30, 2008).

28. Canadian Intelligence Security Service. (2008). Homepage. http://www.csis-scrs.gc.ca/index-eng.asp (accessed August 27, 2013).
29. Warde, I. (2007). *The Price of Fear: The Truth Behind the Financial War on Terror*. Berkeley, CA: University of California Press.
30. Northrup, C. (2003). *The American Economy: A Historical Encyclopedia*, Volume 2. Santa Barbara, CA: ABC-CLIO Publishing, Inc.
31. Rossmo, K. (2000). *Geographic Profiling*. Boca Raton, FL: CRC Press.
32. Foxman, A. (2006). Security and freedom of speech. In Kamien, D. (ed.) *The McGraw-Hill Homeland Security Handbook*. New York: McGraw-Hill Publishing, pp. 1031–1045.
33. Director of National Intelligence. (2008). *Vision 2015: A Globally Networked and Integrated Intelligence Enterprise*. Washington, DC: Office of the Director of National Intelligence. http://www.dni.gov/Vision_2015.pdf (accessed November 30, 2008).

14

The Globalized World and Homeland Security

It has been said that arguing against globalization is like arguing against the laws of gravity.

Kofi Annan

Chapter objectives:

- Understand the concept of globalization
- Gain an understanding of globalization and its impact upon the homeland security of the United States
- Give an overview of the critical issues facing the nation in the areas of transportation and border security
- Examine the historical evolution of globalization
- Identify the salient characteristics of globalization

Introduction

The United States must craft national security policies that incorporate awareness of potential threats that could endanger its economic and financial relationships and functions. Because of the increases in globalism, the US economy and national functioning manifests a myriad of dependencies with other nations around the world. Within its hemisphere, the US enjoys especially close economic and financial relationships with both Canada and Mexico. Therefore, border security is a primary American concern.

The current trends in globalization demonstrate a rapid acceleration of integrated economies. Advances in communication and transportation technology, combined with a free-market ideology, have given goods, services, and capital unprecedented mobility. The vast majority of countries want to open world markets to their goods and take advantage of abundant, cheap labor in other parts of the world. International financial institutions and regional trade agreements, designed to compel the reduction of tariffs, are common among the nations of the world. As a result, many nations witnessed the privatization of state enterprises and the relaxing of both environmental and labor standards. Transnational corporations have become some of the largest economic entities in the world, and their financial and economic performances surpass the financial and economic performances of many states. Their continuous push for liberalization has driven globalization while challenging environmental, health, and labor standards in many countries. The US dollar serves as the standard unit of currency in international markets for many commodities; it is also the world's foremost reserve currency. Given all this, it is evident that the United States manifests a strong, global presence and influence.

Although many people may consider international threats to arise solely from terrorism or rogue states such as North Korea, this notion is naïve. Both man-made and natural threats may arise from a variety of nations and groups that are external to the United States and North America. Globalism has increased the integration and dependency of American society with foreign supply chains and logistics for goods and services. In the words of *New York Times* columnist Tom Friedman,[40] the world has become "flat." Because of globalization, American society is affected by changes and actions throughout the world with increasing magnitude and complexity. Ensuring the security and safety of American society involves considerations of global contexts and geopolitics among nations.

The opening of markets has produced a global supply chain in which raw materials and finished goods routinely travel between countries. This openness produces a record number of imports coming into the United States. In fact, so many goods travel through American ports that only a small percentage is ever examined by customs officials. As a result, experts concur that terrorists could exploit this weakness by introducing a weapon of mass destruction (WMD) that would easily avoid detection through a US port.

Globalization, however, is both a social and economic phenomenon. Today, people move across borders as they never have before. Immigrants and visitors come into the United States in unprecedented numbers. While America has always prided itself on integrating newcomers into its "melting-pot" society, the sheer number of new arrivals severely challenges homeland security and law enforcement officials. While the overwhelming majority of immigrants are law-abiding citizens seeking a better life, a myriad of foreign, criminal organizations have also found their way into the United States (e.g., the case of Mara Salvatrucha). Moreover, many immigrants enter the United States illegally, generally through Mexico. Many officials are concerned that weak border security could be exploited by terrorists entering the United States undetected.

Regardless of the perspectives of social or economic phenomena, globalism will increasingly affect American society. Electronic communications networks facilitate the financial aspects of economic resource allocations among nations. The modernizing of nations has the potential to offset traditional power balances among regions where the United States has global interests. Global dependencies continue to increase among nations, thereby creating complex and intricate relationships internationally. In any case, the United States must understand the potential of globalism to affect homeland security policies.

Globalization explained

There is no single, universally agreed-upon definition of globalization. For example, economist Jagdish Bhagwati[1] defines it as follows:

> …(the) integration of national economies into the international economy through trade, direct foreign investment…short-term capital flows, international flows of workers and humanity generally, and flows of technology…

On the other hand, Held and McGrew[2] define it as follows:

> ...the expanding scale, growing magnitude, speeding up and deepening impact of trans-continental flows and patterns of social interaction.

In order to better understand globalization, it is necessary to trace its history. In fact, the world started becoming globalized when the first explorers and merchants traveled beyond their own borders. In a very real sense, Marco Polo was a "globalist."

However, in the latter part of the 21st century, several factors emerged that would produce what we commonly term "globalization." In the first place, the fall of the Soviet Union introduced capitalism into countries that heretofore had embraced Socialism. The tensions that had existed between nations during the Cold War began to dissipate (although in some cases, the splintering and reformation of national boundaries would not be peaceful; consider the case of Bosnia). As well, countries embracing capitalism signed free-trade agreements, which reduced or eliminated tariffs and encouraged the flow of goods across national boundaries.

However, globalization is more than merely an economic concept—it also includes the free flow of information. Beginning in the 1990s, the evolution of the Internet and the installation of fiber-optic cable permitted instantaneous communication throughout the world. This, of course, has had a large, positive impact on economies; it also has permitted the exchange of cultural, political, religious, and social ideas. Ironically, while the Internet has brought many people closer to one another, it has also allowed individuals to join and form their own niche groups; in some cases, this has caused people to separate from their physical communities. For example, with regard to terrorism, Jensen[3] notes:

> Social scientists have long realized the effects that groups can have on individuals.... although this area has not been subjected to widespread empirical analysis, it is entirely likely that the Internet provides users with a 'cybersense of group.' That is, by engaging in electronic chats and spending large amounts of time communicating via e-mail with others who maintain like interests, one may discover that one's cybergroup exerts influences similar to those found in physical groups. In other words, spending 8 hours a day behind one's computer in cyberspace communicating with fellow 'cell members' may be psychologically similar to meeting with them on a regular basis.... In the opinion of some, technology may play a role in fostering growing ethnic and religious sentiments.... In addition to disseminating information, recruiting members, and concentrating power, the emotional appeal of the messages may stir fervor through the social dynamics of the cybersense of group described above. Members of religious and ethnic groups can be united in cyberspace regardless of where they happen to reside. Therefore, although the Internet may make national boundaries less important, it may make ethnic and religious divisions more pronounced and more important to individuals.

The current levels of globalization are unprecedented and represent a time of unprecedented global interaction. Throughout history, the stages of globalization encompassed a wide range of social, political, and economic changes. Revolutionary advancements in technology, science, industry, agriculture, environmental, and social issues contributed toward the growth of globalization historically and continue to function as primary catalysts for the modern expansion of globalism.

Globalization, then, is a double-edged sword—it can produce much good, but it can also facilitate discord. For example, in 2013, the United States recognized formally "the first Somali national government since 1991 when the Siad Barre dictatorship was overthrown and the country fell into a period of statelessness."[4] This event represents the first elections that occurred "on Somali soil" in over 20 years.[4] However, in that same year, the United States continued to observe the distress in Mexico as a result of its bloody drug wars. As the 2012 year closed, approximately "60,000 people—possibly 100,000—have been killed in violence across Mexico," and thousands of others "have disappeared."[5] Some claim that the opening of borders between the United States and Mexico as a result of the North American Free Trade Agreement (NAFTA) has played some role in facilitating the delivery of drugs into America. The United States now contributes a variety of "drones and sniffer dogs, police trainers and intelligence agents to a country long suspicious of its powerful neighbor."[6]

Overseas powers also have the capacity to affect American society. The nation of China is increasingly becoming modernized and continues to invest economically and financially in the United States. This observation regarding the Chinese situation is an especially important consideration for US security and future American generations. The Chinese own a significant amount of US bond investment debt, thereby contributing vast amounts of money toward the financing of the US government. According to Branigan and Stewart,[26] during the latter part of 2009, the Chinese government signaled a diminishing faith in the potential of the United States economically, and sold approximately $32 billion of its US investments. This investment sale relinquished China's position as the primary holder of US debt globally. However, despite this sale, China retains $755.4 billion of US debt.[26]

Because the United States now relies upon the financial investment of other nations as a method of financing its operations, any loss of faith in American economic potential may have strategic consequences for the United States through time. Such an inability to attract foreign investment would deny the United States access to capital that is necessary for the functioning of the nation. However, despite the Chinese sale of US debt, nations continue to view the United States with some degree of confidence regarding long-term, strategic investments.

Such US reliance upon foreign investment is a strong example of economic and financial integration globally. Given the relationships that bind nations together, varying levels of interdependence have emerged. Therefore, the economic performance of the United States is critical to the successes of its investors regarding their eventual profitability from US investment. This scenario is not the only consideration of interdependence that potentially poses security challenges. As a result, the economies of nations today are inexorably intertwined. If the US economy suffers, so does China.

The Middle East represents a special case with regard to globalization. Among the nations of the world, the the growth of petroleum continues to increase annually to support the needs and wants of emerging economies. Because petroleum is a finite resource for which demand increases annually, it presents a security challenge for the United States. While petroleum conjures up thoughts of oil and gasoline for automobiles, it is also an ingredient in a variety of products that support American lifestyles, such as plastics and medical products.

The dangers of US dependency on international petroleum suppliers, including those of the Middle East, are concerning. The US government is actively advocating the development of alternative fuels and fuel processing systems given the national security issues associated with finite petroleum supplies. Parthemore and Nagl[87] indicate that "up to 77 percent of DOD's massive energy needs—and most of the aircraft, ground vehicles, ships, and weapons systems that DOD is purchasing today—depend on petroleum for fuel." Strategically, this situation represents significant danger regarding the ability of the United States to defend itself and facilitate security functions.

The preceding examples represent a mere subset of the global dynamics facing the world today. Many other situations also present potential security challenges. Garrett and Sherman[42] warn against the dangers of transnational, organized crime within the global economy. According to them, failed states, failing nations, and rouge states are attractive to criminal factions and organizations because of their poor economic conditions; many of these nations succumb to various amounts of chaos, violence, crime, and corruption. The characteristics of these nations include "terrorists and drug lords, seekers of WMDs, incubators of disease, nurturers of religious extremists, and demographic time bombs of growing numbers of unemployed youth."[42] As a method of diminishing the security risks of such detrimental environments, Garrett and Sherman[42] advocate both "international cooperation in counterterrorism and non-proliferation" and "a broad and systematic international effort to help these states move from the category of the failing to the category of the succeeding."

Ramifications of globalization for homeland security

Globalization has had an overall positive effect on the world and among the economies of America. However, it has also redefined the way in which the notion of "security" is conceptualized. What benefits America also benefits those who would harm the nation. The advent of globalization has shifted the balance of power in the world today. Although the United States enjoys the financial benefits of outsourcing services and purchasing cheap imports, the big winners have actually been the countries engaged in these activities. Many experts predict that the emerging superpowers in the world will be China and India. The economies and influences of these nations on the world stage are expected to continue to increase, while those of the United States are expected to simultaneously decline.[68]

China, for one, does not appear content to confine its growth only to the economic arena. It has also increased its military reach accordingly. For example, in 2008, the discovery of a secret Chinese nuclear submarine base has raised concerns that China may attempt to challenge US maritime dominance in the Pacific.[49] China also poses a potential threat, as an aggressor, within the domain of cyber warfare. In 2012, China landed jet aircraft aboard its first aircraft carrier, thereby signaling its increasing military capability and potential ability to project its naval power.[7] Through time, Chinese military modernization may have the potential to offset power alignments within the Asian region.

Another obvious concern in a world of ubiquitous communications and easy travel is the spread of dangerous technologies. Perhaps nothing worries homeland security officials more than the possibility that either a nuclear weapon or nuclear technology will fall into the wrong hands. When the Soviet Union dissolved, there was great concern that some of its nuclear arsenal would make its way to terrorist groups. This scenario was not an unreasonable worry because Soviet nuclear facilities were often poorly guarded during the period following the collapse of its economy. Further, those entrusted with the care of nuclear weapons were poorly paid, if at all. These observances led to speculation that someone might try to sell a nuclear weapon or nuclear material on the black market. In fact, al Qaeda's number two leader, Ayman al-Zawahri, claimed that the group has already purchased a number of "suitcase nukes" from disgruntled Russian scientists. However, Russia has officially denied this claim.[20]

A variety of nations possess nuclear technology and nuclear weaponry. Members of the Nuclear Proliferation Treaty, who are openly known to possess nuclear weapons, include the United States, the United Kingdom, Russia, France, and China. Other known nuclear powers include India, Pakistan, and North Korea. Each of these nations has detonated nuclear weapons. During the time of this authorship, the nation of Israel is classified as an undeclared nuclear weapons state. However, there is the threat of undesirable entities obtaining nuclear weaponry and nuclear technologies necessary for fashioning weapons.

Perhaps a more likely and imminent threat concerns the continued development of nuclear technology on the part of nation–states. As of the writing of this book, Iran is suspected by many of being on the threshold of developing its own nuclear weapon. This would not only lead to the further destabilization of an already volatile Middle East; it would also raise the unpalatable possibility that such a weapon would fall into the hands of an Iranian terrorist surrogate (e.g., Hezbollah).

The 9/11 attacks made it clearly obvious that it is not just nation–states that have the ability to wreak havoc on the United States. Today, technology allows even little groups to act "big." If the Internet has been a blessing for the average citizen, it has proven to be a godsend for international and domestic terrorists and criminals because it allows them to spread their ideology and communicate with one another easily and cheaply. Individuals no longer need to meet physically to swap ideas and plan activities. Many, if not all, of these activities can occur in cyberspace.

The Internet also allows for the rapid dissemination of information of all types. Compared to other forms of deadly technology, information about developing nuclear weapons remains generally secure, at least for the present. However, such security is certainly not the case with chemical, biological, or radiological weapons. For example, documents seized in Afghanistan reveal that al Qaeda possessed crude procedures for producing VX nerve agent, sarin, and mustard gas. Also, recipes for deadly substances like ricin and procedures for making radiological "dirty" bombs circulate freely on the Internet (**Figure 14.1**).[77]

Instructions for making poisons and bombs are not the only advantage the Internet offers terrorist groups. Today, a single individual has the ability to gather and analyze information in a way that only sophisticated intelligence agencies once could. Consider the numerous maps, satellite photos, and information about America's critical infrastructure that currently appear online. The intelligence community recognizes the considerable value of this "open-source" intelligence through the analyzing of such intelligence. Recently, the Central Intelligence

Figure 14.1 *Anthrax letters from 2001.*
(Courtesy of the FBI.)

Agency (CIA) opened its Open Source Center to gather and analyze the vast amount of information that is released to the public daily.[30]

Ironically, it is not merely the information on the Internet that has increased the vulnerability of America. Instead, it is the manifestation of the Internet itself. The original concept for the Internet was developed as far back as Russia's launch of the Sputnik satellite in 1957. Worried about losing its technological dominance over the Soviet Union, the US government opened the Advanced Research Projects Agency (ARPA) in the late 1950s. One of ARPA's projects was the development of a robust network of computers that could survive major losses to the underlying network. This system, dubbed the Advanced Research Projects Agency Network (ARPANET), was the predecessor to today's Internet.[33]

The Internet presents a variety of security challenges among the critical infrastructure of the nation. Many US systems, such as those that control utilities and dams, are run through the Internet. Hackers have already demonstrated the ability to break into these vulnerable systems, worrying officials who fear that terrorists or extortionists may do the same.[21] Within the globalized environment, another major concern is the occurrence of a "Cyber Pearl Harbor." Such an event would represent an attack of epic proportions, disabling major parts of the Internet. Such an attack could have enormous ramifications for business, government, and the average citizen.[62]

Although advanced technologies and open borders benefit nations and terrorist groups, they also make America increasingly vulnerable to transnational criminal organizations. Both organized crime groups and individuals, from as far away as Russia, Asia, Africa, and South America, increasingly victimize US citizens and companies. Also, the revolution in communications and technology has created whole new types of criminal activity. The primary example of such new forms of crime is identity theft. Currently, identity theft is the fastest-growing crime in America. American law enforcement agencies have demonstrated an inability to stop this type of crime and to arrest perpetrators. Because many of these perpetrators operate, with impunity, beyond US borders, it is difficult to locate, identify, and bring to justice such criminals. Today, because of the power they wield and the sophisticated tactics they can employ, some criminal organizations are even considered threats to American national security.[39]

A major theme of globalization is the increasing empowerment of even small groups. One may consider the case of al Qaeda, a relatively small organization. In the wake of the 9/11 attacks, the United States has been forced to respond to its activities the way it historically reacted to foreign enemy states. Technology and the unrestricted movement of personnel have proven to be force multipliers for al Qaeda and have allowed it to wield a level of global influence that was unthinkable years ago.

Perhaps the greatest challenge facing homeland security officials comes not from outside the organization but from inside. Those who study globalization note that, in a world of speedy computers and ever-changing cultural and social networks, it is the swift and flexible, and not the big, who usually survive. Many criminal and terrorist organizations understand this concept. They have "flattened" their organizational structures, thereby exploiting the power of the computer age. Not all agree that the US government has completed a similar form of restructuring its agencies. For example, the Department of Homeland Security was created after the attacks of 9/11 to allow for better sharing of information and resources across agencies. Although the agency is beneficial, some critics contend that the creation of this agency produced a greater bloated bureaucracy that is both slow and fundamentally incapable of keeping up with a rapidly evolving enemy.[73]

Clash of civilizations

One scholar, Samuel Huntington, produced a provocative body of research that suggests that the struggle of the future will not involve countries as much as it will involve cultures and religions. Huntington's premise generates much debate. His commentary appears consistent with the current fight between the al Qaeda movement and the West, and its tenets fit nicely with the realities of the globalized world. However, Huntington is not without critics, and his commentary has produced a variety of debates and discussions.

Huntington calls his theory the "Clash of Civilizations." He wrote it in response to a 1992 book, authored by former RAND Corporation social scientist Francis Fukuyama, titled *The End of History and the Last Man*. Fukuyama's premise was that, with the end of the Cold War, liberal democracy had "triumphed" over all other forms of government and would forever reign as the final form of governance.[41] However, Huntington disagreed with the notions of Fukuyama. Within a 1993 article, contained within the journal *Foreign Affairs*, he declared:

> It is my hypothesis that the fundamental source of conflict in this new world will not be primarily ideological or primarily economic. The great divisions among humankind and the dominating source of conflict will be cultural. Nation states will remain the most powerful actors in world affairs, but the principal conflicts of global politics will occur between nations and groups of different civilizations. The clash of civilizations will dominate global politics. The fault lines between civilizations will be the battle lines of the future (pp. 45–57).[51]

The rise of al Qaeda in the 1990s and the attacks of 9/11 may indicate that Huntington was prescient in his analysis. However, not everyone agrees with this assessment. Some claim that Huntington has misidentified the cultures that exist in the world. Others argue that people may embrace many identities simultaneously (e.g., religious, national, ethnic) within a global society. Such differences may coexist or clash, even at the individual level. Finally, some question exists regarding whether conflict is inevitable. Basically, will different groups be forever consigned to fighting, or can some lasting peace emerge across cultures?

Some views contrast with those of Huntington. Goel offers a different view involving religious ideology and extremism.[8] According to Goel, the "fundamental conflict" that will define the 21st century will occur "between radical Islam and greater part of the rest of humanity" (p. 4).[9] Goel notes, "Militant Islamic anger is directed against Christians, Buddhists, Hindus, Jews, Slavs and animists," and he offers the following list as an itemizing of the factions that military Islam wages war against during modern times (p. 4)[9]:

- Roman Catholics in Mindanao in the Philippines
- Roman Catholics in Timor in Indonesia
- Confucians and Buddhists in Singapore and Malaysia
- Hindus in Bangladesh
- Hindus in Kashmir and within India itself
- Russian Orthodox Catholics in Chechnya
- Armenian Christians in Nagorno-Karabakh
- Maronite Christians in Lebanon
- Jews in Israel and in all other parts of the world
- Animists and Christians in Sudan
- Ethiopian Orthodox Christians in Eritrea
- Greek Orthodox Catholics in Cyprus

- Slavs in Bosnia, Kosovo, and Albania
- Coptic Christians in Egypt
- Ibos in Nigeria
- Christians and Jews in the United States
- Moderate Islamic Regimes in Egypt, Jordan, and Turkey

Other perceptions of future challenges exist that are contrary to the paradigm of Huntington. Voll[10] offers a perspective of modernity regarding contemplations of current global conflicts. According to Voll,[10] current global tensions and conflicts are unrelated to "clashes of civilizations." Instead, they involve a consideration of "profound clashes of culture and life visions."[10] According to Voll,[10] "Competition among different modes of modernity and efforts to define a distinctive modernity for specific societies are part of the foundation of the major conflicts visible around the world today."

Despite these contrasting viewpoints and criticisms, Huntington's view has proven resilient. It provides those involved in homeland security with a theoretical template from which to consider the present and near-term future. Other paradigms will undoubtedly emerge, and they should be considered with equal seriousness. No human can predict the long-term future with certainty or accuracy. However, as globalism continues to increase through time, American preparedness must be vigilantly robust to safeguard against the potential threats that endanger society.

Terrorism: A backlash to globalization?

Whenever there is a rapid change in the social order, there are often groups or individuals who oppose such change. For example, during the early part of the 19th century, a group of British textile workers protested against changes brought about by the industrial revolution by destroying mechanized weaving looms. This group, dubbed the Luddites, felt that their livelihoods were threatened by new technology. This form of human behavior is not confined to historical accounts of balking. Instead, modern human behavior, expressed through acts of terror, may be a modern equivalent of such balking.

Similar to the antitechnology stance of the Luddites, much of modern terrorism can be seen as a response against globalization. Certainly, most terrorist groups embrace and readily use new technologies, such as the Internet. However, many object to other aspects of globalization, particularly the increasing power of international business and the movement of people and culture throughout the world. For example, during the 1990s, many militia groups spoke against the "New World Order" that they thought was secretly being installed. They believed that the new order consisted of a one-world government along the lines of a dictatorship of the wealthy over all others, and they viewed globalized business as a particular enemy. Al Qaeda can also be seen as having an antiglobalization agenda. Osama bin Laden was clear in his desire to remove representatives of foreign governments and un-Islamic leadership from Muslim lands and clear in his disdain for the "decadent" culture of the West. Instead, he favored a return to the "perfect" times of the 7th century, when the Prophet Mohammed lived. Finally, environmental and anarchist groups direct much of their anger against international business concerns. They envision and perceive such business entities to be polluters of the earth and exploiters of poor and indigenous people.

Americans can expect little relief from terrorism and other forms of pushback, at least in the near term. Because the threats of terrorism shall continue during future times, the United States and its allies must be prepared to address future incidents of terrorism (**Figure 14.2**).

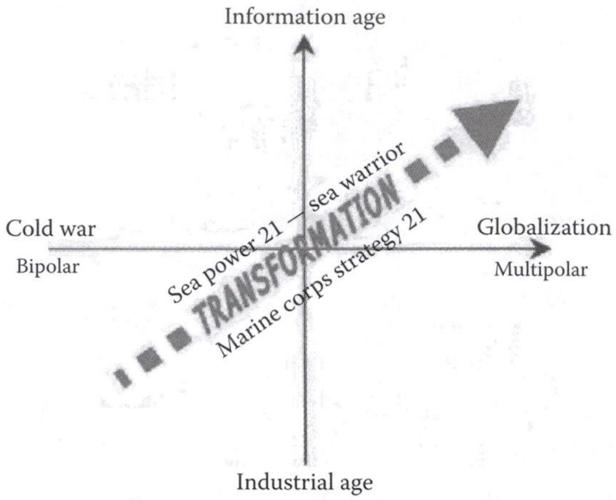

Figure 14.2 Transformation and globalism. (Courtesy of the US Navy.)

Globalism: US security along the US–Mexican border

During the period of the authorship of this textbook, some argue that the nation of Mexico is demonstrating the characteristics of a failing state. At the very least, the nation is experiencing a drug war that impacts commoners as well as the elite factions of its government and society. Corruption is rampant among Mexico's law enforcement, military, judicial, and government entities. Among townships and municipalities, public officials continue to be murdered; their bodies mutilated; and their families terrorized, harassed, or killed. The violent impact of the Mexican drug trade cannot be ignored. According to the *Los Angeles Times*, over 28,228 individuals have perished since the instigation of the Mexican drug war in 2007.[61] The kidnapping and murder of private citizens, vacationing foreigners, law enforcement officials, and government officials is unprecedented.

The murder and beheading of public officials, grenade attacks against civilians, attacks against the clientele of Mexican drug rehabilitation centers, carjackings, and vehicle bombings are not uncommon events facilitated by the drug cartels.[61] Discoveries of the clandestine graves of masses of victims, whose deaths occurred in conjunction with bondage, torture, and dismembering, also occur sporadically.[85]

Hostilities related to the drug war have increasingly affected the US–Mexican border and the US–Mexican national relationship. In 2010, approximately 3500 acres of the border territory, encompassing nearly 80 miles within the Buenos Aires National Wildlife Refuge, were closed to US citizens because of violence.[80] Both US citizens and US law enforcement officials became the targets of this violence, and warnings were issued by US Fish and Wildlife officials warning the American populace against the dangers posed by armed drug traffickers.[80] Such violence increasingly targets US citizens both within Mexico and along the border. In March 2010, an American employed with the US consulate in Mexico and a rancher were murdered within the border city of Juarez.[24] According to the *Washington Times*, by 2010, 79 US citizens had been killed within Mexico; 23 of them were killed in Juarez.[24]

Violence extends in varying degrees across the entire length of the US–Mexican border; many officials fear that this violence will increase over time and spill over into the United States.

Janet Napolitano, the US homeland security secretary, has admitted that "Mexican drug cartels pose a terrorist threat to the United States."[67] The US Department of Justice (DOJ)[38] indicates that Mexican drug-trafficking organizations (DTOs) "represent the single greatest drug-trafficking threat to the United States" and are increasing their influence and distribution among outlets within the domestic United States. In 2009, the DOJ reported that "midlevel and retail drug distribution in the United States was dominated by more than 900,000 criminally active gang members representing approximately 20,000 street gangs in more than 2500 cities." McCaffrey[59] (p. 4) indicates that "before the next eight years are past—the violent, warring collection of criminal drug cartels could overwhelm the institutions of the state and establish de facto control over broad regions of northern Mexico."

Both Arizona Governor Jan Brewer and Senator John McCain have voiced concerns about security along the US–Mexican border. Governor Brewer stated the US government has failed to fulfill its "obligation and moral responsibility" of maintaining security along the border; in response, she has proposed a security plan, involving the use of the National Guard, to protect Arizona from the threats of border violence.[44] In April 2010, Governor Brewer approved and signed immigration legislation that immediately generated much debate regarding its constitutionality. According to the *Arizona Central*,[17] the primary points of this legislation

- Made it a state crime to be in the country illegally and required local police to enforce federal immigration laws
- Required anyone whom police suspect of being in the country illegally to produce "an alien registration document," such as a green card, or other proof of citizenship, such as a passport or an Arizona driver's license
- Made it illegal to impede the flow of traffic by picking up day laborers for work

This legislation immediately prompted a variety of lawsuits. Resistance from both Mexico and the American Civil Liberties Union quickly followed. The most significant rejection of the Arizona legislation, however, came from the US federal government. The Obama administration filed a lawsuit against the state of Arizona seeking to halt its enactment. Governor Brewer's immediate response was a strong defense of the legislation:

Today I was notified that the federal government has filed a lawsuit against the State of Arizona. It is wrong that our own federal government is suing the people of Arizona for helping to enforce federal immigration law. As a direct result of failed and inconsistent federal enforcement, Arizona is under attack from violent Mexican drug and immigrant smuggling cartels. Now, Arizona is under attack in federal court from President Obama and his Department of Justice. Today's filing is nothing more than a massive waste of taxpayer funds. These funds could be better used against the violent Mexican cartels than the people of Arizona. The truth is the Arizona law is both reasonable and constitutional. It mirrors substantially what has been federal law in the United States for many decades. Arizona's law is designed to complement, not supplant, enforcement of federal immigration laws. Despite the Department of Justice's claims in paragraph 62 of today's lawsuit, Arizona is not trying 'to establish its own immigration policy' or 'directly regulate the immigration status of aliens.'[57]

The Arizona debate continues, and there is little agreement among the affected factions regarding the best methods of ensuring border security. In 2010, challenges to the lawsuit of the Obama administration were issued and rejected. During the time of this authorship, legal proceedings are forthcoming that shall introduce court arguments against the Arizona legislation.

The seriousness and potential security threats associated with illegal aliens entering the United States are not unfounded. According to Hedgecock,[50] "Mexico announced it had arrested Jameel Nasr, the reputed Hezbollah leader in Latin America, at his home in Tijuana, a stone's throw from the border separating that Mexican city and San Diego." Hedgecock[50] also indicates that "gang members" among "U.S. prisons" have "tattoos in Farsi (the national language of Iran)," that "Hezbollah agents are teaching the Mexican drug cartels the art of the car bomb," and that "other than Mexican" individuals are increasing being discovered by the Border Patrol. Hedgecock[50] indicates that "Nasr recently spent a month in Venezuela" and that "Iranian agents and Hezbollah members" train in Venezuela to "learn Spanish" and to learn methods of integrating themselves with "the waves of illegals crossing the border."

Within the context of globalization, the relationship between the United States and Mexico is one of mutual interdependence. Both nations are significant trading partners with each other, and their economies are interdependent. Both rely on each other to provide varying percentages of goods and services that are necessary for the continuance of their respective lifestyles and national infrastructures. However, the current drug crisis represents a threat both along the border and, increasingly, within American cities. For example, in 2013, the city of Chicago announced its new "Public Enemy Number One":[11]

> For the first time since Prohibition, Chicago has a new Public Enemy No. 1—a drug kingpin in Mexico deemed so menacing that he's been assigned the famous label created for Al Capone. Joaquin 'El Chapo' Guzman was singled out for his role as leader of the powerful Sinaloa cartel, which supplies the bulk of narcotics sold in the city, according to the Chicago Crime Commission and the Drug Enforcement Administration.

In addition to the threats from drugs and the possible smuggling of terrorists into the United States, Mexico represents another potential threat to the United States. Should the drug war spin sufficiently out of control to represent an existential threat to Mexico, that could present the possibility that a failed state would border the United States. The resultant chaos and economic distress that would ensue could pose a substantial challenge.

Globalism: US security along the US–Canadian border

Defensively and militarily, the United States and Canada have long existed as strategic partners during a variety of mutual civilian and government initiatives. According to the US Department of State, the mutual participation of US and Canadian defense initiatives is "more extensive than with any other country."[19] Based on the information presented by the US Department of State, the closeness of this shared, defensive framework includes the following considerations:

- The Permanent Joint Board on Defense, established in 1940, provides policy-level consultation on bilateral defense matters, and the United States and Canada share North Atlantic Treaty Organization (NATO) mutual security commitments.
- US and Canadian military forces have cooperated, since 1958, on continental air defense within the framework of the North American Aerospace Defense Command (NORAD).
- The military response to the September 11, 2001, terrorist attacks in the United States both tested and strengthened military cooperation between the United States and Canada.

- The new NORAD Agreement that entered into force on May 12, 2006, added a maritime domain awareness component and is of indefinite duration, subject to periodic review.
- Since 2002, Canada has participated in diplomatic, foreign assistance, and joint military actions in Afghanistan. Canadian Forces personnel are presently deployed in southern Afghanistan under a battle group based at Kandahar and as members of the Canadian-led Provincial Reconstruction Team (PRT) at Camp Nathan Smith in Kandahar. The Canadian Parliament has approved the extension of this mission in Kandahar through 2011.

Loucky et al.[56] (p. 25) consider "cross-border regions," such as the Pacific Northwest United States along the Canadian border, to be "central economic and environmental" entities. Hakam and Litan[47] (p. 8) consider border security from a post-9/11 perspective and indicate that "security cooperation [is] essential to sustain normal cross-border commerce, capital flows, and the movement of people."

From the perspective of terrorism, the US border with Canada presents a variety of national security risks. According to Leiken and Brooke[54] (p. 513), "Canada is the most worrisome terrorist point of entry, and Al Qaeda training manuals advise agents to enter the U.S. through Canada." According to them, Canada deserves "top priority among U.S. points of entry."

The Canadian perspective of border security differs from the US perspective. According to Nicol[70] (p. 778), the "greatest risk is not terrorism, but U.S. domination"; the US–Canadian border demarks the "largest trade relationship in the world," and national trading, between the United States and Canada, is "essentially three times more important to the Canadian economy than it is to the U.S. economy." According to the US Department of State,[19] the volume of trading between the United States and Canada represents approximately a daily amount of US "$1.5 billion" involving approximately 300,000 daily physical border crossings. Given this alternative perspective of security, lengthy or significant disruptions of economic activity would significantly impact the living standards and trade potentials of both nations.

The effects of impeded border trade are varied and impact both businesses and individuals. According to Vance[83] (p. 240), the effects of US security measures, after the events of September 11, 2001, instigated "negative externalities" economically through "increased insurance premiums, higher shipment rates, reduced productivity, loss of profits, delayed cross-border shipments, inflated prices, pressure to invest in costly voluntary compliance programs, and damaged commercial relationships between firms on the basis of their relative location with respect to the border." Although such externalities may have lessened during the succeeding years, the dangers associated with the slowing of commerce are viable threats to the economies of both nations. Therefore, considerations of border security must encompass the economic characteristics and functions of both nations.

Regardless of the perspective, the US–Canadian border presents a variety of security challenges and potential threats that impact the national security paradigms of both nations. Although the economic and financial considerations of the US–Canadian border are indicative of globalism, the movement of goods and services across the border are imperative to satisfy the respective human needs and wants of both nations. The US–Canadian relationship is one of peacefulness and provides a basis for mutual investments bilaterally through time. However, a myriad of potential threats may endanger the activities of the US–Canadian border. Therefore, as a method of facilitating border security, both the United States and Canada must craft national security policies that accommodate the potential dangers of terrorism and

Figure 14.3 For those who travel frequently between the United States and Canada, a US passport card can be issued, and that may be used along the US–Canadian border. (Courtesy of the US Department of State.)

the influences of organized crime while allowing for the effective and efficient carrying on of business (**Figure 14.3**); it is not an easy task.

Case study: The rise of a theocratic Iran

Although the United States and the Soviet Union competed for global power and influence during the Cold War, both nations made missteps. For the United States, policy decisions related to Southeast Asia, Central America, the Middle East, and Northern Africa, in some cases, proved to be disastrous. Fortunately for the United States, the foreign policy of the Soviet Union also fell short of its desired goals. In the effort to expand international influence, many nations found themselves drawn into the competition between the superpowers. Iran was one of those nations.

Mohammed Reza Shah Pahlavi came to power as the Shah of Iran in classic Cold War style. In 1951, the Iranian people elected Mohammed Mosaddeq as the prime minister of Iran. His threat to nationalize the massive Iranian oil industry and his friendship with the Soviet Union concerned the United States and Britain. In 1953, with substantial assistance from the CIA, the popular Mosaddeq was deposed in a coup, and Pahlavi, thereafter referred to as the Shah, became the leader of Iran.

The Shah would prove a great friend to the United States. He supported the modernization of his country, maintained cordial relations with the West, and was the first leader of a Muslim nation to recognize the state of Israel. However, these attributes did not endear him to many of his subjects. Further, the wealth in Iran was not evenly distributed. Those close to the Shah enjoyed great prosperity, while most received little. In order to maintain control, the Shah employed a brutal secret police called the Sāzemān-e Ettelā'āt va Amniyat-e Keshvar (SAVAK), which imprisoned and tortured several thousand political prisoners during his reign.

By 1979, the people of Iran had suffered enough. The Shah was convinced to leave the country for his own safety. Suffering from cancer, he stayed for short periods of time in several different countries before succumbing to the disease in 1980 within the United States. The fact that he had been strongly supported by the United States, and was allowed to die there, infuriated many Iranians.

In his place, the people installed the Grand Ayatollah Seyyed Ruhollah Musavi Khomeini as the first supreme leader of Iran. Khomeini had served all his life as a religious leader. However, because of his opposition to the Shah, he had been exiled to Paris. Upon his triumphant return and appointment as leader, he declared Iran to be an Islamic Republic, with all facets of government guided by his very conservative Shi'a interpretation of Islam. Unlike the Shah, Khomeini was no friend of the United States. In 1979, when several of his followers took over the US embassy in Teheran and held its occupants hostage for 444 days, Khomeini, at first, did nothing. Later, he supported the captors of the hostages. The Ayatollah continued to rule Iran until his death in 1989. After he died, the country continued as a theocracy, with power primarily invested in Iran's Shi'a leadership.

Today finds Iran and the United States facing each other in a tense struggle that involves many issues including WMDs, global energy, sponsorship of global terrorism, and influence in the Middle East. For Iran, the United States, once a strong partner, is not the greatest challenge to their power in the region. With United States air and ground military forces in Iran's neighbors, as well as Iraqi and Afghanistan and strong naval forces off its coast in the Persian Gulf, the relationship between the two nations is difficult, with no resolution in sight. Adding to the potential of escalation is the danger a nuclear Iran is believed to pose in the region to its neighbors, especially the strong American ally, Israel.

Case study: Mara Salvatrucha

For many, the word "gang" conjures up an image of a group of disaffected young people engaged in criminality to gain identity, raise money, and acquire and maintain "turf." However, many modern gangs are better described as true transnational criminal organizations. An example is the case of Mara Salvatrucha, also known as MS-13, which the Federal Bureau of Investigation (FBI) describes as "one of the greatest threats to the safety and security of all Americans."[39]

MS-13, which originated in Los Angeles during the 1980s, was started by El Salvadorian immigrants. Many of these individuals participated in or had been victimized by the country's bloody civil war. Unusually violent, MS-13 members engage in drug distribution, murder, rape, prostitution, robbery, home invasions, immigration offenses, kidnapping, carjacking/auto theft, and vandalism. They are also known for violently assaulting law enforcement officers.

With an estimated 10,000 members currently located throughout the United States and an estimated 100,000 members worldwide, they are truly a transnational entity. Their members travel freely among the nations of the United States, Canada, Mexico, Guatemala, Colombia, Spain, Great Britain, and Germany. Their ability to travel freely, coupled with the level of fear and intimidation they bring to their communities, provides a difficult challenge for security officials. Recently, extensive international task forces have been developed to address the dangers posed by this organization. The United States is concerned because international terrorist groups, such as al Qaeda, may attempt to establish alliances with MS-13 to facilitate the movement of terrorists into the United States.

Globalization and organized crime

Globalization certainly produced legal markets for innumerable goods and services flowing across national boundaries. Such products are traded and taxed in accordance with existing laws both domestically and internationally. However, globalism also has facilitated opportunities for illegal markets (i.e., black markets) to exist, ranging from drug smuggling and human trafficking to the producing and selling of counterfeit products. Such activities also provide opportunities for organized crime entities to increase their scope of operations. Though such criminal organizations and their associated networks, numerous threats are posed to American society.

Globalization contributes toward the mellowing of relationships among nations through which the freedom of exchanges across borders increased since the ending of the Cold War. For example, Russian criminal organizations exploited the "increased ease of international travel, the liberalization of emigration policies, the expansion of international trade, the spread of high-technology communications systems, and the underregulation of international financial networks (via sophisticated money laundering techniques) to extend their criminal enterprises well beyond the borders of their own country."[12] Although the Cold War ended, threats to American society still existed. Many other criminal organizations have exploited the diminishing of trade restrictions globally.

Numerous criminal organizations leverage black markets through which financial resources are obtained and laundered to support a variety of crimes. Examples include migrant smuggling and human trafficking; cocaine trafficking through South America into North America; firearms trafficking; wildlife smuggling and trafficking; and a variety of others.[13] **Figure 14.4** depicts many of these dangers arising from the international and global activities of organized crime entities. Such activities cross US borders via land, air, and sea modalities. Ensuring the safety and security of society is a daunting task given the immensity of criminal activity that transcends national boundaries. Even the "most efficient of law enforcement agencies" are able to interdict fewer than approximately 20% of drug-related products.[14] Despite the best efforts of law enforcement agencies, the activities of organized crime represent a continuous danger to American society.

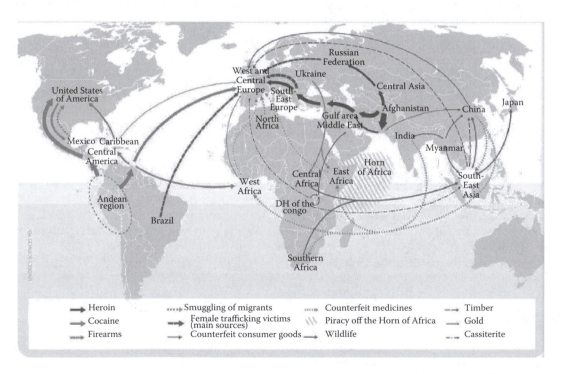

Figure 14.4 *Organized crime activities and network flows globally. (From the United Nations Office on Drugs and Crime,* The Globalization of Crime: A Transnational Organized Crime Threat Assessment, *2010. Reprinted with permission.)*

Conclusion

The Cold War ended at an opportune time in history. Even as economic markets opened, new technologies such as the Internet enabled a series of worldwide changes that have come to be known as "globalization." In short, globalization represents the integration of national economies into an international economic entity that facilitates the rapid, easy movement of people, goods, culture, and ideas. The concept of globalization is not new—international economic trade existed for many centuries. However, global growth and expansion have accelerated drastically given the advances and improvements of modern technologies and the dissolution of the bipolar world.

While globalization is generally viewed as an economic construct, it produces many challenges for homeland security. The Internet allows terrorist groups to communicate and share ideas (e.g., recipes for WMDs) efficiently and effectively. It also quickly facilitates growth among their organizations. Open borders provide opportunities for terrorists and criminals to travel internationally with little difficulty. The very concept of globalization has spurred the formation of new terrorist groups who object to international economies as well as the dispersion of people and culture into previously closed societies.

During the preceding century, the United States was blessed with unprecedented economic growth and influence despite experiencing the Great Depression and other recessionary periods. The global US influence has spawned a backlash that produces challenges for the nation and its allies. However, the integrity of the US economic and financial systems must be protected to ensure the operational capacity and continuance of the nation and to supply its human needs and wants through time. Therefore, any crafting of national security strategy must be mindful of the importance of the US economic and financial systems.

The world continues to change. Future challenges to homeland security will come from a variety of sources, some of which are presently recognized. Examples include rogue states, transnational criminal organizations, natural disasters, terrorist groups, and others that have yet to emerge. Therefore, it is incumbent upon those entrusted with the protection of the American homeland to remain ever vigilant to the dynamic threats that endanger the nation and its interests. Otherwise, the nation is doomed to repeat the mistakes of its past.

Key terms

Globalization
Transnational corporations
Flat world
Free flow of information
Cybersense of group
North American Free Trade Agreement (NAFTA)
Alternative fuels
Nuclear Proliferation Treaty
ARPANET
Cyber Pearl Harbor
Clash of Civilizations
North American Aerospace Defense Command (NORAD)
Mara Salvatrucha

QUESTIONS FOR DISCUSSION

1. The primary consideration of economic theory involves the notion of satisfying the unlimited wants and needs of humans through the availability and distributing of scarce resources through time. Given the proliferation of globalization since the end of the Cold War, how do you believe US foreign policy has impacted the national economy from a homeland security perspective? Write a brief essay that discusses this issue.

2. Some advocates of free trade staunchly believe that free-trade agreements, such as NAFTA, Central America Free Trade Agreement (CAFTA), and so forth, are good economically for the United States, whereas others argue that such policies have undermined and weakened the American economy. Given these notions, write a brief essay that supports your position regarding the effects of globalization and free trade concerning the American economy. Please author this essay from the perspective of homeland security.

3. This chapter introduced arguments that conflict with Huntington's Clash of Civilizations paradigm. Locate some recent materials that either support or refute Huntington's paradigm. Write a brief essay that discusses your findings.

4. This chapter introduces some of the modalities that organized crime entities implement to leverage the attributes of globalism for illegal purposes. Do some research, and locate some items that consider the growth of criminal activity and logistics systems versus increases of globalism through time. Write a brief essay that summarizes your findings. Within your essay, discuss some recommendations that you believe could be used to mitigate the effects of these criminal activities.

References

1. Bhagwati, J. (2004). *In Defence of Globalization*. Oxford, UK: Oxford University Press, p. 3.
2. Held, D. and McGrew, A. (2007). *Globalization/Anti-Globalization: Beyond the Great Divide* (2nd ed.). Cambridge: Polity Press, p. 1.
3. Jensen, C. (2001). Beyond the tea leaves: futures research and terrorism. *American Behavioral Scientist,* 44(6): 914–936, 922–924.
4. Somalia, a State Again. (2013). *The Levin Institute*. http://www.globalization101.org/somalia-a-state-again/ (accessed February 6, 2013).
5. Tuckman, J. (2013). Mexico drug war continues to rage in region where president fired first salvo. *The Guardian.* http://www.guardian.co.uk/world/2012/nov/30/mexico-drug-war-tierra-caliente-calderon (accessed February 6, 2013).
6. Wilkinson, T., Fausset, R. and Bennett, B. (2012). U.S.–Mexico drug war partnership under Calderon broke new ground. *The Los Angeles Times*. http://articles.latimes.com/2012/nov/28/world/la-fg-us-mexico-drug-war-20121129 (accessed February 6, 2013).
7. China Lands J-15 Jet on Liaoning Aircraft Carrier. (2012). *BBC News*. http://www.bbc.co.uk/news/worldasia-china-20483716 (accessed February 6, 2013).
8. Goel, M. The clash of civilizations and radicalism. *University of West Florida*. http://www.uwf.edu/lgoel/Clash_of_Civilizations_and_Radicalism.doc (accessed February 5, 2013).
9. Voll, J. (2013). The impossibility of the clash of civilizations in a globalized world. *Georgetown University*. http://acmcu.georgetown.edu/135378.html (accessed February 7, 2013).
10. Tarm, M. (2013). Cartel kingpin Chicago's new public enemy no. 1. *USA Today*. http://www.usatoday.com/story/news/world/2013/02/14/chicago-cartel-public-enemy/1919117/ (accessed 3 May 2013).
11. Bagley, B. (2001). Globalization and transnational organized crime: The Russian mafia in Latin America and the Caribbean. http://www.as.miami.edu/international-studies/pdf/Bagley%20GLOBALIZATION%202.pdf (accessed February 6, 2013), pp. 2–3.
12. United Nations. (2010). The globalization of crime: A transnational organized crime threat assessment. *United Nations Office on Drugs and Crime*. http://www.unodc.org/documents/data-and-analysis/tocta/TOCTA_Report_2010_low_res.pdf (accessed February 6, 2013).

13. Oliver, I. (2006). The cost of failure. *Journal of Global Drug Policy, 4*(2), 19–22.

14. ABC 5. (2006). MS-13/Al-Qaeda connection. http://www.newschannel5.tv/2005/2/28/1671/MS-13-Al-Qaeda-Connection (accessed August 15, 2008).

15. Adams, R. (2009). *Continental Divides: Remapping the Cultures of North America*. Chicago, IL: University of Chicago Press.

16. Arizona. (2010). Arizona governor signs immigration law; foes promise fight. http://www.azcentral.com/news/articles/2010/04/23/20100423arizona-immigration-law-passed.html (accessed October 31, 2010).

17. Avalos, F. and Garmon, M. (2010). Basic info and online sources for NAFTA and CAFTA research. http://www.nyulawglobal.org/Globalex/NAFTA_CAFTA_Research.htm#_NAFTA (accessed October 29, 2010).

18. Background Note. (2010). Background note: Canada. http://www.state.gov/r/pa/ei/bgn/2089.htm (accessed October 31, 2010).

19. Badkhen, A. (2004). Al Qaeda bluffing about having suitcase nukes, experts say. *San Francisco Chronicle*. http://www.sfgate.com/cgi-in/article.cgi?file=/chronicle/archive/2004/03/23/MNG8D5PM7L1.DTL (accessed August 15, 2008).

20. Baschuk, B. (n.d.). Hackers can use internet search to take down utilities, other companies. *Washington Internet Daily*. http://www.infragardmembers.org/modules/articles/article.php?id=33 (accessed August 15, 2008).

21. BEA. (2010). National income and product accounts table. *U.S. Bureau of Economic Analysis*. http://www.bea.gov/national/nipaweb/TableView.asp?SelectedTable=5&ViewSeries=NO&Java=no&Request3Place=N&3Place=N&FromView=YES&Freq=Year&FirstYear=2009&LastYear=2009&3Place=N&Update=Update&JavaBox=no#Mid (accessed October 28, 2010).

22. Bissett, J. (2008). Does Canada Pose a Security Threat to the United States? *Fraser Forum*, http://www.fraserinstitute.org/uploadedFiles/fraser-ca/Content/research-news/research/articles/does-canada-pose-a-security-threat-to-US.pdf (accessed August 27, 2013).

23. Border Violence. (2010). Border violence threatens Americans. http://www.washingtontimes.com/news/2010/apr/01/violent-mexican-drug-gangs-pose-rising-risk-to-ame/ (accessed October 31, 2010).

24. Bradbury, S. and Turbeville, D. (2008). Are enhanced trade and enhanced security mutually exclusive? The Western Canada–U.S. borderland in a post-9/11 world. *American Review of Canadian Studies, 38*(3), 317–340.

25. Branigan, T. and Stewart, H. (2010). China sells $34.2bn of US treasury bonds. http://www.guardian.co.uk/business/2010/feb/17/china-sells-us-treasury-bonds (accessed October 29, 2010).

26. Brief History. (2010). A brief history of the U.S. foreign-trade zones program. *Foreign Trade Resource Center*. http://www.foreign-trade-zone.com/history.htm (accessed October 28, 2010).

27. Bringing Down. (2010). Bringing down four high-tension wires across the west: High probability, high impact. *The Futurist*. http://www.wfs.org (accessed June 23, 2010).

28. Buultjens, J. (2005). *Economics: Your Step by Step Guide to HSB Success*. Glebe, NSW: Pascal Press.

29. CIA. (2005). Establishment of the DNI Open Source Center: DNI and D/CIA announce establishment of the DNI Open Source Center. https://www.cia.gov/news-information/press-releases-statements/press-release-archive-2005/pr11082005.html (accessed August 15, 2008).

30. Congresswoman. (2010). Congresswoman raises red flag on Hezbollah-Cartel Nexus on U.S. border. http://www.foxnews.com/politics/2010/06/25/congresswoman-raises-red-flag-hezbollah-cartel-nexus-border/ (accessed October 31, 2010).

31. Corey, S. (1998). Revolutionary suicide. *Salon*. http://www.salon.com/news/1998/01/21news.html (accessed September 10, 2008).

32. Defense Advanced Research Projects Agency. (1981). *A History of the ARPANET: The First Decade* (prepared by Bolt, Beranek and Newman). Washington, D.C.: Defense Tech. Info.

33. Dopson, S. (2009). Early warning infectious disease surveillance. *Biosecurity & Bioterrorism: Biodefense Strategy, Practice, & Science, 7*(1), 55–60.

34. Drache, D. (2008). Canada–U.S. relations and the impermeable border post 9/11: the co-management of North America. *CONfines, 4*(7), 69–83.

35. Edwards, P. and Auger, M. (2004). *The Encyclopedia of Canadian Organized Crime: From Captain Kidd to Mom Boucher*. Toronto, Canada: McClelland and Stewart Publishing.

36. Embassy. (2010). The embassy of the United States in Canada. http://canada.usembassy.gov/content/content.asp?section=can_usa&document=general (accessed October 31, 2010).

37. Executive Summary. (2010). Executive summary–national drug threat assessment 2010. http://www.justice.gov/ndic/pubs38/38661/execSum.htm#Top (accessed October 31, 2010).

38. FBI. (2005). Statement of Chris Swecker, Assistant Director, Criminal Investigative Division, Federal Bureau of Investigation, before the Subcommittee on the Western Hemisphere House International Relations Committee, April 20, 2005. http://www.fbi.gov/congress/congress05/swecker042005.htm (accessed August 15, 2008).

39. Friedman, T. (2007). *The World is Flat: A Brief History of the Twenty-First Century* (3rd ed). New York: Macmillan (Farrar, Straus and Giroux).
40. Fukuyama, F. (1992). *The End of History and the Last Man*. New York: Free Press.
41. Garrett, B. and Sherman, D. (2006). Why non-globalized states pose a threat: Increasing interdependence is key concern. http://www.bus.wisc.edu/update/winter03/globalization.asp (accessed October 30, 2010).
42. General Motors. (n.d.). About GM. http://www.gm.com/corporate/about/ (accessed August 15, 2008).
43. Governor. (2010). Governor Brewer announces border security plan. http://azgovernor.gov/dms/upload/04-22-10%20Governor%20Brewer%20Announces%20Border%20Security%20Plan.pdf (accessed October 31, 2010).
44. Grayson, K. (2008). *Chasing Dragons: Security, Identity, and Illicit Drugs in Canada*. Toronto, Canada: University of Toronto Press.
45. Green, K. (2008). To Stop Global Warming, End Eco-Extremism: Pragmatic Solutions Provide the Best Options, *Fraser Forum*, http://www.fraserinstitute.org/uploadedFiles/fraser-ca/Content/research-news/research/articles/to-stop-global-warming-and-eco-extremism.pdf (accessed August 27, 201).
46. Hakam, P. and Litan, R. (2002). *The Future of North American Integration: Beyond NAFTA*. Washington, DC: The Brookings Institution.
47. Hamilton, D. (2006). *Inside Canadian Intelligence: Exposing the New Realities of Espionage and International Terrorism*. New York: Dundurn Press.
48. Harding, T. (2008). Chinese nuclear submarines prompt 'new Cold War' warning. http://www.telegraph.co.uk/news/newstopics/uselection2008/1920917/Chinese-nuclear-submarines-prompt-'new-Cold-War'-warning.html (accessed August 15, 2008).
49. Hedgecock, R. (2010). Iran threatens U.S. with proxy terrorists on border. http://www.humanevents.com/article.php?id=37975 (accessed July 7, 2010).
50. Huntington, S. (1993). The clash of civilizations? *Foreign Affairs, 72*(3): 44–57. Excerpt retrieved from http://www.foreignaffairs.org/19930601faessay5188/samuel-p-huntington/the-clash-of-civilizations.html.
51. Huntington, S. (1998). *The Clash of Civilizations and the Remaking of World Order*. New York: Simon and Shuster.
52. Kurzweil, R. (2000). *The Age of Spiritual Machines: When Computers Exceed Human Intelligence*. New York: Penguin.
53. Leiken, R. and Brooke, S. (2006). The quantitative analysis of terrorism and immigration: an initial exploration. *Terrorism & Political Violence, 18*(4), 503–521.
54. Liddick, D. (2004). *The Global Underworld: Transnational Crime and the United States*. Westport, CT: Praeger Publishing.
55. Loucky, J., Alper, D. and Day, J. (2008). *Transboundary Policy Challenges in the Pacific Border Regions of North America*. Alberta, Canada: University of Calgary Press.
56. Malcolm, A. (2010). No state give on Obama illegal immigration lawsuit; Arizona gov. Jan Brewer fires back defiantly. http://latimesblogs.latimes.com/washington/2010/07/arizona-governor-jan-brewer-illegal-immigration-lawsuit.html (accessed October 31, 2010).
57. Marshall Plan. (2010). Marshall Plan. *Encyclopedia Brittanica*. http://www.britannica.com/EBchecked/topic/366654/Marshall-Plan (accessed October 28, 2010).
58. McCaffrey, B. (December 29, 2008). Memorandum for Colonel Michael Meese and Colonel Cindy Jebb. http://www.mccaffreyassociates.com/pdfs/Mexico_AAR_-_December_2008.pdf (accessed August 16, 2009).
59. (2012). Mexico drug war: tens of thousands dead as battle rages on. *The Huffington Post*, http://www.huffingtonpost.com/2012/08/27/mexico-drug-war_n_1832954.html (accessed February 6, 2013).
60. Mexico Under. (2010). Mexico under siege: The drug war at our doorstep. http://projects.latimes.com/mexico-drug-war/#/its-a-war (accessed October 31, 2010).
61. Miller, J. (2007). Feds take 'cyber Pearl Harbor' seriously. http://www.fcw.com/print/13_17/news/102825-1.html (accessed August 15, 2008).
62. Collacott, M. and Moens, A. (2008). Rights versus risks, *Fraser Forum*, http://www.fraserinstitute.org/uploadedFiles/fraser-ca/Content/research-news/research/articles/rights-versus-risks.pdf (accessed August 27, 2013).
63. Mueller, R. (2009). Does the statue of liberty still face out? The diversion of foreign students from the United States to Canada in the post 9/11 period. *Canadian Journal of Higher Education, 39*(1), 15–43.
64. Muller, W., Kälin, C. and Goldsmith, J. (2007). *Anti–Money Laundering: International Law and Practice*. Hoboken, NJ: John Wiley and Sons Publishing.
65. MSNBC. (2006). MS-13' is one of nation's most dangerous gangs. http://www.msnbc.msn.com/id/11240718/ (accessed August 14, 2008).

66. Napolitano. (2010). Napolitano to McCain: Yes, Mexican cartels pose terror threat to U.S. http://www.cnsnews.com/news/article/75789 (accessed October 31, 2010).
67. National Intelligence Council. 2005. *Mapping the Global Future: Report of the National Intelligence Council's 2020 Project*, Honolulu, HI: University Press of the Pacific.
68. NARA. (2010). The Marshall Plan. *National Records and Archives Administration*. http://www.archives.gov/exhibits/featured_documents/marshall_plan/ (accessed October 28, 2010).
69. Nicol, H. (2005). Resiliency or change? The contemporary Canada–US border. *Geopolitics, 10*(4), 767–790.
70. 9/11 Commission. (2004). *Final Report of the National Commission on Terrorist Attacks upon the United States*. Washington, DC: National Commission on Terrorist Attacks upon the United States/Government Printing Office.
71. Over. (2010). Over 200,000 people leave Mexican border city due to violence. http://laht.com/article.asp?ArticleId=367604&CategoryId=14091 (accessed October 31, 2010).
72. Paul, R. (2007). Security, Washington-style. http://www.lewrockwell.com/paul/paul386.html (accessed August 15, 2008).
73. Schultz, S. and Tishler, W. (2010). World war II: The impact at home. *The University of Wisconsin–American History 102*. http://us.history.wisc.edu/hist102/lectures/lecture21.html (accessed October 28, 2010).
74. Serafino, N., Tarnoff, C. and Nanto, D. (2006). U.S. occupation assistance: Iraq, Germany, and Japan compared. *CRS Report for Congress*. http://www.fas.org/sgp/crs/natsec/RL33331.pdf (accessed October 28, 2010).
75. Shanty, F. and Mishra, P. (2008). *Organized Crime: From Trafficking to Terrorism*, Volume 2. Santa Barbara, CA: ABC-CLIO Publishing.
76. Stratfor. (2004). Al Qaeda and the threat of chemical and biological weapons. http://www.stratfor.com/al_qaeda_and_threat_chemical_and_biological_weapons (accessed August 15, 2008).
77. Switzer, J. (2003). *Environmental Activism: A Reference Handbook*. Santa-Barbara, CA: ABC-CLIO Publishing.
78. The Roots. (2010). The roots of the WTO. http://www2.econ.iastate.edu/classes/econ355/choi/wtoroots.htm#History (accessed October 28, 2010).
79. Uptick. (2010). Uptick in violence forces closing of parkland along Mexico border to Americans. http://www.foxnews.com/us/2010/06/16/closes-park-land-mexico-border-americans/ (accessed October 31, 2010).
80. USCC. (2010). Canada–U.S. trade relationship. http://www.buyusa.gov/canada/en/traderelationsusacanada.html (accessed October 31, 2010).
81. U.S.–Mexico. (2010). U.S.–Mexico at a glance. http://www.usembassy-mexico.gov/eng/eataglance_trade.html (accessed October 30, 2010).
82. Vance, A. (2008). Strategic responses by Canadian and U.S. exporters to increased U.S. border security measures: A firm-level analysis. *Economic Development Quarterly, 22*(3), 239–251.
83. Walby, K. and Monaghan, J. (2010). Policing proliferation: On militarization and atomic energy Canada limited's nuclear response forces. *Canadian Journal of Criminology & Criminal Justice, 52*(2), 117–145.
84. Wilkinson, T. (2010). Mexico grave yields 51 bodies. http://articles.latimes.com/2010/jul/25/world/la-fg-mexico-bodies-20100725 (accessed October 31, 2010).
85. Wilson, C. (n.d.). What's good for the country is good for General Motors, and vice versa. http://www.answers.com/topic/what-s-good-for-the-country-is-good-for-general-motors-and-vice-versa (accessed August 15, 2008).
86. Winter, J. (2010). Feds issue terror watch for the Texas/Mexico border. http://www.foxnews.com/us/2010/05/26/terror-alert-mexican-border/ (accessed on July 7, 2010).
87. Parthemore, Christine and John Nagl. (2010). *Fueling the Future Force: Preparing the Department of Defense for a Post-Petroleum Era*, Washington, DC: The Center for a New American Security.

15

The Future of Homeland Security

A homeland that is safe, secure, and resilient against terrorism and other hazards.

Department of Homeland Security Strategic Plan FY 2012–2016

Chapter objectives:

- Gain insight into the future of homeland security
- Speculate on the future of homeland security both domestically and internationally
- Understand the potential of emerging threats

Introduction

The term *homeland security* is sufficiently broad to encompass a large array of entities that threaten the stability and security of the United States. Examples include terrorism, war, espionage, pandemics, natural disasters, environmental changes, world politics, limited quantities of natural resources, organized crime, and street crime. These entities are merely a subset of the overall superset of threats that endanger the modern United States. Such entities permeate history with accounts of destruction and devastation. Unfortunately, given the imperfections of man and the fallibility of human nature, the future shall manifest threats that are commensurate with the threats of history.

The only constant aspect of both historical and modern times may be expressed through a solitary concept: Human nature is static, whereas human technologies are dynamic. This notion expresses the unchanging characteristics of humanity that both inflict harm and render benevolence through time. Throughout history, humans have both unleashed massive destruction and unselfishly assisted others. This concept also expresses a very important observation: It acknowledges the notion that technology changes, improves, and matures. Technology, such as weapons of mass destruction (WMDs), may be used to incite massive lethality, thereby killing and devastating entire populations. In contrast, technology may also be used to both save lives and spare humans from tremendous suffering (e.g., the polio vaccine). Regardless of any detrimental or benevolent uses of technology or whether humans decide to cause harm or provide benefits among their fellow man, change is a salient aspect of history and the future.

It is impossible to predict future events with complete accuracy and certainty. Many variables exist that affect the outcomes of situations and events. Although one may speculate regarding probabilities of events and formulate strategic contingencies, no one can predict the future with complete accuracy. The future is currently unwritten, and its unknown characteristics will become the histories of future generations. Through time, current speculations either will be proven to be factual or will be discarded as falsehoods. Regardless, situations exist that challenge future generations of Americans.

An understanding of history assists one in conceptualizing the potential events that may impact future generations. The preceding chapters of this text described a myriad of histories regarding terrorism, the United States and its allies, world history, law enforcement, legislation, government and private organizations, a myriad of individuals, and many other topics. Throughout the majority of the historical periods considered within this textbook, all of the considered events occurred on land, at sea, or in the air above the Earth. However, the preceding chapters did not consider vastly the potentials of space that may affect future generations. Because of globalization and the modernization of nations globally, space exploration presents a variety of opportunities and threats that may impact future generations of Americans. Therefore, a brief history of the US and Soviet space programs, as well as commentaries regarding the contemporary space programs of other nations, are included within this chapter.

In order to understand future challenges, it is important to understand how the world is changing. According to Smart,[24] with respect to the precedence of importance, the drivers of change, during the near future, will be technology, economics, and politics. Technology represents the tools through which human functions may improve their efficiency and effectiveness. Economics is concerned with the optimal allocation of resources with respect to the primary economic question: How does one satisfy the unlimited wants and needs of humans with the availability of limited, scarce resources? The economics of resource management and allocation shall continue to challenge future generations. Further, political concerns may be manifested globally, regionally, and locally with respect to the future influences of governmental ideologies and philosophies.

There is one other variable we must consider when forecasting future events: people. Global demographics are shifting, with declining birthrates in developed countries, "youth bulges" in some of the poorest areas of the world, seniors living longer and healthier in wealthy countries, and unprecedented levels of immigration.

Given such notions, this chapter considers some of the threats to homeland security, as they exist today and as they may exist during the future. This chapter does not consider any threat to be of any greater or lesser significance than any of its peers. Instead, this chapter discusses briefly the potential threats that may endanger the United States, its interests, or allies during the upcoming decades.

Future role/mission of the Department of Homeland Security

According the Department of Homeland Security's (DHS's) Annual Financial Report, the department's five key mission areas are preventing terrorism and enhancing security, securing and managing our borders, enforcing and administering our immigration laws, safeguarding and securing cyberspace, and ensuring resilience to disasters.[1]

The FY 2012–2016 Homeland Security Strategic Plan, Mission 1, is the protection of the United States from terrorists. It is the cornerstone of homeland security. DHS's counterterrorism responsibilities focus on three goals: preventing terrorist attacks; preventing the unauthorized acquisition, importation, movement, or use of chemical, biological, radiological, and nuclear materials and capabilities within the United States; and reducing threats to, and vulnerabilities of, critical infrastructure, key resources, essential leadership, and major events from terrorist attacks and other hazards.[2]

To remain viable, the efforts of homeland security must continue to adapt to changes in the threat environment. Strategy must reflect the adaptations and continue to provide futuristic vision for next steps. This is not a static environment. According to the DHS's FY 2012–2016 Strategic Plan, three priority goals are identified for the FY 2012–FY 2013 time frame.

- Priority goal 1: Strengthen aviation security counterterrorism capabilities by using intelligence-driven information and risk-based decisions. By September 30, 2013, the Transportation Security Administration (TSA) will expand the use of risk-based security initiatives to double the number of passengers going through expedited screening at airports, thereby enhancing the passenger experience.
- Priority goal 2: Improve the efficiency of the process to detain and remove criminal illegal immigrants from the United States. By September 30, 2013, reduce the average length of stay in immigration detention of all convicted criminal aliens prior to their removal from the country by 5%.
- Priority goal 3: Ensure resilience to disasters by strengthening disaster preparedness and response capabilities. By September 30, 2013, every state will have a current, DHS-certified threat and hazard identification and risk assessment (THIRA).

These goals are primarily reactive, although the concepts of deterrence, prevention, and ultimately "recovery" are all stated components. Reactive agencies are usually passive and generally need an incident—an interruption of the routine—such as finding forged credentials, questionable documents, and/or suspicious travel plans to respond.

Regardless of any events that occur during future times, it is almost a certainty that the organizational structure of the DHS will change in due time. Government agencies, resources, and technologies were altered after the events of September 11, 2001. Throughout the history of American government, numerous agencies were formed and dissolved. The characteristics of future problem domains will influence the crafting and refining of organizational structures that are necessary to accommodate future threats. Only time will reveal the true instantiation of future DHS hierarchies, components, and services.

Changes for the future in local and state police initiatives for homeland security

One resource, established through DHS funding, is known as the fusion center. Fusion centers are multiagency groupings of federal, state, local, and tribal personnel operating under local authority, supervision, and guidelines. The fusion centers are generally established at the state level. Some of the urban areas have created regional fusion centers that integrate with the state centers. Some states and regional centers have federal partners represented in their centers. The DHS is placing intelligence analysts in state fusion centers to enhance their capability to analyze and exchange intelligence both vertically and horizontally. These centers are authorized to distribute both classified and unclassified intelligence in accordance with federal regulations. The main role of fusion centers is to assimilate, analyze, and disseminate information to public safety and critical infrastructure partners in the community at large. In 1829, Sir Robert Peel established the London Metropolitan Police Department. He introduced several principles to guide policing in those early days. These principles established metropolitan police strategy and the new police department's hierarchy. It also set the stage for all contemporary policing. Its priorities included the following:

- Interacting positively with the community
- Reporting of crime-related news to the public, as an essential service
- Using crime prevention as the primary factor through which policing should be evaluated

Unfortunately, it is difficult to measure prevention because one cannot measure that which did not happen. One can stop a crime or a terrorist act just before it is completed and have a measured event, but it is quite difficult to judge a police officer's effectiveness by looking solely at the absence of criminal activity on the patrol beat.

Policing has gone through many changes during the last several years—random patrol versus "directed" patrol, reactive patrol versus proactive patrol, as well as many other designators. For the last three decades, we have experienced community-oriented policing, problem-oriented policing, CompStat (short for computer statistics or comparative statistics), intelligence-led policing, and neighborhood-driven policing, and now, with Citizen Corps programs in place, the government is recommending community-based homeland security programs. The governments of Great Britain and Canada, as well, have effectively used the intelligence-led policing approach in dealing with both domestic (Irish) and international insurgents within their borders.

Whether the approach is labeled as community policing or intelligence-led policing, there is recognition that the average citizen, living in an average city, should work as a partner with the salaried police in both general crime prevention and community safety, a component of homeland security.

The input of usable, real-time intelligence is absolutely necessary in modern policing. The New York City Police Department has now assigned investigators as liaison officers in at least 20 cities abroad. Their primary job is to assist in the sharing of intelligence information relating to terrorism incidents. After 9/11, the New York City mayor began to look outside the traditional police community for expert assistance. He employed experienced Central Intelligence Agency (CIA) operatives and terrorism unit Federal Bureau of Investigation (FBI) agents, some of whom were retiring from the federal service.

One New York City Police Department assistant police commissioner was employed from a high-level position within the CIA. The unit received the logistical support that it needed with analysts and those familiar with sensitive information. New York City will never again rely exclusively on federal authorities and have to deal with continuing information-flow problems in the federal system. Terrorism avoidance and homeland security are not just federal problems, and they require universal public safety diversity in jurisdictions from the smallest borough to the largest city and state, as well as national agency responsibilities.

The Los Angeles County Sheriff's Department has also taken a lead on the Pacific coast. They have a task force initiative involving police officers, from all the inner jurisdictions of the county, including federal, state, and private security professionals. The task force is now called the Terrorism Early Warning Group. Information is freely shared, threat assessments are accomplished, and cooperative arrangements are made for special events and visits by foreign dignitaries.

Because of past excesses, the domestic intelligence activities of all United States–based local, regional, state, federal, and international agencies are carefully reviewed. While recent legislation has enlarged the intelligence community and has increased discretionary levels of these agents, the courts will be carefully monitoring the use of this information. Abuses could result in landmark decisions from the appellate courts, hurting the intelligence data acquisition process.

There are many challenges remaining in the continued development of a national intelligence infrastructure that incorporates federal, state, local, tribal, and private sector partners. This initiative alone requires substantial funding, time, and planning to integrate the mandates of the diverse agencies involved in the intelligence community. The commitment to continue to support the networking of information sharing, through intelligence initiatives, is essential to the future of homeland security.

Community-based homeland security

The community preparedness approach is formidable, and it comes from traditional anticrime programs associated with community policing. A basic tenet of the national homeland security program is developing methods that will identify who is in a community, what is in a community, and how we assimilate that information into usable data sets for planning on a national basis. For example, the 9/11 hijackers were in various local communities living and, in some cases, learning piloting skills. Who knows the local community better than the residents of each neighborhood? Residents may know, and usually do know, who belongs in their neighborhood and who does not. This local information is at the core of homeland security and its relationship to local communities. While this concept may seem overly simplistic in terms of community-based homeland security programs, there is a strong similarity to traditional programs such as neighborhood watch.

Community preparedness through the Citizens Corps program is an extremely effective and popular program for citizens. Through the Citizens Corps program, local jurisdictions teach the Community Emergency Response Team (CERT) concept. Recently, this program has expanded to include a program called "Teen CERT."[3] Homeland security is about preparedness. This is no more evident that in the local communities in local neighborhoods. Preparedness is about neighbors being neighbors, neighbors helping neighbors. The Citizens Corps program as funded and outlined by the DHS simply amplifies the neighbor-to-neighbor relationship into a degree of knowledge relative to being prepared for crisis and into basic skills at surviving during a crisis. Just as the CERT Program has now expanded to include Teen CERT, it is anticipated that the community preparedness priority will continue to be innovative and support the training and education of the citizenry at large.

Private sector partnerships in securing the nation

This text, thus far, has discussed the partnerships necessary to support the national preparedness program through homeland security. However, one crucial member of this partnership that has not been mentioned is the private sector. Private sector interests have long been engaged in aggressive risk management programs. These programs are often more visionary in their planning approaches than is government. The private sector is most visible in the critical infrastructure/key resource protection initiatives than in other components of the homeland security partnerships.

Today, there are more private police, private investigators, security contractors, and proprietary security than there are public police officers. Worldwide, the contractual security business is one of the, if not the, fastest-growing service businesses in the world. There are at least three times more employees in the private police sector than the public police arena, with a total of more than 1.8 million private police, private security, private investigation, and technical specialists familiar with alarms, closed-circuit television (CCTV) systems, and other security technology.[4]

The future of homeland security is unwritten. Collaboration between the public and private sectors is an essential component of facilitating the safety and security of future generations. Because of the newness of homeland security, conceptually, regarding an all-hazards paradigm, numerous opportunities exist for entrepreneurs to develop futuristic homeland security business models. These business models may be appropriate for both for-profit and nonprofit sectors and may be supplements for governmental organizations.

Threats and challenges of the future

The United States must strive to secure itself from terrorist threats and to enhance security. It must further contribute toward the securing of its borders and the enforcing of immigration laws. Additional requirements will necessitate the securing of cyberspace and building resilience to disaster.[2] This section addresses some of these potential future concerns.

Natural threats

In the future, resources must be put toward a coordinated, comprehensive response in the event of a natural disaster or other large-scale emergency while working with state, local, and private sector partners to ensure a swift and effective recovery effort. The department's efforts to build a ready and resilient nation include bolstering information sharing; providing grants, plans, and training to our homeland security and law enforcement partners; and facilitating rebuilding and recovery where disasters strike.[2]

The threat of terrorism

DHS's counterterrorism responsibilities focus on three goals: preventing terrorist attacks; preventing the unauthorized acquisition, importation, movement, or use of chemical, biological, radiological, and nuclear materials and capabilities within the United States; and reducing the vulnerability of critical infrastructure and key resources, essential leadership, and major events to terrorist attacks and other hazards.[2]

Change is a component of terrorist strategy

Americans need the best intelligence services the world can offer. The future of homeland security is dependent upon a functional intelligence system encompassing both the human and technological components for a comprehensive fusion mechanism. The system cannot be stagnant. Instead, it must have the ability to change and adapt with the times. Intelligence data must also be assimilated, analyzed, and disseminated in a way that it can be used promptly by public safety, private sector, and security professionals.

Historically, some of the beliefs associated with the primary reasons or motivations for terrorism were as follows:

1. Land acquisition, the control of the land, and other nationalistic interests
2. Ethnic-minority interests such as the American Indian Movement or that of an indigenous tribe in Latin America or the Philippines
3. Economic interests (usually along revolutionary Marxist or Maoist themes)

As a change in motivation affects the course of terrorism today, we need to review our knowledge base, beliefs, values, and interpretations to ensure that the truths of yesterday are still true today. The stringent violence of radical Islam is forcing us to review our viewpoints on the issue of religious terrorism. Increasingly, indications of radical Islam, fighting a worldwide Jihad, a religious war, are common. According to Hoffman,[5] almost half (46%) of all modern terrorist groups have motivations stemming predominantly from religion.

Megalomania terrorism

Changes in terrorism venues have occurred—from the Middle East and Africa to Latin America and now to the domestic United States. Trends may also exist regarding the changing of targets, from diplomats to the military, and from mega-business operatives to small business representatives, missionaries, nongovernmental agency humanitarian workers, and on to tourists. Researchers may investigate these notions to examine any potential ramifications for the future of homeland security.

The tactics of terrorism have evolved, from bombings to assassinations, to train hijackings, skyjackings, and barricade hostage situations, and back to bombings. Bombers are increasingly targeting locations offering mass casualties, whereas in years past, the general terrorism statement was "terrorists want a lot of people watching, not a lot of people dead."[6] The former emphasis on limited casualties has changed significantly. Terrorism scholar Bruce Hoffman uses the term *spectacular* versus *megalomania terrorism*. According to Hoffman, "terrorism spectaculars" may be considered as "dramatic, attention-riveting, high-lethality acts that effectively capture the attention of the media and public alike" (p. 12).[18]

Timothy McVeigh, an American military veteran, at odds with the US government, wanted a high-casualty consequence in the Oklahoma City bombing. His murderous act of terror caused a death toll of 168 and inflicted some 674 injuries.[7] Osama bin Laden turned passenger airlines into flying bombs, thereby achieving the highest terrorism single-incident death, destruction, and casualty toll ever achieved, including 2,986 fatalities and 2,337 casualties.[8] Fatalities at the World Trade Center alone were 2,595.[8]

These incidents depict acts of increasing lethality and may be performance measures, unfortunately, for a potential future attack. It is now clear that higher death rates are a primary goal. Any spectacular event, such as the attack on the USS *Cole* or the attacks on the American embassies in Kenya and Tanzania, receive a lot of attention and provides recognition for the perpetrators. Success feeds on success, so there is no indication that "spectacular" terror will lessen during the immediately foreseeable future.

Certainly, global demographic forecasts support fears of future attacks. For example, in the early part of the 21st century, large birthrates were realized in the Middle East and Sub-Saharan Africa, two fertile recruiting grounds for radical Islamic terrorist organizations. Compounding this problem, these areas also suffer from extreme poverty. Individuals born in these "youth bulges" will be reaching maturity over the course of the next several years, providing a potential new generation of terrorists.

Technology offers benefits to those who wish to engage in spectacular events. For example, some experts believe that it has allowed al Qaeda to shift from a hierarchical to a net-centric organization, using the Internet to recruit, inspire, communicate, and plan. For example, al Qaeda has recently begun to produce *Inspire*, a Web-based magazine written in English designed to radicalize potential homegrown US terrorists.

The Internet represents today's technology—what awaits us is difficult to imagine. One noted futurist has observed that technology increases not in a neat, linear fashion but exponentially, doubling and tripling at an alarming speed. According to him:

> [W]e won't experience 100 years of progress in the 21st century—it will be more like 20,000 years of progress (at today's rate).[9]

While future technology will no doubt help terrorist organizations, the authorities can also employ it to maintain peace and stability. The ability to engage in surveillance and mine data, when used in a legal manner that respects civil liberties, can provide law enforcement and intelligence agencies with decided advantages.

Western Hemisphere—US policy and strategy

According to the 2010 US National Security Strategy (NSS),[27] economic and regional concerns are a paramount consideration of American strategy and policy within the Western Hemisphere. This concept is manifested within the following excerpt (NSS, p. 41):[27]

> The strategic partnerships and unique relationships we maintain with Canada and Mexico are critical to US national security and have a direct effect on the security of our homeland. With billions of dollars in trade, shared critical infrastructure, and millions of our citizens moving across our common borders, no two countries are more directly connected to our daily lives. We must change the way we think about our shared borders, in order to secure and expedite the lawful and legitimate flows of people and goods while interdicting transnational threats that threaten our open societies.
>
> Canada is our closest trading partner, a steadfast security ally, and an important partner in regional and global efforts. Our mutual prosperity is closely interconnected, including through our trade relationship with Mexico through NAFTA. With Canada, our security cooperation includes our defense of North America and our efforts through NATO overseas. And our cooperation is critical to the success of international efforts on issues ranging from international climate negotiations to economic cooperation through the G-20. With Mexico, in addition to trade cooperation, we are working together to identify and interdict threats at the earliest opportunity, even before they reach North America. Stability and security in Mexico are indispensable to building a strong economic partnership, fighting the illicit drug and arms trade, and promoting sound immigration policy.

When compared to the excerpts of the 1980s, the preceding passage is indicative of change regarding national security and policy paradigms. The demographics of modern world threats are significantly different from those that were manifested during the 1980s. During modern times, the United States is endangered by terrorist organizations, the severity of organized crime, rogue states, economic functions, and a myriad of other threats. National security policy and strategy must accommodate these issues and incorporate collaboration internationally within a long-term context.

Canada and Mexico share borders with America. This fact is a significant aspect of US national security and policy given the advent and proliferation of globalism during the preceding decades. The successes of the Canadian and Mexican nations affect long-term US interests through time because of the integration of economic interests among these nations. The nations of Canada and Mexico represent two of America's largest trading partners economically and financially. Therefore, US policy and security must be crafted to provide for mutual benefits among the nations of North America and must predominantly ensure the strategic benefit of the United States through time. Certainly, these considerations are appropriate for a Western Hemispheric worldview.

The preceding chapters highlighted the dangerousness of Canadian and Mexican terrorist entities that pose risk for the United States and its interests. These concepts must be accommodated within US national policy and strategy. According to the US Department of State,[28] the United States must collaborate with the nations of Canada and Mexico regarding issues of terrorism. Both Canada and Mexico are "key counterterrorism partners" of the United States with respect to collaborative efforts among government law enforcement agencies and entities.[28] During upcoming decades, the United States and Mexico must cooperate regarding organized crime and terrorist infiltration. The relationship between the United States and Canada must also be cooperative.

Currently, efforts between the United States and Canada include collaboration through the "terrorism subgroup of the Cross Border Crime Forum, the Shared Border Accord Coordinating Committee, and the Bilateral Consultative Group on Counterterrorism" for the purposes of coordinating "policy on bioterrorism, information sharing, and joint counterterrorism training on an annual basis." (Country Reports)[28] given the potential dangers of terrorism that threaten American interests, future American policy and strategic initiatives must incorporate future collaboration among the nations of Canada, Mexico, and the United States.

Other collaborations must occur between the United States and the nations of the Western Hemisphere. With respect to the future of US policy and strategy, cooperation must exist between the United States and South America. This notion is expressed by the US government within its Congressional Committee on Foreign Affairs (CCFA). According to the CCFA,[29] the South American nation of Brazil has the capacity to be a strong partner within the context of US policy and strategy. This observation is expressed within the following excerpt of the CCFA:[29]

> A key to US policy in South America must be our relationship with Brazil, given its size and weight in hemispheric affairs, and its desire to play a greater role in global affairs. For example, Brazil offers a rare example of a nation that, by voluntarily giving up its nuclear program, literally turned swords into plowshares, while also re-making its space-launch program for commercial purposes. As Iran's nuclear ambitions continue, active partnership with Brazil within the International Atomic Energy Agency, if explored fully, could directly assist the global effort to deny Iran's ability to acquire nuclear weapons. Brazil can also serve as an example to Arab countries that favor the promotion of atomic energy for peaceful purposes. And 'leftist' Brazil has itself served as a breakwater against the more populist, anti-US wave sweeping much of South America.

This excerpt is indicative of the potential benefits of collaboration between the United States and South America to affect future interests not only within the Western Hemisphere but also within the Eastern Hemisphere. Future strategic initiatives and policy endeavors of the United States must incorporate meaningful relationships among the nations of South America. According to the CCFA,[29] the following recommendations are offered regarding the strengthening of the relationship between the United States and South America:

- The most obvious recommendation would be to pay more and better attention to the region—not in order to increase our popularity but because it would be in the national interests of the United States. The United States should listen carefully to the voices of the continent.
- The United States should change the way it talks and thinks about Latin America—not as a *patio trasero* given to unpredictable passions and troublesome leaders but as an important area with critical issues and serious problems.
- Outside Venezuela, the United States should undertake to weaken the continental Coalition of Chavez. The United States should court his allies, rather than isolate them. The United States should remember that they are democratically elected leaders. They do not all appreciate Chavez's bombastic style or his transcontinental ambitions. Indeed, Lula of Brazil seeks to establish his nation as the indisputable leader of South America and is therefore more a rival than an ally for Chavez.

Relationships with South America must also be considered from the contexts of illegal activities that transpire between the geographic expanses that separate the United States from South America. Criminal factions exhibit numerous trafficking logistics routes between North America and South America through which black markets within the United States are accessed. These issues will not disappear and will remain a challenge for future American governments.

The nations of Latin America must also be considered among future US strategic initiatives and policies. According to the Council on Foreign Relations (CFR),[30] the region of Latin America represents the "largest foreign supplier of oil to the United States and a strong partner in the development of alternative fuels." Further, the region of Latin America represents a quickly emerging trading partner of the United States and is the "biggest supplier of illegal drugs." Latin America is also the largest source of U.S. immigrants, both documented and not. (Barshefsky)[30] these concepts are indicative of the "strategic, economic, and cultural" relationships that exist between the United States and Latin America. Because of the geographic closeness, economic integration, social histories and relationships, and cultural relationships, the region of Latin America must be a salient consideration of future US strategy and policy during upcoming decades.

Although these endeavors are legal, Latin America represents a conduit through which an amalgamation of trade routes exists for smuggling and trafficking both humans and illegal substances. These issues must be addressed by both current and future governmental administrations.

A variety of additional recommendations are offered by the CFR regarding American policy and strategy initiatives with respect to Latin America. These recommendations involve the nations of Latin America. According to the CFR,[30] the following recommendations are examples, regarding future policy and strategy concerning Latin America, of courses of action that may benefit the United States through time:

- Proactively support the liberalization of textile and agricultural policies, including reducing and eventually eliminating tariffs and subsidies on agricultural commodities, including tariffs on ethanol, and relaxing rules of origin requirements on textiles.

- The United States should establish a comprehensive drug policy that addresses both supply and demand. To combat supply, the United States should continue to work closely with Latin American governments and regional organizations on eradication and interdiction and, in line with these recommendations, on targeting US aid to institution-building, anticorruption, and poverty-alleviation efforts.
- Viable immigration policy must improve border security and management; address the unauthorized work force already present in the country; ensure employer security, verification, and responsibility; and expand a flexible worker program to meet changing US economic demands.
- The Western Hemisphere produces 80% of the world's biofuels, and a precedent for collaborative leadership has been established by the US–Brazil initiative, which includes cooperation on standards to facilitate trade, technology distribution, and support for the development of biofuel production in other countries. The expansion of these industries, aided by US domestic and foreign policy incentives, can benefit the environment, foster economic development through technology transfer and adaptation, and aid in poverty reduction through job creation in the hemisphere.
- While the United States maintains productive relationships with the vast majority of Latin American nations, there are a few with which the United States has strained relations. The task force finds that the United States must officially recognize all countries in the region and should work to identify areas of common interest and cooperation in order to advance US interests, regardless of the countries' political identity; this includes Cuba and Venezuela.

Although many considerations of US policy and strategy within the Western Hemisphere are affiliated with Canada and Mexico, the regions of Latin America and South America are also significant entities within the context of US strategy and policy through time. These regions possess many natural resources and demonstrate the capacity to render influence globally, which may embellish US initiatives within the Eastern Hemisphere. The United States demonstrates much economic integration within these regions and must also concern itself with the politics of these regions. Regardless of the consideration, US policy and strategy must accommodate the regions of Latin America and South America as well as the nations of Canada and Mexico.

Border protection and transnational crime

American border security and management efforts focus on three interrelated goals: effectively securing US air, land, and sea borders; safeguarding and streamlining lawful trade and travel; and disrupting and dismantling transnational criminal and terrorist organizations.[2]

One of the biggest challenges to homeland security may come not from terrorism but from crime. Currently, an insurgency rages in Mexico; its genesis is not political. Rather, rival drug cartels are battling each other and the Mexican government for control of billions of dollars of drug profits. The preceding chapters provide greater discussions and details regarding these drug wars.

Just yards from the United States, beheadings, assassinations, and kidnappings have become everyday events. Given the huge profits to be made, corruption is rampant. For example, a military unit called the Zetas was originally formed to combat the narco-traffickers; however, many members soon joined the ranks of the drug lords, serving as their enforcers. In this role, they took their training, tactics, and many weapons with them. Officials worry that Mexican violence and terrorism may extend across the US–Mexican border. Already, local US officials claim to have been confronted by Mexican drug gangs on the American side of the border.

Mexican crime is not the only criminal threat facing the United States. Some years ago, most law enforcement officials would have defined a "gang" as a criminal entity that sought control over a rather limited physical area. Modern gangs, however, are transnational. For example, Mara Salvatrucha, an American–Salvadoran gang that formed after the Salvadoran Civil War, now boasts thousands of members who travel regularly between the United States, El Salvador, Europe, and South America. Clearly, the United States cannot successfully confront these groups alone. Instead, international cooperation must exist at the highest levels.

WMDs

Chemicals manufactured, stored, and transported in and through most local jurisdictions within the United States can cause major incidents such as accidental events. It is startling to consider those same agents becoming "weaponized." Biological agents being dispersed as weapons and "dirty bombs" using radiological units are all potential threats within the WMD scenario. The utterance of WMD conjures up the most frightening scenarios imaginable. Attempts to realize efficient bioterrorism dispersal systems continue. Purchases of military surplus explosives and materials from the former Soviet Empire continue to be grave concerns for the United States and its allies.

WMDs are often referred to as chemical, biological, radiological, nuclear, and high-yield explosives (CBRNE). These weapons are capable of killing significant portions of the population and decimating the economy. Prior to the sarin nerve gas attack at a Tokyo, Japan, subway station by the Aum Shinrikyo terrorist group, chemical weapons were primarily considered weapons of war.

The thought of chemical and/or biological agents being used as weapons within the United States was, at one time, difficult for the Western mentality to comprehend. The use of these agents as weapons is generally considered barbarian and inhumane. However, one week after the attacks of 9/11, letters containing deadly anthrax were mailed to various American media outlets and two United States senators' offices. Five people died in the attack, and several more were injured. The FBI launched one of the largest investigations in its history, concluding in 2008 that the letters had been mailed by Bruce Ivins, a scientist who worked at an Army bioresearch lab. However, before he could be tried in court, Ivins committed suicide.

The activities of training and properly equipping oneself to effectively deal with deadly WMD agents were, at one time, remote and removed from most of the first responders in America; as the anthrax attacks demonstrated, that is no longer the case.

One of the first programs in homeland security was an equipment program in an effort to provide protective equipment and training to the first-response community in the anti-CBRNE environment. These training and equipment programs prioritized the need to prepare for the detection of chemical and biological agents and to prevent personal injury or death. Although these protocols, at one time, were relegated to the military, it is now status quo for America's first responders.

This notion is not without some precedent; for several decades, first responders trained in hazardous materials response. It is common for modern response agencies to have hazmat teams and technicians. In the WMD venue, training and experience were borrowed from the existing hazmat personnel. Capabilities were enhanced to include WMD training, equipment, and exercise. This priority will continue as the nation's responders adapt to changing contingencies.

Fortunately, terrorist organizations, with large bank accounts and extensive scientific resources, find it difficult to obtain weapons-grade materials, whether bacteriological, chemical, or nuclear, in a condition that they can use and disperse efficiently. However, for future analysis, it must be assumed that at some point in time, terrorists will develop the ability to use such resources.

The major obstacle to stealing, purchasing, or manufacturing any of these materials involves the use of known "precursor" chemicals. These chemicals are carefully monitored by the Australia Group. The Australia Group is a cooperative of countries attempting to manage the sale, export, and import of certain precursor chemicals that could be used for chemical, biological, and radiological terror weapons.

Whether potential threat elements can attain these substances, the threat to use or to weaponize the generic form of chemicals and some biological agents invokes fear. Fear is a baseline motivation and result of terrorism. It is a frequent event for responders to respond to "white powder" or "suspicious substance" calls. Most of these are prank calls, and upon identification, the powder is usually determined to be a common substance such as artificial sweeteners, baking soda, or flour. It still requires valuable agency resources to respond, whether the threat is determined to be a contaminant or a prank. It causes fear. And fear is the most effective weapon of terrorism.

Netwar, cyber warfare, and cyber crime

Cybernetics, commonly referred to as cyberspace, is a critical infrastructure that is vulnerable to one of the greatest threats: cyber attacks. Cyber attacks, frequently referred to as cyber war, encompass a new spectrum of conflict that is emerging in the wake of the electronic communications revolution. Netwar relates to networking and social constructs. Jones and Volpe (p. 414)[31] provide this insight: "A social network perspective highlights the structure of social relations that surround an individual (or node), providing communication, information, and feedback to shape an individual's attitudes and behaviors." Arquilla and Ronfeldt[16] (p. 51) identify four areas that affect the strength of a network: (1) organization—what type of network is employed and to what extent the actors are networked; (2) doctrine—what motivates the use of the network form, what keeps it from falling apart, and how the organization operates without central leadership; (3) technology—what communication technology is being used, and how; (4) how much interpersonal trust exists within the network.

Further, Arquilla and Ronfeldt[16] (p. 49) identify three types of networks: "(1) Chain network—typified by smuggling networks, where end-to-end exchanges (information, contraband, etc.) must travel back and forth between intermediary nodes; (2) Hub or star network—disparate actors are tied to a central (though not necessarily hierarchical) node, and all communications travels through that central node; (3) All-channel network—every individual actor is able to communicate fully with all other nodes in the network."

Because of the Internet, these attacks may originate from any location and may target any system—public, governmental, or private. Assistant Director Shawn Henry, of the FBI's cyber division, told a conference in New York that computer attacks pose the biggest risk "from a national security perspective, other than a weapon of mass destruction or a bomb in one of our major cities."

Networks worldwide are in danger. Russian hackers allegedly mounted huge assaults on Internet networks in Estonia and Georgia in 2008, while Palestinian sympathizers orchestrated attacks against hundreds of Israeli Web sites. Financial cyber criminals, who use the Internet to steal identities, siphon billions of dollars, and sometimes paralyze businesses, are also becoming more sophisticated.

In 2009, South Korean authorities expressed concern over possible cyber attacks from the North when the South Korean media reported that North Korea was running a cyber warfare unit that operated through the Chinese Internet network and tried to hack into American and South Korean military networks. United States computer security researchers who examined the attacking software and watched network traffic played down the sophistication and extent of the attacks, but the attacks clearly reflect an emerging area of threats to our homeland security.

Cyber threats are a reality of modern times. In 2013, the Obama administration made outright accusations against the nation of China for "mounting attacks on American government computer systems and defense contractors."[10] The purpose and motive of such aggression was speculated to be the discovery of "military capabilities that could be exploited during a crisis."[10] Such activity is not unusual in recent years. It is estimated that approximately 90% of cyber espionage within the United States has its origins in China.[10] The nation of China also is developing "electronic warfare capabilities in an effort to blind American satellites and other space assets" as resources through which it may intend to slowly push the US military presence into the mid-Pacific, approximately 2000 miles away from the Chinese coastline.[10]

The future of cyber threats must not be discounted given the integration of digital technologies among the industrial, government, and service sectors. Any disruptions or destructions would incite losses of functionality among a myriad of services and organizations. Because of the modern dependence upon digital technologies among a vast variety of infrastructures the United States must strive to ensure the integrity and security of its cyber-based environments. There is clear evidence this is occurring; for example, in 2010, the US Cyber Command was established. Cyber Command is a joint military unit dedicated to protecting Department of Defense computer infrastructure and conducting full-spectrum military cyberspace operations. The preceding chapters discussed numerous methods through which US homeland security endeavors are addressing the issues of digital technologies and the potential threats to their existences.

Information warfare: Cyber war and cyberterrorism

According to Haeni,[32] information warfare is characterized by "actions taken to achieve information superiority by affecting adversary information, information-based processes, information systems, and computer-based networks while defending one's own information, information-based processes, information systems, and computer-based networks." Information warfare, cyber war, and cyberterrorism can only be waged against enemies whose technological infrastructures demonstrate a significant integration of modern, electronic technologies.

Electronic and digital technologies as tools of warfare were used during the Cold War. According to the *Economist*,[33] in 1982, the use of a logic bomb, which was embedded within the coding of a computer-based control system, which the Soviets had stolen from Canada, caused the failure and explosion of a Soviet gas line. This leveraging of digital technology is indicative of the potential of cyber warfare to wreak havoc and destruction upon the infrastructures of an enemy. During modern times, given the advent and proliferation of the Internet, the ability to inflict significant damage, globally, is possessed by practically any technologically advanced nation. One need not be associated with any military or government organization to attempt the infiltration of computer networks that are located around the world.

However, the modern strategic and tactical benefits and dangers of the virtual environment are not unnoticed by nation–states. President Obama proclaimed the month of October as National Cybersecurity Awareness Month. This proclamation occurred because of the observation that "America's growing dependence on information technology has given rise to the need for greater protection of digital networks and infrastructures" (Cybersecurity).[34] The United States responded to this need through the creation of military infrastructures designated solely for the purposes of cyber warfare.

In 2010, cyber war infrastructures were created and implemented within the US Air Force and the US Navy. The US Air Force announced the operational capacity and readiness of the Twenty-Fourth Air Force on October 1, 2010. The function of this organization serves the purpose of "all component numbered Air Force responsibilities in support of combatant commanders for the Air Force's cyberspace mission" (US Air Force).[35] The formation of the US Navy Cyber Forces was announced on January 26, 2010. The mission of this navy organization "is to organize and prioritize manpower, training, modernization and maintenance requirements; and capabilities of command and control architecture and networks; cryptologic and space-related systems; and intelligence and information operations activities; and to coordinate with TYCOMs to deliver interoperable, relevant and ready forces at the right time, at the best cost, today and in the future."[36]

The formations of these infrastructures occurred in conjunction with the development of the US Cyber Command. According to the Department of Defense,[37] the "U.S. Cyber Command possesses the required technical capability and focuses on the integration of military cyberspace operations" for the purposes of integrating "existing cyberspace resources, creating synergy that does not currently exist and synchronizing war-fighting effects to defend the DOD information security environment."

The threats of the multipolar world also exist among virtual environments. During the last few years, much discussion has occurred regarding the potential of Chinese aggressiveness within the virtual environment. According to Barnes,[38] recently, China "has developed ways to infiltrate and manipulate computer networks around the world in what U.S. defense officials conclude is a new and potentially dangerous military capability." During this period, the computer systems and networks of the Pentagon, US agencies, and contractor entities were hacked, and the source of the infiltration appeared to originate from China; the nation of China also appeared to be the source of additional computer system infiltrations in Germany, France, and Britain.[38]

These attacks are indicative of the dangers of the cyber environment. Through the use of modern technologies, both terrorist organizations and nation–states gain the capacity to infiltrate critical infrastructures and inflict significant damage within the nation without necessitating a physical presence near the intended target. Although the United States has successfully waged war among a variety of physical locations and settings, the domain of cyberspace is a new environment in which the government must adapt and learn to exercise warfare dominance against aggressors.

Space: The next frontier

The 1990s witnessed the first significant implementation of space-based technologies. During 1990 and 1991, space-based technologies were used as effective resources within the Persian Gulf conflict. The use of satellite global positioning systems (GPSs) facilitated the navigation and movements of land-based troops among desert areas, assisted naval vessels in mapping and navigating mine fields, and assisted the accurate targeting and delivery of air force and navy weapons.[25] The use of such satellite technologies also "provided commanders with high-resolution, near real-time weather information that was very helpful in planning air and ground operations" and also "detected short-range Scud missiles that Iraq fired at targets in Israel and Saudi Arabia."[25]

The relevancy of space must not be discounted as a future consideration of homeland security. This notion is given credence from the observations of the Gulf War during the 1990s. According to the Federation of American Scientists,[25] the saliency of space-based technologies is summarized through the statements of Lieutenant General (LTG) Donald L. Cromer as follows:

> Lieutenant General Donald L. Cromer, Commander of SSD at the time, pointed out that Desert Storm was the first space war—the first war in which space systems were used by operational commanders and integrated into their daily decision-making processes. This, in turn, influenced the attitude of military leaders toward space. Previously, said General Cromer, 'space people used to be pushed off to the side. We had to fight for everything. We had neither understanding nor strong support for all the things that space could do for the Air Force.' As a result of Desert Shield/Desert Storm, however, commanders acquired a new appreciation of the value of space systems. In the General's words, 'Operations Desert Shield and Desert Storm will be a water shed for recognizing that space is as much a part of the Air Force and military infrastructure as the airplanes, tanks and the ships.... all future wars will be planned and executed with that in mind.'

These notions are both profound and realistic regarding the relevancy and importance of space-based technologies. Certainly, LTG Cromer's statements are indicative of the future uses of space-based technologies. The essences of his statements are also applicable to commercial entities that maintain a presence in space. Contemporary uses of space technologies are both commercial and militaristic. Numerous corporations possess satellites that facilitate the functioning of a myriad of wireless communications platforms that humans rely upon daily for communications, weather information, logistics, shipping, aviation, sea navigation, and a vast array of other uses.

The loss of any of these functions would devastate many industries and services given the modern reliance that exists upon satellite and wireless technologies. Therefore, future considerations of homeland security must consider the space-based technologies that facilitate the functions of a myriad of industries and services.

Space: Contemporary and future considerations

The history of space exploration and leveraging it for the uses of humans is in its primary stages of infancy. Although numerous benefits are derived from the exploration of space, a variety of ominous futures may exist in which American interests are blatantly threatened from space-based resources. During the Cold War, the United States and the Soviets demonstrated to the world the powerfulness that is affiliated with space-based resources. After the end of the Cold War, global and national interests regarding space-based resources were undiminished. Modern interests associated with space-based resources pervade a variety of nations and regions. The nations of China, India, Russia, Japan, and Britain have modern interests in space-based resources.

According to *Newsweek*,[21] the nation of China is quickly maturing its space program. During the last decade, Chinese astronaut Yang Liwei orbited the Earth, and China successfully destroyed one of its orbiting satellites.[21] Further, China is pursuing "robotic moon landings (a data-gathering probe is already in orbit) and even a rumored manned trip to the lunar surface—a prospect that provoked a minor crisis in Washington, culminating in President George W. Bush's State of the Union promise in 2004 to establish a permanent U.S. moon base."[21]

The maturation of the Chinese space program presents serious considerations for future US interests strategically. According to MacDonald[19] the demonstrated ability of China, to successfully implement antisatellite technologies presents national security risks for American interests during upcoming decades. MacDonald[19] indicates that Chinese technologies could be improved to integrate and implement "lasers, microwaves, or cyber weapons," thereby substantially reducing the "effectiveness of U.S. fighting forces." According to MacDonald,[19] the developing of Chinese space technologies may be a method of asymmetrically bolstering China's military inferiorities when compared with the military prowess of the United States. Such observations are not unnoticed by the US government. According to Spillius,[26] the "Pentagon is spending billions of dollars on new forms of space warfare to counter the growing risk of missile attack from rogue states and the 'satellite killer' capabilities of China."

The actions of China were not ignored by the Asian regional powers. The nation of Japan was alarmed regarding the demonstrations of Chinese technologies. Although Japan is primarily a "pacifist country," the Chinese actions prompted Japanese legislators to contemplate overturning "a parliamentary resolution passed in 1969 that limited Japan's use of space to non-military missions." Such change contributed toward the goal of developing and operating "spy satellites and other hardware designed to enhance the country's security." According to Martin,[20] the Japanese legislature passed legislation that permits "Japan, for the first time, to use space for the purposes of contributing to national security." This legislation demonstrated a significant "departure from an almost forty-year-old policy of strict non-military use of outer space."[20] The nation of Japan also operates a space program through which it performs geographic moon mapping missions.[11]

Other Asian powers also pursue the ability to implement antisatellite systems and programs. According to De Selding,[12] the nation of India is currently developing "lasers and an exoatmospheric kill vehicle that could be combined to produce a weapon to destroy enemy satellites in orbit." The necessary infrastructure of such a system is estimated to be available between the years of 2012 and 2014.[12] Rabinowitz[13] indicates that the justification for an Indian antisatellite program involves the developing of an ability to "defend its satellites from threats like China's newly revealed ability to shoot down targets in orbit." The implementation of such a system inevitably fosters an Asian space race.[13]

Modern Russia emerged from the remnants of the Cold War. Although the nation witnessed change after the demise of the Soviet Union, the Russian interest in space-based capabilities is unwavering. According to Hodge,[17] "A group of retired Russian generals has called for an upgrade to the country's space defenses, saying that the Russian defense industry has fallen dangerously behind and that the country has a limited capability to counter possible threats from space." Modernization efforts consist of the pursuits of antisatellite technologies and programs as responses to the actions of other nations.[22] According to Fox News,[23] these efforts are designed to ensure that Russian technologies are commensurate with the capabilities of other nations.

The development of space technologies and weaponries concerns Britain. Recent warnings indicated that "countries that sought nuclear capabilities could attack Britain from the upper atmosphere instead of through more traditional 'nuclear strikes.'"[14] These warnings also considered the potential of terrorists to attack Britain using such methods. Additional concerns involved the notion that "such an attack involving a nuclear detonation would destroy vital electronic systems by producing an electromagnetic pulse."[14] As a result, British planning considers the risk potentials of hostile entities exploding nuclear weapons in space and causing high-altitude electromagnetic pulses above the nation.[14] Although the space program of Britain lags behind those of other world powers, Britain uses Skynet satellites to facilitate its military communications.[15] Therefore, Britain has a vested interest regarding the security of such satellites.

Globally, a variety of nations are now exploring potential space-based systems that may provide strategic and tactical benefits. America must remain vigilant to facilitate its security regarding the potential of space-based threats. Although the exploration of space has not revealed hostilities among the heavens, the future of space exploration and use is unwritten. The economic considerations of space exploration provide a variety of opportunities and threats. Other bodies, such as the moon and Mars, may contain various resources that may satisfy human wants and needs. Additional considerations involve the preceding concepts regarding security initiatives affiliated with antisatellite technologies, atmospheric electromagnetic pulses, and intelligence functions. Regardless of the scenario, considerations of space threats are a valid consideration of homeland security.

Failed states

The world is undergoing a global recession during the time of this authorship. Some of the world's poorest countries also have the highest rates of birth. This scenario represents a potentially deadly combination of conditions that affect both the United States and other nations. It is especially important for those large numbers of impoverished people who also live in areas struggling with ethnic, tribal, and religious conflict. Wars and genocide, which were witnessed with regularity during the early part of the 21st century, could affect the United States in terms of allocating resources and rendering aid to large numbers of displaced and at-risk individuals.

The term *failed* describes a state that has lost its ability to exercise the powers of a sovereign entity. In the case of a failed state, the civil government no longer functions; thus it is impractical if not impossible for the "country" to function as a nation in the world community, and making international negotiations is impossible because it does not have a functioning government. Failing states are invariably the product of a collapse of the power structures providing political support for law and order. Such a condition is representative of a process that is generally triggered and accompanied by "anarchic" forms of internal violence. Therefore, chaos is an attribute of a failing or failed state.

Periodically, both failed and failing states require the intervention of international troops to restore order. As a precedent, the United States has rendered assistance to those governments that have requested assistance. However, one consideration regarding failed states involves examining and determining which failed states are global security threats and which are simply tragedies for their own people. In 2010, international opinion viewed the nations of Somalia, Zimbabwe, Sudan, Chad, Democratic Republic of the Congo, Central African Republic, Guinea, Ivory Coast, Haiti Burma, Kenya, Nigeria, Ethiopia, North Korea, Yemen, Bangladesh, and East Timor as the top nations failing or in danger of failing. With respect to the security interests of the United States and its allies, the nations that have a high probability of failure represent an international and global security threat.

Somalia is an excellent example of a failed state whose failure poses an international threat. Not only are the sea-lanes around Somalia infested by pirates, but also, Somalia is a challenge to international terrorists seeking their support. A recent report by West Point's Combating Terrorism Center, generated after the capture of al Qaeda documents, revealed that al Qaeda experienced difficulty during Somali operations because of terrible infrastructure, excessive violence and criminality, few basic services, and a variety of other factors. These are the same reasons that international peacekeepers found Somali operations unmanageable during the 1990s. Somalia was too failed even for al Qaeda!

Many consider the nation of Mexico to be a failed or failing state. Violence along the US–Mexican border has been intensifying for several years. The violence poses a strategic problem for the Mexican government. A majority of Mexico's effective troops are deployed along the US border—attempting to suppress violence and smuggling. They are also used to counter the well-known smuggling routes elsewhere in the country. The attacks in Mexico raise the question of whether forces should be shifted from these assignments to Mexico City. Such movement may protect officials and break up the infrastructure of the Sinaloa and other cartels. The government also faces the secondary task of suppressing violence between criminal and drug cartels.

Energy and natural resources

Most individuals realize that oil is a finite resource: That is, someday, we will run out of it. Before that happens, we will likely be in fierce competition with developing industrial powers, such as China, to ensure that our oil supplies remain viable. However, there are other resources that are also threatened. According to the National Intelligence Council,

> By 2015 nearly half the world's population—more than 3 billion people—will live in countries that are 'water stressed'—have less than 1,700 cubic meters per capita per year….in the developing world, 80 percent of water usage goes into agriculture, a proportion that is not sustainable; and in 2015 a number of developing countries will be unable to maintain their levels of irrigated agriculture.[39]

Years ago, ranchers in the western part of the United States went to war over water. Because water is scarce and is a requirement for maintaining human life, is it possible that the same thing could happen in the future on a global scale? In addition to water, energy, land, and arable soil are also becoming scarce resources.

Rising powers

The power balance of nations is constantly changing. Nations are linked economically, socially, and politically. Major powers of the past, such as the Romans, the British, or the Soviets, have seen their empires rise and fall. As one power declines, others emerge. The 20th century was a time of major change in international power. Driven by factors such as war and economics and advancements in science and technology, the 20th century was a time of unprecedented change. In 1900, global power centered in Europe; by the end of the century, the world was considered bipolar, with power radiating from Washington, DC, and Moscow.

The end of World War II saw international power shift to the United States and the Soviet Union, with the United States and the Soviet Union competing with each other to become the global leader, economically and politically, during a period referred to as the Cold War. With the fall of the Soviet Union, the United States gained dominance. Those who believed that the end of the Cold War would open a period of world security were mistaken. Rising and emerging powers compete not only for regional power but also globally.

By 2010, the position of the United States as the dominant world power was under challenge by nations including India, China, and recovering powers, such as Russia. At the same time, the international threats posed by nations such as North Korea and Iran endanger international security.

Domestic and transnational crime

Whereas crime has historically been considered a local issue, modern threats demonstrate transnational characteristics. The gangs of yesteryear are now replaced with organized crime factions consisting of thousands of members who operate globally. The actual levels of such criminal activities, including public corruption, human trafficking, and cyber crime, remain unknown. The profits by some criminal organizations rival the gross national products of some countries. Criminal organizations currently threaten the stability of entire countries. Because of the developments in Mexico, which recent government efforts against drug cartels have thrust into the equivalent of a civil war, US officials remain quite concerned that the extreme levels of violence will soon make their way into the United States.

Future challenges to homeland security

The United States has committed significant resources to the reduction of the nation's vulnerability to homeland security–related threats. When considering the future, several observations may be examined regarding the nation's homeland security initiatives. Continuous planning and attention must be given to the training, equipment, and coordination of logistics and planning, which is necessary for responders at all levels, to ensure timely and effective response. Proactive planning is the key to disaster response.

The length of the borders makes them physically impossible to close. Therefore, once access to the nation is achieved, one desiring to harm the United States can move with relative freedom across the nation. Securing the border and transportation systems continues to be an enormous challenge. The US ports of entry encompass approximately 7,500 miles of land border affecting the United States, Mexico, and Canada; 95,000 miles of shoreline and navigable rivers; and an exclusive economic zone of 3.4 million square miles. Each year, more than 500 million people, 130 million motor vehicles, 2.5 million railcars, and 5.7 million cargo containers must be processed at the US border.[40] Therefore, the US border represents a tremendous security risk.

The potential of future threats

No human can accurately and exactly predict future events. It is impossible to imagine and quantify any and all of the sets of permutations and combinations of events that detail and define catastrophic scenarios that could possibly impact the security of the United States, its citizenry, its infrastructure, and its interests. Therefore, any considerations of determining future threats involve numerous assumptions, limitations regarding collected and examined intelligence, and various amounts of speculation and guessing. No magic, crystal ball exists through which one may examine the future with precision, accuracy, and exactness to foretell whether the current security strategies shall be successful through time. However, despite such a constraint, considerations of possible future threats must occur to facilitate the security of the nation, its citizenry, and its interests through time. Therefore, based on available intelligence, some assumptions, and the use of estimated values of variables, predictions may be offered that describe the potential future challenges that may affect the United States through time.

The modern world exhibits a variety of integrated economic activity. It manifests a variety of established, functional nations and groups of emerging nations whose infrastructures are less than desirable with respect to the expectations of a global society. Regardless, the allocations of the planet's resources are a concern among all nations. Therefore, some economic consideration of global resource allocation must be considered among the strategic planning efforts of the United States and its allies.

McConnell and Brue[41] indicate that the primary questions of any economic system pertain to the product or service to be produced, the consumers for whom such production is intended, and the quantities in which production should occur. These considerations are concerned with the basic economic question of how the unlimited wants and needs of humans may be satisfied through the allocation of limited, scarce resources.[41] Regardless of the economic system, geographic region, or considered society, these economic questions pertain to all humans and their behaviors through time. This notion is salient with respect to the observations given within *Global Trends 2025* (Global)[42] regarding future security issues that may impact the United States through time.

A reading of *Global Trends 2025* presents a variety of potential future scenarios that may impact United States national security. The array of such potential situations ranges from considerations of food concerns to considerations of energy issues. Any such considerations necessitate contemplation as potential threats that may impact US security. Based on a reading of *Global Trends 2025*, it is our opinion that the three most salient issues facing the United States are as follows: (1) energy concerns associated with petroleum; (2) concerns associated with the resources of water and food; and (3) the rise of India and China as world powers.

The first consideration is that of potential energy impacts, affiliated with declining fossil fuel reserves (e.g., petroleum, natural gas, etc.), during the coming decades. According to Fanchi (p. 193), fossil fuels are "non-renewable energy types," and only a finite supply of such resources exists given the time required for the processes of nature to generate repositories of such fuels. According to *Global Trends 2025* (Global, p. 41),[42] the production of such fossil fuels "will not be able to grow commensurate with demand." Fanchi (p. 193)[43] provides similar observations and indicates that the disparities of this situation are manifested because the consumption of such fuels occurs "at a rate that exceeds the rate of replenishment." Further, Campbell (p. 60)[41] indicates that discoveries of oil resources have "been in decline for

40 years" and that consumption demonstrates a ratio of "almost four barrels of oil for every one we find."

The diminishing of fossil fuel resources over time is not unnoticed. According to Eccleston,[44] outcomes of the Hubbert studies, performed during the 1960s, indicated that the "world would deplete about 80 percent of its available oil in a period of under 65 years" and that a "peak in world oil production would occur around 2000." Eccleston[44] acknowledges that such estimates are dependent on the estimated quantities of "barrels extracted" but yield a primary conclusion regardless of the estimated quantities substituted among the variables within the mathematical forecasting models: A peak of production shall occur, followed by declines.

The US Department of Energy (DOE) provides similar observations but manifests different estimates of peak periods and declines. According to Hirsch et al.,[45] the ranges of periods regarding world scenarios considered by the DOE encompass estimates of peak periods occurring somewhere between the years 2006 and 2020. Carlson[46,47] provides similar observations regarding peak periods and declines. According to Carlson,[46,67] various peak estimates range between the years 1998 and 2014.

Considerations of fossil fuel resource scarcities may present a variety of threats and challenges during future decades. Elhefnawy (p. 43)[48] indicates that "the scarcity of oil will work to the advantage of some states, and the disadvantage of others." Further, Elhefnawy (p. 43)[48] indicates that "major oil exporters will enjoy higher revenues and greater political leverage, particularly as their number shrinks, reversing the diversification of the world's oil suppliers under way since the 1970s." Given that "America imports nearly 66 percent of its petroleum needs every day," the observations of Elhefnawy[48] are significant.

Such significance may be contemplated from a variety of perspectives. From a financial and economic perspective, regarding pricing, Elhefnawy (p. 48)[48] observes that with "supplies of energy priced out of the reach of consumers, businesses and government, basic services might fail and states cease to be viable." Additional observations are provided within the writings of Frumkin et al.,[49] regarding various facets of the public health system and medical industries. According to Frumkin et al. (p. 124),[49] regarding the impacts of fuel shortages among medical environments, "Direct and indirect effects will be felt on medical supplies and equipment, transportation, energy, and food." Such effects would occur because petroleum is a base product of numerous plastics, pill coatings and medicines and provides fuel for vehicles.[49]

Rhodes[50] considers the possibilities of war involving the United States resulting from competition of resources regarding scarce supplies of fuel. According to Howard (p. 19),[51] numerous "consuming countries" of fossil fuels may "use their military weight to seize diminishing reserves of petroleum and other natural assets." Howard (p. 19)[51] also indicates that military conflicts may ensue "between and within producing countries." Within this context, Howard (p. 20)[51] contemplates whether scenarios involving agreements between "producers like Kuwait, Venezuela, Syria, or Saudi Arabia" and "Western companies," would "provoke a serious, perhaps heavy, nationalist and Islamist reaction." Such a scenario demonstrates significant political and economic ramifications.

Rhodes (p. 59)[50] also considers a "domino effect" that could involve hoarding nationally, the emergence of a "fuel black market," the unavailability of food and medicine because of a "diminished capacity" among systems of distribution, and inefficiency and ineffectiveness among emergency services agencies. Although many other examples and application domains could be identified, these examples serve as indicators of potential impacts that may result because of fossil fuel declines. Given these examples, the possibility of fuel shortages must be neither understated nor ignored regarding their potential effects both domestically and internationally.

However, the issues affiliated with declining fuel resources are not without opportunities and challenges. Despite the projected decreases among fuel resources, a myriad of opportunities exist to develop alternative fuels and energy sources that would satisfy the needs of fuel consumers among domestic and international markets.[52] Dahl[52] considers the developing of nuclear sources, coal, and biofuels as alternatives to the traditional resources of fossil fuels. However, despite considerations of market alternatives, Gautier (p. 97)[53] indicates that the production of such alternative resource "capacity is still minimal at present, and will take many years to come up to speed."

Such considerations of declining fossil fuel resources and investigations of alternative fuels are salient regarding a second potential threat that may impact the United States during future decades: concerns associated with the resources of water and food. According to *Global Trends 2025* (Global p. 52),[42] competition regarding the use of land resources for food production versus energy production may yield a myriad of "difficult-to-manage consequences." Further, according to *Global Trends 2025* (Global p. 51),[42] such scenarios may be exacerbated because an increase of "cropland or freshwater scarce" regions may emerge. Bassam (p. 10)[54] indicates that "food production is closely correlated with energy availability and energy supply." Given such considerations, significant concerns regarding energy resources and agricultural land resource allocation may impact US security during the coming decades.

A variety of considerations may be contemplated regarding such resource allocation issues of water and food versus energy. According to Gautier (p. 196),[53] "It is expected that by 2030, about 60% of all land with irrigation potential will be in use." Gautier (2008)[53] indicates that additional competition for resources will ensue because water will be necessary for agricultural irrigation purposes as well as for potable drinking. Pimentel and Pimentel (p. 67)[55] also indicate that the "expenditure of human and fossil energy" is necessary for the production of "livestock forage and grain." However, land resources "devoted to grain or forage for livestock production" are continuously eroded because of nature and human activities, and require "large inputs of water for grain and forage crops and, to a lesser extent, directly for animal consumption" (Pimentel and Pimentel, p. 67).[55] Therefore, serious concerns are manifested regarding resource allocations and competition for scarce resources.

The considerations of land resources have significant concerns in terms of economic interdependencies regarding petroleum, land, water, and food. The sustenance of humans depends on water and food—however, given the dependence of agricultural production on the use of petroleum fuels, the potentials of food production may be impacted given the anticipated diminishing of petroleum fuel products.[56] Interdependency is also manifested regarding water use—humans require water for nutritional survival, and water is also required among the functions of agriculture to produce food.[56] Interdependency is seen within agriculture because fuel is necessary for the functioning of farm machinery and is also necessary for human functions that are unrelated to agriculture (e.g., aviation, logistics, etc.).[56]

The perplexities of the first consideration, declining fuel production, and the second consideration, concerning food, water, and land use, are heightened given the anticipated increases among populations globally that will necessitate the use of such resources globally. However, such growth is "inevitably constrained by food availability" (p. 12).[57] The considerations of Southgate et al.[57] pose salient considerations for emerging nations and economies whose needs and requirements encompass increased demands and consumptions of fuel, food, water, and land during future decades.

Therefore, the third category of threats and challenges must be considered. This notion concerns the anticipated emergence of both India and China. According to *Global Trends 2025* (p. 29),[42] "If current trends persist, by 2025 China will have the world's second largest economy, and will be a leading military power." Further, *Global Trends 2025* (p. 29)[42] indicates that "U.S. security and economic interests could face new challenges if China becomes a peer competitor that is militarily strong as well as economically dynamic and energy hungry." Considerations of India also present salient considerations for future US interests. According to *Global Trends 2025* (p. 30),[42] the emergence of India may serve "as a political and cultural bridge between a rising China and the United States."

These emerging nations cannot be ignored with respect to their commensurate increases of demands and consumption of scarce resources through time. According to Herman (p. 22),[72] the growths of "India and China will lead to expanding demand for energy," and "global trends in food production and prices, and changing patterns of consumption are going to put increasing pressure on the availability and prices of basic food items." Given such notions, increases among economic competitions for scarce resources will occur to satisfy the needs and wants of both existing and emerging nations.

McConnell and Brue[56] indicate that the primary questions of any economic system pertain to the product or service to be produced, the consumers for whom such production is intended, and the quantities in which production should occur. These considerations are concerned with the basic economic question of how the unlimited wants and needs of humans may be satisfied through the allocation of limited, scarce resources.[41]

The materials contained within *Global Trends 2025*[42] are indicative of these economic contemplations. The contents of *Global Trends 2025*[42] show an increasing population globally during future decades. According to *Global Trends 2025* (p. 19),[42] the global population is anticipated to "grow by about 1.2 billion between 2009 and 2025—from 6.8 billion to around 8 billion people." Given the growths of China and India—coupled with the anticipated declines of fossil fuels and slow developing of alternative energies; the interdependencies of fuel, food, and water to support such growth (both economically and physically); and the competitions among nations for scarce resources—it is our opinion that numerous issues have the potential of impacting US interests during future decades.

Such considerations must be considered within the context of US security and its policies during future decades. According to Er and Wei (p. 134),[59] the emergence of China "is instilling fear in the U.S. which views China as the emerging challenger to American hegemony despite an important and mutually beneficial trading relationship." Er and Wei (p. 135)[59] consider the emergence of China from the perspectives of viewing China as a potential threat and as an economic partner. According to Er and Wei (p. 135),[59] such concerns influence both US policy and US strategy with respect to the pursuits of both "military containment and economic engagement."

Er and Wei[59] also consider the potentials of the Indian economy during future decades. According to them, (2009), "Many argue that India has tremendous potential to emerge as the third largest economy in the world in purchasing power parity (PPP) terms by 2020, next only to the United States and China." However, Er and Wei[59] also consider the world standing of India, with respect to its economic growth. According to them, regarding "India's position in the world," its expansion of "trade has not grown at a faster rate than its economic growth" (p. 32). They indicate that this fact "is an indication of its dependency, and the very complex paradigm of development trajectory" (p. 32). Given these notions, Er and Wei[59] consider the rise of India to be fraught with uncertainties during future decades.

Another consideration of the emergences of China and India involves their international relationships with each other in future decades. According to Er and Wei (p. 32),[59] the relationship between China and India is strengthening, and "India–China relations have already shown considerable improvement during the last two decades" through the "strengthening of economic ties" and "bilateral relations." However, Er and Wei[59] consider the future success of this relationship to be uncertain because of political differences, land disputes, and economic alignments among Asian nations.

Regardless of the mathematical models used to consider future fuel estimates; expectations of population; potentials of food, water, and agricultural projections; and the future potentials of the emergences of China and India, it is our opinion that no model or forecast can accurately predict future events with absolute certainty. However, forecasts and estimates exist that show the potential threats and challenges that are salient considerations of these entities. Overall, given the cumulative writings of the aforementioned authors, it is our opinion that the emergence of India and China, coupled with the economic concerns of food, water, and land, will present policy concerns for the United States through time.

The emergences of China and India will necessitate significant resources over time. Such resource requirements include the use of land to produce food and the use of water for both human and agricultural needs. Underlying these requirements is the need for petroleum to facilitate agricultural functions and other activities (e.g., airlines, transportation, medical uses, plastics, etc.) that are necessary for continued economic growth. However, the availabilities and quantities of such natural resources are scarce, and the economic need for such resources incites competition globally for their acquisition and use.

Given these notions, it is our opinion that US policy must be crafted to accommodate the potentials of such scenarios and dependencies. Preeg (p. 223)[60] considers such aspects of policy from perspectives of negotiation and trade, and he recommends that policies must be "concerted, not unilateral," and should impose limitations regarding "national or regional shifts for sovereign investment funds." Finn (p. 21)[61] considers courses of action that "focus on mechanisms" that influence China internally "while remaining vigilant and attempting to contain PRC foreign policy actions and economic relationships around the world where these threaten U.S. interests." Regardless of the approach taken, the emergences of India and China, and their requirements for natural resources, will necessitate strong considerations of economic resources and US policies through time.

The future of the world is both nebulous and unwritten. New challenges shall emerge that represent dangers for US security and policy. However, the nation must remain vigilant to ensure its security and must seek a method through which its reliance upon finite resources (e.g., petroleum) may be diminished and eliminated. The nation must also balance its policies to accommodate any threats presented by emerging nations and their alliances. Regardless of the conjectured scenario, future national security challenges are uncertain, but preparations may be made to safeguard America against the potential of recognized and anticipated threats.

Conclusion

Those who wish to harm the United States, its allies, and its interests are constantly contemplating, researching, and planning. In the case of terrorists, they would like nothing better than for governments to overreact. They want counteractions, in response to their violence, to be reflexive actions rather than well-planned and coordinated responses. Terrorists know that responses, which consist of inappropriate actions, in response to their violence, endanger any government. They know that spontaneous countermeasures are usually to their advantage rather than to that of the government they have attacked.

One must always focus on the future, on the knowledge that terrorists change, just as technology and society changes. To rely only on the predictors inferred by recent terrorist activity will always prove dysfunctional. The United States must continue to support teaching homeland security among its public schools and in the universities where students prepare for the future. The United States must also continue to promote the preparedness efforts within the first-response and citizen communities.

The future of homeland security will continue to promote America's commitment to the antiterrorism efforts as initiated in the mid-1990s by the Nunn–Lugar–Domenici Act and the Office of Justice Programs. The homeland security preparedness program will always oscillate between the focus on natural disasters and man-caused incidents, which include acts of terrorism and use of WMDs. That oscillation is necessary and inherent in the public safety environment. At times, the requirement is to marshal all resources in response to a disastrous hurricane. At other times, all resources must respond to a catastrophic act of terrorism. And often, the resources are in the "rest" position, waiting on the next call for service to sound.

The homeland security program is a national program. It will continue to sustain efforts in the protection and securing of America. Issues that will be at the forefront of homeland security will be border security, as we attempt to protect the nation from those who would do us harm; port security, where we are dependent on the commerce and upon secure ports; and the protection of critical infrastructure that is the foundation of the nation's business and trade. Cybersecurity efforts will continue to expand as they integrate into utility infrastructure, the financial sector, and the network of communications on a global scale. And, the priority of training, equipping, and exercising the local responders throughout the United States and its territories will continue to be sustained.

Funding may ebb and flow in support of the national preparedness program. Changes in priorities will occur. However, the preparedness landscape within the United States forever changed following the events of 9/11. The nation's response community has enhanced its capabilities significantly since that time. Preparedness is the national goal. A variety of individuals and organizations must continue to prepare for the next call to service through planning, training, and equipping so they will be prepared regardless of whether future scenarios involve a natural disaster or an act of terrorism.

Space represents a frontier that has not been exploited by humanity. The exploration of space represents a variety of opportunities and challenges, but only time will reveal the outcomes of leveraging space for the use of humans. Although the United States and the Soviets endured a space race during the Cold War, conditions are forming that may propel a myriad of nations into a new space race. The characteristics of such a space race may be justified as defensive, among some nations, whereas others may attempt to validate their efforts through benign, scientific applications. Regardless, the potential of weaponry among the heavens is not outlandish.

Homeland security is a maturing concept. The United States favors an all-hazards approach to its homeland security paradigm. Through its organizational components, the DHS facilitates a variety of homeland security functions. However, during future generations, the attributes of future problem domains will define and characterize the threats that affect future generations globally. Organizational change, within the DHS and other entities, must occur to accommodate the dynamics of future threats. Only time will reveal the changes that shall occur among such agencies and entities. The future is unwritten. It is impossible to accurately and fully predict the future threats that shall endanger later generations. However, it is possible to provide various forecasts regarding future scenarios that may endanger and challenge later generations.

Key terms

Change
Cyber attack
Cyber crime
Cyber war
Domestic crime
Energy
Failed State
Man-made disaster
Netwar
Natural disaster
Natural resource
Policy
Rising power
Space
Strategy
Transnational crime
Trend
Weapon of mass destruction

QUESTIONS FOR DISCUSSION

1. This chapter introduces the notion of a trend. Peruse some texts on quantitative analysis, and define this term. Based on your findings, write a brief essay that highlights the saliency of trends with respect to speculating future events that may occur through time. Within your essay, tailor your discussions toward applications of homeland security.

2. The world is constantly changing and is never static for very long. Do some research regarding the Arab Spring that occurred within recent years. How do you believe changes in the Middle East will affect US policy in due time?

3. Technology changes and advances quickly through time. Based on the discussions of this chapter, what emerging technologies do you believe will have a strong impact upon the application of homeland security practices? Write a brief essay that substantiates your opinion.

4. China is an emerging power. Given its expenditures toward military modernization coupled with the historic frictions of the Asia-Pacific region, how do you believe the balance of power will change in time as China becomes stronger? What implications are there for US policy and security? Write a brief essay that substantiates your opinions.

References

1. US Department of Homeland Security Annual Financial Report: Fiscal Year 2012. (2012). http://www.dhs. gov/sites/default/files/publications/dhs-annual-financial-report-fy2012-vol1_0.pdf (accessed January 23, 2013).

2. Department of Homeland Security Strategic Plan Fiscal Years 2012–2016. (February 2012). http://www. dhs.gov/xlibrary/assets/dhs-strategic-plan-fy-2012-2016.pdf (accessed January 23, 2013).

3. New Jersey Office of Emergency Management. (2013). Volunteer. http://www.state.nj.us/njoem/citizen/ teencert.html (accessed May 7, 2013).

4. Michelson, R. (2013). The business of the private security industry. https://www.google.com/url?sa=t& rct=j&q=&esrc=s&source=web&cd=1&cad=rja&ved=0CDAQFjAA&url=https%3A%2F%2Fcourses. worldcampus.psu.edu%2Fwelcome%2Fcrimj304%2Fcorefiles%2Flinks%2FChapter%25202%2520PPT%252 0RM.ppt&ei=qoSJUfL8K4yi8gSg-IDIAg&usg=AFQjCNE9NaKxyuYJVZBtcmHQuINpxi9L0Q&bvm=bv.4622 6182,d.eWU (accessed May 7, 2013).

5. Hoffman, B. (2006). *Inside Terrorism* (2nd ed.). New York: Colombia University Press.

6. Jenkins, B. (1988). Terrorists want a lot of people watching, not a lot of people dead. http://www.lib.uci. edu/quest/index.php?page=jenkins (accessed May 7, 2013).

7. Wishart, D. (2011). Oklahoma City bombing. *Encyclopedia of the Great Plains*. University of Nebraska, http://plainshumanities.unl.edu/encyclopedia/doc/egp.pd.041 (accessed May 7, 2013).

8. Bullock, J., Haddow, G., Coppola, D., Efgin, E., Westerman, L. and Yeletaysi, S. (2006). *Introduction to Homeland Security*, Burlington, MA: Elsevier.

9. Kurzweil, R. (2001). The law of accelerating returns. *KurzweilAI.net*. http://www.kurzweilai.net/articles/ art0134.html?printable=1 (accessed January 30, 2010).

10. Sanger, D. (2013). U.S. blames China's military directly for cyberattacks. *The New York Times*. http://www. nytimes.com/2013/05/07/world/asia/us-accuses-chinas-military-in-cyberattacks.html?_r=0 (accessed May 7, 2013).

11. Japan. (2008). Japan to scrap space weapon rules. *BBC News*. http://news.bbc.co.uk/2/hi/7392544.stm (accessed December 14, 2010).

12. De Selding, P. (2010). India developing means to destroy satellites. *Spacenews.com*. http://www.spacenews. com/military/india-developing-anti-satellite-technology.html (accessed December 14, 2010).

13. Rabinowitz, G. (2008). Indian army wants military space program: regional race between Asian giants could accelerate militarization of space. *MSNBC News*. http://www.msnbc.msn.com/id/25216230/ns/technology_ and_science-space/ (accessed December 14, 2010).

14. Hough, A. (2010). Britain vulnerable to space nuclear attack of 'solar flare' storm, conference told. *The Telegraph*. http://www.telegraph.co.uk/science/space/8014444/Britain-vulnerable-to-space-nuclear-attack-or-solar-flare-storm-conference-told.html (accessed December 14, 2010).

15. Amos, J. (2010). U.K. Skynet military satellite system extended. *BBC News*. http://news.bbc.co.uk/2/ hi/8556585.stm (accessed December 14, 2010).

16. Arquilla, J. and Ronfeldt, D. (Eds.). (2001). The advent of netwar (Revisited). *Networks and Netwars: The Future of Terror, Crime, and Militancy.* Santa Monica, CA.: RAND.

17. Hodge, N. (2010). Russian generals want their space weapons, too. *Wired*. http://www.wired.com/ dangerroom/2010/05/russian-generals-want-their-space-weapons-too/ (accessed December 14, 2010).

18. Lesser, I.O., Hoffman, B., Arquilla, J., Ronfeldt, D. and Zanini, M. (1999). *Project Air Force*. Santa Monica, California: Rand Corporation.

19. MacDonald, B. (2008). *China, Space Weapons, and U.S. Security.* New York: Council on Foreign Relations.

20. Martin, C. (n.d.). Japan opes the way for military use of outer space. *Foreign Policy Digest*. http://www. foreignpolicydigest.org/20080610111/Regional-Archive/Asia-Archive/japan-opens-the-way-for-military-use-of-outer-space.html (accessed December 14, 2010).

21. Real Space. (2010). The real space race is in asia. *Newsweek*. http://www.newsweek.com/2008/09/19/the-real-space-race-is-in-asia.html (accessed December 14, 2010).

22. Russia Building. (2009). Russia building anti-satellite weapons. *The Independent*. http://www.independent. co.uk/news/world/europe/russia-building-antisatellite-weapons-1638270.html (accessed December 14, 2010).

23. Russia Developing. (2009). Russia developing anti-satellite weapons, defense minister says. *Fox News*. http://www.foxnews.com/story/0,2933,505157,00.html (accessed December 14, 2010).

24. Smart, J. (2005). Homeland security: 2015. Presentation before the Futures Working Group, (March, 2005), Phoenix, Arizona.

25. Space Systems. (n.d.). Space systems in the persian gulf war. *Federation of American Scientists*. http:// www.fas.org/spp/military/program/smc_hist/SMCHOV15.HTM (accessed December 14, 2010).

26. Spillius, A. (2007). U.S. plans new space weapons against china. *The Telegraph*. http://www.telegraph.co.uk/news/worldnews/1569339/US-plans-new-space-weapons-against-China.html (accessed December 14, 2010).
27. NSS. (2010). *National Security Strategy of the United States*. Washington, DC: Government Printing Office.
28. U.S. Department of State. (2009). Country Reports: Western Hemisphere Overview, http://www.state.gov/j/ct/rls/crt/2009/140888.htm (accessed August 27, 2013).
29. Farnsworth, E. (2007). Congressional Testimony: South America and the United States–How to Fix a Broken Relationship, http://www.as-coa.org/articles/congressional-testimony-south-america-and-united-states-how-fix-broken-relationship (accessed August 28, 2013).
30. Barshefsky, C., Hill, J., O'Neil, S. and Sweig, J. (2008). U.S.-Latin America Relations, Council on Foreign Relations, http://www.cfr.org/mexico/us-latin-america-relations/p16279 (accessed August 28, 2013).
31. Jones, C. and Volpe, E. (2011). Organizational Identification: Extending our Understanding of Social Identities through Social Networks, *Journal of Organizational Behavior*, 32(2), pp. 413–434.
32. Haeni, R. (1997). *Information Warfare: An Introduction*. The George Washington University. Washington, DC: Cyberspace Policy Institute.
33. War. (2010). War in the Fifth Domain. *The Economist*. http://www.economist.com/node/16478792 (accessed August 28, 2013).
34. Cybersecurity, Cybersapce, and the DOD. (2010). *Military Avenue*, http://www.militaryavenue.com/Articles/Cybersecurity+Cyberspace+and+the+DoD-35405.aspx (accessed August 28, 2013).
35. U.S. Air Force. (2010). 24th Air Force Achieves Full Operational Capability, http://www.af.mil/news/story_print.asp?id=123224589 (accessed December 30, 2010).
36. Strickland, A. (2010). Navy Cyber Forces Established. U.S. Navy. http://www.navy.mil/submit/display.asp?story_id=50853 (accessed August 28, 2013).
37. U.S. Department of Defense. (2010). DOD Announces First U.S. Cyber Command and First U.S. CYBERCOM Commander, http://www.defense.gov/releases/release.aspx?releaseid=13551 (accessed August 28, 2013).
38. Barnes, J. (2008). Chinese Hacking Worries Pentagon, *The Los Angeles Times*, http://articles.latimes.com/2008/mar/04/world/fg-uschina4 (accessed August 28, 2013).
39. National Intelligence Council. (2000). *Global Trends 2015*. http://www.dni.gov/index.php/about/organization/national-intelligence-council-global-trends (accessed December 2, 2008).
40. Office of Management and Budget. (2003). House Report 108-799. http://www.gpo.gov/fdsys/pkg/CRPT-108hrpt799/html/CRPT-108hrpt799.htm (accessed August 28, 2013).
41. McConnell, C. and Brue, S. (2008). *Economics* (17th ed). New York: McGraw-Hill Publishing.
42. National Intelligence Council. (2008). *Global Trends 2025: A Transformed World*. Washington, DC: Government Printing Office.
43. Fanchi, J. (2004). *Energy: Technology and Directions for the Future*. New York: Elsevier.
44. Eccleston, C., March, F., and Cohen, T. (2012). *Inside Energy: Developing and Managing an ISO 50001 Energy Management System*. Boca Raton, FL: CRC Press.
45. Hirsch, R., Bezdek, R., and Wendling, R. (2005). Peaking of world oil production: Impacts, mitigation, and risk management. *U.S. Department of Energy*. http://www.netl.doe.gov/publications/others/pdf/Oil_Peaking_NETL.pdf (accessed July 1, 2010).
46. Carlson, W. (2007a). Sensitivity of predicted oil production to the sigmoid function. *Energy Sources Part B: Economics, Planning, & Policy*, 2(4), 321–327.
47. Carlson, W. (2007b). Analysis of world oil production based on the fitting of the logistic function and its derivatives. *Energy Sources Part B: Economics, Planning, & Policy*, 2(4), 421–428.
48. Elhefnawy, N. (2008). The impending oil shock. *Survival*, 50(2), 37–66.
49. Frumkin, H., Hess, J., and Vindigni, S. (2009). Energy and public health: The challenge of peak petroleum. *Public Health Reports*, 124(1), 5–19.
50. Rhodes, R. (2010). *The Coming Oil Storm: The Imminent End of Oil and Its Strategic Global Role in End-Times Prophecy*. Eugene, OR: Harvest House Publishing.
51. Howard, R. (2009). Peak oil and strategic resource wars. *Futurist*, 43(5), 18–21.
52. Dahl, C. (2004). *International Energy Markets: Understanding Pricing, Policies, and Profits*. Tulsa, OK: PennWell Publishing.
53. Gautier, C. (2008). *Oil, Water, and Climate: An Introduction*. New York: Cambridge University Press.
54. Bassam. (2010). *Handbook of Bioenergy Crops: A Complete Reference to Species, Development, and Applications*. London, UK: Earthscan Publishing.
55. Pimentel, D. and Pimentel, M. (2008). *Food, Energy, and Society*. (3rd ed.). Boca Raton, FL: CRC Press.
56. Cochrane, W. (1993). *The Development of American Agriculture: A Historical Analysis*. Minneapolis, MN: University of Minnesota Press.

57. Southgate, D., Graham, D., and Tweeten, L. (2007). *The World Food Economy*. Malden, MA: Blackwell Publishing.
58. Herman, C. (2008). *Economic Developments in India*. New Delhi, India: Academic Foundation.
59. Er, L. and Wei, L. (2009). *The Rise of China and India: A New Asian Drama*. Danvers, MA: World Scientific Publishing Co., Ltd.
60. Preeg, E. (2008). *India and China: An Advanced Technology Race and How the United States Should Respond*. Arlington, VA: Manufacturers Alliance.
61. Finn, J. (2007). *China-United States Economic and Geopolitical Relations*. New York: Nova Science Publishers.

Appendix A: Major Domestic Terrorism Events in the United States 1865–2013

Although such criminal events have occurred since the origin of the nation, a review of the events succeeding the Civil War highlights the proliferation of domestic terrorism. The following chronological listing shows a variety of these historical events:

1865	Assassination of President Abraham Lincoln perpetrated by John Wilkes Booth.
1881	Assassination of President James Garfield by Charles Guiteau.
1886	Chicago, Illinois—The Haymarket affair involved a public labor dispute that resulted in bombing, rioting, and the deaths of seven police officers and an unknown quantity of civilians.[36]
1901	Assassination of President William McKinley perpetrated by Leon Czolgosz.
1910	Los Angeles, California—A total of 21 people died when the building of the *Los Angeles Times* newspaper was bombed in conjunction with the Los Angeles Iron Workers strike. [27]
1912	Attempted assassination of President Theodore Roosevelt. The plot failed.
1914	Ludlow, Colorado—The Ludlow Mine massacre resulted in the deaths of "18 innocent men, women, and children" within a mining tent colony.[65] Disputes existed regarding mining labor issues, and a strike occurred. According to the United Mine Workers of America,[65] the event was a "carefully planned attack on the tent colony by Colorado militiamen, coal company guards, and thugs hired as private detectives and strike breakers."
1916	Black Tom Island, New Jersey—This incident occurred as a response to prevent the United States from shipping war materials to Allied nations during World War I. The exact death toll is unknown, the Statue of Liberty "sustained $100,000 in damages," and the "reported property damage was over $20 million".[32] Michael Kristoff, a German immigrant, allegedly perpetrated this event.[32]
1919	Washington, District of Columbia—A militant anarchist named Carlo Valdinoci blew up the front of newly appointed attorney general A. Mitchell Palmer's home and blew himself up in the process when the bomb exploded too early. The bombing was just one in a series of coordinated attacks that day on judges, politicians, law enforcement officials, and others in eight cities nationwide. The next day, a postal worker in New York City intercepted 16 more packages addressed to political and business leaders, including John D. Rockefeller. The Palmer Raids were a response to these mailings and bombings.[20]
1920	New York City, New York—Over 30 people died as a result of this financial district bombing.[19]
1921	Oklahoma—William Hale perpetrated the murders of several Osage Indians and prominent members of the local community for the purposes of oil profits.[44]
1921	Tulsa, Oklahoma—The Tulsa Race Riot conflict involved the armed participation of the National Guard and resulted in the deaths of "10 whites and 26 blacks".[42] The event also involved arson and looting and was instigated over an alleged "sexual attack" against a white woman.[42]
1924	Louisiana—Edward Young Clarke was instrumental in facilitating significant increases of Ku Klux Klan (KKK) memberships within Louisiana. During this period, the KKK gained political power within the state and was guilty of criminal acts including murder. Assistance was requested by Governor Parker regarding the necessity of the federal government to protect states from domestic violence. The FBI was instrumental in bringing Clarke to justice.[3]
1927	Bath, Michigan—Andrew Kehoe perpetrated multiple bombings because he believed taxes were too high regarding the formation of consolidated schools.[56] Over 40 people died during this incident.[56]
1933	Chesterton, Indiana—A Boeing 247 exploded during its flight, and the incident was the first proven event of aviation sabotage.[28]

1933	Attempted assassination of President Franklin Roosevelt. The plot failed.
1940	New York — According to Mauro (2010), a time bomb was planted in the British Pavilion at the New York World's Fair of 1939–1940. After it was secured, "two bomb squad detectives, Joe Lynch and Freddy Socha, tried to defuse it," but "the bomb went off in their faces, killing them instantly".[41]
1940–1956	New York — Between the years of 1940 and 1956, George Metesky (i.e., "Mad Bomber") instigated over 30 bombings to protest his personal experience with a utility company.[14]
1950	Attempted assassination of President Harry Truman. The plot failed.
1958	Atlanta, Georgia — According to Webb (2009), "Militant white supremacists expressed their resistance to segregation and civil rights by dynamiting the most prominent symbol of Jewish life and culture in Atlanta."[63]
1960	New York — The Sunday Bomber perpetrated bombings within the subway system and ferries.
1963	Dallas, Texas — Assassination of President Kennedy by Lee Harvey Oswald.
1963	Birmingham, Alabama — Bombing of the Sixteenth Street Baptist Church in which "four African-American girls" and "more than 20 inside the church" were injured.[18]
1964	Philadelphia, Mississippi — The Mississippi Burning incident occurred in conjunction with civil rights efforts to register black voters and involved the murders of civil rights workers. More than a dozen suspects, including Deputy Price and his boss Sheriff Rainey, were indicted and arrested. Following years of court battles, 7 of the 18 defendants were found guilty — including Deputy Sheriff Price — but none on murder charges. One major conspirator, Edgar Ray Killen, went free after a lone juror could not bring herself to convict a Baptist preacher.[62]
1965	According to *Time Magazine* (1965), the Black Liberation Front and Quebec separatists planned to destroy the Statue of Liberty and the Liberty Bell and to attack United States military installations. However, the conspiracy was infiltrated before any plans could be implemented.[43]
1968	Memphis, Tennessee — Dr. Martin Luther King was assassinated, invoking numerous protests nationally.
1968	Los Angeles, California — Senator Robert F. Kennedy was assassinated during his Presidential campaign.
1969–1970	New York City, New York — The Weather Underground perpetrated bombings to protest the Vietnam War. According to Delafuente (2004), "The only fatalities were three of the radicals, who were killed when a townhouse in the Village, described by the police as a bomb factory, exploded."[14]
1970	New York — Jane Alpert, Sam Melville, and John Hughey III pled guilty to bombing conspiracies in New York.[37] During the 1960s, their activities involved the bombing of the New York City Federal Building, a court building, and a United States military induction center.
1970	Madison, Wisconsin — Sterling Hall, at the University of Wisconsin, was bombed, which caused the death of a researcher. This attack was perpetrated by four individuals, three of whom were captured.[40] However, the fourth individual, Leo Burt, was never captured and continues to elude law enforcement.[40]
1970	Portland, Oregon — According to Redden (2002), a "bomb exploded behind Portland City Hall," which "destroyed a heavy bronze replica of the Liberty Bell, shattered the building's large back doors, blew out windows and upended furniture in the council chambers."[47]
1971	Washington, District of Columbia — A bomb exploded in the Capitol building in Washington, District of Columbia, causing an estimated $300,000 in damage but hurting no one. The Weather Underground claimed credit for the bombing, which was done in protest of the ongoing United States–supported the invasion of Laos. The so-called Weathermen were a radical faction of the Students for a Democratic Society (SDS); the Weathermen advocated violent means to transform American society.[39] The philosophical foundations of the Weathermen were Marxist in nature; they believed that militant struggle was the key to striking out against the state, to build a revolutionary consciousness among the young, particularly the white working class.[39]
1972	Long Island, New York — Black September unsuccessfully attempted to assassinate Golda Meir and had planted bombs along New York's Fifth Avenue and at Kennedy Airport.[30]
1973	New Jersey — Three members of the Black Liberation Army were stopped on the New Jersey Turnpike for a motor vehicle violation. They opened fire on two New Jersey State police troopers. One trooper was wounded, and another, New Jersey state trooper Werner Foerster, was shot and killed execution-style at point-blank range.[31]
1973	Chevy Chase, Maryland — Former fighter pilot and cofounder of the Israel Air Force, Colonel Yosef Alon, was murdered in his Maryland home. Beginning in 1970, Alon assigned for 3 years to the Israeli embassy in Washington as the assistant air and naval attaché. He worked vigorously to procure sophisticated American F-4 Phantoms and other weaponry for the Israeli Air Force as his country battled Egypt.[10]

1974	Berkeley, California — Patty Hearst was kidnapped by the Symbionese Liberation Army (SLA). Hearst was mentally reprogrammed to sympathize with the SLA and became a member of the organization. The SLA desired the overthrow of the US government, and committed a variety of crimes including theft and bank robbery. Hearst was witnessed participating during robbery activities. Despite claims of brainwashing, the jury found her guilty, and she was sentenced to 7 years in prison. Hearst served 2 years before President Carter commuted her sentence. She was later pardoned.[46]
1974	New York — According to Delafuente (2004), the "Armed Forces of National Liberation, better known as F.A.L.N., the initials of its Spanish name, began a decade-long bombing campaign in New York that killed five people."[14]
1974	Pittsburgh, Pennsylvania — The Gulf Tower was bombed, resulting in "an estimated $1 million in damage to the building's 29th floor." The attack was allegedly carried out by the Weather Underground.[50]
1974	Los Angeles, California — The Alphabet Bomber, Muharem Kurbegovic, was responsible for "firebombing the houses of a judge and two police commissioners, firebombing one of the commissioner's cars, burning down two Marina Del Rey apartment buildings, and bombing the Pan Am Terminal of Los Angeles International Airport, killing three people and injuring eight."[53]
1974	Baltimore, Maryland — Samuel Byck attempted to commandeer a plane at Baltimore Washington International Airport with the intention of forcing the pilots to fly into Washington and crash into the White House to kill the president. The man was shot by police and then killed himself on the aircraft while it was still on the ground at the airport.[57]
1975	Attempted assassination of President Gerald R. Ford by Lynnette Fromme. The plot failed.
1975	Attempted assassination of President Gerald R. Ford by Sarah Jane Moore. The plot failed.
1975	La Guardia Airport, New York — A bomb exploded at La Guardia Airport, killing 11 people, and the identity of the responsible party is still unknown.[8]
1975	Chicago, Illinois — The Armed Forces of National Liberation (FALN) bombed the Chicago Sears Tower.[17]
1976	Washington, District of Columbia — Car bomb assassination of Chilean activists Orlando Letelier and Ronni Moffitt, allegedly carried out by members of Chile's secret police.[48]
1977	Chicago, Illinois — The FALN bombed the Chicago city–county building.[17]
1978	Chicago, Illinois — The Unabomber, Ted Kaczynski, distributed a mail bomb to the University of Illinois.[1]
1979	Evanston, Illinois — The Unabomber, Ted Kaczynski, distributed a mail bomb to the Northwestern University.[1]
1979	Bomb exploded in cargo hold during American Airlines flight, injuring 12 and forcing emergency landing at Dulles International Airport.[1]
1980	Staten Island, New York — The Statue of Liberty was bombed, resulting in more than $15,000 in damages. The Croatian Freedom Fighters claimed responsibility for this attack.[34]
1980	Chicago, Illinois — The FALN conducted a takeover of the Carter–Mondale campaign headquarters. Workers in that office were held at gunpoint while the office was ransacked and spray-painted. Lists of delegates to the convention were stolen, and threatening letters subsequently were mailed to many of them.[59]
1980	Oak Creek, Wisconsin — The FALN conducted an armed assault on the Oak Creek National Guard armory in Wisconsin. Employees were threatened at gunpoint, and one round was discharged in an unsuccessful effort to obtain access to the weapons vault.[60]
1980	Chicago, Illinois — Package bomb injured United Airlines president Percy Wood at home near Chicago.[1]
1981	Washington, District of Columbia — Attempted assassination of President Ronald Reagan by John Hinckley, Jr. The plot failed.
1981	New York — The Puerto Rican Resistance Army bombed a JFK Airport toilet, resulting in the death of one individual.[29]
1981	Salt Lake City, Utah — Bomb found in business classroom at University of Utah in Salt Lake City was safely defused.[1]
1982	New York — The FALN bombed a federal building and planted a second bomb near a United States Attorney's office.[35]
1982	Nashville, Tennessee — Janet Smith, secretary, injured at Vanderbilt University in Nashville by bomb from the Unabomber addressed to a computer science professor.[1]
1982	Berkeley, California — Bomb injured Diogenes J. Angelakos, electrical engineering and computer science professor, at University of California at Berkeley; Unabomber is suspected.[1]
1984	Oregon — The Rajneeshee Cult attempted to murder United States Attorney Charles Turner and perpetuated a bioterrorism attack at restaurants in The Dalles, Oregon.[13]
1984	Denver, Colorado — Alan Berg, a Jewish talk-show host, was murdered by an anti-Semitic group calling itself The Order.[64]
1985	Santa Ana, California — Alex Odeh, an agent of the American-Arab Anti-Discrimination Committee, was murdered by a bomb, and the Jewish Defense League is suspected of facilitating the attack.[2]

1985	The Unabomber distributed mail bombs to Auburn, Washington; Ann Arbor, Michigan; Berkeley and Sacramento, California.[1]
1987	Salt Lake City, Utah — Bomb injured Gary Wright near his Salt Lake City computer shop. Witness sighting led to first police sketch of the Unabomber.[1]
1989	New York — Bombing of the Riverdale Press occurred as a response to Salman Rushdie's *Satanic Verses*.[4]
1990	New York — US rabbi Meir Kahane, who advocated the expulsion of all Palestinians from the West Bank and Gaza Strip, was murdered by El Sayyid Nosair, an Egyptian-born American.[24]
1990	Tucson, Arizona — Rashad Khalifa, a Tucson mosque leader, who was hated by Muslim extremists opposed to his teachings, was murdered by stabbing.[55]
1993	San Francisco, California — Unabomber bomb injured Charles Epstein, University of California at San Francisco geneticist, at home.[1]
1993	David Gelernter, Yale University computer scientist, was injured by Unabomber bomb.[1]
1994	Washington, District of Columbia — Frank Corder crashed his aircraft into the base of the White House. Corder died in the attack.[15]
1994	Washington, District of Columbia — Francisco Martin Duran fired multiple rounds toward the White House. He then pulled the weapon back from the fence and ran down the sidewalk from west to east, toward 15th Street, continuing to fire through the fence. When Duran paused to empty his magazine and reload, Harry Michael Rakosky, a tourist, tackled him. Two other citizens, Kenneth Alan Davis and Robert Edward Haines, ran over and assisted Rakosky in subduing Duran until Secret Service Uniformed Division officers arrived seconds later.[21]
1994	North Caldwell, Jew Jersey — Unabomber murdered Thomas Mosser via mail bomb.[1]
1995	Sacramento, California — California Forestry Association president Gilbert P. Murray was killed by package bomb in his Sacramento office. Unabomber sent 35,000-word manifesto to the *Washington Post* and *New York Times*. Threatened to bomb unspecified locations if it was not published. In letter to San Francisco Chronicle, Unabomber threatened attack on a flight out of Los Angeles. *Post*, *Times* published manifesto.[1]
1995	Oklahoma City, Oklahoma — Bombing of the Murrah Federal Building by Timothy McVeigh.
1996	Montana — Theodore J. Kaczynski was detained after his brother's tip led FBI to stakeout of Montana shack and discovery of partially constructed bombs. Kaczynski was identified as the Unabomber and charged with a federal weapons violation and fatal Sacramento bombings.[1]
1996	Atlanta, Georgia — Eric Rudolph bombed the Atlanta Olympics, killing one; a second individual died of a heart attack.
1997	New York City, New York — A man opened fire on an observation deck of the Empire State Building, killing one person and wounding six before shooting himself in the head.[26]
1998	Washington — Gallons of diesel fuel and unleaded gas placed in buckets were used to set a fire at an administrative office of the US Department of Agriculture's Wildlife Service Office near the Evergreen State College, in the state of Washington. Eco-terrorists are suspected.[61]
1999	Michigan — Arson perpetrated by the Earth Liberation Front (ELF) significantly damaged the University of Michigan.[61]
1999	Monmouth, Oregon — ELF claimed responsibility for a Christmas Day fire that destroyed a Boise Cascade timberlands management center.[61]
1999	Columbine, Colorado — High school students Eric Harris and Dylan Klebold instigated a shooting spree that killed 13 individuals at Columbine High School.
2000	Bloomington, Indiana — ELF claimed responsibility for setting a luxury home that was under construction on fire. The fire caused an estimated $200,000 in damages. ELF says that the home was targeted because it is within the Lake Monroe watershed. In their written statement, the group stated, "This is the drinking water supply for the town of Bloomington, IN, and the surrounding area. It is already being jeopardized by existing development and roads." Authorities also found the initials "ELF" and the words "No Sprawl" spray-painted near the scene of the attack.[61]
2000	Syracuse, New York — Bombing of the Jewish Temple Beth El.[16]
2000	New York — On the night before Yom Kippur in 2000, two young men of Arab descent hurled crude Molotov cocktails at the Conservative Synagogue Adath Israel in a botched attempt to set it on fire. Early the next morning, a member of the congregation found the fizzled firebombs.[51]
2001	Glendale, Oregon — ELF set a fire at the administrative offices of the Superior Lumber Company. The fire caused $400,000 in damages to the company. There were no reported injuries or fatalities.[61]
2001	Multiple sites — According to the FBI, Bruce Ivins, acting alone, mailed out letters containing anthrax; 5 were killed and 17 sickened.[6]

2002	Washington, District of Columbia — Beltway Sniper killings were carried out by Lee Malvo and John Muhammed. These killings occurred primarily in the areas of Washington, District of Columbia; Maryland; and Virginia. Pervasive fear enveloped these regions as people were randomly shot at gas stations, parking lots, and even a school. The duo also is also suspected of earlier shootings in Maryland, Alabama, Arizona, Georgia, Louisiana, and Washington state.[11]
2002	Cedar Rapids, Iowa — Luke John Helder was arrested and charged with crimes perpetrated by the "Mail Box Bomber" involving a 5-day spree of pipe bomb incidents from Illinois to Texas that injured six people and prompted a manhunt across the heartland of the country.[5]
2003	Chico, California — A McDonald's employee found two incendiary devices near the back door of a McDonald's restaurant. Animal Liberation Front (ALF) left two notes claiming responsibility, and the group's name was written in red spray-paint on the exterior of the building, along with the slogans, "Meat is murder" and "Species Equality." No one was injured.[61]
2003	Albuquerque, New Mexico — ELF is believed responsible for firebombing two McDonalds fast-food restaurants and an Arby's. No one was injured in the attacks.[61]
2003	Emeryville, California — Two small explosive devices detonated at the third-largest biotechnology firm in the United States, Chiron. The blasts blew the windows out of the building but caused no injuries. The second device was primed to detonate after the first, possibly in order to injure emergency responders. Responsibility for the attacks was claimed by ALF Revolutionary Cells.[61]
2004	Oklahoma City, Oklahoma — Attempting to initiate a race war, Sean Gillespie hurled a Molotov cocktail at Temple B'nai Israel. There were no casualties, but the building sustained minor damages.[61]
2004	West Jordan, Utah — ELF claimed responsibility for starting a fire that caused about $1.5 million in damages to a lumber warehouse. A group claiming responsibility asserted that the lumberyard was attacked because of excessive pollutants released by Stock Building Supply's (owner of the lumberyard) forklifts. In October of 2004, Justus Ireland admitted to setting fire to a delivery truck and a pallet full of wood at the lumberyard.[61]
2005	Oyster Bay, New York — In a series of related incidents, perpetrators set a municipal and maintenance building in Theodore Roosevelt Memorial Park at Oyster Bay Harbor on fire. Although no casualties resulted from this incident, extensive property damage occurred. Two individuals, Arthur Gladd and Robert Hurley, both of whom were junior firefighter dropouts, were arrested and charged for this incident.[61]
2005	San Diego, California — In a series of related incidents, unknown perpetrators carried out incendiary attacks on two separate car dealerships. Collectively, the value of the property damage from these related incidents was approximately $167,000. In this particular attack, at 2:45 a.m. local time, the Pacific Nissan car dealership was targeted, and five sport-utility vehicles (SUVs) were set on fire, which resulted in approximately $150,000 in property damage. No casualties result from this incident, and although no group claims responsibility, authorities suspect ELF.[61]
2006	Chapel Hill, North Carolina — Muslim Mohammed Reza Taheri-azar drove his SUV through a group of students, injuring nine people.[58]
2006	Seattle, Washington — One woman was killed and five others wounded in a shooting at the Jewish Federation building in downtown Seattle. The attack was perpetrated by Naveed Afzal Haq. At the time of the incident, witnesses heard Haq exclaim, "I am a Muslim American, angry at Israel".[33]
2007	Portland, Oregon — ALF sabotaged the car and home of an area scientist apparently because he used monkeys in his research. ALF used graffiti and paint stripper in the attack. No one was injured.[61]
2007	Blacksburg, Virginia — Seung-Hui Cho killed over 30 people during his shooting spree at Virginia Tech.
2008	San Diego, California — Downtown federal courthouse bombed. The device consisted of multiple tubes that detonated simultaneously, releasing more than 50 nails.[25]
2008	Knoxville, Tennessee — Jim D. Adkisson opened fire and killed two people at a Unitarian Universalist Church because of its support for liberalism.[38]
2008	Santa Cruz, California — A University of California researcher's home was firebombed because of his research involving animals.[12]
2008	Crockett County, Tennessee — Daniel Cowart and Paul Schlesselman were found guilty of plotting a multistate killing and robbing spree, including targeting a predominantly African American school. The murder spree was allegedly planned to end with an attempt to assassinate presidential candidate Barack Obama with a high-powered rifle.[7]
2009	Washington, District of Columbia — James W. von Brunn, an 88-year-old white supremacist and Holocaust denier, opened fire in Washington's Holocaust Museum, killing a security guard before being shot in the head.[49]
2009	Wichita, Kansas — Dr. George Tiller, an abortionist, was murdered for his work providing "late-term" abortions.[52]

2009	New York City — A homemade bomb, constructed from fireworks explosives, a plastic bottle, and electrical tape was set off outside a Starbucks coffee shop on the Upper East Side.[54]
2009	Little Rock, Arkansas — Abdulhakim Mujahid Muhammad killed Private William A. Long, 23, of Conway and wounded Private Quinton Ezeagwula, 18, of Jacksonville in a United States Army recruiting center. This attack was response to US operations in Iraq and Afghanistan.[23]
2009	Fort Hood, Texas — Army Major Nidal Hasan opened fire on his fellow soldiers, murdering 13 people and injuring 32 others.[22]
2010	Austin, Texas — Joseph Stack flew his aircraft into an Internal Revenue Service (IRS) building.[9]
2010	Silver Spring, Maryland — James Lee attacked the headquarters of the Discovery Channel television network. Lee was armed and wore explosives during this attack. He was killed by police.[45]
2010	Memphis, Tennessee — Two West Memphis Police Officers killed while on a traffic stop of two members of the Sovereign Citizens — an antigovernment domestic group.
2013	Boston Massachusetts — Bombing at the Boston Marathon.

The preceding list is incomplete with respect to the events that demonstrate and characterize the tactics of terrorism domestically. Many other events could be identified and described. However, this list shows the heinous acts that humans perpetrate against others for a variety of purposes. Regardless, they are indicative of a blatant observation: Acts of terror are not new and continue to challenge America.

References

1. 16 Bombs, Three Deaths. (1998). *The Washington Post*. http://www.washingtonpost.com/wp-srv/national/longterm/unabomber/bkgrdstories.ted.htm (accessed August 1, 2013).
2. Anti-Defamation League. (2013). *Chronology: The Jewish Defense League*. http://archive.adl.org/extremism/jdl_chron.asp (accessed August 1, 2013).
3. Anti-Defamation League. (2013). *Ku Klux Klan – History*. http://archive.adl.org/learn/ext_us/kkk/history.asp?xpicked=4&item=kkk (accessed July 31, 2013).
4. Appignanesi, L. and Maitland, S. (1990). *The Rushdie File*. London, England: Institute of Contemporary Arts.
5. Arena, K., Dornin, R., Frieden, T. and Mears, B. (2002). College student charged in pipe bomb cases. *CNN News*. http://archives.cnn.com/2002/US/05/07/mailbox.pipebombs/ (accessed August 1, 2013).
6. Bhattacharjee, Y. (2010). New FBI material delays academy report on anthrax attacks. *Science*. http://news.sciencemag.org/2010/12/new-fbi-material-delays-academy-report-anthrax-attacks (accessed August 1, 2013).
7. Black, C. (2010). Guilty plea in white supremacist plot to assassinate Barack Obama. *CBS News*. http://www.cbsnews.com/8301-504083_162-20001464-504083.html (accessed August 1, 2013).
8. Bolz, F., Dudonis, K. and Schultz, D. (2012). *The Counterterrorism Handbook: Tactics, Procedures, and Techniques* (4th ed.). Boca Raton, FL: CRC Press.
9. Brick, M. (2010). Man crashes plane into Texas IRS office. *The New York Times*. http://www.nytimes.com/2010/02/19/us/19crash.html?_r=0 (accessed August 1, 2013).
10. Burton, F. and Bruning, J. (2011). *Chasing Shadows: A Special Agent's Lifelong Hunt to Bring a Cold War Assassin to Justice*. New York: Palgrave-MacMillan.
11. Calvert, S. (2010). Beltway sniper Malvo claims more shootings, co-conspirators. *The Baltimore Sun*. http://articles.baltimoresun.com/2010-07-29/news/bs-md-malvo-sniper-interview-20100729_1_malvo-and-muhammad-lee-boyd-malvo-john-allen-muhammad (accessed August 1, 2013).
12. Conn, M. and Parker, J. (2008). Terrorizing medical research. *The Washington Post*. http://articles.washingtonpost.com/2008-12-08/opinions/36783337_1_animal-research-biomedical-research-animal-experimentation (accessed August 1, 2013).
13. Crutchfield, J. (2007). *It Happened in Oregon: From the Birth of Crater lake to the Gruesome Kalawatset Massacre, Thirty-Four Events that Shaped the History of the Beaver State* (2nd ed.). Kearney, NE: Morris Book Publishing.
14. Delafuente, C. (2004). Terror in the age of Eisenhower: Recalling the mad bomber, whose rampage shook New York. *The New York Times*. http://query.nytimes.com/gst/fullpage.html?res=9C05E4DF1530F933A2575AC0A9629C8B63 (accessed July 31, 2013).

15. Dowd, M. (1994). Crash at the White House: The overview; unimpeded, intruder crashes plane into White House. *The New York Times*. http://www.nytimes.com/1994/09/13/us/crash-white-house-overview-unimpeded-intruder-crashes-plane-into-white-house.html (accessed August 1, 2013).

16. Explosion and Fire at Temple Prompt an Inquiry in Syracuse. (2000). *The New York Times*. (accessed August 1, 2013).

17. Federal Bureau of Investigation. (2013). *A Brief History*. http://www.fbi.gov/chicago/about-us/history/history (accessed August 1, 2013).

18. Federal Bureau of Investigation. (2007). *A Byte Out of History: '63 Baptist Church Bombing*. http://www.fbi.gov/news/stories/2007/september/bapbomb_092609 (accessed July 31, 2013).

19. Federal Bureau of Investigation. (2007). *A Byte Out of History: Terror on Wall Street*. http://www.fbi.gov/news/stories/2007/september/wallstreet_091307 (accessed July 31, 2013).

20. Federal Bureau of Investigation. (2007). *A Byte Out of History: The Palmer Raids*. http://www.fbi.gov/news/stories/2007/december/palmer_122807 (accessed July 31, 2013).

21. Federation of American Scientists. *Public Report of the White House Security Review*. http://www.fas.org/irp/agency/ustreas/usss/t1pubrpt.html (accessed August 1, 2013).

22. Friedman, S. (2013). Accused Fort Hood shooter paid $278,000 while awaiting trial. *NBC News*. http://www.nbcdfw.com/investigations/Accused-Fort-Hood-Shooter-Paid-278000-While-Awaiting-Trial-208230691.html (accessed August 1, 2013).

23. Goetz, K. (2010). Muslim who shot soldier in Arkansas says he wanted to cause more death: Memphis man drifted to the dark side of islamic extremism and then plotted a one-man Jihad against his homeland. *Knox News*. http://www.knoxnews.com/news/2010/nov/13/muslim-who-shot-solider-arkansas-says-he-wanted-ca/ (accessed August 1, 2013).

24. Green, D. (2012). This day in Jewish history/Meir Kahane is gunned down. *Haaretz*. http://www.haaretz.com/news/features/this-day-in-jewish-history/this-day-in-jewish-history-meir-kahane-is-gunned-down-1.475191 (accessed August 1, 2013).

25. Gross, G. (2008). FBI: Courthouse bomb was simple, but deadly. *Union-Tribune San Diego*. http://legacy.utsandiego.com/news/metro/20080505-1503-bn05bomb.html (accessed August 1, 2013).

26. Gunman Shoots 7, Kills Self at Empire State Building. (1997). *CNN News*. http://www.cnn.com/US/9702/24/empire.shooting/ (accessed August 1, 2013).

27. Hillel, A. (2012). The LA Times terrorist attack. *The Native Angeleno*. http://www.thenativeangeleno.com/2012/09/07/the-la-times-terrorist-attack/ (accessed July 31, 2013).

28. Historic Wings. (2012). *An Act of Air Sabotage*. http://fly.historicwings.com/2012/10/an-act-of-air-sabotage/ (accessed July 31, 2013).

29. History of US Bombings, Failed Attempts. (2013). *ABC News*. http://abclocal.go.com/kabc/story?section=news/national_world&id=9066080 (accessed August 1, 2013).

30. How the plot to assassinate Golda Meir was foiled: Secret documents reveal how the NSA uncovered a Black September terrorist's 1973 plot to bomb New York City. (2009). *Haaretz*. http://www.haaretz.com/news/how-the-plot-to-assassinate-golda-meir-was-foiled-1.266865 (accessed July 31, 2013).

31. Joanne Chesimard on FBI's Most Wanted Terrorists List. (2013). *FoxNews Tampa Bay*. http://www.myfoxtampabay.com/story/22139805/fbi-to-announce-development-in-joanne-chesimard-case (accessed July 31, 2013).

32. Karnoutsos, C. (2013). *Black Tom Explosion*. New Jersey City University. http://www.njcu.edu/programs/jchistory/pages/b_pages/black_tom_explosion.htm (accessed July 31, 2013).

33. KOMO News. (2006). *One Killed, Five Wounded at Seattle Jewish Federation*. http://www.komonews.com/news/archive/4192846.html (accessed August 1, 2013).

34. Kushner, H. (2003). *Encyclopedia of Terrorism*. Thousand Oaks, CA: Sage Publishing.

35. Liddy, T. (2008). Three cops honored for '82 bomb heroics. *The New York Post*. http://www.nypost.com/p/news/regional/item_ArLTi4UFYqQnl2ctyQz3pN;jsessionid=FB6B75D43D95E8B0F21AC66C78803A75 (accessed August 1, 2013).

36. Linder, D. (2006). *The Haymarket Riot and Subsequent Trial: An Account*. http://law2.umkc.edu/faculty/projects/ftrials/haymarket/haymktaccount.html (accessed July 31, 2013).

37. Lipson, E. (1981). A bomber's confessions. *The New York Times*. http://www.nytimes.com/1981/10/25/books/a-bomber-s-confessions.html (accessed July 31, 2013).

38. Mansfield, D. (2008). Jim D. Adkisson charged in Tennessee church shooting that killed 2. *The Huffington Post*. http://www.huffingtonpost.com/2008/07/28/jim-d-adkisson-charged-in_n_115281.html (accessed August 1, 2013).

39. March 1st … A Long Time Ago, Bomb Explodes in Capitol Building. (2013). *The Palookaville Post*. http://www.palookavillepost.com/2013/03/01/march-1st-a-long-time-ago-bomb-explodes-in-capitol-building/ (accessed July 31, 2013).

40. Markon, J. (2010). After 40 years, search for University of Wisconsin bombing suspect heats up again. *The Washington Post*. http://www.washingtonpost.com/wp-dyn/content/article/2010/09/21/AR2010092106588.html (accessed July 31, 2013).
41. Mauro, J. (2010). A forgotten July 4 bombing at the world's fair. *National Public Radio*. http://www.npr.org/templates/story/story.php?storyId=128216755 (accessed July 31, 2013).
42. Montgomery College. (2013). *The Tulsa Race Riot of 1921*. http://www.mc.cc.md.us/Departments/hpolscrv/VdeLaOliva.html (accessed July 31, 2013).
43. New York: The Monumental Plot. (1965). *Time Magazine*. http://www.time.com/time/magazine/article/0,9171,833472,00.html (accessed July 31, 2013).
44. Oklahoma Historical Society. (2013). *Osage Murders*. http://digital.library.okstate.edu/encyclopedia/entries/O/Os005.html (accessed July 31, 2013).
45. Police Kill Discovery Building Gunman. (2010). *NBC News*. http://www.nbcnews.com/id/38957020/ns/us_news-crime_and_courts/t/police-kill-discovery-building-gunman/#.UfoW4W3pwuA (accessed August 1, 2013).
46. Pratt, M. (2013). *Patty Hearst Trial: A Chronology*. University of Missouri. http://law2.umkc.edu/faculty/projects/ftrials/hearst/hearstchrono.html (accessed August 1, 2013).
47. Redden, J. (2002). Tumultuous times fattened the files: Unprecedented activism and real crimes kept intelligence officers busy. *Portland Tribune*. http://www.portlandtribune.com/archview.cgi?id=13820 (accessed July 31, 2013).
48. Robinson, T., Meyer, L. and Dickey, C. (1978). *Eight Indicted in Letelier Slaying*. Transnational Institute. http://www.tni.org/article/eigth-indicted-letelier-slaying (accessed August 1, 2013).
49. Royce, L. (2009). Guard killed during shooting at holocaust memorial. *CNN News*. http://www.cnn.com/2009/CRIME/06/10/museum.shooting/ (accessed August 1, 2013).
50. Smith, C. (2010). Ayers' talk quiet at Pitt. *TRIB Live*. http://triblive.com/x/pittsburghtrib/news/s_673673.html#axzz2agyRMEl6 (accessed August 1, 2013).
51. Stein, B. (2009). *Point of View: Punishing an Act of Bigotry*. http://riverdalepress.com/stories/Point-of-view-Punishing-an-act-of-bigotry,40679 (accessed August 1, 2013).
52. Stumpe, J. (2009). Abortion doctor shot to death in Kansas church. *The New York Times*. http://www.nytimes.com/2009/06/01/us/01tiller.html?pagewanted=all (accessed August 1, 2013).
53. T is for Terror: A mad bomber who stalked Los Angeles in the '70s could be the poster boy for the kind of terrorist the FBI fears today. (2003). *NBC News*. http://www.nbcnews.com/id/3070093#.UfnyIm3pwuA (accessed August 1, 2013).
54. Tao, D. (2009). Manhattan Starbucks bomber inspired by 'fight club,' police say. *The New York Times*. http://www.nytimes.com/2009/07/16/nyregion/16starbucks.html (accessed August 1, 2013).
55. Terrorists Take to Arizona. (2009). *CBS News*. http://www.cbsnews.com/2100-500164_162-316077.html (accessed August 1, 2013).
56. The Bath School Disaster. (2013). *Ancestry.com Community*. http://freepages.history.rootsweb.ancestry.com/~bauerle/disaster.htm (accessed July 31, 2013).
57. U.S. Government. (2004). *The 9/11 Commission Report: Final Report of the National Commission on Terrorist Attacks Upon the United States*. New York: W.W. Norton&Company, Inc.
58. UNC Students to Protest Campus Attack. (2006). *ABC News*. http://abclocal.go.com/wtvd/story?section=news/local&id=3958312 (accessed August 1, 2013).
59. United Press. (1980). Armed Puerto Rican terrorists raid campaign headquarters. *Rome News Tribune*. http://news.google.com/newspapers?nid=348&dat=19800316&id=48NLAAAAIBAJ&sjid=_jIDAAAAIBAJ&pg=5308,2162642 (accessed August 1, 2013).
60. United States Senate Committee on the Judiciary. (2009). *Testimony of Richard Hahn*. http://www.judiciary.senate.gov/hearings/testimony.cfm?id=e655f9e2809e5476862f735da142aa4b&wit_id=e655f9e2809e5476862f735da142aa4b-1-6 (accessed August 1, 2013).
61. University of Maryland. (2010). *Global Terrorism Database*. http://www.start.umd.edu/gtd/ (accessed August 1, 2013).
62. University of Missouri (Kansas City). (2013). *United States vs Cecil Price et. al.: The Jury's Decision*. http://law2.umkc.edu/faculty/projects/ftrials/price&bowers/jury.html (accessed July 31, 2013).
63. Webb, C. (2009). *Counterblast: How the Atlanta Temple Bombing Strengthened the Civil Rights Cause*. Southern Spaces. http://www.southernspaces.org/2009/counterblast-how-atlanta-temple-bombing-strengthened-civil-rights-cause (accessed July 31, 2013).
64. Weiss, P. (1996). Letting go: Jewish Americans are more prevalent than ever throughout the establishment, and anti-semitism is at historic lows. So, is the long-held image of Jews as persecuted outsiders obsolete? *New York Magazine* (January 29, 1996). New York: K-III Magazine Corporation.
65. United Mine Workers of America. (2013). *The Ludlow Massacre*. http://www.umwa.org/?q=content/ludlow-massacre (accessed July 31, 2013).

Appendix B: Major Hijackings Since 1931

Based on historical data (Timelines 2011), given below is a synopsis of aircraft hijackings that gained notoriety from 1931 through 2009.

1931	In Peru, the first aircraft hijacking incident occurred.[2] Byron Rickards, piloting a Pangera aircraft, was detained by soldiers and was informed that his airplane was to serve the purposes of "revolutionaries, and that he was to fly to their orders."[2] He continuously refused until he was told that the revolution had concluded.[2] He was allowed to return to Lima provided that he "took one of the Junta with him."[2]
1939	In the state of Missouri, Earnest Pletch shot Carl Bivens (Pletch's flight instructor) in the back of the head during flight.[6] Pletch was sentenced to a lifetime prison sentence.[6]
1958	A Cubana Airlines aircraft was hijacked, and flown from Miami, Florida towards Cuba.[5] The airplane crashed "in the dark waters."[5]
1959	An aircraft from Cuba to Florida was hijacked by "four old members of the Batista's Army."[1]
1961	Antulio Ortiz was charged with "committing the nation's first act of air piracy" resulting from his hijacking an aircraft from Florida to Cuba.[4]
1966	Angel Maria Betancourt Cueto hijacked a Cuban aircraft in the hopes of escaping to the United States.[1] The hijacking was unsuccessful, and Cueto was executed.[1]
1967	Louis Gabor Babler hijacked an aircraft from Florida to Cuba.[7]
1968	A Miami-bound flight was commandeered to Cuba.[3]
1968	Five Cubans hijacked a US B-727 jet, from Chicago to Cuba.[3]
1968	Three Latins hijacked a US B-707 jet, from New York's Kennedy International Airport to Cuba. Pena Soltren, a US citizen, and two accomplices used weapons hidden in a diaper bag to hijack Pan Am flight 281. In 2009, Luis Armando Pena Soltren (66) voluntarily returned to the same airport to surrender and face prosecution. On January 4, 2011, Soltren was sentenced to 15 years in prison.[3]
1968	Montesino Sanchez, a Cuban, hijacked a Boeing 720 from Miami to Cuba.[3]
1968	Eduardo Castera, a Latin, successfully hijacked a B-727 from Tampa to Cuba.[3]
1968	Two blacks successfully hijacked a DC-8 from St. Louis to Cuba.[3]
1968	A Palestinian terrorist attack in Athens on an Israeli civilian airliner killed one person. Mahmoud Mohammad (25) and Maher Suleiman (19) were later captured by Greek officials. In 1970, a Greek court convicted Mahmoud Mohammad for his role in the attack. In 1987, Mahmoud Mohammed Issa Mohammed entered Canada, where he was ordered to be deported in 1988. In 2007, he was still in Canada after some 30 appeals and reviews.[3]
1969	Byron Vaughn Booth and fellow convict Clinton Robert Smith, also a robber, escaped from the California Institution for Men at Chino. The next day, they bought a ticket for a flight from Los Angeles to Miami with a connection in New Orleans. National Airlines flight 64 was hijacked over the Gulf of Mexico after the plane left New Orleans. The plane ended up landing at Camaguey, Cuba, where Cuban officials removed the hijackers. The flight continued on to Miami. Booth was arrested in Nigeria in 2001 and returned to the United States.[3]
1969	Black Panther Anthony Garnet Bryant, (i.e., Tony Bryant) (d.1999 at 60) hijacked a National Airlines plane en route from New York to Miami and directed it to Cuba. He was arrested in Cuba, spent a year and a half in jail, and was pardoned in 1980. His 1984 book *Hijack* described his experience in Cuban prisons.[3]
1969	Black Panther William Brent (1931–2006) became the 28th person, in 1969, to hijack a US airplane to Cuba. The Cubans put him in jail for 2 years. He published his memoir in 1996 titled *Long Time Gone*.[3]
1970	Yoshimi Tanaka and a group of students of the Red Army Faction, including Shiro Akagi, seized a Japan Airlines jet and flew to Pyongyang, North Korea, in Japan's first ever case of air piracy. In 1996, Tanaka was sentenced to 12 years in prison.[3]
1970	Palestinian guerrillas of the Popular Front for the Liberation of Palestine seized control of three jetliners, which were later blown up on the ground in Jordan after the passengers and crews were evacuated. This triggered a civil war in and the expulsion of Palestinians from Jordan.[3]

1972	Richard McCoy (1942–1974), Vietnam veteran and pilot, hijacked a United Air Lines jet and extorted $500,000 in a copycat version of the D.B. Cooper crime. He parachuted into a Utah desert but was caught with the money in his house and was sentenced to 40 years in prison. He escaped and died in a shootout with Federal Bureau of Investigation (FBI) agent Nicholas O'Hara in November 1974.[3]
1972	A Belgian Sabena aircraft, bound for Tel Aviv, was hijacked by four Palestinians. At Lod International, two hijackers were shot and killed by Israeli military personnel, dressed as ground engineers. One passenger died eight days later as a result of her wounds. The two women hijackers were subsequently sentenced to life imprisonment.[3]
1972	Hijackers of a German Lufthansa passenger jet demanded the release of the three surviving terrorists, who had been arrested after the Fürstenfeldbruck gunfight and were being held for trial. Palestinian guerrillas killed an airport employee and hijacked a plane, carrying 27 passengers, to Cuba. They forced West Germany to release three terrorists who were involved in the Munich Massacre.[3]
1973	The United States and Cuba reached an antihijacking agreement.[3]
1973	The Japanese Red Army and Lebanese guerrillas hijacked a Japan Airlines plane over the Netherlands. The passengers and crew were released in Libya, where the hijackers blew up the plane.[3]
1973	Three Palestinians hijacked a KLM B747 en route to New Delhi to Abu Dhabi.[3]
1974	Samuel Joseph Byck (1930–1974), an unemployed former tire salesman, attempted to hijack a plane flying out of Baltimore–Washington International Airport. He intended to crash into the White House in hopes of killing US President Richard M. Nixon. Byck killed pilot Fred Jones and an aviation officer, George Neal Ramsburg, before he was shot and wounded by gunfire through the door of a Delta DC-9 airplane. Byck then shot himself in the head.[3]
1975	In Austria, there was a terrorist kidnapping of Saudi oil minister Sheik Ahmed Zaki Yamani and other ministers at the Organization of the Petroleum Exporting Countries (OPEC) gathering in Vienna. Three people were killed and 11 taken hostage. The oil ministers were taken to North Africa in a hijacked plane in a $1 billion ransom drama. Carlos the Jackal (i.e., Ilich Ramirez Sanchez) later admitted to planning the attack. In 2001, Germany sentenced Hans-Joachim Klein to nine years for his role in the attack.[3]
1976	An Air France Airbus flight, AF139, from Tel Aviv to Paris, was hijacked shortly after departing Athens and taken to Uganda.[3]
1976	Israel launched its daring mission to rescue 103 passengers and Air France crew members being held at Entebbe Airport in Uganda by pro-Palestinian hijackers.[3]
1976	Jonathan Netanyahu, brother of Benjamin, led and was killed in an Israeli raid called Operation Thunderball that rescued the [105] hostages held at Entebbe Airport in Uganda. The raid was by Sayeret Matkal, Israel's elite counterterrorist unit, led by Muki Betser, and it freed all but 3 of the 104 Israeli and Jewish hostages and crew of an Air France jetliner seized by pro-Palestinian hijackers. A total of 45 Ugandan soldiers were killed during the raid. The events are described by Muki Betser and Robert Rosenberg in *Secret Soldier, The True Life of Israel's Greatest Commando*. The hijacking was linked to Carlos the Jackal, also known as Ilich Ramirez Sanchez.[3]
1976	Uganda asked the United Nations (UN) to condemn Israeli hostage rescue raid on Entebbe.[3]
1976	Five Croatian terrorists captured a Trans-World Airlines (TWA) plane at La Guardia Airport, New York.[3]
1977	The Japanese Red Army hijacked a Japan Airlines plane over India. The Douglas DC-8, en route from Paris to Haneda Airport in Tokyo with 156 people on board, stopped in Mumbai, India. After taking off from Mumbai, five armed Japanese Red Army (JRA) members hijacked the aircraft and ordered it flown to Dhaka, Bangladesh. The Japanese government freed six imprisoned members of the group and paid $6 million in ransom. On October 2, the hijackers released 118 passengers and crew members. The remaining hostages were freed later.[3]
1977	A Lufthansa Boeing 737, bound for Frankfurt, was hijacked by Palestinians shortly after takeoff. The plane was diverted to Rome's Fiumicino Airport. Almost all of the passengers were German vacationers. "This is Captain Martyr Mohammed speaking," announced one of the hijackers to the Rome air traffic controllers. "The group I represent demands the release of our comrades in German prisons."[3]
1977	West German commandos stormed a hijacked Lufthansa jetliner that was on the ground in Mogadishu, Somalia, freeing all 86 hostages and killing three of the four hijackers, Palestinians of the Popular Front for the Liberation of Palestine. In 1996, Suhaila al-Sayeh was sentenced to 12 years in prison by a German court.[3]
1979	Nikola Kavaja (d.2008 at 77) hijacked a US passenger jet with the intention of crashing it into Yugoslav Communist Party headquarters in Belgrade. He abandoned his hijack mission in Ireland, saying that at the time, he was not sure of the exact location of the downtown party office and did not want innocent civilians to die if the jet missed the target.[3]
1981	A Pakistan Airways Boeing 720 was hijacked by three Pakistani terrorists. The passengers and crew were released March 15 in Syria.[3]
1984	A 5-day hijack drama began as four armed men seized a Kuwaiti airliner en route to Pakistan and forced it to land in Tehran, where the hijackers killed American passenger Charles Hegna.[3]
1984	In Iran, a 5-day hijack drama ended when Iranian commandos captured the Kuwaiti plane. Four armed men had seized a Kuwaiti airliner en route to Pakistan and forced it to land in Tehran, where the hijackers killed American passenger Charles Hegna.[3]

1985	The 17-day hijack ordeal of TWA flight 847 began as a pair of Lebanese Shiite Muslim extremists seized the plane with 104 Americans shortly after takeoff from Athens, Greece. The hijackers killed Petty Officer Robert Dean Stethem and dumped his body on the tarmac in Beirut. In 2002, Stethem's family was awarded $21.4 million in compensatory damages from the US Treasury. In 1987, Mohammed Ali Hamadi was arrested at the Frankfurt airport, when customs officials discovered liquid explosives in his luggage. The Lebanese man was convicted and served a life sentence in Germany for the 1985 hijacking of a TWA jetliner and killing of a US Navy diver. In 2005, he returned to Lebanon after being paroled in Germany.[3]
1985	A total of 39 American hostages from a hijacked TWA jetliner were freed in Beirut after being held for 17 days.[3]
1985	Four Palestinian Liberation Organization (PLO) gunmen hijacked the Italian cruise ship Achille Lauro in the Mediterranean and demanded the release of 50 Palestinians held by Israel. A total of 413 people were held hostage for 2 days in the seizure that was masterminded by Mohammed Abul Abbas. American Leon Klinghoffer was shot while sitting in his wheelchair and thrown overboard. A case was filed against the PLO and settled in 1997. The hijackers surrendered to Egyptian authorities and were turned over to Italy, which let Abbas slip out of the country. Abbas was captured in Baghdad in 2003.[3]
1985	The hijackers of the Italian cruise ship Achille Lauro killed American passenger Leon Klinghoffer, dumping his body and wheelchair overboard.[3]
1985	EgyptAir flight 648 was hijacked to Malta by Palestinian militant Omar Mohammed Ali Rezaq, a member of the Abu Nidal terrorist group.[3]
1985	The hijacking of an EgyptAir jetliner parked on the ground in Malta ended violently as Egyptian commandos stormed the plane. Fifty-eight people died in the raid, in addition to two others killed by the hijackers. Ali Rezaq of the Abu Nidal terrorist group was imprisoned in Malta for 7 years and then released. The US FBI apprehended him in Nigeria in 1993, and he was convicted by a US federal jury in 1996 and sentenced to life in prison.[3]
1986	The Pakistan army stormed a hijacked US B-747 in Karachi, and 22 people were killed. In 2001, Zayd Hassan Abd Al-latif Masud Al Safarini, jailed in Pakistan for 15 years, arrived in Alaska and was expected to face a 1991 indictment for the 1986 hijacking of a Pan Am jet. In 2003, Safarini pleaded guilty and agreed to three life sentences plus 25 years. On January 3, 2008, Pakistani authorities freed and deported four Palestinians convicted in the hijacking.[3]
1987	West German police arrested Mohammed Ali Hamadi at the Frankfurt airport, when customs officials discovered liquid explosives in his luggage. The Lebanese man was convicted and served a life sentence in Germany for the 1985 hijacking of a TWA jetliner and killing of a US Navy diver. Although convicted and sentenced to life, Hamadi was paroled by Germany in December 2005.[3]
1988	Three Israelis were killed when three Arab gunmen hijacked a commuter bus in the Negev Desert; the hijackers themselves were killed when Israeli forces stormed the vehicle.[3]
1988	A 15-day hijacking ordeal began as gunmen forced a Kuwait Airways jumbo jet to land in Iran.[3]
1988	The hijackers of a Kuwait Airways jetliner vowed to carry out a "slow, quiet massacre" of their hostages, one day after one captive was killed aboard the plane parked in Larnaca, Cyprus.[3]
1988	Hijackers of a Kuwait Airways jetliner killed a second hostage, dumping his body onto the ground in Larnaca, Cyprus.[3]
1988	A commandeered Kuwaiti jetliner took off from Cyprus for Algeria, after the pro-Iranian Shiite Muslim hijackers on board freed 12 hostages.[3]
1988	Gunmen who had hijacked a Kuwait Airways jumbo jet were allowed safe passage out of Algeria. An agreement also freed the remaining 31 hostages and ended a 15-day siege in which two passengers were slain.[3]
1989	Fawaz Younis, a Lebanese hijacker convicted of commandeering a Jordanian jetliner in 1985 with two Americans aboard, was sentenced in Washington to 30 years in prison.[3]
1991	In Puerto Rico, three prisoners escaped from the Rio Piedras State Penitentiary in a hijacked helicopter with the help of accomplices. Two were recaptured, while a third remained at large.[3]
1992	In Vietnam, Ly Tong hijacked a Vietnam airlines jet from Thailand and dropped 50,000 antigovernment leaflets over Ho Chi Minh City. He parachuted down and was arrested. He was released in a 1998 amnesty.[3]
1993	An Egyptian surrendered peacefully after hijacking a Dutch jet to Germany to demand that the United States release Muslim cleric Sheik Omar Abdel-Rahman.[3]
1993	Wang Zhihua boarded a scheduled flight from Hangzhou to Fuzhou, the capital of Fujian province opposite Taiwan. He showed fake explosives to the crew, saying he had a bomb, and forced the plane to fly to Taiwan. In 2008, Wang was returned to China and sentenced to 12 years in prison.[3]
1994	Armed Islamic fundamentalists hijacked an Air France Airbus A-300 carrying 227 passengers at the Algiers airport; three passengers were killed during the siege before the hijackers were killed by French commandos in Marseille 2 days later.[3]

1994	Four Roman Catholic priests, three French and a Belgian, were shot to death in their rectory in Algiers, a day after French commandos killed four radicals who had hijacked an Air France jet from Algiers to Marseille.[3]
1995	Riot police stormed a hijacked jumbo jet in Hakodate, Japan, freeing all 364 people on board and capturing a lone hijacker.[3]
1995	French commandos stormed a hijacked Air France jetliner on the ground in Marseilles, killing four Algerian hijackers and freeing 170 hostages. The Air France plane was hijacked by the Armed Islamic Group of Algeria on December 24.[3]
1996	Chechens hijacked a ferry with 165 passengers and crew from the Turkish port of Trabzon bound for the Russian city of Sochi. Gunmen in Trabzon, Turkey, hijacked a Black Sea ferry with more than 200 people on board and demanded that Russian troops stop fighting Chechen rebels in Pervomayskaya. The hostages were released 3 days later after the Russian troops stormed Pervomaiskoye.[3]
1996	Seven Iraqis freed their 184 captives aboard a Sudanese airliner at the London airport and asked for political asylum.[3]
1996	An Ethiopian Boeing 767 airliner crashed into the Indian ocean near Grand Comore Island. It had been hijacked after takeoff from Addis Ababa and ran out of fuel under hijacker demands to fly to Australia. Some 54 of 175 people were saved. The plane was destined for the Ivory Coast with stops along the way.[3]
1997	In Russia, three armed hijackers seized an Ilyushin-62 passenger plane from far east city of Magadan with at least 140 people onboard. They demanded $10 million and a flight to Switzerland.[3]
1998	In Spain, a Boeing 727 with 131 people was hijacked and diverted to Valencia.[3]
1998	In Turkey, antiterrorist squads shot an airline hijacker to death and freed 38 passengers.[3]
1998	The US Federal Aviation Authority (FAA) produced reports about a hijacking threat posed by al Qaeda, including the possibility of an attempt to use a commercial jet against a US landmark. This information was part of a September 11 Commission report in 2004 and was made public in 2005.[3]
1999	In Colombia, an Avianca plane was hijacked with 46 people aboard and flown to a guerrilla stronghold in Bolivar province.[3]
1999	In Colombia, rebels released 6 of 46 hostages from a commandeered Avianca airplane.[3]
1999	In Colombia, rebels released 3 more hostages as army units fought to free the remaining 32 captured in the hijacking of an Avianca plane.[3]
1999	In Japan, Yuzi Nishizawa (b.1970) attempted to hijack flight 61 from Tokyo and stabbed to death pilot Naoyuki Nagashima (51). The hijacker was overcome, and the plane landed safely with 516 passengers. On March 23, 2005, Nishizawa was found to be guilty but of unsound mind and thus only partly responsible for his actions. Presiding judge Hisaharu Yasui handed Nishizawa a life sentence in 2005.[3]
1999	In Nepal, 5 Sikh men, members of the Kashmir Harakut ul-Mujahedin, hijacked an Indian Airlines A-300 Airbus with 189 people onboard. After three stops for refueling, it landed in Kandahar, Afghanistan, where it was surrounded by Taliban militia. Twenty-six passengers were released in Dubai. They called for the release of Maulana Massood Azhar, a Pakistani religious leader, and other Kashmiri militants. They later raised their demands to $200 million, the release of 35 jailed guerrillas, and the exhumation of a dead comrade buried in India.[3]
1999	Erik de Mul, the UN Afghan coordinator, reached Kandahar and began negotiations with Sikh hijackers.[3]
1999	In Afghanistan, the Indian Airlines hijackers dropped their demands for a $200 million ransom and the body of a Kashmiri militant but haggled over the number of militants to be released.[3]
1999	In Afghanistan, the hijackers of an Indian Airlines flight 814 released all 150 hostages after India released three jailed militants: Maulana Masood Azhar, leader of the Harkat-ul-Ansar rebel group; Omar Sheikh; and Mushtaq Zargat, an Indian Kashmiri. Four hijackers came off the plane and left one dead hijacker behind. The Taliban gave them 10 hours to leave the country.[3]
2000	It was reported that hijackers in Europe were engaged in killing truck drivers and stealing their new trucks for resale. One 50-member ring confessed to the murder of 10 truckers at a charge of $8500 per head.[3]
2000	In Afghanistan, an Ariana Airlines Boeing 727 was hijacked with 186 people. It flew from Kabul to Uzbekistan, Kazakstan, and Russia before landing in Stansted near London the next day with 179 hostages.[3]
2000	In England, Afghan hijackers at Stansted released 8 passengers, with 157 still trapped on the plane.[3]
2000	At Stansted, England, four men escaped from the Afghan hijacked airline as negotiations continued.[3]
2000	At Stansted, England, nine hijackers surrendered and released all hostages of the Afghan jetliner.[3]
2000	In Afghanistan, 73 passengers from the hijacked jet returned home, while 74 remained in Britain seeking asylum. The passengers reported that nine men had taken over their flight and appeared to be relatives of many passengers.[3]
2000	In Pakistan, Nawaz Sharif was sentenced to life in prison for hijacking and terrorism due to his October 12 refusal to let a passenger plane land with 198 people aboard.[3]
2000	In Brazil, armed men hijacked an airliner and forced it to land in southern Parana state. They escaped with an estimated $3.3 million in stolen money.[3]

2000	A Saudi jetliner was hijacked with over 100 people and landed in Baghdad. Two hijackers were arrested.[3]
2000	A Dagestan Airlines jet was hijacked. The Russian plane was forced to fly to Israel with 58 people aboard. Prime Minister Ehud Barak, en route to Washington, returned to handle the crisis. The hijacker surrendered, and the plane was returned to Moscow.[3]
2000	The US FAA warned carriers and airports that the prospect of a terrorist hijacking had increased. This information was part of a September 11 Commission report in 2004 and was made public in 2005.[3]
2001	In 2007, it was reported that a French Intelligence document warned that al Qaeda was at work on a hijacking plot. The information was passed on to the Central Intelligence Agency (CIA). Documents on Osama bin Laden's terror network were drawn up by the French spy service, the DGSE, between July 2000 and October 2001.[3]
2001	Chechen men, wielding knives and claiming to have a bomb, hijacked a Russian plane carrying 174 people after it left Turkey and forced it to land in the holy Saudi city of Medina. Saudi special forces stormed the plane the following day; a flight attendant, a passenger, and a hijacker were killed.[3]
2001	In Saudi Arabia, Saudi commandos freed over 100 hijacked hostages held by Chechen rebels in a Russian plane. Three people were killed including a hijacker, a flight attendant, and a passenger.[3]
2001	The CIA placed Khalid Al-Midhar and Nawaf Alhazmi under suspicion as part of the investigation in the bombing of the destroyer Cole in Yemen. The two were among the hijackers who commandeered the jet that hit the Pentagon on September 11.[3]
2001	At 8:45 a.m., American Airlines flight 11, a Boeing 767 carrying 92 people, crashed into the North tower of the World Trade Center in New York City. It was en route from Boston to Los Angeles.[3]
2001	President Bush declared a national emergency and summoned as many as 50,000 military reservists. Congress approved nearly $40 billion and gave President Bush war powers an OK. The number of hijackers involved in the September 11 attacks was raised from 18 to 19, and their names were made public. Bush prayed with his cabinet and attended services at Washington National Cathedral then flew to New York, where he waded into the ruins of the World Trade Center and addressed rescue workers in a flag-waving, bullhorn-wielding show of resolve. Americans packed churches and clogged public squares on a day of remembrance for the victims of the September 11 attacks.[3]
2001	Passenger lists were published for the four airplanes that were hijacked and crashed by terrorists on September 11.[3]
2001	It was reported that more than four planes may have been targeted by hijackers on September 11.[3]
2001	Pictures of most of the September 11 hijackers were published along with some personal data.[3]
2001	German authorities arrested Mounir El Motassadeq (27), on suspicion of funneling money to the September 11 hijackers.[3]
2001	In the first criminal indictment stemming from September 11, a US grand jury in Virginia charged Zacarias Moussaoui, a French citizen of Moroccan descent, with conspiring to murder thousands in the suicide hijackings. Moussaoui pleaded guilty to conspiracy in 2005 and was sentenced to life in prison.[3]
2002	Kerim Sadok Chatty, 29, of Tunisian origin, was arrested with a gun in his carry-on luggage at a Swedish airport as he headed to an Islamic conference in Birmingham, England. He had flunked out of a flight school in South Carolina in 1996. Chatty was charged with attempted hijacking on September 2.[3]
2002	French police arrested a man in Lyon after he tried to hijack an Alitalia flight carrying 57 passengers from Bologna to Paris.[3]
2005	It was reported that US Defense Department data-mining operation Able Danger had identified Mohamed Atta and three other September 11 hijackers by name in mid-2000.[3]
2005	In Colombia, Porfirio Ramirez (42) and his son, Linsen Ramirez (22), hijacked a Colombian airline. The father in a wheelchair dodged a checkpoint and smuggled grenades onto a plane. All passengers and crew were eventually freed unharmed. The elder hijacker said he hijacked the plane to bring attention to a case in which he was partially paralyzed by a police bullet during a raid on his house some 14 years ago and had unsuccessfully sought government compensation.[3]
2006	A Turkish Airlines plane carrying 113 people from Albania to Istanbul landed in Italy, where a Turkish man surrendered and released all the passengers unharmed. The Turkish army deserter who hijacked the airliner sought asylum because he feared persecution in his Muslim homeland after his conversion to Christianity and wanted Pope Benedict XVI's protection.[3]
2007	A hijacker seized a Sudanese passenger plane carrying 103 people and forced the pilot to fly to the Chadian capital, N'Djamena, where he surrendered. The gunman wanted the plane to be flown to Britain but, when told there was insufficient fuel, agreed to go to the capital of neighboring Chad. He said he wanted to draw attention to the Darfur conflict.[3]
2007	A fast-thinking pilot with passengers in cahoots fooled hijacker Mohamed Abderraman, a 32-year-old Mauritanian, by braking hard upon landing in Gran Canaria then accelerating to knock the man down. When he fell, flight attendants threw boiling water in his face, and about 10 people pounced on him.[3]
2007	Authorities arrested a man armed with a knife who hijacked a Sudan Airways plane while flying from Libya to Sudan.[3]

2007	In Belgium, two men hijacked a helicopter and forced the pilot to land in a prison courtyard, where they picked up an inmate in a dramatic jailbreak. RTL-TVI identified the fugitive as a Frenchman who was in pretrial detention on charges of fraud and theft.[3]
2007	A pair of heavily armed Cuban soldiers seized a city bus, killed an army officer, and triggered a gun battle in a foiled bid to hijack a charter flight bound for the United States.[3]
2007	Two men hijacked a Turkish passenger plane from Cyprus bound for Istanbul, holding several people hostage for more than 4 hours before surrendering.[3]
2007	The US FBI launched its computerized System to Assess Risk (STAR) to find terrorist suspects. It stemmed from a data processing program developed by Frank Asher following the 9/11 attacks. Asher's program had screened 450 million people and produced a list of 1200 suspicious individuals, including 5 of the 9/11 terrorist hijackers.[3]
2008	In New Zealand, a knife-wielding woman (33), originally from Somalia, tried to hijack a regional domestic flight, stabbing both pilots and threatening to blow up the twin-propeller plane before she was subdued.[3]
2008	Sudanese hijackers commandeered the Boeing 737 jetliner, which was carrying 95 passengers and crew, soon after it took off from the southern Darfur town of Nyala, not far from a refugee camp that the Sudanese military attacked a day earlier.[3]
2008	Two hijackers, who commandeered a jetliner from Sudan's Darfur region and diverted it to a remote desert airstrip in southern Libya, surrendered after a 22-hour standoff.[3]
2008	Turkish media reported that a hijacker attempted to commandeer a Turkish Airlines plane over Belarus but that he was overpowered by passengers.[3]
2009	In Jamaica, Stephen Fray (20) forced his way though Montego Bay airport security and hijacked a Canadian jet, holding six crew members hostage. He fired his father's licensed .38-caliber revolver into the air, stole money from some of the 167 passengers aboard, and demanded to be flown off the island. After 6 hours, police and soldiers stormed the aircraft and captured Fray. On October 8, Fray was sentenced to 20 years in prison.[3]
2009	In Mexico a Bolivian-born man, clutching a Bible and claiming a divine mission, hijacked a plane with more than 100 people aboard after takeoff from Cancun. The incident ended quickly and without bloodshed when police arrested Jose Flores (44) in Mexico City. Police in Morelia said that they had seized eight counterfeit police and rescue vehicles, including an intensive care ambulance with official-looking logos and paint jobs. The vehicles belonged to gang members who planned to use them to conduct illegal activities.[3]
2009	Security guards thwarted an attempted hijacking on an EgyptAir flight from Istanbul to Cairo by overpowering a Sudanese man who threatened crew members with a plastic knife. The man told flight attendants he wanted to "liberate Jerusalem."[3]

This listing is not exhaustive. Many more hijacking incidents exist. Regardless, this listing provides an overview of noteworthy hijackings that provide a basis for understanding the types and dangers of hijacking.

References

1. "From Cuba to the United States After the Revolucion of 1959." n.d. Hijacked Airplanes in the Cuban Civil Aviation. http://web.archive.org/web/20091027143627/http://www.geocities.com/urrib2000/Civ8-e.html (accessed August 1, 2013).
2. "Hijack Part I." 2013. *Air Disaster*. http://www.airdisaster.com/features/hijack/hijack.shtml (accessed August 1, 2013).
3. "Hijacking." 2013. *Timelines*. http://timelinesdb.com/listevents.php?subjid=709&title=Hijacking (accessed August 1, 2013).
4. Perez, Miguel. 1975. "Hijacker: Cuba Suspected Spying." *The Miami Herald*. http://www.latinamericanstudies.org/hijackers/suspected-spying.htm (accessed August 1, 2013).
5. "Relatives Claim Passenger in 1958 Plane Crash off Cuba was a Hijacker." 2008. *The Guardian*. http://www.theguardian.com/world/2008/nov/19/usa-cuba (accessed August 1, 2013).
6. "The Killer Who Fell from the Sky." 2000. *Bloom*. http://www.magbloom.com/PDF/bloom20/Bloom_20_Killer.pdf (accessed August 1, 2013).
7. "Chronology of Incidents: Cuban Political Violence." n.d. *Cuban Information Archives*. http://cuban-exile.com/doc_176-200/doc0180.html (accessed August 1, 2013).

Index